FOUNDATIONS OF BRITISH FOREIGN POLICY
1792 - 1902

FOUNDATIONS OF
BRITISH FOREIGN POLICY

FROM PITT (1792) TO SALISBURY (1902)

Old and New Documents Selected and Edited

by

HAROLD TEMPERLEY

and

LILLIAN M. PENSON

FRANK CASS & CO. LTD.
1966

Published by Frank Cass & Co. Ltd.,
10 Woburn Walk, London W.C.1
by arrangement with Cambridge University Press.

First Edition   1938
New Impression   1966

Printed in Great Britain by
Thomas Nelson (Printers) Ltd., London and Edinburgh.

To

EARL BALDWIN

of

BEWDLEY

Chancellor of the University
of Cambridge

*magis alii homines quam
alii mores*

Tacitus, *Hist.* ii, 95.

CONTENTS

LIST OF PRINCIPAL DOCUMENTS, HERE FIRST PUBLISHED *page* xxvi

PREFACE   xxvii

ACKNOWLEDGEMENTS   xxx

I. PITT, 1783–1801; 1805–6

1. PITT AND GRENVILLE. THE CASE AGAINST THE FRENCH REVOLUTION, 1792–3. Pitt, origins, Duke of Leeds (pp. 1–2); the influence of Lord Grenville (pp. 2–3)

Document 1. *The case against the French Revolution and the Dispatch of* 31 *December* 1792 (pp. 3–8). Aftermath and declaration of war (p. 8)

2. PITT ON THE DELIVERANCE AND SECURITY OF EUROPE. Pitt's views for the future Concert of Europe, 1792, 1805 (pp. 9–10)

Document 2. *Pitt's Memorandum on the Deliverance and Security of Europe,* 19 *January* 1805 (pp. 10–21)

II. CANNING, 1807–9

3. CANNING AND NATIONALITY, 1807–9

(*a*) SPAIN. Pitt's alleged views upon (p. 22); Canning's policy in Portugal and Spain, extracts from speeches, 8 June 1808, 28 April 1823 (pp. 22–4)

(*b*) GERMANY. Canning on nationality in Norway and Poland (p. 25)

Document 3. *Canning on the future of Germany and the danger from Prussia,* 16 *May* 1807 (pp. 25–7)

III. CASTLEREAGH, 1812–22

4. THE APPROACH OF PEACE (pp. 28–9)

Document 4. *The Cabinet Memorandum of* 26 *December* 1813; *or Instructions for Peace-Making* (pp. 29–34)

5. THE CONGRESS SYSTEM. Castlereagh the European, treatment of France after the war; the Tsar and the European Alliance (pp. 34–9)

Document 5. *Memorandum on the Treaties of* 1814 *and* 1815, *Aix-la-Chapelle, October* 1818 (pp. 39–46)

6. CASTLEREAGH AND NON-INTERVENTION (pp. 47–8)

Document 6. *The State Paper of* 5 *May* 1820; *or the Foundation of British Foreign Policy* (pp. 48–63)

IV. CANNING, 1822–7

7. EUROPE. Canning and the Anti-Congress Policy, his Appeal to Public Opinion (pp. 64–6)

Document 7. *Extract from Speech of* 12 *December* 1826, *on the new source of England's power* (pp. 66–7)

8. CALLING THE NEW WORLD INTO EXISTENCE. Canning's fear of French Intervention from Spain; Commercial Recognition of Spanish America (pp. 68–70)

Document 8. *The Polignac Memorandum, October* 1823; *or* "*hands off*" *to Europe in the New World* (pp. 70–6).

Introduction (pp. 76–7). **Document 9.** *Canning's theory of recognition,* 25 *March* 1825 (pp. 77–81)

9. THE OLD WORLD; GUARANTEE. Canning's idea of Treaty obligations (pp. 81–2)

Document 10. *Canning's Doctrine of Guarantee,* 18 *September* 1823 (pp. 82–4)

Constitutions and Constitutionalism. Canning on "holding the balance" between despotism and democracy (pp. 84–6)

Document 11. *Canning on Constitutions and Constitutionalism,* 4 *December* 1824 (pp. 86–7).

V. PALMERSTON, 1830–41

10. PALMERSTON AND BELGIUM, 1831–7 (pp. 88–90)

Document 12. *Palmerston on the designs of France in Belgium,* 7 *January* 1831 (pp. 90–1)

Document 13. *Palmerston on non-intervention in Belgium,* 18 *February* 1831 (pp. 91–2)

Document 14. *Palmerston on the need for French troops evacuating Belgium,* 17 *August* 1831 (pp. 92–3)

Document 15. *Palmerston on intervention in Belgium,* 7 *December* 1831 (p. 94)

Document 16. *Palmerston's estimate of the value of the Belgian Guarantee,* 7 *October* 1837 (pp. 94–8)

Document 17. *Metternich and the Belgian Guarantee,* 22 *September* 1837 (pp. 98–100)

11. PALMERSTON AND CONSTITUTIONALISM, 1830–47 (pp. 100–1)

(*a*) CONSTITUTIONALISM IN PORTUGAL AND SPAIN, 1835–47 (pp. 102–4)

Document 18. *Palmerston on the nature of the interference in Spain, 24 June 1835* (p. 104)

Document 19. *Palmerston on the conflicting principles, c. 9 June 1836* (pp. 104–5)

Document 20. *Palmerston refuses a European Congress on Spain, 9 August 1837* (pp. 105–6)

Document 21. *Palmerston describes his achievement to his constituents, 31 July 1847* (pp. 106–7)

(*b*) PALMERSTON AND THE CONSTITUTION OF GREECE, 1841 (pp. 107–8)

Document 22. *Palmerston argues with Metternich, 18 February 1841* (pp. 108–11)

Document 23. *Palmerston argues with Guizot about promoting Constitutionalism, 19 March 1841* (pp. 111–3)

Document 24. *Palmerston recommends humanitarian policy to Guizot, 19 March 1841* (pp. 113–6)

VI. WELLINGTON, PALMERSTON, 1835–41

THE NEAR EAST AND THE STRAITS CONVENTION

12. WELLINGTON, A DECISION AS TO THE BRITISH FLEET, 1835 (pp. 117–20)

Document 25. *Wellington revokes the "discretionary order" to the British Fleet to proceed to Constantinople, 16 March 1835* (p. 121)

13. PALMERSTON, MEHEMET ALI, AND THE STRAITS (pp. 121–4)

Document 26. *Palmerston warns Mehemet Ali, 7 July 1838* (pp. 124–6)

Document 27. *Palmerston and the Persian Gulf, 29 November 1838* (pp. 126–7)

Document 28. *Palmerston warns Sultan Mahmud, 15 March 1839* (p. 127)

Document 29. *Palmerston makes the British Lion roar, 2 December 1839* (pp. 127–8)

Document 30. *Palmerston and King Louis Philippe, 22 November 1839* (pp. 128–30)

Document 31. *Palmerston and Metternich on France, and the Straits Convention, 10 May 1841* (pp. 130–1)

Document 32. *Palmerston exchanges views with Metternich on the Palmerstonian theory of Guarantee, 10 May 1841* (pp. 131–3)

VII. PALMERSTON, RUSSELL, CLARENDON, 1841–53

THE ORIGINS OF THE CRIMEAN WAR

14. THE CONVERSATIONS OF NICHOLAS (pp. 134–5)

Document 33. *Palmerston instructs Nicholas I in the obligations of the British Constitution, 11 January 1841* (pp. 135–8)

15. THE HOLY PLACES AND RUSSIA'S PROTECTION OF THE ORTHODOX SUBJECTS OF TURKEY (p. 138)

Document 34. *Stratford de Redcliffe instructed to counsel prudence to Turkey and forbearance to Russia, 25 February 1853* (pp. 139–44)

16. CROSSING THE RUBICON (pp. 144–6)

Document 35. *Clarendon justifies the sending of the British Fleet through the Dardanelles, 30 September 1853* (pp. 146–52)

VIII. PALMERSTON AND THE REVOLUTION OF 1848–9

17. THE DELUGE IN EUROPE (pp. 153–5)

Document 36. *Palmerston distinguishes between Treaty and Guarantee, 6–14 March 1848* (pp. 156–7)

Document 37. *Application by Lord John Russell of Palmerston's principle, 14 September 1859* (pp. 157–8)

18. PALMERSTON AND RUSSIA, 1848–9 (pp. 158–9)

Document 38. *Palmerston explains to Russia his reasons for recognizing the new régime in France, 28 March 1848* (pp. 159–60)

Document 39. *Palmerston recommends neutrality to Russia and advises her to give home rule to Poland, 14 April 1848* (pp. 160–1)

Document 40. *Palmerston declares to Nesselrode that he will not be drawn into war, 2 December* 1848 (p. 162)

19. PALMERSTON AND AUSTRIA

(*a*) ITALY (pp. 162–5)

Document 41. *Palmerston recommends the grant of a constitution as a panacea for Italy,* 22 *February* 1848 (p. 166)

Document 42. *Palmerston on Austrian rule in Italy,* 7 *November* 1848 (pp. 166–9)

(*b*) HUNGARY AND THE RUSSIAN INTERVENTION, 1848–9 (pp. 169–71)

Document 43. *Palmerston refuses to protest against Russia's armed intervention in Hungary,* 17 *May* 1849 (p. 172)

Document 44. *Palmerston declares Austria's existence to be essential to the European balance of power,* 21 *July* 1849 (pp. 172–7)

20. PALMERSTON, TURKEY AND THE HUNGARIAN REFUGEES (pp. 177–9)

Document 45. *Palmerston communicates his decision to support Turkey against Russia and Austria over the Hungarian Refugees,* 6 *October* 1849 (pp. 179–80)

Document 46. *Palmerston moralizes after the crisis has ended,* 28 *October* 1849 (p. 181)

IX. GRANVILLE, MALMESBURY, 1852

THE REACTION AGAINST PALMERSTON

21. LORD JOHN RUSSELL AND THE QUEEN (pp. 182–3)

Document 47. *Granville's General Statement of Foreign Policy,* 12 *January* 1852 (pp. 183–6)

22. GRANVILLE AND THE IBERIAN PENINSULA (p. 186)

Document 48. *Granville advises Spain to pursue a Constitutional Policy,* 31 *January* 1852 (p. 187)

23. DERBY REBUKES PALMERSTON (pp. 187–8)

Document 49. *Malmesbury warns France against aggression against Switzerland,* 5 *March* 1852 (pp. 188–9)

Document 50. *Malmesbury's advances to Austria,* 15 *March* 1852 (p. 189)

X. PEEL AND ABERDEEN, 1851–3

ITALY

24. ABERDEEN; GLADSTONE AND NAPLES (pp. 190–2)

Document 51. *Aberdeen and Gladstone on the Naples Atrocities, October 1851 to December 1852* (pp. 192–3)

GLADSTONE AND PALMERSTON AND THE OFFICIAL NEAPOLITAN REPLY (pp. 193–4)

Document 52. *Gladstone on the Naples Government and the Conservative Principle, 7 January 1852* (p. 195)

Document 53. *Aberdeen on a pro-Austrian policy, 29 March 1853* (p. 196)

XI. DERBY AND MALMESBURY, 1859

ITALY

25. MALMESBURY AND ITALY (pp. 197–8)

Document 54. *Malmesbury remonstrates with Sardinia, 13 January 1859* (pp. 198–200)

Document 55. *Malmesbury invites Austria to submit to Arbitration before going to war, 21 April 1859* (pp. 200–1)

Document 56. *Malmesbury in Palmerstonian vein, 29 April, 2 May 1859* (pp. 201–2)

Document 57. *Malmesbury disclaims an annexationist policy, 1 May 1859* (p. 202)

XII. PALMERSTON AND RUSSELL, 1859–63

ITALY

26. THE UNION OF NORTH ITALY AND NAPOLEON'S ANNEXATION OF NICE AND SAVOY (pp. 203–5)

Document 58. *Lord John Russell on the independence of States, ? July 1859* (p. 205)

Document 59. *Lord John Russell gives a history of British Policy at Congresses since 1815, 15 November 1859* (pp. 206–7)

Document 60. *Palmerston's views on a Congress, 6 March 1849* (pp. 207–8)

Document 61. *The British view of French pledges of disinterestedness in respect to Savoy,* 4 *July* 1859 (pp. 208–9)

Document 62. *Lord John Russell on the cession of Nice and Savoy,* 26 *March* 1860 (pp. 210–2)

27. ITALY AND GARIBALDI

(*a*) THE PRE-GARIBALDIAN PHASE, 1857–9 (p. 212)

Document 63. *Palmerston on the King of Naples,* 17 *March* 1857 (p. 213)

Document 64. *Clarendon on the King of Naples,* 2 *January* 1858 (p. 213)

(*b*) THE SECOND OR GARIBALDIAN PHASE, May to November 1860 (pp. 214–7)

Document 65. *Palmerston on Garibaldi and Sicily,* 26 *May* 1860 (pp. 217–8)

Document 66. *Lord John Russell declines to interfere with Garibaldi in Naples,* 29 *August* 1860 (pp. 218–9)

Document 67. *Lord John Russell defends the right of the Neapolitans to change their Government,* 21 *August* 1860 (pp. 219–20)

(*c*) THE THIRD OR POST-GARIBALDIAN PHASE, THE RECOGNITION OF REVOLUTION, October 1860 (pp. 221–2)

Document 68. *Lord John Russell recognizes the Garibaldian Revolution in Naples and Sicily,* 27 *October* 1860 (pp. 222–5)

Document 69. *Palmerston proposes to stop Spain by force from invading Italy,* 29 *October* 1860 (p. 226)

(*d*) THE AFTERMATH (pp. 226–9)

Document 70. *Palmerston on Austrian rule in Venetia,* 21 *September* 1860 (pp. 229–30)

Document 71. *Russell fails to persuade Austria to sell Venetia,* 18 *November* 1863 (pp. 230–1)

XIII. PALMERSTON AND RUSSELL, 1860–3

RUSSIA AND POLAND

28. THE BRITISH SIDE OF THE POLISH QUESTION, 1831–63 (pp. 232–9)

Document 72. *Palmerston takes the first step,* 25 *February* 1863 (p. 239)

Document 73. *Russell and Palmerston disclaim the idea of going to war with Russia*, 21–2 *April* 1863 (pp. 240–1)

Document 74. *Palmerston urges an immediate amnesty*, 15 *May* 1863 (p. 241)

Document 75. *Palmerston suggests an independent Poland with an Austrian Archduke as King*, 31 *May* 1863 (pp. 241–4)

Document 76. *Russell's answer of* 20 *October to Prince Gorčakov's dispatch of* 7 *September—Russell adheres to his draft in opposition to Austria*, 30 *September* 1863 (p. 244)

Document 77. *Palmerston advises moderation*, 2 *October* 1863 (pp. 244–5)

Document 78. *Palmerston amends Russell's dispatch*, 8 *October* 1863 (pp. 246–7)

Document 79. *Palmerston and Russell on the designs of Russia in Asia*, 1–2 *August* 1860 (p. 247)

XIV. PALMERSTON AND RUSSELL, 1860–4

DENMARK AND SCHLESWIG-HOLSTEIN

29. PALMERSTON'S VIEW OF BISMARCK AND PRUSSIA, 1862–3 (pp. 248–9)

Document 80. *Disraeli on Bismarck's designs and the Palmerston Government*, 9 *July* 1862 (p. 249)

Document 81. *Palmerston and Russell on Bismarck and French military strength*, 1860–3 (pp. 250–1)

Document 82. *Palmerston and Russell advise the King of Prussia and Bismarck to be constitutional*, 1863 (pp. 251–2)

Document 83. *Palmerston on the situation in September* 1863 (p. 252)

Document 84. *Palmerston's warning to those who attempt to attack Denmark*, 23 *July* 1863 (pp. 252–3)

30 THE BRITISH REFUSAL OF NAPOLEON'S INVITATION TO A CONGRESS, NOVEMBER 1863 (p. 253)

Document 85. *Palmerston on the general functions of a Congress*, 8 *November* 1863 (pp. 254–6)

Document 86. *Palmerston's particular objections to a Congress*, 18 *November* 1863 (pp. 256–8)

Document 87. *Russell's account of the Cabinet's decision to refuse the Congress*, 19 *November* 1863 (pp. 258–9)

31. THE GERMAN INTERVENTION, NOVEMBER 1863–
JANUARY 1864 (pp. 259–62)

Document 88. *Russell talks to Apponyi on the Schleswig-Holstein
crisis, 19 December 1863* (pp. 262–5)

Document 89. *Palmerston on the obligations of the Treaty of
1852 on Denmark and Germany, 18 January 1864* (p. 265)

Document 90. *Palmerston's advice to Denmark, 19 January 1864*
(pp. 265–6)

Document 91. *Discussion of Cabinet members on hearing that
France will not use force, 26–7 January 1864* (p. 266)

32. THE BRITISH ATTITUDE AT THE LONDON CON-
FERENCE, 25 APRIL–25 JUNE 1864 (pp. 267–8)

Document 92. *Palmerston warns Austria against sending a fleet to
the Baltic, 1 May 1864* (pp. 268–72)

33. DECLINE OF BRITISH PRESTIGE, MAY–JUNE 1864
(p. 272)

Document 93. *The compromise scheme of Lord John Russell,
5 May 1864* (pp. 273–5)

Document 94. *Clarendon's comment, 5 May 1864* (pp. 275–6)

Document 95. *The British Cabinet's decision at the conclusion of
the Conference, 25 June 1864* (p. 276)

Document 96. *Palmerston's comment, 6 May 1864* (pp. 276–7)

34. THE AFTERMATH, 1864–5 (pp. 277–9)

Document 97. *Palmerston to Russell, 13 September 1865* (pp.
279–80)

XV. PALMERSTON AND RUSSELL

GENERAL QUESTIONS; DEFENCE; THE AMERICAN CIVIL WAR; ARBITRATION; SLAVERY

35. PALMERSTON AND RUSSELL; THE LAST PHASE
(pp. 281–6)

Document 98. *Palmerston on the nature of Alliances and a possible
breach with France, 14 December 1856* (pp. 286–7)

Document 99. *Clarendon's comment, 15 December 1856* (p. 288)

36. PALMERSTON ON NAVAL AND MILITARY DE-
FENCE (pp. 288–91)

Document 100. *Count Rechberg on Palmerston and the naval and
military power of France, 30 June 1859* (pp. 291–2)

Document 101. *Lord John Russell on the need of maintaining England's naval strength,* ? *December* 1859 (p. 292)

Document 102. *Palmerston on force as a Peacemaker,* 23 *October* 1864 (p. 293)

Document 103. *Palmerston on war,* 8 *January* 1865 (pp. 293–4)

37. PALMERSTON AND GLADSTONE AND THE AMERICAN CIVIL WAR (p. 294)

Document 104. *Palmerston on the future of Mexico,* 1 *November* 1855 (p. 295)

Document 105. *Palmerston on the advantages of Monarchy in Mexico and an independent South,* 19 *January* 1862 (p. 295)

Document 106. *Palmerston on Slavery and the South* (p. 295)

Document 107. *Gladstone on an independent Southern Confederacy,* ? *July* 1896 (p. 296)

38. PALMERSTON AND RUSSELL, AND WAR WITH THE NORTH, 1862–3 (pp. 296–8)

Document 108. *Argyll's recollection of the Cabinet decision of* 11 *November* 1862 *against intervention,* 7 *April* 1887 (pp. 298–9)

Document 109. *Palmerston and Russell still think war possible between England and the North,* 25 *April* 1863 (pp. 299–300)

39. BRAZIL—ARBITRATION, 1863 (p. 300)

Document 110. *The inapplicability of the principle of arbitration to England,* 12 *June* 1849 (p. 301)

Document 111. *Palmerston compares Brazil to a Billingsgate Fishwoman,* 6 *February* 1863 (p. 301)

Document 112. *Palmerston on Brazil's demand for compensation,* 4 *May* 1863 (pp. 301–2)

Document 113. *The Arbitration Award by Leopold King of the Belgians,* 18 *June* 1863 (p. 303)

40. THE SLAVE TRADE (p. 303)

Document 114. *Palmerston on the Aberdeen Act,* 31 *July* 1862 [1863] (pp. 303–4)

Document 115. *The execution of the Aberdeen Act, his greatest achievement,* 17 *February* 1864 (p. 304)

Document 116. *Palmerston's last utterance on the Slave Trade,* 29 *January* 1865 (p. 304)

XVI. DERBY AND STANLEY, 1866–7

41. DERBY AND STANLEY ON NON-INTERVENTION AND GUARANTEE (pp. 305–6)

Document 117. *An Austrian view of Stanley and the principle of non-intervention*, 3 July 1866 (pp. 306–7)

Document 118. *Stanley applies the principle of non-intervention in the case of the war between Prussia and Austria, July–August 1866; to Italy in 1867 and to Poland in 1868* (pp. 307–8)

42. LUXEMBURG AND THE GUARANTEE (pp. 309–10)

Document 119. *Stanley on the obligations to Luxemburg before the Conference met*, 30 April 1867 (pp. 310–1)

43. DERBY AND STANLEY EXPLAIN THE GUARANTEE AFTER THE CONFERENCE (pp. 311–2)

Document 120. *Derby's interpretation of the guarantee*, 13 May 1867 (p. 312)

Document 121. *Stanley's authoritative interpretation of the guarantee*, 25 June 1867 (pp. 313–4)

Document 122. *Count Bernstorff refused further explanations*, 12 July 1867 (p. 314)

44. THE DERBY DOCTRINE OF COLLECTIVE GUARANTEE, AND ITS AFTERMATH (1867–1914) (pp. 315–6)

XVII. GLADSTONE, CLARENDON AND GRANVILLE, 1868–74

45. NON-INTERVENTION AND THE RULE OF LAW (p. 317)

Document 123. *Gladstone expounds his principles of policy in reply to criticisms by the Queen*, 17 April 1869 (pp. 317–8)

46. CLARENDON AND THE REDUCTION OF ARMAMENTS (pp. 318–9)

Document 124. *Clarendon makes his final effort with Prussia*, 9 March 1870 (pp. 319–23)

47. THE PRUSSIAN CIRCULAR ON ALSACE-LORRAINE (pp. 323–4)

Document 125. *Gladstone discourses on annexations*, 25 September 1870 (pp. 324–7)

48. THE ALABAMA ARBITRATION (pp. 327–8)

Document 126. *Gladstone argues in defence of arbitration, 6 February* 1873 (pp. 328–9)

49. RUSSIA, THE BLACK SEA CLAUSES AND THE STRAITS (pp. 330–1)

Document 127. *Gladstone points out the principles involved in the Russian Circular of 9 November* 1870 (pp. 331–3)

Document 128. *Granville reflects on the Tripartite Treaty of* 1856, 10 *December* 1870 (pp. 333–4)

Document 129. *Gladstone defines the implications of a Guarantee,* 12 *December* 1870 (p. 335)

50. THE NEUTRALITY OF BELGIUM (pp. 335–7)

Document 130. *Granville explains to Lyons the urgency of an Anglo-French Treaty,* 4 *August* 1870 (pp. 337–8)

Document 131. *Gladstone defends his policy to the House of Commons,* 10 *August* 1870 (pp. 338–40)

Document 132. *The Law Officers express their opinion on the character of the* 1839 *Treaty,* 6 *August* 1870 (pp. 340–1)

51. THE DOCTRINE OF ALLIANCES

(*a*) PORTUGAL (pp. 341–2)

Document 133. *Granville acknowledges the British obligations to Portugal under the Ancient Treaties, but reserves judgment as to their interpretation,* 27 *February* 1873 (p. 343)

(*b*) ANDRÁSSY'S OVERTURE OF 1871–2 (pp. 343–5)

Document 134. *Granville declines to pledge the British Government, but promises free communication with Austria-Hungary,* 15 *April* 1872 (pp. 345–6)

XVIII. DISRAELI AND DERBY, 1874–6

THE CENTRAL POWERS

52. THE OPENING MOVES OF FRIENDSHIP, FEBRUARY 1874 (p. 347)

Document 135. *Derby replies to friendly overtures from Austria-Hungary,* 26 *February* 1874 (pp. 348–9)

Document 136. *Derby discusses the international situation with Münster,* 27 *February* 1874 (pp. 349–51)

53. ENGLAND GIVES ADVICE TO BISMARCK IN THE WAR SCARE OF 1875 (pp. 351–2)

Document 137. *Derby instructs Odo Russell to support Russian diplomatic action,* 8 *May* 1875 (pp. 352–3)

Document 138. *Derby's interview with Münster,* 9 *June* 1875 (pp. 353–4)

54. BISMARCK'S OVERTURE OF FEBRUARY 1876 (pp. 354–5)

Document 139. *Derby replies to Bismarck,* 16 *February* 1876 (p. 356)

XIX. BEACONSFIELD, DERBY AND SALISBURY, 1876–80

THE EASTERN CRISIS AND ITS AFTERMATH

55. THE POLICY OF DEFENDING BRITISH INTERESTS

(*a*) DERBY (pp. 357–9)

Document 140. *Derby defines the British position in a secret communication to Russia,* 17 *July* 1877 (p. 359)

(*b*) BEACONSFIELD (p. 360)

Document 141. *Beaconsfield reasserts his intention to maintain the integrity and independence of the Ottoman Empire,* 6 *August* 1877 (pp. 360–2)

56. GREAT BRITAIN ASSUMES LEADERSHIP ON THE ADVENT OF SALISBURY TO THE FOREIGN OFFICE (pp. 363–5)

Document 142. *Salisbury defines British policy on the eve of his appointment to the Foreign Office,* 21 *March* 1878 (pp. 365–6)

Document 143. *Report of the Cabinet Committee on the Treaty of San Stefano,* 27 *March* 1878 (pp. 367–72)

Document 144. *The Salisbury Circular to the Powers,* 1 *April* 1878 (pp. 372–80)

57. BEACONSFIELD AND SALISBURY DEVELOP BRITISH POLICY AT THE CONGRESS OF BERLIN (pp. 381–4)

Document 145. *Salisbury explains to Layard his views on Turkey-in-Asia,* 9 *May* 1878 (pp. 384–5)

Document 146. *Greece and the internal Government of Turkey,* 30 *May* 1878 (pp. 386–7)

Document 147. *Salisbury proposes an agreement with Turkey concerning the Straits,* 16 *June* 1878 (p. 388)

Document 148. *Beaconsfield comments on the work of the Congress,* 2 *July* 1878 (pp. 388–9)

XX. GLADSTONE AND GRANVILLE,
1880–5

THE OTTOMAN EMPIRE

58. GLADSTONIAN PRINCIPLES AND THEIR APPLICATION (pp. 390–1)

Document 149. *Gladstone states his principles of foreign policy,* 27 *November* 1879 (pp. 391–4)

59. GLADSTONE AND GRANVILLE MODIFY BRITISH POLICY IN THE NEAR EAST (p. 394)

Document 150. *Granville announces to the Powers the attitude of the new administration,* 4 *May* 1880 (pp. 395–6)

Document 151. *A private explanation of policy by Granville,* 5 *May* 1880 (p. 397)

Document 152. *Gladstone's reflections on British policy,* 23 *May* 1880 (p. 398)

60. GLADSTONE AND GRANVILLE CONTEMPLATE THE CANCELLATION OF THE CYPRUS CONVENTION BUT DO NOT ACHIEVE IT (p. 399)

Document 153. *Gladstone's comments on the draft dispatch to Goschen,* 9 *June* 1880 (pp. 399–400)

Document 154. *Granville expounds the attitude of the Liberal Government to the Cyprus Convention and earns the disapproval of the Queen,* 10 *June* 1880 (pp. 400–5)

Document 155. *Gladstone suggests handing over Cyprus to Greece,* 17 *December* 1880 (pp. 406–7)

61. THE ENFORCEMENT OF THE TREATY OF BERLIN (p. 407)

Document 156. *Gladstone contemplates the use of force,* 16–19 *September* 1880 (pp. 407–8)

Document 157. *Gladstone explains his policy to the Cabinet,* 30 *September* 1880 (pp. 408–10)

Document 158. *Turkey collapses and Gladstone rejoices,* 4–12 *October* 1880 (pp. 410–1)

62. GLADSTONE'S PYRRHIC VICTORY AND THE DREIKAISERBUND (pp. 411–2)

Document 159. *Gladstone proposes a warning to Austria-Hungary,* 13–28 *December* 1881 (pp. 412–3)

63. GLADSTONE AND GRANVILLE UNWILLINGLY ACKNOWLEDGE THE OBLIGATION INCURRED BY SALISBURY AS TO TUNIS (pp. 413–4)

Document 160. *Granville explains the limits imposed upon his policy,* 22 *April* 1881 (p. 414)

Document 161. *Gladstone recognizes that his hands are tied,* 22 *April* 1881 (pp. 414–5)

XXI. GLADSTONE AND GRANVILLE, 1882–5

THE EGYPTIAN QUESTION

64. GLADSTONE AND GRANVILLE ENTER ON THE EGYPTIAN ADVENTURE (pp. 416–7)

Document 162. *Granville explains the dispatch of ships to Alexandria,* 23 *May* 1882 (pp. 417–8)

Document 163. *Granville issues instructions for the Conference of Constantinople,* 21 *June* 1882 (pp. 418–9)

65. THE BOMBARDMENT OF ALEXANDRIA (p. 420)

Document 164. *Granville explains his attitude to the bombardment,* 12 *July* 1882 (pp. 420–1)

66. OPERATIONS IN THE SOUDAN (pp. 421–2)

Document 165. *Granville defines the attitude of the Government,* 13 *December* 1883 (pp. 422–3)

67. THE EGYPTIAN CONFERENCE AND THE COLONIAL QUESTION (pp. 423–5)

Document 166. *Bismarck uses the Egyptian Conference to bargain with Granville on Colonial Questions,* 14 *June* 1884 (pp. 425–6)

68. THE BRITISH OCCUPATION OF EGYPT (p. 426)

Document 167. *Granville explains the impossibility of fixing a date for the evacuation of Egypt,* 28 *April* 1885 (p. 427)

Document 168. *Turkey complains to Salisbury of the policy of the Liberal Administration,* 30 *June* 1885 (pp. 427–8)

XXII. SALISBURY, ROSEBERY, AND IDDESLEIGH, 1885-6

BULGARIA AND BATOUM

69. SALISBURY ADAPTS HIS NEAR EASTERN POLICY TO THE CIRCUMSTANCES OF THE TIMES (pp. 429-31)

Document 169. *Salisbury gives instructions for the Conference at Constantinople, 28 September* 1885 (pp. 431-2)

Document 170. *Salisbury finds a formula for the Bulgarian situation, 19 November* 1885 (p. 432)

Document 171. *Salisbury defines the British attitude to the Treaty of Berlin, 4 December* 1885 (p. 433)

70. ROSEBERY AND THE CONTINUITY OF BRITISH FOREIGN POLICY (pp. 433-4)

Document 172. *Rosebery maintains the policy of his predecessors in relation to Greece, 8 February* 1886 (pp. 435-6)

71. BATOUM AND THE STRAITS (pp. 436-7)

Document 173. *Rosebery writes a "Blue-Book" dispatch on Batoum, 13 July* 1886 (pp. 437-41)

72. SALISBURY'S ATTITUDE TO THE BULGARIAN QUESTION, 1886 (pp. 441-2)

Document 174. *Confidential Memorandum communicated to Austria-Hungary on 2 October* 1886 (pp. 442-4)

XXIII. SALISBURY, PRIME MINISTER AND FOREIGN SECRETARY, 1887-92

73. WAR CLOUDS IN THE SPRING OF 1887, AND THE FIRST MEDITERRANEAN AGREEMENT (pp. 445-8)

Document 175. *Salisbury's reaction to the Italian overture, 2 February* 1887 (pp. 448-50)

Document 176. *Salisbury defines the limits of co-operation with Italy, 12 February* 1887 (pp. 450-1)

Document 177. *Salisbury's silence on British obligations to Belgium, 26 February* 1887 (p. 451)

74. THE WOLFF CONVENTION (p. 452)

Document 178. *Salisbury defines his attitude to the evacuation of Egypt, 27 April and 3 May* 1887 (p. 453)

Document 179. *Britain obtains the support of the Central Powers and pays the price demanded by Bismarck,* 17 *February,* 14 *April and* 4 *May* 1887 (pp. 453–4)

Document 180. *Salisbury recognizes the need for acknowledging the existence of the Mediterranean declaration,* 26 *May* 1887 (p. 454)

75. THE SECOND MEDITERRANEAN AGREEMENT, DECEMBER 1887 (pp. 454–8)

Document 181. *Salisbury agrees, unwillingly, to strengthen the Accord à Trois,* 2 *November* 1887 (pp. 459–60)

Document 182. *Salisbury communicates his adherence on nine points,* 12 *December* 1887 (pp. 460–2)

76. THE FALL OF BISMARCK (pp. 462–4)

Document 183. *Salisbury on the results of Bismarck's fall,* 9 *April* 1890 (pp. 464–6)

77. THE RUSSIAN VOLUNTEER FLEET AND THE RULE OF THE STRAITS (pp. 466–7)

Document 184. *Salisbury consults with Austria-Hungary as to the reply to Turkey,* 1 *October* 1891 (pp. 467–8)

Document 185. *Salisbury lays down his own principles regarding the Rule of the Straits,* 2 *October* 1891 (pp. 468–9)

XXIV. ROSEBERY AND KIMBERLEY, 1892–5

78. THE LIBERAL ADMINISTRATION AND THE ACCORD À TROIS (pp. 470–3)

Document 186. *Rosebery assures Austria-Hungary of his recognition of Near Eastern interests, and of his control of foreign policy,* 14 *June* 1893 (pp. 473–4)

Document 187. *Rosebery explains his attitude to the Mediterranean Agreements,* 27 *June* 1893 (pp. 475–7)

Document 188. *Rosebery relies on the strength of the British fleet,* 28 *December* 1893 (pp. 477–80)

Document 189. *Rosebery refuses to give binding assurances concerning Constantinople,* 31 *January* 1894 (pp. 480–7)

79. THE BASIN OF THE NIGER (p. 488)

Document 190. *Kimberley adopts an attitude of watchfulness towards Germany in African questions,* 31 *March* 1894 (p. 488)

Document 191. *Kimberley maintains British interests in the Niger Valley,* 11 *April* 1894 (p. 489)

80. ROSEBERY, KIMBERLEY, AND THE POLICY OF THE FREE HAND (pp. 489–91)

Document 192. *Rosebery threatens to return to a policy of the Free Hand,* 13 *June,* 14 *June* 1894 (pp. 491–2)

Document 193. *Kimberley defines his position in relation to Germany and Russia,* 21 *November* 1894 (pp. 492–3)

XXV. SALISBURY, 1895–1900

81. THE "INTEGRITY OF TURKEY"—BRITAIN, RUSSIA AND GERMANY, 1895 (pp. 494–5)

82. AUSTRIA-HUNGARY'S OVERTURE TO BRITAIN, 1896–7 (pp. 495–6)

Document 194. *Salisbury refuses to pledge himself to action,* 20 *January* 1897 (pp. 496–9)

83. BRITAIN'S OVERTURE TO RUSSIA, 1898 (pp. 499–500)

Document 195. *Salisbury makes an overture to Russia,* 25 *January* 1898 (pp. 500–1)

84. THE CONTROL OF THE NILE VALLEY

(i) GREY AND KIMBERLEY (pp. 501–2)

Document 196. *Sir Edward Grey's warning to France against penetration to the Nile,* 28 *March* 1895 (pp. 502–4)

Document 197. *Kimberley reinforces Grey's warning,* 1 *April* 1895 (pp. 504–5)

(ii) SALISBURY AND THE FASHODA CRISIS (pp. 505–6)

Document 198. *Salisbury asserts British interests,* 2 *August* 1898 (pp. 507–9)

COMMENT ON FASHODA BY THE EDITORS (pp. 509–12)

85. THE PROBLEM OF AFRICA (pp. 512–5)

Document 199. *Salisbury confirms British obligations to Portugal under the Ancient Treaties, October* 1899 (pp. 515–6)

86. THE END OF "ISOLATION" (pp. 516–8)

Document 200. *Memorandum by the Marquess of Salisbury,* 29 *May* 1901 (pp. 518–20)

EPILOGUE BY THE EDITORS (pp. 521–2)

NOTE BY THE EDITORS, Canning, Spain and British Trade with the Spanish Colonies 1810–24 (pp. 523–6)

INDEX   *page* 527

LIST OF PRINCIPAL DOCUMENTS, HERE
FIRST PUBLISHED IN WHOLE OR IN PART*

PRIVATE PAPERS

Aberdeen, **Doc. 53**

Clarendon, **Docs. 104, 106, 124**

Gladstone, **Docs. 51, 155–6, 158**

Granville, **Docs. 47, 108, 125, 127–29, 151–3, 157, 159–61, 164**

Layard, **Docs. 79, 81 iv, 82 ii, 102–3, 111, 116, 141, 145–7**

Russell, **Docs. 69–70, 72, 74–5, 77–8, 81 i, ii, iii, 83, 85–6, 89–91,**
93–6, 105, 112, 114

Stratford Canning, de Redcliffe, **Doc. 11**

Tenterden, **Docs. 130, 148**

Wellesley, **Doc. 98**

OFFICIAL ARCHIVES

Austria (Vienna), **Docs. 64, 71, 73, 75, 80, 87–8, 92, 100, 109, 117,**
119, 174, 183–4, 186–9, 192–9

British (London), **Docs. 3, 19, 20, 22–5, 36, 38–43, 48–50, 54–5,**
56 i, ii, 57–9, 61, 63, 65–7, 76, 82 i, 101, 118 *a*, *c*, 121–2
133–8, 140, 143, 150, 154, 162–3, 165–71, 178–80, 190–1

Netherlands (The Hague), **Doc. 36**

* References are to Documents numbered in the text.

PREFACE

THIS volume represents a selection by the Editors of unpublished and published documents dealing with foreign affairs, from the rise of the Younger Pitt to the death of Salisbury. It contains both official papers and private letters; speeches and other public statements of policy. Should the volume be successful, the Editors will consider the editing of a selection from the eleven volumes of the series *British Documents on the Origins of the War*, which they edited in conjunction with Dr G. P. Gooch.

A selection of documents extending over a period of a century always offers problems and difficulties. The Editors have had access to a large number of unpublished materials, public and private, so that many of the documents that they have chosen are new. But a selection of documents dealing with foreign policy offers less difficulty than one relating to internal affairs. Despite opposed parties, and even opposed policies, the continuity of ideas in British diplomacy is striking. The famous State Paper written by Sir Eyre Crowe on 1 January 1907 reproduces what are virtually Canning's ideas on foreign policy eighty years before. Most of the assumptions underlying these views were accepted by all statesmen from Pitt to Salisbury, though their methods of application and interpretation may have differed. The balance of power, the sanctity of treaties, the danger of extending guarantees, the value of non-intervention, the implications of what Castlereagh called "a System of Government strongly popular and national in its character" were understood by all. It is true that Palmerston, in his robust vigour, was ready to interpret 'non-intervention' in a sense which would have surprised Castlereagh and Canning; that Russell glorified the revolutions which Disraeli disliked; that Salisbury hated publicity and parliamentary control; that Gladstone preferred the concert of Europe to the balance of power. But these differences do not prevent us from seeing that there is a great similarity between the views of all these men, despite the illogicality of their methods. There are times when Castlereagh is English, when Canning is European, when Palmerston admits the superiority of moral ideas, when Gladstone relies on the British fleet, and when Salisbury finds public opinion of value. What is more remarkable is that the ideas of Pitt, as stated in the early pages of this book, clearly anticipate the dangers of violent nationalism, and the merits of a League to enforce peace, and the necessity for England to steer a middle course between these alternating policies.

The main principles of selection are simple; and they derive, as it were, from the nature of the soil and from the English character. Englishmen never say all they mean in published documents or in public speeches, so that secret dispatches and private letters must supply the key to what our statesmen thought to be important. We have fortunately been able to make abundant use of materials of this kind, and public and private utterances are equally represented here. Our first principle of selection has been to give representative extracts from different categories of documents; another has been to ensure that the documents should shew what is specifically the British point of view. Foreign policy as a whole is the expression of the contrasted and combined views of a number of different and often opposed nations. The present book aims not at shewing what is universal in the currents or tendencies of diplomacy in the period, but at revealing the British contribution to it. Nothing is omitted, therefore, just because it is chauvinistic—or prejudiced. Such tendencies indeed it is necessary at times to emphasize. A document is inserted not because it expresses or summarizes an international standpoint, but because it expresses a British or national standpoint, in a word, when it reveals the British mentality. The British way of looking at things under Pitt; the British attitude towards congresses under Castlereagh; towards the recognition of revolted states under Canning; the British intervention at a crisis, with Palmerston 'making the lion roar'; Disraeli dreaming of Empire; Gladstone pleading

for arbitration; Salisbury uniting the Bulgarias in face of
Europe's opposition; these are the truest and most characteristic aspects of British policy. The painter must not shrink
from portraying rugged features, and here, as in the case of
Cromwell's picture, realism is the best art.

The principles of selection thus adopted have led the Editors
to seek their materials in widely different sources. They have
used freely the official documents in the Foreign Office
archives, choosing both published and unpublished papers,
including some that were intended for publication from the
start. Where these were curtailed at their original publication,
the omissions have been marked. They have gone, with equal
freedom, to the numerous private letters and private minutes
which are now available for nearly the whole of the period.
Sometimes they have included the record made by a foreign
ambassador of an English statesman's views—for this is on
occasion particularly illuminating. But always they have had
in mind their main object, that of illustrating the ideas of
policy that English statesmen had in mind, and the ways in
which they sought to put their ideas into action.

Each document (or in some cases series of documents) has
been prefaced by a short introduction explaining its significance, and summarizing the policy which it represents. As
far as possible the sources from which further material can
be found are indicated. The Editors have studied a good deal
of the material, most of which is still unpublished, between
the years 1841 and 1896. Their work in collaboration with
Dr G. P. Gooch on *British Documents on the Origins of the War*
has required them to study the whole of the archive material
from the year 1897 and to read freely in the papers of the
preceding years. They are thus enabled to give original
material for this part of the century as well as for the earlier
periods. They have had special permission to publish material
between the years 1885–96 from the archives not yet open to
the public. For no period, however, have they hesitated to
include documents which were more public in character if
they represented essential features of British policy. They hope
that the collection of material, together with the introductory

matter, will afford suggestions for further study, and will give a general view of the most characteristic phases of British policy in the nineteenth century.

HAROLD TEMPERLEY

LILLIAN M. PENSON

June 1938

ACKNOWLEDGEMENTS

The Editors acknowledge with gratitude their indebtedness in many quarters. They owe much to the facilities granted them in the Foreign Office archives, as well as those of Paris, Vienna and the Hague; and in the Public Record Office and the British Museum in London. They wish particularly to put on record their recognition of the help given them by Sir Stephen Gaselee, K.C.M.G., and by the officials of the British Museum and the Public Record Office. They have used freely the private papers of Lord Aberdeen and Sir A. H. Layard, now in the British Museum; and those of Lord Russell, Lord Granville, Lord Tenterden, and Lord Stratford de Redcliffe which are on deposit in the Public Record Office. Much of the rest of their material comes from the official correspondence in the Record Office or the Foreign Office.

They wish further to express their thanks to three owners of valuable manuscripts for allowing them access to documents not open to the public; to the present Earl of Clarendon for the use of the private Clarendon papers, which include invaluable letters of Palmerston and Russell; to the late Lord Gladstone for access to the private Gladstone papers; and to Sir Victor Wellesley for the use of the private Wellesley papers, which contain the correspondence of the second Earl Cowley with Russell and Clarendon.

In some cases the most vivid account of the attitude of British Foreign Secretaries has been found in the reports of the ambassadors of Austria-Hungary in the Vienna archives, from which a number of documents are here quoted. They wish to record their appreciation of the generous help given to them by the distinguished archivists, Dr Ludwig Bittner and Dr Lothar Gross in this connexion.

Material has of course often been taken from printed collections of documents. The Editors wish, in particular, to acknowledge the permission granted to them to reprint documents from the *Life of Stratford Canning* by S. Lane Poole (published by Longmans, Green & Co.), Dr G. P. Gooch's *Later Correspondence of Lord John Russell* (Longmans, Green & Co.), Lord Morley's *Life of Gladstone* (Macmillan & Co.), Lady Gwendolen Cecil's *Life of Robert Marquess of Salisbury* (by permission of Lady Gwendolen Cecil and Hodder and Stoughton), and G. E. Buckle, *The Letters of Queen Victoria* (John Murray).

They wish to thank further Miss A. Ramm, M.A., for her help in the preparation of the manuscript for press.

I. PITT, 1783–1801, 1805–6

1. PITT AND GRENVILLE. THE CASE AGAINST THE FRENCH REVOLUTION,
1792–3

[The name and fame of the younger Pitt are associated with great administrative and legislative reforms. He is acclaimed as the Peace Minister *par excellence*, and he is sometimes held to have ruined his reputation by embarking on a war with the French Revolution.

The loftiness of his character was indeed maintained and the title of the "Pilot that weathered the storm" is deemed to have been deserved. But the comparative failure of his war-administration has blinded historians to the merits of his foreign policy. That policy had been formulated before the storm of the revolution broke, and it continued to be followed by British statesmen after its force had abated.

That Pitt had a foreign policy at all was the discovery of Oscar Browning. All subsequent historians have admitted that it was characterized by boldness and vigour. Coming to power after the humiliations and disasters of the War of American Independence, Pitt made his influence felt at once. And his influence was personal and direct, for his first Foreign Secretary was a mere clerk in his hands. His aim was undoubtedly to restore British prestige in Europe and overseas, and he was not afraid of novelty. A commercial treaty was negotiated with France, to shew that our enmity with her was not eternal. Yet in 1788 he had taken steps along with Prussia to defeat French influence in Holland. In 1790 he successfully braved the wrath of France—and deterred her from backing up Spain in her claims to the Western shore of Canada. Pitt followed up these striking successes by mediating between Turkey on the one side and Russia and Austria on the other. He was at first successful but finally met defeat over the Oczakov incident (1791). He had intended to stop the further advance of Russia in the Black Sea, but he was threatened with defeat in Parliament. The British public had no objection to Russia's advancing along the Western shores of the Black Sea, or to leaving the Turk to his fate. So Pitt gave way. It was his first defeat in diplomacy and it was inflicted by the British public.

This incident ended the political career of the Duke of Leeds, and brought Lord Grenville on the scene as Foreign Secretary. He came to power at a crisis, for the French Revolution, after almost destroying the old monarchy, was threatening all other powers in Europe. Grenville was an aristocrat. He was cold, able, haughty, unbending. He was likely, in fact, to encourage Pitt in resisting, and not in conciliating, the new revolutionary movement in France. The fact was most unfortunate, for the wild doctrines of the revolutionaries were calculated, in any case, to alarm Pitt. His strong turn of abstract thought was opposed to their theories of overturning the existing order and of releasing all peoples from their obedience to Kings. His practical mind deplored their financial and legislative excesses. None the less, Pitt seems to have shewn all the moderation that he dared. He held aloof from the Kings of the Continent when they went to war with France in 1792. He reduced our armed forces, spoke optimistically of prospects of peace in his Budget speech of February 1792, and viewed with relative unconcern the deposition of Louis XVI in August. He kept up unofficial connexion with the Republic which ensued, and made a formal statement that no change in neutrality was intended.

But the invasion of Belgium by the revolutionaries, the threat to Holland,* and the French victory over the Austrians at Jemappes (6 November 1792) all tended to convert Pitt to the view that the French Revolution must be resisted by arms. The French decree of 19 November appealed to subjects to rise against their rulers, in obedience to the law of nature. When France added the declaration that she intended to open the Scheldt contrary to existing treaties, and to annex Savoy (28 November) in defiance of her pledge of no annexation, she completed Pitt's conversion.† The execution of Louis XVI on 21 January 1793 proved to be the decisive occasion, but not the real cause of rupture. Chauvelin had originally been accredited to England as ambassador by Louis XVI. His functions had been suspended on the deposition of the King on 10 August and on the proclamation of a republic, but he remained in England and held unofficial intercourse with the British Government. When, however, the King himself was dead, Chauvelin's functions ceased to exist. Grenville therefore wrote to him on 24 January, handing him his passports and dismissing him from the country. Of course the technical reason for this step was much strengthened by the fact that the French King's execution offered Pitt an unrivalled opportunity for mobilizing British public opinion against a regicide republic.

The document that follows was written when the breach

---

* The word "Holland" is used as consecrated by popular usage, though "the Netherlands" is technically the correct term.

† On 13 November 1792 Grenville gave the Dutch Government a formal pledge to defend them if attacked, and his private letter of 26 November suggests that he regarded France as forcing hostilities on England (v. documents published by J. Holland Rose, E[nglish] H[istorical] R[eview], [1912], 117–23, 324–30. Pitt had come to the same decision early in December.

between England and France was considered by both Pitt and Grenville to be already inevitable. It sums up the case against France in powerful sentences, and indicates the three causes of dispute. There is first the decree of the French Republic of 19 November 1792 which invites all peoples to revolt against their Kings, thereby inciting them to sedition and meddling in their internal affairs. The second is the attempt of the French Republic to force Holland to throw open the Scheldt to navigation. She proposed to overthrow an old treaty-right in the name of the natural right of Belgium to have access to the sea. The third point is a demand that France shall renounce her plans of "aggression and aggrandisement", her attack on the whole system of Europe, as much on treaty-rights as on settled institutions.

The dispatch here reproduced clearly anticipated a refusal, and may be taken as the British case against the French Revolution. Most people have seen in its sentences the hand of Pitt rather than of Grenville. Other letters, however, written by Grenville on about the same date* shew very similar sentiments and a distinct desire to force a crisis while public opinion was favourable. There can be no doubt that the dispatch embraces Grenville's view of the differences between British and French principles.]

Document 1. *The case against the French Revolution and the Dispatch of* 31 *December* 1792†

I have received, Sir, from you a note [of 27th of December], in which, styling yourself minister plenipotentiary of France, you communicate to me, as the king's secretary of state, the instructions which you state to have yourself received from the executive council of the French republic. You are not ignorant, that since the unhappy events of the 10th of August, the king has thought proper to suspend all official communication with France. You are yourself no otherwise accredited to the king, than in the name of his most christian majesty. The proposition of receiving a minister accredited by any other authority or power in France, would be a new question, which, whenever it should occur, the king would have the right to decide according to the interests of his subjects, his own

* *V. Historical MSS. Commission*, Dropmore MSS. of J. B. Fortescue, II, [1894], 359–62.

† Lord Grenville to M. F. Chauvelin, Whitehall, 31 December 1792. This is from the *Annual Register*, 1793, "Chronicle, State Papers...", 116–19. The original dispatch was in French of which the draft is in [Public Record Office], F[oreign] O[ffice], 27/40. But, as this was doubtless written in English first, the above is probably the true version and corresponds exactly with the French.

dignity, and the regard which he owes to his allies, and to the general system of Europe. I am therefore to inform you, sir, in express and formal terms, that I acknowledge you in no other public character than that of minister from his most christian majesty, and that consequently you cannot be admitted to treat with the king's ministers in the quality, and under the form stated in your note.

But observing that you have entered into explanations of some of the circumstances which have given to England such strong grounds of uneasiness and jealousy, and that you speak of these explanations, as being of a nature to bring our two countries nearer, I have been unwilling to convey to you the notification stated above, without at the same time explaining myself clearly and distinctly on the subject of what you have communicated to me, though under a form which is neither regular nor official.

Your explanations are confined to three points:

The first is that of the decree of the national convention of the 19th of November, in the expressions of which all England saw the formal declaration of a design to extend universally the new principles of government adopted in France, and to encourage disorder and revolt in all countries, even in those which are neutral. If this interpretation, which you represent as injurious to the convention, could admit of any doubt, it is but too well justified by the conduct of the convention itself.* And the application of these principles to the king's dominions has been shewn unequivocally, by the public reception given to the promoters of sedition in this country, and by the speeches made to them precisely at the time of this decree, and since on several different occasions.†

* The President of the Convention at the session of 21 November 1792 had denounced Kings in general and England in particular and interpreted the decree as follows: "She [France] has just declared, by the organ of her representatives, that she will make common cause with all peoples resolved to throw off the yoke and obey only themselves." P. J. B. Buchez et P. C. Roux, *Histoire Parlementaire de la Revolution française*, Paris [1835], xx, 378.

† Chauvelin had agreed that the French invitation to peoples to rise against their sovereigns did not apply to neutral states, but only "to those people who, after having acquired their liberty by conquest, may have demanded the fraternity, the assistance of the republic, by the solemn and unequivocal expression of the general will".

Yet, notwithstanding all these proofs, supported by other circumstances which are but too notorious, it would have been with pleasure that we should have seen here such explanations, and such a conduct, as would have satisfied the dignity and honour of England, with respect to what has already passed, and would have offered a sufficient security in future for the maintenance of that respect towards the rights, the government, and the tranquillity of neutral powers, which they have on every account the right to expect.

Neither this satisfaction, nor this security, is found in the terms of an explanation which still declares to the promoters of sedition in every country, what are the cases in which they may count beforehand on the support and succour of France; and which reserves to that country the right of mixing herself in our internal affairs whenever she shall judge it proper, and on principles incompatible with the political institutions of all the countries of Europe. No one can avoid perceiving how much a declaration like this is calculated to encourage disorder and revolt in every country. No one can be ignorant how contrary it is to the respect which is reciprocally due from independent nations, nor how repugnant to those principles which the king has followed, on his part, by abstaining at all times from any interference whatever in the internal affairs of France. And this contrast is alone sufficient to shew, not only that England cannot consider such an explanation as satisfactory, but that she must look upon it as a fresh avowal of those dispositions which she sees with so just an uneasiness and jealousy.

I proceed to the two other points of your explanation, which concern the general dispositions of France with regard to the allies of Great Britain, and the conduct of the convention and its officers relative to the Scheldt. The declaration which you there make, "that France will not attack Holland so long as that power shall observe an exact neutrality", is conceived nearly in the same terms with that which you was [sic] charged to make in the name of his most christian majesty in the month of June last. Since that first declaration was made, an officer, stating himself to be employed in the service of France, has openly violated both the territory and the neutrality of the republic, in going up the Scheldt to attack the capital of Antwerp, notwithstanding the determination of the government not to grant this passage, and the formal protest by which they opposed it. Since the same declaration was made, the convention has thought itself authorized to annul the rights of the republic, exercised within the limits of its own territory, and enjoyed by virtue of the same treaties by which her independence is secured. And at the very moment when, under the name of an amicable explanation, you renew to me in the same terms the promise of respecting the independence and the rights of England and her allies, you announce to me, that those in whose name you speak intend to maintain these open and injurious aggressions.

It is not, certainly, on such a declaration as this, that any reliance can be placed for the continuance of public tranquillity.

But I am unwilling to leave, without a more particular reply, what you say on the subject of the Scheldt. If it were true that this question is in itself of little importance, this would only serve to prove more clearly, that it was brought forward only for the purpose of insulting the allies of England, by the infraction of their neutrality, and by the violation of their rights, which the faith of treaties obliges us to maintain. But you cannot be ignorant, that here the utmost importance is attached to those principles which France wishes to establish by this proceeding, and to those consequences which would naturally result from them; and that not only those principles, and those consequences will never be admitted by England, but that she is, and ever will be, ready to oppose them with all her force.

France can have no right to annul the stipulations relative to the Scheldt, unless she have also the right to set aside equally all the other treaties between all the powers of Europe, and all the other rights of England, or of her allies. She can even have no pretence to interfere in the question of opening the Scheldt, unless she were the sovereign of the Low Countries, or had the right to dictate laws to all Europe.*

England will never consent that France shall arrogate the power of annulling at her pleasure, and under the pretence of a pretended natural right, of which she makes herself the only judge, the political system of Europe, established by solemn treaties, and guaranteed by the consent of all the powers. This Government, adhering to the maxims which it has followed for more than a century, will also never see with indifference that France shall make herself, either directly or indirectly, sovereign of the Low Countries, or general arbitress of the rights and liberties of Europe. If France is really desirous of maintaining friendship and peace with England, she must shew herself disposed to renounce her views of aggression and aggrandisement, and to confine herself within her own territory, without insulting other governments, without disturbing their tranquillity, without violating their rights.†

With respect to that character of ill-will which is endeavoured to be found in the conduct of England towards France, I cannot discuss it, because you speak of it in general terms only, without alledging a single fact. All Europe has seen the justice and the generosity which have characterised the conduct of the king: his majesty has always been desirous of peace: he desires it still, but such as may be real, and solid, and consistent with the interests and dignity of his own dominions, and with the general security of Europe.

On the rest of your paper I say nothing.—As to what relates to me and to my colleagues, the king's ministers owe to his majesty the account of their conduct; and I have no answer to give you on this subject, any more than on that of the appeal which you propose to make to the English nation. This nation,

---

* In his speech on overtures of peace, 3 February 1800, Pitt said: "This [the Scheldt] claim we discussed not so much on account of its immediate importance (though it was important both in a maritime and commercial view) as on account of the general principle on which it was founded."

† This seems to be a reference to the French annexation of Savoy, in deference to the expressed wish of its inhabitants. This had been decided by the French Convention of 28 November 1792 despite the fact that in May of that year the French Government had declared against all annexations or conquests (v. also *supra*, p. 2 and n.).

according to that constitution by which its liberty and its prosperity are secured, and which it will always be able to defend against every attack, direct or indirect, will never have with foreign powers connexion or correspondence, except through the organ of its king; of a king whom it loves and reveres, and who has never.for an instant separated his rights, his interests, and his happiness, from the rights, the interests, and the happiness of his people.

[The reply of Le Brun, the Foreign Minister of the French Republic, to Grenville was delivered on 7 January 1793. He maintained that the French decree of 19 November did not authorize sedition in a country. It merely said that France would go to the aid of a nation "in which the general will, clearly and unequivocally expressed, should call the French nation to its assistance and fraternity". He pointed out that the Dutch were not seditious when they revolted against Spain, and that France and England had aided them. As regards the French decrees for opening the Scheldt, Le Brun argued that its closing had been concluded "by treaty without consent of the Belgians" who "now reenter into the rights which the house of Austria had taken away from them". He suggested that England and Holland should have "a direct negotiation with Belgia [sic]. If the Belgians, by any motive whatsoever, consent to deprive themselves of the navigation of the Scheldt, France will not oppose it. She will know how to respect their independence even in their errors." Grenville seems to have been affected by certain discussions in the French legislature before he gave his answer. On 12 January 1793, a report of Brissot, on behalf of the Committee of Diplomacy and Defence, was presented to the French Convention. It declared its conviction that all means had been exhausted for preserving peace with England and recommended "the most vigorous measures to repel the aggression of the Court of St James". The same day the Convention decided to ask for various explanations, among others, of the meaning of British armaments. Grenville answered (18 January) that the explanation was "insufficient". On the 21st the news of the execution of King Louis XVI was known in England, and, in consequence of this event, Chauvelin was dismissed and handed his passports three days later. His departure was the prelude for a war lasting, with brief interruptions, for over twenty years.]

2. PITT ON THE DELIVERANCE AND SECURITY OF EUROPE

[It is possible to shew that Pitt was thinking of the security of Europe and of the future even in the crisis of 1792–3. As Russia had begun an overture for intervention in France, Grenville instructed his representative, in reply, to distinguish carefully between two kinds of intervention.* There is first "an interference for the purpose of establishing any form of Gov[ernment] in France". And there is also "a concert between other Gov[ernmen]ts to provide for their own security at a time when political interests are endangered both by the intrigues of France in the interior of other countries, and by their views of conquest and aggrandisement". The former policy was favoured by despotic monarchies like Russia, the latter by a parliamentary state like England. The British proposal was in fact to get France to abandon her conquests, withdraw within her borders, and offer to abandon seditious propaganda in the internal affairs of other states. If the proposal was rejected by France Pitt proposed to use a form of pressure by creating a European Concert or League. In fact we have here, in a very rudimentary form, a sketch of the future settlement of Vienna during the years 1814–15.†

Pitt's ideas were modified, but not essentially changed, after his war on the French Revolution began. His attitude during the years that followed was not wholly consistent, for he varied between demands for "security" and a desire to make peace with the new military republic.‡ During his second ministry and towards the end of his life, he formulated views as to the future settlement of Europe not unlike those just quoted. They are of peculiar interest, for they formed his legacy to Castlereagh. What the master first sketched in 1792 and formulated in 1805, the pupil put into practice at the Congress of Vienna in 1815.

Pitt's ideas were marked by no special tenderness to nationality. He was perhaps led to suspect the principle because Tsar Alexander proposed to use it as an excuse for obtaining the whole Kingdom of Poland for himself. Pitt was, therefore, extremely cautious in his reply to Russia on 19 January 1805. But he adds specific proposals here to the general principle of concert formulated in 1792. He was determined to recover from France Holland,

* Lord Grenville to Charles Whitworth, No. 13, of 29 December 1792. This is of great importance, though too long to be reproduced here. B[ritish] M[useum] Add[itional] MSS. 34,446, ff. 292–5.

† These proposals, in more rhetorical form, are repeated in a declaration by Lord Grenville of 12 October 1793 sent to Charles Whitworth at St Petersburgh, *F.O.* 65/25.

‡ *V.* J. Holland Rose, *Napoleonic Studies*, [1906], Chap. II, Pitt's plans for the settlement of Europe.

Belgium and the left bank of the Rhine. He proposed to make a strong independent Holland by adding to it Flanders from Antwerp to Maestricht. The remainder of Flanders, with Luxemburg and Juliers and other territory adjacent between the Meuse and the Moselle, he proposed to give to Prussia.* In this way Holland would be strengthened, and Prussia engaged against France. As regards Italy Pitt was equally opportunistic. He proposed to strengthen the Kingdom of Piedmont with Genoa, to link Milan south-west of the Adda with Parma and with Piacenza. He meant to make Tuscany "virtually Austrian", and to assign Austria all Lombardy and Venetia in return for relinquishing Belgium. Thus the Alps were protected against France by an enlarged Piedmont and an interested great Power (Austria), while on the Rhine and on the Flemish barrier an enlarged Holland and a new great Power (Prussia) stood as sentries. Here we have purely "balance of power" ideas, which were largely applied at the settlement of Vienna. But by suggesting a special guarantee treaty between Russia and England to carry these ideas into effect, Pitt broke new ground and foreshadowed a guarantee system and sanctions such as Castlereagh subsequently developed at Vienna.†]

Document 2. *Pitt's Memorandum on the Deliverance and Security of Europe*, 19 *January* 1805‡

The Result of the Communications which have been made by Prince Czartoriski to His Majesty's Ambassador at St Petersburgh, and of the confidential explanations which have been received from your Excellency, has been laid before His Majesty; and His Majesty has seen with inexpressible Satisfaction, the wise, dignified and generous policy, which The Emperor of Russia is disposed to adopt under the present calamitous Situation of Europe. His Majesty is also happy to perceive, that the views and Sentiments of the Emperor respecting the means of effecting the deliverance of Europe, and providing for its future Tranquillity and Safety, correspond so entirely with His Own. He is therefore desirous of entering into the most explicit and unreserved explanations on every

---

* Castlereagh alludes to this on 1 October 1814, as an idea Pitt was trying to carry out, *v. infra*, p. 25 and n.

† For Castlereagh, *v. infra*, pp. 28–9 *sqq.*

‡ *F.O.* 65/60. First printed *in toto* in C. K. Webster, *British Diplomacy (1813–15)*, [1921], App. I. The passages omitted in the version published by the British Government, 8 May 1815, are given in double square brackets⟦...⟧. Cp. *A & P.*, [1814–15], XIII, 261–6.

point connected with this great object, and of forming the closest Union of Councils and Concert of Measures with His Imperial Majesty, in order, by their joint influence and exertions, to insure the cooperation and assistance of other Powers of the Continent, on a Scale adequate to the Magnitude and importance of an Undertaking, on the success of which the future Safety of Europe must depend.

For this purpose the first Step must be, to fix as precisely as possible, the distinct objects to which such a Concert is to be directed.

These, according to the explanation given of the Sentiments of the Emperor, in which His Majesty entirely concurs, appear to be three:

1st To rescue from the Dominion of France those Countries which it has subjugated since the beginning of the Revolution, and to reduce France within its former limits, as they stood before that time.—

2ndly To make such an arrangement with respect to the territories recovered from France, as may provide for their Security and Happiness, and may at the same time constitute a more effectual barrier in future against Encroachments on the part of France.—

3rdly To form, at the Restoration of Peace, a general Agreement and Guarantee for the mutual protection and Security of different Powers, and for reestablishing a general System of Public Law in Europe.—

The first and second Objects are stated generally, and in their broadest Extent; but neither of them can be properly considered in detail, without reference to the nature and Extent of the means by which they may be accomplished. The first is certainly that to which, without any Modification or Exception, His Majesty's wishes, as well as those of the Emperor, would be preferably directed, and nothing short of it, can *completely** satisfy the views which both Sovereigns form for the Deliverance and Security of Europe.—Should it be possible to unite in Concert with Great Britain and Russia, the two other great Military Powers of the Continent, there

* Underlined in original.

seems little doubt that such an union of Force would enable
them to accomplish all that is proposed.—But if (as there is
too much reason to imagine may be the case) it should be
found impossible to engage Prussia in the Confederacy, it may
be doubted whether such Operations could be carried on in
all the Quarters of Europe as would be necessary for the
success of the whole of this Project. [The chief points however to which His Majesty considers this doubt as applicable,
relate to the question of the entire Recovery of the Netherlands
and the Countries occupied by France on the left Bank of the
Rhine.—His Majesty considers it essential, even on this Supposition to include nothing less than the Evacuation of the
North of Germany and of Italy, the Re-establishment of the
Independence of the United Provinces, and of Switzerland,
the Restoration of the Dominions of the King of Sardinia,
and Security of Naples; But, on the side of the Netherlands,
it might perhaps be more prudent in this case to confine the
views of the Allies to obtaining some moderate acquisition for
the United Provinces, calculated (according to the Principle
specified under the second Head) to form an additional
Barrier for that Country. His Majesty, however, by no means
intends to imply, if very Brilliant and decisive Success should
be obtained, and the Power of France broken and overcome
by operations in other Quarters, the allies might not, in such
a case, extend their views to the Recovery of the whole or the
greater part of these Territories, but as, in the first instance,
it does not appear probable that they can be re-conquered by
the operations of the War without the aid of Prussia, His
Majesty is inclined to think that this object ought in any
Treaty of Concert, to be described in such Terms as would
admit of the Modifications here stated.—]

The Second Point of itself involves in it many important
Considerations. The Views and Sentiments by which His
Majesty and The Emperor of Russia are equally animated in
endeavouring to establish this Concert, are pure and disinterested. [The insular Situation and extensive ressources
of Great Britain, aided by its military Exertions and Naval
Superiority; and the immense power, the established Conti-

nental Ascendency and remote distance of Russia, already give to the Territories of the two Sovereigns a Security against the Attacks of France,—even after all her acquisitions of Influence, power, and Dominion,—which cannot be the lot of any other Country.—They have therefore no Separate Objects of Their own in the Arrangements which are in question—no personal interest to consult in this Concert but that which grows out of the general interest and Security of Europe, and is inseparably connected with it.]]

Their first View therefore with respect to any of the Countries which may be recovered from France, must be to restore, as far as possible, their ancient Rights, and provide for the Internal happiness of their Inhabitants; but in looking at this Object, they must not lose sight of the general Security of Europe, on which even that Separate object must principally depend.

Pursuant to this principle, there can be no question that, whenever any of these Countries are capable of being restored to their former independence, and of being placed in a Situation in which they can protect it, such an arrangement must be most congenial to the Policy and the Feelings on which this System is founded.—But there will be found to be other Countries among those now under the Dominion of France, to which these Considerations cannot apply,—where either the ancient Relations of the Country are so completely destroyed that they cannot be restored, or where independence would be merely nominal and alike inconsistent with the Security for the Country itself or for Europe.—Happily the larger number is of the first description. Should the Arms of the Allies be successful to the full extent of expelling France from all the Dominions she has acquired since the Revolution, it would certainly be the first Object as has already been stated to reestablish the Republics of the United Provinces and Switzerland, the Territories of the King of Sardinia, Tuscany, Modena (under the protection of Austria) and Naples. But the Territories of Genoa, of the Italian Republic, including the three Legations, Parma and Placentia, and on the other Side of Europe, the Austrian Netherlands and the

States which have been detached from the German Empire on the left Bank of the Rhine, evidently belong to the Second Class. With respect to the Territories enumerated in Italy, Experience has shown how little disposition existed in some, and how little means in any, to resist the Aggression or Influence of France.—The King of Spain was certainly too much a Party to the System of which so large a part of Europe has been a victim, to entitle the former interests of His Family in Italy to any Consideration; nor does the past Conduct of Genoa, or any of the other States give them any claim, either of Justice or Liberality.—It is also obvious that these Separate Petty Sovereignties would never again have any solid existence in themselves, and would only serve to weaken and impair the force which ought to be, as much as possible, concentrated in the hands of the chief Powers of Italy.—

It is needless to dwell particularly on the state of the Netherlands.—Events have put out of the question the Restoration of them to the House of Austria—they are therefore necessarily open to new Arrangements, and evidently can never exist Separate and independent. Nearly the same considerations apply to the Ecclesiastical Electorates, and the other Territories on the left Bank of the Rhine, after their being once detached from the Empire, and the former possessors of them indemnified.—There appears therefore to be no possible objection, on the strictest Principles of Justice and Public Morality, to making such a Disposition with respect to any of these Territories as may be most conducive to the general Interests; and there is evidently no other mode of accomplishing the great and beneficent object of re-establishing (after so much misery and bloodshed) the Safety and Repose of Europe on a solid and permanent basis.—It is fortunate too that such a plan of arrangements as is in itself essential to the End proposed, is also likely to contribute, in the greatest degree, to secure the means by which that great end can best be promoted.—

It is evidently of the utmost importance, if not absolutely indispensable for this purpose, to secure the vigorous and effectual co-operation both of Austria and Prussia; but there is little reason to hope, that either of these Powers, and especially Prussia, will be brought to embark in the common Cause, without the prospect of obtaining some important acquisition to compensate for Its exertions. On the grounds which have been already stated, His Majesty conceives that nothing could so much contribute to the general Security as giving to Austria fresh means of resisting the views of France on the Side of Italy, and placing Prussia in a similar Situation with respect to the Low Countries; and the relative Situations of the two Powers would naturally make those the quarters to which their views would respectively be directed.—

In Italy, sound Policy would require that the Power and Influence of the King of Sardinia should be augmented, and that Austria should be replaced in a Situation which may enable her to afford an immediate and effectual Support to His Dominions in case of their being attacked. His Majesty sees with Satisfaction, from the Secret and Confidential communications recently received through Your Excellency, that the Views of the Court of Vienna are perfectly conformable to this general principle, and that the extension at which She aims might not only safely be admitted, but might even be increased, with advantage to the general Interest.—In other respects His Majesty entirely concurs in the outline of the Arrangement which He understands The Emperor of Russia to be desirous of seeing effected in this Quarter.—His Majesty considers it as absolutely necessary for the general Security, that Italy should be completely rescued both from the Occupation and Influence of France, and that no Powers should be left within it, who are not likely to enter into a general system of Defence for maintaining its Independence.—For this purpose it is essential that the Countries now composing what is called the Italian Republic, should be transferred to other Powers. In distributing these Territories, an Increase of Wealth and Power should undoubtedly be given to The King of Sardinia, and it seems material that His Possessions, as well as the Duchy of Tuscany (which it is proposed to restore to The Grand Duke) should be brought into immediate contact, or ready Communication with those of Austria. On

this Principle [the Part of the Milanese to the South West
of the Adda, and] the whole of the Territories which now
compose the Ligurian Republic, [as well as, perhaps Parma
and Placentia,] might, it is conceived, be annexed to Piedmont. [The three Legations might in His Majesty's opinion,
be annexed to the Territories of Austria, and the addition
which may be made to the acquisitions proposed for that
Power, with advantage to the common Cause.—And the
Duchy of Modena, placed as it would be between the new
Acquisitions of Sardinia, and the Duchy of Tuscany (which
may be considered under this arrangement as virtually
Austrian) might safely be restored to its former Possessor.

The observations which have been stated respecting the
Situation of Sardinia in Italy, seem, in a great Measure, to
apply to that of Holland and Prussia, in relation to the Low
Countries; with this difference however, that the Piedmontese
Dominions, affording in themselves considerable means of
defence, they may be perhaps sufficiently Secure in the
possession of The King of Sardinia, supported by Austria;
whereas the Netherlands being more open and exposed seem
scarce capable of being secured unless by annexing a considerable part of them to Prussia, and placing Holland in a
Second line of defence. With this view (supposing France to
be reduced within its ancient Limits) it might be proposed
to annex to the United Provinces, as an additional Barrier,
the part of Flanders lying within a military line to be drawn
from Antwerp to the Meuse at Maestricht, and the remainder
of the Netherlands, together with the Duchies of Luxembourg
and Juliers, and the other Territories between the Meuse and
the Moselle, to Prussia.—

His Majesty indeed fells so strongly the importance both
of augmenting the Inducements to Prussia to take part, and
of rendering it a powerful and effectual Barrier for the
Defence, not only of Holland but of the North of Germany
against France, that He should even consider it as adviseable
in addition to what has been already proposed, to put into
Possession of that Power the Territories which may be recovered from France on the left Bank of the Rhine, Eastward

of the Moselle—and His Majesty entertains a strong conviction that this arrangement (if it not in other respects be
thought liable to insuperable Objections) would be infinitely
more effectual for the protection of the North of Europe, than
any other that can be devised.

His Majesty is however aware, that great difficulties may
arise in regulating the proportionate Acquisitions of Austria
and Prussia, in such a way as to prevent their being the source
of mutual jealousy—and this consideration it is which,
amongst others, has operated as a great additional Inducement
of acquisition for Austria on the side of Italy.

He thinks it also important to remark, that the Acquisition
to be held out to Prussia ought not to be measured merely by
what would be in itself desirable, but by the consideration of
what may be necessary to outweigh the Temptations which
France will not fail to offer to that Power to secure its co-
operation. These will probably be on an extensive Scale, and
in a quarter much more calculated to produce effects injurious
to the Interests of Austria and of Russia herself—While, on
the other hand, if the ambition of Prussia can be gratified in
the Manner proposed at the Expense of France, it will be
diverted from the views which it will otherwise form towards
the North, the Accomplishment of which would tend to
increase, to an alarming degree, its Influence both in Germany, and over the secondary Powers of the Baltic.—But if,
notwithstanding these powerful Considerations, it should still
be thought by His Imperial Majesty that the Augmentation
here proposed to the Territories of Prussia is greater than
ought to be admitted, His Majesty will, (though not without
Reluctance) concur in any other arrangement that may be
thought preferable, by which a larger Portion of the Netherlands may be allotted to the United Provinces, and the
Acquisitions of Prussia confined within narrower Limits; but
He trusts that, at any rate, it will not be necessary to reduce
them to any thing less than the Territories on the left Bank
of the Rhine between the Meuse and the Moselle, and it will,
in this case, require much consideration, in what hands the
Territories on the left Bank of the Rhine, East of the Moselle

can best be placed or whether they may be safely left in the
possession of France.—

In the event of Prussia not being prevailed upon to enter
into the concert, I have already stated His Majesty's Conviction, that the Views of the Allies on this Side of Europe
must be more limited; and in that case probably nothing
more can be expected than to obtain the complete evacuation
of the North of Germany, and the Re-establishment of the
Independence of Holland, together with the Barrier here
stated within the Line drawn from Antwerp to Maestricht,
leaving the other Territories on the left of the Rhine in the
possession of France.]...

[Details, etc. of the plan of campaign and the amount of
force necessary to obtain the objects stated above.]

Supposing the Efforts of the Allies to have been completely
successful, and the two objects already discussed to have been
fully obtained, His Majesty would nevertheless consider this
Salutary Work as still imperfect, if the Restoration of Peace
were not accompanied by the most effectual measures for
giving Solidity and Permanence to the System which shall
thus have been established. Much will undoubtedly be
effected for the future Repose of Europe by these Territorial
Arrangements, which will furnish a more effectual Barrier
than has before existed against the Ambition of France. But
in order to render this Security as complete as possible, it
seems necessary, at the period of a general Pacification, to
form a Treaty to which all the principal Powers of Europe
should be Parties, by which their respective Rights and
Possessions, as they then have been established, shall be fixed
and recognized, and they should all bind themselves mutually
to protect and support each other, against any attempt to
infringe them—It should re-establish a general and comprehensive system of Public Law in Europe, and provide, as far
as possible, for repressing future attempts to disturb the general
Tranquillity, and above all, for restraining any projects of
Aggrandizement and Ambition similar to those which have
produced all the Calamities inflicted on Europe since the
disastrous æra of the French Revolution. [This Treaty

should be put under the Special Guarantee of Great Britain and Russia, and the Two Powers should, by a separate engagement, bind themselves to each other jointly to take an active Part in preventing its being infringed. Such a Treaty might also be accompanied by more particular and specific Provisions, by which the several Powers of Italy might be united in a closer Alliance for their own immediate Defence. How far any similar system could be adopted for giving additional Security for the Germanic Body, is well deserving of Consideration. Their present State is certainly very unsatisfactory, with a view either to their own immediate interests, or to the Safety of Europe. At the same time it appears to His Majesty very doubtful whether, from local circumstances, and other causes, it would ever be possible to consolidate them into any effectual System. Should this be found to be the case, the evils to be apprehended from their weak and exposed State might (as far as relates to the danger from France) perhaps be remedied, by adopting a system (but on a larger Scale) similar to that formerly established by the Barrier Treaty for the Protection of the Netherlands. It might not be difficult to settle some general plan for maintaining, at the joint expense of the different Powers of the Empire, Fortresses of sufficient Strength, and properly garrisoned, along the course of the Rhine from Basle to Ehrenbreitstein, commanding the principal approaches from France to the most exposed parts of Germany; and the Military Custody of these Fortresses (without infringing in other respects on the Territorial Rights of the Power in whose Dominions they might be placed) might be confided to the two great Powers of Germany, according to their respective means of occupying them.

It seems also desirable, in order to give further Security to the United Provinces (under any of the Arrangements which have already been discussed) that they should be called upon to enter into an Engagement jointly with Great Britain and Russia to maintain, at all times, their Army on such a Footing as may be thought necessary to provide for their Defence against sudden Attack. In addition to this Stipulation His Majesty in his Electoral Capacity, might perhaps be induced to keep a considerable Force (in consequence of arrangements with the British Government) ready to be employed on the first Alarm for the Defence of the United Provinces; and His Majesty would also be ready to enter into a Concert with other Powers for defraying the Expense of maintaining at all times an adequate and effective Garrison to consist of German Troops for garrisoning any Fortresses now existing, or here-after to be established, on whatever may be the line ultimately fixed as the Dutch Frontier.

Having thus stated what more immediately relates to the specific objects of the Concert, and to the means to be employed to give it effect, there still remains one great and important Question for Consideration, and that is how far, either now or hereafter, the views of the Allies ought to be directed towards the Re-Establishment of Monarchy in France, and the Restoration of the Bourbon Family on the Throne. His Majesty agrees entirely with The Emperor of Russia in thinking, that such a Settlement is in itself highly desirable for the future both of France and Europe, and that no fair occasion ought to be neglected of promoting it. But He at the same time thinks, that it ought to be considered only a secondary object in the Concert now to be established, and one which could in no case justify the prolongation of the War, if a Peace could be obtained on the Principles which have been stated. It is one with a view to which no active or decided measures can be taken, unless a series of great and signal Successes shall previously have been obtained by the Allies, and a strong and prevailing disposition for the return of their Monarch, shall then manifest itself in the Interior of France. In the meantime, in order to afford every reasonable chance for the attainment of this object, His Majesty entirely agrees with The Emperor of Russia, that it is highly important that in the conduct of the War, and in the public Declarations and Language of the Allied Courts, the greatest care should be taken to prevent any apprehension in the Minds of any part of the French Nation, of any design either to dictate to them by Force any particular Form of Government, or to attempt to dismember the antient Territories of France.

Such are the Sentiments and Observations which His Majesty is desirous of offering to the Consideration of The Emperor on the great Outlines of the important system which They are equally anxious to establish.

His Majesty will receive, with the utmost attention and satisfaction, every fresh Communication of the opinion of His Imperial Majesty on all the Details connected with so extensive a subject. In the meanwhile, from an anxiety to lose no time in laying the foundation of this great Work, His Majesty has directed a Project to be prepared of a Provisional Treaty, conformable to the Sentiments which appear to be entertained both by the Emperor and himself; and which, if it should meet with His Imperial Majesty's concurrence, He is ready immediately to conclude.]

II. CANNING, 1807–9

3. CANNING AND NATIONALITY, 1807–9

(a) SPAIN

["Napoleon", Pitt is related to have said, "would have met with a check whenever he encountered national resistance", and he declared that Spain was the place for it, and that then England would intervene. This was declared to be one of Pitt's latest utterances. If authentic, it might deserve the eulogium of Acton as "the most astounding and profound prediction in all political history".* But the conversation could not have taken place under the circumstances described. It was reported by a Spaniard, whose memory failed him as to both dates and facts. There are further difficulties. That the policy of favouring nationality in order to conquer Napoleon formed no part of Pitt's programme, we know from his private letters, from his official dispatches, and from his public speeches. The man who did adopt that doctrine was Canning. He had been the special pupil of Pitt but here departed from the master's tenets. No one can examine either Pitt's memorandum of January 1805, or Castlereagh's work at Vienna in 1814, and report that they were in favour of nationality. It is hard to study the policy of Canning between 1807 and 1809 and report that he was not.

Portugal and Spain offered the first examples of nations which rose against Napoleon. In 1807 one French force entered Portugal, and towards the end of the year another one entered Spain. By military menaces and a policy of inconceivable bullying Napoleon first secured the abdication of the old Spanish Bourbon King Charles IV, and then of Ferdinand his son. Ferdinand had been proclaimed King in March 1808 at Madrid, but he was lured to Bayonne, where Napoleon bullied him into abdicating (6 May). The old King was then induced to hand over the succession to the Spanish Crown to Napoleon. He indicated his brother Joseph Bonaparte as his choice for King on 13 May, and it was confirmed by a deputation of ninety Spanish grandees to Bayonne (15 June). These proceedings were viewed with the utmost indignation by the Spanish people. They all hated foreigners and had no idea of supporting the candidature of a Frenchman to their throne, whatever Grandees might think. There was no national organ capable of resisting Napoleon. Spanish Kings new and old were captive

* Acton, *Lectures on Modern History*, [1906], 23, 239. It has been shewn by J. Holland Rose, *William Pitt and the Great War*, [1911], 524, etc., that the story cannot be true in the form given, and Pitt's anti-national attitude is well described in the same author's *Napoleonic Studies*, [1906], Chap. ii.

at Bayonne, the Cortes or national assembly did not exist, the French troops garrisoned Madrid. The Spaniards did not care and rose *en masse*. Local and sporadic risings burst out in the provinces, and sturdy local patriots set up juntas or provincial governments. Asturias, Galicia, Andalusia all declared war against Napoleon. The situation was a very peculiar one. Joseph Bonaparte was technically King of Spain, and Spain was technically at war with England. What then was England to do? France had encouraged people to rise against their Kings, was England to do the same? It was certainly something new for a foreign power to ignore the official organ of a state, and to enter into relations with sectional rebels or organizations within that state.

Canning faced the new and complex situation with vigour and boldness. He helped the struggling juntas of each province with money, with arms and with equipment, because they were the only governmental machinery available. But he would not recognize the provincial juntas as political entities, for he earnestly sought to promote the formation of a Spanish national assembly. He thus did everything to make possible national unity. His doctrine, as proclaimed on 15 June 1808, was revolutionary. Canning ignored Joseph Bonaparte and recognized Ferdinand as King. Spain was technically at war with England, and remained so in spite of popular revolts. Canning swept all that aside. "It will never occur to us to consider that a state of war exists [between England and Spain]....We shall proceed upon the principle, that any nation of Europe that starts up with a determination to oppose a power [France] which, whether professing insidious peace or declaring open war, is the common enemy of all nations, whatever may be the existing political relations of that nation with Great Britain, becomes instantly our essential ally."*

This doctrine is at first sight a revolutionary one. It appeals to a people to rise against its government, and therefore interferes in its internal affairs. Now Revolutionary France had done this often enough. It was precisely for that reason that Pitt and Grenville went to war with her in 1793 (*v. supra*, pp. 1–8). Was not England then adopting the methods she had despised and denounced? Every nation is driven into different positions by war and England had already learned a good deal from France. Napoleon was trying to crush and absorb every nation in one uniform military Empire. The process by which he deposed the Spanish Kings and substituted a French one was deemed to be, in itself, a destruction of legitimate right and an interference in Spain's internal affairs. "The unprincipled seizure of the Spanish crown was an act of violence which precluded all explanation or

* 15 June 1808, *Speeches*, ed. R. Therry, [1828], II, 352. *V.* an article by J. Holland Rose, 'Canning and the Spanish Patriots', *Am[erican] Hist[orical] Rev[iew]*, XII, October 1906, 39–52.

comment, and avowed the most determined rapacity. It revealed
to the whole world that his [Napoleon's] robberies would be only
limited by his power. It proclaimed him unanswerably to be what
he was called in His Majesty's Speech from the throne, at the close
of the last session [1808]...'the common enemy of every established government and independent nation in the world'."*

It will be seen that the British Government here links "established government" to "independent nation". The second has
become as "legitimate" as the first and is united with it in resistance to Napoleon and his aggressive imperialism. Napoleon
had deposed the Spanish King against the will of the nation, and
therefore the nation was justified in revolt. It cannot be denied
that this was, in some sense, a new doctrine. It could hardly have
arisen save under pressure of war and without the obvious convenience of allying with the Spanish people. Yet the idea had a
root in the past. Canning, like Burke, understood that a nation
had rights and was embodied law. Burke had protested against
the original partition of Poland on this same ground. "The
present violent dismemberment...of Poland, without the pretence
of war or even the colour of right, is to be considered as the first
very great breach in the modern political system of Europe."†
Canning saw that it was possible to protest against a similar
breach by recognizing and defending the nation. The cause of
Spain, of the nation in revolution, was the cause of legitimacy and
stable government.

There is no doubt that Canning understood what he was doing
and there is no doubt that the measure, if not new in principle,
was new in practice. For it meant allying with a nation not with
a government, it meant breaking with a government which no
Spaniard trusted and negotiating with individuals who were
patriots. In after years Canning did not repent his decision thus
to have recognized the claims of a nation struggling for freedom.
"When the bold spirit of Spain burst forth indignant against the
oppression of Bonaparte...I discharged the glorious duty...of
recognizing without delay the rights of the Spanish nation, and of
at once adopting that gallant people into the closest amity with
England. It was indeed a stirring, a kindling occasion: and no
man who has a heart in his bosom, can think even now of the
noble enthusiasm, the animated exertions, the undaunted courage,
the unconquerable perseverance of the Spanish nation...without
feeling his blood glow and his pulses quicken with tumultuous
throbs of admiration."‡]

* *Quarterly Review*, May 1809, 447. Article by Canning and Sharon Turner.
    † Burke in 1772. *V. A. B. C.* Cobban in *Camb[ridge] Hist[orical] Journ[al]*, II,
No. 1, [1926], 43.
    ‡ *Speeches*, ed. R. Therry, v, 106-7, Speech in the House of Commons on
Negotiations relative to Spain, 28 April 1823.

(b) GERMANY

[Canning asserted this doctrine of national right as to Spain and not as to Spain alone. He was deeply shocked when British ships forcibly compelled Norway to submit to a union with Sweden in 1814. He also seems to have been much preoccupied with the Polish problem and dreamed of the restoration of Poland as a nation at the Congress of Vienna. When holding office between 1807–9 Canning could not attempt to carry out these projects, and he had no part in the Vienna settlement. During his period of office he did, however, frame his definite views for the future of another potential nation, *Germany*. They are given in the paper that follows. They shew that Canning had the idea that the future of Germany should be on federal principles, and that its domination by Prussia, a military power, would be disastrous.* He evidently wanted a system at once federal and representative. It is interesting to note that in 1814 Canning spoke of Germany as "no longer a name but a nation", and he can therefore hardly have welcomed what the Congress of Vienna did for Germany. However that may be, there can be no doubt that the document that follows is of profound importance in the development of Canning's and England's ideas on the subject of nationality.]

Document 3. *Canning on the future of Germany and the danger from Prussia*, 16 *May* 1807†

I have received private Intimations that Mr de Hardenberg immediately upon his return to Power, has been busied in framing a Plan of Pacification for Germany which is founded upon the idea of placing all the States of the North under the superintending Protection and military Authority of Prussia —and that Hanover is specially intended to be comprised in this Arrangement. Your Excellency will seek an Opportunity ...to induce Mr de Hardenberg to open himself fully...upon this subject. And if you should find occasion to believe, that he indeed entertains the extravagant idea of raising Prussia

---

* Castlereagh also had his suspicions. He describes Prussia to Wellington, 1 October 1814, as "a power peculiarly military, and consequently somewhat encroaching" and doubts the expediency of planting her on the left bank of the Rhine. C. K. Webster, *British Diplomacy (1813–15)*, [1921], 196.

† Canning to Lord G. Leveson Gower, No. 6, 16 May 1807, *F.O.* 65/69. This is the draft; the Archives copy (which would have contained the original) is missing.

to that sort of Supremacy over the other States it's neighbours, which France has assured to Herself over the remaining parts of Germany, a Supremacy which in the Case of the House of Austria, from long usage, and ancient prescriptive Veneration, had become as little oppressive in its Exercise, as unfortunately it has proved to be inefficient in its operation, but which in a new Power, and that new Power Prussia,—a Power essentially military, and depending for it's greatness as a Monarchy of the first Order, less upon the good Government of it's People, than upon the extent of its Army; Your Excellency will not hesitate to declare in the most unequivocal terms His Majesty's determination not to consent to the creation of such a predominant Power in Prussia; and the Resolution of the British Government not to suffer the Electoral Dominions of His Majesty to be incorporated in a System so little favourable to the Happiness and Interests of His Subjects.

The Experience which Hanover has had of the Exaction and Tyranny belonging to the Military Laws of Prussia, especially when enforced upon neighbouring States, has excited in that Country a Repugnance to Prussian Protection, which would make any Arrangement, founded upon that Principle, in the highest degree distasteful....

His Majesty is perfectly ready to cooperate for the Restoration of the Prussian Monarchy to all it's own Estates, and to all its former Splendour. He would even gladly consent to any arrangement (not affecting His own Dominions) which might consolidate and improve the Power and Resources of Prussia; and build Her future greatness on a more solid Foundation, than that of a military System, admirable in Theory till it was tried in action; but of which the Vice and the Weakness (long since discovered by some of the best Politicians of Europe, and perhaps not a little suspected by Prussia Herself) have been unfortunately made too manifest to all the World, at the moment when the existence of the Monarchy came to be staked upon it.

But to attempt to re-establish that same factitious Power, and to give it Strength and Support by subjecting to it, in a great degree, the other neighbouring Countries which are as much entitled as Prussia to the recovery and maintenance of their Independence, is a Project in which there would be as little of Policy as of Justice, and which on both Accounts must be laid aside as absolutely impracticable.

The Safety of the North of Germany (when the States of Germany shall have been restored) may be provided for by a federative System, in which as well as Hanover, Saxony and Hesse are entitled to bear their part, not as subordinate Vassals, but as great and independent Members, and they would probably be found willing to do so.

But they are not willing to choose for themselves a Sovereign —and still less a Sovereign whose System is known, and has been felt to be, that of considering Her Allies not so much the Sharers of Her Councils, as the Recruiters of Her Army— a Power who has proved Herself unequal to Her own defence; but who would repair that Instrument which has broken short in Her own Hand, at the Expense of Her Neighbours, and then call upon them to trust exclusively to it for their Protection.

...You will request the Interference of the Emperor of Russia to check and discountenance any such Projects as are attributed to the Prussian Cabinet....

III. CASTLEREAGH, 1812–22

4. THE APPROACH OF PEACE

[The period during which Castlereagh was Foreign Secretary was the most important in British diplomacy. It witnessed the formation of the Grand Alliance, the defeat of Napoleon, the Congress of Vienna, and the reconstruction of Europe. In all of these Castlereagh had a large share. His skill in binding the Great Alliance together and his tact in handling foreign potentates led him to seek for a system of government by Congress and Conference. He thus became ultimately the most "European" of British statesmen.

Doc. 4, here printed, exhibits the views of the British Cabinet as to the resettlement of Europe, after Napoleon had been defeated at Leipzig but before he had fought his immortal campaign of 1814. The suggestions of the British Cabinet were therefore tentative in character, though they were largely realized in fact. Briefly summarizing, we may say that, as a result of the Vienna settlement, France was excluded from the Low Countries and the Rhine. What is now Belgium (with some slight differences) was united to Holland, to make a strong Dutch state. Prussia got the districts South of the Rhine, but France retained Alsace-Lorraine. Piedmont was strengthened with Genoa, Austria with Lombardy and Venetia. Of the colonies England took what she thought necessary, but returned the rich sugar island of Guadeloupe to France, and Java and other fertile Dutch Indian islands to Holland. Thus the ideas of Pitt in 1805, as well as of the Cabinet in 1813, were pretty well carried out.

So far, any British statesmen of the day might have dictated the Vienna settlement. But it is in the arrangements for guaranteeing that settlement that originality was shewn. It is enough to say here that Castlereagh, in accordance with the ten-year-old proposal of Pitt, proposed "*a general accord and guarantee* between the Great Powers of Europe, with a determination to support the arrangement agreed upon, and to turn the general influence, and if necessary the general arms, against the Power that shall first attempt to disturb the continental peace".* The guarantees were not new, the originality lay in applying a guarantee to the whole of Europe and making the Powers subscribe to it. But the Tsar

* To Liverpool, 13 February 1818. *V.* C. K. Webster, *The Foreign Policy of Castlereagh, 1812–15,* [1931], Chap. vii, § 4, Chap. viii, §§ 3–4; the text is quoted on pp. 428–9.

refused to include Turkey in the guarantee, Napoleon returned from Elba, and the guarantee in its original form was abandoned. Ultimately Castlereagh relied on other means, such as periodic reunions, to keep the peace of Europe. The document printed here shews the instructions which Castlereagh received for the peace, and the next one will shew what he considered had been achieved at Vienna and in the subsequent Conferences.]

Document 4. *The Cabinet Memorandum of 26 December 1813; or Instructions for Peace-Making**

PRESENT: The Lord Chancellor, The Lord President, Lord Privy Seal, Earl of Liverpool, Earl of Bathurst, Earl of Buckingham, Earl of Mulgrave, Viscount Sidmouth, Viscount Melville, Mr. Vansittart, Mr. B. Bathurst, Vis[coun]t Castlereagh.

The Three Allied Powers having invited the Prince Regent to send a Plenipotentiary to the Continent charged with full Powers to treat both with Friendly and Hostile Powers in all matters, which concern the general Interests; and His Royal Highness, having previously received from the Ministers of the said Powers in London satisfactory Assurances on the Maritime Question, has been pleased in Compliance with the desire of the said Allies, to direct H[is] M[ajesty]'s Secretary of State for Foreign Affairs to proceed forthwith to the Head Quarters of the Allies in Execution of this Especial Service.

Lord Castlereagh is Charged in the first Instance to enter into such Preliminary Explanations as may be necessary to ascertain with precision the Basis on which it is proposed to Negotiate.

He is to Endeavour to Establish a Clear and definite understanding with the Allies, not only on all Matters of Common Interest, but upon such Points, as are likely to be discussed with the Enemy, so that the Several Allied Powers may in their Negotiations with France act in perfect Concert, and together maintain one Common Interest.

If Call'd on for an Explanation of the views of his Gov[ern]men]t as to Terms of Peace, and the sacrifice of Conquests, which G[rea]t Britain is disposed to make for the general

* *F.O.* 139/1. This has already been published by C. K. Webster, *British Diplomacy (1813–15),* [1921], 123–6.

Interest, he is to State, that with respect to the latter, It must in a great Measure be governed by the Nature of the Conditions with respect to the Continent, which the Allied Powers may be Enabled to obtain from the Enemy.

If the Maritime Power of France shall be restricted within due bounds by the Effectual Establishment of Holland—The Peninsula and Italy in Security, and Independence, G[rea]t Britain consistent with her own Security may then be induced to apply the greater proportion of her Conquests to promote the general Interests. If on the Contrary the arrangement should be defective in any of these Points, G[rea]t Britain must secure a proportionable share of those Conquests to render her Secure against France.

If Call'd on for more detailed Explanation he may State, that the objects sine Quâ Non upon which G[rea]t Britain can venture to divest herself of her Conquests in any material degree are, 1st the Absolute Exclusion of France from any Naval Establishment on the Scheldt, and Especially at Antwerp and 2ndly The Security of Holland being adequately provided for under the House of Orange by a Barrier, which shall at least Include Juliers and Antwerp as well as Maestricht with a Suitable Arrondisement of Territory in Addition to Holland as it stood in 1792. It being understood that Wesel shall also be in the hands of one of the Allied Powers.

It must be understood that the Monarchies of the Peninsula must also be Independent under their Legitimate Sovereigns. Their Dominions at least in Europe being guaranteed against attack by France. The Allied Powers to take Engagements to this Effect, and to Stipulate the Amount of Succours to be actually furnished in such Case.

If none acceptable to the Continental Powers G[rea]t Britain will be prepared to Confine the Casus foederis to the Continent, being nevertheless herself bound to afford the Stipulated Succours, provided Holland and the Peninsula shall be secured.

In consideration of such an Arrangement for Holland and the Peninsula, G[rea]t Britain will be disposed to Stipulate for the Restitution of the Conquests made from France as

Enumerated in the Margin and in this view to render them available for the purposes of Negotiation.

Malta being Always understood to Remain British, The Mauritius and Bourbon—Guadeloupe and the Saintes cannot be restored to France.

The Mauritius is retained as being when in the hands of an Enemy a most Injurious Naval Station to our Indian Commerce, whilst it is of little Comparative Value to France.

Guadeloupe is insisted upon as a debt of Honor to Sweden.

If by the Success of the Allied Arms Holland and the Peninsula shall be secured as above, the Conquests Specified in the Margin may then be applied to Compensate other demands which our Continental Allies may have to bring forward

If the Restoration of Guadeloupe should be made a point Sine Qua Non by France and consequently of War with Sweden, the Latter Power might in an Ultimatum be compensated by Bourbon, or a Dutch Colony, Holland in that Case taking Bourbon.

Holland being Secured by a Barrier as above, the Dutch Colonies as Specified in the Margin to be restored to Holland—

The Cape of Good Hope is excepted, as a Position connected with the Security of our Empire in the East, but in lieu of this Colony G[rea]t Britain to appropriate Two Million Sterling to be applied towards the Improvement of the Dutch Barrier.

With respect to the Danish Conquests, It is proposed they should (with the Exception of Heligoland) be made Instrumental to the Execution of our Engagements to Sweden.

In all Communications on the Expediency of Peace, the same Course to be pursued as heretofore—viz to Evince a desire to Conform as far as possible to the general Interests of the Continent—To give to the Allies the most unequivocal Assurances of a firm determination to support them in Contending for an Advantageous Peace and to avoid everything that might countenance a Suspicion that G[rea]t Britain was Inclined to push them forward in the War for [her] own purposes.

The Utmost Exertions to be used to prevent any relaxation in the Military Operations, whilst Negotiations are pending.

Also to direct Force as much as possible from all Quarters upon Holland and the Low Countries.

To Explain to the Prince of Orange, that the British Force in Holland, (exclusive of 2000 Russians), cannot at present be carried beyond 10,000 Men and must be considered as liable to be withdrawn to Reinforce Lord Wellington.

Should Austria propose the Settlement of the Arch Duke Charles in the Netherlands, the Proposition to be favorably received. It may be proper to remark at the same time, that much must depend on the Success of the War in Flanders. If the Enemy should be driven back within Antient France by Connecting a Considerable part of the German Territory on the Left Bank of the Rhine with Brabant etc. an Intermediary Power of Considerable Importance might be erected, and one which supported by Austria would form a most Important Barrier both for Holland and Germany. If the Successes of the Allies should be more circumscribed or should the object of giving to Holland an adequate Barrier have to be acquired by Negotiation and not by Conquest, it may then not be prudent to aim at More, than such an Extension of Holland as before described.

The Prince of Orange to be discouraged from any attempt to extend Holland on the Side of the Netherland[s] beyond Its Ancient Limits, without the Express Consent of the Allies.

The proposed Marriage to be Confidentially to be Confidentially [sic] open'd to the Sovereigns at Head Quarters, with the intended Limitation of the Succession, the Prince of Orange's Consent being previously obtain'd.

If Barrier for Holland should not be secured to the Extent propose[d], the restitution of the Dutch Colonies to be proportionately Limited.

As the Barrier for Holland is an object most deeply Interesting to all the Allies, G[rea]t Britain is willing to purchase it by a double Sacrifice, by Cessions both to France and to Holland. If the Allies should not carry this Point, so important to their Own Security, as well as to that of G[rea]t Britain, the latter Power will in that Case have no other alternative than to preserve her Colonial Conquests as a

Counterpoise to the dominion of the Enemy and on these grounds to withhold those Cessions which she would otherwise be prepared to make to France—

The Cession of Conquests by G[rea]t Britain being declared to be Contingent upon Equivalent Securities to result from the Continental Arrangements, and Especially on the Side of Holland and the Low Countries, any general Stipulation which does not expressly declare the principle by which it is to be regulated and connect it pointedly with these objects, appears objectionable.

In any Arrangement of Italy, the Military Line of the Alps, and the Roads lately open'd in the direction of Italy to be particularly attended to.

with respect to the Internal Arrangement of Italy, It is highly Expedient that the King of Sardinia should be restored, perhaps receiving Genoa in Exchange for Savoy.

If Austria Connects herself with Murat, the Sicilian Family to have Tuscany and Elba.

The Pope to be restored to the Estates of the Church.

The Milanese, Modena, Parma, Plascentia etc to be subject to discussion.

The Prince Regent's Mediation, if solicited by the Allies in the Arrangement of the Internal Affairs of Germany, to be afforded.

G[rea]t Britain to declare her readiness, should a General Peace be signed, to Sign a Separate Peace with the United States of America on the *Status Quo Ante Bellum*, without Involving in such Treaty any decisions upon the Points in dispute at the Commencement of Hostilities.

A direct Proposition to treat in London having been lately made to the American Gov[ernmen]t this offer not to be stated, unless the Subject should be brought forward.

Should such an offer be made to America, a Time to be limited within which her Acceptance or refusal must be declared.

The Question as to the Arrangement with Denmark to be Subject to discussion with Sweden.

The distribution of the Command in the North, to be reserved for Consideration at Head Quarters.

The 5 Millions Subsidy may be granted under the following Provisos.

1st Reserve as to the sending Home the Russian Fleet.

2ndly The accepting, if required, a proportion of the Same in Credit Bills.

3rdly The Signing of such Engagements and Especially with respect to Holland and the Peninsula, as may Justify both to the British Publick and the Allies so great an Exertion in favor of the three Powers.

The Treaty of Alliance not to terminate with the War, but to Contain defensive Engagements with eventual obligations to support the Powers attack'd by France, with a certain extent of Stipulated Succours.

The Casus Foederis to be an Attack by France on the European Dominions of any one of the Contracting Parties.

Spain and if possible Holland to be included as Contracting Parties.

Sweden being beyond the Baltick is less Interested in being Included, or rather has an Interest not to participate.

Humbly Submitted for your Royal Highness's Sanction.

[Signed] George P[rince] R[egent]*

5. THE CONGRESS SYSTEM

[The Treaties of Paris and Vienna ended the long period of the Revolutionary and Napoleonic wars and transformed the map of Europe. A comparison of the terms with those foreshadowed in the Cabinet Memorandum of 26 December 1813 is useful. The Treaty of Vienna, signed on 9 June 1815, actually before the decisive day of Waterloo, contained no fewer than 121 clauses.†
Its provisions fell into several great groups. The first of these may be best indicated by describing it as the settlement of the Balance of Power. The principle was that each Great Power was to obtain the territory or its equivalent that it had held in 1805. Except in the case of Russia this was fairly carried out. Russia got a large part of Poland, including Warsaw the capital, which she recovered from Prussia, and promised to form a national kingdom of Poland and to endow her with a constitution. In the opinion of both

* An additional paragraph to these instructions says that the Hon. Frederic John Robinson was to be sent as "Assistant, with the rank of Minister Pleni-potentiary, with Full Powers etc....in case of your illness or otherwise".
† V. Hertslet, Map [of Europe by Treaty], [1875], 1, 208–74.

Castlereagh and Metternich this accession of power and population was too great, and upset the Balance of Power. Alarm was increased by the fact that Alexander maintained an army of nearly a million men, which was about twice the number that good judges thought necessary.

As regards Germany the balancing of power was fairly carried out. Prussia complained that she got less than the 1805 standard, and this was true. But she had had a great deal of Polish territory in 1805, and she exchanged this for half of Saxony and for the Rhine Province. It is singular that Prussia at the time showed no special desire for this last acquisition, which made her ultimately the national champion of Germany against France.

Austria adjusted the balance against Prussia in Germany by preventing her from annexing all Saxony as she had desired. Further, Metternich erected Bavaria once more into a powerful state, on whose co-operation Austria could depend. Hanover, from its British connexion, obtained a good accession of territory. The other smaller states of Germany were cut up and carved out to suit Austrian or Prussian convenience, and the total number of German states included in the new Federation was reduced to thirty-nine. Austria retained, in effect, the headship of Germany, though Prussia was not far behind her in authority.

Austria did not aim at gains in Germany, but in Italy. She acquired Venetia and recovered Lombardy. All the other states in Italy were really satellites in her train. Piedmont acquired Genoa, and was helped by this acquisition to defend the North against France. The Papal States were restored, and Naples was again set up as a kingdom under a Bourbon. By a secret treaty made (with Castlereagh's approval) between Metternich and the King of Naples the latter promised not to grant a constitution without Austria's consent. Metternich's avowed object was to break up and dismember Italy, and he regarded a constitution as likely to lead to an agitation against his views.

The next important phase of the settlement concerned Holland and Belgium. These were united into one kingdom, again with the idea of strengthening the resisting power of small states against France. Castlereagh further restored to the United Kingdom of the Netherlands the enormously rich Dutch colony of Java, and lent her two million pounds to fortify her frontier against France.

Switzerland was recognized as independent and guaranteed by all the Powers. Spain and Portugal recovered their old boundaries in Europe. Denmark was deprived of Norway, which was handed to Sweden. This settlement caused heartburnings, as Castlereagh had to threaten Norway with a blockade before she gave way. But, though this incident was an unpleasant one, it was not one for which practical diplomats will blame Castlereagh. At a critical moment Sweden refused to join the coalition against Napoleon unless Norway was promised to her, and Castlereagh was compelled to pay the price.

Certain other settlements were made by, or in consequence of, the Treaty of Vienna. The property claims of individuals who had suffered by the war were fairly met. The vexatious disputes as to diplomatic etiquette and precedence were finally settled. A doctrine as to international rivers was laid down, which was important for the future. The slave trade was declared inhuman and it was abolished by France, Spain, Holland, and Sweden, and promised to be abolished by Portugal. This great concession to humane ideas was almost solely due to Castlereagh, and to the British popular agitation behind him.

It has been customary to denounce the peacemakers of Vienna as reactionary and illiberal in the extreme. It is indeed true that they represented the old régime and were, to a large extent, untouched by the new ideas. But they represented the best and not the worst of the old régime, and their settlement averted any great war in Europe for forty years. According to their lights the settlement was a fair one. The settlement disregarded national claims, forced 'unnatural unions' on Norway and Sweden, on Belgium and Holland. But in each case the ally and the stronger partner (Sweden and Holland) demanded it, and the Allies did not see their way to resist the demand. A more serious criticism was the disrespect paid to the views of smaller powers. Though the settlement was supposed to be in favour of the old order and existing rights, the smaller states were ruthlessly sacrificed for the benefit of the larger. For this side of their activities there is little excuse, and it is the gravest criticism of their actions.

The work of Vienna, interrupted by Napoleon, was completed by two treaties, signed at Paris on 20 November 1815. Of these, one, the Second Treaty of Paris, modified the terms imposed on France by the First Treaty of Paris of 30 May 1814, bound France to carry out the new arrangements, to submit to the frontiers of 1790, to pay an indemnity, and to return the works of art to foreign capitals. The second treaty was the Quadruple Alliance between the Four Great Powers.* They bound themselves to maintain the arrangements of Chaumont, Vienna, and Paris by armed force for twenty years, both as regards the territorial boundaries now fixed and as regards the perpetual exclusion of Bonaparte and his dynasty from the throne of France. Finally, by Article VI, they agreed to 'renew their meetings at fixed periods' to discuss matters 'of common interest'. In this article lay the germ of future international government.

Alexander sought, further, to bind all monarchs together in a Christian union of charity, peace, and love by a solemn declaration, issued on 26 September 1815, and to be signed by kings

* The texts of the First and Second Treaties of Paris are printed in Hertslet, *Map*, [1875], I, 1–28, 342–69; that of the Quadruple Alliance, *ibid.* 372–5.

alone. The Regent of Great Britain was unable to sign it, for constitutional reasons, though he sent a private letter to Alexander, expressing his sympathy with the sentiments. With this exception it was signed by every king in Europe and by the President of the Swiss Republic. It became known, and was regarded by European liberals as a hateful compact of despots against the liberties of mankind. It was not that, nor had it any diplomatic or binding force. Charity and love are not capable of being defined in diplomatic terms, and no one except Alexander thought seriously of the Treaty. Castlereagh called it a 'piece of sublime mysticism and nonsense'. Metternich made profane jests about Christianity in connection with it. Neither regarded himself as in any way bound by it.*

The bond which Castlereagh and Metternich did recognize was that of the Quadruple Alliance. But they differed greatly about its interpretation. According to Castlereagh, England was bound to defend the territorial limits laid down at Vienna for twenty years. She was bound also to meet periodically in congresses with her Allies, but she was not bound to interfere in case of internal revolution in any country (other than an attempt to restore Napoleon). Metternich argued that the Quadruple Alliance did commit its members to armed interference to suppress internal revolution in any country, if the Congress thought it advisable. In the end these two views were bound to come into conflict.

The first meeting of the Powers—in accordance with the provisions of Article VI of the Treaty of the Quadruple Alliance— took place at Aix-la-Chapelle in the autumn of 1818. The published protocols of the Conference dealt primarily with the settlement with France, including the much debated question of her future relations with the Quadruple Alliance Powers. In brief: the Quadruple Alliance was maintained, and France was invited "to take part in their present and future deliberations, consecrated to the maintenance of the peace, the treaties on which it is founded, the rights and mutual relations established or confirmed by these treaties, and recognised by all the European Powers". This note, dated 4 November, was accepted by the Duc de Richelieu on the 12th.† The part taken by the British representatives in these decisions has been fully analysed by Professor Webster,‡ and it is sufficient here to quote his conclusion: "On the whole, Castlereagh was victorious. He kept his country unpledged except to the obligations which she had taken at Paris. Where Alexander was permitted to have his way the objectionable phrase imposed no definite obligation. Moreover, the system of reunions, under Article VI, was maintained in its full vigour, and France was admitted to them. But they were not made automatic except in the case of a revolution occurring in France itself."§

* For text v. Hertslet, Map, [1875], 1, 317–20.
† V. ibid. 557–75.
‡ C. K. Webster, The Foreign Policy of Castlereagh, 1815–1822, [1925], 121–72.
§ V. ibid. 155–6.

The unanimity of the Allies, suggested by the wording of the published documents, covered in fact a wide divergence of views as to the character of the Alliance. This was the subject of critical discussions extending from 12 to 21 October,* the protagonists being Alexander and Castlereagh. The Tsar explained his views in a long memorandum of 8 October† communicated to the Conference on the 14th; Metternich's were embodied in a letter dated 7 October;‡ Castlereagh gave his verbally. The 'abstractions and sweeping generalities' of the Russian paper alarmed both Wellington and Castlereagh, and they thought it would be 'hazardous' to attempt a written answer. They therefore decided 'to invite the Ministers to a free discussion of all that had been written', and in 'an extended conversation', Castlereagh explained his attitude. On 19 October, he wrote home a private and confidential letter§ describing what had taken place, and enclosing, among other documents, a memorandum of his own. As he himself said, he had 'thrown' into it the substance of his statements to the other ministers. The memorandum was written for the information of the Government at home, although, as Professor Webster tells us, it was shown to Metternich.‖ It records the arguments with which Castlereagh tried to meet the 'abstractions' of the Tsar. It explains at length the interpretation which Castlereagh placed on the treaties which governed the Congress system. It was a private document, never intended for formal communication, far less for publication, and may be taken as expressing Castlereagh's most sincere views.

Great interest attaches to it for this reason. It shows the interpretation which Castlereagh placed on the binding character of treaties, and the meaning of a guarantee. It gives his classification of the two treaties of Paris and the Treaty of Vienna—none of which, he said, 'contain any express guarantee'. It argues that these treaties 'cannot be said to form an Alliance, in the strict sense of the word'; while, in contrast, those of the Quadruple Alliance both at Chaumont in 1814 and Paris in 1815 did. It expresses, clearly and with telling emphasis, the British view of the nature of the Alliance and the character of the guarantee, and in both respects sounds the keynote of the policy which was to be developed in the succeeding years.

The differences between the Powers at Aix-la-Chapelle were in themselves a serious warning that the Alliance might not hold for long. Even when the issue seemed settled a Prussian proposal was made for a territorial guarantee which emphasized the breach between Britain and the continental Powers. The fact was that

---

* Cp. Professor Webster's account, *op. cit.* 145–55.

† *V. Supplementary Despatches, Correspondence and Memoranda of the Duke of Wellington, 1858–72*, XII, 743–51.

‡ *F.O.* 92/35. Cited C. K. Webster, *op. cit.* 149.

§ *F.O.* 92/35. Castlereagh to Bathurst, No. 13, Private and Confidential, 19 October 1818.   ‖ C. K. Webster, *op. cit.* 161.

between Russia, Austria and Prussia, the three original members of the Holy Alliance, a bond existed which did not touch Britain —the bond that in the course of time was to make co-operation impossible. It was a bond of autocrats; a bond strengthened by fear of revolution. Alexander alone among them clothed his fear in the language of abstract theory, but the practical limitations which Castlereagh here places on the obligations of the Powers to interfere in the event of revolution were in reality as little to the taste of Metternich. The natural sequel to Aix-la-Chapelle was the policy expressed in the State Paper of 5 May 1820 (**Doc. 6**). Moreover, it is significant that even the measure of agreement which Castlereagh had with the Allies was not shared by all his colleagues at home, and that among his critics the prominent place was taken by his successor, Canning.*]

Document 5. *Memorandum on the Treaties of* 1814 *and* 1815, *Aix-la-Chapelle, October* 1818†

The Benign Principles of the Alliance of the 26th Sept[embe]r 1815, having been either formally or substantially adhered to by all Powers, may be considered as constituting the European System, in matter of political Conscience.‡

It would, however, be derogatory to this solemn act of the Sovereigns, to mix its discussion with the ordinary diplomatick obligations, which bind State to State, and which are alone to be looked for in the Treaties which have been concluded in the accustomed Fórm.

The present Diplomatick Position of Europe may be considered under two distinct Heads: 1st The treaties which may be said to bind its States collectively. 2ly The treaties which are peculiar to particular States.

Under the first Head, may be enumerated, The Treaty of Peace signed at Paris 30th May 1814,—The Act of the Congress of Vienna, signed June 9th 1815, and the Treaty of Peace, signed at Paris, the 20th of Nov[embe]r 1815.

* Cp. Bathurst's long letter to Castlereagh of 20 October 1818, *Correspondence ...of Viscount Castlereagh*, [1853], XII, 55–8.
† Original in *F.O.* 92/35. Printed *in toto* in C. K. Webster, *The Congress of Vienna* (2nd ed. 1934), 166–71.
‡ *V.* Hertslet, *Map*, [1875], I, 317–20. This is the so-called Holy Alliance Treaty signed by the Austrian and Russian Emperors and the King of Prussia, etc. The Prince Regent of Great Britain announced—in reply to an invitation to sign—that "the forms of the British Constitution...preclude me from acceding formally to this Treaty", but expressed his "entire concurrence" with the principles.

These transactions, to which all the States of Europe, (with the exception of the Porte) are at this day either signing or acceding Parties, may be considered as the great Charte, by which the Territorial System of Europe, unhinged by the events of war and Revolution, has been again restored to order. The Consent of all the European States, France included, has not only been given to this settlement, but their Faith has been solemnly pledged to the strict observance of its arrangements.

These Treaties contain some few Regulations not strictly Territorial, but it may be asserted, that the general Character of their Provisions is of that nature, and, that they contain, in no case, Engagements, which have been pushed beyond the immediate objects which are made matter of regulation in the Treaties themselves.

It is further to be observed, that none of these three Treaties contain any express guarantee, general or special, by which their observance is to be enforced, save and except the temporary Guarantee intended to be assured by Article 5 of the Treaty of 1815 which regulates the Army of Occupation to be left in France.

There is no doubt, that a breach of the Covenant by any one State is an Injury, which all the other States may, if they shall think fit, either separately or collectively resent, but the Treaties do not impose, by express stipulation, the doing so, as matter of positive obligation. So solemn a Pact, on the faithful execution and observance of which all Nations should feel the strongest Interest, may be considered, as under the Protection of a moral guarantee, of the highest Nature, but as those who framed these acts did not probably see how the whole Confederacy could, without the utmost Inconvenience, be made collectively to enforce the observance of these Treaties, the execution of this duty seems to have been deliberately left to arise out of the Circumstances of the Time and of the Case, and the offending State to be brought to reason by such of the injured States, as might, at the moment think fit to charge themselves with the Task of defending their own rights, thus invaded.

If this Analysis of these Treaties be correct, they cannot be said to form an Alliance, in the strict sense of the Word. They no doubt form the general Pact, by which all is regulated, which, at that moment was open, in Europe to regulation, but they can hardly be stated to give any special or superior security to the parts of the European system thus regulated, as compared with those parts, which were not affected by these Negotiations, upon which consequently those Transactions are wholly silent, and which rest, for their title, upon anterior Treaties, or publick Acts of equal and recognised Authority.

Under the 2d Head, vizt, that of Treaties which are peculiar to particular States, may be enumerated, the Treaties of Alliance of Chaumont and Paris, as signed by the four great Allied Powers. There was a Treaty of Alliance, deriving its Principle from that of Chaumont, intermediately signed at Vienna, viz on the 25th March 1815, by nearly all the Powers, but as the Stipulations of this Treaty are declared to have been satisfied by the Treaty of Peace of [Paris] of [20] Nov[embe]r 1815, and to have thereby become extinct, it will make the statement more clear, to omit the further mention of it, in the present discussion.

The treaties anterior to that of Chaumont between the same Powers may be usefully referred to, as explaining the events which first gave birth to this combination between the 4 Principal Powers of Europe, as opposed to France, at a moment when the great Mass of those States, who afterwards joined the Allies, and constituted with them the coalitions which, in the years 1814 and 1815, operated against France, were yet under the yoke of that Power.

The treaties of Quadruple Alliance concluded at Chaumont and Paris may be considered as Treaties of Alliance, in the strictest and most enlarged sense of the word; They have a professed object: They define the steps to be taken in pursuit of that object; And they declare the stipulated Force, by which that object is to be attained and secured. These two Treaties form one system, consistent in its purpose, but varying in its means.

The Restoration and Conservation of Europe against the Power of France may be stated to be the avowed Principle and object of both Treaties.

The Treaty of Chaumont in 1814 aimed at effectuating an Improvement in the State of Europe as the preliminary Condition to a Peace with France, and at defending by the force of the Alliance, the terms of that Peace, if made. The Treaty of Paris in 1815 had only to place the State of Things, as established by the Treaties of Paris and Vienna, under the Protection of the Quadruple Alliance.

The treaty of Chaumont gave to this Alliance that Character of Permanence which the deep rooted Nature of the danger against which it was intended to provide, appeared to require, viz twenty years from March 1814, with an eventual Continuance. This Character of Permanence was additionally recognised by the Language of the Paris Treaty, the whole of the Provisions of which proceed, not only upon the admission of a danger still existing, but upon the necessity of keeping alive the precautionary Arrangements of the Treaty even after the Army of occupation shall have been withdrawn.

The [2nd] Paris Treaty also aimed at specifying with Precision, as far as Possible, the Casus Foederis upon which the Contracting Parties should be bound to furnish their Stipulated Succours.

Where that could not be done, the object was, to provide a Mode by which the Case in doubt might be decided at the time it should arise.

Three distinct Cases are provided for in Articles 2 and 3 of the Treaty,* the two first being cases of fact are clear and specifick, the third being a Case of a mixed Nature, dependent for its just Solution upon the Circumstances of the Event which shall be alledged to give occasion to it, is left to be decided in concert by the Allied Courts when the moment shall arrive.†

In construing the obligations of this Treaty, the Recital which its Preamble contains is no doubt to be held in view.‡

* V. Hertslet, Map, [1875], I, 373–4. (i) Art. II—pledges the signatory powers to exclude the Bonaparte dynasty from France. (ii) Art. III—pledges them to maintain a line of military posts in France for a certain number of years.

† This refers to the following passage in (iii) Art. II, "And as the same Revolutionary Principles, which upheld the last criminal usurpation, might again, under other forms, convulse France and thereby endanger the repose of other States" under these circumstances the Powers will "concert...measures", etc.

‡ Preamble: "Considering that the repose of Europe is essentially interwoven with the order of things founded on the maintenance of the Royal Authority

It serves to show the Degree in which the Order of things then established in France operated as a Motive with the Allies in making the Treaty, and the deep Interest they felt in their Consolidation as a Means to the general Tranquillity; —but as it was not required that France should bind herself, in the enacting Part of Her Treaty, to maintain inviolate the political order of things then existing, it does not appear competent for the Allies to consider an Alteration in that order of things, whether legally effectuated, or brought about by indirect means, as in itself constituting such an Infraction of the Peace as the Allies are entitled to take Notice of, independent of the Consideration of how far that Change goes immediately to endanger their own repose and safety.

The Principle of guaranteeing to both King and People the established order of things was much talked of at the time; by some it was contended that a species of guarantee having been given to the King by the arrangement for placing an army of occupation in France coupled with the Instructions to the Duke of Wellington for the employment of the Troops, whilst they should remain there, that the Allies should give the Nation the same security for their liberties by guaranteeing their Charte, but neither Alternative was adopted and no guarantee was given beyond what grew out of the circumstances above alluded to.

A guarantee which was in its nature temporary, and was expressly limited to a period not exceeding five years by the provisions contained in Art[icle] 5 of the general Treaty of Peace.* The 4 Powers, it is true, took further measures of Precaution in their Treaty of Alliance, signed the same day as will appear by reference to the 5th Art[icle],† but this Article proceeds upon the principle that after the army of occupation

and of the Constitutional charter, and wishing to employ all their means to prevent the general tranquility (the object of the wishes of mankind and the constant end of their efforts) from being again disturbed" etc.

* Cp. the 2nd. Treaty of Paris, signed 20 November 1815.

† *Art.* V: "The High Contracting Parties having agreed to the dispositions laid down in the preceding Articles, for the purpose of securing the effect of their engagements during the temporary occupation, declare, moreover, that even after the expiration of this measure, the said engagements shall still remain in full force and vigour, for the purpose of carrying into effect such measures as may be deemed necessary for the maintenance of the stipulations contained in Articles 1 and 2 of the present Act." This is from the Quadruple Treaty of Alliance signed at Paris, 20 November 1815.

should be withdrawn the Allies could only justify an Interference in the affairs of a Foreign State, upon the ground of
considering their own safety compromised and that, independently of such a Consideration, they could not justly claim
any right of interference, or in prudence charge themselves
with the task of redressing violations of the internal Constitution of France; In this Sense the latter part of Art[icle] 3 is
framed, being the only Article in either Treaty which touches
the question,*—The true point therefore for Consideration
under this Article must always be:—Is the safety or Interest
of the Alliance so far compromised by the event as to justify
recurrence to War? or is it a case if not for actual war, at least
for defensive precautions? or finally is it a case which though
more or less to be disapproved, or regretted, neither justifies
the former nor requires the latter Alternative? The Case
admits in good sense, as well as according to the words of the
Treaty, of no other solution; it would have been impossible
to have proposed to France an express Article to preserve
inviolate the order of things as therein established, for no
state of things could be more humiliating than that of a State
which should be bound to its neighbours, to preserve unchanged its internal System, and that any fundamental change
in it, without their consent first had and obtained, should in
itself be cause of War—If such a Principle cannot be maintained, for a moment in argument, the qualification of it that
the change, to be tolerated, must be legally made, is not less
so, for how can foreign States safely be left to judge of what
is legal in another State, or what degree of Intrigue or violence
shall give to the Change the Character which is to entitle
them to interfere—The only safe Principle is that of the Law
of Nations—That no State has a right to endanger its neighbours by its internal Proceedings, and that if it does, provided
they exercise a sound discretion, Their right of Interference
is clear. It is this right upon which the latter part of Article 3
expressly founds itself, and not upon any Covenant supposed
to be made by France.

The Allies are presumed to have a common Interest in
judging this question soundly when it arises—If they are of

* *V. supra,* p. 42, n. 1.

opinion that the Circumstances of the case prudentially considered, constitute the existence of the danger, against which the Article intended to provide, Then they are bound to concur in furnishing the stipulated succours, but till the case arises, none of the Contracting Parties are engaged for more, under this branch of the Art[icle] than an eventual Concert and decision—

Having discussed and endeavoured to state with precision what the existing Treaties have really done, there will remain open to fair discussion the question;—Have they done enough, or does not much remain yet to be done? No question can be more proper for examination and no Gov[ernmen]t more disposed to consider it than that of Great Britain, whenever any clear and specifick proposition shall be brought forward, always holding in view the Inconvenience of agitating in time of Peace, Questions that presuppose a state of war or disturbance. The desire of the Prince Regent always is, to act cordially with His Allies, but in doing so, to stand quite clear in the view of his own engagements not to be supposed to have taken engagements beyond the Text and Import of the Treaties signed.

The Problem of an Universal Alliance for the Peace and Happiness of the world has always been one of speculation and of Hope, but it has never yet been reduced to practice, and if an opinion may be hazarded from its difficulty, it never can; but you may in practice approach towards it, and perhaps the design has never been so far realized as in the last four years—during that eventful Period the Quadruple Alliance, formed upon Principles altogether limited has had, from the Presence of the Sovereigns, and the unparalleled unity of design with which their Cabinets have acted, the power of travelling so far out of the sphere of their immediate and primitive obligations, without at the same time, transgressing any of the principles of the law of Nations or failing in the delicacy which they owe to the rights of other States, as to form more extended Alliances such as that of the 25th March 1815* at Vienna, To interpoze their good offices for the

* The Treaty of Alliance against Bonaparte arranging for 150,000 men to be mobilized by each Contracting Power, signed at Vienna, 25 March 1815. V. Hertslet, *Map*, [1875], III, 2058–9.

settlement of differences subsisting between other States, To take the initiative in watching over the Peace of Europe and finally in securing the execution of its Treaties in the mode most consonant to the Convenience of all the Parties.

The Idea of an "Alliance Solidaire" by which each State shall be bound to support the State of Succession, Government, and Possession, within all other States from violence and attack upon Condition of receiving for itself a similar guarantee must be understood as morally implying the previous establishment of such a System of general Government as may secure and enforce upon all Kings and Nations an internal System of Peace and Justice; till the mode of constructing such a System shall be devised, the Consequence is inadmissable, as nothing would be more immoral or more prejudicial to the Character of Government generally, than the Idea that their force was collectively to be prostituted to the support of established Power without any Consideration of the Extent to which it was abused. Till then a System of administrating Europe by a general Alliance of all it's States can be reduced to some practical Form, all Notions of general and unqualified guarantee must be abandoned and States must be left to rely for their Security, upon the Justice and Wisdom of their respective Systems, aided by such support as other States may feel prepared to afford them, and as Circumstances may point out and justify without outstepping those Principles which are to be found in the Law of Nations, as long recognized and practiced.

The beneficial effects which may be expected to be produced by the four Allied Powers consulting together, and interposing, from time to time, their good offices, as they have hitherto done, for the preservation of Peace and Order, is considered as equally true with respect to five Powers:—The Introduction of France into such a System, not rendering it too numerous for convenient Concert, whilst it must add immensely to the moral Weight and Influence of such a Mediating Power.

6. CASTLEREAGH AND NON-INTERVENTION

[With the year 1820 the tragedy of Castlereagh begins. As was indicated on p. 39, his structure of European governance was collapsing. France had paid her indemnity and was no longer feared. The four Allies could therefore afford the luxury of disagreement. Revolution was abroad in Europe, actually lifting its head in Spain, Portugal, Naples, and about to do so in Greece. In Spain revolution began with the New Year, and presented the three military monarchs of Central Europe with a problem. All of them, being despots, wished to suppress revolutions everywhere by the united force of monarchies. Though this scheme had never been sanctioned at Vienna or by Castlereagh, they proposed an active system of interference in the internal affairs of other States. They invoked the "Holy Alliance" to defend their pretensions. At the time Castlereagh had ridiculed the idea of being bound by it as "too 'sublime'" (cp. p. 37). In addition the Prince Regent had not signed the Holy Alliance Treaty, though he had expressed verbal agreement with its principles (cp. *supra*, p. 37). But this fact had the important result that neither British Cabinet nor Parliament were officially committed. Castlereagh had no intention of allowing England to join a league of despots. His reply therefore was the State Paper of 5 May 1820. It is the most famous State Paper in British history and the one of the widest ultimate consequence. Castlereagh there states the principle of non-intervention, the obligation of England to follow a "system strongly national and popular", her refusal to interfere by force in the internal affairs of other States. It meant therefore the end of that system of European co-operation which Castlereagh had done so much to promote. It was to end because the other Allies would not confine themselves to the objects settled at Paris and Vienna during the years 1814–15. "If they will be theorists, we must act in separation", said Castlereagh. This State Paper explains his reasons at length.

The Paper was drawn up by Castlereagh, in order to define his policy with regard to Spain, on 5 May 1820, and then circulated to the principal Governments of Europe. It was recognized at once by Gentz (*Dépêches Inédites*, [1841], II, 56–7) as of considerable importance. But what entitles it to even greater consideration is that Canning always declared it to have been the origin of his own policy (*v. infra*, p. 48) and published some extracts from it as a Parliamentary Paper in the spring of 1823.* He referred to it

* A[ccounts] & P[apers], [1823], XIX, 69–71. V. Temperley and Penson, *Century of Diplomatic Blue Books*, No. 119. The question has been raised as to whether Canning influenced Castlereagh in drawing up this State Paper. Its

at length in Parliament on 14 April 1823. "It was not with the intention of separating himself in any degree from those who preceded him...nor with the desire of claiming to himself any merit that belonged to them, that he now felt himself called upon to repeat what he had stated on a former day and what had been much misunderstood—narrowed by some, and extended by others —that, applicable to the considerations on which the Congress was to be employed, he had found in the records of his office (and it was also in the records of the country, and known to all the world) a state paper, laying down the principle of non-interference, with all the qualifications properly belonging to it. When, therefore, with whatever degree of courtesy, it had been ascribed to him, that he had applied new principles to a new case, he had thought it just to remind the House of a fact of which it was indeed already in possession. The principle of non-interference with the independence of foreign States, was laid down in the document to which he alluded, as broadly, clearly, and definitely as it was possible for any statesman to wish to lay it down" (Canning, *Speeches*, v, 5–6). Canning in these words definitely claimed this State Paper as the basis of his own foreign policy. It will be found of value to compare this State Paper in its entirety with the more guarded Circular of 19 January 1821, which was made public *in toto* at the time.*]

Document 6. *The State Paper of 5 May 1820; or the Foundation of British Foreign Policy**

The Events which have occur[r]ed in Spain have, as might be expected, excited, in proportion as they have developed themselves, the utmost anxiety throughout Europe.

[The Russian Despatch of March the 3rd, written when

sentiments bear a striking resemblance to those uttered by Canning in the Cabinet in October 1818 (*v. supra*, p. 39, and n., and Castlereagh's *Correspondence*, xii, 56–7). Canning certainly claimed at the time to have had some influence upon it (*v.* S. L. Poole, *Life of Stratford de Redcliffe*, [1888], i, 291). But this evidence is not sufficient to take the main responsibility from Castlereagh. Probably, Stapleton is right when he says (*Political Life of Canning*, [1831], i, 141) : "Whether or not Mr. Canning had any hand in the drawing up of this particular paper, cannot be positively affirmed; but Lord Londonderry himself would, perhaps, scarcely have denied that there had been occasions on which he had received assistance from Mr. Canning."

  * *V. infra*, p. 64, n. 1. The text that follows is from *F.O.* 7/148; it was partly printed in *A. & P.*, [1823], xix, 69–71; the suppressed passages are supplied through the kindness of Professor Webster. The suppressed passages are enclosed here in double square brackets. The full text has been published by Professor Webster in *Cambridge History of British Foreign Policy*, [1923], ii, 623–33. A good deal of commentary on the State Paper of 5 May 1820 is to be found in *F.O.* 7/148. For the January Circular and its results see *F.O.* 7/158.

the first News of the Military Insurrection in Andalusia had reached St Petersburgh, invites the Allied Powers confidentially to discuss what measures They should adopt, or what attitude They should assume,—

1. In case the King's Gov[ernmen]t should be unable to suppress the revolt,—

2. In case the King should spontaneously solicit the Support of His Allies.

3. In case the Insurrection should be protracted.—

The Despatch from Mr. Rose of the 31st March, referring to a later period of the Insurrection, reports that the Russian Minister at Berlin, M. Alopeus, had suggested to the Prussian Gov[ernmen]t the necessity of referring the whole Question of Spain to the consideration of the Allied Ministers at Paris, including the Minister of France.—

Prince Hardenberg in a Letter to Lord Castlereagh of the 31st ult[im]o refers to M. Alopeus's Suggestion and appears to approve of the discussion being referred to Paris.

It is also understood that the Language held at Paris by some of the Allied Ministers is that the Moment is arrived when the Sovereigns themselves should assemble, under the extraordinary Provisions of the Treaty of Alliance.—]

The British Cabinet, upon this, as upon all other occasions, is ever ready to deliberate with those of the Allies, and will unreservedly explain itself upon this great question of common interest; but as to the form in which it may be prudent to conduct these deliberations, They conceive, They cannot too early recommend that course of deliberation which will excite the least attention or alarm, or which can least provoke jealousy in the mind of the Spanish Nation or Gov[ernmen]t. In this view it appears to them advisable studiously to avoid any reunion of the Sovereigns;—to abstain, at least in the present Stage of the Question, from charging any ostensible Conference with Commission to deliberate on the affairs of Spain:—They conceive it preferable that their Intercourse should be limited to those confidential Communications between the Cabinets which are in themselves best adapted to approximate ideas, and to lead, as far as may be, to the adoption of common principles, rather than to hazard a discussion in a Ministerial Conference, which, from the necessarily limited Powers of the Individuals composing it, must ever be better fitted to execute a purpose already decided upon than to frame a course of policy under delicate and difficult circumstances.

There seems the less motive for precipitating any Step of this nature in the case immediately under consideration, as, from all information which reaches us, there exists in Spain no order of things upon which to deliberate, nor as yet any governing Authority with which Foreign Powers can communicate:—

The King's Authority, for the moment at least, seems to be dissolved: His Majesty is represented in the last Despatches from Madrid, as having wholly abandoned Himself to the Tide of Events, and as conceding whatever is called for by the Provisional Junta and the Clubs:—The Authority of the provisional Gov[ernmen]t does not appear to extend beyond the Two Castilles and a part of Andalusia:—Distinct Local Authorities prevail in the various Provinces, and the King's personal Safety is regarded as extremely liable to be hazarded by any step which might lay Him open to the Suspicion of entertaining a design to bring about a Counter-Revolution, whether by internal or external means.—

This important Subject having been referred to, and considered by, the Duke of Wellington, his Memorandum* accompanies this Minute:—His Grace does not hesitate, upon his intimate experience of Spanish Affairs, to pronounce that the Spanish Nation is of all the European People that which will the least brook any interference from abroad:—He states the many instances in which, during the last War, this distinguishing Trait of national Character rendered them obstinately blind to the most pressing Considerations of publick Safety;—He states the imminent danger in which the Suspicion of foreign interference, and more especially of interference on the part of France, is likely to involve the King;

* This is not reproduced here. It is printed in *Despatches of the Duke of Wellington*, New Series, [1867], I, 116–21.

and he further describes the difficulties which would oppose themselves to any military operations in Spain, undertaken for the purpose of reducing by force the Nation to submit themselves to an order of things to be either suggested or prescribed to them from without.

Sir Henry Wellesley has, in coincidence with this opinion, reported the alarm which the intended Mission of M. la Tour du Pin had excited at Madrid; the prejudice which, in the opinion of all the Foreign Ministers at Madrid, it was calculated to occasion to the King's interests and possible Safety;— He also reports the steps which it was in contemplation to have adopted, on the part of the King to endeavour to prevent the French Minister from prosecuting his journey to Madrid, when Intelligence of the abandonment of the Mission was received from Paris.

At all events therefore until Some Central Authority shall establish Itself in Spain, all Notion of operating upon Her Councils seems utterly impracticable, and calculated to lead to no other possible result than that of compromising either the King or the Allies, or probably both.

[The Emperor of Russia, in the several Cases which H[is] I[mperial] M[ajesty] has successively suggested for deliberation, is altogether silent upon the particular Case which has really occurred:—It may therefore be inferred that His Imperial Majesty's reasoning is not meant to be applied to that total change in the order of things previously existing in Spain, which has been effected with the avowed Concurrence and under the formal Sanction of the King:—This Change, no doubt forced by circumstances, has been regularly notified by His Majesty to all Foreign Powers, and is apparently acquiesced in, if not adopted by, the great Body of the Nation.

In these circumstances, can the other States of Europe, in prudence proceed publickly to deliberate upon the King's Acts, much more to call them into question? If not would it be wise to give advice, wholly unasked, which is very little likely too contain any suggestion for the salutary modification of the Constitution of 1812 other than such as will readily occur to those publick Men within the Country who have good Intentions, and whose influence and means of effectuating an amelioration of the Constitution are likely to be weakened rather than strengthened by an interference from abroad?]

The present State of Spain no doubt seriously extends the range of political Agitation in Europe, but it must nevertheless be admitted that there is no portion of Europe of equal magnitude, in which such a Revolution could have happened, less likely to menace other States with that direct and imminent danger which has always been regarded, at least in this Country, as alone constituting the Case which would justify external interference.—If the Case is not such as to warrant such an interference If we do not feel that We have at this moment either the right or the means to interfere with effect by force;—if the Semblance of such an interference is more likely to irritate than to overawe, and if We have proved by experience how little a Spanish Government, whether of King or Cortes, is disposed to listen to advice from Foreign States, is it not prudent at least to pause before We assume an attitude which would seem to pledge us in the eyes of Europe to some decisive proceeding? Before We embark in such a measure, is it not expedient at least to ascertain with some degree of precision what We really mean to do? This Course of temperate and cautious policy, so befitting the occasion and the critical position in which the King is personally placed, will in no degree fetter our action, when, if ever, the case for acting shall arise:—

In the mean time, as independent States, The Allied Powers may awaken through their respective Missions at Madrid, with not less effect than would attend any joint Representation a salutary apprehension of the consequences that might be produced by any violence offered to the King's person or family, or by any hostile Measures directed against the Portuguese Dominions in Europe, for the protection of wh[ich] G[rea]t Britain is bound by specifick Treaty:—

In conveying any such Intimation, however, the utmost Delicacy should be observed, and tho[ugh] It is to be presumed that the Views and Wishes of all the Allied Powers must be essentially the same and that the Sentiments They are likely to express cannot materially differ, it does not follow that They should speak either in their corporate character or through any common Organ;—Both which Expedients would be calculated rather to offend than to conciliate or to persuade.

There can be no doubt of the general Danger which menaces more or less the stability of all existing Governments from the Principles which are afloat, and from the circumstance that so many States of Europe are now employed in the difficult task of casting anew their Gov[ernmen]ts upon the Representative Principle: but the notion of revising, limiting or regulating the course of such Experiments, either by foreign Council or by foreign force, would be as dangerous to avow as it w[oul]d be impossible to execute, and the Illusion too prevalent on this Subject, should not be encouraged in our Intercourse with the Allies.—That Circumstances might arise out of such Experiments in any Country directly menacing to the safety of other States cannot be denied, and against such a Danger well ascertained, the Allies may justifiably, and must in all prudence, be on their guard; but such is not the present Case; fearful as is the Example which is furnished, by Spain, of an Army in Revolt, and a Monarch swearing to a Constitution which contains in its frame hardly the Semblance of a Monarchy: there is no ground for Apprehension, that Europe is likely to be speedily endangered by Spanish Arms.

[The Argument against any ostensible step whatever being taken by the Allies to interpose even their good offices in the affairs of Spain, and the serious difficulties that must present themselves to an armed Interference under any Circumstances in that Country, have been so forcibly detailed in the Duke of Wellington's Paper as to exhaust that part of the Question.

It remains to be considered what Course can best be pursued by the Allies in the present Critical State of Europe, in order to preserve in the utmost Cordiality and vigour, the Bonds which at this Day so happily unite the great European Powers together, and to draw from their Alliance, should the moment of Danger and Contest arrive, the fullest extent of Benefit, of which it is in it's nature susceptible:—]

In this Alliance as in all other human Arrangements, nothing is more likely to impair or even to destroy its real utility, than any attempt to push its duties and obligations beyond the Sphere which its *original Conception and understood Principles** will warrant:—It was an union for the Reconquest and liberation of a great proportion of the Continent of Europe from the Military Dominion of France, and having subdued the Conqueror it took the State of Possession as established by the Peace under the Protection of the Alliance:— *It never was however intended as an Union for the Government of the World, or for the Superintendence of the Internal Affairs of other States:—**

⟦It provided specifically against an infraction on the part of France of the State of Possession then created: It provided against the Return of the Usurper or of any of his family to the Throne: It further designated the Revolutionary Power which had convulsed France and desolated Europe, as an object of it's constant solicitude; but it was the Revolutionary Power more particularly in it's Military Character actual and existent within France against which it intended to take Precautions, rather than against the Democratic Principles, then as now, but too generally spread throughout Europe.

In thus attempting to limit the objects of the Alliance within their legitimate Boundary, it is not meant to discourage the utmost Frankness of Communication between the Allied Cabinets;—their Confidential Intercourse upon all Matters, however foreign to the purposes of the Alliance, is in itself a valuable Expedient for keeping the current of Sentiment in Europe as equable and as uniform as may be: It is not meant that in particular and definite Cases, the Alliance may not (and especially when invited to do so by the Parties interested) advantageously interpose, with due Caution, in matters lying beyond the Boundaries of their immediate and particular Connection; but what is intended to be combated as forming any part of their Duty as Allies, is the Notion, but too perceptibly prevalent, that whenever any great Political Event

* The passages here italicized were quoted by Canning in the Commons in his speech of 30 April 1823.

shall occur, as in Spain, pregnant perhaps with future Danger, it is to be regarded almost as a matter of course, that it belongs to the Allies to charge themselves collectively with the Responsibility of exercising some Jurisdiction concerning such possible eventual Danger.—

One objection to this view of our duties, if there was no other, is, that unless We are prepared to support our interference with force, our judgement or advice is likely to be but rarely listened to, and would by frequent Repetition soon fall into complete contempt. So long as We keep to the great and simple conservative principles of the Alliance, when the dangers therein contemplated shall be visibly realized, there is little risk of difference or of disunion amongst the Allies: All will have a common interest: But it is far otherwise when We attempt with the Alliance to embrace subordinate, remote, and speculative cases of danger;—all the Powers may indeed have an interest in averting the assumed danger, but all have not by any means a common faculty of combating it, in it's more speculative Shapes, nor can they all without embarrassing seriously the internal administration of their own affairs be prepared to show themselves in jealous observation of transactions, which, before they have assumed a practical character, publick opinion would not go along with them in counteracting.—

This principle is perfectly clear and intelligible in the case of Spain: We may all agree that nothing can be more lamentable, or of more dangerous example, than the late revolt of the Spanish Army: We may all agree, that nothing can be more unlike a monarchical Government, or less suited to the wants and true interests of the Spanish Nation, than the Constitution of the year 1812; We may also agree, with shades of difference, that the consequence of this state of things in Spain may eventually bring danger home to all our own doors, but it does not follow, that We have therefore equal means of acting upon this opinion: For instance the Emperor of Russia, from the nature of his authority, can have nothing to weigh, but the physical or moral difficulties external from his own Gov[ernmen]t or Dominions, which are in the way of his giving effect to his Designs:—If H[is] I[mperial] M[ajesty]'s Mind is settled upon these points, His Action is free and His Means are in His own hands. The King of Great Britain, from the nature of our Constitution, has on the contrary all His means to acquire through Parliament, and He must well know that if embarked in a War, which the Voice of the Country does not support, the Efforts of the strongest Administration which ever served the Crown would soon be unequal to the prosecution of the Contest. In Russia there is but little publick Sentiment with regard to Spain, which can embarrass the decision of the Sovereign; In Great Britain there is a great deal, and the Current of that Sentiment runs strongly against the late Policy of the King of Spain. Besides, the People of this Country would probably not recognize (unless Portugal was attacked) that our Safety could be so far menaced by any State of things in Spain, as to warrant their Government in sending an Army to that Country to meddle in it's internal affairs; We cannot conceal from ourselves how generally the Acts of the King of Spain since His restoration have rendered His Government unpopular and how impossible it would be to reconcile the People of England to the use of force, if such a Proceeding could for a moment be thought of by the British Cabinet for the purpose of replacing power in His hands, however He might engage to qualify it. The principle upon which the British Government acted in the discussions with respect to the Colonies, (viz: never to employ forcible means for their reduction) would equally preclude them from any intervention of such a character with regard to Old Spain. The interposition of our good offices, whether singly, or in concert with the Allied Gov[ern-men]ts, if uncalled for by any authority within Spain, even by the King Himself, is by no means free from a like inconvenience as far as regards the Position of the British Government at Home; This species of intervention especially when coming from Five great Powers, has more or less the air of dictation and menace, and the possibility of it's being intended to be ultimately pushed to a forcible intervention is always assumed or imputed by an adverse party. The grounds of the intervention thus become unpopular, the intention of the parties is misunderstood, the publick Mind is agitated and perverted, and the General Political Situation of the Government is thereby essentially embarrassed.—

This Statement is only meant to prove, that We ought to see somewhat clearly to what purpose of real Utility our Effort tends, before We embark in proceedings which can never be indifferent in their bearings upon the Government taking part in them.—In this country at all times, but especially at the present conjuncture, when the whole Energy of the State is required to unite reasonable men in defence of our existing Institutions, and to put down the spirit of Treason and Disaffection which in certain of the Manufacturing Districts in particular, pervades the lower orders, it is of the greatest moment, that the publick Sentiment should not be distracted or divided, by any unnecessary Interference of the Government in events passing abroad, over which they can have none or at best but very imperfect means of controul.— Nothing could be more injurious to the Continental Powers than to have their affairs made matter of daily discussion in our Parliament, which nevertheless must be the consequence of Their precipitately mixing themselves in the affairs of other States, if We should consent to proceed pari passu with them in such interferences. It is not merely the temporary inconvenience produced to the British Government by being so committed, that is to be apprehended, but it is the exposing ourselves to have the publick Mind soured by the effects of a meddling policy, when it can tend to nothing really effectual, and pledged perhaps beforehand against any exertion whatever in Continental Affairs;—the fatal effects of such a false step might be irreparable when the moment at which we might be indispensably called upon by Duty and Interest to take a part should ar[r]ive.

These Considerations will suggest a doubt whether that extreme degree of unanimity and supposed concurrence upon all political subjects w[oul]d be either a practicable or a desirable principle of action among the Allied States, upon matters not essentially connected with the main purposes of the Alliance. If this Identity is to be sought for, it can only be attained by a proportionate degree of inaction in all the States. The position of the Ministers at Paris for instance can never be altogether uniform, unless their language upon Publick Affairs is either of the most general description, or they agree to hold no publick language whatever:—The latter Expedient is perhaps the most prudent, but then the Unanimity of the Sentiment, thus assumed to be established, will not be free from inconvenience to some of the parties, if the Cabinets of other States by their publick documents assign objects to that Concert, to which, at least as described by them, the others cannot conveniently subscribe. The fact is that we do not, and cannot feel alike upon all Subjects:—Our Position, our Institutions, the Habits of thinking, and the prejudices of our People, render us essentially different;—We cannot in all matters reason or feel alike; We should lose the Confidence of our respective Nations if we did, and the very affectation of such an Impossibility would soon render the Alliance an Object of Odium, and Distrust, whereas, if we keep it within its *common Sense* limits, the Representative Governments, and those which are more purely Monarchical, may well find each a common Interest, and a common facility in discharging their Duties under the Alliance, without creating an Impression that they have made a surrender of the first principles upon which their respective Gov[ernmen]ts are founded.—Each Government will then retain it's due faculty of independent Action, always recollecting, that they have all a common Refuge in the Alliance, as well as a common Duty to perform, whenever such a Danger shall really exist, as that against which the Alliance was specially intended to provide.

There is at present very naturally a widespread apprehension of the fatal Consequences to the publick Tranquillity of Europe, that may be expected to flow from the dangerous Principles of the present Day, at work more or less in every European State, Consequences which no human foresight can presume to estimate.

In all Dangers the first Calculation of Prudence is to consider what we should avoid and on what we should endeavour to rely:—In considering Continental Europe as divided into two great Masses, the Western, consisting of France and Spain, the Eastern of all the other Continental States still subsisting with some limited exceptions, under the form of their ancient Institutions, the great Question is, what System of General and defensive Policy (subject of course to special Exceptions arising out of the Circumstances of the particular Case) ought the latter States to adopt with a view of securing themselves against those dangers, which may directly or indirectly assail them from the former.—By the late Proceedings at Vienna, which for all purposes of internal tranquillity, bind up the various States of Germany into a single and undivided Power, a great degree of additional simplicity as well as Strength has been given to this Portion of Europe. By this Expedient there is established on that side of Europe, instead of a multitude of dispersed States, two great Bodies, Russia and Germany, of the latter of which, Austria and Prussia may for purposes of internal tranquillity be regarded as component parts. In addition to these there remain but few Pieces on the board to complicate the Game of Publick Safety.

In considering then how the game can best be played, the first thing that occurs for our Consideration is, what good can these States hope to effect in France or Spain by their mere Councils? Perhaps it would not be far from the truth to say, None whatever:—When the chances of Error, Jealousy and National Sentiment are considered, the Probability of Mischief would be more truly assigned to the System of constant European Interference upon these Volcanick Masses:—

Of this truth the Duke de Richelieu seems fully satisfied, as appears by the manly and earnest Intreaties which he has lately addressed to certain of the Allies' Courts that, they would keep their Ministers quiet at Paris, and that abstaining themselves from all advice or interference, They would leave the French Government to combat for themselves and upon their own views of things, the dangers which surround them.—

What could The Allied Powers look to effect by their Arms, if the supposition of an armed interference in the internal affairs of another State could be admitted? Perhaps as little;

Because in supposing them finally triumphant, We have the problem still to solve, how the country in which such Interference had been successful was to provide for its Self-Government after the Allied Armies shall have been withdrawn, without soon becoming an equal Source of danger to the tranquillity of neighbouring States; but when we consider how much danger may arise to the internal Safety of the rest of Europe, by the absence of those Armies which must be withdrawn to overrun the Country in which the supposed Interference was to take place,—what may be the danger of these Armies being contaminated,—what may be the incumbrances to be added by such renewed exertions to the already overwhelming Weight of the debts of the different States,—what the local irritation which must be occasioned by pouring forth such immense armies pressing severely as they must do upon the resources of Countries already agitated and inflamed, —no rational Statesman surely w[oul]d found his prospects of Security on such a calculation: He would rather be of opinion, that the only necessity which could in wisdom justify such an attempt is, that which, temperately considered, appears to leave to Europe no other option, than that of either going to meet that danger which they cannot avoid, or having it poured in the full tide of military invasion upon their own States.—The actual Existence of such a danger may indeed be inferred from many circumstances short of the visible preparations for attack, but it is submitted that on this basis the conclusion should always be examined.

If this position is correctly laid down, it may be asserted, that the case supposed, not only does not at present exist, but the chances of such a danger have latterly rather declined in proportion as both France and Spain are almost exclusively and deeply occupied by their own internal embarrassments: The military Power in France at this day is circumscribed within those limits which are not more than competent to the necessary duties of the Interior; That of Spain is upon even a more reduced Scale, whilst the military Establishments of all the other European States, and especially that of Russia, were never perhaps at any period of their history upon a footing of more formidable efficiency both in point of Discipline and Numbers;* Surely then, if these States can preserve harmony among themselves, and exercise a proper degree of vigilance with respect to their interior Police, there is nothing in this state of things which should prevent them from abiding with patience and with firmness the result of the great political process to which circumstances have given existence in the States to the Westward of their Frontiers. They may surely permit these Nations to work out by their own means, and by the lights of their own Councils, that result which no doubt materially bears upon the general Interests of the World, but which is more especially to decide their own particular destinies, without being led to interfere with them, at least so long as their own immediate Security is not directly menaced, or until some Crisis shall arise which may call for some specifick, intelligible and practicable interposition on their part.

The principle of one State interfering by force in the internal affairs of another, in order to enforce obedience to the governing authority, is always a question of the greatest possible moral as well as political delicacy, and it is not meant here to examine it.—It is only important on the present occasion to observe that to generalize such a principle and to think of reducing it to a System, or to impose it as an obligation, is a Scheme utterly impracticable and objectionable. There is not only the physical impossibility of giving execution to such a System, but there is the moral impracticability arising from the inaptitude of particular States to recognize, or to act upon it.—No Country having a Representative System of Gov[ernmen]t could act upon it,—and the sooner such a Doctrine shall be distinctly abjured as forming in any Degree the Basis of our Alliance, the better;—in order that States, in calculating the means of their own Security may not suffer Disappointment by expecting from the Allied Powers, a support which, under the special Circumstances of

* It was estimated in 1826 that Russia had a European army of 860,000 men (which exceeded the total forces of France, Prussia, Austria and England in Europe). Wellington said that half that number would have been enough for Russia.

their National Institutions they cannot give:—Great Britain
has perhaps equal Power with any other State to oppose
Herself to a practical and intelligible Danger, capable of being
brought home to the National Feeling:—When the Territorial
Balance of Europe is disturbed, she can interfere with effect,
but She is the last Gov[ernmen]t in Europe, which can be
expected, or can venture to commit Herself on any question
of an abstract Character.

These observations are made to point attention to what is
practicable and what is not.—If the dreaded Moral Contagion
should unfortunately extend itself into Germany, and if the
flame of Military Revolt should for example, burst forth in
any of the German States, it is in vain for that State, however
anxiously and sincerely we deprecate such a Calamity, to turn
it's Eyes to this Country for the means of effectually suppressing
such a Danger:—If External Means are indispensable for it's
Suppression, such State must not reckon for assistance upon
Gov[ernmen]ts constituted as that of Great Britain, but it is
not therefore without it's Resource.

The internal Peace of each German State is by Law placed
under the protection of the Army of the Empire:—The Duty
which is imposed by the Laws of the Confederacy upon all
German States, to suppress, by the Military Power of the
whole mass, Insurrection within the Territories of Each and
Every of the Co-Estates, is an immense Resource in itself, and
ought to give to the Centre of Europe a sense of Security which
previous to the Reunion of Vienna was wholly wanting:—
The Importance of preventing the Low Countries, the Military
Barrier of Europe, from being lost, by being melted down into
the general Mass of French Power, whether by Insurrection,
or by Conquest, might enable the British Gov[ernmen]t to
act more promptly upon this, than perhaps upon any other
Case of an internal Character that can be stated;—But upon
all such Cases we must admit ourselves to be, and our Allies
should in fairness understand that we are, a Power that must
take our Principle of action, and our Scale of acting, not
merely from the Expediency of the Case, but from those
Maxims, which a System of Government strongly popular,

and national in it's character has irresistibly imposed upon us.] We shall be found in our place when actual danger menaces the System of Europe, but this Country cannot, and will not, act upon abstract and speculative Principles of Precaution:—The Alliance which exists had no such purpose in view in its original formation:—It was never so explained to Parliament; if it had, most assuredly the sanction of Parliament would never have been given to it, and it would now be a breach of Faith were the Ministers of the Crown to acquiesce in a Construction being put upon it, or were they to suffer themselves to be betrayed into a Course of Measures, inconsistent with those Principles which they avowed at the time, and which they have since uniformly maintained both at Home and Abroad, [and which were more fully developed in a confidential Memorandum delivered in by the British Plenipotentiaries to those of the Allies, at Aix la Chapelle, bearing date in October 1818, to which Memorandum they now refer as more fully Illustrative of their Sentiments.]*

* The text is given *supra*, **Doc. 5**, on pp. 39–46.

IV. CANNING, 1822–7

7. EUROPE. Canning and the Anti-Congress Policy, his Appeal to Public Opinion

[Castlereagh's State Paper of 5 May 1820 had defined the principles of British Foreign policy to which, as we have seen (p. 48), Canning in theory adhered. But there were important differences in practice. During 1821, the New Holy Alliance (Austria, Russia and Prussia) had intervened in the internal affairs of Naples, threatened to intervene in those of Spain, and declared such intervention to be a duty. Castlereagh protested again in a circular dispatch of January 1821—which was published.* Otherwise he was not able to offer much effective opposition. There were several reasons for this attitude but the main one was that during 1821 the Greek revolt flourished and there was great fear that the excitable Tsar Alexander would go to war with Turkey to bring aid to his co-religionists.†

Castlereagh knew of no way of restraining him but by talking of Union and by proposing a new Congress. He therefore proposed to summon a new Congress at Verona. So up till his death Castlereagh was still using Europe and the Congress idea to keep Alexander at peace with Turkey.

Immediately after Castlereagh's death the Congress opened at Verona. But by this time the danger of war with Turkey had passed and Canning could take a bolder line. The only fear was that France by herself, or Austria, Russia and Prussia in common, might interfere by force to put down the constitutional movement in Spain. Canning's policy is given in his own words. He instructed the British representative (the Duke of Wellington) as follows: "If, as I confess I see reason to apprehend...there is entertained by the Allies a determined project of interference by force, or by menace, in the present struggle in Spain, so convinced are His Majesty's Government of the uselessness and danger of any such interference,—so objectionable does it appear to them in principle, and so utterly impracticable in execution—that, if the necessity should arise, or (I would rather say) if the opportunity should offer, I am to instruct your Grace at once frankly and peremptorily to declare, that to any such interference, *come what may*, His Majesty will not be a party."‡

* Text in *A. & P.*, [1821,] XXII, 1–4; cp. Temperley and Penson, *Century of Diplomatic Blue Books*, No. 95.
† *V.* C. K. Webster, *The Foreign Policy of Castlereagh, 1815–22*, [1925], 363.
‡ Quoted in Temperley, *The Foreign Policy of Canning*, [1925], 64–5.

The Duke of Wellington executed his instructions on 30 October 1823 and, in effect, broke up the Congress of Verona by refusing to commit England to the policies of the Continent. He refused to agree with the New Holy Alliance which had one policy, or with France which had another. "We stand alone," said the Duke, "and we do so by choice." This was in fact the death blow to the Congress system, though, as so often, the effect of the blow was not immediately seen. But in December 1823 Spain asked the Powers to attend a Congress to discuss the question of her revolted American Colonies. Canning refused to attend and said England would take her own course regardless of the Powers. By the end of 1824 he initiated steps for recognizing three Spanish American States as independent (Argentine, Columbia, Mexico). When Tsar Alexander summoned a Congress on Turkey in December 1824 Canning refused in effect to attend, and it broke up in confusion by the May of 1825. That was the last Congress of the old type. Canning had ended it all in three years.

In his State Paper of 5 May 1820 Castlereagh proclaimed separation from Congressional Europe. Canning enforced it. The difference lay not in principle but in the means used. Castlereagh had been hampered by his past relations with despots who affected to believe he was not in earnest, and by having to revert to Congress policy at Verona. In addition "throughout his career, therefore, Castlereagh was impatient of Parliamentary criticism and that of public opinion generally...he could hardly hope to make his fellow countrymen understand his point of view".*

Canning, who came fresh to power without embarrassments, who was a great orator, saw that a breach with despotic sovereigns would be popular, and that the public would support him in breaking off from Congresses. Even during his first ministry he had published Blue Books with unusual frequency and got the popular applause for doing so.† He now evoked rounds of applause when he spoke of "the immediate object of England" as being to "take care that the war should not grow out of an assumed jurisdiction of the Congress; to keep within reasonable bounds that predominating *areopagitical* spirit [of the despots];" and of his desire "to get rid of the Areopagus and all that".‡

That utterance seemed the appeal of an orator. But immediately after he quotes from Castlereagh's State Paper of 5 May 1820 saying that the *Areopagitical spirit* is "beyond the sphere of the original conception and understood principles of the Alliance", which was never "intended for the government of the world or

* C. K. Webster in *Camb. Hist. Journ.* 1, No. 2, [1924], 159.
† Temperley and Penson, *Century of Diplomatic Blue Books*, p. 1.
‡ Speech of 28 April 1823, *Speeches*, ed. R. Therry, v, 63.

for the superintendence of the internal affairs of other States".
What is new, therefore, is not the principle of separation from the
New Holy Alliance, but the popular appeal and the reliance on
public opinion to support England when she stood aloof and
isolated. A British Cabinet, supported by Parliament and the
people, was stronger than a foreign despot, supported by millions
of bayonets. Opinion was stronger than armies and was a thunderbolt in the hand of a British Minister. It was Canning who
discovered this new source of strength and power.]

Document 7. *Extract from Speech of* 12 *December* 1826, *on the new source of England's power**

Sir, I set out with saying that there were reasons which
induced me to think that nothing short of a point of national
faith or national honour I will not say would justify, but would
make desirable at the present moment, any voluntary approxi-
mation to the possibility of a dangerous war. Let me be
understood, however, distinctly, as not meaning to say that
I dread war in a good cause (and in no other may it be the
lot of this country ever to engage!) from a distrust of the
strength of the country to commence it, or of her resources
to maintain it. I dread it, indeed—but upon far other
grounds: I dread it from a consciousness of the tremendous
power Great Britain possesses of pushing hostilities in which
we may be engaged, to consequences which I shudder to
contemplate. Some years ago, in the discussion of the negocia-
tions respecting the French war against Spain, I took the
liberty of adverting to this topic. I then stated that the
position of this country in the present state of the world was
one of neutrality, not only between contending nations, but
between contending principles; and that it was by neutrality
alone that we could maintain that balance, the preservation
of which I believed to be essential to peace and safety of the
world. I then said that I feared that the next war which
should be kindled in Europe, would be a war not so much of
armies, as of opinions. Four years' experience...has confirmed
rather than altered my opinion. It is, to be sure, within
narrow limits that this war of opinion will be confined: but

* Temperley, *Foreign Policy of Canning*, 579–81.

it *is* a war of opinion that Spain (whether as Government or as nation) is now waging against Portugal; it is a war which has commenced in hatred of the new institutions of Portugal. How long is it reasonable to expect that Portugal will abstain from retaliation? I fear that the next war to be kindled in Europe, if it spread beyond the narrow limits of Spain and Portugal, will be a war of most tremendous character—a war not merely of conflicting armies, but of conflicting opinions. (*Cheering.*)

I know that if into that war this country enters (and if she do engage, I trust it will be with a most sincere desire to mitigate rather than exasperate, and to contend with arms, rather than with the more fatal artillery of popular excitation), she will see under her banners, arrayed for the contest all the discontented and restless spirits of the age, all those who— whether justly or unjustly—are dissatisfied with the present state of their own countries. The consciousness of such a situation excites all my fears, for it shows there exists a power to be wielded by Great Britain, more tremendous than was perhaps ever yet brought into action in the history of mankind. (*Hear.*) But, though it may be "excellent to have a giant's power it may be tyrannous to use it like a giant". The knowledge that we possess this strength is our security; and our business is not to seek opportunities of displaying it, but to content ourselves with letting the professors of violent and exaggerated doctrines on both sides feel that it is not their interest to convert an umpire into their competitor. The situation of this country may be compared to that of the Ruler of the Winds.

> "Celsâ sedet Aeolus arce,
> Sceptra tenens; mollitque animos et temperat iras;
> Ni faciat, maria ac terras coelumque profundum
> Quippe ferant rapidi secum, verrantque per auras."*

* This is the text of the speech as actually delivered. A corrected version was subsequently issued owing to the pressure of George IV. The chief point of alteration was that England would find on her side the discontented of *any* country with whom she went to war, not of *all* countries. *V.* Temperley, *Foreign Policy of Canning*, 579–85.

8. CALLING THE NEW WORLD INTO EXISTENCE

CANNING'S FEAR OF FRENCH INTERVENTION FROM SPAIN; COMMERCIAL RECOGNITION OF SPANISH AMERICA

[Canning recognized Latin America, the Argentine, Columbia, Mexico, Venezuela, Honduras, Brazil, as nations. In this sense he "called the New World into existence". The situation in 1823 must be very briefly sketched. For many years the struggle between Spain and her revolted Colonies had been proceeding. They had been loyal until loyalty became impossible, and finally separated from the Motherland because of the corruption and inefficiency of her rule. At the period with which we deal, the year 1823, the States of the Rio de la Plata (the modern Argentine Republic) had been entirely free for many years. Equally free was Columbia (which included the modern Venezuela). The struggle was nearly hopeless in Chile. In Mexico the Spanish loyalists held a castle, veritably a castle in Spain, and the only one. In Peru a balanced contest was still maintained. From 1820 onwards the Spanish Monarchy was in the throes of revolution at home. Ferdinand VII had to appoint a constitutional ministry. It actually negotiated with the Rio de la Plata on the basis of independence, but this attempt was ultimately disavowed by Ferdinand VII. His act convinced England that there could be no reconciliation save on the basis of independence, and that it was hopeless for Spain to attempt the recovery of her authority by force.

Castlereagh undoubtedly took this view and referred to recognition in 1822 as "a matter of time and circumstance". In 1823, however, France precipitated events. Her Government thought that the constitutionalists in Spain were too violent and were endangering peace. The French Bourbon Louis XVIII thought it a duty to prevent the Spanish Bourbon Ferdinand VII from being bullied into too extreme a constitution. So a French army crossed the Pyrenees to "free" the Spanish King. This action was a menace to peace and was regarded with great jealousy by England. But Canning said England would not fight if three conditions were observed. France was not to remain permanently in Spain; she was not to violate the territorial integrity of Portugal (which England was pledged to defend); and she was not to attempt to appropriate any part of the Spanish Colonies to herself.

It is the third of these points with which we are concerned. In the old days the trade with Spanish America had been monopolized by the Mother Country. The Spanish Colonies opened their ports as they revolted, and their trade fell naturally and almost mechanically into England's lap. As Spain herself was clearly incapable of reconquering her Colonies, there was no danger that England would be deprived of this trade. But if French soldiers victoriously subdued Old Spain, French sailors might attempt to reconquer the Spanish Colonies. In that case King Louis might plant French princes in Spanish America and restrict the Spanish colonial trade to French ships. Canning was determined to prevent either possibility.

As the French army advanced into Spain the Spanish constitutionalists retreated before it, dragging the captive Ferdinand along with them. The Spanish people did not like the constitutionalists because they were liberals and opposed to the Church. Hence the French army, this time, was as popular in Spain as Napoleon's had been detested. Within a short time the French army had victoriously advanced to Madrid and finally shut up the constitutionalists in Cadiz. In September its fall was only a question of time. Canning hesitated no longer. "The Pyrenees had fallen, he would maintain the Atlantic." He accredited consuls to various ports of the South American States in order to make clear that he would retain uninterrupted commercial relations with them.*

In the first days of October 1823, before Cadiz had actually fallen, Canning had several interviews with the French Ambassador, the Prince de Polignac. The result is given in **Doc. 8**, which follows. The principles established were three: First, France was definitely warned off any interference "by force or by menace", and Polignac, thus challenged, definitely promised not to interfere. Second (in the part of the memorandum left unpublished at the time), Canning said that he would not enter a Congress on the future of Spanish America unless the United States were invited to become a member of it. Third, England declared she would recognize the Spanish Colonies as independent at once if any attempt was made to restrict her existing trade with them. As regards the first point, it has been suggested that the threat of France to intervene by force of arms in Spanish America was not very real. But this policy was pursued by a strong minority in French governmental circles, and among others by Polignac himself. It might soon have become that of the French Government as a whole. Anyhow Canning's action settled that the New World should develop unhindered by the arms of Europe. It remained under the protection of the British Fleet until the United States was strong enough to put the Monroe Doctrine into practice.

* According to more recent international law, this step would imply ultimate diplomatic recognition, but it was not the intention of Canning to concede more than commercial recognition at the time.

As regards the two other principles Canning shewed distinct originality. The Conferences of Great Powers had hitherto been confined to Europe, but Canning was prepared to include a power from the New World and thus introduce the United States into world politics. The Congress did not meet so the project never materialized. But Europe was horrified and astounded by Canning's proposal to invite a Republic to share the deliberations of Kings. It was an important testimony to the power of the United States rendered by Canning in the very year that President Monroe proclaimed his famous doctrine. As regards his third principle Canning shewed that he would not, in any case, inter- rupt British trade with the Spanish Colonies and that he regarded the question of the recognition of their independence by Great Britain as one of time only.]

Document 8. *The Polignac Memorandum, October* 1823; *or "hands off" to Europe in the New World*

The Prince de Polignac having announced to Mr. Canning, that His Excellency was now prepared to enter with Mr. Canning into a frank explanation of the views of his Govern- ment respecting the question of Spanish America, in return for a similar communication which Mr. Canning had pre- viously offered to make to The Prince de Polignac, on the part of the British Cabinet; Mr. Canning stated that the British Cabinet has no disguise or reservation on that subject:

That their opinions and intentions were substantially the same as were announced to the French Government by the Dispatch of Mr. Canning to Sir Charles Stuart of the 31st of March, which that Ambassador had communicated to M. de Chateaubriand, and which had since been published to the world;

That the near approach of a crisis, in which the Affairs of Spanish America must naturally occupy a great share of the attention of both Powers, made it desirable that there should

* "Memorandum of a Conference between The Prince de Polignac and Mr. Canning, begun Thursday October 9th and concluded Sunday October 12th 1823", enclosure in Canning to Stuart, No. 84 of 9 November 1823, *F.O.* 146/56. Part published in *A. & P.*, [1824], xxiv, 641–53, *v.* Temperley and Penson, *Century of Diplomatic Blue Books*, No. 131. Cp. also *B.F.S.P.* xi, 49–53. The suppressed passages were printed for the first time by Temperley in the *Cambridge History of British Foreign Policy*, [1923], ii, 633–7. Cp. also Temperley, *Foreign Policy of Canning*, 114–18.

be no misunderstanding between them on any part of a subject so important.—

That the British Government were of opinion, that any attempt to bring Spanish America again under its ancient submission to Spain, must be utterly hopeless;—that all Negotiation for that purpose would be unsuccessful;—and that the prolongation or renewal of War for the same object, would be only a waste of human life, and an infliction of calamity upon both parties to no end.

That the British Government would, however, not only abstain from interposing any obstacle, on their part, to any attempt at Negotiation which Spain might think proper to make, but would aid and countenance such Negotiation, provided it were founded upon a basis which appeared to them to be practicable, and that they would, in any case, remain strictly neutral in a War between Spain and the Colonies,—if War should unhappily be prolonged;—But that the junction of any foreign Power in an enterprize of Spain against the Colonies, would be viewed by them as constituting an entirely new question; and one upon which they must take such decision as the interest of Great Britain might require.

That the British Government absolutely disclaimed, not only any desire of appropriating to itself any portion of the Spanish Colonies; but any intention of forming a political connection with them, beyond that of Amity and Commercial Intercourse.

That, in these respects, so far from seeking an exclusive preference for its Subjects over those of other foreign States, it was prepared, and would be contented, to see the Mother Country (by virtue of an amicable arrangement) in possession of that preference; and to be ranked, after her, equally with others, only on the footing of the most favoured Nation.

That, completely convinced that the ancient system of the Colonies could not be restored, the British Government could not enter into any stipulation binding Itself either to refuse or to delay its recognition of their Independence.—

That the British Government has had no desire to precipitate that recognition, so long as there was any reasonable chance of an accommodation with the Mother Country, by which such a recognition might come first from Spain; but that It could not wait indefinitely for that result; that It could not consent to make Its recognition of the New States *dependent* upon that of Spain; and that It would consider any foreign interference by force or by menace in the dispute between Spain and the Colonies, as a Motive for recognizing the latter without delay.—

That the mission of Consuls to the several Provinces of Spanish America, was no new Measure on the part of this Country;—that it was one which had, on the contrary, been delayed, perhaps too long, in consideration of the state of Spain, after having been announced to the Spanish Government, in the Month of December last, as settled; and even after a List had been furnished to that Government of the Places to which such Appointments were intended to be made.*

That such Appointments were absolutely necessary for the protection of British Trade in those Countries.—That the old pretension of Spain to interdict all Trade with those Countries was, in the opinion of the British Government, altogether obsolete;—but that, even if attempted to be enforced against others, it was, with regard to Great Britain, clearly inapplicable.—

That permission to trade with the Spanish Colonies had been conceded to Great Britain in the Year 1810, when the Mediation of Great Britain between Spain and her Colonies was asked by Spain, and granted by Great Britain;†—That this Mediation indeed was not afterwards employed, because Spain changed her Counsel;—but that it was not therefore practicable for Great Britain to withdraw Commercial Capital once embarked in Spanish America, and to desist from Commercial intercourse once established.—

That it had been ever since distinctly understood, that the Trade was open to British Subjects, and that the ancient Coast Laws of Spain were, so far as regarded them at least, tacitly repealed.—

[* Note. Mr. Canning here read to The Prince de Polignac Extracts of Two Dispatches addressed to Sir William à Court, on the 5th and 28th of December 1822, in which that Minister was directed to make these successive communications to the Spanish Government. Note in original.]

† This seems to be inaccurate, *v.* note at end of volume, pp. 523–6.

That, in virtue of this understanding, redress had been demanded of Spain in the Year 1822, for (among other grievances) seizures of Vessels for alleged infringements of those Laws, which redress the Spanish Government bound Itself by a Convention (now in course of execution) to afford.—

That Great Britain, however, had no desire to set up any separate right to the free enjoyment of this Trade;—That She considered the force of circumstances, and the irreversible progress of events, to have already determined the question of the existence of that freedom for all the World;—But that, for Herself, She claimed and would continue to use it; and should any attempt be made to dispute that claim, and to renew the obsolete interdiction, such attempt might be best cut short by a speedy and unqualified recognition of the Independence of the Spanish American States.—

That, with these general opinions, and with these peculiar claims, England could not go into a joint deliberation upon the subject of Spanish America, upon an equal footing with other Powers, whose opinions were less formed upon that question, and whose interests were no way implicated in the decision of it.

That She thought it fair therefore to explain beforehand, to what degree Her mind was made up, and Her determination taken [so far as Mr. Canning had explained it.—]

The Prince de Polignac declared, that his Government believed it to be utterly hopeless to reduce Spanish America to the state of its former relation to Spain;—that France disclaimed, on Her part, any intention or desire to avail Herself of the present state of the Colonies, or of the present Situation of France towards Spain, to appropriate to Herself any part of the Spanish Possessions in America; or to obtain for Herself any exclusive advantages; and that, like England, She would willingly see the Mother Country in possession of superior Commercial advantages, by amicable arrangement; and would be contented, like Her, to rank, after the Mother Country, among the most favoured Nations.—Lastly, that She abjured, in any case, any design of acting against the Colonies by force of Arms.—

〚Mr. Canning having alluded to certain reports in the Newspapers, of some attack, or intended attack, by a French Naval Force against the Independents in Columbia,〛 the Prince de Polignac said, 〚that so far from intending any such hostile act, the French Government had recalled the only Line of Battle Ship in those Seas, the "Jean Bart";—which is on its return to France.—〛

That as to what might be the best arrangement between Spain and Her Colonies, the French Government could not give, nor venture to form, an opinion, until The King of Spain should be at liberty.—That they would then be ready to enter upon it in concert with their Allies, and with Great Britain among the number.

In observing upon what Mr. Canning had said with respect to the peculiar situation of Great Britain in reference to such a concert* the Prince de Polignac declared he saw no difficulty to prevent England from taking part in the Congress* however She might now announce the difference in the view which She took of the Question from that taken by the allies— The refusal of England to cooperate in the work of reconciliation might afford reason to think either that She did not really wish for that reconciliation, or that She had some ulterior object in contemplation, two suppositions equally injurious to the Honour and Good Faith of the British Cabinet.—The Prince de Polignac further declared that he could not conceive what could be meant, under present circumstances, by a pure and simple acknowledgement of the Independence of the Spanish Colonies; since those Countries being actually distracted by civil Wars, there existed no Government in them which could offer any appearance of solidity and that the acknowledgement of American Independence, so long as such a state continued, appeared to him to be nothing less than a real sanction of Anarchy.

The Prince de Polignac observed that in the interest of humanity, and especially in that of the Spanish Colonies, it would be worthy of the European Governments to concert

* In the version printed in *B.F.S.P.* the word "Conference" is substituted for "concert" and "Congress".

together the means of calming in those distant and scarcely civilized regions passions blinded by party Spirit; and to endeavour to bring back to a principle of Union in Government, whether Monarchical or Aristocratical People among whom absurd and dangerous theories were now keeping up Agitation and Disunion.

Mr. Canning without entering into any discussion upon abstract principles contented himself with saying that however desirable the Establishment of a Monarchical Form of Govern-[men]t in any of those Provinces might be, he saw great difficulties in the way of it, nor could his Government take upon itself to recommend it.*

⟦Mr. Canning further remarked that he could not understand how an *European* Congress could discuss Spanish American Affairs without calling to their Counsels a Power so eminently interested in the result, as the United States of *America*,† while Austria, Russia and Prussia, Powers so much less concerned in the subject were in consultation upon it.

The Prince de Polignac professed himself unprovided with any opinion of His Government upon what respected the United States of America; but did not *for himself* see any insuperable difficulty to such an Association. He added, that he saw the less difficulty in a Congress upon this subject, as such a mode of treating it had been proposed at Verona by the Duke of Wellington.

Referring to the Convention said to have been concluded between the Govern[men]t of Buenos Ayres and the Commiss[ione]rs from Spain, and especially to the declaration of the Buenos Ayres Legislature accompanying that Convention which promised a Subsidy to Spain in the War against France; the Prince de Polignac was not prepared to say, how far such a declaration might be considered by his Government

---

* In the version printed in *B.F.S.P.* the final sentence of this paragraph ends as follows: "Saying that,—however desirable the establishment of a Monarchical form of Government, in any of those Provinces, might be, on the one hand, or whatever might be the difficulties in the way of it, on the other hand—his Government could not take upon Itself to put it forward as a condition of their Recognition."

† This proposal so remarkable in that age, as admitting an overseas Republic to a Congress, was of course carefully concealed from the public.

as an act of hostility against France:—But, upon Mr. Canning's observing that the declaration was only eventual and conditional, that it depended for its confirmation on two Circumstances:—1st. The Ratification of the Convention by the King of Spain; and 2dly—The acceptance of the like terms and the conclusion of similar Conventions with Spain by *all* the other States of Spanish America;—neither of which had yet occurred, and further that, even if carried into effect, such a subsidy would have done no more against France, than the Colonies might have been bound to do, if still under the Controul of the Mother Country;—The Prince de Polignac was willing to admit that this case was not one which could be expected to change practically the Views of his Government, with respect to the general question of Spanish America, or much to influence the general principles of Policy, by which that question must be decided.

But upon this point The Prince de Polignac said, that he was speaking only his own individual opinion, and that opinion not formed upon mature reflection.]*

Introduction

[The Polignac Memorandum ended all question of French or European interference by force in the New World, but it was not until the last day of 1824 that Canning completed arrangements for negotiating commercial treaties with the most advanced of the new independent Republics. These were Rio de la Plata (Argentine), Columbia and Mexico respectively. Full political recognition followed in 1825 with the ratification of the treaties. In this way Canning recognized the New World. It will, perhaps, be useful to indicate the rival theories of recognition that prevailed at this time. There were three, and the first two started from ideal bases. The American or United States' view erred a little by excess of zeal. They were too ready to recognize a revolted colony because it was a republic without considering if it was sufficiently stable. The Spanish view, which was held also by Russia, Austria and Prussia, was that a King alone could grant recognition to his revolted subjects. In other words, subjects could only revolt by permission of their King. The objection to this was practical.

* A P.S. of 15 October 1823 is omitted. It deals with Canning's view of the Duke of Wellington's attitude as regards the Spanish Colonies at the Congress of Verona with quotations.

Obviously subjects might in the future, and had in both past and present, revolted and formed a State before Kings were willing to recognize the fact. Such a revolted State was like an illegitimate baby. Its existence could not be denied, whether its father recognized it as his or not. Canning reconciled these two points of view. He admitted the one view of recognition, which came from the King or former sovereign at his own will. This was *de jure*. But there was also a recognition *de facto* which was based on a practical appreciation of whether the new State had shewn a sufficient degree of force and stability first to achieve its independence, and next to discharge internal and external acts of sovereignty. Provided it had, it mattered little whether the State was a monarchy or a republic. Stability was the first test of legitimacy. British recognition of a new State was not the recognition of a right but of a fact, "or rather of an opinion of a fact". The "fact" was that the new State existed and could act for itself.

Any British Ministry would have recognized the Spanish American Colonies in any case within a year or two after Canning recognized them. Englishmen are a practical race and awake to facts. Yet it was owing to Canning's insistence that the Colonies were recognized in 1825. And it was his peculiar power of thinking out principles to their conclusion which laid down the theory of recognition, a theory which has been adopted by every country in the world as a permanent part of international law. There are many illustrations of Canning's views, but the dispatch before us contains them in relatively short compass. It was written in reply to a remonstrance of the Spanish Minister. It is a model of diplomatic argument and an instance of extreme common sense applied to international law. We can only wonder to-day why it was then necessary to point out to Governments that facts could not be ignored, and that recognition of a new state of things could not be indefinitely delayed.]

Document 9. *Canning's theory of recognition,*
25 *March* 1825*

[The dispatch begins by a detailed refutation of the charge that "Britain has uniformly put forward the basis of independence as the *sine quâ non* condition of her counsel and assistance to Spain in negotiation with her Colonies".]

To come now to the second charge against G[rea]t Britain, the alleged violation of general international Law. Has it

---

* Note from George Canning to the Chevalier de Los Rios, Minister Plenipotentiary of His Most Catholic Majesty, 25 March 1825, *F.O.* 72/309. Cp. *B.F.S.P.* xii, 909–15. A few passages of little importance have been omitted, and the argument in them summarized.

ever been admitted as an Axiom, or ever been observed by any Nation or Gov[ernmen]t, as a practical Maxim, that no circumstances, and no time should entitle a *de facto* Gov[ernmen]t to recognition? or should entitle Third Powers, who may have a deep interest in defining and establishing their relations with a *de facto* Gov[ernmen]t, to do so?

Such a proceeding on the part of Third Powers, undoubtedly does not decide the question of right, against the Mother Country.

The Netherlands had thrown off the Supremacy of Spain, long before the end of the 16th Century: but that Supremacy was not formally renounced by Spain till the Treaty of Westphalia in 1648. Portugal declared in 1640, her independence of the Spanish Monarchy; but it was not till 1668, that Spain by Treaty acknowledged that independence.

During each of these intervals, the abstract rights of Spain may be said to have remained unextinguished. But Third Powers did not, in either of these instances, wait the slow conviction of Spain, before they thought themselves warranted to establish direct relations, and even to contract intimate Alliances, with the Republick of the United Netherlands, as well as with the New Monarchy of the House of Braganza.*

The Separation of the Spanish Colonies from Spain has been neither our work, nor our wish. Events in which the British Gov[ernmen]t had no participation, decided that separation: a separation which we are still of opinion might have been averted, if our Counsels had been listened to in time. But out of that separation grew a state of things, to which it was the duty of the British Gov[ernmen]t, (in proportion as it became the plain and legitimate interest of the nation whose welfare is committed to it's charge,) to conform its measures, as well as its language, not hastily and precipitately, but with due deliberation and circumspection.

To continue to call that a possession of Spain, in which all Spanish occupation and power had been actually extinguished

* The Dutch, though they had successfully revolted from Spain in 1580, did not secure *de jure* independence till 1648. Portugal, though conquered by Spain in 1580, had revolted against her in 1640 and had become independent under the House of Braganza.

and effaced, could render no practical service to the Mother
·Country;—but it would have risked the peace of the World.
For all political communities are responsible to other political
communities for their conduct:—that is, they are bound to
perform the ordinary international duties, and to afford
redress for any violation of the rights of others, by their
citizens or subjects.

Now, either the Mother Country must have continued
responsible for acts over which it could no longer exercise the
shadow of a controul; or the Inhabitants of those Countries,
whose independent political existence was, in fact, established,
but to whom the acknowledgement of that independence was
denied, must have been placed in a situation, in which they
were either wholly irresponsible for all their actions, or were
to be visited for such of those actions as might furnish ground
of complaint to other Nations, with the punishment due to
Pirates and Outlaws.

If the former of these alternatives, the total irresponsibility
of unrecognized States, be too absurd to be maintained; and
if the latter, the treatment of their Inhabitants as Pirates and
Outlaws, be too monstrous to be applied, for an indefinite
length of time, to a large portion of the habitable Globe; No
other choice remained for Great Britain, or for any Country
having intercourse with the Spanish American Provinces, but
to recognize in due time, their political existence as States,
and thus to bring them within the pale of those rights and
duties, which civilized Nations are bound mutually to respect,
and are entitled reciprocally to claim from each other.

The example of the late revolution in France, and of the
ultimate happy restoration of H[is] M[ajesty] Louis XVIII,
is pleaded...in illustration of the principle of the unextin-
guishable right in a legitimate Sovereign.

[Examples are then given of how "every power in Europe,
and, specifically, Spain amongst the foremost" not only recognized the successive governments of France, after the monarchy
was overturned, "but contracted intimate alliances with them
all".]

...The appeal, therefore, to the conduct of the Powers of

Europe, and even to that of Great Britain herself with respect to the French Revolution, does but recall abundant instances of the recognition of *de facto* Gov[ernmen]ts by G[rea]t Britain perhaps later and more reluctantly than by others, but by G[rea]t Britain Herself, however reluctant, after the example set to Her by the other Powers of Europe, and specifically by Spain.

... M. Zea declares that The King of Spain will never recognize the new States of Spanish America; and that H[is] M[ajesty] will never cease to employ the force of arms against his rebellious Subjects, in that part of the World.

We have neither the pretension, nor the desire to controul H[is] C[atholic] M[ajesty]'s conduct:—But this declaration of M. Zea comprises a complete justification of our conduct in having taken the opportunity which to us seemed ripe for placing our relations with the New States of America on a definite footing. For this declaration plainly shows, that the complaint against us is not merely as to the mode, or the time of our advances towards those States: It shows that the dispute between us and Spain is not merely as to the question of fact, whether the internal condition of any of those States, be such as to justify the entering into definite relations with them: that it was not merely a reasonable delay for the purpose of verifying contradictory reports, and of affording opportunity for friendly negotiation, that was required of us: It shows, that no extent of forbearance on our part would have satisfied Spain, and that, defer our advances towards the New States as long as we might, we should still have had to make them, without the consent of Spain; for that Spain is determined against all compromise, under any circumstances and at any time, and is resolved upon interminable War with her late Colonies in America.

M. Zea concludes with declaring that H[is] C[atholic] Majesty will protest in the most solemn manner against the measures announced by the British Gov[ernmen]t, as violating existing Treaties, and the imprescriptible rights of the Throne of Spain.

Against what will Spain protest?

It has been proved that no Treaties are violated by us;—and we admit that no question of right is decided by our Recognition of the New States of America.

But if the argument on which this declaration is founded be true, it is eternal;—and the offence of which we are guilty in placing our intercourse with those Countries under the protection of Treaties, is one of which no time and circumstances could, in the view of Spain, have mitigated the character....

9. THE OLD WORLD; GUARANTEES

[The theory of Guarantee generally receives all sorts of reckless applications during and after a great war. It is obviously necessary to give guarantees in war time, which cannot be maintained in peace. Thus, for example, when Napoleon drove the King of Portugal out of Lisbon and forced him to take refuge in Brazil, England guaranteed the succession of the House of Braganza. But this obligation was promptly annulled in 1815 with the arrival of peace. None the less, the theory of general guarantee was widely mooted. Castlereagh had great trouble in persuading the despots of Europe that England would not guarantee Monarchs their thrones. But liberals were equally anxious that England should guarantee constitutions to certain countries, as for instance to Sicily and Spain. When the French invaded Spain in 1823, in order to overthrow its too constitutional Government, the British liberals urged Canning to retaliate by guaranteeing to Spain the eventual restoration of her constitution. Canning was thus urged by despots to assist in the destruction of a constitution, in Spain; and by liberals to assist in the restoration of one. In each case he refused the petition.

In stating his decision Canning laid down the doctrine of guarantee in its most classic form. He points out the dangers of extending such an obligation and the necessity of observing it. He distinguishes between a guarantee and a defensive alliance. He points out the difficulties and dangers inherent in a territorial guarantee, and the enormously increased risks of a guarantee of internal institutions, by an external power. It is safe to say that the doctrine was never so brilliantly expounded before or since.

It is of interest to observe that, despite his objections to guarantee, Canning was sometimes prepared to offer one. But the limits within which he acted shew his prudence. Thus he offered to defend Cuba "for Spain against external aggression", if Spain would accept "British good offices to recognize the independence of the Spanish Colonies". In the case of a dispute between Brazil and Buenos Aires he offered to guarantee the free navigation of the Rio de la Plata estuary, if both Governments desired it. In both cases the Governments concerned refused his offer, which accordingly lapsed. But it should be noted that, in each case, the guarantee was "maritime protection". This was "of the domain of England" and one which she could immediately and practically enforce. On the other hand, while Canning was quite clear that England's treaty obligation to Portugal meant a promise to defend her European possessions against any enemy, he did not admit the extension "to the Colonial Possessions of the Crown of Portugal".* In the case of Greece, he did indeed contemplate a guarantee accepted by all the Powers. But he declined to proceed with it when Austria and Prussia withheld their assent. On the whole Canning was extremely reluctant to give any guarantees, and he never gave one which he could not enforce.]

Document 10. *Canning's Doctrine of Guarantee,*
18 *September* 1823 †

The British Government will not, in any case, undertake any guaranty whatever, either of territory or internal Institutions.

The scrupulousness with which England is in the habit of fulfilling her obligations makes it the more necessary for her not to contract them lightly. A guaranty is one of the most onerous obligations which one State can contract towards another. A defensive Alliance binds the Government contracting it, to come to the aid of its Ally, in case of an unprovoked attack upon his Dominions: and to make in his behalf, every reasonable and practicable exertion,—practicable in extent, and reasonable in duration. But it does not bind the assisting Government to the alternative of either a successful result, or an indefinite prolongation of the War. A guaranty, strictly construed, knows no limits either of time, or of degree. It would be, unless distinctly restricted in that respect, claimable in a War commenced by the Power to whom the guaranty is given, as well as in a War of unjust aggression

---

* Cp. Temperley, *Foreign Policy of Canning*, 539–42, and *v. infra* p. 85.
† Printed in Stapleton, *Political Life of Canning*, [1831], 1, 427–30, with some mistakes. This version is from Temperley, *Foreign Policy of Canning*, 539–40, where the text is taken from the original dispatch, *F.O.* 185/91. Canning to A Court, No. 54, 18 September 1823, received 30 September.

against that Power; and the integrity of the territory of that Power must be maintained, at whatever cost the effort to maintain it is prolonged: nay, though the guaranteed Power itself should contribute almost nothing to the maintaining it. If. . .the engagement is to be restricted in these particulars, it would constitute an unilateral defensive Alliance, but it would cease to be a guarantee. Objectionable as a territorial guaranty is shown to be, the objections to a guaranty of internal institutions are infinitely stronger. It is difficult to say whether these objections apply with greater force to the party giving, or to that which receives such a guaranty.

The very principle on which the British Government so earnestly deprecated the War against Spain, was, that of the right of any Nation to change, or to modify, its internal Institutions.

Is that War to end in His Majesty's consenting to assume to Himself the province of defending, against all Challengers, from within, as well as from without, the Institutions, whatever they might be, which the War may leave standing in Spain?

Is His Majesty to guaranty the Constitution of 1812, indifference to which, to say the least. . ., is the single point upon which anything like an Agreement of opinion has been found to exist in Spain? or is He to guaranty the antient despotism, the restoration of which, with all its accompaniments, appears to be the object of by far the largest party in the Country? or is it to be in behalf of some new system, struck out at a heat, at the winding up of affairs at Cadiz, that the faith of Great Britain is to be pledged, and that Her blood and treasure are to be forthcoming? or is it only to the undoubted right of the Spanish Nation to reform its own Government, that the sanction of His Majesty's guarantee is to be added? If such a guarantee were anything more than the mere affirmance of an abstract proposition, against whom would it have practically to operate? clearly against the Spaniards themselves: and in the endless struggles which might be expected from the then distracted state of parties in that Country, against every party by turns?

Could anything be more unbecoming than the assumption of such a right by a foreign Power? Could anything be more intolerable to the Country with respect to which it was assumed?

It is hardly necessary to add that while His Majesty must decline accepting such a right for Himself, he could not acknowledge it in any other Power.

The exercise of such a right must necessarily lead to an intermeddling with the affairs of the guaranteed State, such as to place it, in fact, at the mercy of the Power who gives the guarantee.

Russia, in former times, guaranteed the Constitution of Poland.

The result is known—and it was inevitable. The natural and necessary course of things must, in such a case, overbear even the most sincere and studied abstinence from interposition on the part of the guaranteeing Power.

There can be no doubt that His Majesty's Allies will feel how little such an arrangement would be compatible with the Engagements by which they stand bound to each other: to maintain the State of territorial possession established at the Peace, and the rights of independent Nations.

Constitutions and Constitutionalism

[It is commonly suggested that Canning was the chief deviser and practiser of the policy of allying with constitutional states against despotic ones. Thus Lord Salisbury says, "Palmerston was the disciple of Canning and with him believed that foreign policy should follow your political proclivities".* This has some truth in respect to Palmerston, very little in respect to Canning.

Canning certainly thought that British public opinion was, in case of war, an enormous force.† He also thought that if England was fighting with a despotic power, she would find the liberals of that country on her side. But he did not apparently wish to unite with the discontented of all countries. His aim was to hold the balance between "the conflicting principles" of despotism and liberty. He did not like despotisms, nor did he like democracies.

---

* Lord Salisbury, 31 August 1896, in Gooch and Temperley, *British Documents on the Origins of the War*, [1930], VI, 780.

† *V. supra*, pp. 65–7.

In "the ancient world Their existence...was in war." He said the same of the democratic or liberal republics of the Middle Ages, whereas "long intervals of profound peace are much more readily to be found under settlements of a monarchical form". He goes on to argue, very much on the lines of the accompanying document, that it is England's freedom and constitution that is her strength, but freedom "ceases to be a distinction, in proportion as other nations become free".* This was on 28 April 1823. Canning was not therefore the champion of constitutionalism as such; in fact it was only with reluctance that he ever accepted any such *rôle*. England only came over to the constitutionalist side because the despots would have none of her. Even so Canning allied England with a despotic state (Russia) and a constitutional one (France) by a treaty signed in the last month of his life. He was thus still "holding the balance".

The chief reason for describing Canning as a champion of constitutionalism is because of his defence of Portugal in 1826.† Portugal had just received a free constitution. For that reason despotic Spain tried to upset it. She used all sorts of methods such as arming, organizing and equipping Portuguese deserters who crossed the border. Finally, when frontier incidents had taken place, Canning held that the British guarantee of territorial integrity arose and must be honoured. He therefore sent troops to defend Portugal. Not unnaturally British troops were considered the defenders of the constitution, as well as of the frontier, of Portugal. But this was the effect, and not the intention, of Canning's move.

There can be no doubt that Canning himself had not desired, and had done nothing to secure, the grant of the Portuguese constitution.‡ He had in fact been embarrassed when he heard the news and was forced willy nilly into supporting it. Early in 1826 he had been concerting measures with despotic Russia to save Greece from Turkey, and it did not suit him to be driven into the constitutionalist camp. He could not avoid taking advantage of the situation for political purposes. But it is noticeable that during the last months of his life he was trying to recall Dom Miguel as Regent to Portugal, and he can hardly have believed that he was a respecter of constitutions. He did believe (and rightly) that the Portuguese public wished for Dom Miguel and, just before his death, was working at a compromise whereby Miguel would accept the constitution in return for being made

* *Speeches*, ed. R. Therry, v, 125–6.
† *V.* his speech *supra*, pp. 66–7.
‡ *V.* on this point Sir R. Peel's speech of 1 June 1829 in the House of Commons: "Nothing could be more express than the disclaimer by Mr Canning, that the [British] army was not sent out for the purpose of supporting political institutions." The testimony is the weightier as Peel was not wholly friendly to Canning. *V. Hans. Deb.*, New Ser., xxi, 1626.

Regent. This scheme never matured, but it shews that Canning
was very far from being an indiscriminate supporter of constitutions. The idea that he was, is due to the polemical arguments of
Stapleton and Lady Canning, who were trying to discredit his
successors. It has been uncritically accepted by historians,
especially by those of Portugal.* But it was not the idea of the
master. His true mind is undoubtedly revealed in the following
conversation which he had with Stratford, "the third great
Canning", a diplomat as imperious and able as himself.]

Document 11. *Canning on Constitutions and Constitutionalism,*
4 December 1824†

General Politics

Great Britain maintains a policy of her own, suited to her
position and Constitution. She will be no party to a general
interference in the concerns of other states; though prepared
to interfere on *special* occasions in her opinion justifying *such*
interference. Why should the Governments, forming the
H[oly] A[lliance] be looking continually to parties in foreign
States, and not to the Governments in their relations with
those States. Gr[eat] Br[itain] is ready to live on terms of
amity with arbitrary Governments, why should they not do
the same with respect to free States, so long as nothing be
done by the latter to violate their rights or to prejudice their
just interests. The principle of British Policy is shewn in
nothing more than in her abstaining from controuling the
interference of the Allied Sovereigns with Spain and Naples,
when She could not herself take part with them. Gr[eat]
Br[itain] in communicating with despotic Governments does
not complain of their principles of Government; why then
should they complain of her free institutions and the spirit of
her nation in dealing with Her? Not, on the other hand, a

* Cp. also Temperley, *Foreign Policy of Canning*, 457–61. The view put
forward by Mr E. Prestage in *Transactions of the Royal Historical Society*, 4th Ser.,
xvii, [1934], 94–7, is based on Portuguese authorities, who certainly misconceive
the situation by representing Canning as the champion of constitutions. This
view is flatly contradicted by the evidence of the British Archives and by the
testimony of Peel given above. *V.* p. 85 note.

† *F.O.* 352/9. "Private: Memoranda of a conversation [of Stratford Canning]
with the Secretary of State and Mr Planta on leaving the Foreign Office
Dec[embe]r 4th 1824, previously to setting out for Petersburg and Vienna.
G[eorge] C[anning]."

British Interest to have free States established on the Continent. Much better and more convenient for us to have neighbours, whose Institutions cannot be compared with ours in point of freedom. The principle of all this [is] a middle course for England between *Jacobinism* and *altruism*, with a view particularly of preventing the extreme parties from coming to an open rupture.*

Austria

Believes her general habitual policy to be what Esterházy states, favourable to connection with England. P[rince] M[etternich] has acquired great influence over the Emp[eror] A[lexander] and is not backward in making professions to this country, but his declarations cannot be depended upon.

* This same thought is indicated in Canning's speech of 28 April 1823. *Speeches*, ed. R. Therry, v, 127 and 129. "Can it be either our interest or our duty to ally ourselves with revolution?...Our station then, is essentially neutral: neutral not only between contending nations, but between conflicting principles."

V. PALMERSTON, 1830–41

10. PALMERSTON AND BELGIUM, 1831–7

[Palmerston undoubtedly looked up to Canning as his master. *The Morning Chronicle*, his press organ up till 1848, never refers to Canning save in terms of reverence. "We do not think that England ever had a minister better qualified to preserve her from war than Mr Canning. Yet certainly never was there a Minister who discussed these difficulties which must arise between countries with more spirit, ability and decision."* Palmerston said much the same in his speeches.† "If I might be allowed to express in one sentence the principle which I think ought to guide an English Minister, I would adopt the expression of Canning, and say that with every British Minister the interests of England ought to be the shibboleth of his policy." In the portrait of Palmerston painted at the height of his power a bust of Canning is noticeable in the background.

Though Palmerston was the pupil, he was far from carrying out the policy of the master. Canning was credited by his secretary with "a system of policy" which is no more than to say that his policy suited the needs of the age. Canning deprecated the laying down of "fixed resolutions for eventual probabilities", and declared that "cases must arise upon facts which it is utterly beyond the powers of human foresight to combine and calculate beforehand".‡ Yet he was supreme in the intellectual conception of policies, and in the following out of their legal implications. The consequences of such doctrines as those of recognition, non-intervention and guarantee were actually more clearly conceived by Canning than by any of his successors. They formed, in fact, a system, though one capable of future modification. Palmerston, "though generally desirous to keep England on the side of liberal opinions", had no system of policy relative to foreign states. He wrote thus, in his bluff fashion, to Clarendon. "When people ask me, as Howden does, for what is called a policy, the only answer is that we mean to do what may seem to be best, upon each occasion as it arises, making the Interests of Our Country one's guiding principle."§ "'England', he said to me once, 'is strong enough to brave consequences.'"‖ Here is the contrast between the two men.

* 2 April 1845.
† *Hans. Deb.*, 3rd Ser., xcvii, 123, 1 March 1848.
‡ Temperley, *Foreign Policy of Canning*, 471.
§ *Pte Clar. Papers*. Palmerston to Clarendon, 20 July 1856.
‖ Sir H. Bulwer, *Life of Palmerston*, [1870], 1, 346. This sentence is preceded by a passage similar to that in the letter from Palmerston to Clarendon just quoted.

There is no case in which Palmerston's departure from principle is more clearly indicated than in the settlement of Belgium. By the Vienna settlement Belgium had been united to Holland and to the House of Orange and both race and dynasty were hateful to her. The Revolution of 1830 in France deposed the absolutist Charles X and set Louis Philippe on the throne. The success of this revolution stimulated the Belgians to revolt against the Dutch. In November, just when Grey and Palmerston came into office, the revolted Belgians in Congress issued a declaration of National Independence (18 November 1830) and subsequently excluded the House of Orange from the throne. The danger was very real. The French had a good case for intervening to restore order and Prussia might take the opportunity to attack her old enemy. France had an idea of setting forward a French royal prince, the Duc de Nemours, as a candidate for the Belgian throne. The Belgians were ready to accept him.

A Congress sat at London to decide the grave question. It had sat in one form or another since November 1830. Its president was Palmerston; Talleyrand, the wisest head in Europe, was the French representative. Finally a settlement, by which Belgium was to be neutral and independent and Prince Leopold of Coburg to become its ruler, was suggested. It was devised by the Great Powers and accepted by Belgium. All would have been well had the Dutch accepted the settlement too. They did not and Leopold's desire for Luxemburg gave them an excuse for intervention. In the first days of August 1831 they invaded Belgian territory and beat the Belgian troops. They were only kept back from Brussels by the advance of a French army into Belgium. The danger was extreme. The French were in Belgium, the British fleet was in the Downs ready for any emergency. Palmerston told the French that they must leave Belgium early in September. They agreed to do so. The crisis was over.

The Dutch King remained to be coerced and was so ultimately, despite Russian disapproval and Prussian and Austrian abstention. A French army and a British fleet proceeded against Antwerp. The fortress, blockaded by sea and bombarded by land, surrendered to the Allies and was handed over to Belgium (May 1833). This success consolidated Leopold's position on the Belgian throne. But it was not until 1839, after endless conferences had met and seventy protocols been signed, that peace came. Then the famous Treaty of London, neutralizing and guaranteeing the independence of Belgium, was signed by Austria, France, Great Britain, Russia and Prussia (19 April 1839). This was the "scrap of paper" which Germany tore up when she invaded Belgium in 1914.

In 1793 Pitt and Grenville went to war with France to keep Belgium and Holland independent of her. The same burning question touched British interests in 1830. All the old suspicions of French aggression had been aroused, and the first breach in the territorial settlement of Vienna was made. No British statesman, of course, would have allowed French influence to dominate in Belgium. So if Belgium was to be made a separate state, she must take rank as a separate nation.

The documents that follow are, in two instances (**Docs. 12** and **14**) quotations from Bulwer's *Life*. His authority is not impeccable but, in this case, the sentiments can be supported from other evidence and are to be inferred from the speeches in Parliament. In **Docs. 16** and **17** Palmerston argues with Metternich about the meaning of guarantee. A reference to *infra*, pp. 156–7, will shew that when defining his meaning in 1848 he actually rose to the height of a general principle. He shews a curiously practical turn of mind in the particular question of Belgium. Provided the French were got out of Belgium he did not object to revising the Treaty of Vienna or to infringing Canning's pet theory of "non-intervention". His easy method of interpreting that policy justifies the famous *mot* of Talleyrand. When asked to define "non-intervention" the latter replied that it was a word signifying much the same as "intervention". That is the result of not having a "system".]

Document 12. *Palmerston on the designs of France in Belgium,*
7 January 1831*

In a conversation which I had a few days ago with Talleyrand, about the affairs of Belgium, I mentioned to him an idea which had occurred to me, as an arrangement which might probably smooth some of our difficulties. The King of the Netherlands would wish his son to wear the crown of Belgium; the Belgians want much to have Luxembourg. Could not the King give up Luxembourg to his son, on condition of his being elected by the Belgians? and might not the Belgians choose the Prince of Orange, on condition that he should bring Luxembourg with him? Talleyrand looked very grave, and said he thought his Government would not like to see Luxembourg united to Belgium. I asked why, inasmuch as it had been so united hitherto, and would not be more inconvenient to France when united to Belgium alone, than when united to Belgium joined with Holland. He said, the fact was that their frontier in that direction is very weak and exposed, and Luxembourg runs into an

---

* Palmerston to Viscount Granville, Private, 7 January 1831, Bulwer, *Life of Palmerston*, II, 27–9.

undefended part of France. He then said, Would there be no means of making an arrangement *by which Luxembourg might be given to France?* I confess I felt considerable surprise at a proposition so much at variance with all the language and professions which he and his Government have been holding. I said that such an arrangement appeared to me to be impossible, and that nobody could consent to it. I added that England had no selfish objects in view in the arrangements of Belgium, but that we wished Belgium to be really and substantially independent. That we were desirous of living upon good terms with France, but that any territorial acquisitions of France such as this which he contemplated would alter the relations of the two countries, and make it impossible for us to continue on good terms. I found since this conversation that he had been making similar propositions to Prussia about her Rhenish provinces, in the event of the possibility of moving the King of Saxony to Belgium and giving Saxony to Prussia. To-day he proposed to me that France should get Philippeville and Marienburg, in consideration of France using her influence to procure the election of Leopold for Belgium. I do not like all this; it looks as if France was unchanged in her system of encroachment, and it diminishes the confidence in her sincerity and good faith which her conduct up to this time had inspired. *It may not be amiss for you to hint, upon any fitting occasion, that though we are anxious to cultivate the best understanding with France, and to be on the terms of the most intimate friendship with her, yet that it is only on the supposition that she contents herself with the finest territory in Europe, and does not mean to open a new chapter of encroachment and conquest.*

Document 13. *Palmerston on non-intervention in Belgium,* 18 *February* 1831*

There was nothing in the principle of non-interference, fairly and reasonably laid down, which prescribed to a State the absence of all interference in what passed in a neighbouring country, when that which was passing concerned the interests of the other party: and if Belgium chose a Sovereign

* *Hans. Deb.*, 3rd Ser., II, 702–3, 18 February 1831.

who might become dangerous to the neighbouring States, those States had a right to say "Such a person to us will be dangerous, and such a person we refuse to recognise". He said, therefore, that the Powers of Europe had a right to say to France, "You cannot consistently, with your relations with other Powers, accede to the appointment of the Duc de Nemours as King, and thereby virtually attach Belgium to yourself". On the one hand they had a right to say this to France; and on the other, they had a right to say to Belgium, that if the Duc de Leuchtenberg was elected, because he, from the circumstances of his family, would make Belgium the centre of political intrigues, him they would not acknowledge. He said, that this was not interfering with Belgium in any sense inconsistent with sound and rational principles.

Document 14. *Palmerston on the need for French troops evacuating Belgium, 17 August 1831* *

I like not your letter nor your despatches,† nor those which Talleyrand read to me to-day by desire of Sebastiani.

The despatches which Talleyrand himself writes to Sebastiani are perfect, and evidently written that he may read them to me. What else he writes I cannot tell, but I am not so sure that what he reads to me is all he sends, and that the rest is in the same tone.

One thing is certain—the French must go out of Belgium, or we have a general war, and war in a given number of days. But, say the French, we mean to go out, but we must choose our own time and our own terms. The time, however, they have agreed shall be settled by the conference, and it must be as early as is consistent with the objects for which they professed to go in.

They came in at the invitation of an allied sovereign, whose neutrality and independence they have agreed to guarantee, and they marched for the accomplishment of the objects which the five Powers have all been aiming at. What terms then are

* Palmerston to Granville, Private, 17 August 1831, Bulwer, *Life of Palmerston*, II, 108–10.

[† They stated that the French would not go out of Belgium without some previous arrangement as to the fortresses. Note by Bulwer.]

they entitled to make as to their retreat? None! With regard to the fortresses, make them understand that their pretensions are utterly inadmissible. The very basis upon which we can agree to the demolition of any of these fortresses is the security derived from the guarantee of France and of the other Powers.

That guarantee, then, must be given in the fullest and most formal manner before we can stir a step; and to dismantle these fortresses while the French have them in possession would be a disgrace to all the five Powers; and as to making France a party to the treaty for their demolition, that is impossible. Nothing shall ever induce me to put my name to such a treaty, and I am quite sure the Cabinet never would sanction it.

We have had no Cabinet to-day upon your letter and your despatches, because we want to learn the result of my letter and Grey's of Saturday last. Sebastiani and Soult apparently want to pick a quarrel with all their neighbours, or to compel everybody to submit to their insolence and aggressions.

They miscalculate their chances, however, I think; and they will find that a war with all the rest of the world, brought upon them by a violation of their word, will not turn to their advantage, nor redound to their honour. They will not be the better able to carry on the war on the Continent for losing all their commerce, and for being deprived of the revenue arising therefrom. The ruin of their seaports will create general distress throughout the country; the Chambers will soon be sick of barren glory if they succeed, or of defeats brought needlessly upon them if they fail; the ministry will be turned out, and the King may go with them. The Carlist party will make an effort, and with the Republicans may give much embarrassment. Austria and Prussia are well prepared for war.

The Belgians will not join the French.*

[* This decided language, which a less resolute minister would have avoided as likely to provoke war, really prevented it, as will be seen by the following extract from a letter of Lord Granville, dated Paris, August 15 1831: "My representations and Talleyrand's despatches of the state of public feeling in

Document 15. *Palmerston on intervention in Belgium,* 7 *December* 1831*

He must altogether deny, that the Government of this country had been instrumental in imposing upon Belgium a Government inconsistent with the wishes of the people of that country. On the contrary, the people of Belgium had chosen their own form of government, and had elected their own sovereign. The circumstances under which the Government of this country had interfered were simply these:—Both Holland and Belgium were anxious to be separated, but it was impossible for them to agree upon the terms of such separation, and the inevitable consequence of being left to themselves would have been, that Europe must have been involved in war. By the interference which had taken place, peace was preserved, and Europe saved from the horrors of war. It would have been a war of principle too, into which it was probable England would soon have been brought. By the interference which had taken place this consequence was averted.

Document 16. *Palmerston's estimate of the value of the Belgian Guarantee,* 7 *October* 1837†

... Her Majesty's Government is inclined to think that Prince Metternich is mistaken in supposing that the question as to the Fortifications at Diest is with Prussia a question of Peace or War: The Prussian Government is much too enlightened not to see that War upon such grounds would be wholly unjustifiable; and it has too much foresight not to be aware of the inconvenient consequences to Prussia herself which a War so commenced would inevitably produce: But if Prussia

England have alarmed them (Périer and Sebastiani) a little, and produced the half-measure, which Talleyrand is instructed to announce, of the immediate return to France of 20,000 men, and of the retreat of the remainder into that part of Belgium between Nivelles and the French frontier." Note by Bulwer.]

* *Hans. Deb.*, 3rd Ser., IX, 106–7, 7 December 1831.

† Palmerston to Sir F. Lamb (Vienna), No. 127, 7 October 1837, *F.O.* 120/160. Palmerston is replying to a protest by Metternich as to the erection of fortifications at Diest by the King of the Belgians. A report of Metternich's views is added in **Doc. 17.**

were to be so infatuated as to begin such a War, She must abide by it's results; and upon Her and Her advisers the responsibility of those results would exclusively fall.

... With regard to the necessity of such a defence for Belgium as the proposed Works at Diest would afford against an Attack from Holland, the slightest glance at the Map is sufficient to shew that those Works have not been resolved upon by the Belgian Government without good and sufficient reasons. Prince Metternich indeed is of opinion that the Guarantee of Austria, England, France and Prussia ought to be to Belgium a sufficient security, without any Fortifications; and he has written down as a Memorandum a Sentence recording some Declaration said to have been made at some time or other by those four Governments to The King of the Netherlands, and to The King of the Belgians, to the effect that the former would not be permitted to make any attack upon the latter. But Prince Metternich is too experienced a Statesman, and is too conversant with international Transactions, to lay much stress upon a mere Memorandum of such a Declaration, without any date of time, or any statement of the formalities which rendered it an engagement binding on the four Powers, and to which the Belgian Government could appeal in case of need. There exists however a much more formal Guarantee of the integrity and independence of Belgium in the 25th Article of the Treaty of November 1831, to which Russia, as well as the other four Powers, was a Party; and there can be no doubt that if Paper securities could be taken as standing in stead of military defences, Belgium might by virtue of that Guarantee, consider Herself one of the safest Countries in Europe.

But unfortunately the History of the World abounds with instances to shew, that it is unwise for any State to rely entirely for it's defence, even upon the most solemn engagements of other Powers, and Her Majesty's Government regret to say that the conduct of Austria Russia and Prussia with respect to the Affairs of Belgium has not formed any striking exception to the warning to be derived in this respect from the experience of preceding Times. It is impossible to put into words in any language a Declaration more precise, positive, and unqualified, than that which was drawn up by the Russian Plenipotentiaries in the Conference, and made an Annex to the 49th Protocol of the 14th of October 1831;— That Document, after referring the Belgian Plenipotentiary to the communication which had been made to him of the 24 Articles, proceeds thus:—"Les cinq Cours se reservant la tâche, et *prenant l'engagement* d'obtenir *l'adhésion de la Hollande* aux Articles dont il s'agit, quand même Elle commencerait par les rejeter; *garantissant de plus leur* execution; et convaincus que ces Articles, fondés sur des principes d'equité incontestables, offrent à la Belgique tous les avantages qu'Elle est en droit de reclamer; ne peuvent que déclarer içi leur ferme determination de s'opposer, par tous les moyens en leur pouvoir, au renouvellement d'une lutte qui, devenue aujourd'hui sans objet, serait pour les deux Pays, la source de grands malheurs, et ménacerait l'Europe d'une guerre générale, que le premier devoir des cinq Cours est de prevenir. Mais plus cette détermination est propre à assurer la Belgique sur son avenir, et sur les circonstances qui y causent maintenant de vives alarmes, plus elle autorisera les cinq Cours à user également de tous les moyens en leur pouvoir pour amener l'assentiment de la Belgique aux Articles ci-dessus mentionnés, dans le cas où, contre toute attente, Elle se refuserait à les adopter, et pour faire cesser les sacrifices qu'une telle résolution de sa part imposerait à la Hollande."

A similar Declaration was at the same time made to The King of the Netherlands.

The Belgians relying upon this Declaration accepted, though with much reluctance, the 24 Articles thus sent them; but The King of the Netherlands rejected those Articles.

The Denunciation in the Annex has been doubtless prepared by the Russian Plenipotentiaries in the belief that the 24 Articles would be at once accepted by The King of Holland to whom they were highly favourable; and that the repugnance to subscribe to them would come from the Belgians; and if such had been the result, the three Powers would have been ready enough to carry the Denunciation into effect.

But when the reverse of what they expected took place, when the 24 Articles were accepted by Belgium, and refused by Holland, from that moment the three Powers resolved to consider the Denunciation of the Annex as a dead Letter; and no persuasion or argument has ever been sufficient to induce them to take one single step in execution of their solemnly recorded pledge, to obtain the assent of Holland to those Articles. Nay more; the five Powers in Nov[embe]r 1831 signed a Treaty with The King of the Belgians by which They formally acknowledged Him as King, and solemnly guaranteed to Him the Territory described in that Treaty. But for a long time after that Treaty was signed, neither Austria nor Prussia sent any Minister to Brussels; and even up to the present day, Russia professes to have only partially acknowledged The King of the Belgians, and refuses to hold any diplomatic intercourse with Him.

Moreover for some time after the Treaty of 1831 was concluded, the Dutch continued to retain possession of the Citadel of Antwerp, which by that Treaty the five Powers had guaranteed to Belgium; and when at last in 1832 Great Britain and France invited the other 3 Powers to unite with them in carrying into execution those territorial arrangements of the Treaty, upon which all the five were agreed, and to which none of the Reserves accompanying the Ratifications applied, the Three Powers positively refused to fulfil their engagements, and retired in consequence from the Conference; and when afterwards Great Britain and France, faithful to their own stipulations, employed the necessary means for compelling the Dutch to evacuate the Citadel of Antwerp, a Prussian Army assembled upon the Frontier of the Prussian Rhenish Provinces, placing itself in a position and attitude much calculated to encourage the resistance of the Dutch.

It cannot then be surprizing if The King of the Belgians with the experience of these facts present to His mind, should think it better to provide means of His own to resist the constantly threatened Attack of the Dutch, than to trust for his safety to the already broken Guarantee of the three

Powers; and it must be remarked, that all the arguments which are used to shew that the projected Fortifications are unnecessary, would equally tend to prove that any Belgian Army is needless, and that the whole military force of Belgium might safely be disbanded. But if for want of an Army, or for want of fortified positions to support an Army, Belgium were again overrun by a sudden irruption of the Dutch, and if the Troops of The King of the Netherlands were in possession of Brussels, and the other great Towns of Belgium, it may well be doubted whether the three Powers would take any steps to expel the Dutch, and whether their boasted Guarantees would be proof against a "Fait accompli"....

Document 17. *Metternich and the Belgian Guarantee, 22 September* 1837*

Prince Metternich in speaking upon the fortifications of Diest said that it was for Prussia a question of Peace or War.— I asked in reply why he said more than Prussia herself; and insisted upon the necessity of a security to the Kingdom of Belgium against the possibility of an attack from Holland?—

This security the Prince said was to be found much more complete in the guarantee given by the Four Courts of Austria, England, France and Prussia to that of Belgium than in the fortification of a point of the frontier.—

Upon my expressing a doubt as to the existence of this guarantee, he offered to shew it me in the acts, and at my request wrote down what it is. I copy his words—

"Les Cours ont déclaré aux Rois des Belges et des Pays-Bas, qu'elles ne souffriroient pas, que le dernier commette des actes d'hostilité contre la Belgique et qu'elles sauroient deslors les empêcher"—

When the Prince had given this paper in, I said that supposing the King of Belgium to have full confidence in this Guarantee, still it would not prevent the Dutch from marching to Brussels, if there was nothing in the way to stop them....

[He then said that the fortifications were offensive.]

* Lamb to Palmerston, No. 63, 22 September 1837, *F.O.* 7/265.

...All his reasonings repose upon the idea that in case of War the Belgick fortresses would probably fall into the hands of France, and that the Northern ones, if Diest were added to them, would form a formidable basis for offensive operations against the Territory of the Confederation. He represents himself to have had a similar discussion with the Duke of Wellington and Lord Castlereagh in the year 1815 with regard to the erection of the fortresses on the Southern frontier of Belgium, which he persisted in regarding as built for the profit of France, while they defended them on the ground that England would always have time to come to their defence. The event, he contends, proved the soundness of his views, and he now implores Her Majesty's Government to look beyond the policy of the moment; to consider the great chances there are of France being the first to occupy Belgium in the event of a war, and to consider the formidable position, in which the occupation of a secure basis for operation on the Meuse would place her, and the extent of Territory which it would lay at her mercy. As I have no means of estimating the value of these considerations, which can hardly be appreciated without reference to competent Military Judges and as the means of security which Prince Metternich holds out to Belgium coincides in part with the views taken in Your Lordship's No. 14 to Sir Hamilton Seymour, I have thought it best to submit his reasonings to the consideration of Her Majesty's Government without entering into further controversy upon them. All I think necessary to add is, that the Prince's manner has impressed me with the conviction that his objections are made in good faith. It is to be remarked that he fully admits the right of King Leopold to be secured against attacks from Holland. The only question then that remains, relates to the nature of that security.

I am unacquainted with the guarantee which Prince Metternich asserts to exist, but if it does exist, which I cannot doubt after the manner in which he has pledged himself to it, I cannot but feel that if conjoined with the diminution and removal of the Dutch force from the frontier, it will give a

better security to Belgium—and in the interests of England—
a safer one than the erection of new fortresses which may
hereafter be turned to other uses than those for which they
were designed.*

11. PALMERSTON AND CONSTITU-
TIONALISM, 1830–47

[That Palmerston was "generally desirous to keep England on
the side of liberal opinions" is admitted by his biographer. That
was in fact his nearest approach to a "system". He derived from
Canning the view that any war of the future would be a war of
opinion. It was to be between the "two great parties...one
which endeavours to bear sway by the force of public opinion;
another which endeavours to bear sway by the force of physical
control.... There is in nature no moving power but mind...in
human affairs this power is opinion; in political affairs it is public
opinion; and he who can grasp this power, with it will subdue the
fleshly arm of physical strength, and compel it to work out his
purpose."† He thought that, if the Belgian trouble had involved
Europe in war, "it would...have been a war of opinion, and the
consequences must have been most lamentable".‡ One reason
for this approaching conflict was that the despots of Europe had
promised constitutions in their hour of need and broken these
promises in their hour of triumph. "When Bonaparte was to be
dethroned, the Sovereigns of Europe called up their people to
their aid; they invoked them in the sacred names of Freedom and
National Independence; the cry went forth throughout Europe:
and those, whom Subsidies had no power to buy, and Conscrip-
tions no force to compel, roused by the magic sound of Constitutional Rights, started spontaneously into arms. The long-suffering
Nations of Europe rose up as one man, and by an effort tremendous
and wide spreading, like a great convulsion of nature, they hurled
the conqueror from his throne. But promises made in days of
distress, were forgotten in the hour of triumph."§
Palmerston planned therefore to support constitutional monarchies everywhere against despotic ones, to promote the growth
of constitutional and parliamentary government, so as to restrict
by opinion the military forces of despots and the Neo-Holy
Alliance. He proclaimed this principle quite openly towards the

* For Palmerston's doctrine on the general nature of guarantee v. **Doc. 32**
infra, where he convicts Metternich of inconsistency.
† *Hans. Deb.*, New Ser., xxi, 1668, 1 June 1829.
‡ *Hans. Deb.*, 3rd Ser., ix, 966, 26 January 1832.
§ *Hans. Deb.*, New Ser., xxiii, 82, 10 March 1830.

end of 1832. "I am prepared to admit, that the independence of constitutional States, whether they are powerful, like France or the United States, or of less...importance, such as the minor States of Germany, never can be a matter of indifference to the British Parliament, or, I should hope, to the British public. Constitutional States I consider to be the natural Allies of this country; and...no English Ministry will perform its duty if it be inattentive to the interests of such States."* Now here we have a curious and almost sentimental idealism revealed in a man supposed to represent the business instincts and hard-headedness of John Bull. He is prepared definitely not to be an umpire, as Canning was, "between the conflicting principles of despotism and democracy". He means to take sides. He has forgotten the master's dictum "not, on the other hand, a British Interest to have free States established on the Continent". His course is his own and it is a very different one, despite the fact that his biographer claims it as "the full completion of Mr. Canning's policy".†

One of Palmerston's reasons for supporting constitutionalism was that it would separate parliamentary France from despotic Russia. Over the Belgian affair the three Eastern despots of Russia, Prussia and Austria had shewn dangerous tendencies. Palmerston, who had worked in the War Office for twenty years, knew the extent of their military power, but he knew that it stopped at high-water mark. The sea was the domain of England on which her navy rode supreme. The military despots were only to be feared if France joined them, with a navy powerful in the Mediterranean. "It must not be forgotten that one great danger to Europe is the possibility of a combination between France and Russia."‡ In that case the most formidable military power in the world would advance to India overland, while France was obstructing England in the East on the sea. That danger could only be avoided if France were separated from Russia.

Palmerston intended to keep France "in the right track". And the right track was that of constitutional liberty, to which Russia was utterly opposed. His chance came in 1834 when a prospect appeared of forming a constitutional *bloc* in the West. There was a chance to make Spain, Portugal, France and England one in a constitutional alliance and Palmerston took it.]

* *Hans. Deb.*, 3rd Ser., xiv, 1045, 2 August 1832. *V. supra*, p. 88.
† Bulwer, *Life of Palmerston*, ii, 188.
‡ Palmerston to Granville, 8 June 1838, quoted in Bulwer, *Life of Palmerston*, ii, 268; in italics in original.

(a) CONSTITUTIONALISM IN PORTUGAL AND SPAIN, 1835–47

[The situation in the Iberian peninsula was a very peculiar one. In Portugal and Spain there was a war, in each case of girl nieces against wicked uncles. Each of the girl nieces had a constitutional policy, each of the wicked uncles a despotic one. The triumph of innocence and constitutions was therefore in the interests both of England and of sentiment. In Portugal virtue had almost triumphed already. In 1826 Canning had sent troops to defend Portugal but they had in effect helped the constitutionalists. On their withdrawal the young Maria II became unpopular and was ultimately deposed by her uncle Dom Miguel (1829). But the constitutional party had raised a rebellion in the Azores, and finally had received reinforcements from Brazil and England. They landed in Portugal and seized Oporto (1832). Miguel, though absolutist, was popular and for a time confined them to the coast. But matters changed in 1833 when the British captain Napier was put in command of the constitutionalist fleet. It was tiny but its crews were mostly British mercenaries and desperate blades. Napier sallied boldly out, destroyed or captured Miguel's whole fleet, and returned to Oporto in triumph. The constitutionalist forces, elated by this success, moved on Lisbon and captured it. Their success was startling and the young Queen entered her capital in triumph. But the battle was not yet won. Miguel was still in the field and drawing great assistance from the absolutists over the border in Spain. He and the absolutist pretender in Spain also drew money and assistance "from the Despotic Powers of Europe", i.e. from Austria, Prussia and Russia. There was thus, in Palmerston's view, a world struggle of opinion and he must take sides. "Maria's cause has won the day in Portugal", wrote Palmerston (8 October 1833), "though the race is not quite over.... The triumph of Maria [in Portugal], and the accession of Isabella [in Spain], will be important events in Europe, and will give great strength to the Liberal [and constitutional] party. England, France, Belgium, Portugal, and Spain, looked upon merely as a mass of opinion, form a powerful body in Europe."* He decided to make it still more powerful by constitutionalizing Spain, and allying with constitutionalist France.

In Palmerston's view the Spanish and Portuguese problems were one, and despotism must be crushed simultaneously in both countries. Some outside assistance was necessary. In Spain the

---

* Palmerston to Temple, 8 October 1833, Bulwer, *Life of Palmerston*, [1870], II, 168–9.

situation was critical. Ferdinand VII, the old absolutist King, died in the autumn of 1833. Isabella, a child Queen, succeeded. Her mother Christina became Regent and adopted a mildly constitutional policy. Don Carlos, Isabella's uncle, claimed the throne, raised a rebellion and appealed to reactionaries throughout Spain. Palmerston thought the situation so grave as to demand a veiled intervention by England. He did it by negotiating a treaty between Great Britain, France, and the constitutional Governments of Spain and Portugal, for the pacification of the peninsula.* The girl Isabella and the girl Maria were to help one another to expel Miguel, the Portuguese, and Carlos, the Spaniard, pretenders from the Iberian peninsula. England was to lend naval aid; France also promised help. This was the treaty finally signed on 22 April 1834.

According to Palmerston "it was a capital hit and all my own doing" (12 May 1834). It certainly was immediately effective in driving out the Portuguese wicked uncle and forcing him to leave the country he had misgoverned. Even before the ratifications were exchanged the Miguelists laid down their arms. Miguel had undoubtedly a good many thousand men still under arms, and if he had marched into Spain and taken Carlos with him, there might have been serious trouble. But he and his army surrendered without bloodshed.†

It took longer, however, to deal with Don Carlos. France disconcerted Palmerston by tending to favour Don Carlos in deference to Austria, Russia and Prussia. All sorts of methods, none of them consistent with non-intervention, were tried, but Palmerston stopped short of direct intervention. His justification was that none of his methods would have succeeded unless the Spanish nation had desired them to do so. He relaxed the Foreign Enlistment Act to enable a volunteer military legion to be raised in England for service in Spain, which became the best aid of Isabella. He allowed arms and equipment to be exported to the constitutionalists and prevented their going to the Carlists. The British navy cut off Carlist supplies and occasionally bombarded their coast towns. Finally he lent the Queen Regent half a million pounds for military expenses. The Carlist movement lived on in the Basque provinces, but finally flickered out in 1839. It seemed as if Palmerston had triumphed.

The four documents that follow shew Palmerston's opinions well. **Doc. 18** shews his peculiar view of intervention; **Doc. 19**, his view of the nature of the conflicting principles; **Doc. 20**, his refusal to submit to a European Congress; **Doc. 21** is a broad popular account of the whole transaction to his constituents on the hustings.

* Text in Hertslet, *Map*, [1875], II, 941–4.
† Palmerston to Temple, 27 June 1834, Bulwer, *Life of Palmerston*, II, 197.

The sequel proved that Palmerston's triumph was a barren one. The constitutions of Spain and Portugal fully justified the scepticism which Canning had always extended to institutions "struck out at heat". The constitutional *bloc* in the West failed to balance the three despotic monarchies in the East. Portugal and Spain proved no more important when endowed with constitutions than when without them. Both proved unable to restrain France or even to keep her in the Alliance. By 1840 France and England were estranged. In 1846 Spanish affairs caused a serious breach between England and France. It would probably have been better in the end to have adhered to Canning's doctrine of non-intervention with more strictness, and to have left Portugal and Spain to their own futile and sordid disputes. The cause of constitutionalism succeeded in Belgium just because a people were ready and able to receive it. For exactly the opposite reason it failed in Portugal and Spain. There is perhaps no episode of Palmerston's career more to his credit than his Belgian achievement, and none less to it than his building of castles in Spain and his adventures in the country of Don Quixote.]

Document 18. *Palmerston on the nature of the interference in Spain, 24 June* 1835*

In the first place, the present interference (for he took it to be generally allowed that it was in principle an interference) was founded on a treaty arising out of an acknowledgement of the right of a sovereign, decided by the legitimate authorities of the country over which she ruled. In the case of a civil war, proceeding either from a disputed succession or from a long revolt, no writer on national law denied that other countries had a right, if they chose to exercise it, to take part with either of the two belligerents.

Document 19. *Palmerston on the conflicting principles, c.* 9 *June* 1836†

Draft prepared June 9/36

Entirely approve the Language held by L[or]d Granville on this unexpected suggestion of Mons[ieu]r Thiers.

* *Hans. Deb.*, 3rd Ser., xxviii, 1162–3, 24 June 1835.
† Rough note by Palmerston, 9 June 1836, *F.O.* 96/18. The draft on which it comments is by "B", i.e. Backhouse, Permanent Under-Secretary, 1827–42.

It is well known that from the Commencement of the Civil war in Spain the 3 Courts and Especially that of Vienna have Entertained the notion of putting an End to the Contest by a Marriage between the Infant Queen and the Son of Don Carlos.

If the Contest now going on in Spain were merely a Rival-ship between Two Individuals such a Proposal for uniting in a Common Interest the Conflicting Claims might appear plausible and specious. But any Person who takes so limited a view of the Events which have been passing in the Peninsulas, must indeed be a very superficial observer of human affairs.

The struggle in Spain is not between Persons but between Principles—Carlos and Isabella are the names which have been put forward as the rallying Cry of the Two Parties, but the real Question at issue is, whether Spain shall fall back under the arbitrary System of Gov[ernmen]t which has so long paralized [sic] the Natural Energies of the Spanish Nation, or whether a Constitutional System similar to that which exists in England and in France and in Portugal shall be established also in Spain—between these opposing Principles no alliance can take Place; one or other of them must pre-dominate, and it is sufficiently obvious that the Scheme of Marrying the Infant Queen to the Son of Don Carlos now 18 or 19 years old, is founded upon the Hope that such an arrangement would give Predominance to the Party of Don Carlos that is to the supporters of absolute Government....

P[almerston]

Document 20. *Palmerston refuses a European Congress on Spain, 9 August 1837**

Mr. Villiers' No. 201.

Mr. Villiers [is] to be instructed to assure The Queen of Spain that nothing but a State of Things in Spain of which at present there are no Symptoms, and which we fervently hope never will arise, could induce the British Gov[ernmen]t to become Parties to a European Congress for the Purpose of regulating the affairs of Spain; and it is needless to say

* Rough note by Palmerston, 9 August 1837, *F.O.* 96/19.

that no such Congress could have any practical Results as long as Great Britain declined to belong to it, and refused to acquiesce in its Resolutions....

The Queen may therefore confidently reckon upon a continuance of the cordial sympathy and active assistance of G[rea]t Britain, and upon having France to a certain degree with her in measures whatever may be the Secret Feelings of the French Cabinet—Thus supported by the two great Powers who are more immediately in contact Geographically and Politically with Spain, The Queen has nothing to apprehend from the Despotic Powers of Europe except a continuance... of those supplies of money with which it is well known they have for the last two years furnished Don Carlos.

The Patriotism and Energy of the Spanish Nation will therefore not be controuled by any Foreign Interference in Favour of the Pretender and if that Energy and Patriotism shall succeed as we trust it will in firmly establishing the Queen Isabella on her Throne without any Interference of Foreign Armies in her Favour, although the struggle may on that account be somewhat longer, and although the Sacrifices which the Spanish Nation will have been required to make may on that account be somewhat greater, still the Result will be more honourable to the Nation and more advantageous to the Queen; For a Throne which is founded upon the spontaneous attachment of a Loyal People, and which has been established by their own national exertions rests upon a far firmer Basis than one which has been raised under the Protection of foreign Bayonets.

P[almerston] 9/8–37.

Document 21. *Palmerston describes his achievement to his constituents, 31 July 1847**

...We took part with the people of Spain—with those who wanted constitutional liberty, equal laws, a Parliament, justice, no Inquisition—against those who were for having no Parliament, no justice, but much Inquisition. We succeeded;

* Speech of Palmerston to the electors of Tiverton, 31 July 1847. *Pamphlet*, 2nd ed., 25–6.

and by means of very trifling assistance, which could not possibly have determined events, if the Spanish people had not been on that side, we enabled them to work out their liberties with smaller sacrifices than they must otherwise have submitted to, and with less suffering than they must otherwise have encountered.... There was a struggle in Portugal very similar to that which I have mentioned as taking place in Spain... Did we set up Dom Miguel? No; we put him down. We threw our influence into the scale of liberty, freedom, and constitutional rights; and, by our assistance, that cause conquered, and the Portuguese nation became possessed of a Parliament, and of all those rights which are essential for securing the liberties of a nation.

(b) PALMERSTON AND THE CONSTITUTION OF GREECE, 1841

[The documents that follow are a compendium of Palmerston's views on constitutionalism which, as has already been noticed, differed considerably from those of Canning.* He had a real and sincere belief in the efficacy of constitutions, which the Master did not share. Thus, in his argument with Metternich in **Doc. 22**, he plainly regards the Prince's attitude as absurd. He shews Metternich that the persistence in absolutism is persistence in folly, when the King, like Otto of Greece, is a fool. In **Doc. 23** he informs Guizot that "Her Majesty's Government do not happen to recollect any country in which a constitutional Government has been established that has not on the whole been better off in consequence". The style of reasoning is now different. For Guizot, being a professed Parliamentarian, can be twitted for his reluctance to press a policy which is an article of his faith. In **Doc. 24** Palmerston takes up the humanitarian ground and departs even further from the Canning doctrine of non-intervention. The principle, to which he refers in **Doc. 23**, that under which the Three Powers (France, Great Britain and Russia) guaranteed "a real and *bona fide* Constitution to Greece", was an extremely dangerous one. It justified exactly that sort of meddling interference in the internal affairs of other States against which Canning had warned the despotic Governments of Europe. The despots of Europe had wished to interfere to suppress constitutions in Spain or Naples, because they disliked constitutional principles. Palmer-

* *V. supra*, pp. 84–6, 88.

ston wished to interfere in countries already endowed with constitutions, if he thought they worked badly or were in danger of
coming to grief. Yet, in practical fact, the danger of Great Powers
interfering in the internal affairs of small States is always real and
serious, whether they wish to promote or to suppress constitutions.

A study of these documents shews that Palmerston proposed to
insist on a *bona fide* constitution being erected in Greece. He wanted
Guizot to join him in enforcing "the removal of the Bavarian
Camarilla and the entire abolition of the irresponsible Referen-
daires,...interposed between the King and the Ministers of
State". In **Doc. 24**, inflamed by a real humanitarian zeal, he
goes even further. He proposes to prevent the Government of
Greece from placing soldiers at free quarters, from poisoning
brigands, from torturing prisoners, from conniving at "the Slave
Trade". Of these only the last could, by any conceivable argument, be considered other than a purely internal affair of Greece.
Palmerston, acting in a spirit of genuine benevolence, is thus
advocating a policy of "restless meddling activity". Greece was
too feeble to resist him, but the consequences of this policy were
ultimately serious to Europe, to England and to Palmerston
himself.]

Document 22. *Palmerston argues with Metternich,*
18 *February* 1841*

I have to acknowledge the Receipt of Your Excellency's
Despatch No. 19 of the 5th Instant inclosing a copy of a
despatch addressed by Prince Metternich to Prince Esterhazy
on the Affairs of Greece, and a copy of a Private Letter to
Your Excellency on the same subject.

With reference to the wish expressed by Prince Metternich,
that the English Minister at Athens should receive directions
to place himself on a footing of perfect confidence with the
Austrian Minister, I have to state to Your Excellency that
I have reason to believe that those Two Ministers are already
on perfectly good and confidential terms, and that the best
understanding exists between them; and Her Majesty's
Government have moreover been informed that the opinions
of Colonel Prokesch as to the Evils Existing in Greece, and as
to the Remedies which ought to be applied to them do not
differ very widely from the opinions of Sir Edmund Lyons.

* Palmerston to Lord Beauvale, No. 38, 18 February 1841, *F.O.* 120/193.

But Prince Metternich, admitting the Existence of these Evils, seems to think that the only remedy is to "renforcer l'attitude Royale".

Now if the Evils of Greece arose from the weakness of the Royal Authority, and from encroachments made upon it by popular Power, such a remedy might be just and appropriate; but the present Evils of Greece arise precisely and solely from the "attitude Royale"; they are occasioned by the obstinate pertinacity with which a King devoid of all capacity for governing insists upon grasping and retaining in his own hands, not only all the Powers of the State, but all the details of the Administration of every Department.

In this state of things to "renforcer l'attitude Royale", if indeed it were possible to do so, (which seems doubtful, for absolute Power could not well be carried further,) would only be to increase the cause of the present Evils, and therefore to aggravate the Evils themselves.

The Evils being universally known to arise from want of any controul upon the Royal will, the only practical remedy must consist in Some Machinery which would afford such a controul. Prince Metternich seems to think that such a controul would be found in the appointment of able Ministers who would give King Otho good advice in the Secret recesses of his Closet.

But, in the first place, who is to appoint those Ministers? They can be appointed only by King Otho himself; and it is not likely that King Otho would of His own accord chuse Persons who would give him advice different from his own opinions; But supposing that out of deference to the urgent Representations of Great Britain and Austria such Ministers were to be appointed; who is to guarantee that King Otho would take the advice they would give Him? The probability is that He would not do so. What would these good Ministers then have to do? Why of course resign!—But in that case King Otho would be delighted; He would accept their Resignations without Hesitation, and would appoint in their stead the bad Ministers whose advice would be more suited to his taste.

It seems then that the only real Controul which can be established upon the obstinate but wrong headed opinions of King Otho, must be found in some institution which would render the effects of his own will imperfect, unless supported by the concurrence of other Persons, whose will He should not be able intirely to command. But such an arrangement, though it might afford an effectual Controul over King Otho, might not always controul His will in a manner advantageous to the real interests of the Greek Nation; unless the Persons in whom this Power of Controul was vested, were themselves liable to be controuled by the opinion of their fellow subjects; because, otherwise, they might pursue their own private and separate interests or prejudices without regard to the general Interests of the Greek Nation.

Therefore, in order that the measures of the Government should be calculated to promote the general welfare, it seems indispensable that the Power of the Executive should be limited, so that new Laws should not be made, that new Taxes should not be imposed, and that Publick Expenses should not be incurred, without the consent of some bodies of men answerable to the Country at large for the manner in which they might give or withhold their consent on such matters.

But this is what in common parlance is called a Constitution; for such bodies can only be assemblies more or less numerous according to the Circumstances of the case, chosen by Publick Election, or holding their privileges by a Tenure placing them in a state of Independence of the Crown; and invested with a share in the power of Legislation, and authorized to take cognizance of the Revenue and Expenditure of the Country.

What particular form of an Institution of this kind would be best adapted to the present wants and condition of Greece Her Majesty's Government do not pretend to be able at once to say; but it does appear to them that unless some Institutions of this kind be established, King Otho will never have able and proper Ministers;—and that neither the allotment of Lands, nor any other great measure which may be required for the welfare of Greece can stand the slightest chance of being adopted.

There may be in assemblies of this Kind, as alleged by Prince Metternich, much idle and unprofitable talk; but, nevertheless, in such assemblies the true interests of a Nation are sure to be brought into publick discussion; abuses and Evils of all kinds are made publickly known, remedies are publickly proposed and examined, the general intelligence of the nation is brought to bear practically on the General welfare, and the Country is sure to advance in the Career of improvement.

Document 23. *Palmerston argues with Guizot about promoting Constitutionalism,* 19 *March* 1841*

I have the honour to acknowledge the receipt of your Excellency's despatch No. 89, of the 12th Instant, stating that Mons[ieur] Guizot had read to you a despatch upon the Affairs of Greece, which he has addressed to the Baron de Bourqueney, and reporting the substance of a Conversation which you held with Monsieur Guizot upon that subject.

The Baron de Bourqueney read to me two days ago the despatch in question, and I intend to have a further Conversation with him upon the Subject. In the meanwhile, I have to state that your Excellency has correctly expressed the sentiments and views of Her Majesty's Govern[men]t on this matter.

Her Majesty's Govern[men]t is not pedantically attached to any particular Form of political Constitution; and although they may be of opinion that the Form which, with some variations in each Country, has been established in England and France, is, on the whole, the best, they by no means wish to press the immediate adoption of that Form upon the King of Greece. But, on the other hand, the Three Powers did, by their Proclamation of the 30th of August, 1832, pledge themselves to the Greek Nation that a Constitution should be given, and a similar promise was made by the King of Bavaria in

* Palmerston to Lord Granville (Paris), No. 84, 19 March 1841, *F.O.* 27/619.

the name of His son in a Letter from Baron Gise to the Greek Secretary for Foreign Affairs.

Under these circumstances, it certainly appears to Her Majesty's Govern[men]t that the Three Powers are bound in honour not to allow this matter to rest as it does, and that however gradual the steps by which a real and *boná fide* Constitution is arrived at, such a Constitution is the end which the Three Powers ought to resolve to reach.*

As to the practicability of establishing a Constitution in Greece, it is always easy to say, with regard to any Country in which men do not wish to see Constitutional Government established, that such Country is not fit for it, and that it would not work there; but Her Majesty's Government do not happen to recollect any Country in which a Constitutional system of Government has been established that has not on the whole been better off in consequence of that system than it had been before.

However there is no reason that because Two Parties are willing to go different distances in the same Road, they should not go on together as far as both are disposed to go; and although the French Government has for some time past been less constitutional in its view of Greek Affairs than the British Government has been, Her Majesty's Government will be glad to cooperate with that of France in effecting those preliminary Improvements which at all events would pave the way for the further measures which Her M[ajesty]'s Government think ultimately necessary; and H[er] M[ajesty]'s Gov[ernmen]t would be glad to know what steps Monsieur Guizot would propose to take, in order to carry his views into effect.

Your Excellency will state to Mons[ieu]r Guizot that one indispensable preliminary to any improvement in Greece is the removal of the Bavarian Camarilla, and the entire abolition of the irresponsible Referendaires, who, after the Bavarian

---

* Cp. Palmerston, on 2 March 1848, in *Hans. Deb.*, 3rd Ser., xcvii, 138. He there refers to this obligation of 1832 as "giving a pledge that that Sovereign should give to the Greek nation a constitutional system of government. We, therefore, do stand in the position of parties who have undertaken certain obligations towards the people of Greece; and those obligations...we are bound in honour to see carried out."

Model, have been interposed between The King and the Ministers of State. It is absolutely necessary that the Greek Ministers who are at the head of the various Departments of the public Service, should come in personal contact with the King, should themselves explain to him the measures they propose, and should in person receive his Pleasure thereupon.

You will give a Copy of this despatch to Mons[ieur] Guizot.

Document 24. *Palmerston recommends humanitarian policy to Guizot, 19 March 1841** *

I have the honour to acknowledge the receipt of Y[our] E[xcellency's] Despatch No. 93, of the 15th Instant, enclosing a Copy of the Reply of M[onsieur] Guizot to the Communication which you had addressed to him renewing the proposal of H[er] M[ajesty]'s Gov[ernmen]t that a joint Representation should be made to King Otho by the Representatives of the Three Powers at Athens, relative to the system of cruelty and torture practised by the Agents of the Greek Gov[ernmen]t.

I have in reply to instruct Y[our] E[xcellency] to present a Note to Mons[ieur] Guizot, expressing the sincere regret of H[er] M[ajesty]'s Gov[ernmen]t to find the sentiments of the French Government so different from those of H[er] M[ajesty]'s Government upon questions such as the employment of Torture to extort confession, and the stationing Troops at free Quarters on the Population of a Country as a means of punishing Families for an assumed connivance at the Offences of their Relations. The French Government considers that any Representation to King Otho upon such matters as these would give him just offence by exhibiting the Appearance of a wish to "intervenir *à tout propos dans les moindres actes*" of his Administration.

Her Majesty's Govern[men]t on the contrary, cannot look upon these as small and minute details of Administration, but as great crying enormities involving important and fundamental Principles of Government, and, in the opinion of H[er]

* Palmerston to Granville, No. 85, 19 March 1841, *F.O.* 27/619.

M[ajesty]'s Government, the Powers, who being specially authorized and invited by the Greeks to choose them a Sovereign, placed King Otho on the Throne of Greece, are bound out of a regard for their own honour to express unreservedly to King Otho the strong disapprobation which they must necessarily feel at measures so repugnant to the practice of civilized Nations in the present times, in the hopes of being able thereby not only to rescue the Greek Nation from such Oppressions now, but also to prevent the recurrence of such abuses of Power in future.

H[er] M[ajesty]'s Gov[ernmen]t are concerned to have further to state, that the African Slave Trade is notoriously carried on to a considerable extent in the Mediterranean in Greek Vessels and without any attempt on the part of the Greek Government to prevent or to punish it; and charges have been made against the Greek Government to which no Reply or Denial has yet been made that the Agents of that Govern[men]t have been in the habit of endeavouring by stratagem to poison Persons accused of being Robbers, instead of resorting to those means which are used in other Countries to arrest the Offenders, and to punish them by due process of Law.

With regard to the employment of Torture to extort Confession, Mons[ieur] Guizot says, that the French Minister at Athens acknowledges that it has been practised, but M[onsieur] Lagréné alleges that it has been practised only in two cases, the one, that of a Maltese Subject of Her Majesty, the other, that of a Turkish Subject of the Porte.

Now, upon this, Her Majesty's Government would beg to remark, that the facts admitted by Mons[ieur] Lagréné do not seem to warrant the conclusion he draws from them, but would rather lead to a contrary inference. For how can Mons[ieur] Lagréné know that these two cases are the only ones in which Torture has been thus used, and might he not with more justice have said that these two cases were the only ones to which public attention had been called; and why? because these had probably been the only cases in which the Greek Police had ventured so to torture men, who being entitled to claim the protection of the Ministers of Foreign Powers had the means of making their suffering known by appealing to Advocates placed in a situation authoritatively to demand redress; and is it not fair to suppose that the Persons who have been in the habit of thus inflicting Torture, must have carried their practice to a great extent upon native Greeks before they could have become so regardless of consequences as to hazard its infliction upon a subject of the Sultan, and a subject of Her Britannic Majesty.

Monsieur Guizot says however that the Greek Government has relieved Itself from all responsibility in this respect, by ordering the Persons who inflicted these Tortures to be criminally prosecuted. H[er] M[ajesty]'s Gov[ernmen]t regret that they cannot concur in this view of the matter; because, as long as M[onsieur] Tzinos and the other Persons of higher station than him by whose advice and orders these Tortures have been inflicted, are retained in their respective Offices, it is impossible to consider the prosecution of the Gens d'Armes, who were the immediate Instruments of the cruelty, as anything but a measure of evasion.

With regard to the stationing the Troops at free Quarters, H[er] M[ajesty]'s Gov[ernmen]t know, that the Edict under which it was done has nominally been rescinded but they have not yet been informed whether the practice has actually ceased.

Monsieur Guizot seems to think that, to address to King Otho a remonstrance against Acts so revolting as those which have been adverted to in this Note, would be a greater Interference with the Independent action of King Otho than to point out to him the Measures of Government which they think it would be most for his advantage to adopt. Her Majesty's Government certainly cannot, upon any general principle, concur in this view. Her Majesty's Gov[ernmen]t are undoubtedly ready to join with that of France in recommending such measures of improved Administration as may tend to secure to the Greek Nation that civil and political Freedom which the Treaty of 1827 was destined to secure for them. But H[er] M[ajesty]'s Gov[ernmen]t cannot but think, that to recommend to The King of Greece new arrangements of his Provincial Councils, or a new organisation of his Council of State is a step which requires stronger and more peculiar grounds to justify it than would be necessary to authorize a Remonstrance against the employment of Torture, the placing Troops at free Quarters, the protection of Slave Trade, and the secret destruction of supposed Robbers by Poison.

VI. WELLINGTON, PALMERSTON,
1835–41

THE NEAR EAST AND THE
STRAITS CONVENTION

12. WELLINGTON, A DECISION AS TO
THE BRITISH FLEET, 1835

[Few persons recollect that Wellington was once Foreign Secretary, fewer still understand that, in that capacity, he performed one of his most memorable services. The circumstances of his doing so were peculiar. In November 1834, William IV became dissatisfied with the Whig Ministry and expelled them from power. Peel, whom he wished to head the new Ministry, was absent in Rome. The King, therefore, made Wellington temporarily First Lord of the Treasury and Secretary of State. In that capacity he absorbed all offices of the Crown until Peel's return. There were murmurs as to his unconstitutional position, though a Secretary of State could legitimately transact all business of the Crown and act for every department of Government. The Duke was as unconcerned by the murmurs as he had once been by bullets, and the murmurs soon changed to admiration when the crowds watched the old hero riding from office to office every day, and transacting alone and with such care the business which had previously taxed the energies of four active Ministers. Peel returned late in December and Wellington, though abandoning his other offices, remained Foreign Minister. Palmerston himself admitted that the affairs of that office were never more punctually and correctly handled. In one direction Wellington did make a change and a momentous one. This does not seem to have been due to any question of party, for in regard to supporting the constitutionalists in Spain he carried out Palmerston's measures of which he was known to disapprove. In the instance in question he altered the policy of the previous Government because the change appeared to him essential. The change was due to his sagacious judgment and cool practical mind. It was taken in reference to policy at Constantinople.

Palmerston had already won fame in his handling of the affairs of the Near East. He had started well in 1832 by enlarging the boundaries of Greece. But towards the end of 1832 his policy became hesitating and uncertain. Mehemet Ali, the ambitious

Pasha of Egypt, threw off his allegiance to the Sultan and attacked him in Asia. His warlike son, Ibrahim, advanced into Syria, winning victories everywhere. In July 1832 he beat the Turks at Homs, entered Aleppo and conquered Syria. In December he advanced into Asia Minor and won his "crowning mercy". The Turkish forces were utterly routed, the Grand Vizier was captured at Konieh, the Egyptian troops occupied Adana and Cilicia. They might soon be at Smyrna or even at Constantinople, unless the Great Powers intervened.

Stratford Canning wrote from Constantinople and begged the British Government to send the fleet to Constantinople. The Sultan would be reassured, for Ibrahim would never dare to attack either Constantinople or Smyrna with the British flag flying or British ships in the harbour. Above all, the Russians would have no excuse for intervention. Such was Stratford's plan and Metternich from Vienna pressed the same advice. Palmerston himself would like to have adopted it. But it did not suit his more timid colleagues in the Cabinet. And Palmerston was now reaping the fruits of his resolute and restless policy elsewhere. The biggest British fleet was coercing the Dutch over the Antwerp affair (*v. supra*, p. 89), another British squadron was observing affairs in Portugal. There literally were not the ships to send. If sent at all they must go in such commanding force as to overcome the Egyptians, and at the moment such force was not available. Palmerston therefore refused the Sultan's request for aid and flung him into the arms of Russia.

Russia did not refuse the Sultan's appeal. It was not to her interest to do so. Tsar Nicholas had decided on a new policy at the time of the Treaty of Adrianople (1829).* It was that a weak neighbour (Turkey) was better than a strong one, and that a speedy collapse of the Turkish Empire would bring in France and England to share the spoils. If, however, it gradually dissolved Russia might absorb the "lion's share". This was the Tsar's policy and Ibrahim looked like upsetting it altogether. He appeared suddenly from the blue and threatened to smash the Turkish Empire at a blow. He must therefore be resisted at all costs. If Palmerston would not give aid, Nicholas would. In response to the frenzied appeal of the Sultan, Nicholas sent a naval squadron and transports with a Russian army aboard them. By the end of February they arrived in the Bosphorus, and for the first and last time in history the Russians were in friendly occupation of Constantinople. The Tsar's ships anchored in the Bosphorus just opposite the windows of the British Embassy. His soldiers paraded its shores fraternizing with their Turkish comrades-in-arms. The

* The text of the protocol of 16 September 1829, recording the decision taken by Russia, is printed by R. J. Kerner in 'Russia's New Policy in the Near East after the Peace of Adrianople', *Camb. Hist. Journ.*, v, No. 3, [1937], 286–9.

result was decisive for Ibrahim. He was merely a dashing soldier, but his father Mehemet Ali said that the game was up. His "bluff" was definitely "called", and he threw down the cards. He secured the administration during his lifetime of Syria and Palestine, he also obtained a veiled control over Adana and thus got a gate into Asia Minor. On these terms the Egyptians made peace with the Sultan (5 May 1833).

Russia did not intend to save Turkey for nothing, and Turkey was ready to pay a definite price for the service rendered. The Sultan considered (and with some justice) that France favoured the Egyptians, he thought (and again with some justice) that England had failed him in the hour of need. Russia had not and to Russia he was correspondingly grateful. Count Orlov, the Tsar's representative, shewed the most delicate courtesy and insinuating address. He won the assent of all the Turkish Ministers, as some said, by golden arguments. At any rate, he induced the Turks to sign the celebrated Treaty of Unkiar Skelessi (8 July 1833). It provided for mutual alliance between Russia and Turkey and defence of each other's territories, during eight years. A secret article provided that Russia would not ask Turkey for armed aid in case of war. She would only require Turkey to close the Dardanelles to ships of war, i.e. to prevent a British or French fleet from entering them. This treaty was interpreted by Palmerston and by France as placing Turkey in a state of vassalage to Russia. They tried, and vainly, to prevent the ratification of the treaty.

Turkey seemed bound to Russia, pledged in case of need to admit Russian ships into the Bosphorus and to stop British and French ships at the Dardanelles. A violent anti-Russian agitation arose in England which Palmerston did nothing to restrain. Lord Ponsonby, the British Ambassador at Constantinople, whose windows had been commanded by Russian naval guns for three months, was more violent still. As a result of all this popular agitation and ministerial excitement, Palmerston addressed an instruction to Ponsonby (10 March). This informed him that a secret Admiralty order had been issued to Sir Josias Rowley, commanding the Mediterranean Squadron. By this "discretionary order" he was authorized to comply with any request of the Turkish Government, addressed to him through Ponsonby. He was to sail to Constantinople, if so ordered by Ponsonby, to defend it "against any threatened attack of the Russians". The only restriction on him was "provided that, in a naval point of view, he should consider his force adequate to the emergency".* The French had given similar orders to their Admiral, but Ponsonby was not compelled to consult the French Minister before sum-

* Palmerston to Ponsonby, 10 March 1834, endorsed: "App[rove]d William R."*F.O.* 78/234. *V.* C. W. Crawley, *Camb. Hist. Journ.*, III, No. 1, [1929], 61; Temperley, *England and the Near East, The Crimea*, [1936], 76–7.

moning the fleet. The power thus given him was dangerous. Ponsonby, an extreme anti-Russian, had it in his power to summon the British fleet and produce war, without consulting his own Government first.

It was this "discretionary order" which Wellington studied during his brief tenure of the Foreign Secretaryship. Like Washington and Marlborough, he had a profound understanding of sea power. But it was inconsistent with his ideas that control over it should be exercised at one of the extremities, and not at the heart of the British Empire. Neither did it accord with his ideas that an Ambassador should commit the Foreign Minister to a course of policy or plunge England into war, without the Cabinet itself being consulted on the issue. He also saw, with a good deal of sagacity, that the "discretionary order" had been issued during a period of great excitement, and that much of that excitement was now allayed. He knew well enough too that Lord Ponsonby was a fanatical anti-Russian and that the thunderbolt, if in his hand, might be launched without due consideration. He brought the matter before the Cabinet, who thereupon revoked the order. The dispatch that follows is the draft not, as usual, the original. This draft was in Wellington's own hand, a fact which shews the importance attached to it, and is endorsed with the approval of William IV. "The Sailor King" was as fanatical and anti-Russian as Ponsonby himself, and had approved the original instruction. But he doubtless now saw the naval objections to placing the fleet at the discretion of an Ambassador.

What is still more interesting is the sequel. In those days a change of ministry was often followed by a reversal of foreign policy. But even Palmerston would have hesitated to change openly so deliberate a revocation of orders and a revocation formally approved by the King. After he returned to office in 1835 Palmerston did nothing for some time. Ponsonby remonstrated against "the fatal dispatch" of Wellington and intimated that he would have resigned had he not thought Wellington would soon be out of office. But Palmerston seems to have appreciated the *douche* of cold common sense which Wellington had applied. He waited until May 1836 before cancelling the "fatal dispatch". But, even when he renewed the "discretionary order", it was with considerable limitations. He warned the ardent Ponsonby that there was no immediate danger. When, in 1838, Ponsonby suggested ordering up the fleet, he was promptly snubbed by Palmerston. Even in 1839, when Mehemet Ali was again attacking the Sultan, Palmerston warned Ponsonby to be "sparing" of using his power, and insisted on his not acting save in concert with the French Ambassador. It is obvious, therefore, that Wellington's one important action, while Foreign Secretary, was to teach Palmerston a lesson in prudence and moderation.]

Document 25.   *Wellington revokes the "discretionary order" to the British Fleet to proceed to Constantinople,* 16 *March* 1835*

...I have received H[is] M[ajesty]'s Commands to inform Y[our] E[xcellency] that it does not appear to H[is] M[ajesty] that Affairs in the Levant are at this period in such a State as to require that the Discretion should be vested in the Ambassador at the Porte and the Responsibility imposed upon that Officer of placing this Country in a State of War with Russia.

Under these Circumstances the King's Servants have decided that the Directions contained in a Despatch from the Secretary of State to Sir Josias Rowley dated 31st Jan[uar]y 1834, and that those from Lord Palmerston to Your Lordship dated 10th March 1834 containing a Copy of the abovementioned Instructions should be countermanded, and I have to signify to Your Lordship His Majesty's pleasure accordingly.

The Instruction under which the operations of the Fleet in the Mediterranean and its Relations with the Embassy at the Porte are to be directed in future, are contained in a Despatch to Your Lordship dated 15 Feb[ruar]y 1834.

The Instructions to the Admiral dated Sept[ember] 19 1834 referable to the Conduct of H[is] M[ajesty's] Naval Forces in the Mediterranean in case of a Collision between the Naval Forces of the Ottoman Porte and those of Mahomed Alli will likewise be countermanded.

13. PALMERSTON, MEHEMET ALI, AND THE STRAITS

[Palmerston is generally admitted to have scored a great success in dealing with Mehemet Ali. He won a victory over Mehemet Ali, over France, over Turkey, and over the majority of his colleagues in the British Cabinet. "The bold conception and the brilliant performance were worthy of that name; but the domestic difficulties with which Lord Palmerston had to struggle place the

* Wellington to Lord Ponsonby, No. 5, 16 March 1835, *F.O.* 78/251. The draft is endorsed "App[rove]d William R."

exploit beyond the happiest achievement of the Elder Pitt. The expulsion of the Egyptians from Turkey remains a great monument alike of diplomatic skill and administrative energy." So Disraeli in *Tancred*, and the utterance is not only important in respect to Palmerston, but because Disraeli himself in after days attempted to achieve the same results in the Near East.

The facts may be simply related. Mehemet Ali and his son Ibrahim had grown more formidable than ever. The old Sultan Mahmud was anxious to reduce his rebellious vassal, and to take from him Adana, Syria and Palestine. Finally, in April 1839 the Turkish forces began the struggle by crossing the Euphrates. Two months later, at Nisibin, they were annihilated by Ibrahim. The Turkish fleet sailed to Alexandria and surrendered without striking a blow. Mahmud died (1 July) before the news of either disaster reached Constantinople. Abdul-Medjid, a seventeen-year old boy, became Sultan, without an army, without a fleet and without money. Palmerston endeavoured to get up a European combination to restrain Mehemet Ali from profiting by his conquests. This plan was defeated by the obvious reluctance of France to engage in any measures of coercion against Mehemet Ali. Egypt had, since Napoleon, been the dream of French ambition and Mehemet Ali would prefer to be the vassal of France rather than of Turkey. And the Egyptian fleet, added to the French, would threaten British sea power in the Mediterranean.

Palmerston was not deterred by the reluctance of France, and he found a willing partner in Austria. But Russia at first refused to join a European Conference. The Five Powers (Austria, France, Great Britain, Russia, Prussia) presented a joint Note to the Turks on 27 July 1839, the object of which was to stop future hostilities between Egypt and Turkey. Immediately afterwards Russia approached England and Palmerston made a desperate effort at a compromise with France. It broke down because France wished Mehemet Ali to retain more of his conquests than Palmerston was ready to admit. Nevertheless he was probably genuinely anxious to avoid separation from France. Finally, as France remained recalcitrant, he concluded a Convention between the four Powers (Austria, Great Britain, Prussia and Russia) on 15 July 1840. By this agreement Mehemet Ali was to be expelled from the Holy Cities of Arabia, from Crete, from Adana and from North Syria. South Syria and Acre, plus Egypt, he was to retain as a hereditary pashalic. If Mehemet Ali did not accept these terms he would be confined to Egypt; England and Austria pledged themselves to naval intervention to subdue him. All the Four Powers signing the Quadruple Treaty agreed to defend Constantinople if Ibrahim attacked it.

France was left out of this treaty. It was a mortal affront to her and many persons thought that war with England would follow.

But Palmerston had completely measured the gravity of the crisis. He did not believe there would be war, for the British navy was too strong. Though he could not avoid leaving France out of the treaty* he was as prudent as he could afford to be in public. As Mehemet Ali refused to accept the terms, the consuls of the four Powers concerned notified him of his deposition (23 September). He received the news with calmness. He announced that "this was the fourth [time he had been deposed], and that he hoped to get over it as well as he had done the other three, with the help of God and the Prophet".† Probably he counted less on the Prophet than on the French. But he was doomed to disappointment. The French offered the angriest of protests but they were not ready to fight.

Even in August 1840 Admiral Stopford was off the Syrian coast with a naval squadron. Stimulated by his presence the Lebanon revolted, for all Syria hated Ibrahim's tyranny. Stopford captured Beyrouth (3 October) and then Acre (3 November), which had once baffled Napoleon. Before the end of the month Napier, Stopford's lieutenant, appeared at Alexandria and forced Mehemet Ali to sign a Convention submitting to the Powers and restoring the Turkish fleet. The agreement was disavowed but the result was decisive. Ibrahim and his hitherto invincible army were meanwhile moving back to Egypt along inland roads. He had no further thought of armed resistance to the Powers.

The liquidation of the whole affair took place by a solemn publication of firmans on 10 June 1841. Mehemet Ali became hereditary pasha of Egypt and of Nubia, etc. with an obligation to pay tribute and to limit his army to 18,000 men. France still held aloof. But her game was lost. She was finally induced to join the Straits' Convention of 13 July 1841, in conjunction with all the Great Powers and Turkey. It was signed just after the expiry of the Russo-Turkish Treaty of Unkiar Skelessi. The preamble of this Convention paid a vague homage to the "inviolability" of the Sultan's "sovereign rights". The articles pledged the Sultan to close both Bosphorus and Dardanelles to ships of war (with specified exceptions as to light vessels) "according to the ancient rule of the Ottoman Empire". Russia thought she had gained an advantage by stopping British and French war ships at the Dardanelles, England and France by stopping Russian ships at the Bosphorus. The vague general recognition of sovereign rights pledged all powers in support of Turkey. It also released Palmerston and the French from all fear of the effects of the Treaty of Unkiar Skelessi. It had, in fact, not only expired by efflux of time but a purely Russo-Turkish connexion had been superseded

* Palmerston has a lengthy defence of his treatment of France in a private letter of 27 July 1843. Bulwer, *Life of Palmerston*, [1875], III, 426–33.
† Quoted in *Cambridge Modern History*, x, 570.

by a general European agreement. It was an important European settlement and one for which Palmerston can claim a good deal of credit.

The documents selected are representative and not complete, but they are of great interest and importance. **Doc. 26**, dated 7 July 1838, is a solemn warning by England to Mehemet Ali that she speaks only for herself. None the less any attempt by Mehemet Ali to throw off the Turkish yoke will not only be impossible but will ultimately produce British intervention. One reason for the British attitude is shown in **Doc. 27**. Palmerston announces England's determination navally to control the Persian Gulf, which led next year to the British occupation of Aden (1839). **Doc. 28** warns the Sultan (as it proved vainly) not to attack Mehemet Ali. **Doc. 29** may be described as a roar of the British lion. It shows that England was prepared to act alone even in December 1839. **Doc. 30** details the attitude to Louis Philippe and to France about the same time, and is important as shewing the approach to Russia, which ultimately resulted in the Treaty of 15 July 1840, signed without France. In **Doc. 31** Palmerston exchanges views with Metternich on the Straits' Convention and in **Doc. 32** on the theory of guarantee.* This last is of much importance as Metternich's theory is a different one from that he previously held. *V. supra*, **Doc. 17**, pp. 98–100.]

Document 26. *Palmerston warns Mehemet Ali,* 7 *July* 1838†

Her Majesty's Government have received the Communication made through You of the Intention of the Pasha of Egypt to throw off his Allegiance to the Sultan, and to declare himself the Independent Sovereign of those Provinces of the Turkish Empire, which he has been appointed by the Sultan to govern.

The British Government have received this announcement with extreme Regret; and You are instructed to express to the Pasha the deep concern which this Intelligence has occasioned them, but at the same time to state that Her Majesty's Government do not yet abandon the hope that fuller Consideration of the subject, and more mature Reflection, both upon the nature of the contemplated step, and upon its inevitable Consequences, may lead the Pasha to come to a more just and prudent Resolution.

Two Motives are represented as impelling the Pasha thus

---

* *V. supra*, the dispatch of Canning, pp. 82–4.
† Palmerston to Colonel Campbell, No. 21, 7 July 1838, *F.O.* 78/343.

to rebel against his Sovereign and to attempt to dismember the Turkish Empire. The one is a Regard for his own Fame, the other an anxiety for the future Fate of his Family.—But, in the opinion of Her Majesty's Government, both these Motives ought on the contrary strongly to operate to dissuade the Pasha from adopting the contemplated Course.

For, with respect to his own Fame, he ought to recollect that if he has hitherto risen progressively in the esteem of the Nations of Europe, it has been in consequence of the Pains he has taken to establish the authority of the Law among the People whom he has governed, and by reason of his successful exertions to give the ascendancy to Justice in all the Transactions between Man and Man, so as to secure to every man the Possession and enjoyment of what rightfully belongs to him.

But if now the Pasha should himself set all these Principles at naught, and should give to the world by his own Conduct a signal example of violent Injustice and of wrong deliberately done, instead of leaving behind him a name to be respected by future ages, he will tarnish the Reputation he has already acquired, and be included in the List of Men who, according to the extent of their means, have, upon a larger or smaller scale, endeavoured to appropriate to themselves by Force Things which belonged of Right to others.

But equally erroneous would be the expectation that by such an attempt he would improve the Condition of his Family. Far different would be the Result. For, success in such an enterprize being impossible, He would only involve his Family in the inevitable Ruin which He would bring upon Himself; and thus He would destroy those very Persons for whose future welfare He feels so strong an Interest.

Her Majesty's Gov[ernmen]t at once and decidedly pronounce the successful execution of the attempt to be impossible; and its inevitable Consequence to be Ruin to the Pasha; because they know that the Conflict which must necessarily be brought on by such an attempt, would not be between the Pasha and the Sultan singlehanded, but between the Pasha and the Sultan aided and supported by all the Powers of Europe.

Were the Contest indeed to lie between the Turkish and Egyptian Forces left to themselves, it would not in the present state of Things be safe for the Pasha to reckon upon obtaining the same success as that which attended his arms in 1832; But it is needless to say that if the Great Powers of Europe shall determine to assist and uphold the Sultan, the Result of the Contest must be the overthrow and expulsion of the Pasha.

The British Government, however, speaks only for itself; but feels itself bound, in return for the frank and unreserved Communication which it has received from the Pasha, to declare to him, in a manner equally unreserved and explicit, that, if He should unfortunately proceed to execute his announced Intentions; and if Hostilities should (as they indisputably would) break out thereupon between the Sultan and the Pasha, The Pasha must expect to find Great Britain taking Part with the Sultan in order to obtain Redress for so flagrant a Wrong done to the Sultan, and for the Purpose of preventing the Dismemberment of the Turkish Empire; and the Pasha would fatally deceive himself if he were to suppose that any Jealousies among the Powers of Europe would prevent those Powers from affording to the Sultan, under such Circumstances, every assistance which might be necessary for the Purpose of upholding, enforcing, and vindicating his just and legitimate Rights.

Document 27. *Palmerston and the Persian Gulf,* *29 November* 1838*

You stated in your despatch No. 5 of this year, that Mehemet Ali, in reply to a communication which by my despatch No. 25, of the 8th of December, you had been directed to make to him, had assured you that he had not the least idea of extending his authority towards the Persian Gulf.

You also stated in your despatch No. 54 of this year that the Pasha's forces had been entirely successful in Arabia, and particularly in the Nedjib Country and the Hedjaz; and that

* Palmerston to Colonel Campbell, No. 30, 29 November 1838, *F.O.* 78/343. It was largely in consequence of this suspected danger that Aden was occupied by the British Government in 1839.

the Assii tribe of Arabs had entirely submitted to the Pasha's forces under Achmet Pasha and you added that you considered these successes to have afforded a very great relief to Mehemet Ali, as Arabia will in consequence no longer drain Egypt of men, money, and provisions.

The advices however which Her Majesty's Government have recently received from Bagdad, represent the Egyptian forces as being about to cross the Peninsula of Arabia to Lahsa and Katif, with the ultimate Purpose of taking Possession of the Island of Bahrein in the Persian Gulf.

I have to instruct you to ask Mehemet Ali whether the fact is so; and you will add that Her Majesty's Government hope and trust that he will upon full consideration abandon any intention of establishing himself on the Persian Gulf, because, as you have already declared to him, such a scheme on his part could not be viewed with indifference by the British Government.

Document 28. *Palmerston warns Sultan Mahmud, 15 March 1839**

Her Majesty's Government entirely approve the language which, as reported in your despatch No. 28, you have held with the view of inducing the Sultan to avoid committing himself in any way at present; and I have to instruct Your Excellency to press strongly on the Sultan that while, on the one hand, Great Britain would undoubtedly assist him to repel any attack on the part of Mehemet Ali, it would, on the other hand, be a different question if the war was begun by the Sultan.

Document 29. *Palmerston makes the British Lion roar, 2 December 1839†*

I have to instruct Your Excellency to continue to urge the Turkish Government to remain firm, to make no concession to Mehemet Ali, but to trust to the support of its Allies. The British Government has taken its line; and the course of the

* Palmerston to Lord Ponsonby, No. 38, 15 March 1839, *F.O.* 195/155.
† Palmerston to Lord Ponsonby, No. 180, 2 December 1839, *F.O.* 195/158.

negotiation during the last few Months ought to inspire the Turkish Government with confidence in Great Britain. For it has been the British Government which has mainly prevented the Porte from being pressed by the Five Powers to submit unconditionally to all the demands of Mehemet Ali. France has for some time declared her opinion, that such a settlement is the only one that is practicable; and she has laboured to persuade the other Powers to adopt her views. If Great Britain had given way to France, and had consented to support the French propositions, Austria, and Prussia, and Russia would probably have acquiesced in them also: because those Powers have intimated that they would support any arrangement which England and France should have agreed upon. But England has stood firm to the Principles which she laid down in the outset of the negotiation, and her steadiness has encouraged Austria to adhere to the same line, while it has made it impossible for Russia to adopt the views of France, even if she had been disposed to do so; because Russia having contracted special engagements to protect Turkey, could not appear to be less friendly to that Power than England is. In like manner the avowed desire of France to support the pretensions of Mehemet Ali has led to no result, and will lead to none as long as the Porte is true to its own Interests.

Document 30. *Palmerston and King Louis Philippe,* *22 November* 1839*

With reference to Your Excellency's Despatch of the 18th Instant, marked "Secret and Confidential", reporting a Conversation which Your Excellency had held with The King of the French, on the subject of the Turkish and Egyptian Question, I have to observe to Your Excellency, that the upshot of the remarks of His Majesty upon that occasion appears to be, that in proportion as the course of events have rendered the active assistance of the Powers of Europe necessary for maintaining the Integrity and Inde-

* Palmerston to Lord Granville, No. 371 Secret and Confidential, 22 November 1839, *F.O.* 146/211.

pendence of the Turkish Empire, exactly in that proportion and precisely for that reason, the French Government has become unwilling to afford to the Sultan any assistance at all.

With respect to the notion that the Five Powers acting in union with the Sultan, have not the means of compelling the Pasha of Egypt to evacuate Syria, that opinion is one which it can scarcely be worth while seriously to argue; the disparity of Forces between the two Parties in such a contest, being so infinitely great, that resistance on the part of the Pasha must necessarily be vain.

The King of the French, however, seems to be of opinion, that the Sultan would be more seriously injured in his Independence by receiving Assistance from Russia, than by having his Empire practically dismembered, and by being deprived permanently of the resources of a large portion of his own Territories. In this opinion, Her Majesty's Government cannot concur. It is undoubtedly a misfortune for a Sovereign to be under the necessity of receiving Military or Naval Aid from another Sovereign to defend him against hostile attack. The receiving of such Aid is a publick and undeniable proof of great weakness on the part of him who receives it; and real Independence is not compatible with great weakness. Such aid also, if given by the single Act of the Sovereign who affords it, entitles that Sovereign to ask in return, favours and influence, which must trench upon the future Independence of the Sovereign who has been protected. But if Russia were to give Assistance to the Sultan, not as acting upon her own single Decision, but as acting in pursuance of a Concert between the Five Allied Powers, such Assistance would of course not bring after it any favours or concessions from Turkey to Russia, that would be injurious to the Independence of Turkey; and then, the only question would be, whether the Independence of the Turkish Empire would permanently and for the future, be most affected, by the temporary occupation of some part of the Turkish Territory by a friendly Russian Force, which would come in to restore that Territory to the Sultan, and which would go out again, when that purpose was accomplished; or by the permanent occupation of such Territory by a hostile Egyptian Force, which having come in to conquer, would stay in to retain; and would by retaining, practically sever such Territory from the Turkish Empire. But surely there can be no doubt how that Question must be answered.*

[France refused to respond to this appeal and the Convention of 15 July 1840 was signed by the four other Powers without her at London. Execution followed by England and Austria. Ibrahim was defeated (10 October) and Acre taken on 3 November. By 9 December Mehemet Ali in effect submitted. But the usual tedious delays supervened and it was not until 13 July 1841 that France signed the Straits' Convention with the other Powers.]

Document 31. *Palmerston and Metternich on France, and the Straits' Convention,* 10 *May* 1841†

With reference to Your Excellency's despatch No. 79 of the 22d Ultimo, reporting Prince Metternich's opinion as to the moment at which it would be most expedient that France should affix her signature to the Convention, the Draft of which was initialled on the 15th of March, I have to state to Your Excellency that Her Majesty's Government have felt great pleasure at learning the very sound and judicious view taken by Prince Metternich of the matters treated of in this despatch. It is perfectly true, as His Highness observes, that the Isolation of France can only cease when that Treaty in the execution of which the four Powers are engaged, and to which France is not a party, shall have been fully carried into effect; for the Isolation of France arises from the fact, that the four Powers have undertaken a political operation which France declined to take part in; and when that operation is finished, and the four Powers fall back into the ordinary state of quiescence in which all Powers are when they are not actively engaged in any combined measures with Allies, then the Four Powers and France will all be equally

* Palmerston has a lengthy defence of his whole attitude to France in a private letter of 5 July 1840. *V.* Bulwer, *Life of Palmerston*, II, 356–61; Temperley, *England and the Near East, The Crimea*, [1936], n. 196, pp. 429–32.

† Palmerston to Lord Beauvale, No. 97, 10 May 1841, *F.O.* 120/194. Cp. Temperley, *England and the Near East, The Crimea*, [1936], Chap. v *passim.*

isolated: and this is a distinction which seems to have been either overlooked or not understood in France.

The French think that the Isolation of France will cease by the signature of the proposed Treaty, and that this Treaty will make France enter again into "the European Concert" but the proposed Treaty contains no stipulations for action or for concert; it merely records the determination of the Great Powers to respect the decision and intention of the Sultan in a matter with regard to which he is intitled as an independent Sovereign to declare his will.

Document 32. *Palmerston exchanges views with Metternich on the Palmerstonian theory of Guarantee, 10 May 1841**

With reference to Your Excellency's despatch No. 80 of the 22d Ultimo, reporting Prince Metternich's opinion that it would not, in the present state of things, be expedient for the Powers of Europe to enter into a guarantee of the Integrity of the Turkish Empire, I have to inform Your Excellency that Her Majesty's Government intirely agree with Prince Metternich in that opinion. But Her Majesty's Government cannot quite concur with Prince Metternich in the reasons which, in his despatch to Baron Stürmer, he gives for that opinion.

Prince Metternich argues that a State which is guaranteed loses thereby its Independence and becomes a Mediatized State; that the guaranteeing Power becomes a protecting Power, and that, while it is inconvenient to have even one Protector, to have several would be an intolerable Burthen; that in fact there is but one form of guarantee free from these inconveniences, and that is a defensive Alliance.

Now Her Majesty's Government quite admit, that when a single Power guarantees another, such an engagement does place the weaker Power in a situation of dependence upon the stronger, which must derogate from the Freedom of Action, and from the intire Independence of the weaker

* Palmerston to Lord Beauvale, No. 98, 10 May 1841, *F.O.* 120/194. This dispatch should be carefully compared with Canning's classic utterance, *v. supra*, pp. 82–4, and Palmerston's of 1848, *v. infra*, pp. 156–7.

Power, and must give the stronger one a preponderant influence. But this effect cannot be produced in the same degree when the guarantee is given by several Powers; because it is probable that those Powers would all have different views and wishes; and these opposite and conflicting impulses would destroy each other.

At all events Austria has not always held these opinions; because She joined with the other four Powers in guaranteeing, not merely the Integrity, but the Independence of Belgium, proving thereby that She did not consider a guarantee of Integrity as being necessarily destructive of Independence; and the result, in the case of Belgium, has not shewn that the guarantee deprived Belgium of any portion of her Independence.*

Again; France Great Britain and Russia guaranteed the integrity and Independence of the Kingdom of Greece, and although Foreign Influence has, during the reign of King Otho, exerted a most injurious sway in Greece, yet this evil has had no connection with the guarantee.

The evil of a guarantee to the State to which it is given is, that it leads such State to rely upon Foreign Aid for its defence; and then, when the moment comes when that aid is wanted, it may upon some pretence or other be withheld, or it may arrive too late.

In the present case of Turkey, if the status quo of 1839 had been maintained, and if Mehemet Ali had been left in occupation of Syria, the Sultan would have been constantly exposed to an imminent and serious danger and there might have been a reason why the four Powers should have entered into engagements to come to his assistance against Mehemet Ali whenever wanted; but now that Mehemet has been driven back into Egypt, and the Sultan has recovered possession of Syria and of his Fleet, and may by good management and perseverance make himself stronger by Sea and by land than Mehemet Ali can possibly be, there seems to be no standing danger against which it can be necessary for the Allies to guarantee the Sultan; and therefore it would, on many

* V. supra, Doc. 17, pp. 82–4.

accounts, be better that Turkey and the other Powers of Europe should stand towards each other in the ordinary relation in which independent States reciprocally stand.

But Prince Metternich's observation as to the effect which a guarantee of the integrity of the Turkish Empire by the Five Powers, France included, would have, seems perfectly wellfounded; and that would alone constitute a weighty reason why the Sultan should not desire to have such a guarantee.

As to that part of Prince Metternich's despatch to Baron Stürmer, in which he expresses an opinion that the Sultan would do better to revert to the old system of selling Pashaliks and farming His revenues, rather than adhere to the newly introduced Plan of collecting the Taxes by receivers of his own, Her Majesty's Government cannot concur in that opinion, and would see with extreme regret it's adoption by the Sultan. They look upon the change which the Sultan has made in this part of his administration as an improvement of the very greatest importance as regards both the Interests of the Sultan and the welfare of the people; and though this Reform, like many others which involve great changes of System, may require some time to come fully and completely into operation, there cannot be a shadow of doubt that it would be calamitous to rescind it.

VII. PALMERSTON, RUSSELL, CLARENDON, 1841–53

THE ORIGINS OF THE CRIMEAN WAR

14. THE CONVERSATIONS OF NICHOLAS

[The origins of the Crimean War really go back to Russia's signing the Treaty of Unkiar Skelessi with Turkey in 1833. This was abrogated and the Straits' Convention was substituted in 1841 as a European, rather than a Russian, protection of Turkey, but the integrity and independence of Turkey were not, in fact, guaranteed by the Powers. The most immediate result of the Straits' Convention was that Tsar Nicholas, delighted at the separation of England from France over Egypt, tried to make that separation lasting. In effect, he asked England to enter with him into a secret alliance against France in the winter of 1840. Palmerston refused and in his reply of 1841 laid down the whole doctrine of obligations by which a British Cabinet and Parliament can be bound. This is a doctrine of fundamental importance to the understanding of British diplomacy. It would have been well if Nicholas had appreciated and acted on his advice. Had he done so—he would not have endeavoured by his conversations with Aberdeen in 1844, and with Seymour in 1853,* to obtain results which only decisions of the Cabinet or of Parliament could give. Had he marked Palmerston's warning the Crimean War might have been avoided. The Tsar's conversations with Aberdeen, 1844, and with Seymour in 1853, discussed in more detail the partition of the Turkish Empire and in 1853 specific proposals were made. These were as follows, and may be compared with proposals on the same subject outlined by the Tsar in a memorandum to Field-Marshal Paskievic. In the following table the former are designated as (S) and the latter as (P).†

Constantinople.
   (*a*) Not to be a permanent possession of Russia, but might be temporarily occupied (S).
   (*b*) To be a free port but no annexation (P).

Moldo-Wallachia.
   (*a*) Independent under Russian protection (S).
   (*b*) "Not independent but Russian" (P).

---

* For the two latter, *v.* G. B. Henderson in *History*, October 1933, 240–7; and Temperley, *England and the Near East, The Crimea*, [1936], Chap. x *passim.*
† Quoted from Temperley, *England and the Near East, The Crimea*, [1936], 461.

Servia.
   (*a*) Independent under Russian protection (S).
   (*b*) Independent (P).

Bulgaria.
   (*a*) Independent (S).
   (*b*) Northern part and Constanza to be Russian (P).
       Most of Bulgaria to be independent (P).

Greece.
   Not to be enlarged (S).

Straits.
   Russia to garrison Bosphorus, and Austria to garrison the Dardanelles (P).

Turkish coasts of Adriatic and Archipelago.
   To go to Austria (P).

Crete.
   (*a*) Crete and other isles to go to France. England to have Cyprus or Rhodes (P).
   (*b*) Crete to go to England, if she wanted it (S).

Egypt.
   Egypt to England (S and P).

It should be noted, however, that Nicholas, neither in 1841 nor in 1844 nor in 1853, provoked the suspicions of British Ministers, though they regarded secret agreements with him as potential developments in the future as absurd. But they believed in his disinterestedness and accepted his pledge as to not wishing to break up the Turkish Empire. In March 1853 even Palmerston regarded Nicholas as "a gentleman" whose pledge could be trusted. The later misinterpretation of the Seymour and Aberdeen conversations was a phase of war psychology and of war propaganda. The theory that Nicholas invited England to rob Turkey of Egypt in the South, while he robbed her in the North, should be relegated to the sphere of legend. It is nevertheless true that he would have done well to heed Palmerston's warning given in 1841.]

Document 33. *Palmerston instructs Nicholas I in the obligations of the British Constitution,* 11 *January* 1841*

I have received Your Excellency's despatch No. 76 of the 22nd of December, marked "Confidential", reporting the wish expressed to You by The Emperor of Russia that some engagement should be entered into between England and the

* Lord Palmerston to the Marquis of Clanricarde, No. 6, 11 January 1841, *F.O.* 181/168.

other three Great Powers who are Parties to the Treaty of July, with the view of providing for the contingency of an attack by France upon the liberties of Europe: and I have to instruct Your Excellency thereupon to state to His Imperial Majesty that Her Majesty's Government are much gratified by the confidence which he reposes in the Government of England, and by the frank and open manner in which he has been pleased to communicate his views and opinions to Your Excellency. Her Majesty's Government will be equally open with The Emperor, and will state to His Imperial Majesty exactly their sentiments on the subject on which he has touched in his conversation with Your Excellency.

One of the general principles which Her Majesty's Government wish to observe as a guide for their conduct in dealing with the relations between England and other States, is, that changes which foreign Nations may chuse to make in their internal Constitution and form of Government, are to be looked upon as matters with which England has no business to interfere by force of arms, for the purpose of imposing upon such Nations a Form of Government which they do not wish to have, or for the purpose of preventing such Nations from having Institutions which they desire. These things are considered in England to be matters of domestic concern, which every Nation ought to be allowed to settle as it likes.

But an attempt of one Nation to seize and to appropriate to itself territory which belongs to another Nation, is a different matter; because such an attempt leads to a derangement of the existing Balance of Power, and by altering the relative strength of States, may tend to create danger to other Powers; and such attempts therefore, the British Government holds itself at full liberty to resist, upon the universally acknowledged principle of self-defence.

Now, it is quite true, as stated by The Emperor, that any Country, such as France, for instance, may, under the plea and pretext of altering its own Institutions, seek to overthrow the existing Governments of other Countries, for the purpose of adding those Countries to its own Territories, or of associating them with its own aggressive system; and such proceedings would cease to be domestic changes of arrangement, and would assume the unquestionable character of external aggression.—Such attempts England has in former times on many occasions resisted; and it is highly probable that if a similar case were again to arise, England would again pursue a similar course.

But it is not usual for England to enter into engagements with reference to cases which have not actually arisen, or which are not immediately in prospect: and this for a plain reason. [All formal engagements of the Crown, which involve the question of peace and war, must be submitted to Parliament; and Parliament might probably not approve of an engagement which should bind England prospectively]* to take up Arms in a contingency which might happen at an uncertain time, and under circumstances which could not as yet be foreseen.

It is true that His Imperial Majesty has spoken of an understanding which need not be recorded in any formal Instrument; but upon which He might rely if the Turn of Affairs should render it applicable to events. But this course would not be free from objections. For, in the first place, it would scarcely be consistent with the spirit of the British Constitution for the Crown to enter into a binding engagement of such a nature, without placing it formally upon record, so that Parliament might have an opportunity of expressing its opinion thereupon, and this could only be done by some written Instrument; and to such a course the objection which I have alluded to above, would apply. [But if the engagement were merely verbal, though it would bind the Ministers who made it, it might be disavowed by their successors; and thus the Russian Government might be led to count upon a system of policy on the part of Great Britain, which might not eventually be pursued.

Under these circumstances, it seems to Her Majesty's Government that the Cabinet of St. Petersburgh should be

* The passages enclosed in brackets have already been published by Major John Hall, *England and the Orleans Monarchy*, [1912], 320, and there has been a fuller publication by Professor F. S. Rodkey since. *V.* also Temperley, *England and the Near East, The Crimea*, [1936], 251–3.

satisfied to trust to the general tendency of the policy of Great Britain, which leads her to watch attentively, and to guard with care the maintenance of the Balance of Power:] and Her Majesty's Government hope that His Imperial Majesty will not think that this policy is the less deeply rooted in the minds of Her Majesty's Government, if they should not think it expedient to enter at the present moment into engagements such as those mentioned by The Emperor.*

15. THE HOLY PLACES AND RUSSIA'S PROTECTION OF THE ORTHODOX SUBJECTS OF TURKEY

[The real grounds of England's going to war with Russia was the pressure of British public opinion, which ultimately regarded Turkey as a lamb and Nicholas as a brutal and ravening wolf. But that was not the first opinion of the British Government on the dispute as to the Holy Places, between Napoleon and Nicholas. As will be seen from **Doc. 34** the first impression of the British Government in 1853 was that the French had, by undue influence, obtained an unfair decision from the Sultan in December 1852 and that England's influence must be used to redress the balance in favour of Russia, by putting pressure on Turkey. It will also be seen that the influence of the Tsar's conversations with Seymour had caused the British Government to be distinctly favourable to him and to believe that he did not desire to seize Constantinople. It is also important to note that Stratford de Redcliffe, who had been reappointed Ambassador, had a large share in drawing up his own instructions† and seems to have been quite friendly to the Tsar.]

* Cp. *F.O.* 65/262. From Clanricarde, No. 76, 22 December 1840. "The Emperor said he did not require a Treaty—a clear understanding would suffice him—the assurance of Ambassadors—my word would be ample security to him, if I was authorized to pass it." The subsequent history of this offer, which is connected with the Tsar's conversations with Aberdeen in 1844, and with Seymour in 1853, will be found in Temperley, *England and the Near East, The Crimea*, [1936], Bk IV, Chap. x.

† The instructions that follow were based on a memorandum given by Stratford himself, qualified by some suggestions from the new Prime Minister Aberdeen. They are dated 25 February and the draft is actually signed by Lord John Russell, but he had asked his successor to draw them up, and the Blue Book gives them as Clarendon's. *V.* Temperley, *England and the Near East, The Crimea*, [1936], 314–15.

Document 34. *Stratford de Redcliffe instructed to counsel prudence to Turkey and forbearance to Russia,* 25 *February* 1853*

The Queen has been pleased to direct that at this critical
period of the fate of the Ottoman Empire, Your Excellency
should return to your Embassy for a special purpose and
charged with special instructions.

Your Excellency is aware that the preservation of the
independence and integrity of Turkey enters into the general
and established system of European policy: that the principle
is solemnly declared and sanctioned by the Convention of
1840,† and is acknowledged by all the Great Powers of Europe.

[But while the general principle is acknowledged, the
inclination of different Powers is very different, and must be
carefully borne in mind.

Great Britain adopts it in all sincerity, without mental
reservation; is animated by sincere friendship for Turkey;
and has no after-thought on the subject.

France is likewise desirous to maintain it, partly from the
traditions of her policy, partly from jealousy of the Powers
which, being the nearest neighbours to Turkey, would claim
to possess the fairest portion of the inheritance in case of her
dissolution.

Austria is likewise disposed from policy and interest to
maintain the independence of the Porte; but several causes of
dissention have arisen of late years, and her passions may lead
her to depart widely from the road of her true interest, and
her conservative policy.

The case of Russia is altogether different. The possession
of Constantinople was a favourite dream of The Empress
Catherine. The wars which Russia has waged with Turkey,
both during Her reign, and down to the period of the peace
of Adrianople, have all ended in the aggrandizement of

---

* Clarendon to Stratford de Redcliffe, No. 1, 25 February 1853, *F.O.*
195/396. Published with some omissions in *A. & P.*, [1854], LXXI, [1698],
96–8. Cp. Temperley and Penson, *Century of Diplomatic Blue Books*, No. 460.
The omissions made in the Blue Book are indicated above by the use of double
square brackets.

† The date is given in the Blue Book as 1841. On the relevance of the 1840
and 1841 conventions from this standpoint cp. Temperley, *England and the Near
East, The Crimea*, [1936], 146.

Russia, and the depression of the Mahometan Power. The conquest of Constantinople is a favourite object of national ambition. Millions of Christian Subjects of the Porte long to reverse the triumphs of the Fifteenth Century, and to make the Crescent inferior to the Cross.

But the possession of Constantinople by Russia, giving her a commanding position at once on the Baltic and the Mediterranean, would not be seen with complacency by other Powers. The difficulty of arranging this point prevented a cordial Alliance between Napoleon the First and The Emperor Alexander: an attempt to cut the knot by Russia would at this moment unite against her all the Powers of Europe. The Emperor Nicholas is conscious of this difficulty, and with a moderation at once magnanimous and wise is content to forego the prospect of this brilliant prize.

But the weakness of the Turkish Empire and the presumption of its rulers may bring on a danger which no one seems willing to invite, and hasten a crisis which no one is anxious to precipitate.]

The object [therefore] of Your Excellency's Mission at this time is to counsel prudence to the Porte, and forbearance to those Powers who are urging her compliance with their demands. You are instructed to use every effort to ward off a Turkish war, and to persuade the Powers interested to look to an amicable termination of existing disputes.

[The disputes which more immediately demand attention are those which relate to Montenegro and the Holy Places.

The defence of Montenegro may be prolonged or the Mountaineers may submit to the Turkish force; and in either case the Sultan may be unwilling to return to the status quo that has been peremptorily insisted upon by Austria.

But] the question of the Holy Places in Syria offers [more] danger to the Peace of Turkey. However indifferent to their respective merits, the Porte is now unavoidably exposed to the rival pretensions of Russia and France, each animated by a political interest, as well as by religious zeal, and both appealing to engagements alleged to have been contracted towards each of them by the Porte. Threatened from both sides, and unable to satisfy one party without displeasing the other, the Sultan is placed in a position of embarrassment and danger, rendered more critical by the internal weakness of the Empire, and the special character of the points at issue.

It is therefore to be feared that if the Three* Governments do not modify Their demands, and should continue to maintain towards the Porte the dictatorial, if not menacing attitude they have lately assumed, they may, without any deliberate intention of departing from those principles of European policy to which I have above alluded, accelerate the dissolution of the Turkish Empire, and produce the catastrophe that all are concerned in averting.

England however is in a position to neutralize by her moral influence these alarming contingencies; [for England has the important advantage of having no special interest in the pending questions, and of being viewed by the Porte with less mistrust and stronger hopes of eventual assistance than any other Power in Christendom;] and the Porte will learn with satisfaction that even before your arrival at Constantinople the best efforts of Her Majesty's Government have been directed to restrain encroachment and to obtain every fair concession calculated to settle the existing differences.

With this object Your Excellency is instructed to proceed to Constantinople by way of Paris and Vienna.

You will inform the French Minister for Foreign Affairs that Her Majesty's Government have great satisfaction in believing that the interests of France and England in the East are identical; and that nothing therefore need prevent their cordial cooperation in maintaining the integrity and independence of the Turkish Empire. In communicating with M. Drouyn de Lhuys respecting the Holy Places in Syria, Your Excellency will govern Yourself by the language of the despatches of Lord John Russell to Lord Cowley and Colonel Rose, copies of which are herewith enclosed; and You will explain to him the fatal embarrassment to which the Sultan may be exposed, if unduly pressed by France upon a question

* "Two" in the Blue-Book version.

of such vital importance to the Power from which Turkey has most to apprehend.

At Vienna Your Excellency will state to Count Buol that Her Majesty's Government have received with sincere pleasure the assurances that the friendly disposition of Austria towards the Porte was unchanged; and that her conservative policy in the East would be rigidly adhered to; that the increasing tendency to disorder and weakness in the Turkish Empire calls for moderation and forbearance on the part of the Sultan's Allies, and in such a policy the cordial cooperation of Her Majesty's Government may be relied upon by Austria; [and that with reference to Montenegro You are instructed to support the demands of the Austrian Minister at Constantinople in as far as they may be consistent with the honour and independence of the Sultan.]

To the Sultan you will say that Her Majesty, in directing Your Excellency to proceed forthwith to Constantinople, manifests the feelings of friendship by which She is animated towards His Highness, and at the same time Her opinion of the gravity of the circumstances in which Her Majesty has reason to fear the Ottoman Empire is now placed.

[With respect to Montenegro Your Excellency will state that Her Majesty's Government do not dispute the rights of the Porte, but are of opinion that those rights should be asserted with extreme moderation, considering the slight authority that the Sultan can exercize over the wild inhabitants of that distant portion of His dominions; and You will recommend that the force now employed against the Montenegrins, which is maintained at such great cost for no adequate object, shall be withdrawn at the earliest opportunity that is consistent with the honour and dignity of the Sultan.]

As regards the Holy Places, Her Majesty's Government are unwilling to give you any special instructions, and prefer to leave Your Excellency unfettered in the exercise of your judgment and discretion, as much may depend on your communications with M. Drouyn de Lhuys, and upon the state in which you find the negotiation between Russia and the Porte on Your arrival at Constantinople.

[In using your best endeavours for bringing to a successful termination this unseemly dispute which reflects so little credit on the two denominations of Christians engaged in it, Your Excellency will bear in mind that Her Majesty's Government without professing to give an opinion on the subject, are not insensible to the superior claims of Russia both as respects the Treaty obligations of Turkey, and the loss of moral influence that The Emperor would sustain throughout His dominions if, as the Ecclesiastical Head of His Church, He were to yield any privileges it has hitherto enjoyed, to the Latin Church of which the Emperor of the French claims to be the Protector.]

Your Excellency will [then], with all the frankness and unreserve that may be consistent with prudence and the dignity of the Sultan, explain the reasons which lead Her Majesty's Government to fear that the Ottoman Empire is now in a position of peculiar danger. The accumulated grievances of Foreign Nations which the Porte is unable or unwilling to redress, the mal-administration of its own affairs, and the increasing weakness of executive Power in Turkey, have caused the Allies of the Porte latterly to assume a tone alike novel and alarming, and which, if persevered in, may lead to a general revolt among the Christian Subjects of the Porte, and prove fatal to the independence and integrity of the Empire, a catastrophe that would be deeply deplored by Her Majesty's Government, but which it is Their duty to represent to the Porte is considered probable and impending by some of the great European Powers.

Your Excellency will explain to the Sultan that it is with the object of pointing out these dangers, and with the hope of averting them, that Her Majesty's Government have now directed You to proceed to Constantinople. You will endeavour to convince the Sultan and His Ministers that the crisis is one which requires the utmost prudence on their part, and confidence in the sincerity and soundness in* the advice They will receive from You, to resolve it favourably for their future peace and independence.

* "Of" in the Blue Book.

Your Excellency's long residence at the Porte, and intimate knowledge of the affairs of Turkey, will enable you to point out those reforms and improvements which the Sultan, under His present difficulties, may have the means of carrying into effect, and in what manner the Porte may best establish a system of administration calculated to afford reasonable security for the development of its commercial measures, and the maintenance of its independence recognized by the Great Christian Powers on the presumption of its proving a reality and a stable bond of peace in their respective relations with the Porte, and generally throughout the Levant. Nor will you disguise from the Sultan and His Ministers that perseverance in their present course must end in alienating the sympathies of the British Nation; and making it impossible for Her Majesty's Government to shelter them from the impending danger, or to overlook the exigencies of Christendom exposed to the natural consequences of Their unwise policy and reckless mal-administration.

It remains only for me to say that in the event, which Her Majesty's Government earnestly hope may not arise, of imminent danger to the existence of the Turkish Government, Your Excellency will in such case despatch a Messenger at once to Malta,* requesting the Admiral to hold himself in readiness, but you will not direct Him to approach the Dardanelles without positive instructions from Her Majesty's Government.

16. CROSSING THE RUBICON

[Stratford de Redcliffe reached Constantinople on 5 April 1853, and had settled the Holy Places dispute, in accordance with his instructions, by 5 May. Unfortunately on that very day the Russian Prince Menšikov, who had been sent on a special mission to Constantinople, presented a far-reaching set of demands, which even Aberdeen declared to be "unreasonable" and which were considered equivalent to a demand for a Russian protectorate over Turkey.† Menšikov's terms were ultimately refused and he

* "Archipelago?" is pencilled in the margin of the MS. original.
† V. Temperley, *England and the Near East, The Crimea,* [1936], Chap. XII *passim.*

retired in dudgeon on 21 May. A crisis then supervened. The Tsar had caused alarm by his activity in armaments in January and Napoleon excitement by sending the French naval squadron to Salamis, in consequence of the first report of Menšikov's activity in Constantinople. In this demonstration England had refused to join, but on 1 June she agreed to join with France in sending the French and British squadrons to Besika Bay, just outside the Dardanelles. The reasons for this move were that British public opinion had resented Menšikov's conduct at Constantinople. On 27 May the Tsar, by an independent and almost simultaneous decision, sent orders to his troops to cross the Turkish frontier and occupy the Principalities of Moldavia and Wallachia. This created a tense situation—which the four other Powers tried to avert by a Conference at Vienna during June and July. Their representatives there drew up a note which, they hoped, would satisfy both Russia and Turkey. Unfortunately the Ambassadors of the Powers were negotiating an agreement with Turkey at Constantinople at the same time. The two propositions killed one another. The Tsar accepted the "Vienna Note". The Turks refused it because they were annoyed at the refusal of the Powers to accept their proposition. The Turkish refusal took place on 19 August. The British Government at first thought of forcing the Turks to accept the "Vienna Note", and of recalling Stratford if he failed to secure Turkey's submission. But on 16 September Clarendon received an authentic version of an interpretation of the "Vienna Note" by Nesselrode, the Russian Chancellor, which would have given to Russia all the superiority over other Powers at Constantinople which Menšikov had claimed. This interpretation was professedly based on Article VII of the Treaty of Kutchuk Kainardji, but was wholly opposed to the views of the other four Powers at the Vienna Conference. Clarendon described it as "violent" and next day (the 17th) abandoned all intention of pressing the "Vienna Note" further upon Turkey, as did France. Rumours of the "violent interpretation" leaked out in the press and Clarendon expected a storm. On 23 September he and Aberdeen were informed by the French Ambassador that a sedition had broken out in Constantinople, endangering the lives of Europeans and of the Sultan. Aberdeen and Clarendon thereupon, without even waiting for confirmation from Stratford and without consulting the Cabinet, sent orders to Stratford to call up the British fleet outside the Dardanelles to Constantinople, thereby violating the Straits' Convention. Such a step required considerable defence, so by way of anticipating this movement and justifying it beforehand, Clarendon wrote the dispatch which follows. It sums up the whole case against Russia and the attitude of Great Britain on the Eastern question. It accuses Russia of "seeking to obtain a virtual protectorate over the Christian subjects of the Porte", and states generally the British view on the whole Eastern question and on the need of supporting the integrity of Turkey.

War was declared by the Turks on Russia on 4 October, and the Turks began hostilities in Europe on 23 October, and extended them to Asia. The British and French naval squadrons passed the Dardanelles on 22 October—a day before the Turks began hostilities. Russia still maintained a defensive attitude and declared she was not at war with Turkey. Finally she intervened and destroyed a Turkish naval squadron at Sinope (30 November). This decided the British Government to join with France on 24 December in sending their naval squadrons into the Black Sea, and in turning back Russian vessels found there. This was the final cause of war. This decision is explained in a dispatch of 24 December (*A. & P.*, [1854], LXXI, [1699], 753–4), but it contains no new statement of principle.]

Document 35. *Clarendon justifies the sending of the British Fleet through the Dardanelles, 30 September* 1853*

I have already informed you that two Desp[atche]s from C[oun]t Nesselrode to B[aro]n Meyendorff were communicated to me by B[aro]n Brunnow announcing that the Turkish Modifications of the Vienna Note had been rejected by the Cab[ine]t of St Petersburg, and stating the grounds upon which that decision was founded.

These despatches would appear to preclude the hope of an amicable arrange[men]t between Russia & Turkey, and as their effect may consequently be desastrous [*sic*] to Europe, they have rec[eive]d the serious attention of H[er] M[ajesty]'s Gov[ernmen]t and I shall now proceed to state the opinion that has been formed of them, with reference to the intentions of the Conference of Vienna in framing the Note, to the motives of the Ottoman Gov[ernmen]t in proposing amendments, and to the repeated declarations of the Emp[ero]r that he desired no new right nor any extension of influence in Turkey.

In his first Desp[atc]h C[oun]t Nesselrode alludes to the terms in w[hic]h the Note had been accepted at St Petersburg, and the understanding that if any changes were intro-

* Clarendon to Seymour, No. 222, 30 September 1853, *F.O.* 195/402. The original text is in *F.O.* 181/290. Published in *A. & P.*, [1854], LXXI, [1699], 555–8. Cp. Temperley and Penson, *Century of Diplomatic Blue Books*, No. 460 a.

duced at Constan[tino]ple, the Russian Gov[ernmen]t would be at liberty to withhold its assent.—

The Russian Gov[ernmen]t had of course a right to make this condition, or to suggest amendments to the Note. The Turkish Gov[ernmen]t, possessing a similar right, exercised it by proposing certain modifications. The Conference had no power to impose the Note on either party. Its position was that of a mediator endeavouring to do equal justice to both parties, & its intention was to guard the honor & independence of the Sultan, & secure to Russia what She was entitled to claim, but no more: viz: the maintenance of existing Treaties, and the status quo in matters of religion. The Conference therefore could not refuse to entertain the modifications of the Porte, altho' regretting the loss of time w[hic]h they occasioned. They were not looked upon as altering the sense of the Note, nor at variance with the intentions of the Conference; & they were unanimously recommended to the acceptance of the Russian Gov[ernmen]t, the Russian Minister at Vienna, it is understood, concurring in the recommendation.

They have been rejected but the Russian Gov[ernmen]t did not take its stand upon the condition on w[hic]h the note had been accepted; viz. that of no change being made, but has fully entered into the objections to w[hic]h it considered the modifications were liable, & w[hic]h showed that inferences were drawn from the note, and claims were to be established by means of it hereafter altogether inconsistent with the views and intentions of the Four Powers. The frankness of this proceeding on the part of the Russian Gov[ernmen]t, and the determination that its intentions should not be misapprehended, are doubtless very proper; but, on the other hand, H[er] M[ajesty]'s Gov[ernmen]t feel that, even while retaining their own original interpretation of the Note, it would now be highly dishonorable to press its acceptance on the Porte, when they have been duly warned by the power to whom the Note is to be addressed, that another & a totally different meaning is attached to it by that Power. And even if this were not dishonorable, it would be

in the highest degree impolitic for the reasons stated in
C[oun]t Nesselrode's first desp[atc]h with ref[erence] to
admitting of any amendment, viz: that the Emp[ero]r would
expose himself "to renew political relations with Turkey under
unfavorable auspices w[hic]h would deprive them of all
solidity for the future, and inevitably bring about a fresh and
more decided rupture".

H[er] M[ajesty]'s Gov[ernmen]t earnestly desire to see the
relations between Russia & the Porte reestablished on a
friendly and permanent footing; and they consequently can
be no party to an arrangement w[hic]h the Cab[ine]t of
St Petersburg has shown would frustrate the object w[hic]h
they have at heart.

C[oun]t Nesselrode declares* that the modifications are by
no means so insignificant either in their spirit or their "arrière
pensée" as might at first sight be supposed; but he appears
not to be aware that this declaration goes far to justify the
Turkish Gov[ernmen]t in proposing them; and H[is]
Ex[cellency] altogether fails to show by what right or in
reparation of what injury Russia claims admissions and concessions from the Sultan who is unwilling to make them, and
whose independence Russia together with the other Powers
of Europe has determined to respect.

With regard to the first objection in Count Nesselrode's
note, I have to observe that the Conference at Vienna in
adverting to the active solicitude at all times displayed by
the Emp[ero]rs of Russia for the maintenance of the privileges
& immunities of the Greco-Orthodox Church, simply intended
to record the anxiety w[hic]h every Sovereign must feel for
the welfare in a foreign Country of the religion he himself
professes. But the Conference by no means intended to
affirm that the immunities and privileges in question were
solely due to the solicitude of the Emperors of Russia, and
the Porte is justified in asserting that many of these privileges
are of a date anterior to the existence of diplomatic relations
between the Two Countries.

Count Nesselrode alludes to other grievances but specifies

* Altered to "appears to think" in the Blue Book.

none except that regarding the Holy Places, w[hic]h has been satisfactorily settled. Nor have any other grievances connected with religious matters at any time been put forward by Russia, and it was not for the Conference to assume the existence of wrongs of w[hic]h they had no knowledge. But C[oun]t Nesselrode asks, where then was the object of P[rin]ce Menchikoff's mission? the answer to that is the assurance repeatedly given that it was to settle the question of the Holy Places, and to obtain a guarantee for its not being again disturbed. That question has been settled to the satisfaction of all Parties, and the Vienna Note contains a guarantee against w[hic]h Russia raises no objection. The modification proposed by the Porte with reference to the Treaty of Kainardji appeared to H[er] M[ajesty]'s Gov[ernmen]t wholly uncalled for, until they read the objection made to it by Count Nesselrode's Note. H[er] M[ajesty]'s Gov[ernmen]t considered that the stipulations of the Treaty of Kainardji and the maintenance of religious privileges had been dis-connected in the Note in a manner not to be mistaken; and indeed this is admitted by C[oun]t Nesselrode. But the Russian Gov[ernmen]t, while disclaiming all pretension to exercise a protectorate yet affirms that all these religious privileges and immunities are direct consequences of the Treaty, which was doubtless a solemn engagement taken by Turkey towards Russia; and the fulfilment of that engagement, but no more it was the object of the Conference to secure. By C[oun]t Nesselrode's interpretation of the Note however, Russia would under the Seventh Article of the Treaty be entitled to superintend all these privileges and immunities, w[hic]h are of that peculiar character that She would be constantly able, if so minded to interfere between the Sultan and his subjects; and thus the religious Protectorate w[hic]h is abjured, and the new rights and extended influence w[hic]h are equally dis-claimed would be established.

It is superfluous to say that no such intention was entertained by the Conference; nor can the Treaty of Kainardji, by any subtlety of reasoning, be so construed. By the 7th Art[icle] of that Treaty the Porte promises to protect the

C[hris]tian religion in all its Churches throughout the Ottoman dominions; but in the same Article the Min[iste]rs of Russia are permitted to make representations in favour of a new Church, and its Ministers; and this Clause would have been wholly unnecessary if Russian diplomacy had also been allowed to make representations on every matter connected with religion.* If the Article bore the sense that C[oun]t Nesselrode now seeks to attach to it, and if the two Contracting Parties had been agreed upon it, it is reasonable to suppose that at the signing of the Treaty a stipulation so important as that of maintaining the privileges & immunities of the Greek Church would not have been omitted.

The third objection raised by Count Nesselrode is even more than the two w[hic]h precede it, at variance with the intentions of the Conference, w[hic]h assuredly was not that the Sultan should enter into an engagement with Russia to concede to the Greek Church all such advantages as might be granted to other C[hris]tian denominations but only those advantages which were conceded to Communities who, like the Greeks, were Ottoman Subjects. The spiritual head of the R[oman] Catholics in Turkey, as elsewhere, is a foreign Sovereign, and if it pleased the Sultan to enter into a Concordat with the Pope, conferring privileges upon R[oman] Catholics, not subjects of the Porte, surely that ought to confer no right upon the Emp[ero]r of Russia to claim all the benefits of that Concordat for the Greek Community, Subjects of the Porte, whose spiritual Head, the Patriarch of Constan[tino]ple is also a subject of the Sultan.

No C[hris]tian community being subjects of the Sultan would have any right to participate in the privileges and advantages that the Sultan might confer upon Russian Convents, Ecclesiastics or laymen; such for example as the Russian Church and Hospital about to be built at Jerusalem:—and in the same manner the Greek Community consisting of many millions would have no right to participate in advantages granted to foreign Convents or Ecclesiastics, and w[hic]h

---

* For the text of this article and the different Russian and British interpretations v. Temperley, *England and the Near East, The Crimea*, [1936], 467–9.

might not for many and obvious reasons be fitting for a
C[hris]tian Community subject to the Porte.

In fact if the Sultan has at any time, in the exercise of his
Sovereign Authority conferred religious privileges upon a
community not subject to Him, or if He at any future time
should think proper to do so, C[oun]t Nesselrode claims that
Russia should have a right to demand that several millions
of Greeks who are subjects of the Porte should at once be
placed upon the footing of Foreigners, and should enjoy,
through the intervention of Russia, all the advantages w[hic]h
the Sultan, for reasons of w[hic]h he is the only competent
judge, may have granted to such Foreigners.

How such a claim can be reconciled with the professed
desire for the maintenance of existing Treaties, and the strict
status quo in religious matters, it is not for H[er] M[ajesty]'s
Gov[ernmen]t to explain; but they consider it exhibits a total
disregard for the feelings and interests of the European Powers
who, in common with Russia, have declared that They will
uphold the independence of Turkey, and who, cannot therefore see with indifference that Russia should thus surrepti-
tiously seek to obtain a virtual Protectorate over the C[hris]tian
Subjects of the Porte.—

And with respect to C[oun]t Nesselrode's supposition that
some new privilege not mentioned in the recent Firmans might
be granted to the R[oman] Catholic Establishments in
Palestine to the prejudice of the Native Communities H[is]
Ex[cellency] appears to have overlooked that by the Vienna
Note the Porte engages that no change shall be made in the
order of things lately established at Jerusalem, without previous communication with the Gov[ernmen]ts of Russia and
France.

I have now fully stated in what spirit & with what intentions the Vienna Note was framed; but in interpreting it as
C[oun]t Nesselrode has done by his objections to the modifications, H[is] Ex[cellency] not only does not prove, but he
does not even advert to, any obligation by w[hic]h the Porte
is bound to make concessions utterly irreconcilable with its
independence. But H[er] M[ajesty]'s Gov[ernmen]t are

compelled to consider that the claims put forward by Russia are equally irreconcilable with the assurance that no extended power or influence is sought in Turkey. They deeply regret that such claims should have been made for even were they successful they would be useless to Russia if She sincerely desires the independence of the Ottoman Empire; but under any circumstances they must produce feelings of suspicion & distrust on the part of the Porte; & differences between the two Powers will thus in future, as of late, be a source of anxiety to Europe and expose the general peace to constant danger of disturbance.

You will communicate this Desp[atc]h to C[oun]t Nesselrode, or to M. de Séniavine should C[oun]t Nesselrode be still absent, and also give him a Copy.—

VIII. PALMERSTON AND THE REVOLUTION OF 1848-9

17. THE DELUGE IN EUROPE

[The policy of Palmerston during 1848-9 may be made clearer by a very brief sketch of general movements in Europe. On 25 February 1848, Louis Philippe, the King of the French, fled to England. There had been a long battle with the parliamentary opposition which had ended in street fighting by revolutionaries. The Government had fallen because of its unpopularity and the King's nerve had failed at the crisis. A Republic was declared, and the famous Lamartine became Foreign Minister. This Republic was soon occupied with its internal troubles, and Lamartine declared that France did not intend to interfere with other nations. His utterance was a little ambiguous as he suggested that the Treaty of Vienna needed revision at the same time as he disclaimed interference with other States. Palmerston viewed that utterance with sympathy. He knew the difficulties of reconciling different parties in a Cabinet and accepted the declaration in good faith. He thought that a recognition of the new régime would be the best way to help France and to pacify Europe. He cheerfully recommended this course to other Governments (*v. infra*, pp. 159-60) and adopted it himself as soon as possible. France herself electrified Europe not by her interference but by her example. Germany, Austria-Hungary, and Italy had long groaned beneath the iron rule of Metternich and autocracy. Germany, Italy and Hungary all wanted to be nations and all wanted to be free. France had shewn the liberals and patriots of Central Europe that a government could be overthrown. The example fell like a spark on gunpowder.

In March an earthquake wave of revolution swept over all Central Europe. There was never anything like it in suddenness; there was no resisting it. Every King or princelet in Central Europe either had to promise a liberal constitution or to appoint a liberal ministry. Most of them ran away from their capitals. Every one of them yielded to his people. Metternich, who refused to yield, was forced to resign and fled from Vienna on 13 March exclaiming "after me the deluge". The foolish Emperor, whom he left, yielded everything for the deluge was indeed at hand. Ferdinand issued an Edict giving liberal constitutions both to Austria (15 March) and to Hungary (17 March). Frederick William IV did the same in Prussia on the 18th and declared for a Pan-German policy. Even before that (on the 16th) the King of Bavaria had abdicated in favour of his son. By the end of March a *Vorparlament* had met at Frankfurt to arrange for the union of all Germany in one state. A National German Assembly met in May and appointed the Archduke John, a popular Habsburg, *Reichsverweser* or Imperial Vicar. Germany seemed already one.

But the unity of Germany did not depend on talkers at Frankfurt. It depended on whether the rulers of the two strongest German States could assert themselves and restore order in their German territories. The Austrian Emperor twice fled from turbulent Vienna to Innsbrück. But by the end of October 1848 Vienna was restored to order and the feeble Emperor abdicated (December) in favour of the eighteen-year-old Franz Joseph. Prince Schwarzenberg, who was the real ruler of Austria, soon ended the power of the Austrian Germans in parliament or in executive. In November (1848) the Prussian King finally summoned his soldiers to his aid and reduced the Prussian Parliament to impotence. So early as September Prussian and Austrian troops had quelled disorder and intimidated the Pan-German National Assembly at Frankfurt. At any rate by the end of 1848 it was clear that the German revolution, in itself, was likely to be mastered by the older and more reactionary forces.

England had some very slight repercussions of Continental unrest. On 10 April a monster demonstration of Chartists on Kennington Common ended in a complete fiasco. "Yesterday", wrote Palmerston, "was a glorious day, the Waterloo of peace and order." He was secure at home and refused to be dismayed by events on the Continent. Palmerston had always told Metternich that his system would tumble into ruins, and was delighted at his fall and flight. "Feebleness and decay were the inevitable consequences" of his system. But Germany now had aspirations for national unity, she might become free and liberal. He recommended constitutions, whether for separate States or for all Germany, as a speedy cure for all her ills. Queen Victoria and Prince Albert, the rest of the Cabinet and the world might protest and lift up hands of horror, but he was unmoved.

As has been very well said, Palmerston "judged the movements of 1848 at their proper value. He did not fall into panic fear at what was happening, and many of his dispatches are filled with the undisguised note of jubilation of a prophet justified in his prophesying at the last. He knew that the end of social order had not come in England, and, in spite of barricades and fugitive royalty, believed that the same was true of Europe. There was probably only one man, apart from himself, on whose judgment he placed any reliance, and that man strongly corroborated this belief....Sir Stratford Canning...saw shivering burghers relieve the guard with white-gloved students in a deserted Berlin, and witnessed nocturnal disturbances at Vienna; and yet he wrote home his firm belief that Central Europe was sound at heart.

What was true of Germany was true of the rest of Europe; and, if there was trouble ahead, it was the fault not of the peoples, but of the Courts."* That was Palmerston's view from Downing Street too. He saw and judged more accurately and coolly than anyone else there. If "not a great man" he was "the right man". He was indeed the one sane statesman, the one cool head, among the Foreign Ministers of the Great Powers.

While Queen Victoria and the other Ministers were deploring the fall of thrones and sovereigns, Palmerston was urging the upholding of treaties. At an early date in 1848 he took care to lay down his idea of the treaty obligations which England was prepared to maintain. It was as well to do this when a revolution was sweeping over Europe, threatening the territorial integrity of every State and appearing to obliterate every old landmark. In **Doc. 36** Palmerston himself specifically and narrowly limits the treaty obligations of Vienna to those affecting Saxony, Savoy and Switzerland. In fact, he had very recently taken the line that England would not even necessarily be bound by her guarantee to Switzerland. When Switzerland was in revolution in 1847 and the Powers were threatening to intervene, Palmerston minuted as follows. "Instruct Mr. Peel to say whenever the matter may be mentioned, that L[or]d Minto made no Declaration... as to what England would or would not do in the Event of any Foreign Power interfering by Force of Arms in the internal affairs of Switzerland. The British Gov[ernmen]t have reserved to itself unfettered Freedom to act as it may think fit on such an occasion if it should unfortunately happen."† He seems to be getting near the sentiment expressed with much greater cynicism by Lord John Russell in the Commons (8 May 1856): "If a treaty be found injurious to the interests of a country and some means of violating it are obvious, I do not know of what country in Europe we could predicate a strict observance of the Treaty."‡

By March 1848, however, Palmerston seems prepared, in British interests, to maintain by force the integrity of Saxon Prussia, and the neutrality of Switzerland and of Belgium against all comers. He was particularly resolute as to defending the latter.§ But he will not do the same for the Prussian Rhine province or for Austrian Lombardy, on the ground that in neither case is he pledged by guarantee. His view of England's obligations was strictly confined to guarantee, and he further shewed prudence in refusing to be drawn into the European imbroglio by his liberal sympathies or opinions.]

* C. Sproxton, *Palmerston and the Hungarian Revolution*, [1919], 8.

† *F.O.* 96/21, Minute signed "P[almerston] 2/10/47".

‡ Cp. a curious minute by Lord Hardinge in 1908 where he gives certain circumstances under which it is "doubtful whether England or Russia would move a finger to maintain Belgian neutrality". Gooch and Temperley, VIII, 378.

§ *V.* also Ashley, *Life [of Palmerston]*, [1876], I, 92.

Document 36. *Palmerston distinguishes between Treaty and Guarantee, 6-14 March 1848**

With reference to your Lordship's dispatch No. 52 of the 9th instant reporting Baron Canitz's version of a conversation I had held with the Chevalier Bunsen, I have to observe that the latter seems to have overstated what I stated to him in the conversation of which he gave an account.† I did not say "That England would unflinchingly maintain the arrangement of the Treaty of Vienna"; but on the contrary I especially guarded myself against being understood to make any declaration as to what England would or would not do in any case which has not yet happened. I distinctly said that I had no Power or Authority to give any such pledge in a matter which, if ever the case occurred would have to be considered and determined by the Government and by Parliament. I moreover drew the attention of Chev[alie]r Bunsen to the distinction between Treaties without and Treaties with a guarantee observing that the first Description of Treaties gave the contracting parties a *Right* to maintain all the Stipulations which such Treaties contained, but imposed no *obligation* to do so; and I pointed out that the Treaty of Vienna of 1815 contains no guarantee except in regard to the portion of Saxony which was allotted to Prussia, and in regard to some of the arrangements connected with Switzerland.

[This next document, dated 6 March 1848, actually reports Palmerston's *ipsissima verba* in a conversation with Baron de Bunsen. The report was received by a Dutch diplomat at the time from Bunsen and is here subjoined.‡ It agrees with Palmerston's own account, but is fuller, vivider and in the first person.]

I [Palmerston] distinguish between a *Treaty* and a *Guarantee*. The fact of having been one of the signatory powers

* Palmerston to Westmorland (Berlin), No. 50, 14 March 1848, *F.O.* 64/282.
† *V. F.O.* 64/285, Westmorland to Palmerston, No. 52, 9 March 1848. Canitz approves of Bunsen's report "in which you [Palmerston] state that the interests of England in the territorial arrangements of Europe were now the same as they had been in the years 1814 and 1815, and that you would unflinchingly uphold them".
‡ *V. Nederlands Rijks Archief*, Constantinople, From Zuylen de Nyevelt, No. 172, 9 November 1854. He transmits "a communication made at the time" (6 March 1848) and requests that his name may not be mentioned, or that of Baron de Bunsen.

of such a treaty gives the right to intervene, but does not impose on it the obligation to do so, in the case in which the state of possession has been changed.*

It is otherwise with a guarantee which involves the obligation of maintaining the state of possession.

Similar guarantees have been given by England to the *King of Prussia* for the province of Saxony; to *Switzerland* and to *Belgium* for their neutrality and integrity.†

England has guaranteed neither Lombardy to Austria, nor the Rhine Provinces to Prussia. It has the right of aiding them in case of attack but has no obligation to do so.

Document 37. *Application by Lord John Russell of Palmerston's principle,* 14 *September* 1859‡

[Palmerston's distinction between guarantee and obligation was later explained by John Russell with retrospective reference to Cracow (1841) and actual application to Parma and Modena (1859).]...Rights acquired or confirmed under the Treaty of Vienna and which do not form the subject of a special guarantee give to G[rea]t Britain as a contracting party a right but do not impose on her an obligation to interfere. For instance the Republic of Cracow had a separate existence secured to her by the Treaty of Vienna; that separate existence was annulled, and Cracow was annexed to Austria [1846], but although H[er] Majesty considered

---

* Sir James Headlam-Morley, *Studies in Diplomatic History*, [1930], quotes (pp. 121–2) an utterance of Gladstone as to Palmerston's holding this view. Gladstone suggests that it was well known that he held it. It ought to be mentioned that Palmerston, who in 1848 accepts the guarantee as binding England to interfere as e.g. in the case of Belgium, is quoted elsewhere as having expressed a different doctrine (*v. infra*, p. 339). The probable explanation is that he did actually say different things at different times. Indeed, as quoted *supra*, p. 155, he had declared on 2 October 1847 that he reserved "unfettered freedom" to England, if Switzerland's neutrality were violated. Yet, according to his statement on this page to Bunsen, the guarantee to Switzerland imposed an obligation.]

† *Prussia and Saxony*, Arts. XV and XVII of Final Act of Congress of Vienna, 9 June 1815, Hertslet, *Map*, [1875], I, 221–3; *Switzerland*, Art. LXXXIV, *ibid.* I, 64–5, 259–60; *Belgium*, Art. II of Belgian Treaty of 19 April 1839, *ibid.* II, 981.

‡ Lord John Russell to Fane (Vienna), No. 74, 14 September 1859, *F.O.* 7/564.

that annexation a manifest violation of the Treaty of Vienna H[er] Majesty did not consider herself bound to defend by force of arms the independence of Cracow.

So also the Powers of Europe acknowledged, by the Treaty of Vienna, the addition of Belgium to Holland, but the rights thereby acquired by the King of the Netherlands did not avail when an insurrection of the Belgian people made it expedient in the eyes of Austria, as well as of other Powers to sanction the separation of Belgium from Holland.

The reasons which then prevailed against the rule of Holland in Belgium appear to H[er] M[ajesty]'s Gov[ern-men]t to be applicable to the rights of reversion of Austria in Tuscany and Modena.

The abstract right of Austria to interfere in Tuscany and Modena on account of her right of reversion ought in the opinion of H[er] M[ajesty]'s Gov[ernmen]t to yield to the interest of Europe. The renewal of a contest in Italy for Austrian supremacy on the one side, and Italian independence on the other would be so great an evil that some sacrifice ought to be made to avert it.. . .

18. PALMERSTON AND RUSSIA, 1848–9

[Palmerston's dealings with the Tsar in the period of revolutions are most revealing. Nicholas I, the great religious and political autocrat of the day, the great upholder of legitimacy and divine right, was horrified by the way thrones had tumbled down in Central Europe and the manner in which Kings had run away from their capitals. He had determined to restore order wherever he could. He was therefore most unwilling to recognize a new régime in France. He did not admit that even the deposed Louis Philippe had been legitimate and was most unwilling to recognize a republic. He increased the rigidity of his rule in his own police-governed dominions and particularly in the danger spot of Poland. His troops entered Moldavia and Wallachia with the express view of restoring the authority of the princes and of preventing any chance of a republic being proclaimed. Then in May 1849 he sent Russian troops into Hungary. The Magyars had beaten the armies of the Imperial Habsburg and would, in all probability, have formed for themselves an independent republic but for the intervention of the Imperial Romanoff. After a gallant resistance Hungary was crushed and, as the Tsar's Marshal informed him, lay "at the feet of Your Majesty". The powerful intervention of the Tsar had finally crushed revolution everywhere in Central Europe.

Such is the briefest outline of Nicholas' policy. Palmerston's communications are highly characteristic. **Doc. 38** indicates clearly the intention of the British Government to recognize the new régime in France as soon as it is stable. This is pure Canningite doctrine and it is excellent common sense. But in **Doc. 39** Palmerston not only recommends Russia to be neutral but actually suggests Nicholas' granting some form of self-government to Poland, in spite of a previous contention that every State [even Russia presumably] "has the right" to decide such a matter for itself. This was very rash counsel and certain to make Nicholas more anti-Polish still. In **Doc. 40** Palmerston shews pretty clearly that, whatever may be England's liberal sympathies, she is not going to be drawn into war.]

Document 38. *Palmerston explains to Russia his reasons for recognizing the new régime in France, 28 March 1848**

[Lord Bloomfield to thank Count Nesselrode for his communication.† On the abdication of King Louis Philippe official relations were broken off with France. But the British Ambassador, Lord Normanby, remained at Paris to deal with events. As soon as a Government is established in France, new credentials will be given to our Ambassador, and diplomatic intercourse regularized.]

...But independently of these considerations belonging to the local interests and geographical position of Great Britain, it may be right to remind Count Nesselrode that it is an Established Principle of the British Government in regard to its Foreign relations, to acknowledge the right of every State to decide what shall be its own form of Government; and therefore the Government of Great Britain is in the habit of acknowledging any Government established in a Foreign State when such Government shall appear to be firmly and permanently established.

* Palmerston to Bloomfield (St Petersburgh), No. 70, 28 March 1848, *F.O.* 65/343.
† This is referred to, *infra*, **Doc. 39**.

With regard to the great difference which Count Nesselrode points out between the recent Revolution in France and that of July 1830, Her Majesty's Government entirely concur in the distinction so well and so clearly pointed out by Count Nesselrode. The late revolution is certainly a much greater internal convulsion than the former one; but it seems to Her Majesty's Government that the causes of the two events have not been so dissimilar as the extent of their results. Both events were brought about by a blind disregard, on the part of the Monarch and His Ministers, of public opinion—In each case the Government shut its eyes and its ears to the timely warnings which were afforded by a great variety of significant indications; and in each case the Government found the military force upon which they relied for support, fail them when They wanted to bring that force into conflict with the People in a cause which public opinion had pronounced to be unjust.

Document 39. *Palmerston recommends neutrality to Russia and advises her to give home rule to Poland,* 14 *April* 1848*

I inclose for Your Lordship's information a Copy of a Despatch dated the $\frac{17}{29}$ Ultimo from Count Nesselrode to Baron Brunnow, which has been communicated to me by the latter, containing a statement of the opinions and determinations formed by the Emperor of Russia on the subject of the recent events in France and other parts of Europe.

I have to instruct Your Lordship to say to Count Nesselrode, with reference to the inclosed Despatch, that nothing can be wiser or more dignified than the determination which His Imperial Majesty has taken to maintain a neutral attitude with regard to the events which are passing in other Countries, and to confine himself to such defensive measures as in his judgment he may deem necessary for the protection of his own Dominions; and Her Majesty's Government have the more reason to applaud this course on the part of the Russian

* Palmerston to Bloomfield, No. 94, 14 April 1848, *F.O.* 65/344.

Government, because it is the course which the British Government also has resolved to follow.

His Imperial Majesty may rest assured that the friendly sentiments which Count Nesselrode expresses towards Great Britain, are fully reciprocated by Her Majesty's Government towards Russia; and Her Majesty's Government will at all times feel great pleasure to communicate without reserve with the Russian Government on the progress of events, and are convinced that a good understanding on these matters between the British and Russian Governments must have an important and beneficial influence on the maintenance of the Peace of Europe.

With regard to any plots which might be carried on in the United Kingdom with a view to disturb the internal tranquillity of any part of the Emperor's Dominions, His Imperial Majesty may be assured that Her Majesty's Government will at all times endeavour to prevent the hospitable shelter which this Country affords to Foreigners from being perverted so as to serve as a means for disturbing the tranquillity of other Countries.

Of course it is not for Her Majesty's Government to suggest to His Imperial Majesty any course of policy with reference to matters which more peculiarly concern the internal affairs of his own Dominions, although such affairs may by reason of peculiar circumstances have a close bearing on the general interests of Europe; but His Imperial Majesty will no doubt in the exercise of his own enlightened judgment well and maturely consider whether it would not be possible for him to direct that some arrangements might be made in regard to the Kingdom of Poland, which might avert the danger of conflicts, the results of which must in any case, and however they may end, be lamentable and afflicting.*

* Cp. another letter to Bloomfield of 11 April 1848, Ashley, *Life*, [1876], I, 91 and note.

Document 40. *Palmerston declares to Nesselrode that he will not be drawn into war, 2 December 1848**

I have received your despatch No. 69 of the 20th Ultimo, reporting a conversation with Count Nesselrode on the affairs of Sicily and Lombardy, and with reference to the opinions expressed by Count Nesselrode that England would eventually be drawn in to take part with one or other Belligerent in any European War, I have to instruct you to say to Count Nesselrode, if he should recur to these opinions, that the Continental Powers would be much mistaken if they reckon upon drawing Great Britain into a war brought on by them by pursuing a course diametrically opposite to the counsels of Great Britain, and of the dangers of which the British Government had unavailingly warned them.

19. PALMERSTON AND AUSTRIA

(a) ITALY

[The revolution of 1848 ran a violent course in Italy. It was, in essence, a national uprising against foreign or uncongenial domination. Italy wanted to be one nation just because she was so hopelessly divided. Naples and Sicily were ruled by one tyrant, Parma and Modena by another, Tuscany by a third. Lombardy and Venetia were controlled by the foreign soldiers of the detested Austrians. There were only two rulers whom a patriotic Italian could tolerate. The new Pope, Pius IX, for once was a patriotic Italian, and shewed liberal tendencies in the Papal States. But, as the revolution developed he proved a broken reed. The Papacy is international, not national, and no Pope could work long for the freedom and unity of Italy. Salvation was to come from the North, from the King of Sardinia, who also ruled Piedmont and Savoy. Charles Albert, though a wavering politician, was a genuine Italian patriot who hated the Austrians. At the critical moment in February 1848 he came down at last on the right side. Not only did he declare war against Austria and fight for the union of Italy, but he granted a constitution to his subjects. This decision led him to defeat, to deposition, to exile and to death, but it made his son King of a united Italy. It was the supreme justification of Palmerston's contention that a constitution was the cure of all ills.

* Palmerston to Buchanan (St Petersburgh), No. 62, 2 December 1848, *F.O.* 65/346.

The course of events may be briefly described. In February 1848 Charles Albert granted a constitution, and the one truly Italian prince in Italy thus identified national independence with political liberty. Metternich had long been hated by Italians as a bloody tyrant, and his fall (13 March) produced uprisings in Lombardy and Venetia. After five days' street fighting Milan was occupied by Italians, and the Austrians withdrew from Venice. On 23 March Charles Albert issued a proclamation that he would aid the people of Lombardy and Venice against their tyrannical oppressors. His army crossed the Ticino and the fight for the union of Italy really began. It is not correct to say, although the charge was subsequently made by Queen Victoria and in the Commons, that Palmerston addressed no word of caution to Charles Albert before he declared war.* But, once the declaration was launched, he hoped it would succeed.

For a time it looked as if the liberals and patriots of the other States of Italy would co-operate with Savoy and a united Italian front be shewn. Naples and Sicily rose and their miserable King promised them a constitution and all sorts of liberal reforms, with every intention of breaking his word at the first opportunity. The Grand Duke of Tuscany made promises likewise and was a little more sincere about keeping them. Pope Pius IX did the same, but the stormy course of revolution speedily frightened the timid old man into reaction. Disunion ruined everything. Even had the rulers been more amenable, the patriots were divided. Mazzini, who displaced the Pope at Rome, wanted a republic and had an immense following everywhere. The Tuscans wanted a federation, Charles Albert a constitutional monarchy. The net result was failure. On 25 July 1848, Charles Albert was heavily defeated at Custozza. This meant the Austrian reconquest of Milan and the defeat of the national idea. The Pope finally sent French troops to the Papal States. They crushed Mazzini's Roman Republic and, distrusting Austria, remained in military occupation of the Papal States. Reaction triumphed everywhere else. The Grand Duke broke his promises in Tuscany; King "Bomba" returned to Naples and brutally mishandled the patriot leaders. These rulers seemed to have won, but their triumph was as inglorious as it was brief. There was to be no place for them in a free and united Italy.

Among all the lawful rulers of Italy Charles Albert alone remained faithful to his word and to his ideals. He had been defeated and his troops expelled from Austrian territory, but he would not give up the idea of a united Italy. Austria demanded the *status quo*, Charles Albert refused. The sword was drawn again, and the Austrian army under Radetzky moved on the Sardinian. On the field of Novara (23 March 1849) Charles Albert sought

* V. C. Sproxton, *Palmerston and the Hungarian Revolution*, [1919], 23 n.

death in vain, and his army was hopelessly defeated. He abdicated and left Italy. His son Victor Emmanuel made peace and retired within his own territories. There he remained true to his ideals. Despite pressure from Austria and other reactionaries in Italy, he steadily maintained the constitution to which he had sworn. And the one Italian ruler, who had kept his vows, was one day to rule over all Italy.

Palmerston understood that the revolution of 1848 was due to strong national impulses in countries like Italy. With those national aspirations he had much sympathy, for he understood their strength. Queen Victoria and the more conservative British statesmen viewed uprisings and revolutions with horror. They saw in them nothing but a breach of treaties, a defiance of sovereigns, a destruction of the old order. Palmerston was more optimistic because he did not predict long life for an Empire like the Austrian in Italy, which was based on force, not on the consent of the governed. He thought a Government based on force a sham thing, and one based on consent a real thing. In his view concessions and constitutions were the only safety for the petty rulers of Italy. This is clearly indicated in **Doc. 41.** His only remedy for Austrian rule in Italy was that it should cease. He did not think that even his favourite remedy of a constitution would succeed in Lombardy or Venetia. It might have done if tried in time. But national feeling was at last awake in Italy, and would never be allayed until the Austrian had left her soil.*

Palmerston was undoubtedly right, as events have proved. But his doctrine was too revolutionary for contemporaries. It was not, however, by any means so revolutionary as it seemed. Even in the Treaty of Vienna England had never guaranteed her Italian possessions to Austria, as Palmerston was at pains to point out. "The Treaty of Vienna they [the Austrians] themselves set at nought when they took possession of Cracow, and they have never fulfilled their engagement to give national institutions and a national representation to their Polish subjects. They cannot claim the treaty when it suits their purpose, and at the same time, when it suits their purpose, reject it."† This was good sense though unpalatable advice.

As regards the cession of territory it meant a disturbance in the European balance of power but, as Palmerston pointed out, that was the lesser evil. The real danger was that France would intervene and attack Austria in Italy. She had already sent troops to support the Pope. Austria could not defend Milan against France and was much safer behind the Alps. The Austrian reactionaries thought that, if they yielded to revolution in Milan, they would

* For a discussion of Palmerston's policy in Italy *v.* Taylor, *The Italian Problem in European Diplomacy, 1847–1849*, [1934], 89–90, 238–42.
† Ashley, *Life*, I, 107, private letter to Ponsonby of 31 August 1848.

never recover power in Budapest or Vienna. They were reactionaries everywhere and by instinct. Palmerston himself thought that the expulsion of the Habsburg from Italy would not "diminish the real strength nor impair the real security of Austria as a European Power". He wanted Charles Albert to rule over a Kingdom of North Italy, including Parma, Venetia and Lombardy. Austria would not go so far. She wished to retain Venetia under her direct rule, and to give a kind of home rule to Lombardy under an Austrian prince.* These negotiations failed, and after Custozza in July 1848 Austria raised her terms and ended all hope of peaceful solutions.

On the day that Charles Albert was defeated at Custozza, Victoria wrote thus to her Prime Minister: "The Queen must tell Lord John [Russell] what she has repeatedly told Lord Palmerston, but without apparent effect, that the establishment of an *entente cordiale with the French Republic*, for the purpose of driving the Austrians out of *their dominions* in Italy, would be a *disgrace* to this country."† Yet Palmerston succeeded by much tact in confining French intervention to the Papal States. His own point of view was very clear. "I do not wish to see Italy emancipated from the Austrian yoke by the help of French arms, but perhaps it would be better it should be so done than not done at all; and if it were so done at a time when England and France were well together, we might be able to prevent any permanently bad consequences from resulting from it. But the great object at present is to keep things quiet; to reestablish peace in Northern Italy, and to trust to future events for greater improvements"‡ (28 December 1848).

The same spirit inspires **Doc. 42.** Palmerston addresses an eleventh hour counsel to Austria, just before her final and successful campaign against Charles Albert was undertaken. His advice was disregarded and the young Emperor Franz Joseph went forward in Italy to a brief triumph and a lasting defeat. Palmerston clearly foresaw this result, for he wrote (9 September 1849): "He [Franz Joseph] holds Italy just as long as and no longer than France chooses to let him have it. The first quarrel between Austria and France will drive the Austrians out of Lombardy and Venice."§ His prediction was right, though his time-table was a little amiss. In ten years Napoleon III drove the Austrians from Lombardy. Seven years later, by the aid of Bismarck, the Austrians were expelled from Venetia.]

---

* Ashley, *Life*, 1, 98–100.
† Quoted by C. Sproxton, *op. cit.* 23. Queen Victoria to Lord John Russell, 25 July 1848.
‡ Ashley, *Life*, 1, 114. Private letter to Abercromby of 28 December 1848.
§ Ashley, *Life*, 1, 141.

Document 41. *Palmerston recommends the grant of a constitution as a panacea for Italy, 22 February 1848**

With reference to the Conversation which your Lordship had with Baron Canitz on the affairs of Italy as reported in your Despatch No 30 of the 14th Instant, I have to desire that Your Lordship will take an opportunity of observing to Baron Canitz that the example of what has happened at Naples would seem strongly to shew the wisdom with which The King of Sardinia has acted in yielding betimes to the reasonable desires of His Subjects. For if The King of Naples had made timely concessions, and had sent over to Sicily by the 12th of January the Scheme of moderate reform which the Sicilians were then expecting, the outbreak which subsequently happened would not have taken place, and the same reforms which would in that case have satisfied the Sicilians would also have contented the Neapolitans. But The King of Naples has by his own delay and obstinacy brought upon himself the necessity of going far beyond the point to which he had previously refused to advance.—

For the subjects of the King of Naples this result is no doubt very advantageous, and thus out of evil good has come; but to other Sovereigns who are desirous of keeping the direction of their own affairs in their own hands and of retaining with regard to their people the gracious character which belongs to those who voluntarily grant, instead of being reduced to the more or less humiliating position which belongs to those who reluctantly yield to physical or moral coercion, the late events in Naples and Sicily ought to serve as a useful warning.—

Document 42. *Palmerston on Austrian rule in Italy, 7 November 1848†*

Send Copy to L[or]d Ponsonby with Instructions to communicate it to B[aro]n Wessembergh and at same Time to request that most serious attention to the Statements contained in this and in other Reports wh[ich] have been

---

* Palmerston to Westmorland (Berlin), No. 30, 22 February 1848, *F.O.* 64/282.   † Minute by Palmerston, 7 November 1848, *F.O.* 96/22.

rec[eive]d from the Same Quarter. He will at same Time say that H[er] M[ajesty]'s Gov[ernmen]t are persuaded that These simple Statements of Facts must surely convince B[aron] Wessemberg that it is impossible to expect that a Province in which there exists throughout the whole Population both in the towns and in the Country District and from the Noble to the Peasant such deeply rooted Hatred of Austrian Domination can ever become either a secure or useful Possession of the Imperial Crown. It cannot reasonably be imagined that any national Institution which the Emp[ero]r may grant to the People of Lombardy can alter their National antipathy to Foreign Rule, or have any other effect than that of affording them greater Facilities of throwing off the yoke from which they are so anxious to get free.

If indeed such Institutions as are now promised had been granted to the Lombards Ten or Fifteen years ago there is no saying to what Extent practical Independence might have reconciled them to nominal Subjection but matters have now gone much too far between the Italian and the Austrian Gov[ernmen]ts to make it possible that any such connection could be permanent; and if the whole of Lombardy is in a state of either passive or active Resistance to Austrian Rule now when the Province has been recently reconquered, and is occupied by an overwhelming Austrian Force exercising authority by all the Powers and Severities of Martial law, what sort of obedience can the Austrian Gov[ernmen]t expect to meet with from the Lombards when the Austrian Troops shall have retired, when the local Gov[ernmen]t shall be administered by the very Italian Nobles who are now in voluntary Exile to avoid any Contact whatever with the Foreign Invader, and when there shall be assembled a Parliament composed of Italians, and elected by the People who are now under Circumstances of the most extreme Difficulty engaged in a desperate because wholly unequal Struggle with the regular Force of Marshall [*sic*] Radetsky.

...The present moment is a most favourable one for Austria to make an arrangement by which Lombardy would be released from Austrian Rule. The armies of Austria have reoccupied Lombardy and therefore the Concession would manifestly be the result of choice and not of local compulsion.

[Mentions the danger from France.]

...It is impossible to doubt that an efficient and powerful French Army aided and supported by a general Rising of the Italians would be too strong for the Austrian Forces in Italy, and the Probability is that in such a Case Austria would lose everything to the South of the Alps. It may be said indeed such a Conflict might bring on a more Extensive war in Europe and other Powers might take Part with Austria. But is the Austrian Gov[ernmen]t sure that the Sympathies even of Germany would be with Austria and her attempt to rivet her yoke upon the Italians, and would not the Principle of nationality which is now the rallying Cry of Germany tell against Austria in such a struggle? Nor would the Principle of antient Prescription be much more in her Favor, because although that Principle may be pleaded by her in the Case of that small Part of Lombardy which as the Duchy of Milan has long been connected with the Imperial Crown, yet that Principle would be strongly invoked against the Republic of Venice, a State which has played a distinguished Part in history during nearly Fourteen Centuries of Freedom, and the Austrian Title to which goes no further back than the Treaty of Vienna and its transfer to her by Buonaparte by the Treaty of Campo Formio.

H[er] M[ajesty's] Gov[ernment] have good Reason to believe that the Administrator of the German Empire himself an Austrian Arch Duke [John], and known to be passionately attached to the State which was the Country of his Birth and the Residence where he has passed the greater Part of a long life, is strongly of opinion that Austria ought to Emancipate Lombardy; and if H[er] M[ajesty's] Gov[ernment] are not misinformed that same opinion prevails Extensively in many Parts of Germany.

H[er] M[ajesty's] Gov[ernment] would earnestly entreat the Austrian Gov[ernmen]t to take these matters into its most serious but early Consideration; and if it should upon Reflection arrive now at the Same Conclusion to which it had come some months ago when M. de Hummelauer presented his second Memorandum there are many obvious and weighty Reasons on account of which it would be most desirable that the P[leni] P[otentiaries] whom the Austrian Gov[ernmen]t is about to send to the Conference of mediation should be instructed at once to make known the Intentions of the Austrian Gov[ernmen]t on this Subject.

P[ALMERSTON] 7/11/48.

(b) HUNGARY AND THE RUSSIAN INTERVENTION, 1848–9

[The revolution in Hungary was the most remarkable event of 1848, for it had a unique and peculiar character. Perhaps for that reason Palmerston's policy towards it was then, and is now, frequently misunderstood. Except in some aspects it was not a liberal revolution; it was the uprising of a very strange nation which had a strangely conservative character. The Magyars ruled the Kingdom of Hungary, but formed less than one half of the population. The other and larger half was Slav or Ruman and anti-Magyar in both cases. But the Magyars proper were a strongly legal and conservative nation, who had inherited from ancient times a constitution and a sturdy tradition of self-government. Thus in its early stages the Hungarian revolution was a demand for what we should call Dominion Status or Responsible Government. But there was this difference. The Kingdom of Hungary was older than the Habsburgs or Austria and, in demanding self-government, the Magyars were demanding not the revolutionary rights of man but the historic rights of Hungary. It was only by a series of accidents that they were driven into a revolutionary position. What Hungary asked was not a constitution, "which they had possessed since the days of Magna Carta", but freedom to work it.

On 15 March 1848 the Emperor Ferdinand, in his capacity of King of Hungary, conceded freedom of the press and responsible government. These reforms were in action in April. The Hungarian executive became patriotic and national, and the German bureaucracy were expelled. It looked as if the Hungarians might still remain conservative. Kossuth, however, an orator of burning power, a real revolutionist, formed the idea of supporting a liberal and united Germany, thus checkmating Habsburg absolutism or reaction. To this movement the reactionaries of Vienna were naturally opposed, and they found ways of exciting opposition to the Magyar in the discontented Slavs and Rumans of Hungary. At the end of October a Slav Imperialist army united with a

German one in front of revolutionary Vienna. They entered it and reaction triumphed. In the first days of October the Vienna reactionaries had already dissolved the Hungarian Parliament and sent troops against Kossuth and the Revolutionary Government. They found willing allies in the Slavs of the Hungarian Kingdom, who were only too delighted to attack their Magyar masters. In December the Emperor Ferdinand was removed and Franz Joseph succeeded. The struggle went on and Budapest was recaptured by the Austrians in January 1849. But it was very far from being over.

Kossuth was an avowed revolutionary, yet the Hungarians had a strong case for resistance on constitutional grounds. They took a legal and a quite defensible line that Ferdinand was still King of Hungary. Schwarzenberg replied to this by publishing a *constitution octroyée* (4 March 1849) which, in effect, annihilated the Hungarian constitution. It was six centuries old, and the promises of Vienna to observe it had recently been again broken. The patriotism and valour of the Magyars were displayed to the full. At first they had some successes and Kossuth finally issued a declaration of Independence (14 April) declaring the perjured Habsburgs deposed. This bold step thoroughly frightened the Austrians, who appealed to Russia for aid. It was known on 11 May that the Tsar would give it. Against the well-equipped Russian army resistance was hopeless, though a gallant struggle continued. Finally on 13 August the main Hungarian army surrendered and by October all resistance ended. Long before that executions and a reactionary reign of terror had begun.

Palmerston's attitude to all this was incomprehensible to Hungarians. That is intelligible enough. Kossuth saw that Palmerston was anti-Austrian in Italy and wished the Austrians to be expelled from the plains of Venetia and Lombardy. But it was a great mistake to suppose that Palmerston was anti-Austrian in Hungary and wished to expel Austria from the plains between the Danube and the Theiss. Palmerston feared that, if Austria went out of Hungary, Russia would come into it. Russia—already established in Moldavia and Wallachia—would add Hungary, with its half-Slav population, to her other domains, dominate the Danube from its mouth to Budapest and control all Eastern Europe. Palmerston could not therefore wish for an independent Hungary. That is why he steadily declined all official intercourse with Kossuth and refused even to interest himself in the question, until Russia intervened. Russia was Palmerston's bogey, so her intervention made his interest in Hungary acute.

Russia was one thing to which Palmerston was alive, British public opinion was another, and British public opinion had gradually been stirred by the gallant resistance of the Magyars. Palmerston had therefore to conciliate British public opinion and, so far as possible, to restrain Russia. He knew it was no good protesting against her intervention. He refused point blank to do so, as **Doc. 43** shews. He had, in fact, anticipated the possibility of Russian intervention by some months. The increase of Russian forces in Moldavia and Wallachia, plus at least one incursion across the frontier, had warned him of what was likely to happen. He thought that Russian intervention meant the restoration of Hungary to Austria intact, and that he could not but approve. **Doc. 43** indeed represents Palmerston as regretting Russian intervention. But in this, as in so many other cases, he may have had regard to future publication. Other dispatches suggest that he accepted, if he did not welcome, Russian intervention.*

Palmerston's idea seems to have been to reconcile the British public to the Russian intervention by inducing Austria to give generous terms to Hungary. A large-hearted amnesty, plus a restoration of her constitution, would, he thought, solve all difficulties. These are the ideas behind the famous speech he delivered on 21 July 1849, of which extracts are reproduced in **Doc. 44.** It never attained the popular repute of his *Civis Romanus Sum* speech of 1850, but is, diplomatically, of far greater interest. He puts the case for the survival of Austria on the ground of British interests, he expresses the hope that Hungary may receive her old constitution. Politically the speech was a masterpiece, for its sentiments brought the liberals to his side, while its realism won over the conservatives.

By August the struggle was over and in September the bloody and brutal reprisals began. They were of a very horrible character. Noble Hungarian women were flogged on their bare backs, thirteen Generals were shot, scores of patriots died on the scaffold. All this caused deep indignation to Palmerston. He thought such acts as politically foolish as they were barbarously cruel. "The Austrians are really the greatest brutes that ever called themselves by the undeserved name of civilised men. Their atrocities in Galicia, in Italy, in Hungary, in Transylvania are only to be equalled by the proceedings of the negro race in Africa and Haiti."† He was therefore delighted to receive delegations or petitions from Upper Tooting or Camden Town, protesting against these inhumanities, or describing the Emperors of Austria and Russia as "odious and detestable murderers and assassins". The Queen, as usual, protested, but Palmerston had gauged the public aright. If protests from fifty British cities could teach Austria humanity, he would have rejoiced. If Austria would not give Hungary home rule, then one day Austria would suffer as many calamities as she had in 1848. Meanwhile Austria was anchored once more as an element in the balance of power.]

* Several are quoted in C. Sproxton, *op. cit.* 82–6.
† Ashley, *Life*, I, 139, Palmerston to Ponsonby, 9 September 1849.

Document 43. *Palmerston refuses to protest against Russia's armed intervention in Hungary, 17 May 1849**

I have to acquaint you that Her Majesty's Government approve the language which you held to Count Nesselrode, as reported in your despatch No. 151, of the 2d instant, relative to the military assistance to be afforded by Russia to Austria.

Much as Her Majesty's Government regret this interference of Russia, the causes which have led to it, and the effects which it may produce, they nevertheless have not considered the occasion to be one which at present calls for any formal expression of the opinions of Great Britain on the matter.

Document 44. *Palmerston declares Austria's existence to be essential to the European balance of power, 21 July 1849†*

...Austria has been our ally. We have been allied with Austria in most important European transactions; and the remembrance of the alliance ought undoubtedly to create in the breast of every Englishman, who has a recollection of the history of his country, feelings of respect towards a Power with whom we have been in such alliance. It is perfectly true, that in the course of those repeated alliances, Austria, not from any fault of hers, but from the pressure of irresistible necessity, was repeatedly compelled to depart from the alliance, and to break the engagements by which she had bound herself to us. We did not reproach her with yielding to the necessity of the moment; and no generous mind would think that those circumstances ought in any degree to diminish or weaken the tie which former transactions must create between the Governments of the two countries. But there are higher and larger considerations, which ought to render the maintenance of the Austrian empire an object of solicitude to every English statesman. Austria is a most important element in the balance

---

* Palmerston to Buchanan, No. 141, 17 May 1849, *F.O.* 65/361.
† *Hans. Deb.*, 3rd Ser., cvii, 808–15.

of European power. Austria stands in the centre of Europe, a barrier against encroachment on the one side, and against invasion on the other. The political independence and liberties of Europe are bound up, in my opinion, with the maintenance and integrity of Austria as a great European Power; and therefore anything which tends by direct, or even remote, contingency, to weaken and to cripple Austria, but still more to reduce her from the position of a first-rate Power to that of a secondary State, must be a great calamity to Europe, and one which every Englishman ought to deprecate, and to try to prevent....I firmly believe that in this war between Austria and Hungary, there is enlisted on the side of Hungary the hearts and the souls of the whole people of that country.* I believe that the other races, distinct from the Magyars, have forgotten the former feuds that existed between them and the Magyar population, and that the greater portion of the people have engaged in what they consider a great national contest. It is true, as my honourable and gallant friend has stated, that Hungary has for centuries been a State which, though united with Austria by the link of the Crown, has nevertheless been separate and distinct from Austria by its own complete constitution. That consti-tution has many defects; but some of those defects were, I believe, remedied not long ago, and it is not the only ancient constitution on the continent that was susceptible of great improvement. There were means, probably, within the force and resources of the constitution itself to reform it; and it might have been hoped that those improvements would have been carried into effect. But, so far as I understand the matter, I take the present state of the case to be this: without going into the details of mutual complaints as to circumstances which have taken place within the last year, or year and a half, I take the question that is now to be fought for on the plains of Hungary to be this—whether Hungary shall con-tinue to maintain its separate nationality as a distinct king-dom, and with a constitution of its own; or whether it is to

* A notable mistake. Large numbers of Serbs and Croats fought under Jellačić against Hungary and the Rumans of Transylvania and the Slavs rose in rebellion against her.

be incorporated more or less in the aggregate constitution
that is to be given to the Austrian empire? It is a most
painful sight to see such forces as are now arrayed against
Hungary proceeding to a war fraught with such tremendous
consequences on a question that it might have been hoped
would be settled peacefully. It is of the utmost importance
to Europe, that Austria should remain great and powerful;
but it is impossible to disguise from ourselves that, if the war
is to be fought out, Austria must thereby be weakened,
because, on the one hand, if the Hungarians should be successful, and their success should end in the entire separation
of Hungary from Austria, it will be impossible not to see that
this will be such a dismemberment of the Austrian empire as
will prevent Austria from continuing to occupy the great
position she has hitherto held among European Powers. If,
on the other hand, the war being fought out to the uttermost,
Hungary should by superior forces be entirely crushed, Austria
in that battle will have crushed her own right arm. Every
field that is laid waste is an Austrian resource destroyed—
every man that perishes upon the field among the Hungarian
ranks, is an Austrian soldier deducted from the defensive
forces of the empire. Laying aside those other most obvious
considerations that have been touched upon as to the result of
a successful war, the success of which is brought about by
foreign aid—laying that wholly aside, it is obvious that even
the success of Austria, if it is simply a success of force, will
inflict a deep wound on the fabric and frame of the Austrian
empire. It is therefore much to be desired, not simply on
the principle of general humanity, but on the principle of
sound European policy, and from the most friendly regard
to the Austrian empire itself—it is, I say, devoutly to be
wished that this great contest may be brought to a termination by some amicable arrangement between the contending
parties, which shall on the one hand satisfy the national feelings
of the Hungarians, and on the other hand, not leave to Austria
another and a larger Poland within her empire. . . . It is most
desirable that foreign nations should know that, on the one
hand, England is sincerely desirous to preserve and maintain

peace—that we entertain no feelings of hostility towards any nation in the world—that we wish to be on the most friendly footing with all—that we have a deep interest in the preservation of peace, because we are desirous to carry on with advantage those innocent and peaceful relations of commerce that we know must be injured by the interruption of our friendly relations with other countries: but, on the other hand, it is also essential for the attainment of that object, and even essential for the protection of that commerce to which we attach so much importance, that it should be known and well understood by every nation on the face of the earth, that we are not disposed to submit to wrong, and that the maintenance of peace on our part is subject to the indispensable condition that all countries shall respect our honour and our dignity, and shall not inflict any injury upon our interests. Sir, I do not think that the preservation of peace is in any degree endangered by the expression of opinion with regard to the transactions in Hungary or other countries. I agree with those who think—and I know there are many in this country who entertain the opinion—that there are two objects which England ought peculiarly to aim at. One is to maintain peace; the other is to count for something in the transactions of the world—that it is not fitting that a country occupying such a proud position as England—that a country having such various and extensive interests, should lock herself up in a simple regard to her own internal affairs, and should be a passive and mute spectator of everything that is going on around. It is quite true that it may be said, "Your opinions are but opinions, and you express them against our opinions, who have at our command large armies to back them—what are opinions against armies?" Sir, my answer is, opinions are stronger than armies. Opinions, if they are founded in truth and justice, will in the end prevail against the bayonets of infantry, the fire of artillery, and the charges of cavalry. Therefore I say, that armed by opinion, if that opinion is pronounced with truth and justice, we are indeed strong, and in the end likely to make our opinions prevail; and I think that what is happening on the whole surface of the continent

of Europe, is a proof that this expression of mine is a truth.
Why, for a great many years the Governments of Europe
imagined they could keep down opinion by force of arms, and
that by obstructing progressive improvement they would
prevent that extremity of revolution which was the object of
their constant dread. We gave an opinion to the contrary
effect, and we have been blamed for it. We have been accused
of meddling with matters that did not concern us, and of
affronting nations and Governments by giving our opinion
as to what was likely to happen; but the result has proved,
that if our opinions had been acted upon, great calamities
would have been avoided. These very Governments that used
to say, "The man we hate, the man we have to fear, is the
moderate Reformer; we care not for your violent Radical, who
proposes such violent extremes that nobody is likely to join
him—the enemy we are most afraid of is the moderate
Reformer, because he is such a plausible man that it is difficult
to persuade people that his counsels would lead to extreme
consequences—therefore let us keep off, of all men, the
moderate Reformer, and let us prevent the first step of improvement, because that improvement might lead to extremities and innovation,"—those Governments, those Powers
of Europe, have at last learned the truth of the opinions
expressed by Mr. Canning, "That those who have checked
improvement, because it is innovation, will one day or other
be compelled to accept innovation, when it has ceased to be
improvement." I say, then, that it is our duty not to remain
passive spectators of events that in their immediate consequences affect other countries, but which in their remote
and certain consequences are sure to come back with disastrous effect upon us; that, so far as the courtesies of international intercourse may permit us to do, it is our duty,
especially when our opinion is asked, as it has been on many
occasions on which we have been blamed for giving it, to
state our opinions, founded on the experience of this country—
an experience that might have been, and ought to have been,
an example to less fortunate countries. At the same time,
I am quite ready to admit that interference ought not to be

carried to the extent of endangering our relations with other countries. There are cases like that which is now the subject of our discussion, of one Power having in the exercise of its own sovereign rights invited the assistance of another Power; and, however we may lament that circumstance, however we may be apprehensive that therefrom consequences of great danger and evil may flow, still we are not entitled to interpose in any manner that will commit this country to embark in those hostilities. All we can justly do is to take advantage of any opportunities that may present themselves in which the counsels of friendship and peace may be offered to the contending parties.... Sir, to suppose that any Government of England can wish to excite revolutionary movements in any part of the world—to suppose that any Government of England can have any other wish or desire than to confirm and maintain peace between nations, and tranquillity and harmony between Governments and subjects, shows really a degree of ignorance and folly which I never supposed any public man could have been guilty of, which may do very well for a newspaper article, but which it astonishes me to find is made the subject of a speech in Parliament.

20. PALMERSTON, TURKEY AND THE HUNGARIAN REFUGEES

[Palmerston proved "a daring pilot in extremity". He had steered the British ship with wonderful skill through the stormy waters of 1848–9. What is more, by August 1849 all seemed over. Palmerston had averted war from England during the stormiest of all periods for Europe. Yet the crisis for England was still to come. Within two months Palmerston had actually to risk war in defence of a weaker State against the two greatest Powers of Eastern Europe.

The question that arose was apparently a trivial one, yet it brought four Powers to the verge of war. When nerves are frayed and passions high, slight incidents often produce serious results. In the same way a fly or an insect may cause disaster by obstructing the delicate mechanism of a great engine. In this case the quarrel was about political refugees who had fled to Turkey. One of them was the Hungarian revolutionary, Kossuth, who carried with him the historic Hungarian crown and buried it on the borders of his native land. In addition to Hungarian refugees there were many

Poles, some of them Russian subjects like Generals Bem and Dembinski, and all of them revolutionaries. The Emperors of Russia and Austria thirsted for the blood of revolutionaries and demanded the surrender of their rebels from Constantinople.

The Turks did not feel at all inclined to surrender these political refugees. They have a traditional friendship for Hungarians and so did not want to surrender them to the Habsburg. They well understood that the Poles are the enemies of the Russians and did not want to surrender them to the Tsar. They knew that to surrender either was to abdicate their independence for ever. But in the last resort the Turks were weak and knew that they could not resist Russia and Austria without help from outside. "The Sultan", wrote Stratford Canning, is "accessible to secret information and he is always more or less fearful of Russia."* The Tsar sent him a stately letter (which was presented on 7 September), asking him to give up the Polish refugees. "Russia", he explained, "has intervened in Hungary in virtue of the same...principle which was present when I spontaneously offered aid to Your Majesty to establish order [in Moldavia and Wallachia] last year."† Could the Sultan, or dare the Sultan, resist the pleading of this masterful protector?

On 16 September Stratford Canning reported that the Austrian and Russian representatives had sent peremptory notes demanding the surrender of the "rebels". They had, said he, the full intention of "consigning the most illustrious to the Executioner". If they were not surrendered they would break off diplomatic relations with the Porte. The Ambassadors of England and France both advised the Porte to stand firm and not surrender the refugees. They declared that the Austro-Russian demands were not justified by previous treaties. But they could not of course pledge the Governments of France and England to the support of the Turks without orders from home. So the decision had to be made in Paris and London.

Palmerston seems to have had no doubt as to the decision, and for once the Queen was with him. She generally was for resisting the pretensions of Russia. The Cabinet also concurred and on 6 October the decision was taken and embodied in a dispatch. The Turks were to be supported, the British Mediterranean squadron was to go to the Dardanelles, and the French Government to be asked to send their fleet as well.‡ Such was the im-

---

* Stratford Canning to Palmerston, No. 257, 25 August 1849, *F.O.* 78/778.
† Stratford Canning to Palmerston, No. 271, 5 September 1849, *F.O.* 78/779.
‡ This dispatch is printed in the Blue Book (*A. & P.*, [1851], LVIII, [1324], 440–2) with one passage omitted. But it is there dated 6 October by mistake. The original is in *F.O.* 195/325, Palmerston to Canning, No. 241, 7 October. It is endorsed "Recd Oct. 24 Waring". The draft dispatch (*F.O.* 78/771) has "V.R." against it in pencil. Cp. Temperley, *England and the Near East, The Crimea*, [1936], 264, where the passage suppressed in the Blue Book is given.

portance of the dispatch that three couriers carried copies of it by different routes. A gallant courier, who half killed himself in the effort, arrived on the 26th with one copy. He had made a record ride from Belgrade, but he lost the race by two days. The one that actually reached Constantinople first was that carried by Messenger Waring, who came by steamer from Marseilles and arrived on the 24th.*

This dispatch carried the day. Stratford Canning bore it exultantly to the Sultan, saying "the cause of honour and humanity has been vindicated". In fact the Tsar had already given way at St Petersburgh. Russia and Austria, involved as they were elsewhere, had no desire to try conclusions with the Franco-British fleet. They withdrew their pretensions, the Turks were triumphant and the Hungarian refugees were saved.

The whole incident is a good example of Palmerstonian diplomacy. By his skilful management he had kept public opinion behind him throughout the whole period. It was now that he had his reward. The British Cabinet saw that, if Turkey once yielded up the refugees at the demand of two powerful foreign despots, her independence would be gone. They were determined to protect the sovereignty and independence of the Sultan. The British public, not understanding this rather subtle point, was determined to protect gallant refugees against alien tyrannical despots. As Palmerston wrote: "The Sultan has clearly right upon his side. That is the universal opinion of all men of all parties, and of all newspapers in this country."† With this backing Palmerston knew he would be triumphant. But he did not, in fact, believe that Russia and Austria would fight. He thought that "a little manly firmness" would do the trick. And it did. So Palmerston concluded the year 1849 and his handling of the whole problem of those stormy years with a spectacular success.

Docs. **45** and **46** are private letters. They have been selected as being, among all the papers of the period, the most revealing as to Palmerston's views on the crisis.]

Document 45. *Palmerston communicates his decision to support Turkey against Russia and Austria over the Hungarian Refugees, 6 October 1849‡*

I send you a despatch to be communicated to Schwarzenberg.§ We have endeavoured to make it as civil as possible, so as not to leave him any ground for saying that he cannot

* Lane Poole, *Life of Stratford Canning*, [1888], II, 197–9, is a little misleading.
† Private letter to Lord Bloomfield, 6 October 1849, quoted in Sproxton, *op. cit.* 126–7.
‡ Palmerston to Ponsonby (Vienna), 6 October 1849, Ashley, *Life*, I, 153–5.
§ The real ruler of Austria.

yield to threats. We make none; and in my verbal communications with Brunnow and Colloredo* I have said nothing about our squadron being ordered up to the Dardanelles. But it is right that *you* should know and understand that the Government have come unanimously to the determination of taking this matter up in earnest, and of carrying it through. We have resolved to support Turkey, let who will be against her in this matter. It is painful to see the Austrian Government led on in its blindness, its folly, and its passionate violence into a course utterly at variance with the established policy of Austria. If there is one thing more than another which Austria ought to do, it is to support Turkey against Russia; and here is Schwarzenberg, in his fondness for bullying the weak, co-operating with the Russian Government to humble Turkey, and to lay her at the feet of Russia.

But you understand these questions so thoroughly that you will no doubt have been able to lay before the Austrian Government and Camarilla the full extent of the mistake they are making. They are besides uniting England and France in joint action, which is not what Austrian Governments have hitherto been particularly anxious to do. I cannot believe that the two Governments will push this matter further. The rights of the case are clearly against them. Both Colloredo and Brunnow, though I beg they may not be quoted, acknowledge that the Sultan is not bound by treaty to do what is required of him. Metternich,† I am told, says it is a great mistake.

What could Austria hope to gain by a war with Turkey, supported, as she would be, by England and France? Austria would lose her Italian provinces, to which she seems to attach such undue value, and she never would see them again.... I cannot conceive that, in the present state of Germany, it would suit Austria to provoke a war with England and France; and I do not think that such a war would be of any advantage even to Russia....‡

* Respectively the Russian and Austrian diplomatic representatives at London.
† The ex-Austrian Chancellor was now an exile residing in England.
‡ The similar private letter to Bloomfield (St Petersburgh), 6 October 1849, should be studied in Sproxton, *op. cit.* 126–7.

Document 46. *Palmerston moralizes after the crisis has ended,*
28 *October* 1849*

...All things however have turned out well. The English Government and nation have shewn a spirit, a generosity, and a courage which does us all high honour. We have drawn France to follow in our wake, after much division and difference of opinion in the French Cabinet and public. We have forced the haughty [Russian] autocrat to go back from his arrogant pretensions; we have obliged Austria to forego another opportunity of quaffing her bowl of blood; and we have saved Turkey from being humbled down to absolute prostration. All this will be seen and felt by Europe; all this should be borne in mind by ourselves, and ought to be treasured up in grateful remembrance by Turkey; but all this *we* ought not to boast of, and on the contrary we must let our baffled Emperors pass as quietly and decently as possible over the bridge by which they are going to retreat.

* Private letter to Stratford Canning, 28 October 1849, Lane Poole, *Life of Stratford Canning*, [1888], II, 202. An article on Great Britain and Kossuth by D. A. Janóssy, with many extracts from British documents, is in *Archivum Europae Centro-Orientalis* ed. Lukinić, Budapest [1937], Tome III, 53–190.

IX. GRANVILLE, MALMESBURY, 1852

THE REACTION AGAINST PALMERSTON

21. LORD JOHN RUSSELL AND THE QUEEN

[When Lord Palmerston's resignation was demanded in December 1851, Queen Victoria, after accepting Lord Granville as his successor, asked Lord John Russell as Premier to get the new minister to prepare a general statement of foreign policy. This was done to commit the Cabinet in future in regard to the manner in which such policy was to be "*practically applied*". Lord John, who did not wish to be so committed, replied on December 29 with studious generalities, e.g. "it is very difficult to lay down any principles from which deviations may not frequently be made".* He instructed Lord Granville in the very driest style—as follows:

"I send you a letter from the Queen which imposes upon you the duty of preparing a programme. I have told H.M. that it is not the policy of this country to make engagements except on a view of the circumstances of the moment and that any rule may be broken through.† That the best rule after all is to do to others as we wish they should do unto us. Still you may write a sketch of what you conceive our foreign policy should be."‡

The memorandum, of which the text is here subjoined, is only an unsigned draft and was perhaps not even presented to Lord John Russell or to the Cabinet. It was evidently not presented to the Queen for there is no copy at Windsor. A further memorandum, for reasons shortly to be explained, was apparently never even drafted.

Charles Greville, to whom Granville shewed his draft, described it as "a series of commonplaces",§ but there is one section in which real change was foreshadowed. Choice of men of ability

* These two documents are in *Queen Victoria's Letters*, ed. A. C. Benson and Lord Esher, 1st Ser., end of Chap. xx. Cheap ed., [1908], II, 351-3.
† Here is an illustration. He proposed to adopt a certain interpretation of a Treaty of 1854 between Turkey and Sardinia "even if the Law of Nations and the general necessity of every Government to provide in particular cases for its security did not override that Treaty" (*F.O.* 195/663, Lord John Russell to Sir H. Bulwer, No. 219, 8 April 1861).
‡ Russell to Granville, 29 December 1851.
§ Greville, *Journal*, [1885], 2nd Part, III, 442-3, *ap.* 14 January 1852.

and stricter discipline for ambassadors meant something novel, and "new measures to secure the efficiency of those" entering diplomacy were a revolution. They portended tests by examination "no doubt" to "please the educational propensities of the Prince [Consort]".*

Even the "commonplaces" are worthy of study, for they conceal a humour as dry as that of Lord John himself. There are hints at the overbearing conduct of Palmerston, and an obvious reference to the Don Pacifico case and the *Civis Britannicus Sum* policy. By implication also Lord Granville disclaims active interference in the internal affairs of other nations of the Palmerstonian type. On the other hand, however, the principles of Mr Cobden are condemned in the assertion that "non-intervention" does not always mean a policy of negation or Free-Trade a policy of aggression. Apparently Granville proposes to steer the Cabinet ship between the Palmerstonian Scylla and the Cobdenite Charybdis.

The practical application of his general principles seems to have given Lord Granville pause for thought, and he had apparently not written a line of his further memorandum by the third week in February. By that time it was unnecessary to write it, for Palmerston carried a motion against the Government on the 20th, and Lord John Russell handed in his resignation on the 25th.

The draft that follows is therefore one of the few memorials of one of the weakest of ministries.]

Document 47. *Granville's General Statement of Foreign Policy,*
12 January 1852†

In obedience to Her Majesty's gracious Commands transmitted by you, I will endeavour to state, altho' very imperfectly, the views of Her Majesty's present Government with respect to the Foreign Policy of Great Britain. I will point out what I conceive to be the objects of that Policy, the principles of action, by which those objects are to be obtained, and the application of those principles to our relations with the principal countries of Europe.

In the opinion of the present Cabinet, it is the duty and the interest of this country, having possessions scattered over the whole globe, and priding itself on its advanced state of civilization, to encourage moral, intellectual and physical progress among all other nations.

* Greville, *Journal*, [1885], 2nd Part, III, 442–3, *ap.* 14 January 1852.
† *Pte Granville Papers*, Granville to Lord John Russell, London, 12 January 1852.

For this purpose the Foreign Policy of Great Britain should be marked by justice, moderation, and self-respect, and this country should in her relations with other States do by others as it would be done by. While the Cabinet do not believe that all considerations of a higher character are to be sacrificed to the pushing our manufactures by any means into every possible corner of the globe, yet considering the great natural advantages of our Foreign Commerce, and the powerful means of civilization it affords, one of the first duties of a British Gov[ernmen]t must always be to obtain for our Foreign Trade that security which is essential to its success.

British subjects of all classes, engaged in innocent pursuits, are entitled abroad as well as at home to the protection of their Gov[ernmen]t. Where they have been treated with injustice, they have a right to expect that redress should be demanded in strong but dignified language, followed if necessary by corresponding measures; where they may, by their own wanton folly or misconduct, have got into difficulties in a Foreign Land, they have no right to expect assistance, and even where they unwittingly but imprudently subject themselves to the penal laws of the country in which they find themselves, they can only claim those good offices, the efficacy of which must depend upon the friendliness of our relations with the country in which the difficulty has arisen.

The Cabinet adhere to the principle of non-intervention in the internal affairs of other countries, as one tending most to maintain the dignity of the Crown, the security of the Country, and to strengthen the lasting influence of this Nation upon the opinion of the world.

They do not attach to the word "non-intervention" the meaning implied by some who use it, viz. that Diplomacy is become obsolete, and that it is unnecessary for this country to know, or take a part in what passes in other countries. H.M.'s Gov[ernmen]t ought to be informed accurately and immediately, by their Agents, of every important event which may arise.

With regard to occurrences likely to have international consequences, no general rule can uniformly be applied. In each case, the Gov[ernmen]t must exercise its own discretion, whether it shall interfere at once, or remain aloof till its arbitration or good offices be required. The latter course may often be advisable when, as at present, opinion abroad is in extremes, and the Foreign Policy of England has obtained, whether justly or unjustly, the reputation of interfering too much. It will also often be found advisable to combine with other great Powers, when no sacrifice of principle is required, to settle the disputes which may arise between other nations.

With respect to those internal arrangements of other countries, such as the establishment of Liberal Institutions and the reduction of Tariffs, in which this country has an indirect interest, H.M.'s Representatives ought to be furnished with the views of H.M.'s Gov[ernmen]t on each subject, and the arguments best adapted to support those views, but they should at the same time be instructed to press these views only when fitting opportunities occur, and when their advice and assistance are required. The intrusion of advice which is suspected to be not wholly disinterested, never can have as much effect as opinions given at the request of the person who is to be influenced.

With reference to the support to be given to those Countries which have adopted Liberal Institutions similar in Liberality to our own, it will be the endeavour of H.M.'s Gov[ernmen]t to cultivate the most intimate relations with them.

It will be the duty of H.M.'s Gov[ernmen]t to inform them of all that may expose them to danger, and to give them, when required, frank and judicious advice. It will exert its influence to dissuade other Powers from encroaching on their territory, or attempting to subvert their institutions, and there may occur cases in which the honour and good faith of this country will require that it should support such Allies with more than friendly assurances.

H.M.'s Cabinet believe that every assistance, within the one competency of Gov[ernmen]t should be given to all those undertakings which tend to promote a more rapid interchange of knowledge and opinions among various countries; they believe that such increased intercourse will tend more than anything else to promote the Peace of the world.

The Cabinet is also of opinion that new measures should be taken to secure the efficiency of those who enter into the diplomatic career, and who are promoted in that profession— that a stricter discipline should be established among the members of each mission, and that those persons who combine those personal qualities which engage respect and popularity with activity in obtaining information, and zeal in executing their instructions, should be selected to represent Her Majesty, at the different Courts.

I will now endeavour to show how the principles which I have laid down as adopted by H.M.'s Gov[ernmen]t can be applied to our relations with the different European Nations and the United States; but it must be remembered that one unforeseen event may, like a move on a chessboard, necessitate perfectly different arrangements.*

22. GRANVILLE AND THE IBERIAN PENINSULA

[In view of the implied condemnation of Palmerstonian policy in the "General Statement", **Doc. 48** is amusing. Granville, in one of the very few decisions of his brief Ministry, advocated interference in Spain, with the view of encouraging constitutional tendencies on true Palmerstonian lines. In point of fact, such interference was not required, but the fact that it was contemplated is instructive. This was all against the Canningite tradition. Another instruction was thoroughly Canningite. Lord Granville, fearing a possible Spanish attack on Portugal, stated: "The Spanish Government must...be well aware that were any Spanish Military Force to be directed to enter Portugal without the consent, and against the Will, of the Constitutional Organs of that Country, G[rea]t Britain would be bound by Faith, by Honour, and by regard for Her own Interests, practically to fulfil the obligations imposed upon Her by the stipulations of those [Anglo-Portuguese] Treaties."†]

* We have to thank the Dowager Countess Granville and the present Lord Granville for permission to publish the text of this memorandum, and Lord Fitzmaurice for advice and information in connexion with the incident. He published in his *Life of 2nd Earl Granville*, [1905], I, 49–52, a careful summary, with comments, of the memorandum, and Lord John Russell's letter reproduced above is in *ibid.* I, 49. Section 21 was originally published in *Camb. Hist. Journ.*, II, No. 3, [1928], 298–301.

† Granville to Howden, No. 23, 31 January 1852, *F.O.* 72/801.

Document 48. *Granville advises Spain to pursue a Constitutional Policy, 31 January 1852**

Your Lordship's reports respecting the state of things at the Madrid and the fears which you have expressed of organic changes in the system of Gov[ernmen]t in Spain, have caused some anxiety to H[er] M[ajesty]'s Gov[ernmen]t.

I have to instruct Your Lordship to state to the Spanish Gov[ernmen]t, that while H[er] M[ajesty]'s Gov[ernmen]t do not think it right or expedient to tender advice to other countries, as to the changes which may be adopted in them with respect to their internal administration, yet the very intimate nature of our relations with Spain, and the share which we happily have had in establishing the present dynasty on the Throne, would make us deeply regret that any changes should be made which would affect the constitutional character of the Spanish Gov[ernmen]t, with which the reign of H[er] Cath[olic] Maj[est]y has hitherto been identified, and which was one of the main considerations which induced H[er] Majesty's Gov[ernmen]t to give assistance to Queen Isabella in the long continued struggle with Don Carlos.

You will also point out, that should this difference between Her Cath[olic] M[ajest]y and Don Carlos be effaced, the partisans of Don Carlos would enter upon a renewed struggle with advantages they do not now possess. On the other hand, the friends of the Constitution would no longer defend the Throne with the zeal and enthusiasm they have hitherto displayed.

23. DERBY REBUKES PALMERSTON

[On the fall of Russell's Government, as the result of Palmerston's motion in the Commons, Derby came into power. On 27 February 1852 Derby delivered a speech in the Lords, obviously repudiating Palmerston's policy and especially his expressions. He recommended "observing to all Foreign Powers—whether powerful or weak—a calm, temperate, deliberate and conciliatory course of

* Granville to Howden (Madrid), No. 24, 31 January 1852. Enclosure in Granville to Sir H. Seymour, No. 45, 9 February 1852, *F.O.* 181/280. Original text in *F.O.* 185/252.

conduct, not in acts alone, but in words also".* Again he suggested: "Not indulging in vituperation and intemperance of language, but submitting equally to the honour and justice of other countries the claim we should be the first to acknowledge ourselves."† Aberdeen, it is interesting to note, not only "entirely acquiesced" but declared there was no "shade of difference" between him and Derby nor had been "for the last ten or twelve years".‡ The real incident, which Derby and Aberdeen had in mind, was at the end of the reception of Kossuth, when Palmerston received addresses reflecting on the Tsar and the Austrian Emperor as murderers and assassins.]

Document 49. *Malmesbury warns France against aggression against Switzerland, 5 March* 1852§

[Mentions the anxiety of the new Government as to a report that the French intend to march into Switzerland.]

After the Speeches respectively made by the Earl of Derby and Lord John Russell at the opening of the present Parliament, neither the members of the late, nor of the present Gov[ernmen]t of Her Majesty can be exposed to the suspicion of approving virulent strictures on the part of any National Press against Gov[ernmen]ts in alliance with Great Britain; and it is needless to add that H[er] M[ajesty's] Gov[ernment] can only look upon Socialist Doctrines as revolting in their nature; but H[er] M[ajesty's] Gov[ernment] feel strongly that to occupy and [*sic*] Independent, and Neutral Country, with a Military Force for the Suppression of such Strictures and Doctrines, is to establish an entirely new Principle.

If admitted it will put an end to all the smaller States to which it may in turn be applied, inasmuch as it will make their internal Government dependent upon the momentary interest and arbitrary demands of their more powerful neighbours.

...The first object of H[er] M[ajesty]'s Gov[ernmen]t will be to preserve the Peace of Europe; and believing that an abstinence from all interference openly or indirectly with the

---

* *Hans. Deb.* 3rd Ser., cxix, 892.
† *Ibid.* 893.   ‡ *Ibid.* 912–13.
§ Malmesbury to Cowley (Paris), No. 9 Confidential, 5 March 1852. Enclosure in Malmesbury to Sir H. Seymour, No. 14, 16 March 1852, *F.O.* 181/267. Original text in *F.O.* 146/436.

choice of nations as regards their own Gov[ernmen]ts be these despotic or Constitutional, is the Policy most efficient for this result, they are not less anxious to see this course adopted by other countries, and especially by one whose alliance, and amity is so much valued by H[er] M[ajesty]'s Gov[ernmen]t as that of France: and if H[er] M[ajesty]'s Gov[ernmen]t may be allowed to speak in a frank and friendly spirit to that important Power, so remarkable for its History and love of* Glory, it would ask of France and of the remarkable man whom she has chosen for her Leader,† whether under almost any circumstances a military movement initiated by so great a nation against the smallest of European States will contribute to her Renown....

Document 50. *Malmesbury's advances to Austria, 15 March 1852‡*

...In proportion to the value which H[er] M[ajesty]'s Gov[ernmen]t place upon the maintenance of a cordial friendship with Austria, the oldest Ally of England, cemented not only by the tie of mutual interest, but by the recollection of past efforts in a common cause, was the regret with which H[er] M[ajesty]'s present Gov[ernmen]t on succeeding to office, found that the result of the events of the last few years had been to substitute for these friendly relations a tone of mutual suspicion, if not of actual alienation, and to give to their diplomatic correspond[en]ce a character quite at variance with the dispositions which ought to subsist between them....

* The text in *F.O.* 146/436 has "love of military Glory".
† Napoleon III.
‡ Malmesbury to Buol, 15 March 1852. Enclosure in Malmesbury to Sir H. Seymour (St Petersburgh), No. 22, 16 March 1852, *F.O.* 181/268. Original text in *F.O.* 120/265.

X. PEEL AND ABERDEEN, 1851–3

ITALY

24. ABERDEEN; GLADSTONE AND NAPLES

[Aberdeen had not been fortunate as a negotiator in his first diplomatic essay in 1814, when he dismayed Castlereagh by offering the Rhine frontier to Napoleon; nor were his negotiations in regard to Portugal or Greece happy during his first period at the Foreign Office. But his second period was marked by considerable success in regard to the United States. In 1846 the Queen regretted that the Government had resigned for internal reasons just when they had achieved a decisive success in foreign politics. They had concluded the Oregon Boundary Treaty with the United States (1846), and solved a problem which had baffled all negotiators since the days of Canning.

In respect to Europe Aberdeen was pacific. He tried to maintain friendly relations with France through his friend Princess Lieven, who had the ear and the heart of Guizot. He did not indeed avoid a very serious dispute with France over Tahiti in 1844, nor did he emerge from it with much credit. He was involved in the early stages of the sordid dispute about the Spanish Marriages but can hardly be held responsible for the *dénouement*, and indeed might perhaps have averted it.* But he had definite ideas in respect to conciliating two, at least, of the despotic powers of Europe. These had been alienated both by Palmerston's manners and by his intervention in favour of constitutionalism in Portugal, Spain, Greece and Belgium. Aberdeen, whose nature was gentle and trustful, believed that the establishment of personal relations with the Ministers and Sovereigns of these Courts might really improve diplomatic intercourse. He was an old friend of Metternich and Nesselrode, he knew Schwarzenberg, he knew the Tsar. His attempts to improve relations with Russia are described above (pp. 134–5); here we may confine ourselves to those with Austria. The difficulty of reconciling political with personal friendships was there strikingly revealed; but, paradoxically enough, the revelation came when Aberdeen had ceased to be Foreign Minister. It was only in 1853 that the full development of his pro-Austrian policy was seen.

Aberdeen had sharply criticized Palmerston during 1849 for his attitude towards Naples and for his attempts to prevent its King

* Cp. Jones Parry, *The Spanish Marriages*, [1936], *passim*.

from indulging in barbarous and savage reprisals towards his subjects. Palmerston described his action later thus: "The English Government went so far as to break off diplomatic relations with Naples avowedly on the ground of the tyrannical Government of the late King."* Aberdeen had particularly attacked Palmerston for saying that such grievances, when unredressed, were the true cause of revolution. In 1850 he returned to the charge, asserting that Palmerston had deeply injured Austria by his attacks on her in Italy, and that "Naples, like other Governments, was entitled to manage her own internal affairs". In 1851 Aberdeen was suddenly confronted with an indictment of Naples more severe than any that even Palmerston had made. It came from a man who was no advocate of Italy, from a "stern unbending Tory", from a Peelite and a personal friend. And this intervention was the first time that a name, afterwards renowned throughout Europe, was mentioned with reverence or enthusiasm by Liberals.

Gladstone had gone to Naples on a pleasure trip, and had remained to investigate the state of the prisons and the treatment of political criminals. He saw what the crushing of the revolution had meant in Naples, he saw the fruits of King "Bomba's" tyranny. The King had sworn to a constitution, promising to all his subjects parliamentary government, freedom of speech, and freedom from arbitrary arrest. The constitution was still in existence, though over half of the members of the Parliament thus created were in gaol or in exile. These political prisoners were loaded with chains, and, though usually professional men or learned persons, were coupled with the vilest felons. Thousands of political Liberals remained in gaol, without knowing their offences, and without any prospect of being brought to trial. The filthy and loathsome cells were seldom visited by officials and never by the doctors. Gladstone saw with his own eyes the "sick prisoners, men almost with death in their faces". He estimated that some twenty thousand were in prison for political offences, and modern research deems this figure too small and his other charges fully made out.†

Worse than all this cruelty and corruption, in Gladstone's view, was the moral atmosphere. The judges, the police, the Ministers were terrorized or vile. Not only was the practice of the Government unspeakable, but the very doctrines it inculcated were those of perjury. This truth was well illustrated not only in the publications enjoined for use in the schools, but in the *Official Reply of the Neapolitan Government* to Gladstone's assertions. That denounced "the unhappy constitution of 1848", and spoke of the

* G. & D. 22/20, *Pte Russell Papers*. Palmerston to Russell, 19 June 1859.
† V. G. M. Trevelyan, *Garibaldi and the Thousand*, [1909], Chap. III, *passim*. He relates some horrors which Gladstone did not discover.

"warm desire" for its abolition. It declared that the constitution was obtained by "agitators alone". Yet "the King of Naples told the world, on the 10th of February 1848, that he granted it [the constitution] 'to the unanimous desire of Our Most beloved subjects'".*

Gladstone was determined that these iniquities should either end or be revealed to the world. He consulted Lord Aberdeen and agreed with him to try private remonstrance in the first instance. Failing its success, Gladstone intimated that he would appeal to the public. He prepared a pamphlet for the purpose. Impressed by the enormities there related, Aberdeen at length wrote to Prince Schwarzenberg (2 May). Gladstone waited for a reply for seven weeks, then became impatient and published his first letter to Lord Aberdeen, together with a second. Aberdeen says that, two days after the publication, Schwarzenberg at length answered saying that he would make private remonstrances at Naples. As soon, however, as Schwarzenberg heard of the appeal to the public, he declined any further assistance and expressed deep indignation at Gladstone's pamphlet.

Doc. 51 shews Aberdeen's view of the situation after publication. Attached to it are a series of extracts shewing the sequel.]

Document 51. *Aberdeen and Gladstone on the Naples Atrocities, October* 1851 *to December* 1852†

You will probably have seen the Neapolitan Statement in the "Debate" in three numbers of which it is contained. I would send it to you, if I did not conclude that you must already have received it. I have not yet seen it in a pamphlet form. The best feature of this Defence, is the tone in which it is written. It is dignified, and considering the nature of the accusation, sufficiently courteous. This is calculated to produce a favourable impression; but although some points are satisfactorily disposed of, the worst of your accusations remain unanswered.

The question of foreign interference is delicate; because it must be one of degree, and must involve a right of reciprocity. To be successful, with any Government which respects itself,

---

* Gladstone,*Gleanings*, [1879], IV, 126. *The First Letter*, to Aberdeen, dated 7 April 1851; *The Second Letter* dated 14 July; and the *Examination of the Official Neapolitan Reply*, 29 January 1852. For Aberdeen's side of the case, *v.* Stanmore, *Life of Aberdeen*, [1893], 203–5. For Gladstone's, *v.* Morley, *Life*, Bk III, Chap. VI.

† *Pte Gladstone Papers.* Aberdeen to Gladstone, 29 October 1851.

it is clear that friendly and confidential expostulation offers the best chance. As we have lost this in a great measure, we must see how we may best now go to work. For my part, I shall always be ready and happy to do anything in my power calculated to diminish human suffering, and to promote improvements in the Neapolitan, or any other Government, for which I am well aware there may be ample grounds.

With your disinterested and benevolent views, I am sure you must be distressed at the practical encouragement given to the promotion of revolution throughout Europe....

[After saying that he has just received a new letter from Prince Schwarzenberg, Aberdeen goes on] The substance is plain enough and pretty much what I anticipated. He says that the publicity given to these accusations has entirely deprived him of the means of exercising any influence, even in the most confidential manner. He takes no notice of my appeal founded upon the admitted sufferings of individuals, without reference to their guilt or innocence; but enters into a sort of justification of the Neapolitan Government.

[When Gladstone informed Aberdeen that he was preparing an *Examination of the Official Neapolitan Reply* Aberdeen asked him to see that it was not addressed to him. "I cannot bear the thought of seeing you practically united with Kossuth and Mazzini."* Gladstone replied: "You need not be afraid, I think, of Mazzinism from me, still less of Kossuthism, which means the other *plus* imposture, Lord Palmerston and his nationalities" (1 December 1852).† Aberdeen closed the controversy mournfully: "My only difference with you relates to the mode of your proceeding."]

Gladstone and Palmerston and the Official Neapolitan Reply

[What is interesting about the whole matter is that "the mode of proceeding" had been forced on Gladstone by the horrors of Neapolitan rule. Though he was still far from supporting Palmerston's idea of nationalism in Italy it was utterly impossible to keep silence on such enormities. Here was a man with a respect for governments "as the representatives of a public, nay of a Divine authority", denouncing a government in terms that even Palmerston had never used. "It is such violation of human and written

* *Pte Gladstone Papers.* Aberdeen to Gladstone, 29 November 1852. Gladstone's reply is in Morley, *Life*, [1903], 1, Bk III, Chap. VI.
† *Pte Gladstone Papers.* Gladstone to Aberdeen, 1 December 1852.

law as this, carried on for the purpose of violating every other law, unwritten and eternal, human and divine;...The effect of all this is, total inversion of all the moral and social ideas....I have seen and heard the strong and too true expression used, 'This is the negation of God erected into a system of Government.'"*
Gladstone had in his controversy with Naples reached the position of Hildebrand in his contest with the Empire. The secular power was Evil, visible and personified.

The Naples Government met the charge with an "Official Reply". It attempted to refute Gladstone's statements point by point, and was able to find a few errors. Gladstone admitted these in his *Examination of the...Neapolitan Reply*, and shewed in the most damaging fashion how that *Reply* was full of errors and inconsistencies. But, before the *Examination* had been published, Palmerston (then in the last days of his second Foreign Secretaryship) intervened. He caused his diplomatic agents to distribute copies of Gladstone's *Letters* on Naples to every Government in Europe. The Neapolitan Minister in London asked that copies of the *Official Reply* should likewise be circulated. Palmerston grasped the chance of telling a Neapolitan official something of what England thought of his Government. He repeated his familiar views on its badness and warned him of the revolution which its excesses would produce. He flatly declined to circulate the *Official Reply*. It consisted he said "of a flimsy tissue of bare denials and reckless assertions mixed up with coarse ribaldry and common-place abuse".

Remonstrances as to the treatment of prisoners by a foreign state do not often benefit the prisoners themselves. It is quite possible, as Aberdeen contended, that Gladstone and Palmerston actually injured the prisoners whom they tried to help. But they had evoked sympathy throughout the world for their sufferings. This example had at least the effect of changing a Conservative into a Revolutionary. Gladstone now argued that the existing order in Naples was more dangerous than any revolution, and that Palmerston's attacks on it had been right. Any Government, like Austria, condoning and supporting such an order, was condoning a system certain to end in disorder. This point of view is embodied in the first document that follows (**Doc. 52**). In the second (**Doc. 53**) Aberdeen (just after becoming Prime Minister at the end of 1852) reiterates his old idea that Austria must be supported, whether she supports wrong or wickedness or not. Thus the doctrines of new and old conservatism in foreign policy are opposed. It is easy to see why Aberdeen's policy was a failure, why Austria was driven from Lombardy, and why King "Bomba's" heir fled from Naples before Garibaldi.]

* *First Letter* in *Gleanings*, [1879], IV, 6–7.

Document 52. *Gladstone on the Naples Government and the
Conservative Principle, 7 January 1852**

...The principle of conservation and the principle of progress
are both sound in themselves; they have ever existed and must
ever exist together in European society, in qualified opposition, but in vital harmony and concurrence; and for each of
those principles it is a matter of deep and essential concern,
that iniquities committed under the shelter of its name should
be stripped of that shelter.... Nor has it ever fallen to my
lot to perform an office so truly conservative, as in the
endeavour I have made to shut and mark off from the
sacred cause of Government in general, a system which I
believed was bringing the name and idea of Government into
shame and hatred, and converting the thing from a necessity
and a blessing into a sheer curse to human kind.

For I am weak enough to entertain the idea that, if these
things be true—if justice be prostituted, personal liberty and
domestic peace undermined, law, where it cannot be used as
an engine of oppression, ignominiously thrust aside, and
Government, the minister and type of the Divinity, invested
with the characteristics of an opposite origin,—it is not for the
interests of order and conservation, even if truth and freedom
had no separate claims, that the practical and effective
encouragement of silent connivance should be given either to
the acts or to the agents. This policy, in the extravagant
development of it which I have stated, is a policy which,
when noiseless attempts at a remedy have failed, ought, on
the ground of its mere destructiveness, to be stripped, beneath
the public gaze; and this, too, before the strain it lays upon
human nature shall have forced it into some violent explosion....

* *Examination of the Official Neapolitan Reply*, 7 January 1852. *Gleanings*, [1879],
IV, 116–17.

Document 53. *Aberdeen on a pro-Austrian policy,*
29 *March* 1853*

[Aberdeen instructs Clarendon to suppress a sharp despatch
to Count Buol.] . . . I think the greatest misfortune of the
present day is our alienation from Austria. It is an entirely
new feature in our foreign policy, and deranges all our
calculations. Austria is a State with which I should have
thought it impossible to quarrel; and however desirable to be
on the best terms with France and Russia, is the only Power
on whose friendship I should have thought that we could confidently rely.

I fully admit that the irritation and hostility on the part of
Austria are most unreasonable, and that we may be justified
in shewing our resentment. But the most difficult task in
politicks is the exercise of forbearance, especially when we have
most reason to complain. We must make some allowance too,
for the recollection of past injuries, on the part of Austria,
which are probably not yet forgiven. If we add the attempt
on the life of the Emperor, the outbreak at Milan, and the
machinations of the Refugees, of which the centre is supposed to be in London, the irritation of the Austrian Government may be accounted for; and as all this however irrationally,
is connected with English policy, we are made, more or less,
responsible.

Our first object ought to be to convince the Austrian
Government of our sincerity, and to lead them to believe that
we have no object in view but their own real welfare.

* B.M. Add. MSS. 43,188, *Pte Aberdeen Papers*. Aberdeen to Clarendon,
29 March 1853.

XI. DERBY AND MALMESBURY, 1859

ITALY

25. MALMESBURY AND ITALY

[Lord Malmesbury, the new Foreign Secretary, had already served in that capacity during 1852–3 (*v. supra*, pp. 187–9). He emphasized the difference between his own and the Palmerston Government by filling vacant diplomatic posts with men of his own party;* but otherwise his policy did not differ much. "I assume", he said three years later, "that the general principles are the same, by which I mean that we wish always to support constitutional governments, and to support them and encourage them as much as possible; and the principle of non-interference is generally recognized now."† He was soon to illustrate the difficulty of reconciling "non-interference" with "the support" and "encouragement" of "constitutional Governments".

The documents subjoined shew admirably his attitude. **Doc. 54** is written after Victor Emmanuel, as King of Sardinia, had informed his Parliament that he would redress the wrongs of Italy. He was confident, of course, of the secret support of France. The document is a very mild version of the real sentiments of Malmesbury. "I can muster no patience towards that little conceited mischievous State now called 'Sardinia'" for whom "Europe should be deluged in blood".‡ Malmesbury suggested to Sardinia that a constitutional state owes obedience to the rule of law in its relations not only with its own subjects but with its neighbours. He followed this up by suggestions in Paris of a general disarmament. Count Rechberg said that if "England should give to Austria a formal guarantee of security against attack from France, Austria would agree to stop armaments". She would go to a Congress and there settle her difficulties with Sardinia.§ As England refused so extensive an obligation,

* This was the view of Vienna on whom Lord Augustus Loftus was imposed. The Austrian Ambassador in England was extremely unfavourable. Thus "I found him [Malmesbury] more mediocre and feeble than usual....I pronounced a monologue as usual." W.S.A. viii/55, Berichte aus England. From Apponyi, 9 February 1859.

† Diplomatic Service, Report of the Select Committee, [1861]. *A. & P.*, [1861], vi, 459, p. 199, § 1932.

‡ *Papers of 1st Earl Cowley*, [1928], ed. by Col. F. A. Wellesley, private letter, Malmesbury to Cowley, January 1859, p. 175.

§ W.S.A. viii/53, Weisungen nach England. Count Rechberg to Count Apponyi, 9 April 1859.

Austria lost patience, refused to disarm, and threatened Sardinia. Malmesbury, in **Doc. 55**, then invoked that interesting provision for mediation introduced by Clarendon into the protocols of the Treaty of Paris (1856). Austria declined and went to war. This result (as **Doc. 56** shews) caused Malmesbury to assume an attitude hardly consistent with neutrality or the sentiments of an exponent of arbitration. But in **Doc. 57** he recovers himself and shews a singular aversion from annexing new territory.

It is worth noting that the Neapolitan Government in 1852 suggested that Gladstone's *Letters* are "but a part of a covert scheme cherished by England for obtaining territorial acquisitions in the Mediterranean at the expense of the Two Sicilies". Gladstone replied: "The prevalent, and the increasingly prevalent, disposition of this country is against territorial aggrandisement." He added in 1878: "This salutary disposition was, in no small degree, perhaps, due to the steady policy and action of all the various Administrations between the peace of 1815, and the date of this Tract [1852]."* It will be seen that Lord Malmesbury pursued the same policy during 1859.

As soon as Malmesbury retired and Russell succeeded him, Palmerston wrote exultantly as follows: "How refreshing it must have been to the people of the Foreign Office to have to read two such despatches as yours to Bloomfield and Elliott after Malmesbury's milk and water." (22 June 1859.)†]

Document 54. *Malmesbury remonstrates with Sardinia,* 13 *January* 1859‡

The Telegraphic despatch which you have sent to this Office and the Public Journals give so nearly the same report of The King of Sardinia's Speech to His Chambers that Her Majesty's Government have no reason to doubt that these statements are correct.

Assuming them to be so, I cannot for a moment conceal from the Sardinian Government the apprehensions which that address has caused in Her Majesty's Government, while every subsequent hour has brought to them tidings from abroad indicating that the Public Mind shares deeply in those apprehensions.

Her Majesty's Government are surprised that the Sardinian

* *Gleanings*, [1879], IV, 131, 133 and note.
† G. & D. 22/20, *Pte Russell Papers*. Palmerston to Russell, 22 June 1859.
‡ Malmesbury to Sir James Hudson (Turin), No. 10, 13 January 1859, *F.O.* 167/105.

Government, by whose advice His Majesty's Speech was delivered, did not foresee the effect that it was likely to produce in a Country, so easily agitated as Italy has ever been by either her just or exaggerated hopes of changes in her internal policy.

The language uttered from the Sardinian Throne, if accurately reported by you, is calculated to excite those who are oppressed and those who indulge in impossible theories to look to Sardinia as the Champion of both and to trust to the Sword of Savoy for a realization of their desires.

None more than Her Majesty's Government sympathize with the wrongs which portions of the Italian People have endured on the part of their Rulers. Her Majesty's Government know them to be almost intolerable, but they are equally convinced that it is not by provoking the terrible curse of a European War that any part of Europe will acquire real freedom, or her people obtain happiness.

If a consequence so fatal to the prosperity of all Countries should arise as a war, I wish you to point out to the Sardinian Government the utter blindness as to its results in which we must all be involved.

The only certainty that Her Majesty's Government can foresee is, that considering the elements which it must upheave, its duration and its miseries will be prolonged to an incalculable period.

In a War so begun the Republicans of every possible hue, the dreamers of every impracticable theory, the exiled Pretenders to Thrones, and all in short who seek Gain, Power or Revenge, will expect to find their account.

If Sardinia believes that from such a struggle She will come forth in a more prosperous and honorable position than She occupies at present, Her Majesty's Government believe she will be utterly deceived in this deadly lottery.

England has always viewed in Sardinia the model for Europe of a young Constitutional State daily increasing in prosperity, as the fruit of her liberty so wisely granted by a Politic Sovereign, and so reasonably enjoyed by an intelligent and grateful People.

It was a sincere satisfaction to Her Majesty's Government equally felt by every successive Administration to point out Sardinia as a living argument to refute the statements of those who maintained that Constitutional States were impossible in Italy. The experiment has been tried and until now has vindicated those Principles of Civil and Religious liberty which both England and Sardinia represent.

But if Sardinia should unfortunately be the first to provoke by either imprudence or ambition a calamity which Providence has averted from the most important and richest territory of Europe for forty three years, Sardinia will show the World that a popular Government may be as unwise and as grasping as the single mind of an ignorant or despotic Ruler.

Such a consummation to a career so brilliantly begun as that of Sardinia would be most deeply deplored by Her Majesty's Government for the sake of Sardinia Herself. But for the interests of humanity in general Her Majesty's Government must be still more anxious, and you will frankly show Count Cavour the terrible responsibility of the Minister who unassailed by any Foreign State, and with no point of honor at stake, appears to invite a European War by addressing himself through his Sovereign to the suffering subjects of other Powers.

This imprudent act has however been committed, and in the panic which has followed Count Cavour may already read public opinion: Her Majesty's Government have nevertheless thought it a duty which they owe to Europe to express without reserve their sentiments of concern and anxiety at an address for which, not only to Her Allies, but to the God whom in that address She invokes, Sardinia is deeply responsible.

Document 55. *Malmesbury invites Austria to submit to Arbitration before going to war, 21 April 1859**

A meeting of the Cabinet was held as soon as possible after the receipt of Your Lordship's telegram of Yesterday after-

---

* Malmesbury to Loftus (Vienna), No. 282, 21 April 1859, *F.O.* 7/563.

noon, announcing that a summons to Sardinia to disarm had been despatched from Vienna in the previous night; and on its breaking up I desired Your Lordship by telegraph to acquaint Buol that Her Majesty's confidential Servants had determined to protest in the strongest manner against the step taken by Austria which they looked upon as inevitably involving the early breaking out of War in Italy.

By this precipitate step the Cabinet of Vienna forfeits all claim upon the support or sympathy of England whatever may be the consequences that may ensue from it, and Her Majesty's Government see only one means of averting the calamities with which Europe is threatened. That result might possibly be attained if the Austrian Government would declare its readiness to act on the principles to which its plenipotentiary acceded in the Conference of Paris of 1856, and H[er] M[ajesty]'s G[overnmen]t still cherish the hope that Austria may even now be induced according to the terms of the 23d Protocol of the 14th April to refer her differences with other Powers to the friendly mediation of an impartial and disinterested Ally.*

Document 56. *Malmesbury in Palmerstonian vein, 29 April, 2 May* 1859

i. *29 April* 1859.†

...I understand from them [your despatches] that you are convinced there is no treaty offensive and defensive between France and Russia. If so the war may be localized but you may as well let it be known as y[ou]r private opinion that we must be involved in it if it reaches the Baltic by blockades or other commercial annoyances.

* *A. & P.*, [1856], LXI, [2073], 143–8. Protocols of Conferences held at Paris relative to the General Treaty of Peace (1856). This protocol contains the discussion at which Cavour made himself very objectionable to Count Buol. But "the Plenipotentiaries do not hesitate to express, in the name of their Governments, the wish that States between which any serious misunderstanding may arise, should, before appealing to arms, have recourse, as far as circumstances might allow, to the good offices of a friendly Power".

† Malmesbury to Cowley (Paris), Private telegram of 29 April 1859, D. 1.5 p.m., *F.O.* 96/26.

ii. 2 *May* 1859.*

I should prefer entering into an agreement with Russia and France and Austria for the neutrality of the Adriatic and Baltic; if you cannot get that,—for East Shore of the Adriatic up to Trieste; if not the Adriatic,—at all events the Baltic. You will see at once that if the Baltic was made safe, we could, with comparative ease, keep out of the War—but if France or Russia act in a hostile manner in that sea, it will be hardly possible for us not to interfere.

Document 57. *Malmesbury disclaims an annexationist policy,*
1 *May* 1859†

Although a serious refutation of the speculation mentioned in your telegram of yesterday‡ that England looks to obtaining possession of Sicily as a result of the present commotion in the South of Europe, seems nearly as absurd as the imputation itself, it may nevertheless be desirable that you should be able to say on the direct authority of instructions from home that if all the great Powers of Europe were to combine to offer to this Country the possession of Sicily, the offer would be unhesitatingly declined.

* Malmesbury to Sir John Crampton (St Petersburgh), No. 181, 2 May 1859, *F.O.* 65/532. The sense of this document is considerably expanded in a private letter to Lord Cowley of 2 May 1859, Malmesbury, *Memoirs of an Ex-Minister*, [1885], 482.
† Malmesbury to Sir J. Crampton No. 182, 1 May 1859, *F.O.* 65/532.
‡ Sir J. Crampton to Malmesbury, No. 198, 30 April 1859, *F.O.* 65/535. "One of my Colleagues has told me in strict confidence that the Emperor of Russia intimated to him the suspicion that England had been playing a double game, and wished for war in Italy in hopes of obtaining Sicily for herself."

XII. PALMERSTON AND RUSSELL, 1859–63

ITALY

26. THE UNION OF NORTH ITALY AND NAPOLEON'S ANNEXATION OF NICE AND SAVOY

[The union of North Italy had become a possibility when Palmerston and Lord John Russell took office (18 June 1859). A week later Napoleon III and the Sardinians heavily defeated the Austrians at Solferino (24 June). On 8 July an armistice was signed, and on the 11th Napoleon made a preliminary peace with Austria at Villafranca without consulting the Sardinians. By this peace Napoleon held Austrian Lombardy in trust to deliver to Sardinia, which he very soon did. So much was gained. But it was intended to restore Parma, Modena and Tuscany to their detested rulers; and the Romagna was to go back to the Pope, who had so disgracefully misgoverned it. But none of the peoples of these areas intended to return to slavery. They all summoned assemblies, and began demanding the rule of the constitutional King of Sardinia, Victor Emmanuel. Russell, as **Doc. 58** shews, generally supported the idea that "consent of the governed" should be the principle for the rearrangement of North Italy. He and Palmerston were denounced as revolutionaries for taking this line, just as the latter had been for a similar Italian Policy in 1848. They were not popular with the Queen or their colleagues.* But the fact is, both men were now thoroughly convinced that it was more revolutionary to restore Lombardy to Austria or the princelets to the thrones of North Italy than to hand the territories over to Victor Emmanuel. For Victor Emmanuel at least had popular support. The times were full of peril, but on a balance of chances it was safer to back the peoples than to restore the kings. For the first might ensure peace, while the second must engender war.

Lombardy was annexed to Sardinia, but the fate of the rest of North Italy hung in the balance. The usual expedient of a European Congress was suggested, as a solution of these ills. But to a Congress few Powers were willing to agree. The Pope did not want it, because Napoleon III had inspired a pamphlet suggesting the reduction of his temporal estates to a minimum. Austria was hostile. So was Lord John Russell, for precisely opposite reasons,

* V. supra, pp. 163–5, 182.

as **Doc. 59** shews. He announced them in a dispatch full of historical allusions, after his manner. He decided against the intervention of England in any Congress on Italy likely to impose a settlement of the disputed areas, which was contrary to the will of the people inhabiting them. This attitude helped ultimately to unite all North Italy under the King of Sardinia. There remained only Venetia, which Austria retained, and the Romagna, which French troops continued to garrison.

But there was to be one excessively unpleasant incident for England. Napoleon agreed to the British proposal, formulated on 15 January 1860,* that the States of Central Italy should decide their destinies. But, whereas Lord John Russell wanted assemblies, he insisted on plebiscites, as the instruments of decision. Napoleon prevailed and the districts concerned voted by over-ruling majorities for union under the King of Sardinia (March 1860). The first Italian Parliament, including representatives from Parma, Modena and Tuscany, met at Turin in April 1860 only to find itself called on to discuss the cession of Savoy and Nice to France. Plebiscites were taken here in April and the vote was for union with France. Despite assertions to the contrary, the wish of the inhabitants of both areas was probably to be annexed to France. It was, however, the view of Lord John Russell and of Palmerston that the verdict of the plebiscites was secured by a trick. In this they were probably in error.† But no incident proved more harmful to Franco-British friendship in this era as this.

Palmerston and Russell had cause for their irritation. For the annexation of Savoy to France affected the treaty dispositions of Vienna in certain districts adjoining to Switzerland. It was, moreover, as Palmerston and Russell conceived, a flagrant breach of previous pledges. Even if it were possible to explain away the promises of 1859, there were others of an earlier date which could not be dismissed. Thus Derby, who was out of office and no friend to Russell and Palmerston, wrote: "we shall be quite justified in stating, if necessary, the positive assurances which we had from Louis Napoleon [in 1852].... He does not, however, deny these assurances, but rests his demand of Savoy on the readjustment which is taking place of the territorial limits of Northern Italy. The plea is futile enough; but it relieves him from the necessity of denying his former engagements, while it leaves him free, in his own mind, to dispense with them."‡

* These proposals are really anticipated by a private letter of Palmerston of 4 December 1859 to Persigny, v. *Cowley Papers*, ed. by F. A. Wellesley, [1928], 189–91. *V.* also Russell to Cowley, 15 January 1860, *F.O.* 27/1322, and from Cowley of 27 January 1860, *F.O.* 27/1332.

† Sarah Wambaugh, *Plebiscites*, [Carnegie Endowment, New York, 1920], 58–101, 370–725.

‡ Malmesbury, *Memoirs of an Ex-Minister*, [1885], 514. Private letter, Derby to Malmesbury, 5 March 1860.

Doc. 61 shews the British idea as to the nature of Napoleon's pledge in 1859. Matters came to a head when Napoleon made a violent attack on British policy to Cowley at a *levée*. This was on 6 March and provoked strong private remonstrances.* Russell made an excessively long remonstrance.† He also made a violent speech to the Commons openly expressing distrust of Napoleon on 26 March (Doc. 62). Palmerston told Flahault that he agreed with every word, knowing that he would report the interview to Napoleon. An acrimonious discussion took place about which much dispute has arisen. There does not seem any doubt that Palmerston said the Emperor's conduct rendered confidence impossible. Flahault then said that would mean war, and Palmerston answered that war would be accepted if the price of peace was toleration of the Emperor's misdeeds.‡ The breach between Palmerston and Napoleon was complete, and became a serious hindrance to their future joint action in Europe. Over a year later Palmerston told an Austrian agent that "he would like an alliance with us [Austria] more than any one". His judgment on Napoleon was not modified. "He continues to watch his [Napoleon's] progress with the same mistrust." He was "against a Congress which, he knows, Napoleon wants".§]

Document 58. *Lord John Russell on the independence of States, ? July* 1859‖

...The balance of power in Europe means in effect the independence of its several States. The preponderance of any one Power threatens and destroys this independence. But the Emperor Napoleon by his Milan proclamation, has declared that the "enemies" of the Emperor represent him as making war to aggrandize the territory of France.... The independence of States is never so secure as when the sovereign authority is supported by the attachment of the people.

J[OHN] RUSSELL.

* *Cowley Papers*, ed. by F. A. Wellesley, [1928], 200, refers to it but does not quote the dispatch. It makes clear that Russell replied to these "extraordinary and insolent terms" in a dispatch he directed "to be kept *out of the office*". The original account is in *Letters of Queen Victoria*, 1st Ser., [Cheap ed. 1908], III, 390–4.
† The most important is to Cowley, No. 288, 22 March 1860, *F.O.* 146/892.
‡ The two main authorities are Palmerston's note of the conversation at the time (27 March 1860), Ashley, *Life*, II, 190–2, and Flahault's report of what Palmerston told him, *Cowley Papers*, ed. by F. A. Wellesley, [1928], 202–3. *V.* also, Spencer Walpole, *Life of Lord John Russell*, [1889], II, 321; Malmesbury, *Memoirs of an Ex-Minister*, [1885], 517–8; Vitzthum von Eckstaedt, *St Petersburg and London*, [1887], II, 52–4.
§ W.S.A. VIII/62, Berichte aus England. From Apponyi, 13 July 1862.
‖ No date, but after the Milan Proclamation of Napoleon III, *F.O.* 96/24.

Document 59. *Lord John Russell gives a history of British Policy at Congresses since* 1815, 15 *November* 1859*

It may be useful at the present moment to recall to mind the conduct which Great Britain has pursued since the peace of 1815, both when she passively abstained from, and when she actively participated in European affairs.

In 1818 pretensions were put forward by some of the Great Powers to regulate and direct the internal affairs of all other countries.

In 1821 these pretensions were put in practice at the Congresses of Troppau and Laybach. A large Austrian army was sent to Naples in order to change the internal government of the Two Sicilies and 40,000 Austrian troops were stationed there in order to suppress free institutions in that Kingdom.

Against the principle upon which this aggression was based, Lord Castlereagh, in the name of Great Britain, protested.

In 1823 another interference was sanctioned by the Congress of Verona in the case of Spain, whose form of internal government was not agreeable to the theories of the Great Powers.

The Duke of Wellington went to Verona, but remonstrated. Mr Canning declared that the principles laid down by the allies struck at the root of the British Constitution.

Thus far England did not concur and protested. But in 1825 England acknowledged two or more of the Republics of South America, and the Northern Powers in their turn protested.

In 1827 was signed the Treaty between Great Britain, France and Russia which led very speedily to the independence of Greece.

In 1830 Belgium rose against Holland, and Great Britain was active, both in the Cabinet and on the sea, in concerting the measures which led to the establishment of the independence of Belgium.

* Russell to Cowley, No. 498, 15 November 1859, *F.O.* 27/1287.

Thus in these five instances the policy of Great Britain appears to have been directed by a consistent principle. She uniformly withheld her consent to acts of intervention by force to alter the internal government of other nations; she uniformly gave her countenance and, if necessary, her aid, to consolidate the de facto Governments which arose in Europe or in America.

There is every reason why we should pursue a similar course in regard to the affairs of Italy; namely by withholding our assent to any measures of intervention by force to regulate the internal government of Italian States; and by using our influence to maintain and consolidate any regular and orderly governments which the Italians may form for themselves.

[It is of interest to compare the above with Lord Palmerston's view of ten years before, **Doc. 60**, and also with that of four years later, **Doc. 85**.]

Document 60. *Palmerston's views on a Congress,* 6 *March* 1849*

This notion of a European Congress to settle all pending matters and to modify the Treaty of Vienna so as to adapt it to the interests and necessities of the present time sounds well enough to the ear, but would be difficult and somewhat dangerous in its execution. First in regard to pending matters, some of them relate to parties who did not sign the Treaty of Vienna and who perhaps might not chuse to submit their affairs to the decision of the new Congress; and the new Congress would not have the power and assumed right which recent conquest vested in the Congress of 1814–1815. At that time all Europe may be said to have been occupied by the armies of the allies. Nations counted for nothing, sovereigns submitted to the decisions of the Congress, and its resolves became easily law. But nowadays sovereigns count for little, and nations will submit to no external dictation without the actual employment of overruling force; and a Congress

* G. P. Gooch, *Later Correspondence of Lord John Russell*, [1925], I, 351–2. Palmerston to Russell, 6 March 1849.

might not find it easy to give effect to its resolutions without establishing a European *gendarmerie*. Then in regard to France, the notion of modifying the Treaty of Vienna implies some intention of asking for cessions to France which the other Powers would not be disposed to consent to. If the modifications in question related to the past only, and were to be stipulations giving a European sanction to violations heretofore committed of the Treaty of Vienna, such as what has been done about Poland and Cracow, neither England nor France would much like to give their sanction to things which they have protested against and condemned. If the proposed modifications relate to future changes of still existing arrangements, it seems to me that such a chapter had better not be opened. On the whole therefore I should be for giving a civil but declining answer, pointing out the many difficulties which would arise in such a course.

Document 61. *The British view of French pledges of disinterestedness in respect to Savoy, 4 July 1859**

I have afforded Count Walewski an opportunity of giving me as much information as he might choose, respecting the intentions attributed to The Emperor of annexing Savoy to France, to which Capt[ai]n Harris despatch No. 4 of the 1st inst[ant] forwarded by this Messenger, relates.

I regret to say that His Excellency's language was not over satisfactory. He stated, indeed, that he could give me the positive assurance that there was no understanding whatever upon the subject between France and Sardinia, but he did not deny that the question had been more than once discussed, and that The Emperor had entertained the idea that if Sardinia was to become a large Italian Kingdom, it was not unreasonable to expect that she should make territorial concessions elsewhere.†

I said that I trusted that The Emperor for his own sake, and

---

* Cowley to Russell, No. 101, 4 July 1859, *F.O.* 27/1299.

† A good deal of information as to how far pledges were given in 1859 will be found in the Debate in the Lords, on 23 April 1860, quoted in *Cowley Papers*, ed. by F. A. Wellesley, [1928], 203–6; cp. *Hans. Deb.*, 3rd Ser., CLVII, 2112–39.

for the sake of his reputation with Europe would abandon any such idea of territorial aggrandisement, if he still harboured it. I called to Count Walewski's recollection the suspicions which had been excited in Europe on the breaking out of the present war as to The Emperor's intentions suspicions which had been somewhat allayed by His Majesty's posterior proclamations, but I ventured to predict, that if after his solemn declarations that he had no selfish interests in the war, His Majesty were now to endeavour to obtain an increase of territory, every Government would condemn him, while if he wished for peace, he might seriously compromise the chances of an early arrangement. If His Majesty desired to recover the confidence of Europe, let him beware of all attempts at aggrandisement.

Count Walewski replied that as far as his personal opinion was concerned, he agreed with me, but there were others who considered that France ought to be indemnified for the expenses of the war. I said that I was sorry to hear this, for that I had hoped that the same course would have been followed as at the end of the Crimean war, when it was agreed that no indemnities should be asked of Russia by the belligerents. If, however, Austria was to be required to add a pecuniary compensation to the territorial concessions she would probably be called upon to make, I saw but little hope of an early peace. The fact also that Austria was so much impoverished that she could hardly pay her own expenses, ought not to be lost sight of.

Count Walewski, however, contended that the cases of Russia and Austria were very different, and he went on to argue that the expenses incurred by France, ought to be paid in some way or other; if not by Austria, by Sardinia and Italy in general, and if this could not be effected in money, it might be taken into account whenever the territorial distribution of Italy should come under consideration.

Although I feel persuaded that Count Walewski is not favourable to any project for the annexation of Savoy to France, his language leads me to apprehend that some attempt of the kind may be made.

Document 62. *Lord John Russell on the cession of Nice and Savoy,* 26 *March* 1860*

. . . I do not follow the right hon. Gentleman [Mr. Horsman] in his depreciation of the character of the Emperor of the French; but it is obvious that the course he has pursued, as I expected, and as I said from the first, frankly and fairly to the French Government, has already produced a great deal of distrust. I believe myself that if when the war was begun last year the Emperor of the French and the King of Sardinia had said openly to the world, "The King of Sardinia has to sustain a great war against the empire of Austria; he cannot sustain it alone; the Emperor of the French has determined to help him, but the Emperor of the French expects, and has stipulated by treaty with the King of Sardinia, that if the territories of that King are very much increased in Italy that portion of the territories of the King close neighbouring on France and on the French side of the Alps shall be given to the Emperor of the French"—if that bargain, not so unlike many others which have occurred in the history of Europe, had been openly declared, I will not say what amount of indignation would have been entertained in regard to it; but I must say, looking to the circumstances under which the question has been brought forward, and with which it has been attended, especially after the declaration of the Sardinian Government that they would neither sell, exchange, nor surrender this territory, the course that has been pursued has produced great distrust in this country, and I believe it will produce great distrust all over Europe. Sir, I very much doubt whether strong Resolutions, or even strong language, on the part of this House would have produced any great effect upon the ultimate issue of this affair. We have been told that the passionate language held in this House made it necessary for the French nation to insist on their Government doing what has been done. That is rather a pretext than a true representation. It is evident that it is a plausible pre-

* *Hans. Deb.*, 3rd Ser., CLVII, 1257–8, 26 March 1860.

text to say, "We should have negotiated or conceded this point, but the insulting language used is such that our honour is at stake and we can no longer give way." I say that is a plausible pretext; but, be this as it may, there has been declared from the beginning of these discussions, immediately after the first debate that took place in the House of Lords—and the declaration was carried by *The Times* newspaper all over Europe—that, although strong language might be used on the subject, there was no intention of going to war on account of it. The right hon. Gentleman the Member for Stroud (Mr. Horsman) said in one of his speeches that we might be quite sure no man in this House wished to go to war for Savoy; now, if there had been entire liberty to Her Majesty's Government to negotiate on this subject—although certainly they would not have threatened war—although they would still less have pledged the Government and the country to go to war, still it is a different thing, not saying anything on the subject, and declaring from the commencement of the negotiations that whatever may be the issue we will not go to war. Sir, my opinion as I declared it in July and January I have no objection now to repeat—that such an act as the annexation of Savoy is one that will lead a nation so warlike as the French to call upon its Government from time to time to commit other acts of aggression; and, therefore, I do feel that, however we may wish to live on the most friendly terms with the French Government, and certainly I do wish to live on the most friendly terms with that Government—we ought not to keep ourselves apart from the other nations of Europe, but that, when future questions may arise—as future questions may arise—we should be ready to act with others and to declare, always in the most moderate and friendly terms, but still firmly, that the settlement of Europe, the peace of Europe is a matter dear to this country, and that settlement and that peace cannot be assured if it is liable to perpetual interruption—to constant fears, to doubts and rumours with respect to the annexation of this one country, or the union and junction of that other; but that the Powers of Europe, if they wish to maintain that peace, must respect each other's rights, must respect each other's limits, and, above all, restore and not disturb that commercial confidence which is the result of peace, which tends to peace, and which ultimately forms the happiness of nations.

27. ITALY AND GARIBALDI

(a) THE PRE-GARIBALDIAN PHASE, 1857-9

[The Naples question had two distinct phases. The first was due to the situation created by the misgovernment of King "Bomba" after 1848, and in no way alleviated by his successor Francis II (1859), whom Palmerston called "Bombalino". The second was due to that created by Garibaldi's arrival in Sicily. During the first phase Palmerston considered the situation so bad as to justify foreign intervention in the internal affairs of Naples (v. **Doc. 63**). Clarendon (v. **Doc. 64**) used language of extraordinary violence to the Austrian Ambassador, and declared England would not lift a finger to save the tyrant. Thus the indignation of Prime Minister and Foreign Secretary was as great as that of Gladstone* and led equally to revolutionary conclusions. It had led in fact already to strong action. In October 1856 the British and French Legations had been withdrawn from Naples, because that Government had disregarded their remonstrances as to the ill-treatment of political prisoners and other abuses. Russia had remonstrated at this step on the ground that "to endeavour to obtain from the King of Naples concessions as regards the internal government of his States by threats, or by a menacing demonstration, is a violent usurpation of his authority, an attempt to govern in his stead; it is an open declaration of the right of the strong over the weak".† Now this is a case for intervention upon humanitarian grounds, and raises a problem still hotly debated by jurists.‡ What is interesting, however, is that this problem was raised during the first period, before any question of Garibaldi's going to Naples had arisen. It is also interesting that Clarendon had already decided to do nothing to prevent "the chastisement of the crimes" of King Bomba. That was a stage on the way to applauding the venture of Garibaldi, and to recognizing Victor Emmanuel as King of Italy.]

* V. supra, pp. 191–5.
† T. Martin, Life of Prince Consort, [1877], III, 510–11, n.
‡ V. infra, pp. 227–8.

Document 63. *Palmerston on the King of Naples,*
17 *March* 1857*

The Two Governments might have objected to withdraw
their Missions from Naples upon the ground that the King of
Naples governs like a Tyrant, but as the Two Gov[ernmen]ts
have taken that step and have broken off diplomatic Relations with Naples they would render themselves perfectly
ridiculous if they sent their Missions back without having
obtained some more changes in the Neapolitan system.

P[ALMERSTON] 17/3/57.

Document 64. *Clarendon on the King of Naples,*
2 *January* 1858†

[After Apponyi, the Austrian Ambassador, had referred to
Muratist plots, Clarendon spoke thus to him.] I hold the
King of Naples to be the most execrable monster who ever
sat upon a throne. I find him not only the shame of humanity
but also that of his own class of sovereigns, and I shall not
raise a finger to prevent the just chastisement of his crimes
coming to him. We shall not give a coin or a man or express
a wish to defend him. Certainly we should not look kindly on
a Murat on the throne of Naples but, when you add up the
account, anything is better than what now exists and I quite
understand that these poor Neapolitans want to be rid of him
at all costs. [Apponyi says] I could only laugh, shrug my
shoulders and say passion blinded him. [Clarendon replies]
...They are five centuries behind all Europe in education,
roads, railways, posts. Oh it is a detestable government and
it is all one to me if they change it.

* Minute by Palmerston, 17 March 1857, on Cowley to Clarendon, No. 422,
16 March 1857, *F.O.* 27/1192.
† W.S.A. viii/50, Berichte aus England. From Apponyi, No. 1. B., 2 January
1858.

(b) THE SECOND OR GARIBALDIAN PHASE, MAY TO NOVEMBER 1860

[Russell attained office on 18 June 1859, just before Solferino was fought. Italy was the one subject of foreign policy about which Russell was better informed than Palmerston. Like him he was wholly in favour of a strong and compact Kingdom of Italy, formed by uniting Florence and Modena to Piedmont. It "would I believe, be an excellent thing for that mechanical contrivance, the balance of power. At all events it is enough for us that the Tuscan people wish it, and that there is no strong reason against it." But he saw no advantage in a union of all Italy. "I dare say the dreamers wish to unite Naples and Sicily, and make a kingdom of the whole of Italy. But that is wild and foolish. It would make a despotism instead of a free government, an unwieldy power instead of a compact one, and it would increase tenfold the European difficulties."* He was very anxious to make the King of Naples reform his Government, he was far from wanting to take his Kingdom from him. He thought of giving him half the Romagna, and Piedmont the other half. Palmerston himself held the same views at this time. He wished the Kingdom of the Two Sicilies to be well instead of badly governed. He did not wish it to form part of a united Italy. He thought it better for the interests of England that it should remain separate, for, in the case of war between France and England, it would "side, at least by its neutrality, with the strongest Naval Power".†

Garibaldi was the active agency which induced Russell and Palmerston to acquiesce in the absorption of Naples and Sicily in a united Italy. Russell at least admitted that the example of the revolution of 1688 justified the deposition of sovereigns for misgovernment. When the Queen wrote that she "could not make out what the doctrines of the Revolution of 1688 have to do with this", he explained at length.‡ The correspondence lasted four months and concluded with special reference to Naples. Russell compared her King to the last Stuart, and the King of Sardinia to William III. He implied that a revolution was at hand. "Of course the King of Sardinia has no right to assist the people of the Two Sicilies, unless he was asked to do so, as the Prince of Orange was asked by the best men in England to overthrow the tyranny of James II—an attempt which has received the applause of all our great public writers and [with a significant thrust at his German

* G. P. Gooch, *Later Correspondence of Lord John Russell*, [1925], II, 238–9, 25 August 1859.

† *Letters of Queen Victoria*, 1st Ser., [Cheap ed. 1908], III, 428. Palmerston to the Queen, 10 January 1861. He admits having held this view in the summer of 1860.

‡ G. P. Gooch, *Later Correspondence of Lord John Russell*, [1925], II, 253–5, 12 January 1860. *V. Letters of Queen Victoria*, 1st Ser., III, Chap. XXIX, *passim*.

sovereign] is the origin of our present form of Government."
Russell then wrote to the Queen, "he cannot see anything morally
wrong in [the King of Piedmont] giving aid to an insurrection in
the Kingdoms of Naples and Sicily. But he admits that to do so
for the sake of making new acquisitions would be criminal" (30
April 1860).

Before Garibaldi ever started on his expedition, Russell was
prepared to applaud it. Palmerston had an even more advanced
view, as **Doc. 65** shews. A day before Garibaldi entered
Palermo with his red-shirted "Thousand", Palmerston suggested
that Sicily might be united to Sardinia if the Sicilians wished it.
But he drew the line at Naples. Napoleon drew the line at
Sicily. By the end of July he was thoroughly alarmed at Garibaldi's progress. Sicily was already Garibaldi's by a conquest
which seemed miraculous. Napoleon feared a Garibaldian descent
on the mainland which would encourage the King of Sardinia to
attack Austrian Venetia. He therefore instructed his Ambassador
to suggest that England and France "should not remain passive
spectators" and "that the Commanders of our naval forces
should at once be authorised to declare to General Garibaldi that
they had orders to prevent him from crossing the Strait".

The proposal was not in itself unreasonable. Napoleon thought
he had done enough for Italy. He was threatened by Prussia on
the Rhine, and by Austria from Venetia. French troops were
holding the Romagna, and he did not want to be embarrassed by
Garibaldi's marching on Naples and Rome. Palmerston too feared
the results of further Garibaldian enterprise. Garibaldi's invasion
of the mainland might upset the balance of power and destroy the
condition of peace which was slowly being attained in North
Italy. The new King, Francisco, in his terror at Garibaldi's
success, was promising all sorts of constitutional reforms at
Naples. A mild but firm intervention by France and England
might confine Garibaldi to Sicily and confirm King Francisco in
the path of virtue.

The decision to support Napoleon in preventing the Gari-
baldians from crossing to the mainland had almost been taken by the
British Cabinet. But Cavour, who had some inkling of what was
going on, sent a warning to Lacaita in London. This distinguished
Italian exile, who had aided Gladstone in exposing the horrors
of Neapolitan prisons, was now begged by Cavour to intervene.
He was a friend of the Russell family, and managed to get a private
interview with Lady John Russell, who was ill in bed. She sent a
message to her husband, who was actually closeted with the
French Ambassador, discussing the details of the Franco-British
scheme to prevent Garibaldi from crossing the Straits. Lord John
was lured from the French Ambassador to his wife's bedside.
There he was assailed by the entreaties of a sick woman and by the

passionate eloquence of Lacaita. If Garibaldi crossed to Calabria, Italy was made. If Lord John prevented him, he would be for ever hated by the Liberals of Europe.* The great Liberal listened, was moved, and gave way.

It is certain at least that on 23 July Lord John tried to send a private message to Garibaldi that he "ought to be content with the whole of Sicily and not stir any further the fire of...insurrection".†
It is also certain that the Cabinet on the 25th came to a decision which greatly surprised the French, and this "on Lord John's recommendation".‡ He informed Cowley at Paris that the Cabinet had decided that "no case had been made out for a departure on their part from their general principle of non-intervention. That the force of Garibaldi was not in itself sufficient to overthrow the Neapolitan Monarchy. If the navy, army and the people of Naples were attached to the King, Garibaldi would be defeated; if on the contrary, they were disposed to welcome Garibaldi, our interference would be an intervention in the internal affairs of the Neapolitan Kingdom." After casting doubts on the sincerity of the King of Naples in his constitution-alism Lord John ended: "If France chuses to interfere alone, we should merely disapprove her course, and protest against it. In our opinion the Neapolitans ought to be the masters, either to reject or to receive Garibaldi." This dispatch, dated 26 July, settled the course of British policy, prevented France from inter-fering, and allowed Garibaldi to pursue his glorious march to Naples.

Doc. 66, which is here given under date of 29 August, repeats the phrases of this dispatch of 26 July. The line taken in **Doc. 67** moreover shews that England was not unfriendly to Austrian rule in Venetia, and still not wholly friendly to a union of both Naples and Sicily with the now enlarged dominion of Victor Emmanuel in North Italy. But Lord John's hostility to the King of Naples was extreme. "I suppose", he wrote to our Minister at Naples, "that Garibaldi, if not killed or wounded, will succeed at Naples. In that case you must suspend your functions and await instructions. But do not follow the King to Gaeta or any other place where he may lay his false head on his

---

* G. M. Trevelyan, *Garibaldi and the Making of Italy*, [1911], 105–9, and App. A, 315, which seem to prove the authenticity of the tale.

† G. P. Gooch, *Later Correspondence of Lord John Russell*, [1925], II, 265, Russell to Elliot, 23 July 1860.

‡ Spencer Walpole, *Life of Lord John Russell*, [1889], II, 324. Lord John in his *Selections from Speeches...and from Despatches...*, [1870], II, 224, does not admit the Lacaita incident, but this is intelligible. There is no letter from Palmerston at the critical date, but he and the rest of the Cabinet were much preoccupied with the Syrian question, in which they had refused to join France in a military expedi-tion. It was therefore intelligible that they accepted the advice not to join in a naval enterprise with France.

uneasy pillow"* (6 August). A month later to the very day, the much abused monarch fled from Naples to Gaeta. For the Garibaldian troops had landed on the mainland on 19 August and were threatening the capital. Twenty hours after the King had left, Garibaldi with half a dozen redshirts entered Naples. He defied the guns of the forts and received the surrender of six thousand armed men. Here was a living proof of Palmerston's doctrine that "opinions are stronger than armies". Here Russell was justified. "If the King of the Two Sicilies had not been misled by bad advisers, Garibaldi could not, with 2000 men, have overthrown the Monarchy" (24 October).

On 15 October Garibaldi, who had become dictator, signed a decree, transferring the whole heritage to the King of Sardinia. "I decree that the Two Sicilies, who owe their redemption to Italian blood and who elected me freely as Dictator, shall form part of Italy, one and indivisible, with its constitutional King Victor Emmanuel." On 21 October plebiscites in Sicily and Naples endorsed this transfer by immense majorities. Meanwhile Victor Emmanuel himself had taken a hand, his army had advanced into South Italy, his fleet had bombarded the poor King of Naples at Gaeta. On 26 October Garibaldi met Victor Emmanuel in the Abruzzi, and saluted him as King of Italy. On 8 November Victor Emmanuel received in Naples the formal decision of the plebiscites and assumed the sovereignty of the Two Sicilies. Garibaldi was still at his side. On 9 November a British ship sailed from the Bay of Naples. Garibaldi was on board and was leaving for his solitary home on the rocky isle of Caprera. He was poorer than when he had left it. All honours had been refused, a dowry for his daughter, a castle, an estate and a Dukedom. But he carried with him a seed bag of corn for his farm, his only reward for making Victor Emmanuel King of Italy.]

Document 65. *Palmerston on Garibaldi and Sicily,*
26 *May* 1860†

I conceive that it is the Interest of England and therefore the object of the Policy of the English Gov[ernmen]t that Sicily should remain attached to Naples forming with Naples one Monarchy, but that cannot be expected unless the Kingdom of the Two Sicilies is better governed than it has

* G. P. Gooch, *Later Correspondence of Lord John Russell*, [1925], II, 266, Russell to Elliot, 6 August 1860. At the end of the month Palmerston was writing—"we expect every Day to hear of Bombalino's Flight from Naples". G. & D. 22/21, *Pte Russell Papers*. Palmerston to Russell, 31 August 1860.

† Note by Palmerston, 26 May 1860, *F.O.* 96/26, on Cowley to Russell, No. 611, 21 May 1860, *F.O.* 27/1338.

hitherto been—If Garibaldi succeeds it is probable that Sicily will declare itself separated from Naples and united to Sardinia. That union would be very difficult in its practical and permanent working, but neither England nor France would do well to endeavour to constrain the will of the Sicilians on such a Question.*

P[ALMERSTON] 26/5/60.

Document 66. *Lord John Russell declines to interfere with Garibaldi in Naples, 29 August* 1860†

...The substance [of a letter read to me by M. de Jancourt] appears to have been the same as that of Monsieur Thouvenel's conversations with you, and it is not of vital importance whether the interference suggested was to prevent Garibaldi from landing in Neapolitan territory, or from invading Roman territory. In either case forcible interference is suggested in the internal affairs of Italy, and to such forcible interference Her Majesty's Government strongly object.

Her Majesty's Government do not deny that the consequences may be serious, but in their opinion the Emperor of the French and the King of Sardinia may avert the worst of those consequences by refraining from any attack on the Venetian frontier of the Empire of Austria....

It appears to Her Majesty's Government that this course is clear and simple; namely that the Italians should be allowed to maintain or to change the Governments of Naples and Sicily, and of Rome, according to their wishes, but that France should discourage an attack upon Venetia by Sardinia, for France is bound to maintain Sardinia in the possession of Lombardy, and therefore the contest could not be an equal one, and it must also be borne in mind that if, Sardinia being worsted in the war, France were to come to her assistance, it is possible that the German Powers might move to the assistance of Austria, and that thus the War

* A much longer argument on these lines is in Russell to Cowley (Paris), No. 555, 4 June 1860, *F.O.* 27/1325.

† Russell to Cowley (Paris), No. 833, 29 August 1860, *F.O.* 146/907.

might assume European dimensions. Austria, on the other hand, cannot be again permitted to occupy and govern Naples and the Roman States without a renewal of the miseries of the last forty years for Italy, and a prospect of disturbance of the peace of Europe.

Document 67. *Lord John Russell defends the right of the Neapolitans to change their Government,* 21 *August* 1860*

In reply to the enquiries made by Count Rechberg and reported in your despatch No. 19 of the 9th instant, I will give you, as far as the present uncertain aspect of affairs in Italy admits, an answer to Count Rechberg's questions.

The project of Italian Unity has found great favour among high and low in Italy. The reason why Italy has long been merely a geographical term is supposed to be found in its division into separate states. The wish for independence which has long prevailed is therefore now connected with a wish for Unity.

Her Majesty's Government are alive to the dangers which endeavours to accomplish that Unity may produce by disturbing political relations between other States exciting national ambition among the Italians and leading to events which might injuriously alter the existing Balance of Power in Europe.

Her Majesty's Government have on these grounds urged the King of Sardinia to use his influence with General Garibaldi to induce that chief to refrain from invading the Kingdom of Naples.

But they are convinced if the King of Naples possesses the attachment of his people, he will run no risk from Garibaldi's incursion, even supported by the cry for Unity.

If on the other hand the affections and confidence of his Neapolitan subjects are alienated from him, and if the Neapolitan nation desire to form part of a united Kingdom of Italy, Her Majesty's Government would not feel justified in attempting to impose upon them a Government in which

* Russell to Fane (Vienna), No. 9, 21 August 1860, *F.O.* 7/587.

they can have no confidence, and under which they can enjoy no security. But even if all Italy comprising more than twenty millions of Inhabitants were formed into one Kingdom, Her Majesty's Government would see in that change no reason for any further aggrandizement of France.

In any future European war Italy thus enlarged would be free to join France, or to unite with the adversaries of France or to remain neutral. But Her joining in any coalition against France would not be probable unless her independence were threatened by French ambition.

Her Majesty's Government therefore would oppose any further annexation of Italian Territory to France on the pretence of Danger to France by the incorporation of Italy into one state.

It is impossible however not to fear that Italy, formed into one Kingdom comprising Naples, Sicily and the States of the Pope, in addition to the present Dominions of the King of Sardinia might threaten the position of Austria in Venetia, and any menace of this kind might be supported by discontent and even by insurrection in Venice, and in the Italian Towns in the Province of Venetia.

Her Majesty's Government would discourage as much as possible any such aggressive tendency, and would use all their influence at Paris to dissuade the Emperor of the French from assisting Sardinia in an aggressive war against Austria.

More than this Her Majesty's Government cannot engage to do. They are persuaded that Austria is more than a match for Italy singlehanded, and they do not believe that unless other complications arise the Emperor of the French will incur the cost of blood and treasure which would be the certain result of his participation in a fresh war in Italy. Nor can they think it probable that the King of Sardinia would lightly engage singlehanded in an enterprize, the end of which would be doubtful and the Dangers of which would be certain.

(c) THE THIRD OR POST-GARIBALDIAN PHASE, THE RECOGNITION OF REVOLUTION, OCTOBER 1860

[Before Garibaldi actually set out for Caprera, but after he had saluted Victor Emmanuel as King of Italy, England took two diplomatic decisions of great importance. The Russian and the French Emperors had expressed their displeasure at Victor Emmanuel's proceedings by withdrawing their Ministers from his court. The Prince Regent of Prussia expressed strong disapproval of his actions. At this critical moment Lord John Russell came out with his famous dispatch of 27 October, printed here as **Doc. 68**. This, in effect, justified the proceedings both of Garibaldi and of Victor Emmanuel in language so bold and on principles apparently so revolutionary as to stagger the world of diplomacy. The dispatch was published at once so that the whole world saw the discomfiture of the pundits of reaction. They saw also that England intended to recognize Victor Emmanuel as King of Italy at the earliest possible moment.*

The authorship is undoubtedly that of Russell. The arguments about the revolution of 1688 and the quotations from Vattel had been employed by Lord John in his correspondence with the Queen, ten months before.† But the principles that the Neapolitans had won the right to choose their own King, and that the British Government supported them, were fully concurred in by Palmerston.

Doc. 69 refers to an incident which is as obscure as the first is renowned. It has always been held that England's influence in promoting Italian unity was moral not actual. Here we have definite proof that Palmerston warned off Spain from armed interference in Italy by a threat of force. This transaction, though hidden from the public, was well known to diplomatists. It probably contributed to prevent Napoleon III from interfering by force to relieve King Francisco at Gaeta. The actual aid rendered by England at the end of October was, therefore, material as well as moral.

Lord John Russell remained throughout his period of office a warm friend of Italy. His friendship took unconventional ways of expressing itself. On one occasion Count Apponyi, the Austrian

---

* The recognition actually took place on 30 March 1861, after the opening of the first Italian Parliament. Napoleon III recognized Victor Emmanuel on 25 June.

† *V.* two letters of Lord John Russell to Queen Victoria, 11 January 1860, and her reply; and two of 30 April and her reply. *Letters of Queen Victoria*, 1st Ser., [Cheap ed. 1908], III, 383–4, 397–8. Spencer Walpole in his *Life of Lord John Russell*, [1889], II, 327, finds the arguments only in a dispatch of nearly *eight weeks before*.

Minister, admired a handsome stick that Lord John carried. "I am glad you like it," said Lord John with a quick upward look, "it belonged once to Garibaldi." On another occasion the whole diplomatic *corps* were entertained by Russell's brother, the Duke of Bedford, at Woburn Place. Apponyi's son, who was in attendance, could not find his hat as he was leaving. Russell said: "I'll give you one." He brought out one of his own, fitted it on to the young man's head, crushing it down. "There," said he, "I hope it will get some good liberal ideas into your head."* The same unconventional style is visible in the dispatch of 27 October 1860.]

Document 68. *Lord John Russell recognizes the Garibaldian Revolution in Naples and Sicily, 27 October* 1860†

It appears that the late proceedings of the King of Sardinia have been strongly disapproved of by several of the principal Courts of Europe. The Emperor of the French, on hearing of the invasion of the Papal States by the army of General Cialdini, withdrew his minister from Turin, expressing at the same time the opinion of the Imperial Government in condemnation of the invasion of the Roman territory.

The Emperor of Russia has, we are told, declared in strong terms his indignation at the entrance of the army of the King of Sardinia into the Neapolitan territory, and has withdrawn his entire Mission from Turin.

The Prince Regent of Prussia has also thought it necessary to convey to Sardinia a sense of his displeasure; but he has not thought it necessary to remove the Prussian Minister from Turin.

After these diplomatic acts, it would scarcely be just to Italy, or respectful to the other Great Powers of Europe, were the Government of Her Majesty any longer to withhold the expression of their opinion.

In doing so, however, Her Majesty's Government have no intention to raise a dispute upon the reasons which have

* These two anecdotes were told to Professor Temperley by Count Alexander Apponyi, who was at that time chargé d'affaires to his father in London. In Spencer Walpole, *Life of Lord John Russell*, [1889], II, 329, we learn that Garibaldi exchanged sticks with Russell on his visit to London in 1864.

† Lord J. Russell to Sir J. Hudson, 27 October 1860. Russell, *Selections from Speeches...and from Despatches...*, [1870], II, 328–32, *A. & P.*, [1861], LXVII, [2757], 241–3.

been given, in the name of the King of Sardinia, for the invasion of the Roman and Neapolitan States. Whether or no the Pope was justified in defending his authority by means of foreign levies; whether the King of the Two Sicilies, while still maintaining his flag at Capua and Gaeta, can be said to have abdicated—are not the arguments upon which Her Majesty's Government propose to dilate.

The large questions which appear to them to be at issue are these:—Were the people of Italy justified in asking the assistance of the King of Sardinia to relieve them from Governments with which they were discontented? and was the King of Sardinia justified in furnishing the assistance of his arms to the people of the Roman and Neapolitan States?

There appear to have been two motives which have induced the people of the Roman and Neapolitan States to have joined willingly in the subversion of their Government. The first of these was, that the Governments of the Pope and the King of the Two Sicilies provided so ill for the administration of justice, the protection of personal liberty and the general welfare of their people, that their subjects looked forward to the overthrow of their rulers as a necessary preliminary to all improvement in their condition.

The second motive was, that a conviction had spread since the year 1849, that the only manner in which Italians could secure their independence of foreign control was by forming one strong Government for the whole of Italy. The struggle of Charles Albert in 1848, and the sympathy which the present King of Sardinia has shown for the Italian cause, have naturally caused the association of the name of Victor Emmanuel with the single authority under which the Italians aspire to live.

Looking at the question in this view, Her Majesty's Government must admit that the Italians themselves are the best judges of their own interests.

That eminent jurist Vattel, when discussing the lawfulness of the assistance given by the United Provinces to the Prince of Orange when he invaded England, and overturned the throne of James II, says, "The authority of the Prince of Orange had doubtless an influence on the deliberations of the States-General, but it did not lead them to the commission of an act of injustice; for when a people from good reasons take up arms against an oppressor, it is but an act of justice and generosity to assist brave men in the defence of their liberties."

Therefore, according to Vattel, the question resolves itself into this:—Did the people of Naples and of the Roman States take up arms against their Governments for good reasons?

Upon this grave matter Her Majesty's Government hold that the people in question are themselves the best judges of their own affairs. Her Majesty's Government do not feel justified in declaring that the people of Southern Italy had not good reasons for throwing off their allegiance to their former Governments; Her Majesty's Government cannot, therefore, pretend to blame the King of Sardinia for assisting them. There remains, however, a question of fact. It is asserted by the partizans of the fallen Governments that the people of the Roman States were attached to the Pope, and the people of the Kingdom of Naples to the Dynasty of Francis II, but that Sardinian Agents and foreign adventurers have by force and intrigue subverted the thrones of those Sovereigns.

It is difficult, however, to believe, after the astonishing events that we have seen, that the Pope and the King of the Two Sicilies possessed the love of their people. How was it, one must ask, that the Pope found it impossible to levy a Roman army, and that he was forced to rely almost entirely upon foreign mercenaries? How did it happen, again, that Garibaldi conquered nearly all Sicily with 2,000 men, and marched from Reggio to Naples with 5,000? How, but from the universal disaffection of the people of the Two Sicilies?

Neither can it be said that this testimony of the popular will was capricious or causeless. Forty years ago the Neapolitan people made an attempt regularly and temperately to reform their Government, under the reigning Dynasty. The Powers of Europe assembled at Laybach resolved, with the exception of England, to put down this attempt by force. It was put down, and a large foreign army of occupation was left in the Two Sicilies to maintain social order. In 1848 the Neapolitan people again attempted to secure liberty under the Bourbon Dynasty, but their best patriots atoned, by an imprisonment of ten years, for the offence of endeavouring to free their country. What wonder, then, that in 1860 the Neapolitans, mistrustful and resentful, should throw off the Bourbons, as in 1688 England had thrown off the Stuarts?

It must be admitted, undoubtedly, that the severance of the ties which bind together a Sovereign and his subjects is in itself a misfortune. Notions of allegiance become confused; the succession of the Throne is disputed; adverse parties threaten the peace of society; rights and pretensions are opposed to each other, and mar the harmony of the State. Yet it must be acknowledged on the other hand, that the Italian revolution has been conducted with singular temper and forbearance. The subversion of existing power has not been followed, as is too often the case, by an outburst of popular vengeance. The extreme views of democrats have nowhere prevailed. Public opinion has checked the excesses of the public triumph. The venerated forms of Constitutional Monarchy have been associated with the name of a Prince who represents an ancient and glorious Dynasty.

Such having been the causes and concomitant circumstances of the revolution of Italy, Her Majesty's Government can see no sufficient ground for the severe censure with which Austria, France, Prussia, and Russia have visited the acts of the King of Sardinia. Her Majesty's Government will turn their eyes rather to the gratifying prospect of a people building up the edifice of their liberties, and consolidating the work of their independence, amid the sympathies and good wishes of Europe.

P.S. You are at liberty to give a copy of this despatch to Count Cavour.

Document 69. *Palmerston proposes to stop Spain by force
from invading Italy,* 29 *October* 1860*

[Letters of 26 and 28 October shew that Napoleon III had
suggested to England that Spain was preparing to intervene
by force in favour of Francisco King of Naples.]

There is no Force in the Queen's argument. It does not in
the least follow that because we prevent Spain from invading
Italy we are therefore bound to assist or Countenance France
in invading Austria or any other Part of Germany.

I think it is quite impossible for us with a powerful Fleet
in the Mediterranean to stand by and see Spain crush by
Force of arms the nascent Liberties of Italy; our Preventing
such an outrage would in no fair sense of the word be
deemed Interference in the affairs of Italy; and I am confident from the little which I have seen in those Parts of the
public Feeling on the Italian Question that if we were to
shrink from taking our Line on such a Question if it should
arise, we should be deemed to be betraying our own Principles
and abdicating the Position which this Country ought to
hold among the Nations of the world....

[As a result of the inquiries instituted Spain disclaimed all
idea of interference by force.]

(*d*) THE AFTERMATH

[The consequences to international diplomacy of Lord John
Russell's famous dispatch of 27 October 1860 are worth studying.
Its popular success was immediate and resounding. Russell's dispatch was published everywhere, his name was blessed by millions
of Italians. It made it possible for Italy to be one and powerful.

But the ultimate question is whether this immense gain was
effected by a loss of too much. England approved the dissolution
of the bonds between monarch and subject, sanctioned the force
exercised by a revolutionary dictator against a sovereign at peace
with all other powers, and disregarded the Great Powers of
Europe. All of them viewed her with horror and amazement.

The despots of Europe, Alexander II of Russia, Franz Joseph
of Austria, the Prince Regent of Prussia, met in conclave in

---

* G. & D. 22/21, *Pte Russell Papers*. Palmerston to Russell, 29 October 1860.

October. The latter informed the Prince Consort of his views. "He seems very unhappy about Lord John Russell's last published Despatch, which he calls a tough morsel to digest, in which he sees a disruption of the Law of Nations as hitherto recognised, and of the holy ties which bound people and sovereigns, and a declaration on the part of England, that, wheresoever there exists any dissatisfaction among a people, they have the privilege to expel their sovereign, with the assured certainty of England's sympathy. The Prince sees great difficulty in the way of future agreement with England, if that is to be the basis of her policy." The saying went abroad: "Any Emperor or President...who entertained an inconvenient sympathy for Canada, for Ireland, for India, or for the Channel Islands, will remember that Vattel and Lord John Russell approve of foreign intervention against oppressive and unpopular governments." *

The real objection of rulers to Russell's action was to a foreign power's applauding the deposition of a ruler by his subjects. Queen Victoria and the Prince Consort were evidently affected by this argument, though far from believing in the divinity of kings. Russell had been, in fact, compelled to rely on Vattel and general principles, because Victoria had asked him to quote precedents for his action in applauding a breach of international law. He had therefore to justify himself in her eyes and in those of the world. He would have done much better to repeat the views he expressed to Granville on general principles of foreign policy: "There is no rule which may not be broken through."

Vattel, as Russell said, considered it permissible to succour a people oppressed by its sovereign; other jurists such as Wheaton and Bluntschli defend the right of aiding an oppressed race.† But the particular case in point was stronger than the general principle. The oppression exercised by King Bomba had been unspeakable, but Francisco had promised reforms after the loss of Palermo, and had appointed a constitutionalist Ministry. Russell took the view that Francisco could not be trusted, and that Garibaldi and his Thousand could not have overthrown a kingdom with 90,000 soldiers, unless the people had supported him. From this point of view the argument was fairly good. It might be argued, in fact, that Victor Emmanuel, who had established the rule of constitution and law in Piedmont, would establish it in Naples and in Sicily if he ruled there. Russell could therefore justly claim that he was disavowing a royal system of disorder and lawlessness and recognizing a royal system of order and law. His oft-repeated analogy of William III's descent upon England had a basis of fact. "I come among you", said William, as he landed in England, "to secure your liberties." He received a very old

* T. Martin, *Life of Prince Consort*, [1880], v, 226–7.
† Cp. Hall, *International Law*, [1924], Part II, Chap. VIII, 340 n.

man, who said to him: "But for your Highness, I should have survived the Law." With these professions William, though not an English prince, invaded England. With the same professions Victor Emmanuel, who was an Italian, invaded Naples.

Other justifications can be found, the best based on the model of the Treaty of Vienna. The argument is thus put by Lord Acton. "In 1815 the Germans wanted territory (from France). Alexander (Emperor of Russia) decided that a better security would be (the adoption by France of) a popular constitution. It was imposed on France as an alternative for territory (restored to her). It (the constitution) was the security of European peace. By how much more popular founded on general opinion, by so much more valuable in the eyes of Europe."* The inclusion of Naples and Sicily within Piedmont meant to Palmerston and Russell the extension of constitutionalism and therefore of peace, order and legality.

But this way of looking at it was not wholly sound. Canning believed that a nation had a right to depose its ruler; or that a portion of it, like one of the Spanish colonies, had a right to throw off the sovereignty of a parent state like Spain. In such case, when the rebels had acquired a certain degree of force and consistency, England would recognize the state as a republic or as independent. But he never admitted that this could be done against treaty rights, and the union of Naples and Sicily to Piedmont violated the Treaty of Vienna and disturbed the balance of power. It was a strong step to assume that the will of Naples and Sicily overrode those treaty rights when that will was aided to success by Piedmont from without. "Burke says the nation must be able to do its will. Yes, but not its criminal will. In that case it loses its right to independence." Again, the ideal of the unity of Italy meant revolution. Were Palmerston and Russell justified in promoting it? "Revolution is the right to make one's own government, who has the right? Not every part of (the) country. Not (La) Vendée for instance but Ireland."† It is therefore a fair question whether Naples and Sicily, a part of the Italian peninsula, had the right to disturb the whole of it.

To these questions no direct answer can be given. Palmerston later stated, in connexion with Schleswig-Holstein, "If the Duchies had forced themselves from Denmark by their own exertions, they would have acquired a right to dispose of themselves" (19 September 1865).‡ This was good Canningite doctrine. But Naples and Sicily had only done this with the armed aid of the King of Sardinia, and their action disturbed the whole peninsula. But Palmerston and Russell argued that as the

* Acton MSS. 5443, Cambridge University Library.
† Acton MSS. 5462, Cambridge University Library.
‡ G. P. Gooch, *Later Correspondence of Lord John Russell*, [1925], II, 316.

return of Francisco to Naples was "impossible" the union to Piedmont was the solution most likely to lead to peace. It was to be defended therefore not on general principles but as a special case.

What Palmerston and Russell do not seem to have faced is the ultimate consequences of justifying the irregularities of Victor Emmanuel and Garibaldi, which were opposed to all conventional notions of law or right. This harvest was bound to bear bitter fruits, which the British Ministers soon tasted. Rattazzi said to Layard, "Against Austria all methods are good", and Russell and the Queen were shocked to hear such expressions in the mouth of a "regular government".* Palmerston did not, indeed, believe that Venetia could remain permanently part of Austria. He, therefore, proposed to her the common-sense expedient of selling it to the enlarged Piedmont for money. He actually contemplated sending Clarendon to Vienna on a special mission for that purpose at the end of 1860. In mid-July 1862 Palmerston told Apponyi: "There were only two ways to sell it [Venetia] or govern it in a conciliatory way. You [Austria] did neither." Russell also indulged in plain speaking: "In case of an attack on Venetia no English minister could ever take part and lot with us, in face of so pronounced a public opinion in his country."†

Doc. 70 shews Palmerston's view of the hopelessness of Austria's permanently retaining Venetia. **Doc. 71** shews the final failure of Russell's well-meant attempt to give her compensation elsewhere.]

Document 70. *Palmerston on Austrian rule in Venetia,* 21 *September* 1860‡

...Pray observe what Perry says of the state of Venetia and of the system of Austrian Government in his Despatch No. 8, of the 14th of this month. What a Picture he gives. People arrested and kept in Prison some without Trial, others including a Lady of Rank and Family, after acquittal. The whole Population ripe for Revolt; The Garrison who are to defend the Place against attack, on the Point of melting and spiking the guns they are expected to fire off! all this in addition to the wholesale sequestration of Property as a

* W.S.A. viii/66, Berichte aus England. From Apponyi, No. 1 B of 3 January 1863, ff. 7–9. Russell gave him this information.
† W.S.A. viii/64, Berichte aus England. From Apponyi, Nos. 52 A and B of 16–17 July 1862.
‡ G. & D. 22/21, *Pte Russell Papers*. Palmerston to Russell, 21 September 1860.

Punishment for evading arrest and Imprisonment by leaving the Country, and the minute Interference with the Shirt Pins of men and the Finger Rings of women.*

Can any Man believe that the occupation of a Country on these Conditions can be a source of Strength to any Government or Empire; and can any Man believe that an occupation on these Conditions can be lasting...every liberal minded man will rejoice when the day of its overthrow arrives.

It is an act of political Infatuation in Austria to cling to the Possession of a Country which it cannot hold without crushing it and Treading with her Iron Heel on the Necks of the resentful Population....Austria as long as she holds Venice will have every Italian her bitter Foe...Cavour and Victor Emmanuel may say and promise what they will, but when Italy shall have been well organized as one and undivided, which it soon will have been, barring Rome and its immediate neighbourhood, They will be forced into a Quarrel with Austria about Venice, and the sympathies of Europe will go with them, and Military success will crown their efforts....

Document 71. *Russell fails to persuade Austria to sell Venetia,*
18 November 1863†

Not without visible embarrassment Lord Russell tried to introduce the second question...as one which might be treated in [European] Congress. He called to his help a letter of the King of the Belgians which he had just received and which, mentioning the difficulties raised by Napoleon III's project, contained among others the following passage "If there was question of an abandonment by Austria of her Italian provinces, it is clear that this could only be effected in return for ample compensations [elsewhere]."

This was the point which Lord Russell wished to reach and I resolved to settle this question once and for all...."We are

---

* *V.* Letter of 13 September. An Austrian Edict sequestrated the property of 500 persons in Venetia if they did not return at once. Men were punished for wearing tie-pins of three colours (the Italian tricolor) and women for wearing rings with white marks on them, called "the tears of Italy".

† W.S.A. viii/67, Berichte aus England. From Apponyi, No. 86B of 18 November 1863.

often slow. . .in deciding. . .but on this point we have not had
a moment's hesitation and I have been charged by the Emperor and his Government not to leave a shadow of doubt on
a resolution which is irrevocable, whatever may happen. We
might lose a province as the result of an unfortunate war, we
have a sad instance of this, but to sacrifice one lightheartedly,
while sitting round a green table, to satisfy caprices and I do
not know what imaginary need for reshapings of the map of
Europe. Never! We prefer to run the risks of war." "That is
very plain language", my interlocutor contented himself
with saying. He had heard me with attention mixed with
surprise. "I rather expected this point of view, [he said] but
it is another question if it is a wise one."

"It is the language England would undoubtedly hold",
replied I, refusing to be disconcerted, "if a Congress arro-
gated to itself the right of disposing of one of its possessions.
Do you agree?" The minister remained silent.

"As for compensations," replied I, "allow me to tell you,
Austria recognizes no-one, not even a European Areopagus,
who has the right to offer them. It could only be at the
expense of its neighbours, and I repeat to you we do not wish
to despoil others, in order to be despoiled ourselves."

"Yet", said Lord Russell, "there are examples. The
House of Lorraine renounced its Duchy to obtain Tuscany."

"And now", cried I, "its successors possess neither the
one nor the other. If that is what you call compensations,
your historical quotation is not a happy one. . . .Do you not
see that the Danubian provinces (Moldavia and Wallachia)
are the only compensation that could be offered to us for
Venetia and would not (the cession of) these provinces imply
the Eastern question and the dismemberment of the Ottoman
Empire?"

This observation made Lord Russell think and after some
moments of silence he said, "If for one reason or another we
decline to enter the Congress, can we reckon on Austria
following our example?" "I believe I can say so", said I,
and these words seemed somewhat to impress him. . . .

XIII. PALMERSTON AND RUSSELL, 1860–3*

RUSSIA AND POLAND

28. THE BRITISH SIDE OF THE POLISH QUESTION, 1831–63

[The British side of the Polish question has hitherto had very little light thrown on it. There are a good many official dispatches in the Blue Books of 1863,† but neither Sir Spencer Walpole nor Dr Gooch has published anything material from the private papers of Russell, nor has Ashley from those of Palmerston. These gaps can be at least partly filled from the Russell MSS., from Palmerston's rough notes in the Record Office, and from the Archives of Vienna. The Editors have also been fortunate in being able to quote some unpublished opinions of that great authority, Sir Ernest Satow, on the diplomatic bearing of the questions really at issue.

Russell treated the Polish question in 1863 much as Palmerston treated it during 1831–2. In 1815 the Tsar Alexander I had signified his intention of granting a constitution to Poland in the Treaty of Vienna and the Powers of Europe signatory to the Treaty had taken note of the fact. These were England, France, Austria, Prussia, Russia, Sweden, Portugal and Spain. In fact the first four were the only ones who counted apart from Russia. The relevant Article of the Treaty of Vienna runs as follows:

"Article Ier. Le Duché de Varsovie, à l'exception des Provinces et Districts, dont il a été autrement disposé dans les Articles suivants, est réuni à l'Empire de Russie. Il y sera lié irrévocablement par sa Constitution, pour être possédé par Sa Majesté l'Empereur de toutes les Russies, Ses Héritiers et Ses Successeurs à perpétuité. Sa Majesté Impériale se réserve de donner à cet État, jouissant d'une Administration distincte, l'extension intérieure qu'elle jugera convenable. Elle prendra avec ses autres Titres, celui de Czar, Roi de Pologne, conformément au Protocole usité et consacré pour les Titres attachés à Ses autres Possessions.

Les Polonois, Sujets respectifs de la Russie, de l'Autriche et de la Prusse, obtiendront une Représentation et des Institutions

---

* The authors wish to acknowledge help received in the past from an unpublished thesis by W. F. F. Grace (Ph.D., Cantab.), though this has not been consulted in the present instance.

† Cp. Temperley and Penson, *Century of Diplomatic Blue Books*, Nos. 643–643h.

Nationales, réglées d'après le mode d'existence politique que chacun des Gouvernements, auxquels ils appartiennent jugera utile et convenable de leur accorder."

The question of the meaning of "Constitution" is certainly obscure. The Article quoted above as printed in *B.F.S.P.* (*1814–15*), II, 11, has a capital "C", which may have led the Foreign Office in 1831 and 1863 to suppose that a detailed written constitution was thereby promised to Poland.* Even this is a disputable point, for at this period "Constitution" was a word of varied and disputed meaning. But probably the Tsar himself was actually thinking of granting a constitution of the modern representative type to Poland in connexion with this Article of the Treaty. The first part of the text of the Polish constitution which he actually granted suggests the above interpretation of the Treaty. Once the constitution had been granted, the Article of the Vienna Treaty was executed, and that ended the matter. It is not easy to see what right the Great Powers (other than Russia) had to interfere so long as Poland formed a government and administration separate and distinct from Russia, and was held by a personal tie. That at least was the opinion of our Ambassador at St Petersburgh during the crisis.†

After the rebellion of the Poles against Russia in 1831 the Tsar (and not unnaturally) deprived them of most of their constitutional privileges. His son destroyed almost all that remained in 1863. On both occasions the question arose as to whether the consent of the guaranteeing Powers of the Treaty of Vienna (France, England, Prussia and Austria) was necessary to these changes, or whether these Powers had in fact guaranteed the constitution to Poland. Was it the duty of these Powers to interfere to make Russia restore the constitution intact to Poland? In 1831 Heytesbury, as has been shewn, thought not. But the governments, both of England and of France, thought differently. France, constitutional, bourgeois, notoriously friendly to Poland since the days of Napoleon, wished to protest. England of the Reform Bill in the heyday of furious zeal for constitutions, under Whigs like Russell, Durham and Grey, wished to do the same. Palmerston is believed personally to have deprecated protest. But he sent off one, none the less. "The Constitution once given, became the link which, under the Treaty, binds the Kingdom of Poland to the Empire of Russia; and can that link remain unimpaired, if the Constitution should not be maintained?" This passage reveals the British Government as prepared to contend that, if Russia reduced Poland "to the state and condition of a

* This fact doubtless influenced British statesmen but no argument can properly be based on it, for the "British and Continental modes of using capitals is quite distinct" [Satow].

† Heytesbury (St Petersburgh) to Palmerston, Separate and Secret, 1 October 1831, *F.O.* 65/193.

Province", England might refuse to recognize Russia's title to that country. "It cannot be admitted that the revolt of the Poles... can absolve the Emperor...from his obligation to adhere to that Constitution."* From this position England never wavered.

Nesselrode's reply to Palmerston expresses exactly the opposite view. It started by asserting that the constitution was "not a necessary consequence of the treaty of Vienna, but a spontaneous act of his [Alexander's] sovereign power". "If it had been the intention of the contracting Powers to stipulate in favour of the [Polish] Kingdom a special charter, and to guarantee it, there can be no doubt that such a stipulation would be expressed in a manner more explicit and formal." When the text of the constitution was published, none of the signatory powers attempted to examine or comment upon it. "All of them, on the contrary, recognized, either expressly or by their silence on the subject, that in granting this Constitution to his new subjects, the Emperor had followed the dictates of his free will." † This is perhaps straining the meaning for the intention to give a constitution was noted by the signatory powers. It does not appear, however, that they were judges of the performance of the Tsar's intention. The case is like the Declaration made by Italy at Versailles in 1919 when she annexed a part of the German Tyrol. Italy published a Declaration that she intended "to adopt a broadly liberal policy towards its new subjects of German race, in what concerns their language, culture, and economic interests".‡ This Declaration was quoted by the signatory powers of the Austrian Treaty in their official reply to Austria of 2 September 1919. The Italian Government fulfilled their promise by making linguistic and other concessions to Germany in the Italian Tyrol. When, however, some years later they withdrew these concessions because of real or alleged sedition, the other Powers made no protest or comment. The Declaration was not indeed formally embodied in the Austrian Treaty, as was Alexander's in the Treaty of Vienna, but in both cases the other signatory powers possessed a right of remonstrance.

The Polish constitution was actually granted by Alexander on 24 December 1815. Later some restrictions were introduced by him, but the constitution was not withdrawn until after the revolt of 1830. The reasons for withdrawing it are thus stated by Nesselrode in the dispatch already quoted, of 1832. "The Polish constitution was annulled by the very fact of the rebellion. Will it be necessary for us to prove it? It is a recognized fact that between government and government, the Treaties and conventions freely consented to by both parties are put an end to by a state of war

* Palmerston to Heytesbury, 23 November 1831, No. 52, *F.O.* 65/190; printed in Hertslet, *Map*, [1875], II, 875-80.
† Nesselrode to Lieven, 3 January 1832, *F.O.* 65/204.
‡ V. Temperley, *History of the Peace Conference*, [1921], IV, 284.

and must be renewed, or at least expressly confirmed on the conclusion of peace. All the more is it so with an act which is not two-sided, but granted by a sovereign to his subjects, and the first condition of which is the obedience and faithfulness of the latter. All the more so, I say, is such an act annulled by a state of war when the war is the necessary consequence of insurrection and treason?" So far Nesselrode's argument. Sir Ernest Satow deemed it "unanswerable". He adds the comment: "I don't see that there is anything [in the Article of the Treaty] to hinder them [the Russians] from modifying these [the articles of the constitution] from time to time, in the way of extension or contraction, as might seem desirable.* Surely it cannot be argued that they were bound to maintain unaltered for all time the shape they had given them when they started on this paragraph" [Article I of Vienna Treaty].

In 1832 the Russian Government adhered to the line given above, and refused all concessions to the remonstrances of England and of France. A generation later, when Russell was Foreign Minister, Palmerston is found supporting him in a series of protests exactly like the old ones. The arguments were, in fact, the same on both sides. It is extraordinary that Palmerston, having received a severe rebuff thirty years before, should have courted another. It is the more remarkable since he is supposed personally to have disapproved of the protest, which he signed for the British Cabinet, in 1832. One explanation is that the almost octogenarian Palmerston was overborne by the more vigorous Lord John Russell. This thesis is hardly sustained by the facts. In 1848 Palmerston suggested to the Tsar that he might enlarge the constitutional freedom of Poland (**Doc. 39**), and Russell, who was Premier, may have concurred in this suggestion. The latter could not, however, have shared in the developments of 1856, for he was not then in the Government. It was then that Palmerston got Clarendon privately to raise the Polish question at the Congress of Paris. The Russians managed to prevent him from putting it officially before the Congress by giving the assurance that the new Tsar intended immediately to grant again to the Poles their national constitution and the use of the national language. When, after the outbreak of revolution in 1863, the fear arose that the Polish constitution would again be annulled, Palmerston had a strong motive for interference. For the Russian promises to him had been broken. As he could not remind the Russians of these officially he had to invoke the Treaty of Vienna. In the course ultimately taken Palmerston and Russell were entirely at one. The first wrote to the second when unable to

---

* In point of fact, as Heytesbury had pointed out to Palmerston (*F.O.* 65/193, 1 October 1831): "This Constitution has already been altered and modified upon several occasions, without the slightest reference to Foreign Powers, and without the slightest remonstrance on their part."

attend a Cabinet meeting: "I give you my Proxy, for I think our views and Policy on pending Questions are identical."*

Alexander II had made some half-hearted attempts to conciliate Poland. But the Poles were angry and suspicious and perhaps concessions actually encouraged them to revolt. When concessions were succeeded by harsher measures, revolt began. In January 1863, the Russian Government introduced conscription into Poland, and took care to conscript the leading members of the Opposition. Revolt actually began on 22 January 1863 and developed thereafter into a futile and bloody civil war. The revolution merely exhibited a frantic and active hatred of two nations for one another. It was part of the old and irreconcilable conflict between Pole and Russian, Catholic and Orthodox, Latin and Byzantine. The revolt had no chance of success and was drowned in blood.

In February Bismarck improved the occasion by negotiating a convention (that of Alvensleben) between Prussia and Russia.† This, though never actually ratified, proved the beginning of a permanent understanding between Russia and Prussia. The news of this *entente*, if not alliance, greatly excited the French. Napoleon wished to protest along with England in an identic note. Palmerston opposed this, as he thought it "a trap" which would lead to war.‡ Napoleon then dropped his protest against a Russo-Prussian alliance, and took up the cause of Poland direct. His proposal for an Anglo-Austro-French suggestion for conciliatory measures to Polish rebels coincided with a milder initiative from Palmerston himself on 25 February (*v.* **Doc. 72**). This joint suggestion, which was presented in three separate communications, was eventually rejected by Russia in mid-April. The British communication of 10 April had laid stress on the Treaty of Vienna and refused to acquiesce in the doctrine that Poland's revolt in 1830 justified the suspension of her constitution. This was "so contrary to good faith, so destructive of the obligation of Treaties, and so fatal to all the international ties which bind together the community of European states". The revolt of the Poles could not release the Tsar from the contracted obligation. But a passage added at the end said "the condition of things" in Poland "is a source of danger, not to Russia alone, but also to the general peace of Europe...which might, under possible circumstances, produce complications of the most serious nature".§ To this

* G. & D. 22/22, *Pte Russell Papers.* Palmerston to Russell, 25 May 1863. Russell says [*Selections from Speeches...and from Despatches...,* [1870], II, 235]: "Lord Palmerston himself took a large part in framing the despatches."

† *V. Die Auswärtige Politik Preussens,* Bd. III, von R. Ibbeken [Oldenburg, 1932], Nos. 164–9.

‡ To the King of the Belgians, 13 March 1863, Ashley, *Life,* [1876], II, 232.

§ Russell to Lord Napier, 10 April 1863, *Selections from Speeches...and from Despatches...,* [1870], II, 393–7.

menacing conclusion Prince Gorčakov replied by a refusal of the terms proposed and a polite reiteration of the old arguments of 1832.

On the previous day (9 April) Russell made a still more astonishing suggestion to the Russian Ambassador. He proposed dealing thus with the difficulty that the Tsar could not give representative institutions to Poland and deny them to Russia: "Why should they [representative institutions] not be granted at one and the same time to the kingdom of Poland and to the Empire of Russia?" Russell adds, with almost touching *naïveté*, "Baron Brunnow had no information as to the intentions of the [Russian] Emperor on this subject, and I did not press him further". This was magnanimity indeed!

England had a case, based on the Treaty of Vienna, as to recommending representative institutions for Poland. But the recommendation to give them to Russia was an astonishing attempt to interfere in her internal affairs, for which no treaty right could be pleaded.

But this interview of 9 April was even more menacing in its tone than astonishing for its suggestions. Brunnow asked, as well he might, "whether the communication Her Majesty's Government were about to make at St Petersburgh was of a pacific nature. I [Russell] replied that it was, but that as I did not wish to mislead him I must say something more. Her Majesty's Government had no intentions that were otherwise than pacific, still less any concert with other Powers for any but pacific purposes. But the state of things might change. The present overture of Her Majesty's Government might be rejected as the representation of March 2 had been rejected by the Imperial Government. The insurrections in Poland might continue and might assume larger proportions.... If in such a state of affairs the Emperor of Russia were to take no steps of a conciliatory nature, dangers and complications might arise not at present in contemplation."* This seems to be almost a threat of war to Russia if she did not attend to England's remonstrances.

War was not, however, intended by either Palmerston or Russell. They made this fact quite clear by their declarations to the Austrian Minister at the end of April, which are given in **Doc. 73.** But on this fact the Blue Book is silent and there are no dispatches at all published between 2 May and 17 June. The next step was actually taken by Palmerston in mid-May when he suggested pressing Russia to grant an amnesty to the Polish rebels (**Doc. 74**). The overture of Palmerston on 31 May (**Doc. 75**), in which he suggested an Austrian Archduke as King of an independent Poland, is remarkable for its rashness. Only the refusal of Austria averted grave consequences. On 17 June Russell sent a

* Russell, *Selections from Speeches...and from Despatches...*, [1870], II, 397–9.

dispatch demanding six points, an amnesty plus a settlement of
Poland on the lines of the Treaty of Vienna. Austria and France
endorsed this programme. Russia replied by saying that she would
consent only to a conference of the powers directly interested in
Poland. These were Prussia, Austria and Russia and, as Prussia
and Russia were allies, they would always outvote Austria. For
the rest Russia promised to consider the six points and report the
results to France and England (13 July 1863). Austria refused a
conference on these terms and England and France were left out
in the cold.

Napoleon, who was the most rebuffed of the three sovereigns,.
wished now for a real intervention. He proposed an identic note
from Austria, France and England. Austria declined and England
decided, on Palmerston's urging, to keep "within the limits of
reciprocal diplomatic communication".* War was thus averted.
Russell would have done well to say little more, for the Russian
reply had been sharper to France than to England. But he
addressed a dispatch in his best lecturing style to St Petersburgh
(11 August).† This pointed out that the Polish clauses of the
Treaty of Vienna included all the signatory powers, and that a
conference, which excluded France and England, would be
contrary to its terms. He added: "It would not be open to Russia
to enjoy all the benefits of a large addition to her dominions, and
to repudiate the terms of the instrument upon which her tenure
depends." This can hardly bear any other meaning than that
England will now refuse to recognize Russia's title to the Kingdom
of Poland as defined at Vienna in 1815 if she continued to refuse
to restore the constitution.

Russia was now secure. Prussia sided with her, Austria was
obviously very timid, England was ready enough with words but
France was not ready with swords. Prince Gorčakov ultimately
addressed a dispatch dated 7 September to Russell denying his
conclusions. This provoked the final reply of Russell of 20
October.‡ It is interesting to see how Russell wished still to be
defiant and how Palmerston succeeded in watering down his
wine. The difference is a real one. For Palmerston saw the
"bluff" had failed and wished to extricate himself without further
loss of dignity. Russell still wished to continue a controversy in
which England had already been humiliated. What is even more
astonishing is that, in an interview with the Austrian Minister on
17 November, Russell tried to raise the question again. He asked
if a European Congress met and decided on the separation of
Poland from Russia under a foreign or a Russian prince, would

* So announced to the Queen, 11 August 1863. *V. Letters of Queen Victoria*,
2nd Ser., [1926], I, 103.
† Russell, *Selections from Speeches...and from Despatches...*, [1870], II, 410–17.
‡ This dispatch is printed in *A. & P.*, [1864], LXVI, [3243], 582.

Austria agree to use force against Russia to secure her consent? Apponyi answered that he would like to know if England would use force. "As I had foreseen, Lord Russell told me that this eventuality had not been examined yet and that, not being ready to answer me, he begged me for the present to consider his question as not having been put (comme non avenue)."* In this way even Lord Russell was at last reduced to silence about Poland.]

Document 72. *Palmerston takes the first step,* 25 *February* 1863†

[On 25 February Palmerston saw the Austrian Ambassador and suggested that the Russians should give an amnesty to the revolted Poles and return to the situation created by the Treaty of Vienna in 1815. "The idea only came to me this morning, I have spoken to no-one not even to Lord Russell."‡ What follows is what he advised to Russell.]

...Our communication in conjunction with France ought to be mainly addressed to Russia the real culprit rather than to Prussia an incidental accomplice, and who might reasonably say "mea res agitur paries cum proximus ardet". I daresay that cunning old Fox, Brunnow does his best to persuade us not to say anything to his Government, but public opinion in this country as well as in France is getting strong upon this subject, and we shall not stand well if we do not do something. In past times personal influence did much to embarrass the action of the British Gov[ernment], Mad[am] Lieven had great influence over Lord Grey and put much water into my wine, while at Petersburg Durham's inordinate vanity and desire to be well with the Russian Court entirely gagged him as our mouth piece about Polish affairs; and accordingly we do not I think stand quite satisfactorily as to our Language and Course in those times.

* W.S.A. VIII/67, Berichte aus England. From Apponyi, No. 86A of 18 November 1863.

† G. & D. 22/22, *Pte Russell Papers*. Palmerston to Russell, 26 February 1863. A letter of 25 February is to the same effect and commends the suggestion that the Powers who signed the Treaty of Vienna should approach Russia.

‡ W.S.A. VIII/66, Berichte aus England. From Apponyi, No. 15C of 25 February 1863.

Document 73. *Russell and Palmerston disclaim the idea of going to war with Russia, 21–2 April 1863*

...The answers of Lord Russell [21 April] can be briefly stated. As for desiring or meaning to make war on Russia, the Minister answered with an absolute *No*. But as to what England would do in case the Emperor Napoleon took the initiative in such a war, and as to knowing whether England had the firm resolution to prevent such a war the Chief Secretary of State was much less explicit....[Some discredit is then thrown on Hennessy's report, though Palmerston did not think he had invented it all.]

Lord Palmerston said [22 April] "Mr Hennessy is deceived in thinking that Parliament in a given case, would drag the [British] Government into war; he believed the contrary would happen, if the Government gave Parliament and the nation sufficient reasons. For despite the uncontested and unanimous sympathies of the British public for Poland, a war is not desired by the country and is against its interests.

...The diplomatic *démarche* [of 10–11 April] we made at St Petersburgh in concert with France and Austria is enough at present...who knows what the future will bring? You know we do not like to pledge ourselves beforehand and in this business our best policy is to keep our liberty of action, except in so far as our interests and circumstances limit it."

APPONYI. "But have you at least a *strong* intention of preventing war" said I to him, "if that could be attained by a strict understanding between our two cabinets."

PALMERSTON. "How do you mean to prevent it?"..."The only means would be to threaten France by putting ourselves on Russia's side and that is and will always be absolutely impossible for us. Neutrality is *the least* that we could do, and you see that according to your version, that is all France would ask of us. The Emperor Napoleon is strong enough to

---

* W.S.A. viii/68, Varia. Lettre particulière. From Apponyi, 22 April 1863. Apponyi started by reading the contents of a private letter from Rechberg, of the 16th, which related to Napoleon III's interview with Mr Pope Hennessy in which he hinted at creating an independent Poland by making war on Russia.

make war alone "....[Palmerston then discussed the question of Polish resistance.]

[Apponyi comments]..."The plans of the Emperor Napoleon do not seem to surprise Lord Palmerston, he seems to expect anything. What has surprised me is that I have found the [Prime] Minister more disposed to suffer, or even to second, to some degree, the projects of this Sovereign than resolutely to oppose them."...

Document 74. *Palmerston urges an immediate amnesty,* 15 *May* 1863*

Might it not be well to say that all these Questions would require much Time for Consideration and Discussion, that in the meanwhile a great Effusion of Blood much sacrifice of Life, and all the Calamities incident to civil war would be going on, and that therefore we wish to suggest whether as a first step towards other arrangements, and indeed as a necessary preliminary to other arrangements it would not be well to propose to the Contending Parties an armistice to last for a sufficient time.

P[ALMERSTON] 15/5–63.

Document 75. *Palmerston suggests an independent Poland with an Austrian Archduke as King,* 31 *May* 1863†

[On 25 May Palmerston wrote a letter to Russell proposing that a European Conference on Poland should be held and attended by the eight Powers who signed the Treaty of Vienna. "Nothing can now be expected to produce Tranquillity but that which the British G[overnmen]t avowed its Desire to see in 1815, namely a separate and independent Kingdom of Poland."‡ This idea seemed so pleasing to Palmerston that he proposed to secure it by Austrian support and by putting an Austrian Archduke on the throne. Austria had suggested that Russia should govern as she had done in Galicia. This idea did not suit Palmerston. So he sent for Apponyi (31 May) and expounded his new and rash policy. He deprecated suggesting to Russia that she should institute in her Congress Kingdom of Poland a constitution and assembly on the model of that in Austrian Poland, i.e. Galicia.]

* G. & D. 22/22, *Pte Russell Papers.*

† W.S.A. VIII/66, Berichte aus England. From Apponyi, No. 38C of 1 June 1863.

‡ G. & D. 22/22, *Pte Russell Papers.* Palmerston to Russell, 25 May 1863.

...We have reasons for claiming that the Emperor of Russia should fulfil the engagements of his predecessor. For the Russian interpretation of the treaties of 1815 with reference to Poland is the constitution given spontaneously [octroyée] by Alexander I. That, and not the legislative assembly [Diète] of Galicia must be taken as the starting point of negotiation. We must invoke a Russian, not an Austrian, precedent. If this constitution led to the revolution of 1830, it was not because it was bad, but because it was not observed; because the Grand Duke Constantine [the Viceroy] was a man without faith or law [sans foi ni loi], the National Assembly [Diète] was only convoked at long intervals and all the promised institutions little by little became dead letters. If the constitution were re-established now, it could not be in this position again, for this time it would be placed, so to speak, under the moral guarantee of Europe, as a result of formal engagements taken by the Emperor of Russia....

[Palmerston then discussed the question of an armistice and amnesty, expressing the belief that the Polish revolt was extending.]...The national enthusiasm, which Russia attempts to excite, is purely artificial [factice], and were it genuine would make her task more difficult. A party is beginning to form which favours a cession of Poland, as being only an embarrassment and source of weakness for Russia and there is even a report that they had the idea of ceding the Kingdom to Prussia.

"To say truth", continued Lord Palmerston, "my inner feeling is that the best solution of this inextricable question would be to reconstitute an independent Poland beneath the sceptre of a foreign Prince, and I believe an Austrian Archduke would be the arrangement most welcome to Poland."

I begged my interlocutor not to speak to me of such venturesome projects, which my court was in no way disposed to favour. The empty glory of seating one of its princes on the throne of Poland would in no way make up to the Imperial House for the loss of a fair and rich province of which the western Powers could certainly not offer us the territorial equivalent.

"I do not see" [replied Palmerston] why Austria should

not keep Galicia and Prussia Posen. You would only have to give up Cracow, a 'holy city' of the Poles, and this sacrifice would be amply compensated by the presence of a friendly and allied Kingdom on your frontiers. It would separate you from Russia and rid Europe of this 'Muscovite promontory' which juts into the centre of civilization. Besides, I believe more than you do in the power of dynastic ties, especially when the interests of peoples are identical. But, I repeat, I here only give my personal opinion and, if Austria is against it, let us speak no more of it and return to the actual situation.". . .

[Apponyi then explained that, in respect either to armistice or to imposing the Polish constitution of 1815 on Russia, "We should never associate ourselves with putting compulsion on Russia to adopt a programme which we should think incompatible with our own interests".]

Lord Palmerston answered that the refusal of Russia, however regrettable, would not necessarily bring war along with it. If one could not negotiate without fighting, diplomacy would be useless, and we should then need only generals and admirals. . . . The danger of doing nothing is, in his view, greater than that of acting. He believes in truth that, for the time being, the Emperor Napoleon desires sincerely to avoid a war. Those of the Crimea and of Italy gave him and the French nation glory enough. . . . A war against Russia would soon assume colossal and incalculable proportions, and the Emperor would only resolve on it at the last extremity. But once the expedition to Mexico ended, it was possible for him to turn his eyes to Poland. If the horrors of war still continued there, he might say to France "I have tried in vain to come to an understanding with England and Austria. They have turned their backs on me. Let us finish alone an enterprise worthy of a great nation, the liberation of the Polish people." Lord Palmerston draws the conclusion that it is best to go with France up to a certain point, for in this way she is grouped and controlled. . . . [Palmerston in response to inquiry said his remarks applied to the kingdom of Poland as defined for Russia in 1815.] . . . Your Excellency will see from this interview that if the ideas of Lord Palmerston are clear enough as to the proposals he has to make, they are vague and illusory as to the consequences likely to result. I think he has not here revealed his whole thought, perhaps so as not to discourage Austrian cooperation. Lord Palmerston has too strong a dose of British pride to imagine that England could remain inactive beneath the blow that a Russian refusal would give her. He believes too strongly in the final triumph of the Polish cause to let himself be discouraged. He will therefore let himself be gently forced to follow France in any steps she takes forward, and will end by being dragged into making common cause with her, while leaving her with the largest share of the risks and expenses of a hazardous enterprise.

Document 76. *Russell's answer of 20 October to Prince Gorčakov's dispatch of 7 September—Russell adheres to his draft in opposition to Austria, 30 September* 1863*

State to Count Rechberg that if a contract is violated on one side, it can hardly be held to bind the other. Poland is united to Russia in the first article of the Treaty of Vienna by its Constitution. Where is this Constitution? Russia rules only by the sword of the executioner, England has no wish or intention to go to war for Poland. The dispatch is very moderately expressed, and the British Gov[ernmen]t cannot consent to say less if it says any thing.   RUSSELL

Document 77. *Palmerston advises moderation,*
2 October 1863†

Is not this Draft superseded by a later Despatch from Paris stating that the [French] Emperor agrees to our proposed Communication to Russia? If that is so this Despatch is unnecessary and need not be sent.

But if it is to go I should much recommend its being greatly shortened.

* Rough draft by Russell, *F.O.* 96/27, for telegram to Bloomfield, No. 145, 30 September 1863, *F.O.* 7/649. He is remonstrating with Rechberg for wanting to moderate his dispatch.
† G. & D. 22/22, *Pte Russell Papers*. Palmerston to Russell, 2 October 1863.

All that is therein said might be well said in a Conversation which was not to be made public and which bound nobody to any Conclusions, but much of this Draft seems to me inexpedient in a Document which is liable to be laid before Parliament and to be published to the World.

In the first Place I think much is to be said against the opinion herein expressed that the Poland of 1815 could not be erected into a Separate State independent of Russia. My own opinion is that such an arrangement would be practicable if Russia willingly or unwillingly was brought to consent to it, and that such an arrangement would be a great Gain to Europe—There seems to be no Reason Why Such a Kingdom should not Stand as well as Saxony, Wurtemberg or Hanover. The Difficulty would be, not to maintain Such a Kingdom but to prevent it from trying to absorb Posen and Gallicia. It would be better therefore I think not to commit the Government in a Despatch to an opinion on which all do not agree, and on a Point on which we are not called upon to record or form a Decision.

Secondly all you propose to Say about the Difficulties of making war against Russia for Poland is no Doubt full of weight, but there is much to be said the other way, and I am inclined to think that if England and France were really determined to force Russia to give up the Kingdom of Poland they would be perfectly able to do so without the Co-operation of Austria; and in that Case instead of our having to defend Sweden, Sweden would probably give us effective assistance. But assuming that all that is said in this Draft about the Difficulties of such a war to be unanswerable Surely there is no use in proclaiming this to the World and telling it to Russia, and we should be doing so by sending this Despatch to Paris.

If Such a Despatch is to go in answer to Drouyn's* first opinion it ought I think to be confined simply to Saying that Drouyn's object appears to be war, and that the British Gov[ernmen]t have not at present any Intention of making war for Poland.

 * Drouyn de Lhuys—Foreign Minister of Napoleon III.

Document 78. *Palmerston amends Russell's dispatch,*
8 *October* 1863*

I see that Rechberg vehemently objects to the concluding
Passage in your proposed Draft to Napier on Polish affairs,
in which you purpose to say that Russia by leaving unfulfilled the Engagements taken by her with Regard to the
Kingdom of Poland by the Treaty of Vienna will lose all the
International Right to Poland which She had acquired by
that Treaty.

I know that the Poles have always urged us to say something to that effect, but I own I never could see that they
could derive any advantage from our doing so. If we were
prepared to take measures for wresting the Kingdom of
Poland from Russia, it would be very proper to lay the
Foundation for such a Measure by telling Russia that She has
lost her international Title to Poland; but as we have no such
Intention, and Austria has no such Intention and as I much
doubt whether France has any such Intention or has easy
means of executing Such an Intention if She had it, I do
not see what practical advantage is to be gained by Such
a Declaration to Russia, however true and just it may in
itself be. In Fact Russia might take advantage of it to Say
in Reply, Well and Good. If I no longer hold Poland by
the Treaty of Vienna, I am released from all the obligations
which you Say the Treaty of Vienna imposed upon me.
I now by your own admission hold Poland by my own Strong
Hand and Stark Sword; I am at Liberty to deal with Poland
henceforward as I chuse, and you have no Right to Say any
Thing to me about Warsaw any more than about Moscow or
Siberia. You might I think give way to Austria on this Point
without any real Sacrifice.

[The crucial part of the dispatch, as finally sent on 20 October,
was modified as follows: "Her Majesty's Government acknowledge that the relations of Russia towards European Powers are
regulated by public law; but the Emperor of Russia has special
obligations in regard to Poland.

* G. & D. 22/22, *Pte Russell Papers*. Palmerston to Russell, 8 October 1863.

Her Majesty's Government have, in the despatch of August 11 and preceding despatches, shown that in regard to this particular question the rights of Poland are contained in the same instrument which constitutes the Emperor…King of Poland." Gorčakov, in reply to this, acknowledged "the friendly disposition" and "moderation" of the British Government.*]

Document 79. *Palmerston and Russell on the designs of Russia in Asia, 1–2 August 1860†*

The Russian Gov[ernmen]t perpetually declares that Russia wants no increase of Territory that the Russian Dominions are already too large and that the whole attention of the Gov[ernmen]t is directed to internal Improvement. But while making in the most solemn Manner these Declarations the Russian Gov[ernmen]t every year adds Large Tracts of Territory to the Russian Dominions, and the only Shadow of Foundation for the above Disclaimer is, that these yearly acquisitions are not made for the Purpose of adding so much Territory to an Empire already too large but are carefully directed to the occupation of certain Strategical Points, as Starting Places for further encroachments or as Posts from whence some neighbouring States may be kept under Controul or may be threatened with Invasion.

With regard to such matters at least, the assertions of the Russian Gov[ernmen]t are not entitled to the slightest Confidence. P[ALMERSTON] 1/8/60.

Lord Palmerston has returned the Draft to St. Petersburg about Russian Designs in Central Asia without alteration but with this comment. [L]

This is all true enough but yet the transport of an army from Tiflis to the Punjab is no slight matter. Let the Despatch go tomorrow to Petersburg and the next day to Brunnow.

AUG[UST] 2 R[USSELL].

* Russell, *Selections from Speeches…and Despatches…*, [1870], II, 419–20. The statement in Salisbury, *Essays on Foreign Politics*, [1905], 202–4, that the dispatch was amended because of a suggestion of Gorčakov himself seems quite unfounded.

† B.M. Add. MSS. 38,991, *Pte Layard Papers*, f. 170. Minutes by Palmerston, 1 August 1860, Layard and Russell, 2 August 1860.

XIV. PALMERSTON AND RUSSELL, 1860–4

DENMARK AND SCHLESWIG-HOLSTEIN

29. PALMERSTON'S VIEW OF BISMARCK AND PRUSSIA, 1862–3

[The failure of Palmerston over Schleswig-Holstein was his greatest diplomatic defeat. The question was one about which the Austrian Minister reported Russell as knowing very little. Palmerston had studied it for years and knew it in all its details. Yet in this contest Bismarck deceived this Nestor of diplomacy and outfaced a veteran practised in the calling of "bluffs".

A warning signal had been given by Bismarck to Disraeli (**Doc. 80**), but it cannot be proved that it ever came to the ears of Palmerston or Russell. The other documents shew why, if it did, these warnings were disregarded. Palmerston, whose military knowledge was considerable, did not think that England's twenty thousand soldiers could stop three hundred thousand Prussians and Austrians. As will be seen, he thought the French army infinitely superior to the Prussian, a military misconception prevalent in England until 1870 and held by so great a foreign military authority as Todleben. Now, during 1863, Palmerston hoped for French co-operation in favour of Denmark, until the very end of the year.

Apart from this fact Palmerston, full of his belief in constitutionalism, believed that the arbitrary course of the King and Bismarck's defiance of the Prussian Parliament must end in disaster. Public opinion would not only stop Bismarck from war, it would lead him and his King to abdication, to exile and to the block. Palmerston believed not only that the French army would beat the Prussian but that the majority in the Prussian Parliament would ultimately reduce Bismarck and his King to submission. He was thus the victim of a double blunder, as the documents shew. They suggest that Bismarck is "crazy", that his unconstitutional methods stimulate assassins to murder his King, and risk the loyalty of the Rhine province. Between July and August 1863 Palmerston and Russell were obsessed by the notion that France would destroy Prussia if it came to blows, and that Bismarck and his King would be drowned by the rising tide of parliamentarianism. It is easy to understand then why Palmerston made his fatal boast that if certain (i.e. German) Powers attacked Denmark, it would not be "Denmark alone" with whom they might have to fight. This utterance was at the time a fair representation of the political situation. Napoleon was anxious to act with England, Russia was not yet alienated. But before the end of the year British policy over Poland had estranged both Russia and France. Napoleon had also been deeply wounded by a British refusal to attend a Congress. It was at that unfortunate juncture that Palmerston's boast was remembered.]

Document 80. *Disraeli on Bismarck's designs and the Palmerston Government, 9 July 1862**

[Bismarck visited England in June 1862. The famous conversation he is alleged to have had with Disraeli has sometimes been discredited. He is said to have used these words: "As soon as the army shall have been brought into such a condition as to inspire respect, I shall seize the first best pretext to declare war against Austria, dissolve the German Diet, subdue the minor States, and give national unity to Germany under Prussian leadership."† Apponyi's account makes it probable that the substance of this utterance is authentic. Only the insistence on the "I" is different. Apponyi makes Bismarck give his policy as one for Prussia, not necessarily one for himself.]

What I know is that he [Bismarck] has seen Mr Disraeli and said to him that Germany could only find her safety in the supremacy of Prussia, and that according to him the only policy for Prussia to follow was to do in Germany what Sardinia had done in Italy.

Mr Disraeli in relating these proposals to one of my colleagues added that he had enough confidence in the existing English Cabinet to be convinced that they would reject such insinuations and never lend a hand in projects of this kind.

---

* W.S.A. viii/64, Berichte aus England. From Apponyi, No. 51 B of 9 July 1862, ff. 24–5. The usual account is that given by Vitzthum von Eckstaedt, *St Petersburg and London*, [1887], ii, 172. W. H. Dawson, *The German Empire*, [1919], i, 158–61, questions the account on the ground that Bismarck said he was about to become Minister-President of Prussia, a fact not then certain. But it will be seen that, according to Apponyi, he made no such claim.

† Buckle, *Life of Disraeli*, [1916], iv, 341.

Document 81. *Palmerston and Russell on Bismarck and French military strength*, 1860–3

i. 8 *October* 1860.*

...I had no Idea that Prussia had such serious Intentions of attacking France during the late Italian war as these Papers disclose. Ma Foi elle l'a échappée belle. She would have been fairly Trounced if she had carried her Intentions into execution, and her Rhenish Provinces would by this Time have been Part of the French Empire....

ii. 21 *January* 1861.†

...It may be doubtful whether Prussia is not falling into a Trap about her Quarrel with Denmark and whether France may not be lying in wait for a Rupture between those Parties to side with Denmark and threaten Rhenish Prussia....

iii. 3 *March* 1863.‡

...The French probably thought that Prussia would not or could not back out of their agreement with Russia, and that if She did not do so upon the Representation of England France and Austria France would have a fine opportunity of occupying the Rhenish Provinces, ostensibly as a Measure of Coercion but intending that Measure to end in Conquest.

People say that the Conduct of the King of Prussia is making his Subjects in those Rhenish Provinces turn their Thoughts much towards France.

iv. 27 *June* 1863.§

This is highly probable and indeed more than probable, and the gentlemen at Frankfurt and the crazy Minister at Berlin

* G. & D. 22/21, *Pte Russell Papers*. Palmerston to Russell, 8 October 1860. Palmerston had just seen papers relating to Prussia's military preparations on the Rhine in 1859.

† G. & D. 22/21, *Pte Russell Papers*. Palmerston to Russell, 21 January 1861.

‡ G. & D. 22/22, *Pte Russell Papers*. Palmerston to Russell, 3 March 1863. At this time there was a secret Treaty between France and Russia. *V.* B. H. Sumner, 'The Secret Franco-Russian Treaty of 3 March 1859', *Eng. Hist. Rev.* XLVIII, [January 1933], 65–83.

§ B.M. Add. MSS. 38,989, *Pte Layard Papers*, f. 147. Palmerston to Russell, 27 June 1863, with note by Russell, 10 July. It is not clear to what "This" in the first line refers. A similar letter (26 December 1863) from Palmerston to Russell says "the French would walk over" the Prussian army, *v.* Spencer Walpole, *Life of Lord John Russell*, [1889], II, 388 n.

[Bismarck] should have this impressed upon them. Any aggressive Measure of Germany ag[ains]t Denmark would most likely lead to an aggressive move of France ag[ains]t Germany, and specially ag[ains]t Prussia the main instigator of such aggression. The Prussian Provinces would at once be occupied by France and in the present state of the Prussian army its system of drill Formation and movements, the first Serious Encounter between it and the French would be little less disastrous to Prussia than the Battle of Jena.

P[ALMERSTON] 27/6–63.

Baron Gros told me that the Pr[ussian] Gov[ernment] was about to make representations in Germany similar to Mine. A war of France ag[ain]st Germany would be no light matter.

R[USSELL] 10 JULY [1863]

Document 82. *Palmerston and Russell advise the King of Prussia and Bismarck to be constitutional, 1863*

i. *Palmerston, 27 June 1863.**

   a. C[oun]t Bismarck might be privately told that if The King's Life is in Danger C[oun]t B[ismarck] and the unwise and unconstitutional system he is persuading the King to adopt were the true Causes of that Danger.

P[ALMERSTON] 27/6/63.

   b. C[oun]t Bismarck might be reminded that the Insurrection in Poland was provoked by the notorious violation of the Treaty of Vienna by Russia, and that it does not seem [fit] for Prussia one of the Parties to that Treaty to assist Russia in maintaining her violation of that Treaty.

P[ALMERSTON] 27/6/63.

ii. *Russell, 17–19 August 1863.†*

   ...What will the King of Prussia do? but abdicate, I guess.

R[USSELL] 17 AUG. 63.

---

* *F.O.* 96/27. Rough Notes by Palmerston under this date.
† B.M. Add. MSS. 38,989, *Pte Layard Papers*, f. 254, Russell to Layard, 17 August 1863.

[Russell gives instructions to write privately to Lowther regretting the King of Prussia's decision to refuse to attend the Council of German Princes summoned by the Emperor of Austria.]

There can be no Germany without Prussia.

R[USSELL] AUG. 19 63.*

Document 83. *Palmerston on the situation in September* 1863†

...These German Gentlemen appear to be determined to mettre le feu aux Etoupes, as Bulow used to say. When we remonstrate with them it is the old story of the shoulder of mutton which one Thief had not got and which the other had not stolen. Austria and Prussia say that execution depends on the other Members of the Diet, and the other Members say it all depends on Austria and Prussia. But they ought all to understand that they are beginning an affair the end of which may be different from the Beginning, and not by any means agreeable to them.

Document 84. *Palmerston's warning to those who attempt to attack Denmark,* 23 *July* 1863‡

...There is no use in disguising the fact that what is at the bottom of the German design, and the desire of connecting Schleswig with Holstein, is the dream of a German fleet, and the wish to get Kiel as a German seaport. That may be a good reason why they should wish it; but it is no reason why they should violate the rights and independence of Denmark for an object which, even if accomplished, would not realize the expectation of those who aim at it. The hon. Gentleman [Mr Seymour Fitzgerald] asks what is the policy and the course of Her Majesty's Government with regard to that dispute. As I have already said, we concur entirely with him, and I am satisfied with all reasonable men in Europe, including those

* B.M. Add. MSS. 38,989, *Pte Layard Papers*, f. 258, 19 August. Note by Russell.

† G. & D. 22/22, *Pte Russell Papers*. Palmerston to Russell, 29 September 1863.

‡ *Hans. Deb.*, 3rd Ser., CLXXII, 1252, 23 July 1863.

in France and Russia, in desiring that the independence, the integrity, and the rights of Denmark may be maintained. We are convinced—I am convinced at least—that if any violent attempt were made to overthrow those rights and interfere with that independence, those who made the attempt would find in the result, that it would not be Denmark alone with which they would have to contend.

30. THE BRITISH REFUSAL OF NAPOLEON'S INVITATION TO A CONGRESS, NOVEMBER 1863

[No event affected Europe in general, or England in particular, more than the British refusal of Napoleon's invitation to a European Congress. It divided France and England just when their united strength was needed to oppose Austria's and Prussia's attempt on Schleswig-Holstein.

By the end of 1863 Napoleon was sorely embarrassed. There were hints of disaster over his venture in Mexico; Prussia had rudely repelled his attempt at intervention in Poland. He blamed England for failing to support him in both cases. He therefore proposed to redeem his reputation by summoning a European Congress at Paris. He would settle the problems of Italy, Schleswig-Holstein, Rumania, Poland. He hoped that England would help him to restore his damaged reputation. Palmerston saw in this proposal a trap. His distrust of Napoleon, since the annexation of Nice and Savoy, had been increased since the Polish imbroglio. A Congress might enable Napoleon to carve Europe and escape from all the remaining bonds of the Treaty of Vienna. Palmerston began his attack on the proposal by a historical sketch. This was on the lines of previous arguments both by himself (1849) and by Russell (*supra*, pp. 206–8). On this occasion, moreover, Russell was not wholly unfavourable to the idea of a Congress until 18 November. But the arrival of a new letter from Palmerston clinched his decision, and on the 19th he informed the Austrian Minister of the British decision.

Prussia had already accepted Napoleon's invitation, though with some reservations. Austria ultimately refused though with some courtesy. England's refusal, which was proclaimed to the world, completed the final severance between Napoleon and England, and it was Schleswig-Holstein which felt the results of that severance.]

Document 85. *Palmerston on the general functions of a Congress, 8 November* 1863*

This Proposal of a Congress seems to require very serious Consideration. We might simply accept, or simply refuse or ask what Questions would be considered, and what excluded. At the End of a war when States of Territorial Possession have been forcibly changed, a Congress may be necessary in order to Settle what should thenceforward be the Boundaries of States and the Rights of Sovereigns; and so it was in 1815, and to a less Degree in 1856 after the war with Russia. But what are the unsettled Territorial Questions of the present Day? The arrangements of Vienna of 1815 have in many Instances it is true been modified, and in some violently set aside, the modifications were sanctioned at the Time by Treaties, are we prepared now to legalize the violations—to some we should willingly give our Sanction from others we should withold it. The Separation of Belgium from Holland was a modification regularly Sanctioned at the Time and not requiring any fresh assent. The Elevation of Napoleon to the Throne was a setting aside, not of the general Treaty of 1815, but of a separate Engagement, but it has been sanctioned by the acknowledgement of all civilized Nations and requires no Confirmation. The Transfer of Lombardy to Pie[d]mont was an alteration of the Treaty of Vienna, but was sanctioned by the Treaty of Villa Franca. The Cession of Nice and Savoy to France were alterations of the Vienna Treaty, but were regularized by Treaty, only that in the Case of Savoy the Stipulation of Vienna about the Neutrality of Chablais and Fraucigny has been dropped. The Cession requires no Confirmation, and we should not sanction the leaving out of the neutrality Condition. These are the Changes made by formal Compacts at the Time. There are some made without proper Sanction, some of which we could...not sanction. The annexation of Tuscany, Parma Modena Emilia Naples and Sicily to the Kingdom of Italy, were all Breaches of the Treaty of

* G. & D. 22/22, *Pte Russell Papers.* Palmerston to Russell, 8 November 1863.

Vienna which have as far as I recollect received no direct European sanction by any formal Treaty. To these Transactions however we should most willingly give our sanction. Cracow has been swallowed up by Austria in violation of the Vienna Treaty, are we prepared to give our formal sanction to that absorption? perhaps it was sure to happen sooner or later, for a little Republic could hardly be long lived between Three Military Powers. The Kingdom of Poland has been misgoverned in violation of the Vienna Treaty but Russia does not seem inclined to govern it better.

Well then there are Two Functions which the Congress would, or might have to perform. The first to make regular, the Changes that have practically been accomplished and those are chiefly what I have just mentioned. The other Function would be to bring about and to sanction changes which are wished for, or which would be desirable. This last Function might range over a wide Field, and would give Rise to more Difference than agreement.

Many Sovereigns and States wish to have what belongs to their Neighbours, but are there many of those neighbours who would consent to the Cessions asked of them, and is the Congress to be invested with the Power possessed by that of Vienna in 1815: to compel submission to its Decrees? Does the Emperor conceive that his Congress would give its Seal to his Map of Europe of 1860? If there was any chance that a Congress would give Moldo Wallachia to Austria and Venetia and Rome to Italy and incorporate Sleswig with Denmark, and separate the Poland of 1815 from Russia and make it an independent State not touching the Question of The Rhine as a French Frontier nor the relieving Russia from what was imposed upon her by the Treaty of Paris such a Congress would be a well doer by Europe but such Results can scarcely be expected. The Congress—if it met would probably separate without any important Results. But there would be France and Russia on one side, England and Austria on the other and the other States acting according to their views of the Questions discussed. What States are to be represented? of Course the 5 who signed the Vienna Treaty, and probably Turkey in addition as well as Italy. But I see the German Confederation, and the Swiss Confederation are to be invited. Switzerland is an independent aggregate, but the German Confederation consists partly of Delegates from Powers who would have Representatives of their own. Would Belgium and Holland be represented. Here would be 13 or 14 States some of them no Doubt with Two Representatives. What a Babel of Tongues and what a Confusion of Interests. It is not likely that war would follow out of it, but there would not be much Chance of any considerable Results. I doubt whether we should even get Spain to give up her Slave Trade, or France to abide [by] and faithfully to execute her abandonment of that Crime.

Document 86. *Palmerston's particular objections to a Congress, 18 November 1863**

[Russell, in an interview with the Austrian Ambassador two days after (*v.* **Doc. 87**), also deprecated a Congress. Count Apponyi indicated that Austria would be unfavourable. Russell seems to have been converted by Palmerston's letter and this interview (*v. supra*, p. 253).]

I think your proposed Line of answer to the Emperor is the safe and the true one. A Congress meeting to discuss the Affairs of Poland, Italy, Denmark and Moldo Wallachia, could come to no other Result than that of formally recording, and making more irreconcileable, fundamental Differences of Interests and Opinions.

Why should we expect Russia to be more willing to concede to Europe about Poland in verbal Controversy round a Table, than she has been in courteous diplomatic Communications, and if the Congress were to obtain no Concession from Russia, Europe would have no Choice except submitting to Humiliation or reverting to war.

Italy would be an equally unpromising Subject of Discussion. Would the Congress have merely to record and establish by European Sanction the present Condition of Italy, as to territorial Possession, or would it be asked to restore some

* G. & D. 22/22, *Pte Russell Papers*. Palmerston to Russell, 18 November 1863.

Parts of Italy to former owners, or would it be invited to urge and to Sanction further Transfers and Changes. The first of these arrangements would not suit Austria, the Pope or the King of Italy. Austria and the Pope would not like to sanction by Treaty the changes and Transfers already made; The King of Italy would not like to record by such a Treaty his abandonment of all Pretension to Venetia and Rome.

The second alternative would suit Austria and the French Emperor, especially the latter who is bent upon separating Naples from the Italian Kingdom, and on restoring a Separate Monarchy of the Two Sicilies. But this would not suit the Italians if they are wise, though from what I have heard from some of them, I suspect that in their present shortsighted Turn of mind, they would give up the Ten Million Neapolitans and Sicilians in Exchange for Venetia if they could so get it. But this would be a bad European arrangement. Naples and Sicily ought to remain as they now are, a Part of united Italy.

As to the last alternative the Task would be hopeless. Who can expect that at present at least Austria would give up Venetia, or that the Emperor would throw over the Pope. As to Austria we know that if any Proposals were made about a Cession of Venetia, She would leave the Congress. If indeed the Scheme which you say Aali is inclined to, could be effected, and the Moldo Wallachian Provinces could be given to Austria in Exchange for Venetia, Italy making money Compensation to Turkey, such a Scheme would be good for Austria, Italy, and Turkey, but would no Doubt be much opposed by Russia, and probably objected to by the Moldo Wallachians.

The Two really European Questions being thus put aside there remain only the Dispute between Denmark and the Diet and the Contumacy of Prince Couza and neither of these Matters, as you justly observe seem to be in their nature of sufficient Magnitude and Importance to require that Europe should assemble in Congress, in order to settle them.

The State of Europe in 1815 was wholly different from what it is now. At that Time the Success of French arms had

swept away most of the territorial Boundaries, and separate
Sovereignties which existed before 1792; The Tide of Conquest which at first ran from West to East, then returned
back from East to West and swept away almost all that
France had established. Europe was a political Waste, and
required the action of a Body of Inclosure Commissioners to
allot the Lands and to give holding Titles. This was done at
Vienna in 1814 and 1815. But nothing of the Kind exists
in 1863, and nobody wants an improved Title to any Possession except those who ought not to get it, as for Instance
Russia to the Kingdom of Poland, Austria to Cracow,
France to Savoy without neutrality and the Pope to what he
holds and as much as he could get back.

It is quite certain that the Deliberations of a Congress
would consist of Demands and Pretensions put forward by
some, and resolutely resisted by others and that there being
no Supreme Authority in Such an assembly to enforce the
Opinions or Decisions of the Majority, The Congress would
separate leaving Many of the Members on Worse Terms with
Each other than when they met.*

Document 87. *Russell's account of the Cabinet's decision to
refuse the Congress, 19 November 1863†*

[Palmerston's letter (**Doc. 86**) was written to Russell the day
before the Cabinet meeting of 19 November. On the 20th Count
Apponyi came to tell him formally what he had already privately
indicated on the 18th, that Austria would refuse to attend, and
Russell addressed him as follows.]

It was essential...to know the questions which Napoleon
III meant to submit to the deliberations of the Congress.
We have lately had confidential but certain information on
the subject. They were first, Poland; then the relations of
Germany and Denmark; then the affairs of Italy; finally
those of the Danubian principalities. I admit these to be the

* There are two other letters from Palmerston printed in Ashley's *Life*,
[1876], ii, 236–44, one of 15 November 1863 to Leopold King of the Belgians
and the other of 2 December to Russell.

† W.S.A. viii/67, Berichte aus England. From Apponyi, No. 87A of 22
November 1863, ff. 434–9, reporting an interview with Russell of the 20th.

four most important questions and that a Congress could not assemble without occupying itself with them. On the other hand, not one of these questions could hope to be satisfactorily solved in a Congress, or would not lead, after estrangement of interests and irremediable disputes, inevitably to war. We could no longer hesitate when we once had this conviction, and in the cabinet council of yesterday we decided to decline to take part in the Congress. I had already prepared a despatch giving our motives; it was approved by Lord Palmerston and my other colleagues and this morning I have submitted it to the Queen, who gave her cordial assent.*

[The dispatch was ultimately sent under date of 25 November 1863. It was actually published in the *Gazette* on the 27th before the French Government received it. This circumstance and the sharpness of the dispatch itself were deeply resented by Napoleon.†]

31. THE GERMAN INTERVENTION, NOVEMBER 1863–JANUARY 1864

[Palmerston's boast of July 1863 had suggested that England would defend the integrity of Denmark. England's refusal to join Napoleon's Congress made it unlikely that France would support Palmerston in any such defence. It was soon to be revealed that neither Queen, Cabinet nor Parliament would support him either.

It is necessary to explain the situation by a few brief words.‡ The essential point is to realize that the Danish kingdom had attached to it three Duchies, Schleswig, Holstein and Lauenburg. All these were juridically distinct from Denmark proper, that is they had certain rights and privileges of their own. Holstein and Lauenburg were overwhelmingly German and Holstein, as a member of the Bund or German Diet, was entitled to its protection. The Danish attempt to interfere with the rights, or to alter the status of Holstein, was therefore certain to be resented and likely to lead to war. There had been actual war between the German powers and Denmark after the revolution of 1848 and it is of historic importance that it was Russell and Palmerston who

* The Queen had already told King Leopold "this Congress is in fact an impertinence" [12 November 1863], *Letters of Queen Victoria*, 2nd Ser., [1926], I, 114.
† The text is in Hertslet, *Map*, [1875], II, 1583–8.
‡ The general situation is very well summarized in Gooch, *Later Correspondence of Lord John Russell*, [1925], II, Chap. xv—and generally *v.* L. D. Steefel, *The Schleswig-Holstein Question*, Harvard Press, [1932].

patched up a peace and avoided a general war. It was a case in which a good temporary settlement produced a permanent unrest. And the two British negotiators paid the price by seeing their patchwork torn to pieces.

The instrument which pacified the north was signed at London by Malmesbury for England on 8 May 1852. It really represented the ideas of Palmerston and Russell.* This settlement was a good one for the time being, but it had several defects. It was not signed by the German Bund, but by Austria and Prussia as individual powers. It did not guarantee the settlement, it merely acknowledged the integrity of the Danish monarchy and declared it an important element in the Balance of European Power. Similarly, Prince Christian of Glucksburg was simply acknowledged as heir to the childless King Frederick. There was no guarantee but merely an acknowledgment by the signatory powers (i.e. Austria, England, France, Russia, Prussia and Sweden). This amounted merely to a suggestion that none of the signatory powers (e.g. Austria or Russia) were likely to disturb the integrity of Denmark. If they did, France and England gave no pledge to defend Denmark by force of arms. If France were friendly and public opinion favourable in England the two together would doubtless prevent Russia and Austria from attacking Denmark. That is what Palmerston hoped would happen when he made his boast in July 1863.† But, if France were estranged from England and Palmerston was opposed in his own Cabinet or by the majority in Parliament, Denmark would be at the mercy of Austria and Prussia. That is what actually happened in 1864.

The second point left doubtful was the nature of the settlement. It was hoped of course that Denmark would govern Schleswig and Holstein according to their old privileges. But there was nothing except their own promises which could compel the Danes to do so. Holstein was predominantly German, Schleswig was receiving an increasing quantity of German settlers, German nationalism was a rising tide. A violent chauvinism reigned in Denmark of which the childless King Frederick had to take notice. He finally tried to solve the difficulty by granting self-government to Holstein and incorporating Schleswig in Denmark. This compromise pleased nobody.

Palmerston and Russell had at first been by no means friendly to the Germans. When Mr John Ward produced a memorandum favourable to their claims, Palmerston would not publish it as a

---

* Text of the Treaty of 8 May 1852 in Hertslet, *Map*, [1875], II, 1151–5. It is really a formal recognition of the protocol already signed under Palmerston's mediation by all the Powers above mentioned except Prussia, 2 August 1850, cp. *ibid.* II, 1137–8.

† *V. supra*, p. 249.

Blue Book.* In the autumn of 1862 Lord John Russell went to Gotha, came under German influences, and wrote the famous "Gotha dispatch". This was really a settlement of the Schleswig-Holstein difficulties on moderate German lines. The attempt failed and the crisis became graver. The Prince of Wales became betrothed to a Danish Princess in the autumn of this year, and married her in March 1863. In the same month King Frederick issued a declaration proclaiming his intention to take action against the Duchy of Holstein, which was practically in revolt. Russell pressed King Frederick to abandon his purpose. He not only refused, but prepared a new constitution unifying all the provinces. He proposed to unite Schleswig, Holstein and Lauenburg under the Danish Crown, and destroy all their separate rights and privileges.

Frederick VII died suddenly leaving his new unifying and revolutionary constitution unsigned. The Prince of Glucksburg succeeded with the title of Christian IX and, after a few days of hesitation, signed and issued the new constitution, unifying all his dominions, on 18 November 1863. He would probably have lost his throne if he had not thus given way to Danish public opinion. Yet it was impossible for the German Bund as a whole, or for Austria or Prussia separately, to accept such a defiance. Holstein was a member of the Bund and obviously the German powers could not let her be treated as an integral part of Denmark. It was the moment for her to free herself from what she thought unjust coercion. The Duchy of Holstein refused allegiance to the new King. The Prince of Augustenburg claimed both Schleswig and Holstein and many Germans supported him. Austria declined to receive the Danish envoy sent to announce the accession of the new King. Prussia followed suit. No one seems to have doubted that the German Bund had determined on a Federal Execution, which meant that German troops would occupy Holstein. The Danish King revoked the March patent on 4 December, but this step, urged by Russell, passed almost unnoticed. The furies were unloosed and concession was too late to affect the situation.

Russell sent Lord Wodehouse as special envoy to Denmark to congratulate the new King on his accession. He seized the opportunity to define British policy. There seem to have been struggles in the Cabinet, because Russell's original draft implied "a threat of war". Eventually the instructions recommended "patience and impartiality" to the Great Powers, and instructed Wodehouse (No. 4 of 9 December) to "point out to M. de Bismarck the dangers of any execution in Holstein by German

* I.e. in 1857. It was only published in pursuance of an address in 1864, v. A. & P., [1864], LXV, [3292], 729-41; cp. Temperley and Penson, Century of Diplomatic Blue Books, No. 660.

troops at the present time, but you will not press this point, if it should appear inexpedient to do so".* Wodehouse in his interview with "M. de Bismarck" tried to stress the binding character of the Treaty of 1852, as pledging the Powers to preserve the integrity of Denmark. But Bismarck met him with the telling argument that the King of Denmark had already broken the pledges with regard to the position of Schleswig, Holstein and Lauenburg. Article III of the 1852 Treaty said "the reciprocal Rights and Obligations of His Majesty the King of Denmark, and of the Germanic Confederation [Bund], concerning the Duchies of Holstein and Lauenburg, Rights and Obligations established by the Federal Act of 1815, and by the existing Federal Right, shall not be affected by the present Treaty".† The Bund found it impossible to give way over this and on 24 December the German Bund troops entered Lauenburg and Holstein for purposes of Federal Execution.

Doc. 88 shews what Russell thought, just before the Federal troops had entered Holstein, but when he regarded their invasion as inevitable. It will be seen that, while he does not propose to take action because of the German occupation in Holstein, he hints that a German occupation of Schleswig will be a *casus belli* for England. Events moved quickly. Austria and Prussia decided to occupy Schleswig. The Bund wanted to support the claims of the German prince Augustenburg, Austria and Prussia to uphold the Treaty of 1852. The Bund refused to occupy Schleswig, Austria and Prussia decided to do so—and sent an ultimatum to Denmark on 16 January demanding the withdrawal of the November Constitution in forty-eight hours.]

Document 88. *Russell talks to Apponyi on the Schleswig-Holstein crisis, 19 December 1863‡*

The question of Schleswig-Holstein played a great part in my last interview with the Principal Secretary of State.... While taking into account the difficulties which involve the

* The dispatches are in *F.O.* 211/110. To Lord Wodehouse, Nos. 4 & 5 of 9 December 1863 (*v.* also *F.O.* 22/306, which shews that both were seen by the Cabinet and the Queen). G. & D. 22/27, *Pte Russell Papers*, contains a series of comments by members of the Cabinet modifying the original dispatch. These are not given by L. D. Steefel, *The Schleswig-Holstein Question*, [1932], 137–8.

From Wodehouse, No. 3 of 12 December 1863, reporting Bismarck, No. 6 of 13 December, reporting King William, *F.O.* 211/110. Bismarck repeated this argument to Austria—"no fulfilment of the Danish obligations of 1851–2, no Treaty of London", L. D. Steefel, *The Schleswig-Holstein Question*, [1932], 100.

† Hertslet, *Map*, [1875], II, 1153.

‡ W.S.A. VIII/67, *Berichte aus England*. From Apponyi, No. 93A of 19 December 1863.

position of the two great German powers [Austria and Prussia] and doing justice to their moderation, at least as compared with the exaggerations of ultra-German fanaticism, Lord Russell deeply regrets and is seriously alarmed at the determination of the Cabinets of Vienna and Berlin to consider the Treaty of London as invalid in their eyes, unless the Danish constitution of 18 November [1863] is withdrawn, in so far as it relates to Schleswig, between now and the 1st of January. He hopes, in fact, that this concession will be made and that the Cabinet and Rigsraad [Parliament] of Copenhagen will be induced by the efforts of European diplomacy to make this concession easy for the [Danish] King who is personally in favour of it. But if this arrangement fails, would that be reason enough to consider the Treaty as null and to deliver Denmark to anarchy, thus opening anew the question of the succession with all the train of different claims and more or less contested or contestable rights? In such conduct England would only see the manifest violation of a solemn treaty and a greater danger for Austria and Prussia than that which they would run by resisting the tide of German popular passions.

Lord Russell hopes that the measure of federal execution will be limited to Holstein: but even in such case can they prevent the separatist party organizing itself, under the protection of federal bayonets, and proclaiming the Prince of Augustenburg? Can they prevent the Pretender himself from entering the Duchy and putting himself at the head of his partisans? Can they avoid a conflict with the Danish troops near the bridgeheads of Frederichstadt and Rendsburg which the Danes seem determined to defend? Those are the complications to be feared and the Principal Secretary of State fears Austria and Prussia will be drawn further than they intended at the outset, and without wishing to be. In such case the affair would assume very disturbing proportions, the British Government could not answer, from now onwards, for the attitude which circumstances might impose on it.

Having pressed my interlocutor to know if he saw a possible case in which the Government would actively take part in favour of Denmark he answered me, begging me however to consider his words confidential and private, that if the German Powers, for example, repudiated the Treaty of London, contested King Christian's sovereignty over Denmark, invaded Schleswig, and supported there the rights of the Duke of Augustenburg, England might consider these acts as a *casus belli*, and lend Denmark the aid of her fleet.* The sympathies of the British public for the Danish cause were stronger than was generally believed, especially since the marriage of the Prince of Wales and despite the desire and interest the country had in the maintenance of peace, he would not be astonished to see public opinion on fire for this cause as for that of Poland and of Italy.

Lord Russell does not doubt our goodwill nor even that of the Cabinet of Berlin, to circumscribe the question as far as possible within reasonable and moderate limits, and he still hopes these dispositions, joined to the efforts of British French and Russian diplomacy, will succeed in producing a peaceful solution.

He told me that, so far as he knew, General Fleury† had no precise instructions and was only charged to declare that, whatever happened, Denmark ought not to count on the material support of France....

[Palmerston expressed views in January 1864 when he had just learnt of the Austro-Prussian ultimatum. They shew that his fear was a German unification of Schleswig-Holstein. They shew also that, despite his boasts, he had no intention of going to war for Schleswig alone. Moreover, by 27 January one thing was quite clear to the whole Cabinet—France would not join England in using force to defend Denmark.‡ Palmerston, however, still recommended trying to obtain "the co-operation of France in diplomatic [i.e. not military] action". It was all in vain. On 1 February the Prussian forces crossed into Holstein followed after

* This seems to be the extent of Russell's threat, *v. infra*, pp. 274–5; also G. & D. 22/23, *Pte Russell Papers*, Gladstone to Russell, 1 July 1864. "I apprehend that your 'menaces', as far as they were specific, had reference wholly to the invasion of Schleswig; and that they were confined to the period before you [Russell] were aware that there would be no cooperation beyond a moral one by France and Russia in maintaining the Treaty of 1852."

† French diplomatist on special mission.

‡ G. & D. 22/27, *Pte Russell Papers*. Minute by George Grey, 26 January 1864, initialled by Gladstone, 27 January 1864.

a short time by the Austrians. This step was not opposed by the German Bund, which remained content with "Federal Execution" in Holstein. Now the seriousness of this step lay in the fact that Austria and Prussia were signatories of the Treaty of 1852, which the Bund was not. Hence they were breaking the Treaty, relying on the pretext that Denmark had broken it first. Austria and Prussia maintained, however, that they were merely occupying Schleswig as a "material guarantee" to induce Denmark to see reason.]

Document 89. *Palmerston on the obligations of the Treaty of 1852 on Denmark and Germany, 18 January 1864**

...I took great Pains in the Negotiations which led to the Treaty of 1852 to obtain from the Germans an abandonment of this Pretension to a Sleswig-Holstein State; and you will see by looking back to the Correspondence that in the Negotiations and Interchange of Engagements in the Course of which Denmark promised not to incorporate Sleswig with Denmark, the Germans renounced their Demand for the Union of Sleswig with Holstein. The Germans cannot with Justice or Reason claim the Engagement of Denmark not to incorporate Sleswig and in the same Breath retract their Engagement not to ask for the union of Sleswig with Holstein....

Document 90. *Palmerston's advice to Denmark, 19 January 1864†*

...What has happened about Holstein ought to be a Lesson to them [The Danes]. If they had revoked the Patent of March 63 in proper Time, Holstein would not have been occupied by German Troops...If they now quickly repeal the new Constitution as it regards Sleswig, Austria and Prussia will have no Pretence for invading Sleswig....Denmark must not suppose that any of its non German Allies would go to war with all Germany in order to expel the Austrian and Prussian Troops from Sleswig upon the mere Question of

* G. & D. 22/15, *Pte Russell Papers*. Palmerston to Russell, 18 January 1864. For Russell's view of the German violation of their pledges *v. infra*, pp. 273–5.

† G. & D. 22/23, *Pte Russell Papers*. Palmerston to Russell, 19 January 1864. The Danish King had revoked the "March Patent" on 4 December 1863, but too late.

whether Sleswig and Holstein should be administratively united into one Duchy to be held by the King of Denmark or whether they should remain with separate internal organization. Great Powers like Russia may persevere in wrong doing, and other States may not like to make the Effort necessary for compelling it to take the right Course. But no such Impunity in wrong is possessed by a small and weak State like Denmark. Such a State is sure to be coerced by its Stronger Neighbours, and common Prudence and a Regard for its own Interests and safety must counsel it to set itself right with the least possible Delay. . . .

Document 91. *Discussion of Cabinet members on hearing that France will not use force, 26–7 January* 1864*

I do not think that these Despatches deprive us of the Hope of the Cooperation of France in diplomatic [i.e. non-military] action for the Maintenance of the Treaty and of the Integrity of Denmark, and if no diplomatic action was ever to take Place unless there was beforehand a formed Intention to follow it up by Force there would be an end to all Negotiation and it would be better to begin by an Ultimatum and follow it up by an immediate Blow. . . .   P[ALMERSTON] 26/1/64.

We now know that France will not join us in the use of force in defence of Denmark. . . .

> G[EORGE] G[REY] 26 JAN[UARY] 1864.
> W. E. G[LADSTONE] 27 JAN[UARY] 1864.

It is quite clear. . .that France will not risk war in order to support the treaty of 1852—that is the integrity of the present Danish territory. But I do not think that Lord Russell ever proposed that we sh[oul]d do so. His original proposal was to offer material assistance in the event of an attempt to place the Duke of Augustenburg directly or indirectly in possession of Schleswig. . . .

> C[HARLES] W[OOD] [26 JANUARY 1864].

* G. & D. 22/27, *Pte Russell Papers*. The final conviction as to the refusal of France to use force was due to a dispatch of 25 January 1864 from Cowley.

32. THE BRITISH ATTITUDE AT THE LON-DON CONFERENCE, 25 APRIL–25 JUNE 1864

[The Cabinet had considered and rejected the use of force early in January. On 2 February Derby, the leader of the Opposition, made a pacific speech, largely under royal influence. But the invasion of Holstein by Austro-Prussian forces on 1 February created a new situation. Palmerston even thought that the Austro-Prussians might occupy Copenhagen and on 21 February the Channel fleet was ordered home, and the intention to send a British squadron to Copenhagen was made known to France and Russia.* They were asked to join in the naval demonstration. Here, however, Russell had gone too far, and the Cabinet took steps to check any demonstration. On 24 February they decided in effect to revoke their previous decision and inform France and Russia that there was no more question of sending the fleet to Copenhagen. They were satisfied with Austro-Prussian assurances and did not believe that an attack by the Austrian fleet was any longer contemplated. As England thus subsided France became more bellicose, especially as the Austro-Prussian troops went beyond Holstein into pure Danish territory and invaded Jutland. This fact was known in Paris on 21 February. It created a new situation once more. Denmark, with her own kingdom invaded, was at last really at war with Austria and Prussia. But none the less, as before related, the British Cabinet had decided against sending the fleet on 24 February, with no dissentients save Palmerston and the Chancellor.† On the same day Russia, in ignorance of this decision, refused the previous British request to join in a naval demonstration. Her attitude was due partly to the fact that Russian ships were bound in ice in the Gulf of Finland till mid-May. It was also due to the Tsar's hatred and suspicion of Napoleon III, whom he wished to keep in isolation, and to his friendly feeling for Bismarck.

Austro-Prussians had invaded Jutland on 20 February. This advance may have been an accident due to military ardour or strategic reasons, but it had the important result of clarifying the situation. Austria agreed reluctantly to support the invasion of Jutland in a Convention of 6 March which she signed with Prussia. As hostilities had already begun at sea between Denmark and the German lands the whole basis of things was changed. War dissolves treaties and thus destroyed the great aim of Russell, which had been to maintain the integrity of the Treaty of 1852.

* V. L. D. Steefel, *The Schleswig-Holstein Question*, [1932], 178.
† *Ibid.* 179, 199–200; *v.* also *Letters of Queen Victoria*, 2nd Ser., [1926], I, 160–8.

All he could do, therefore, was to press on the negotiations for a Conference of the Powers at London. Clarendon, who had just entered the Cabinet, went on a private mission to Paris, but Napoleon declared quite frankly he was not prepared to go to war with Germany. Russell's only resource would have been to offer France compensation on the Rhine—and that was all against his and Palmerston's ideas.* Then finally on 18 April the Prussians captured Düppel, thus securing a bridge-head into the isle of Alsen.

The Conference opened at London on 25 April 1864. It included representatives from Great Britain, Austria, Denmark, France, the German Bund, Prussia, Russia and Sweden. All of the territory of Lauenburg and Holstein was occupied by German troops; Austro-Prussian troops occupied all Schleswig except Alsen and part of Poland. An Austrian naval squadron was, it was thought, about to proceed through the Channel and North Sea to reinforce the German fleet in the Baltic. Palmerston, always sensitive as to naval movements, determined to stop this one and had an interview with Apponyi, the Austrian Minister, for the purpose, on 1 May. This is what he called "a notch off my own bat". It was followed by heated discussion in the Cabinet as to how far the incident should be recorded in a dispatch. There were remonstrances from the Queen and the whole ended in a rather feeble compromise between Russell's direct demands and the milder views of the Cabinet. The account of the conversation here given is that of Apponyi, which confirms, but considerably amplifies, Palmerston's own version.† A careful study of the whole incident shews how far England's reputation had already sunk, if even Palmerston could speak of her as being considered "poltronne" in Germany. There is something pathetic in his claim to divine the instincts of that public in England which had so recently deserted him.]

Document 92. *Palmerston warns Austria against sending a fleet to the Baltic,* 1 *May* 1864‡

The First Minister opened the interview by saying he wished to have a frank explanation with me on the subject of our [naval] squadron. "You know our opinion", said he,

* Cp. Palmerston to Queen Victoria, 22 February 1864: "If the Rhenish provinces of Prussia should be added to France, everybody in England would say that it served Prussia right; but everybody would feel that it was a severe blow to English interests through such a change in the balance of Power." *Letters of Queen Victoria,* 2nd Ser., [1926], I, 165.

† Palmerston to Russell, 1 May 1864, Ashley, *Life,* [1876], II, 249–52.

‡ W.S.A. VIII/70, Berichte aus England. From Apponyi, No. 42 C of 3 May 1864. In the original the dispatch is almost without paragraphs. These have been inserted at appropriate places.

"about your conduct towards Denmark. You think it right, we think it unjustifiable and I maintain that glory, if there is any in this war, belongs to the conquered not to the conquerors. However that may be since the war began our first impulse was to side [de prendre fait et cause] with the Danes. But it was winter, our fleet was condemned to inaction. Our army is small and British direct interests are not sufficiently engaged for immediate action to appear indispensable. We decided then to wait and to confine ourselves to representations to which I must say, you have paid no attention. We hoped that you would be moderate and conciliatory. Instead of that you occupied Schleswig, after occupying Holstein; next you invaded Jutland and now, not content with your victory on land, it is said that you are going to send your naval forces into the Baltic and reunite them to the Prussian boats, perhaps with the aim of occupying the Danish isles one by one, and ending the war by un coup d'éclat, by dictating peace at Copenhagen.

Look here, there are things which can be suffered (des choses qu'on peut passer), and things which cannot. I consider the passage of an Austrian squadron through our Channel and past our ports, to give help in a war which we strongly condemn, as an insult to England, and I am resolved, for my part, to leave the Cabinet rather than suffer such an affront. I am convinced that the country shares my views in this respect, for I flatter myself that I can divine the instincts and opinions of my countrymen. It is generally thought, and especially in Germany that England is cowardly [poltronne], that it wishes to avoid war at any price; you can easily be deceived. You know the price I attach to good relations with Austria; but if you enter the Baltic a struggle is inevitable, and that means war. A war between England on the one side and Austria and Germany on the other—for I doubt not that Germany would join you—would be a great calamity. We have no army to invade Germany with, nor one comparable with yours, but our navy is strong and we can do you much harm. There are ports in the Adriatic and Baltic and there are other enemies who only wait for the opportunity to fall upon Austria. All this deserves to be seriously considered, and I thought it more loyal to warn you in a friendly way of our mode of thought, so as to avoid disastrous consequences." [So far the conversation agrees with Palmerston's own version, what follows is much fuller.]

I thanked Lord Palmerston for his frankness and said that, although nothing which he had just said was new to me, it was valuable to hear it from his own mouth. I had long since known, I added, that England objected to our going into the Baltic. This eventuality had been more than once the subject of my conversations with Lord Russell, with the King of the Belgians and several [British] Ministers * had spoken to me in the same sense. I had always answered that there was no question of crossing the North Sea. I had given the most formal assurances, read dispatches, communicated the instructions given to our Admiral, and I was only surprised that after all this they seemed to attach more credence to reports, of which they might find a difficulty in disclosing the source, than to the word of an Ambassador speaking in the name of his Government.

"But", exclaimed Lord Palmerston, "your assurances are not conclusive, at bottom they are limited to saying that *for the moment* you have no intention of crossing the Baltic; but if circumstances altered, a new order from Vienna might modify your resolve. This can only satisfy us for *the present.* Also we have arranged that Russell should address you an official communication to let you know that if your intentions change, we can rely on your warning us *in time*, for in that case also we should change our intentions too. It seems to me that in answering such a communication you would in no way detract from your dignity by informing us that you do not intend to go into the Baltic."

I observed to Lord Palmerston that, as regards the question of dignity, my government was the sole judge, but that the answer we should make would depend in part on the tone of the English note, as that kind of document was in general

* This fact is not mentioned in Palmerston's version. The rest of this para-graph, and the whole of the next three, are also new.

dry, imperious and little calculated to evoke a friendly answer. I did not know whether my government would give a formal engagement, but I could assure my interlocutor that we were far from sharing the opinion that England had decided to avoid a contest at all costs. We knew perfectly well her superiority at sea and consequently, whatever we determined to do, we should take it into account especially after what he had just said to me.

He [Palmerston] might well consider that we were not attracted by running the risk of having our ships fired on by the British fleet, or of being obliged to retrace our steps at the summons of a British admiral. This argument, based on common sense, seemed to offer a stronger guarantee of our intentions, than all the written declarations that could be demanded. The English [i.e. Palmerston's] move seemed to me also inopportune, on the eve of the time when hostilities would probably be suspended by land and sea.* Besides, I must say that Denmark had taken the initiative in a maritime war and had thus obliged us to take in hand the defence of our commercial interests. It was therefore unjust to accuse us of extending a war which, on the contrary, we wished to confine within the narrowest limits.

[Lord Palmerston then asked Apponyi what he thought of the prospects of the conference. Apponyi dwelt at length on the strength of national feeling in Germany.]

"For Germans", added I, "this question is as much one of *right* as of nationality. You will never make a German understand that a dozen plenipotentiaries have the right to sit round a green table and dispose of the fate of a million of their compatriots contrary to pre-existing rights of succession and without consulting the estates of the Duchies or of the German Diet [Bund]. Hence the unanimous sentiment with which the German Governments are obliged to reckon, and with which we ourselves dare not wholly break, though try-ing to restrain it within the bounds of moderation." . . . If I went so far, it is because I wished to prepare Lord Palmerston

* The paragraph so far is similar to Palmerston's version. All the rest of the report is new.

for the worst and see what he would say. But I found the same indifference with him that struck me in the case of Lord Russell. He made no objections nor interruptions, and abstained from speaking of the *casus belli* if the Treaty of London [of 1852] were not kept. This reserve is explained if it is true that Clarendon only got five words out of Paris. The alarming vagueness which veils Napoleon's policy, to a certain extent, gives the key to the hesitation of the British Ministers.

33. DECLINE OF BRITISH PRESTIGE, MAY–JUNE 1864

[The British plan of settlement (**Doc. 93**) was drawn up by Russell on 5 May 1864. The memorandum was prepared by one British Foreign Minister and subjected to the criticisms of two other Ministers who had held this office. There is considerable interest in Russell's declaring that every nation has a right to regulate its own internal affairs, but cannot allow "a free choice of the form of government to every part of its dominions". Clarendon contested this, and Palmerston supported Russell, arguing that Holstein was disturbed by foreign adventurers. This was rather sophistical, for the foreign adventurers were received with a great deal of enthusiasm in the Duchies. Palmerston, in fact, used a much better argument to the Queen. "Your Majesty says that the people of Holstein and Schleswig were not consulted about the succession. Have they formally remonstrated during the ten years which have elapsed since the Treaty?"* These speculations by Victorians as to what we should call "self-determination" are really interesting.

Russell's actual plan seems to have been based on the untenable idea that the Danewerke was still a military barrier. It corresponded to no racial line and was therefore contrary to ethnic justice. It violated all the canons of historical and genealogical right. It was therefore a political compromise, only likely to be accepted when both sides were cool-headed. But the Danes saved Bismarck all trouble by refusing to accept this scheme. They also refused every project which protected Schleswig and Holstein from interference by Denmark or would have substituted a personal union with the Danish Crown for the one that existed. Bismarck and Austria therefore went out from the Conference. The day that it broke up Russell formulated the British policy anew in a Cabinet minute (**Doc. 95**) making clear England would not fight about Schleswig-Holstein alone.]

* Palmerston to Queen Victoria, 4 January 1863, *Letters of Queen Victoria*, 2nd Ser., [1926], I, 140.

Document 93. *The compromise scheme of Lord John Russell,*
5 May 1864*

In considering the terms of a solid and permanent arrangement of the dispute long continued between Germany and
Denmark, we must take into account the principles we have
maintained, the force we can use, and the allies upon whose
co-operation we can reckon. The matter of principle is not a
simple one. On the one side is the principle of undoubted
justice of allowing every nation to regulate its own internal
affairs according to its own views and opinions. This is the
principle which has guided us in regard to the affairs of
Italy. But in the application of this principle we are soon
met by another equally valid, namely that a Nation cannot
allow this free choice of its form of government to every part
of its dominions without hazard to its own existence. Thus
when the direct line of succession from William and Mary,
and from the Princess Anne failed the Parliament of England
settled the Crown upon the Electress Sophia and her des-
cendants, without consulting the people of Ireland, who
would in all probability have decided by a great majority in
favour of a Prince of the House of Stuart. Thus at the end of
the war of the Spanish succession the Catalans a brave and
spirited race would have preferred an Austrian Archduke to a
French Prince, but Spain could not allow a rich maritime
province to be torn from her side. Thus when in 1793 the
French Nation adopted a Republican form of government, it
is clear that Toulon and La Vendee [*sic*] would have given a
popular vote in favour of Monarchy, but the Republic could
not allow such a dismemberment, and established by force
the integrity of France.

Austria has lately acted on the same principle in regard to
Hungary. Such being the principles involved let us see how
they can be applied to the case before us.

Holstein is a German Duchy; it has a Diet of its own, and

* G. & D. 22/27, *Pte Russell Papers.* Memorandum on the German question of
5 May 1864. The memorandum is marked for circulation to Viscount Palmerston,
Earl of Clarendon, Duke of Somerset, Earl Granville, Chancellor of the Exchequer.

Germany has long maintained that it should have the right of voting its own laws, and its own taxes.

Its possession by Denmark is useful for the maintenance of the balance of power, but not essential to the existence of Denmark.

It is otherwise with Sleswig—Sleswig contained in 1860 according to the calculations of the Almanach de Gotha founded on an estimate made in 1849 by Adam de Biernatzki of Altona—of persons speaking

Low German	146,500
Danish	135,000
Frisian	33,000
German and Danish	85,000
	399,500

Thus of 400,000 inhabitants only 146,000 spoke German only—and 135,000 might be reckoned as Danish—and the remaining 118,000 as much Danish as German.

But apart from any detailed calculation which is always liable to dispute, it may be safely said that if South Sleswig is German, North Sleswig is decidedly Danish. But if it is a hardship to place Germans under a Danish administration it is equally a hardship to place Danes under a German administration. It cannot be assumed that the Danes are all wolves, and the Germans all lambs.

But besides this consideration, it may be safely affirmed that the separation of South Sleswig from Denmark whether under the title of Personal Union, or the bolder scheme of Dynastic Separation, would be incompatible with the safety of Denmark—Jutland and the Islands would form too strong a temptation for the Duke of Sleswig-Holstein backed and supported by Germany.

Thus a permanent peace would not be obtained.

If we pass from these considerations of justice and general policy to the urgent practical questions of the force of which we can dispose, and the Allies upon whom we can count, it must be observed—That we can act only by sea, and that only in the Summer time. It would not be safe to shut up a

British Fleet in the ice of Copenhagen harbour during the winter.—That France who could aid us by land shews a positive and persistent determination not to use force to save the Danish Monarchy—

That Russia is divided between her wish to save Denmark, and her unwillingness to break with the conservative Monarchies of Austria and Prussia.

It seems to me that a tolerable arrangement in these circumstances would be,

1. To add to Holstein the Southern part of Sleswig as far as the Slie and the Dannewerke.

2. To give to the Duchies of Holstein and Lauenburg thus augmented a power of self-government embracing legislative and administrative independence, and providing that no Danish or German troops in the service of other German States should ever enter it except with the joint consent of the German Confederation and of Denmark.

3. The rest of Sleswig to be joined to Denmark, and to be represented in the Danish Parliament for general affairs, and in a Sleswig Diet to be chosen by the people at large, for local affairs.

4. The Holstein troops to be commanded by the Lieutenant of the King in Holstein—The Lieutenant to be selected by the King out of three names to be presented to him by the Diet of Holstein. The Lieutenant in the absence of the King to have a Conseil of Administration chosen from among the members of the Diet.

MAY 5 1864. R[USSELL].

Document 94. *Clarendon's comment, 5 May 1864**

It can hardly be said that the principle w[hic]h guided us in regard to the affairs of Italy has been observed with respect to Holstein as the views and opinions of the people of that Duchy were not considered when the order of succession was altered and settled, and if they are now disregarded, after the events of the last four months, no form of arrangement will be peaceful or lasting.

* G. & D. 22/27, *Pte Russell Papers.*

Undoubtedly a nation cannot allow every part of it's dominions to choose it's own form of Gov[ernmen]t, but the supreme Gov[ernmen]t must be able to assert it's own authority, as was the case in Ireland Catalonia and La Vendée and dismemberment was thus prevented. Without foreign aid the K[ing] of Denmark w[oul]d be unable to establish or to maintain his authority in Holstein. . . .

MAY 5/64. C[LARENDON].

Document 95. *The British Cabinet's decision at the conclusion of the Conference, 25 June 1864**

We do not propose to engage in a war for the settlement of the present dispute, so far as the duchies of Holstein and Sleswig are concerned: but if the war should assume another character and the safety of Copenhagen or the existence of Denmark as an independent Kingdom should be menaced, such a change of circumstances would require a new decision on the part of the [British] Government.

Document 96. *Palmerston's comment, 6 May 1864†*

There is one additional Circumstance and Element in the Condition of those Things which is not mentioned in L[or]d Russells Mem[orandum], and that is, that all the Powers now called upon to Settle these Matters are bound by Treaty Engagement, to respect and Maintain the Integrity of the Danish Monarchy including Holstein Lauenbourg and Sleswig. This may not compel those Parties to go to war for the Integrity of Denmark, but it surely is a Bar shutting out any of the Powers from proposing in Conference a Dismemberment.

As to the scheme of asking the Duchies who they would like to belong to, none of the Precedents of former Cases apply. The Duchies were quiet and orderly till foreign Forces

* G. & D. 22/27, *Pte Russell Papers*. Minute in Russell's hand, 25 June 1864. There are several drafts.
† G. & D. 22/27, *Pte Russell Papers*. Palmerston on Lord John Russell's Memorandum, 6 May 1864.

came violently in, put down the legal authority and made a Revolution.

In the Italian and other Cases as of Greece for Instance, Insurrections were spontaneous and immediately connected with the Flight of the reigning Sovereign—and when it is said that Holstein if restored to Denmark could not be kept without Foreign aid I should rather say that it could not be wrested from her without Foreign aid, but it must be admitted that in the present excited State of Germany, volunteer Bands w[oul]d not be wanting to back up a Holstein Insurrection.

As to a Plan for a permanent Settlement I intirely Concur with L[or]d Russell, and I think the Scheme he has Sketched out is the one which we ought to aim at in Conference and except from Prussia and the Diet I should not expect much objection to it. The only modification which might be suggested is that The King Duke should have the Choice of his own Holstein Lieutenant instead of having three names presented to him. Of course he ought to chuse a Holsteiner or a German Sleswiger or a Lauenburger. There would be reasonable objection to Establishing foreign Garrisons at Rendsburg and at Kiel under the Pretence of making them federal Fortresses.

P[ALMERSTON]. 6/5–64.

34. THE AFTERMATH, 1864–5

[With the conclusion of the Conference England's share in events practically ended. The Prussian seizure of Düppel, which had caused such grief to the Prince of Wales, had already determined the issue. Hostilities were resumed and the isle of Alsen was quickly seized. Denmark, thus isolated and helpless, was forced to terms. There was an Armistice on 18 July, and preliminaries of peace were signed at Vienna on 1 August, the definitive peace being signed on 30 October. To this treaty only Denmark, Prussia and Austria were parties. Thus not only was Europe, but the German Bund itself, excluded from the settlement. Schleswig and Holstein were ceded to Austria and to Prussia, without mention of self-government or special treatment of Danish minorities. Apart from Lauenburg, Schleswig and Holstein, the integrity of Denmark was preserved, and with it "the safety of

Copenhagen". But Austria and Prussia had a condominium in the Duchies.

England does not seem to have divined whither this arrangement would lead. In his memorandum of 5 May 1864 Russell plainly feared that the Duke of Augustenburg would become ruler of Schleswig-Holstein. Palmerston feared rather the absorption of a dismembered Denmark into Sweden and that English interests would be endangered by the keys of the Baltic being in the hands "of one Power [Sweden] and that Power ruled by a Sovereign by race and descent a Frenchman"* (22 February 1864). The danger was German not French. In the end Prussia got both Schleswig and Holstein and the Kiel Canal as well, and ultimately expelled Augustenburg and Austria and the German Bund, as well as Denmark, from all share in either.

It has been very well said by a Danish writer (cited by Mr Cruttwell) that the conflict was "one between the historical and dynastic rights of the Danish crown and the assertion of the idea of nationality; both of which", Mr Cruttwell adds, "were inextricably interwoven with international threads".

Finally, these international threads were cut and a solution imposed which swept away Danish sovereignty and compromised those claims of nationality, which had been the ostensible cause of armed intervention. This result, which so much alarmed and disgusted European diplomacy, was due to the fact that Bismarck alone of all the actors engaged saw clearly both the end and the means by which it must be secured."†

Palmerston and Russell were greatly shaken by the course of events. When the great debate ended on 9 July 1864 in a narrow victory for the Government, Apponyi reported Palmerston and Russell as "jubilant". He compared Palmerston to Kaunitz, another statesman who had won victories at eighty. Palmerston won a victory by making an immense draft on his old popularity, and by tactics worthy of an old parliamentary hand. After perfunctory references to Denmark he dwelt on the thriving state of the finances. Everyone knew that this result was due to Gladstone's economies which Palmerston was generally (and rightly) thought to have opposed. All men listened, hardly believing their ears, and by their confusion Palmerston made sure of their votes.‡ But he could not so prevail in Europe. There the fall of his and of England's prestige was almost total.

What completed the discredit of Palmerston was the Convention of Gastein, signed between Austria and Prussia on 14 August 1865. The settlement of 1864 held out a faint hope that the

---

* The King of Sweden was a Bernadotte.

† C. R. Cruttwell, *History*, xviii, [April 1933], 69.

‡ *V.* Sir A. W. Ward, *Germany, 1815–1890*, [1917], ii, 182, and n. He was an eye-witness.

arrangements of that year would be temporary. The Gastein Convention settled everything on a permanent basis. Austria sold the Duchy of Lauenburg outright to Prussia, Schleswig was handed over to Prussia and Holstein to Austria for permanent administration. England was thus disregarded, and, for all her boasts, had been completely impotent to influence the issue. The Queen and Russell exhausted their vocabulary of invective against Bismarck and King William. Russell's protest was expressed in a circular to British diplomats which is remarkable for its violence. "The dominion of Force is the sole power acknowledged and regarded" (14 September 1865).* Palmerston's views hardly differed from those he had expressed to the Queen early in 1864. "There cannot be a principle more dangerous to the maintenance of peace, or more fatal to the independence of the weaker Powers, than that it should be lawful for a stronger Power, whenever it has a demand upon a feebler neighbour, to seize hold of part of its territory by force of arms, instead of seeking redress in the usual way of negotiation" (8 January 1864).† In fact he felt the shock to European public law as much as Russell. But he set aside all querulous complaints, and viewed the question in a large way, with an eye on the future. This, almost the last of his many incisive letters, shews a view of foreign policy as clear as of old. Even humiliation cannot blind him to reality or prevent his view from being statesmanlike. He sees that a strong Prussia will balance a Franco-Russian alliance. In the moment of defeat Palmerston, unlike the Queen or Russell, shews a certain greatness.]

Document 97. *Palmerston to Russell, 13 September 1865‡*

...It was dishonest and unjust to deprive Denmark of Sleswig and Holstein. It is another Question how those two Duchies, when separated from Denmark, can be disposed of best for the interests of Europe. I should say that, with that view, it is better that they should go to increase the power of Prussia than that they should form another little state to be added to the cluster of small bodies politic which encumber Germany, and render it of less Force than it ought to be in the general Balance of Power in the world. Prussia is too weak as she now is, ever to be honest or independent in her action,

---

* Hertslet, *Map*, [1875], III, 1645-6.
† *Letters of Queen Victoria*, 2nd Ser., [1926], I, 146.
‡ G. & D. 22/15, *Pte Russell Papers*. The letter is printed in Ashley, *Life*, [1876], II, 270-1. For the first part of this letter, not printed here, see G. P. Gooch, *Later Correspondence of Lord John Russell*, [1925], II, 314-15.

and, with a view to the Future, it is desirable that Germany, in the aggregate, should be strong, in order to controul those Two ambitious and aggressive powers, France and Russia, that press upon her west and east. As to France, we know how restless and aggressive she is, and how ready to break loose for Belgium, for the Rhine, for anything she would be likely to get without too great an Exertion. As to Russia, she will, in due Time, become a Power almost as great as the old Roman Empire. She can become Mistress of all Asia, except British India, whenever she chuses to take it, and when enlightened arrangements shall have made her Revenue proportioned to her Territory, and Railways shall have abridged distances, her Command of men will become enormous, her pecuniary means gigantic, and her power of transporting armies over great distances most formidable. Germany ought to be strong in order to resist Russian aggression, and a strong Prussia is essential to German strength. Therefore, though I heartily condemn the Whole of the Proceedings of Austria and Prussia about the Duchies, I own that I should rather see them incorporated with Prussia than converted into an additional asteroid in the system of Europe.

XV. PALMERSTON AND RUSSELL

GENERAL QUESTIONS; DEFENCE; THE AMERICAN CIVIL WAR; ARBITRATION; SLAVERY

35. PALMERSTON AND RUSSELL; THE LAST PHASE

[Palmerston came to his last period of office with thirty years of diplomatic triumph behind him. He had never had such popularity before. Russell, one of his most formidable political rivals, was now his friend, colleague and supporter. Yet a few years of partnership between the old rivals destroyed the reputation of both. Palmerston's death came at the time that his foreign policy was deeply discredited. Russell, who succeeded him as Premier, could not keep either the Cabinet or the new Foreign Minister in the old ways. His failure shewed that Palmerston's death had ended an epoch in foreign policy.

This singular pair were thus criticized by Count Apponyi, the Austrian Minister. He thought "reserve inherent in his [Russell's] nature and perhaps in the tradition of the Foreign Office". "The difficulty of getting an answer from Lord Russell is proverbial in the diplomatic corps." For the rest, he was "indolent and guided by agents".* Towards Palmerston he was more favourable. Russell was unwilling to state his opinion at once, Palmerston was quick, open, decisive and frank. Few Prime Ministers have ever had as much direct concern with the Foreign Office as Palmerston had on this occasion. Russell sent him not only foreign diplomats, but draft dispatches, in profuse abundance. Both benefited by their contact with the higher authority. Palmerston not only cut and altered drafts galore, but exercised great freedom of criticism. "I have great Doubts as to the expediency of such a Despatch as this. It would make a good leading article in an irresponsible newspaper, but is hardly of the character of a government Despatch."† Thus the octogenarian to the septuagenarian, and the reproof seems in no way to have disturbed their friendly relations. The criticism applied to both of them. For it was the irresponsibility of these old men which betrayed them.

* W.S.A. VIII/73, Berichte aus England. From Apponyi, No. 27B of March 1861; No. 36A of 23 April 1861; No. 18 of 10 May 1861.
† G. & D. 22/22, *Pte Russell Papers*. Palmerston to Russell, 13 September 1863.

Palmerston's diplomatic experience was immense. Poland, Schleswig-Holstein, Latin America and France hid few secrets from him. In one respect alone was Russell superior. His wife's influence and her extensive knowledge of political refugees proved a better source of information to him about Italy than any official dispatches. And in Italy, curiously enough, the one undisputed success of the period was won. Russell, with much less of Palmerston's knowledge, had most of his defects. He had the same love of sharp retorts, the same propensity to lecture, the same irritating air of superiority. He had a little less courage but an even more restless and interfering disposition. He had none of his occasional breadth of view and largeness of mind. Palmerston actually encouraged Russell to become a kind of living caricature of himself. For he was quite blind to his own defects when they appeared in another.

Both men were living in a new age and handling weapons they did not understand. Their physical vigour was still great, but their mental arteries had hardened. Each of them had once been the master of England's, perhaps even of Europe's, policy. They were now no longer masters even in their own Cabinet, but they took long to understand that bitter truth. Palmerston was not always effective as a Premier. No one had brought a measure before Peel's Cabinet without consulting him beforehand; "nobody thought of consulting Palmerston first".* Palmerston complained to Russell that the Cabinet was different from those of old. Had men such as Hardinge, Goulburn or Westmorland composed it, "you and I might have our way on most things". But the Cabinet was one of "All the Talents", with men of intellectual calibre like Gladstone, Lewis and Westbury, or of culture and distinction like Granville and Clarendon. They cared little for the eloquence of Russell or for the popularity of Palmerston, needing hard argument or harder facts. Palmerston said the others are "often too busy...to follow up foreign questions so as to be fully master of them, and their conclusions are generally on the timid side."† Russell and Palmerston sometimes prevailed. Over Italy, for instance, they won by springing a series of surprises on Cabinet and Queen. But the Cabinet soon learned the lesson. "Our old men (two) are unhappily our youngest", said Gladstone, and the Cabinet curtailed their pranks in future. The Cabinet as a whole decided against recognizing the Confederate States, against interfering in Poland, and against protecting Denmark in the possession of Schleswig-Holstein. And they decided thus against the will of its two most important members.

* Phillimore, 12 August 1860. Morley, *Life of Gladstone*, [1903], ii, Bk v, Chap. ii, 35.
† Palmerston to Russell, 11 September 1864, Ashley, *Life*, [1876], ii, 257–8.

Such old hands as Palmerston and Russell knew the Cabinet could be influenced from without. But the majority in Parliament was seldom stable or secure, and was apt to turn against Palmerston in a fury of petulant independence. It did so over Brazil (*v.* p. 300). It failed him at the crisis over Poland and over Denmark. The opposition might have been a resource but did not prove so in this case. Disraeli had spent over thirty years in coining sarcasms about Palmerston and Russell, and could not abandon his habit. Derby was always "on the timid side", more so than even the greatest intellectual in the Cabinet. Victoria thought Palmerston and Russell "two dreadful old men", and the Prince Consort held them in deep suspicion. At the Danish crisis the Queen found ways of influencing the opposition both in Cabinet and Parliament, unknown to Palmerston and Russell. It was a new experience for them both.

Europe, as well as England, provided other experiences for this aged pair. Palmerston had successfully rebuked or defied a generation of Continental Kings and statesmen. He did not admit that another generation had arisen. Yet Franz Joseph had more capacity than Ferdinand; Alexander II was cooler than Nicholas; Napoleon more powerful than Louis Philippe. The world had not only new rulers, but new forces were controlling it. Neither Palmerston not Russell overlooked the dynamic strength of nationalism. But they did not understand that Piedmont and Prussia were directing it for their own ends. In his prime Palmerston had baffled Metternich, Thiers, Guizot, Nesselrode, Buol. He was not to baffle Cavour and Bismarck.

Palmerston and Russell were in fact misled by the one political theory in which they really believed. They thought that nationalism was no danger to Europe but a blessing, provided always that nationalism was associated with constitutionalism. Their creed has been summed up in four propositions. "First, that a people with Nationalist aspirations will, once these are gratified, become a Liberal constitutional state. Second, that a country with a constitutional government will pursue a peaceful, and not an aggressive, foreign policy. Third, that a Nationalist government will favour Nationalism in other countries. Fourth, that a British Government should be friendly to the progress of the National and Liberal parties abroad."* These were in substance their aims. Free scope to constitutionalism would promote the rule of law in Europe; free scope to nationalism would produce stability.

The fallacies of this conception are obvious. Clarendon said sarcastically: "A representative system...is his [Palmerston's] great panacea for all evils everywhere."† Constitutionalism was neither a universal movement, nor a universal type in Europe. It worked

* A. A. W. Ramsay, *Idealism and Foreign Policy*, [1925], 25.
† *Pte Wellesley Papers*, Clarendon to Cowley, 1 January 1856.

so differently in different countries that Hammond, the Permanent Under-Secretary of Foreign Affairs, declared publicly that he did not know what constitutionalism meant.* This utterance was not due to prejudice, for Hammond was an advanced liberal. It was a simple statement of fact. For constitutional monarchy, despite Palmerston's efforts, had been a decided failure in Portugal, in Spain, in Brazil and in Greece. In Belgium and Piedmont it was successful, but the constitutionalism of Piedmont did little to restrain nationalist excesses. Above all in Prussia Bismarck was forging a new weapon. Constitutionalism was to be overthrown by national autocracy. Palmerston thought otherwise. Prussia he considered a Mazeppa, whirled away on the mad horse of Bismarck's ambition. At the very moment that Palmerston thought her destruction certain, Bismarck was dispatching Prussia on that triumphant march, which began when her cavalry crossed the Holstein frontier and ended when they rode beneath the Arc de Triomphe at Paris.

Defence and armaments were not neglected by either of these ardent constitutionalists. Palmerston's ideas were somewhat crude and original. He believed that other governments, and particularly Napoleon's, would be peaceful in proportion as England's forces were strong. Neither Russell nor Palmerston favoured a European standpoint, nor resort to arbitration. Sir Ernest Satow, who spoke with unrivalled authority on the East, thought Palmerston's treatment of China and Japan indefensible. In respect to Brazil their record (as shewn in **Docs. 111–113**) is not much to their credit. But it must be remembered that Brazil, like Spain, was peculiarly obnoxious to Palmerston because of its connivance at the Slave Trade. Against that traffic both men fought like crusaders. It would be wrong to overlook the strong humanitarian strain in both men. The cheeks of these old men flush and their hearts burn as they write of the cruelties done in Naples or of the agonies suffered by Poland. They had not the calm judgment of Castlereagh or the intellectual power of Canning. But they were valiant warriors in the cause of freedom.

The gravest defect of the pair was not their lack of discretion. Nor was it even their irresponsibility. It was their failure to find contact with reality. The great days of Palmerston were when he solved the Syrian question and flung Mehemet Ali back on Egypt. His policy had been a mixture of bravado, audacity, and common sense. It had succeeded because the elements were carefully mixed. He could afford to be resolute, for he shrewdly guessed that the enemy did not want to fight. Now in the 'sixties Russia and Prussia were determined to fight if England went too far. Yet England went very far, and Palmerston was

---

* *Select Committee on Diplomatic and Consular Services*, [1870], in *A. & P.*, [1870], VII, 382, p. 342, §§542–3.

reckless enough to tempt Austria with the offer of a Habsburg Archduke on the throne of an independent Poland (*supra*, **Doc. 75**). Even this rash suggestion was less culpable than his conduct over Schleswig-Holstein. Russell's dark hints of interference by force were as futile as Palmerston's attempt to make Austria give a written pledge not to send a fleet to the Baltic (*supra*, **Doc. 92**). There is a wildness in these schemes which shewed that Palmerston failed to distinguish between speech and action, between realities and dreams.

Palmerston and Russell during this period persistently applied all the rules to other nations and claimed all the exceptions for England. They were most insistent that Russia and Austria should respect the integrity of the Turkish Empire. But, when the Austrian Minister pointed out that England had annexed Perim and Aden, they found nothing to say. Palmerston invoked the principle of non-intervention to prevent all foreign powers from interfering in Italy. But when Spain proposed to do so Palmerston declared he would prevent her by force. This action would involve a departure from non-intervention indeed, but it was an exception made by England and therefore not worth mentioning. The claim that England should always have the plums was one which the new world would not admit. This aged "enfant terrible" was checked by the unsentimental majority in the Cabinet, or by contact with new realities in Europe.

The cause of failure was always the same in these later years. Palmerston had been a true realist at his best. He had understood how to play on the moods of the public and bring these to bear on his colleagues in the Cabinet or on the sovereigns of Europe. His whole policy depended on that success. He took up a cause when the public pressed him to do so, as he did that of Poland. He was equally ready to abandon a cause, if the public wanted it. There was nothing in which he believed more than the support of the Ottoman Empire. Yet he confessed in private to Russell, "our Power" of maintaining the Turkish Empire "depends on Public Opinion in this Country and that public opinion would not support us unless the Turkish Gov[ernmen]t exerts itself to make Reforms".* The master speaks no longer with the old confidence and pride. He has lost his sureness of touch and his instinct for driving the popular wishes. So he ceased to be the leader, and became the victim, of public opinion.

Long ago Metternich had said that Canning was wrong in relying on public opinion, for that was a force inconstant, unstable and impossible to drive or to direct. Canning had understood well enough how to do it; so had Palmerston for thirty years.

---

* G. & D. 22/21, *Pte Russell Papers*. Palmerston to Russell, 13 December 1860; and on the Suez Canal, G. & D. 22/15. Palmerston to Russell, 8 July 1865.

Now he failed because he had forgotten how to trim his sails to the moods and gusts of public opinion. He moved a little too soon or a little too late; he mistook a light breeze for a strong wind, or a public meeting for the voice of the nation. "If we look at the questions relating to Poland, and Italy, and Denmark," said an English diplomat bitterly, "what really happened was that a sort of strong and violent public sympathy, expressing itself in public meetings, and articles in the press, and so forth, reacted upon the imagination of foreigners and the people concerned, so as to make them believe that what a public meeting with a popular chairman, in England, decided, would be ratified by Parliament.... We forget altogether, or we do not sufficiently consider that what a great free people like the people of England expresses vociferously at a public meeting, people abroad take for good coin."* Russell and Palmerston trafficked in this dubious currency. First the British Cabinet, and finally all Europe, found out that the coinage was debased. They turned upon Palmerston and Russell and held them up to obloquy as the utterers of false coin. It was forgotten that Greece and Switzerland had been strengthened, Italy helped on the road to unity, and Turkey twice saved from destruction. It was remembered that Prussia had united Germany in the teeth of British opposition. It was remembered that China, Brazil and Japan complained of being oppressed, Poland and Denmark of being betrayed, by England.]

Document 98. *Palmerston on the nature of Alliances and a possible breach with France, 14 December 1856†*

[The great fault of Palmerston and Russell in their last ministry was the breach with France over her annexation of Savoy. During the next five years France and England were never really friends, and the results were seen in their failures over Poland and Schleswig-Holstein. It is quite plain that a strong Franco-British combination might have held Prussia and Russia in check. It is, moreover, curious that in an inspired moment in 1856 Palmerston anticipated the end of the Franco-British alliance and laid down the principles governing the continuation of successful alliances in a private letter full of shrewd and homely wisdom.]

As to the altered feelings of the French Court towards us I look upon that change with calmness and composure. It is in the nature of things and might have been expected sooner or later.

* Mr (afterwards Sir) R. B. Morier, *Select Committee on Diplomatic and Consular Services*, [1870], in *A. & P.*, [1870], VII, 382, p. 621, § 4395.
† *Pte Wellesley Papers*. Palmerston to Clarendon, 14 December 1856. (Copy enclosed in Clarendon to Cowley of 15 December 1856.)

Unaccountable circumstances have made us for the last two years the compliant followers of France. What she determined to do we did, what she disliked doing we agreed not to do. This state of things could not longer outlive the war. It is quite necessary that we should resume our independent action and position and it was inevitable that the Emperor should be annoyed at the change. Moreover during the war all the separate interests and feelings of the two Governments and countries were forgotten in their common exertions for a common and paramount object. That object attained, the separate interests and feelings again come into play, just as the stars become visible when the moon ceases to shine. The conflict of opinion first made itself felt on the occasion of events in Spain which led the Emperor to think of marching across the Pyrenees. Then besides other smaller matters came the present difference about the Treaty of Paris, and when that is over something else will spring up. We shall long continue to be at peace with France, because it is the interest of France as well as of England that peace should continue between the two Countries, but intimate Alliances cannot long subsist between equal Powers. These Relations can be lasting only between a stronger and a weaker state, when the weaker allows itself to be guided by the stronger. The close Alliance between Austria Prussia and Russia lasted long because Austria and Prussia allowed themselves to be ruled by Russia. That alliance continues as to Prussia, because she is still subservient, but has ceased as to Austria, because she has become selfwilled.

It would not answer for us to be sacrificing real interests or important points under the idea of thereby maintaining the French Alliance, for if that alliance is to be maintained only by such means, the British Nation would soon feel it to be a yoke, which ought to be shaken off. I take it that the Emperor and the English Government are much about in the relations of Pompey and Caesar of whom Lucan says: nec jam ferre potest Caesare priorem Pompeius ne parem. We like Caesar, will not submit to a superior. The Emperor like Pompey, does not like an equal.

Document 99. *Clarendon's comment, 15 December 1856.**

I am not prepared to abandon the French alliance as lightly as Palmerston seems to be. We cannot of course go on in peace as we have done in war for even if divergent interests did not interfere the tortuous ways resorted to by the French Government and which are not distasteful to the Emperor would make it impossible for the two Countries to march hand in hand together, but I want to keep up something of the prestige of the Alliance and at all events to avoid a public separation because I know how much our difficulties with the U[nited] S[tates] would be increased if we were thought to be ill with France and moreover several Governments in Europe in order to shew their hostility to England would be offering the incense to the Emperor which they know he relishes and there might in the course of a little time spring up a sort of League against us.

36. PALMERSTON ON NAVAL AND MILITARY DEFENCE

[No aspect of Palmerston's foreign policy was more important than that of armaments and defence. He had been in the War Office for nearly twenty years (1808–28) and knew by experience the military situation. He was also well acquainted with the naval one. After the war of 1815 the army was cut down to the narrowest limits by the economy campaign. Indeed, the only way of preserving it at all was to do what Wellington did, and hide the army in garrisons overseas. As a result seventy thousand redcoats were scattered all over the globe, while the heart of the Empire was thinly guarded by a few poor thousands. Lord Wolseley says that London must have fallen if the French had landed in England in 1837. It was assumed, however, that the British navy was supreme, and assured England's safety. But the rapid development of steam communication (more readily promoted in the French navy than in the British) destroyed much of our immunity. On 9 January 1847 Wellington wrote his famous letter to Sir John Burgoyne, declaring that steam propulsion had rendered England "assailable" at all times from the sea and that the military forces were insufficient for defence. "If it be true that the exertions of the fleet are not sufficient to provide for our defence, we are not

* *Pte Wellesley Papers*, Clarendon to Cowley, 15 December 1856.

safe for a week after the declaration of War." He avowed quite openly that the danger and the enemy came from France.

The publication of Wellington's letter in the press caused an immense sensation. His concrete proposal to raise a new force of one hundred and fifty thousand men as a militia was ultimately adopted within six years. And this success was due to the special urgency of Palmerston. It was finally made law in 1852 under the Derby-Malmesbury Ministry. Thereby was provided a reinforcement without which the British force in the Crimean War could not have been kept up to strength. It was a measure due to panic and believed to be essential to save us from France. It was concurred in by all parties. Aberdeen, in most alarmist tones, had admitted the danger to the Russian Ambassador. "If he [Napoleon III] thinks us divided, he will fall on us.... We should begin by being beaten even with equal numbers. Fifty thousand Frenchmen would beat fifty thousand Englishmen; and we have not so much to oppose to a sudden invasion." He claimed that Lords Derby and Lansdowne, and Lord John Russell, thought as he did. He declared: "These considerations make us doubly feel the need of strengthening our ties with the Continent." Tsar Nicholas, when he heard of these views, could not conceal his contempt and he spoke of the "cowardice" of the British Government.*

But the alarm in England was ultimately due not so much to Palmerston's insistence on the smallness of the British force, nor to Wellington's insistence on the changes in naval warfare introduced by steam. It was due to the fact that France's steam fleet was increasing almost as rapidly as the British. In 1859 the total British fleet was 95 sail of the line to 51 French, and 96 frigates to 97 French ones. But many of the British big ships were old sailers and not considered of much fighting value. England and France had each over 30 screw battleships of the line. Measures were being taken whereby the British in this class would soon number fifty to forty.† In this class there was no longer any question of a two-power superiority. England's naval supremacy might be considered as seriously challenged. The naval competition of

* Report of Brunnow of 29 November 1852. Aberdeen was just about to become Prime Minister; the Derby Government fell on 24 December 1852. Zaionckovski, *Vostochnaiá Voina*, etc., St Petersburg, [1908–13], I, 277–8. The whole question is discussed at length between an economist and a man experienced in war in Guedalla's invaluable *Gladstone and Palmerston...Correspondence...*, [1928]; *v.* esp. 113–18, 123, 142–3, 157–64, 172–4, 181–7, 293–308, 310–15. Practically all the arguments on both sides are given here in a nutshell.

† These statistics are taken from H. Busk, *Navies of the World*, [1859], App. pp. 51, 88, 108–9. He had visited every dockyard in France and considered his information more exact than the British Government's. The naval competition was considered so serious that even the Austrian Ambassador produced elaborate statistics; *v.* W.S.A. VIII/52, Berichte aus England. From Count Apponyi, No. 18 E of 4 March 1859.

France with England had been strenuous for a decade and was palpably increasing. Moreover, Napoleon himself admitted it. Malmesbury declared the Emperor said to him at Cherbourg: "'In 1860 I reckon to have fifty ships of the line of one thousand horse power.' And, added he, striking me [Malmesbury] on the shoulder, 'I promise you I'll double them'."*

Palmerston was not the man to suffer such policies or utterances without counter measures at a time when public opinion was ready to support him. The measures taken were first a costly system of coast defence and fortification. Then (1859) came the creation of the Volunteers or riflemen, a voluntary organization providing a second line of defence to the Regulars, the already existent militia being the first.

"Form, form, riflemen, form!" is the title of one of Tennyson's poems of this era. It was against the French they were to form and against Napoleon, "such an ally that only the devil can tell what he means". The response was one hundred and seventy thousand civilians exercised in arms. The last measure was to increase the race in naval armaments, and to cause great opposition from Gladstone at the Exchequer. But the measure soon told on Napoleon. A cartoon in *Punch* of 23 March 1861 represented the Emperor as playing his last card at "Beggar my neighbour" with Palmerston looking firmly at him, a straw as always in a corner of his mouth; Palmerston had just laid down "The Warrior" as a *riposte* to Napoleon's "Gloire". This year was the culminating one of naval expenditure, and thereafter the naval competition died down. Sir George Lewis's effort to increase army expenditure, pushed during 1861-2, actually failed in the latter year. Gladstone estimated naval and military expenditure at over thirty millions during 1860-1 (of which four millions was due to the Chinese War), at £26,345,000 during 1863-4, and almost at the same amount during 1864-5. In 1866 it was twenty-four millions. By 1863 the danger point of naval competition with France was passed, but that there had been a real peril does not seem to be open to question. It was not a question of a two-power standard of safety but whether France would not actually surpass England in iron ships.† Palmerston insisted throughout, as against Gladstone, that England's rate of shipbuilding must vary with that of France.

Palmerston's attitude towards naval matters generally is interesting. Russia was only less dangerous than France as a naval power. That is why it was important to prevent her from pressing Turkey and forcing the Dardanelles, and from pressing on Denmark and forcing the Sound. That is why the British fleet

* W.S.A. viii/55, Berichte aus England. From Count Apponyi, 19 January 1859, f. 166. Reporting a conversation of Malmesbury.

† *Gladstone and Palmerston...Correspondence...*, ed. Guedalla, [1928], 181-7, 310-15.

entered the Black Sea in the autumn of 1856 to enforce the execution of the Treaty of Paris. In the Mediterranean France was watched with great jealousy. Palmerston's own belief was that smaller naval powers like Naples and Sicily or Greece were comparatively innocuous because likely to side with England as the bigger naval power in the case of a Franco-British war. But at times he doubted whether he should enlarge their territory or power in case they fell victims to stronger states. As has been seen (p. 215) he hesitated as to whether to support the incorporation of Naples and Sicily into Italy. For he feared the enlarged Piedmont, being contiguous to, might be dependent on, France. However, he ultimately came down on the side of the Union of Italy. In a somewhat similar way he at the time thought of retaining Corfu as a naval base for England, though he ultimately added it and the other Ionian Isles to Greece.

Doc. 100 gives the Austrian Count Rechberg's views on the effect Palmerston's arrival to power would have on the naval and military preponderance of France. In **Doc. 101** Lord John Russell expresses the tradition of the British navy. In **Doc. 102** and **103** Palmerston sums up his philosophy of naval defence with his usual vigour. It is quite in accordance with his airy dismissal of Cobden's scheme of an agreement between England and France "about the number of ships of war which each of the two countries should maintain". He answered: "It would be very delightful if your Utopia could be realized....But unfortunately man is a fighting...animal" (8 January 1862).* When the argument was used that it would be better to rely on accumulating wealth instead of arms he said: "That would only be offering to the butcher a well-fatted calf instead of a well-armed bull's head." It is worth remembering that even he believed that moral forces sometimes outweighed material ones. "Opinions are stronger than armies. Opinions, if...founded in truth and justice, will in the end prevail against the bayonets of infantry, the fire of artillery, and the charges of cavalry" (21 July 1849).† Also presumably against the big guns of any navy.]

Document 100. *Count Rechberg on Palmerston and the naval and military power of France, 30 June 1859‡*

...England in particular seems to me to a still superior degree and more immediately interested that the power of Austria should remain intact and strong enough to form in

* Ashley, *Life*, [1876], II, 221. Private letter to Richard Cobden. Cobden's scheme is in App. V, 335–41.
† *Hans. Deb.*, 3rd Ser., CVII, 813.
‡ W.S.A. VIII/55, Varia. Mission en Angleterre et à Paris de...P[rinc]e Esterházy. To Esterházy, 30 June 1859, Private.

the East the counterpoise necessary to the ambitious views of
Russia and the intrigues of France. So I cannot share the
apprehensions of those who, inspired with the memory of
1848, deplore the reentry into power of Lord Palmerston in
the complications of the moment. On the contrary I think
that we have—instead—to congratulate ourselves, for if the
policy of this statesman has not always been convenient
to us, we must do him the justice that he has never had
any aim save the great interests of his Nation which he
not only recognizes with remarkable accuracy but makes
them prevail by his uncommon energy. Lord Palmerston is a
guarantee to us that he will not lend a hand to establish the
preponderance of France in the concert of Europe, already
so much to be feared by its military power and the quite
extraordinary development of its marine in the last years....

Document 101. *Lord John Russell on the need of maintaining
England's naval strength, ?December* 1859*

H[er] M[ajesty's] Gov[ernmen]t find it impossible to
reconcile the wish expressed by Baron Schleinitz for the continuance of the preponderance of the naval power of Great
Britain with the favour he is disposed to shew to the views of
the U[nited] S[tates]. It is obvious that if these views were to
prevail a State with two men of war would be as strong as
one with two hundred. Naval preponderance would be an
empty Name, entailing a very real burden. Transport ships
full of sailors might hover on the coasts of an enemy, and
could not be captured, or interfered with. But a week after
they might come back full of troops, who might land in a
commercial town, and levy such contributions as the French
levied in Hamburg in 1812–13. All this too in the name of a
respect for private property!

Not only the power, and the greatness, but the very safety
and independence of Great Britain depend on her maritime
strength. It is a matter of great concern to H[er] M[ajesty's]
Gov[ernmen]t to find that Prussia listens to these insidious
proposals.   J. R[USSELL]

* Rough Note by Russell for Bloomfield, ? December 1859, *F.O.* 96/26.

Document 102. *Palmerston on force as a Peacemaker, 23 October 1864**

...As long as we are strong and prosperous we may reckon upon a good understanding with France upon all matters on which they may not find it easy to deceive us, as they have done about Tunis. Murchison gave me the other day a Buffalo Hide Whip from Africa called in those Regions a Peace Maker and used as such in The Households of Chieftains. Our Peace Makers are our Armstrongs and Whitworths and our Engineers...[It is perhaps fair to add two other brief quotations. "Peace and good understanding between France and England are most likely to be permanent when France has no Naval Superiority over England" † and "The Mole, Trafalgar, the Peninsula, Waterloo and St. Helena are Records which Frenchmen would gladly seize fair opportunity of counterbalancing."]

Document 103. *Palmerston on war, 8 January 1865‡*

I return you this with Thanks. I daresay Bulwer is right as to some Designs of France about the Islands he mentions. The standing Policy of France is to make the Mediterranean a French Lake, and they steadily pursue it on every favourable occasion. If we maintain our Superiority at Sea which we *must* do in spite of Economists and Radicals, we should probably be able, in the Event of War to drive them out of most of the Positions they might acquire; but to do so would cost us great efforts, many lives and much money and therefore Prevention is better than Cure. Our Business consequently ought to be to unravel their Plots, to see through their Intrigues, and to defeat their schemes by Counteraction steadily and Systematically applied; and as the French

* B.M. Add. MSS. 38,990, *Pte Layard Papers*, f. 328. Palmerston to Layard, Private, 23 October 1864. Part of this has been quoted in Guedalla, *Palmerston*, [1926], 451.
† *Gladstone and Palmerston...Correspondence...*, ed. Guedalla, [1928], 187.
‡ B.M. Add. MSS. 38,991, *Pte Layard Papers*, ff. 3–5. Palmerston to Layard, Private, 8 January 1865. Bulwer's letter has not been found.

Gov[ernmen]t though bent upon Encroachment and acquisition will always wish to avoid a Rupture with England unless it be unavoidably forced upon them, will generally give way if firmly resisted, and if we shew them we are not disposed to shrink from Thwarting them. They also know, and have learnt by experience, that when England and France are at variance Austria Russia and Prussia are much more disposed to join with us than with France, and what the French wish most to avoid is a European Coalition against them.

I do not understand the "Victoria" Passage in Bulwer's Letter.

37. PALMERSTON AND GLADSTONE AND THE AMERICAN CIVIL WAR

[This has been the subject of infinite discussion most of which has now been fairly settled. But here is some interesting unpublished material which adds a little to the story. One letter of Palmerston's shews how he feared that Mexico would be absorbed by the United States in 1855 (**Doc. 104**), and another (**Doc. 106**) shews that he anticipated Lincoln in thinking of proclaiming the emancipation of the slaves as a war-measure against the South. But this was before the Civil War began. The main data in the situation after war broke out are these. During the middle of 1862 the South, under the leadership of Lee, had not only repelled the North from Richmond but was invading Northern territory. Napoleon III had made unofficial suggestions as to recognition of the South, and there was a large body of opinion in England in favour of it owing to the desire to import cotton from the South. Russell was much more favourable to action than Palmerston. The latter hit off the situation thus (13 June 1862): "I may say that no Intention at present exists to offer Mediation. In Fact it would be like offering to make it up between Sayers and Heenan [two famous pugilists] after the Third Round."* In June therefore Palmerston was thus not prepared for anything until the fighting had proved more decisive. At the same time (as **Doc. 105** shews) he was by no means friendly to the North and saw the advantages to England from a division between it and the South.]

* G. & D. 22/22, *Pte Russell Papers*. Palmerston to Russell, 13 June 1862.

Document 104. *Palmerston on the future of Mexico,*
1 November 1855*

I think we may assume its [Mexico's] annexation is
written in the Book of Fate, for England and France would
not go to war to prevent it [from being annexed to the
United States] and would scarcely be able to prevent it if
they did go to war.

Document 105. *Palmerston on the advantages of Monarchy*
in Mexico and an independent South, 19 January 1862†

...As to the Monarchy Scheme [in Mexico], if it could be
carried out it would be a great Blessing for Mexico and a
Godsend for all Countries having anything to do with
Mexico, as far at least, as their Relations with Mexico are
concerned.

It would also stop the North Americans whether of the
Federal or Confederate States in their projected absorption
of Mexico. If the North and South are definitely disunited,
and if at the same Time Mexico could be turned into a
prosperous Monarchy I do not know any arrangement that
would be more advantageous for us....

Document 106. *Palmerston on Slavery and the South‡*

The U[nited] S[tates] Gov[ernmen]t cannot by their
constitution make war without the consent of the Senate and
Congress does not meet till December. But I take it that they
are mere swaggering Bullies. If moreover they should push
matters to extremities we should be quite able to meet them.

I cannot think that their own people would allow it. We
have a deeply piercing blow to strike at their Southern
States if ever we should be at war with them.

Freedom to the Slaves proclaimed by a British force landed
in the South would shake the Union to its Base.

---

* *Pte Clarendon Papers.* Palmerston to Clarendon, 1 November 1855.
† G. & D. 22/22, *Pte Russell Papers.* Palmerston to Russell, 19 January 1862.
‡ *Pte Clarendon Papers.* In Palmerston's hand, but unsigned and apparently
of the year 1855.

Document 107. *Gladstone on an independent Southern Confederacy, ? July 1896**

...I was not one of those who on the ground of British interests desired a division of the American Union. My view was distinctly opposite. I thought that while the Union continued it never could exercise any dangerous pressure upon Canada to estrange it from the empire—our honour, as I thought, rather than our interest forbidding its surrender. But were the Union split, the North, no longer checked by the jealousies of slave-power, would seek a partial compensation for its loss in annexing, or trying to annex, British North America. Lord Palmerston desired the severance as a diminution of a dangerous power, but *prudently held his tongue....*

38. PALMERSTON AND RUSSELL, AND WAR WITH THE NORTH, 1862–3

[Palmerston may be accused of a Machiavellian calculation in desiring severance between North and South, but his realism was to be of considerable advantage to the North in the end. Russell suggested to Palmerston on 6 August that "we should make some move in October".† It was finally arranged to hold a Cabinet to settle the matter on 23 October. In mid-September Russell started to sound Napoleon on the subject but found him at the moment unexpectedly cool. Thouvenel emphasized "the serious consequences" to France of recognition, and, though Napoleon was capable of overruling him, this was a momentary obstacle. Palmerston, however, declared that Russia must also be consulted. That imposed delay. Then on 16 September the battle of Antietam was fought in which Lee was severely checked and had to retreat from Northern territory. On 23 September Palmerston was in favour of immediate mediation only "if the Federals sustain a great defeat". Next day Palmerston wrote to Gladstone that he and Russell agreed on an offer of mediation but that "no actual step would be taken without the sanction of the Cabinet", i.e. until 23 October. This intimation set Gladstone off on a course of his own.

Gladstone had a strong predilection for the South and, great orator as he was, could not resist the opportunity of a master-

* Note by Gladstone in Morley, *Life of Gladstone*, [1903], II, Bk v, Chap. v, 81–2. The italics at the end are the Editors'.

† E. D. Adams, *Great Britain and the American Civil War*, [1925], II, 32. See Chap. XI, *passim*, for other details given below.

stroke. On 7 October at Newcastle he uttered the fateful words: " We may have our own opinions about slavery; we may be for or against the South; but there is no doubt that Jefferson Davis and other leaders of the South have made an army; they are making, it appears, a navy; and they have made what is more than either, they have made a nation."* This utterance was an indiscretion because Gladstone was a Cabinet Minister and thus seemed to be giving notice of the Government's intentions to accord recognition to the South. As he had been told by Palmerston that such intention depended on a Cabinet decision, his action was unwarranted. On 12 October Palmerston wrote to Russell: " We must I think hear something of a decisive character before our Cabinet on the 23rd, but it is clear that Gladstone was not far wrong in pronouncing by anticipation the National Independence of the South."† Russell, doubtless encouraged by the Prime Minister, circulated a Memorandum to the Cabinet on the 13th. He urged that the Great Powers should consider whether they ought not to propose a "suspension of arms" between North and South, for the purpose of "weighing calmly the advantages of peace".

It seemed that the battle was won. Russell and Gladstone, each with a strong hold on the public, were for something active. Palmerston, with a stronger hold than either, had hitherto shewn more caution. Now he seemed at last to have come down on their side. But on 14 October Sir George Lewis, a minor member of the Cabinet with a strong grasp of international law, made a public speech. He said that the South had not established a *de facto* independence, and was therefore not entitled to recognition. This utterance seems to have been made independently, but it was naturally taken to mean that the Cabinet had as yet made no decision.‡ Palmerston no sooner heard of it than he asked Clarendon to consult Derby, the leader of the Opposition. Derby shewed himself opposed to any action. Lewis, who was Clarendon's brother-in-law and close friend, was probably cognizant of these facts when he circulated a most able counter memorandum to that of Russell of the 13th. He summed up the technical objections to an armistice and advised against all immediate action. On 22 October, the day before the fateful Cabinet, Palmerston expressed his views on the two documents. He was "much inclined to agree with Lewis.... I am therefore inclined to change the opinion on which I wrote to you when the Confederates seemed to be carrying all before them, and I am very much come back to our original view of the matter, that we must continue merely to be

* These words are differently reported, but the above is the version of Morley, *Life of Gladstone*, [1903], II, Bk v, Chap. v, 79.
† G. & D. 22/22, *Pte Russell Papers*. Palmerston to Russell, 12 October 1862.
‡ It was wrongly assumed that Palmerston had put Lewis up to make the speech. V. E. D. Adams, *Great Britain and the American Civil War*, [1925], II, 50-1.

lookers-on till the war shall have taken a more decided turn."*
It might now be the seventh or eighth round but it was not yet
time to make it up between Sayers and Heenan.

Palmerston's action, or inaction, was decisive. The Cabinet of
23 October was postponed. Palmerston was not there himself, but
a few members turned up for an informal discussion. Russell
found himself opposed by Lewis and the majority of those present.†
A fiasco like this was enough to decide most questions and to
silence most men. But Russell and Gladstone persisted in trying
to reopen the question. Each circulated a memorandum to the
Cabinet. These might have produced no result but Napoleon III,
having replaced Thouvenel by Drouyn de Lhuys, suddenly
proposed intervention to secure an armistice and a suspension of
the Northern blockade of the South. This could only have been
procured by armed naval force executed by England and France
combined. This overture was made at the end of October and
Palmerston, who still wavered a little, summoned the Cabinet
for 11 November. Lewis, valiant as ever, circulated a second
memorandum which was even more effective than the first. The
Cabinet declined the French proposal of joint intervention when
it met on 11 November. "Russell rather turned tail...Palmerston
gave...a feeble and half hearted support" noted Gladstone in his
diary. The decision was immediately made public. As it proved,
that ended the whole matter.

Doc. 108 is Argyll's recollection of the Cabinet discussion on
intervention. He appears to be referring to Lewis's second
memorandum and the full Cabinet of 11 November 1862. Other
accounts of this Cabinet support his view,‡ but the poignant
details are his own. It seems clear that, at the last, Palmerston
was not very strong for intervention.]

Document 108. *Argyll's recollection of the Cabinet decision
of 11 November 1862 against intervention, 7 April 1887*§

My recollection is distinct and painful upon that subject.

1. That the French Emperor wished and tempted us (in
some form or other) to "recognize" the South. I don't
recollect *how* the communication was made—whether as a
para[graph] on the [Gladstone's] speech or not.

* G. P. Gooch, *Later Correspondence of Lord John Russell*, [1925], II, 327-8.
† *V.* E. D. Adams, *Great Britain and the American Civil War*, [1925], II, 55-7.
Gladstone's Memorandum of 25 October is in *Gladstone and Palmerston...
Correspondence...*, ed. Guedalla, [1928], 239-47. There were, ultimately, two
memoranda from Russell and Lewis, respectively, and one from Gladstone.
‡ Quoted in E. D. Adams, *Great Britain and the American Civil War*, [1925], II, 62-5.
§ G. & D. 29/29, *Pte Granville Papers*. Argyll to Granville, 7 April 1887.

2. That several members of our Cabinet were Ayes and inclined only too much to assent.

3. That Gladstone was one of these. I have a *mild* recollection of a conversation with him culminating in the *Dark Passage* from the Park to Downing Street in which he expressed his strong feeling that the Recognition must come soon.

4. That the Ayes party were smashed up by a very able paper from *Cornewall Lewis* after which it was no more heard of.

5. It never came to a division in the Cabinet. Of this I feel very sure.

Document 109. *Palmerston and Russell still think war possible between England and the North,* 25 *April* 1863*

[It will be seen from this document that neither Palmerston nor Russell thought the question decided on October 1862.]

In my late interviews with Lord Russell and Lord Palmerston,† in order to try the ground I observed to them that a war between England and America seemed to be more probable than a war with Russia. Both completely agreed but the Prime Minister added, that he could not believe that the Federals, whose position is already critical, would out of lightness of heart engage in addition in a war with England.

I do not however doubt that Lord Palmerston seriously contemplates such a war as possible, and this supposition is the key to the language he held the other day on the question of Poland. In saying that England reserved her liberty of action, and would take counsel of circumstances and events, whether to remain neutral or to be allied with France, he doubtless thought of the possibility of an American war. It is thus also that I explain the indifference with which the Prime Minister contemplated an isolated war of France against Russia and a demonstration on the Rhine which, in other circumstances, he would not have regarded so lightly. Were

* W.S.A. viii/66, f. 358, Berichte aus England. From Apponyi, No. 29B of 25 April 1863.
† 21–2 April 1863. *V. supra*, pp. 240–1.

she once engaged in America, England would no longer be able to prevent anything happening in Europe and that is one of the dangers of the situation and a grave consideration for the [Austrian] Imperial Cabinet.

39. BRAZIL—ARBITRATION

[In regard to Brazil Russell and Palmerston are usually admitted to have been in the wrong in the disputes that arose in 1862. These disputes concerned two points. First there was the case of a British ship wrecked on a solitary part of the Brazilian coast, in which four seamen were found under suspicion of being murdered. But the crime was "not proven" and no criminal was ever found. It was followed by a case in which three naval officers of H.M.S. *Forte*, ashore in civil costume, were locked up in gaol after a hilarious dinner at a country inn. Russell and Palmerston demanded compensation and punishment of the officials concerned. When Brazil resisted, British ships blockaded Rio. But when the matter came before Parliament both Houses criticized these proceedings severely. Brazil finally paid compensation for the lost ship and Palmerston and Russell referred the other case to arbitration. They did this under pressure from Parliament. The matter has been touched by the vitriolic pen of Salisbury;* his account is by no means friendly but his facts cannot be substantially impugned.

The documents here given on arbitration shew Palmerston's attitude towards it in 1849, but it should not be forgotten that he suggested a treaty of arbitration with the United States in 1848.† Further, in agreeing to the famous Declaration of Paris in 1856, Palmerston shewed considerable friendliness to the United States, and a desire for pacific solutions of difficulties with them, which was not shared by all his colleagues. Palmerston's hostility to Arbitration is not likely to have been assuaged by "the Brazil Award". The Alabama Arbitration took place after his death, but it was believed that it was one to which he would not have assented. Certainly Russell, in later years, shewed dissatisfaction with it.‡]

* Lord Salisbury, *Essays on Foreign Politics*, [1905], 158–69.
† Palmerston to Russell, 20 January 1848. Ashley, *Life*, [1876], I, 59–60.
‡ *V.* Russell, *Recollections and Suggestions, 1813–73*, [1875], Chap. xii.

Document 110. *The inapplicability of the principle of arbitration to England,* 12 *June* 1849*

...I confess also that I consider it [arbitration] would be a very dangerous course for this country itself to take, because there is no country which, from its political and commercial circumstances, from its maritime interests, and from its colonial possessions, excites more envious and jealous feelings in different quarters than England does; and there is no country that would find it more difficult to discover really disinterested and impartial arbiters. There is also no country that would be more likely than England to suffer in its important commercial interests from submitting its case to arbiters not disinterested, not impartial, and not acting with a due sense of their responsibility...

Document 111. *Palmerston compares Brazil to a Billingsgate Fishwoman,* 6 *February* 1863†

The Conduct of the Brazilian Gov[ernmen]t resembles that of a Billingsgate Fishwoman Seized by a Policeman for some misdeeds. She scolds and kicks and swears and Raves and call [*sic*] on the Mob to help her and vows she wont go to the Lockup House but will sooner die on the spot: but when she feels the strong grip of the Policeman and finds he is really in Earnest she goes as quiet as a Lamb though still using foul mouthed Language at the Corner of each street.

P[ALMERSTON] 6/2. 63.

Document 112. *Palmerston on Brazil's demand for compensation,* 4 *May* 1863‡

I suppose the note from Moreira which you sent me with other Letters to be forwarded to the Queen relates to the answer you are preparing to his Demand for Compensation and apology for our Reprisals. I hope that you will be firm

* *Hansard Deb.*, 3rd Ser., cvi, 90. Speech by Palmerston of 12 June 1849.
† B.M. Add. MSS. 38,989, *Pte Layard Papers*, f. 43. Note by Palmerston, 6 February 1863.
‡ G. & D. 22/22, *Pte Russell Papers*. Palmerston to Russell, 4 May 1863.

with him and that you will properly maintain the Dignity and guard the Interests of the Country. It is all very right to use civil Language in your Communication to him but the Reprisals were deliberately ordered by us and were very forbearingly carried into Execution by Christie, and there is nothing connected with the Transaction for which the slightest Regret can be expressed unless it be that the Brazilians should by a pertinacious Denial of Justice, have compelled us to resort to Force. As to any Demand for Compensation that is too preposterous to be seriously dealt with. The real way to deal with Moreira, if we did only what he and his Government deserve, would be to say to him as I once said to Bourqueney who came to complain of a French officer having been put under arrest at the Mauritius for breaking the Rules of the Port, "my good Fellow put your Despatch in your Pocket and go Home with it and let us hear no more about the matter," and that advice was taken.

It would not be amiss to take this opportunity of reminding the Brazilian Gov[ernmen]t who say they want to reestablish friendly understanding with us, of their habitual and Systematic Discourtesy towards England by neglecting to give answers to Representations made to them by our Representatives at Rio, and you might exemplify that, by enumerating the Dates of the many unanswered applications made to them for Information about the Condition of the Negroes Emancipated by Decrees of the Mixed Courts at Rio, and still held in Slavery after the Lapse of many years.

It would also be well to remind the Brazilians that we have unsatisfied Claims of long standing amounting if I mistake not to between £3 and 200,000.

It is a little too Much for the offending Party to pretend to be the offended one, and we must not allow ourselves to be worked upon by the various Influences which the Brazilians set to work to play upon us, to induce us to take towards these Brazilians an Attitude not worthy of our Country.

If Moreira is to go unless we do that which it is unbecoming for us to do, let him go, and wish him a good voyage.

Document 113. *The Arbitration Award by Leopold King of the Belgians,* 18 *June* 1863*

...We are of opinion that in the mode in which the laws of Brazil have been applied towards the English officers there was neither offence, nor premeditation of offence, to the British navy. 18th day of June 1863. [Signed] Leopold I.

40. THE SLAVE TRADE

[In the debate on arbitration of 12 June 1849 Palmerston took care to dispel the impression that "England is not ready, as she is ever, to repel aggression and resent injury, and that she will never be found acting aggressively against any power". There is a bad side to this, but there was a good side, too, in the sense that England was ready to redress wrong not wrought against herself and to denounce cruelty and oppression. The noblest and most sincere side of Palmerston and Russell is their hatred of cruelty, and in particular of what John Wesley called long before "that execrable sum of all villainies, the Slave Trade". It was because Brazil, more deeply than most nations, had aided and abetted it that Russell and Palmerston were so moved against her.]

Document 114. *Palmerston on the Aberdeen Act,*
31 *July* 1862 [1863]†

Denman my Colleague at Tiverton has sent me the accompanying Letter from Livingstone giving an account not very clear indeed, of the Portuguese Doings in Slave Trade on the East Coast of Africa.

When the Brazilians ask us to repeal the Aberdeen act which produced in 1851 and 52 the Miraculous Conversion from Slave Trade of a Nation which up to that Time had committed that Crime to the greatest Extent of any Nation, and in Spite of the Strongest Remonstrances which the English Language could convey, and when they tell us to accept a Slave Trade Treaty as a sufficient Substitute for our act, it is impossible not to reflect that the Slave Trade Treaty with Spain does not prevent some 15 or 20,000 Negroes and perhaps more from being every year imported into Cuba;

* V. *B.F.S.P.*, (1862–3), LIII, 150–1.

† G. & D. 22/22, *Pte Russell Papers.* Palmerston to Russell, 31 July 1862, [1863]. Partly printed in H. C. F. Bell, *Lord Palmerston,* [1936], II, 411–12.

That our Slave Trade Treaty with Portugal does not prevent an extensive Exportation of Slaves from the Portuguese Possessions in Africa East and West, and that the abolition of Slave Trade and of Slavery itself by France has not prevented the Rizis Contract which was real Slave Trade, and that even the abolition of that Contract does not prevent a considerable Export of Slaves from the East Coast of Africa to the Island of Reunion. If we were to repeal the Aberdeen act the Slave Deluge would again inundate Brazil.

Document 115. *The execution of the Aberdeen Act, his greatest achievement,* 17 *February* 1864*

...There are no two men in England more determined enemies of the slave trade than Lord Russell and myself, and certainly we are neither of us bigoted enthusiasts nor West Indian proprietors, but we have both laboured assiduously and with much success for the extirpation of that abominable crime.

During the many years that I was at the Foreign Office, there was no subject that more constantly or more intensely occupied my thoughts, or constituted the aim of my labours. ... The achievement which I look back to with the greatest and purest pleasure was the forcing the Brazilians to give up their slave trade, by bringing into operation the Aberdeen Act of 1845. The result, moreover, has been greatly advantageous to the Brazilians, not only by freeing them from a grievous crime, but by very much improving their general condition...

Document 116. *Palmerston's last utterance on the Slave Trade,* 29 *January* 1865†

One Evil arising from the annexation of the Uruguay or any Part of it to Brazil, would be, that Slavery would be introduced into Territory in which at present it is forbidden.
P[ALMERSTON] 29/1/65.

* Palmerston to Sir John Crampton, 17 February 1864. Ashley, *Life*, [1876], II, 263–4.
† B.M. Add. MSS. 38,991, *Pte Layard Papers*, f. 32. Rough note by Palmerston. There is a letter by Palmerston of 27 December 1864, in B.M. Add. MSS. 38,990, on the Slave Trade in Brazil.

XVI. DERBY AND STANLEY, 1866-7

41. DERBY AND STANLEY ON NON-INTERVENTION AND GUARANTEE

[Russell became Prime Minister on Palmerston's death with Clarendon as Foreign Secretary (3 November 1865). Even Russell was conscious of the discredit caused by the restless and meddling policy of the past and Clarendon soon shewed his hand. He failed to avert the war between Prussia and Austria which began early in June 1866. He was asked by Vitzthum von Eckstaedt what England would do if Prussia invaded Saxony which was guaranteed by England under the Treaty of Vienna of 1815. He replied, correctly but cautiously, that only a part of Saxony was thus guaranteed.* Here was an obvious reaction from Palmerston's system. It became more pronounced when Russell's Ministry fell and a Conservative Government took office.

Stanley took office in the new Government as Foreign Secretary on 6 July 1866, and remained there till December 1868. Disraeli, its most brilliant member, was almost wholly occupied with "dishing the Whigs" over Parliamentary Reform. Foreign policy was shared between father and son, between Derby as Prime Minister and Stanley as Foreign Secretary. When Derby retired in February 1868 Disraeli became Prime Minister, but the control of foreign policy was hardly altered. In fact, also, the critical decisions over the Austro-Prussian War and Luxemburg question had already been made.

The father and son worked in general accord over foreign policy, but for somewhat different reasons. On the face of it their first utterances were reasonable enough. Derby put the matter thus in the House of Lords over the Austro-Prussian War: "though not wishing to adopt non-interference in an absolute manner, we [England] would yet abstain from armed intervention". Stanley said: "I am not a supporter of the system of advising foreign governments. I think this right has not only been used but abused of late and that we have lost not gained by it."† Stanley viewed the matter with a radicalism which he owed to Cobden's theory of

* W.S.A. VIII/74, Berichte aus England. From Apponyi, No. 45B of 22 June 1866.

† W.S.A. VIII/74, Berichte aus England. From Apponyi, No. 51B of 24 July 1866.

non-intervention and with a cynicism which he owed to himself.
When the Cretan revolt broke out in 1867, Stanley professed
"neither sympathy nor special interest for the Turks. If they dis-
appeared from Europe he would not be inconsolable, the difficulty
is to know what to put in their place." Derby, though anything
but radical or cynical, was very timid in the face of public opinion.
He "did not conceal the fact that he is struck by seeing several
newspapers, and principally 'The Times' give the Party the advice
to give up Crete, and he avows 'assez naïvement' that, if the
public opinion of the country pronounced itself for such a solution,
he could only yield to its pressure".* Thus both men were willing,
though for different reasons, to abandon even such a cherished
Palmerstonian dogma as the integrity of the Ottoman Empire.
The same motives led Stanley to regard the obligations of the
Vienna Treaty in reference to Poland as outworn, and to view
all the guarantees of that instrument as obsolete (v. **Doc. 118** (a)).
The way was thus prepared for the Stanley-Derby interpretation
of the Luxemburg guarantee.]

Document 117. *An Austrian view of Stanley and the principle of non-intervention, 3 July 1866†*

Lord Stanley is the only one [of the Cabinet] whose nomination has been welcomed in England with general satisfaction...no one contests his honest and honourable character
and talents. [He] belongs to that school of statesmen (still
few, but enjoying all the sympathies of the British public)
who make a dogma of the most complete non-intervention
and the most absolute abstention of Great Britain from the
affairs and quarrels of Europe. According to Lord Stanley
the only great interest of this country consists in the pacific
development of its prosperity and its colonial and commercial power, and as England could not attain this goal and
at the same time interfere actively and influentially in the
affairs of Europe she ought not to hesitate between the two
courses, but choose that which best assures her riches and
prosperity. Consequently foreign affairs should only have a

* W.S.A. viii/75, Berichte aus England. From Apponyi, No. 69 of 25
September 1867, ff. 468–9, reporting Stanley. W.S.A. xii/87, Weisungen nach
Türkei. Beust to Prokesch-Osten, enclosing a report of Kálnoky in January
1867 on Derby's views.

† W.S.A. viii/74, Berichte aus England. From Apponyi, No. 48 of 3 July
1866.

secondary place in English policy, and the true interests of the country being engaged in none of the different questions agitating the Continent it is better to abstain from all advice or interference when one has decided that no result can follow and to retire into complete passivity and neutrality.

...[He said recently to a friend of mine] that "the post did not suit him at all, he understood nothing of diplomacy and would have to make serious studies...". [He possesses] a serious and reflective mind; a complete and upright character; very strong convictions, his opinions are a mixture of Toryism and Radicalism.

Document 118. *Stanley applies the principle of non-intervention in the case of the war between Prussia and Austria, July–August 1866; to Italy in 1867 and to Poland in 1868.*

(a) *To Austria.**

[The Austrian Ambassador, Count Apponyi, said a strong power in North Germany involved a future risk of war with France and Russia.]...I [Stanley] thought, on the contrary, that the danger of disturbance to the peace of Europe lay in the weakness rather than in the strength of Germany.

An allusion having then been made to the Treaties of 1815, I did not hesitate to express my belief that in the actual state of Europe, it was useless to appeal to those Treaties as being still binding....

(b) *To Russia.*

[Baron Brunnow (the Russian Ambassador) in relation to the Treaty of Vienna submitted that the Preliminaries of Peace]...would involve a departure from the Treaties which had been signed by Great Britain and Russia.

By right, no Treaty could be modified without the participation of all the Contracting Parties.

The Imperial Cabinet of Russia held to this principle; and he, Baron Brunnow, was instructed to inform his Court whether the British Government had the same intention as Russia, in order to maintain and to reserve its right to take

* Stanley to Lord Bloomfield, No. 12, 21 July 1866, *F.O.* 7/702.

part, as a signing party to the Treaties which it is proposed
to modify.* [Stanley in reply deprecated any proposal to
adhere to the Treaties of 1815, and refused to join in a declaration to that effect. When asked in 1868 by Apponyi
whether he considered the obligations of the Treaty of Vienna
binding as to Poland he answered] He [Stanley] could not
deny a certain value to the argument of Baron de Brunnow,
according to which Poland having been twice conquered by
Russian armies since the Treaty of Vienna, these treaties—
elsewhere only a historic dream for Europe—were virtually
abrogated for Russia. [Apponyi commented] The theory of
the right of the strongest and of the absorption of small
nationalities by great, has always a certain attraction for the
eminently practical and positive mind of Lord Stanley.†

(c) To France.‡

[Lord Cowley was instructed] That Her Majesty's Government will not join in any such declaration as may have the
appearance of a Protest against what is passing in Germany:
    That they reserve to themselves entire freedom of judg-
ment as to the future.
    And that while on the one hand they are not responsible
for the steps that Prussia has taken to increase her Power at
the cost of other States, they have, on the other hand, no
cause to object to such increase of Power on her part.

(d) re Italy.

[Austria had been informed that we could not use our
good offices to induce Italy to abandon her claims to the
Trentino.§
    When in 1867 Prussia informed Stanley that she could not
see "with indifference" Italy attacked by France, and asked
for a statement of England's intention, Stanley declined to
commit himself beforehand.‖]

* Stanley to Buchanan, No. 29, 6 August, F.O. 65/696.
† W.S.A. viii/77, Berichte aus England. From Apponyi, No. 25B of
7 April 1868.
‡ Stanley to Cowley, No. 118, 8 August 1866, F.O. 27/1608.
§ Stanley to Cowley, No. 123, 9 August 1866, F.O. 27/1608.
‖ Stanley to Loftus, No. 233, 23 October 1867, F.O. 64/616.

42. LUXEMBURG AND THE GUARANTEE

[The Luxemburg question proved the crucial test for Derby and Stanley. By it they became celebrated, or at least known, in diplomatic history, for they laid down an original doctrine. Clarendon said that the 14th Earl of Derby "understands nothing about them [foreign affairs] and never thinks or cares about the effect which his speeches may produce on foreign countries".* This is a judgment from an opponent and it would probably be unfair to include Derby's son Stanley in the condemnation. For he was a genuine non-interventionist—on grounds of principle and not from indifference to foreigners.

The Grand Duchy of Luxemburg, on the settlement of 1839, had remained subject to the King of the Netherlands. But it had a dual capacity. Though Dutch, it was garrisoned by Prussian troops; like Holstein it was a member of the German Bund. But the Bund had been destroyed by the Austro-Prussian War of 1866 and thus the right of the Prussians to garrison the citadel was legally ended. Napoleon, in consequence, showed unmistakable signs of desiring to annex Luxemburg to France. Finally he proposed to buy it from the King of the Netherlands. Bismarck was aware of these designs and made a most able speech on the subject to the North German Reichstag. This was on 1 April 1867, Bismarck's birthday. It was not the day on which he was befooled. He declared that the new North German Bund did not wish to include Luxemburg as a member, and that the Prussian right of garrisoning the citadel had expired. He wished good relations with France but, while discrediting the designs on Luxemburg attributed to her, he said that a settlement could only be achieved by agreement between the signatory powers of the Treaty of 1839. And he intimated that Luxemburg, if evacuated, would be neutralized under a European guarantee.

There was some danger of war as German national feeling was much excited against French aggression. It was allayed by the expedient of a Conference meeting in London which endorsed Bismarck's idea of guarantee. Recent unpublished German documents throw a new light on the affair.† They prove that in April Stanley informed Bernstorff that England did not regard Luxemburg as on a par with Belgium and that no British Foreign Minister could get England to fight for the former (*D.A.A.P.*, VIII, No. 410). The report of 30 April (**Doc. 119**) shews exactly what Stanley's views were before the Conference met. It proves that he wished to avoid mention of a guarantee altogether. It

* *Pte Wellesley Papers.* Clarendon to Cowley, 21 April 1857.
† *V. Die Auswärtige Politik Preussens*, Bd. VIII, von Herbert Michaelis, [Oldenburg, 1934]. The references in the text are cited as *D.A.A.P.* with the number of the volume and of the document following.

seems to be pretty clear therefore (and this is a revelation from the German documents) that Bismarck knew the guarantee meant little, but wished England to give it for purposes of assuaging German public feeling and reconciling it to Prussia's evacuation of Luxemburg.]

Document 119. *Stanley on the obligations to Luxemburg before the Conference met, 30 April* 1867*

...His Lordship [Stanley] was less reassuring in his answers when I asked him if it was understood that England would take her part in guaranteeing the neutrality of Luxemburg. He told me I should know how unpopular any obligation of that kind was in England and what strong objections a new guarantee would consequently encounter from public opinion. For these reasons, and considering himself personally the "Trustee" of British interests he could not take the engagement to defend Luxemburg by armed force, if such was the interpretation given to the word *guarantee*. But he thought that this word might be avoided and that an engagement taken by the Great Powers to *respect the neutrality of Luxemburg* would suffice. That would then be a *moral guarantee* which England is ready to share and which would attain the same goal, since it would protect neutralisation from all attempts on it. Even if it did not what would England's forty or fifty thousand men avail against Powers who had four or five hundred thousand? We had never, went on Lord Stanley, claimed to play the part of a military power on the Continent. We are a maritime State, we have great commercial and political interests to defend in Belgium, which explains the guarantee taken up in regard to this Kingdom which, in our eyes, is summed up in the position of Antwerp. But Luxemburg has not the same importance for us, and that is why, we should wish to limit ourselves in this business to the minimum of engagement indispensable to assure the maintenance of peace.

I observed to Lord Stanley that M. de Bismarck had made

* W.S.A. vIII/75, Berichte aus England. From Apponyi, No. 33C of 30 April 1867.

a neutralisation *guaranteed by the Powers* a condition of the [Prussian] evacuation, and that it was to be feared the reservation made by England would not solve the difficulty.

His [Stanley's] answer was that he understood perfectly that, if Prussia was not to be trusted in her pacific intentions, she could make use of this pretext; but he flattered himself that things would not turn out thus, and that there would be no opportunity to discuss this delicate question, as to which England could hardly make concessions.

43. DERBY AND STANLEY EXPLAIN THE GUARANTEE AFTER THE CONFERENCE

[On 4 May, before the Conference met, Bernstorff reported Stanley as telling him that the British Parliament "would give no guarantee containing a pledge which might ultimately lead to war" (*D.A.A.P.*, VIII, No. 577). At the Conference itself, contrary to Stanley's desire, Bismarck pressed hard on the subject of guarantee. He wished clearly to have something, which appeared to be real and effective, before consenting to evacuate the Prussian garrison and demilitarizing the fortress of Luxemburg, and this was clearly reasonable. Stanley tried to evade the issue by proposing the following text for Article II of the proposed Treaty: "Le Grand Duché de Luxemburg, dans les limites déterminées par l'Acte annexé aux Traités du 19 avril 1839 sous la garantie des Cours de la Grande Bretagne, d'Autriche, de France, de Prusse, et de Russie, formera désormais un État perpétuellement neutre.

Il sera tenu d'observer cette même neutralité envers tous les autres États.

Les Hautes Parties Contractantes s'engagent à respecter le principe de neutralité stipulé par le présent Article."

Count Bernstorff, the Prussian representative, then said that a European guarantee of Luxemburg was the basis on which Prussia had accepted the invitation to the Congress. He therefore pressed for an amendment as follows: "le principe [de neutralité] est et demeure placé sous la sanction de la garantie collective (ou commune) des Puissances signataires du présent Traité, à l'exception de la Belgique, qui est elle-même un État neutre". Stanley resisted the amendment, but he was outvoted by the majority of the members. He then referred the matter to the British Cabinet. On the 9th he returned to the Conference with the news that they had accepted the amendment, which was accordingly inserted in the Treaty signed at London on 11 May* by Austria, Belgium,

* English text in Hertslet, *Map*, [1875], III, 1801-5.

France, Great Britain, Italy, Holland, Prussia and Russia. It is the main Article of the Treaty.

It will thus be seen that Stanley and the British Cabinet were negotiated, even pressed, against their will, into a guarantee. But Stanley's previous private explanations to Bernstorff shew clearly that a British guarantee of Luxemburg meant little and would differ from the Belgian one.* The matter came up and was debated on several occasions in the Lords and Commons, when both Derby and Stanley spoke. Stanley, when asked by Count Bernstorff officially for an interpretation, discredited the report of his father's speech, and indeed the authority of all parliamentary speeches. But in private he gave an authoritative explanation of his own speech (*v.* **Doc. 121**). This utterance, hitherto unpublished (and not the speeches so frequently quoted by jurists and by historians), is the really binding document. He did in substance adopt the view that a collective guarantee means nothing, because it disappears when any signatory power violates it. This is much the same as the Derby doctrine, and as the explanation given by Stanley to the Commons on 14 June.† But it differs from the latter in being much more explicit as to the true reason for whittling away the force of the collective guarantee. He says that it would be wrong to regard the guarantee as "purely illusory", but that you cannot, in fact, bind the British Parliament in advance to a question involving peace or war. In other words Stanley hoped the guarantee would be honoured but would not bind himself to such a view. The German revelations, above alluded to, threw a new light on the question. Instead of *perfide Albion* deceiving Bismarck, it would be more true to say that Bismarck and Stanley agreed on a formula which, in effect, deceived the German public.‡]

Document 120. *Derby's interpretation of the guarantee,*
13 *May* 1867§

[In answer to a question] The guarantee is not a joint and separate guarantee, but is a collective guarantee, and does not impose upon this country any special and separate duty of enforcing its provisions. It is a collective guarantee of all the Powers of Europe...

* *V.* esp. *D.A.A.P.*, viii, Nos. 410, 577. These discussions of April and May were prior to the Conference.

† *Hans. Deb.*, 3rd Ser., CLXXXVII, 1921–3, 14 June 1867.

‡ For the older view *v.* Sir E. Satow, 'Pacta Sunt Servanda', *Camb. Hist. Journ.* I, No. 3, [October 1925], 306–18; for the modern view *v.* Temperley in *Eng. Hist. Rev.* L, [October 1935], 730–1; and *D.A.A.P.*, viii, Nos. 385, 391, 409–10, 473, 577.

§ Lord Derby on 13 May 1867, *Hans. Deb.*, 3rd Ser., CLXXXVII, 379.

Document 121. *Stanley's authoritative interpretation of the guarantee, 25 June 1867**

[After Count Bernstorff had referred to the reply of Lord Derby to a question in the Lords (*v.* **Doc. 120**)] I told Count Bernstorff that discussions in the House of Lords were, from the difficulty of hearing, often imperfectly reported; and that I could not undertake to defend words attributed to Lord Derby, without knowing whether they had been really used or not; but that I would explain to him my idea of the obligations involved in a Collective Guarantee.

I said that it was absurd to suppose that each of the Powers that had signed such a guarantee could be made singly and separately responsible for its being enforced. Supposing (to take an extreme case) that France and Prussia came to an understanding involving a violation of the territory of Luxemburg that the King Grand Duke appealed to the Guaranteeing Powers, that Austria, Russia and Italy held aloof, would it be contended that England, single-handed, was bound, on that account to go to war with France and Prussia combined? It seemed to me, I said, impossible to define with legal strictness the amount of obligation really incurred; but whatever that might be, I could not see that the binding force of the engagement which we had signed, was in any degree lessened by comments made in debate upon it, even by its authors. The construction to be placed upon an international document was to be inferred from the words employed, and from the general usage of Europe. Once it was signed, the individual opinion of the Ministers signing was of no more weight than that of any other person. In a country like ours, no absolutely valid engagement could be entered into as to the course to be adopted at a future period, and under circumstances not now foreseen.

Questions of war or peace must be decided by the Parliament of the day.

* Stanley to Loftus, No. 200, 25 June 1867. Draft corrected and initialled by Lord Stanley and endorsed "seen by Lord Derby and the Queen". *F.O.* 64/615.

I would however add, as I had stated in the House of Commons, that if I had regarded the Guarantee which we had given as purely illusory, neither I nor my colleagues would have had anything to do with it.

With these explanations Count Bernstorff appeared partly satisfied: he however expressed his satisfaction that the question was to be raised again in the House of Lords, where he hoped that a full and clear explanation would be given.

Document 122. *Count Bernstorff refused further explanations,*
*12 July 1867**

[Count Bernstorff referred to the discussions in Parliament as having "caused some surprise and even some anxiety to the Cabinet of Berlin".] The Prussian Government do not accept the interpretation given by the Earl of Derby of a collective guarantee, which would amount to this, that if anyone of the guaranteeing Powers broke the Compact, no other could be required to enforce it. Such an interpretation would in their opinion weaken the force of Public Law, and relax international obligations.†

The Prussian Government do not however think it necessary to continue the discussion at present, as no practical result can follow.

I told Count Bernstorff that the question had already been argued between us more than once, and that I agreed with his Government in thinking further discussion upon it useless.

* Stanley to Loftus, No. 209, 12 July 1867. The draft is corrected in Stanley's own hand and endorsed "seen by Lord Derby and the Queen". *F.O.* 64/616.

† This interpretation is not quite a fair one. Stanley, in his authoritative interpretation, says that he *hopes* the British Parliament of the day would uphold the guarantee but that he could not pledge it in advance. This is very different from signing a treaty with no intention of keeping it and deceiving other signatories accordingly; it is, in fact, a warning to other signatories that Great Britain may be unable to keep it.

44. THE DERBY DOCTRINE OF COLLECTIVE GUARANTEE, AND ITS AFTERMATH (1867–1914)

[The "Derby doctrine" of collective guarantee would be more correctly called the "Stanley doctrine". For his statement of the case, endorsed by Derby and the Queen, is alone authoritative. What is more he appealed to the word "collective" as being interpreted according to "the general usage of Europe", not according to the whim of an "individual" Minister or by "comments in debate". Unfortunately, Stanley and Derby have been able to find few jurists to support them. They sought to apply their "collective" doctrine retrospectively to the guarantee in the Treaty of Paris of 1856, and this was certainly not the view of Cowley, who drafted the article in question.* Further, the idea that "collective" responsibility excluded "individual" responsibility is flatly contradicted by the use of the word "solidairement" in the guarantee article of the Triple Alliance Treaty of 1856. The authorized English rendering of "solidairement" is there given as "jointly and severally". The terms are technical ones in both French and English law. It is almost certain that both mean collective and individual responsibility. It is certain that they do not mean "collective responsibility" in Derby's sense. "Collective guarantee" is not a technical law term at all in English. Derby's statements in debate that the Treaties of 1831 and 1839 embody "several and individual" guarantees, and not collective ones, were inaccurate. Until Derby tried to draw the distinction, the Powers plainly had regarded the Treaty of Luxemburg as implying pledges of exactly the same nature as those given in 1831, 1839 and 1856.† The argument from the Treaty of 1856, or from the "general usage" of the past, is therefore all against the Derby interpretation.

Derby's almost meaningless interpretation of the "collective guarantee" was contested by three great authorities at the time, by Earls Russell and Granville and the Duke of Argyll. It was supported by Lord Clarendon. It has generally been rejected by jurists since its proclamation.‡ Bismarck at a later date (1885) complained that "the Minister of the day [Derby]... had explained

---

* H. Temperley, 'Treaty of Paris 1856', *Journal of Modern History*, IV, No. 4, [December 1932], 526–7, and notes.

† *V.* Sir E. Satow, 'Pacta Sunt Servanda', in *Camb. Hist. Journ.*, I, No. 3, [1925], 309 n., 312 n., 316.

‡ *V.* A. D. McNair, ed., Oppenheim, *International Law*, 4th ed., [London, 1928], I, 772–3; Hall, 8th ed. [1924], 400–2; Dr G. Quabbe, *Die Völkerrechtliche Garantie*, [Breslau, 1911], 159; C. P. Sanger and H. T. J. Norton, *England's Guarantee to Belgium and Luxemburg*, [1915], 87–90.

away [the Luxemburg Treaty] almost as soon as it was signed".*
Yet it must be said that Bismarck, in view of the new evidence
here brought forward, could hardly have been deceived at the
time, though he dared not enlighten the German public. This
explains why the Derby-Stanley doctrine as regards Luxemburg
became an accepted canon of the British, and of no other,
Foreign Office. When in 1914 Germany violated both the territory
of Belgium and of Luxemburg, France forwarded protests in both
cases; England confined her protest to Belgium. On 2 August
Monsieur Cambon asked Sir Edward Grey what attitude the
British Government meant to assume about the German violation
of Luxemburg. "I told him", said Sir Edward, "the doctrine
on that point laid down by Lord Derby and Lord Clarendon in
1867."† Grey is reported by Cambon as saying "that the Convention [sic] of 1867, referring to Grand Duchy [of Luxemburg],
differed from the Treaty referring to Belgium, in that Great
Britain was bound to require the observance of this latter Convention without the assistance of the other guaranteeing Powers,
while with regard to Luxemburg all the guaranteeing Powers
were to act in concert".‡ The influence of Stanley and Derby
reached far. Owing to the doctrine laid down by them in 1867,
England did not protest about Luxemburg in 1914 and went to
war for Belgium alone.]

* Lady Gwendolen Cecil, *Life of Salisbury*, [1931], III, 259.
† Gooch and Temperley, *British Documents on the Origins of the War*, [1926],
XI, 275, No. 487.
‡ *Collected Diplomatic Documents*, [1915], French Yellow Book, 235, No. 137,
Cambon to Viviani, 2 August 1914, in *A. & P.*, [1914–16], LXXXIII, [Cd. 7860],
33–601, cp. also the text in *D[ocuments] D[iplomatiques] F[rançais]*, IIIme Sér., XI,
469, No. 612.

XVII. GLADSTONE, CLARENDON AND GRANVILLE, 1868–74

45. NON-INTERVENTION AND THE RULE OF LAW

[The Gladstone administration, which came into office at the close of 1868, is more associated with the enunciation of principles for the conduct of foreign affairs than with specific achievements. During the first eighteen months Clarendon was at the Foreign Office, and the Queen had expressed suspicions about his appointment and his views as to British obligations. "She would deeply regret", the Queen wrote to Clarendon, "to think that either Portugal or Belgium should be led to imagine that they must not look to England for support in case of need. If it were to be generally understood that we could not any longer be relied upon, except for moral support, England would soon lose her position in Europe."* Clarendon's explanations partly removed the Queen's anxieties, but at her direction the correspondence was sent to Gladstone, and he replied with an important and characteristic exposition of policy (**Doc. 123**).

Most of the ideas which Gladstone enumerated in this letter were illustrated by the events of the ensuing period. Granville, like Clarendon, was called upon to define his attitude to the Portuguese treaties; Gladstone and Granville together worked out a scheme for the maintenance of Belgian neutrality; the use of "firm but moderate language" to deter the strong was tried more than once in connexion with Prussia, and the attempt to develop a public opinion in Europe and to forward the interests of international justice was the keynote of the Gladstonian policy.]

Document 123. *Gladstone expounds his principles of policy in reply to criticisms by the Queen, 17 April 1869†*

...I do not believe that England ever will or can be unfaithful to her great tradition, or can forswear her interest in the common transactions and the general interests of Europe. But her credit and her power form a fund, which

* *Letters of Queen Victoria*, 2nd Ser., [1926], 1, 589. Queen to Clarendon, 15 April 1869.

† Gladstone to General Grey, 17 April 1869. Morley, *Life of Gladstone*, [1903], II, Bk VI, Chap. IV, 317–18.

in order that they may be made the most of, should be
thriftily used....

...As I understand Lord Clarendon's ideas, they are
fairly represented by his very important diplomatic communications since he has taken office. They proceed upon
such grounds as these:—That England should keep entire
in her own hands the means of estimating her own obligations upon the various states of facts as they arise; that she
should not foreclose and narrow her own liberty of choice by
declarations made to other Powers, in their real or supposed
interests, of which they would claim to be at least joint
interpreters; that it is dangerous for her to assume alone an
advanced, and therefore an isolated position, in regard to
European controversies; that, come what may, it is better for
her to promise too little than too much; that she should not
encourage the weak by giving expectations of aid to resist the
strong, but should rather seek to deter the strong by firm but
moderate language, from aggressions on the weak; that she
should seek to develop and mature the action of a common,
or public, or European opinion, as the best standing bulwark
against wrong, but should beware of seeming to lay down the
law of that opinion by her own authority, and thus running
the risk of setting against her, and against right and justice,
that general sentiment which ought to be, and generally
would be, arrayed in their favour....

46. CLARENDON AND THE REDUCTION OF ARMAMENTS

[Clarendon's abortive attempt to persuade Bismarck to reduce
his "monster armaments" is now well known.* France had vainly
asked Stanley, when he was Foreign Secretary, to take the initiative
in the matter. Clarendon was already interested in the idea before
he came into power and, after conversations at Berlin and Paris
in the autumn of 1869, he approached Prussia in the following
January. The overture was a secret one, recorded in private letters
and unknown to Lord Sanderson, who was then in charge of the

* Cp. Morley, *Life of Gladstone*, [1903], II, Bk VI, Chap. IV, 321–3; *Letters of Queen
Victoria*, 2nd Ser., [1926], II, 8–9; H. Oncken, *Die Rheinpolitik Kaiser Napoleons
III...*, [1926], III, 299 n.; Newton, *Lord Lyons*, [1913], I, 246–79; A. A. W. Ramsay,
Idealism and Foreign Policy, [1925], 277–9; P. Knaplund, *Gladstone's Foreign Policy*,
[1935], 44–5.

German Department at the Foreign Office. He wrote privately: "Lord Clarendon's endeavour in the spring of 1870 to promote a mutual reduction of armaments by France and Prussia was conducted by private letters, and was entirely unknown to me until the publication of Lord Newton's *Life of Lord Lyons*." * In fact all communications with Bismarck on the subject remained personal in character. When this issue seemed doubtful, the French Minister for Foreign Affairs, Daru, suggested that Clarendon should correspond officially with Prussia. Bismarck might, he thought, be more ready to listen if the possibility that the dispatches might be laid before Parliament were present in his mind. Clarendon, however, was not ready to use this weapon, and the final communication to Bismarck on 9 March was made privately like the rest (**Doc. 124**). It had no better fortune than its predecessors. Bismarck suggested that England was acting the part of a "cool friend"; the overture utterly failed to lessen the tension in Europe.]

Document 124. *Clarendon makes his final effort with Prussia, 9 March* 1870†

I have delayed writing to request that you would convey to C[oun]t Bismarck my cordial thanks for the courtesy and frankness with wh[ich] in a private letter dated Feb[ruary] 9th and communicated to me by C[oun]t Bernstorff he answered my letter to you on the subject of partial disarmament.

This delay has been occasioned by my endeavour to ascertain correctly the relative forces of the great Military Powers and I hope that C[oun]t Bismarck will not consider that I trespass unduly on his time and his confidence if I again resort to a subject wh[ich] more than any other I have at heart and wh[ich] an Eng[lis]h Minister may have some claim to discuss without suspicion of his motives because Eng[lan]d is not a military Power but is deeply interested in the maintenance of peace and the progress and prosperity of the Continent.

I am as convinced as C[oun]t Bismarck himself can be that no German Gov[ernmen]t w[oul]d wish to impose upon its People the maintenance of an army in excess of that proportion for wh[ich] the requirements of its safety imperatively calls

* *Pte letter.* Lord Sanderson to Dr Temperley, 11 August 1922.

† Clarendon to Loftus, Private, 9 March 1870. *Pte Clarendon Papers, F.O.* 361/1; Newton, *Lord Lyons*, [1913], I, 267–70.

and I w[oul]d not desire the reduction of a single regiment if I thought it w[oul]d impair the independ[en]ce and the power of Prussia the maintenance of wh[ich] in their plenitude I regard as essentially beneficial to Europe.

But can it be correctly affirmed that the power and independ[en]ce of Prussia are menaced from any quarter and if not surely the military force of Prussia is excessive and entails upon other Countries the unquestionable evil of maintaining armies beyond the requirements of their safety.

The only Countries from wh[ich], owing to her geographical position, Prussia c[oul]d anticipate danger are Russia, Austria and France and can it be said that from either there is any real cause for apprehension?

In the conversation I had with C[oun]t Bernstorff when he commun[icate]d to me the letter of C[oun]t Bismarck he dwelt at some length upon the ill will of Russia towards Germany wh[ich] might take an active form on the death of the present Emp[ero]r and for wh[ich] Prussia ought to be prepared, but C[oun]t Bismarck must know better than myself that Russia has long since and wisely ceased to aim at influence in Germany or intervention in German affairs and that all her energies are now directed Eastward with a view of extending her territory and her commerce in Asia. Whatever sentiments may be suggested in other quarters by a rapid development of the present policy of Russia wh[ich] has the entire support of public opinion in that Country it appears certain that Germany can have no danger to guard ag[ain]st from Russia whatever may be the personal feelings or opinions of the reigning sovereign.

On paper, and only on paper, Austria has an army of 800,000 but she c[oul]d not even on the most pressing emergency bring 250,000 men into the field—her finances are dilapidated and her internal disorganization affords just cause of alarm—danger to Prussia from Austria must for many years to come be a chimera.

The military peace establish[men]t of France is nominally greater than that of Prussia the former being 400,000 and the latter being 300,000 but the number of troops stationed in the costly and unproductive Colony of Algiers is not and cannot ever be less than 60,000 men. Other Colonial possessions require military protection and the garrisons in Lyons and other great towns necessary for the maintenance of order have not less than 40,000 men. The establishments of the two Countries are as nearly as possible upon an equality. Can this state of things in France be regarded as a menace or a danger to Prussia? I am greatly mistaken if any Pruss[ia]n Statesman or General w[oul]d answer this enquiry in the affirmative.

The question then to my mind appears quite simple. The military forces of the first Continental Powers have a certain proportion to each other—in order to maintain that proportion very heavy burdens were imposed upon each Country but if by common agreement each reduces its army by a certain number of men the same proportions will be maintained while the burthens wh[ich] are fast becoming intolerable will be alleviated and this w[oul]d in no way weaken the important declaration made by the King in His M[ajesty]'s speech on opening the Federal Parl[iamen]t viz that the legitimate purpose of the military force of the country is to guard its own and not to endanger the independ[en]ce of other Nations.

C[oun]t Bismarck however thinks that if the question of diminishing the military strength of Prussia is entertained it will be necessary carefully to enquire what guarantees can be given by neighbouring Military Powers in compensation to Germany for a decrease in the amount of security wh[ich] she has hitherto owed to her armies.

Upon this I w[oul]d respectfully beg to observe that a minute discussion of guarantees w[oul]d be endless and dangerous—the legitimate rights and precautionary measures of independent Gov[ernmen]ts w[oul]d be analyzed in a spirit possibly of unfriendly criticism and if agreements were arrived at constant vigilance over their faithful fulfilment w[oul]d be necessary and this might possibly give rise to the quarrels that the agreements were intended to avert and wh[ich] w[oul]d at once put an end to the compacts.

It is upon a dispassionate consideration of the probable course of events that the question of partial disarmament sh[oul]d in my opinion be decided and in France (the only country with wh[ich] we need concern ourselves) what do we find? a nation resolutely pacific—a Gov[ernmen]t depending on popular support and therefore equally pacific—a responsible Min[iste]r declaring that France will not interfere with the affairs of her neighbours and the Sovereign willingly assenting to a diminution of 1/10th of the annual conscription without asking for reciprocity on the part of Germany and thereby showing his confidence in the King's declaration.

I venture to think that the present state of opinion in France founded as it is upon a true estimate of French interests is a more solid guarantee than any that the respective Gov[ernmen]ts of Fr[anc]e and Germany c[oul]d effect for their own security.

C[oun]t Bismarck will admit, and I am sure that a Statesman so liberal and far sighted will admit without regret that the people every where are claiming and must obtain a larger share in the administration of their own affairs and that in proportion as they do so the chances of causeless wars will diminish. The people well understand the horrors of war and that they and not their rulers are the real sufferers—they equally understand and will daily become more impatient of the taxation for those costly preparations for war wh[ich] in themselves endanger peace and I believe that there is at this moment no surer road to solid popularity for Gov[ernmen]ts than attending to the wants and wishes of the people on the subject of armaments.

I have reason to know that the reduction in the French army w[oul]d have been carried further if the Gov[ernmen]t c[oul]d have hoped that the example w[oul]d be followed by Prussia—sooner or later however this reason will be publicly assigned and then upon Prussia will rest the responsibility not only of maintaining so large a force herself but of compelling other Countries reluctantly to do the same.

It w[oul]d be to me a matter of most sincere pleasure to

think that no such responsibility will rest on Prussia but I should hardly have presumed to recur to the subject if I had not gathered from the private letter of C[oun]t B[ismarck] that further discussion was not absolutely precluded and I had not therefore been encouraged to hope that he might think proper to make my suggestions known to his Sovereign.

47. THE PRUSSIAN CIRCULAR ON ALSACE-LORRAINE

[Prussia's intention to annex Alsace and Lorraine was made known to England by a circular, dated 13 September 1870 and communicated on the 22nd. Gladstone was greatly shocked at the idea of annexing a people against their will, and he clung as long as he could to the thought of action, though in fact he did not wish to act alone. In his view there were only two courses open to Britain—to protest on the ground of "the sense of the inhabitants"; or to consider the communication *non avenu*. The paper here printed (**Doc. 125**) was sent to Granville for his personal information, and was greeted with polite disagreement.* Goschen supported Gladstone at the Cabinet on the 30th; but Granville won "after the longest fight I ever had against Gladstone". Granville tried to console the Premier: "Palmerston", he said, "wasted the strength derived by England from the great war by his brag, I am afraid of our wasting that which we at present derive from moral causes by laying down general principles, when nobody will attend to them." The cue was quickly taken. "In moral forces, and in their growing effect upon European politics," wrote Gladstone, "I have a great faith: possibly on that very account, I am free to confess, sometimes a misleading one." † But he found the Cabinet decision "rather indigestible", and feared that "a most mischievous wrong will have been done and will be beyond recall, without a word from anybody".‡ Even then he was not finally convinced. In October he wrote an article in the *Edinburgh Review* in which he stated publicly, though anonymously, his objection to forcible annexation. "To wrench a million and a quarter of a people from the country to which they have belonged

---

* Cp. P. Knaplund, *Gladstone's Foreign Policy*, [1935], 55–8, where an extract from Gladstone's memorandum is printed, and his correspondence with Granville on the subject cited. Professor Knaplund points out (*ibid.* 56 n.) that in Morley, *Life of Gladstone*, [1903], II, Bk VI, Chap. V, 345, there is a confusion between this memorandum and Gladstone's article in the *Edinburgh Review*, CXXXII, 564–93, October 1870.

† Fitzmaurice, *Life of Granville*, [1905], II, 62–3; cp. Morley, *Life of Gladstone*, [1903], II, Bk VI, Chap. V, 346–8; G. & D. 29/58, *Pte Granville Papers*. Gladstone to Granville, 8 October 1870.

‡ G. & D. 29/58, *Pte Granville Papers*. Gladstone to Granville, 4 October 1870.

for some two centuries, and carry them over to another country of which they have been the almost hereditary enemies, is a proceeding not to be justified in the eyes of the world and of posterity by any mere assertion of power, without even the attempt to show that security cannot be had by any other process." And a little later in the article he asks: "Can Germany afford, and does she mean, to set herself up above European opinion?" and finally he closes with his favourite doctrine: "Certain it is that a new law of nations is gradually taking hold of the mind, and coming to sway the practice, of the world; a law which recognises independence, which frowns upon aggression, which favours the pacific, not the bloody settlement of disputes, which aims at permanent and not temporary adjustments; above all, which recognises, as a tribunal of paramount authority, the general judgment of civilised mankind."* In November Gladstone wrote a second memorandum, but failed to get the necessary support in the Cabinet.† His attitude was wholly without effect on this issue—a marked contrast to the effectiveness of his action for the defence of Belgium and his establishment of the principle of the sanctity of treaties in the Black Sea question.]

Document 125. *Gladstone discourses on annexations,*
25 September 1870‡

The Chancellor of the North German Confederation announces, in his memorandum of the th [*sic*] current, the intention of the Confederation to demand from France, as a condition of peace, the cession of Alsace and a portion of Lorraine, countries inhabited by more than $1\frac{1}{4}$ million of inhabitants.

In signifying this intention as matter of fact, he likewise states the ground on which the demand is to be enforced. It is not to be for the mere augmentation of German Territory: nor is it to be for the purpose of improving the facilities for an attack by Germany upon France. It is to be a defensive acquisition exclusively, and is simply to make it more difficult for France to attack Germany.

* *Edinburgh Review*, CXXXII, 554–93, October 1870. Reprinted in *Gleanings of Past Years*, IV, 197–257. The passages cited above are on pp. 241, 242 and 256.
† Cp. P. Knaplund, *Gladstone's Foreign Policy*, [1935], 59–61. The memorandum is printed in full, pp. 270–9, App. I.
‡ G. & D. 29/58, *Pte Granville Papers*. The first memorandum enclosed in a letter from Gladstone to Granville, 24 September 1870. Part printed in Knaplund, *Gladstone's Foreign Policy*, 55–6.

Avoiding all collateral and secondary matters, the British Government feels itself required, by the communication it has received, to consider briefly

1. Who it is that makes the demand
2. What it is that is demanded
3. Why it is that the demand is made.

As respects the first.

The demand of a belligerent people, expressed by its constituted organ, must be taken as the authentic expression of its will.

But this expression may vary greatly in moral weight and authority, according as it may in given cases express the free and ascertained sentiment of the nation, or on the other hand only the sentiment of those who, thinking in accordance with the governing power, are allowed to speak their minds, while others who differ are put to silence by the action of the Government.

In order that we may give to the demand announced by the Chancellor of the Confederation its full moral weight, we must absolutely assume that the formation and expression of opinion upon that demand in Germany are free: that the public enunciation of the opinion opposite to that of the Government, besides encountering no hindrances, entails no legal penalties to person property or otherwise, more than that of an opinion coinciding with that of the Government. Otherwise we could not tell whether this condition is one really desired by the German nation, or whether it only represents the opinion which is held by persons in authority, and is supported by the greatest degree of physical force.

2. The thing that is demanded is, that a country with its inhabitants shall be transferred from France to Germany. More than a million and a quarter of men who, with their ancestors for several generations, have known France for their country, are henceforth to be severed from France, and to take Germany for their country in its stead.

The transfer of the allegiance and citizenship, of no small part of the heart and life, of human beings from one sovereignty to another, without any reference to their own consent, has been a great reproach to some former transactions in Europe; has led to many wars and disturbances; is hard to reconcile with considerations of equity; and is repulsive to the sense of modern civilization.

All these considerations would apply with enhanced force, if there were any sort of foundation for a rumour, which has gained some currency, that it was intended to constitute and govern the territory of Alsace and Lorraine after cession, not for itself, nor upon terms of perfect equality (whether incorporated or not) with the rest of Germany, but in some special and artificial manner, on behalf of Germany as a whole, and in a state of qualified civil or political inferiority.

The British Government must therefore presume it to be a *sous-entendu* in the memorandum of Count Bismarck, that the transfer of Alsace and a portion of Lorraine to Germany is only to take place upon its being ascertained to be conformable to the wishes of the population of those districts.

3. Thirdly and lastly, with reference to the reason, for which, and for which alone according to the Chancellor's memorandum, the transfer is to take place.

It needs no argument to shew that according to the common opinion a river is a bad strategic frontier, and that Metz and Strasburg afford to the French great facilities for the invasion of Germany.

It is however rational to ask whether were the fortresses of Alsace and Lorraine in the hands of Germany, they might not afford considerable facilities for the invasion of France by Germans?

It is difficult to carry the conviction to mankind in general, that any one country, whatever it may be called, is by a special charter of Nature exempt under all circumstances from all temptation to political excess; however freely it may be admitted on the other hand, that Germany is entitled to take ample securities against France, and that this cannot be done without materially impairing her rights and powers.

It would appear, however, that no greater harm ought now to be inflicted upon France, than is sufficient to meet the demand of Germany for ample security.

If then there is a method of proceeding which, with less of injury, and of future danger, to France, would give to Germany in substance the same guarantees against France as the appropriation of French territory, it would seem that that much ought to be preferred to such appropriation.

It seems to be worth while to consider, whether the military neutralization of the territory in question, and the destruction of all its fortresses, would not, without its being withdrawn from French allegiance attain the object of giving security to Germany.

The base of any military operations to be effected against Germany must then lie in France west of the proposed frontier, just as much as if the territory were transferred to Germany.

The exercise of civil Government from Paris in Alsace and Lorraine could not it is apprehended, be made to subserve the purposes of military aggression.

The disadvantages to France would be great. It may be uncertain whether she would submit to them. But the question now is why should the German demand extend beyond the condition of a military neutralization, of an interposition between the two countries of a space strategically void and exempt, and this wholly at the expense of France.

There may be other more eligible methods of proceeding: or there may be a perfect answer to the question which has been put. But as at present advised the demand of the Chancellor seems to have been pushed, and if so then inadvertently without doubt, beyond the scope of the argument on which it is founded, and within the true limits of which they cannot doubt it would if necessary according to reason, be reduced.

48. THE ALABAMA ARBITRATION

[Gladstone's application of principle to the conduct of foreign affairs was put to the severest test in the matter of the Alabama Arbitration. The details of the case were fully represented in Blue Books at the time,* and they fall outside the scope of the present volume. An extract only is given here from Gladstone's speech in the debate on the Address in February 1873, after the award had

* *V.* Temperley and Penson, *Century of Diplomatic Blue Books*, 241–3, 246–8.

been published. His defence of its acceptance was couched in terms similar to those which he used in connexion with the Black Sea Conference, and here again the keynote of his utterance was the establishment of a rule of law in international relations.

It is noteworthy that Gladstone in the earlier stages of the arbitration was doubtful of its desirability. But the experiment, despite its unpopularity in England, seems to have convinced him. Some years later, in his second ministry, when France and Italy were disputing about Assab Bay, he wrote that "the question of territorial right in this case is one for arbitration", and proposed that Britain ought "decidedly to recommend to both parties to hold their hands with a view to a settlement of that kind".*]

Document 126. *Gladstone argues in defence of arbitration,*
6 February 1873 †

...Sir, as was to be expected, the interest...of the evening's discussion, has turned chiefly upon that paragraph of the Speech which refers to the Arbitration at Geneva....I am bound to say that, in my opinion, if we had unhappily the same circumstances again before us, it would be our duty to meet them in the same manner....It is not as an alternative for the independent communication of independent countries that arbitration is to be preferred. The serious question is, whether arbitration is not a comparative blessing when, being resorted to without the slightest sacrifice of honour, it becomes the means by which worse, far worse, results are to be avoided? And by those far worse results I do not only refer to the contingency of war,...but I refer to the planting of habitual and perpetual discord between countries that every consideration of interest and duty ought to lead into the closest alliance....Arbitration is not a novel invention. Arbitration has undoubtedly its own grave and serious and characteristic difficulties; but what I think we are justified in saying—not wishing to make either too much or too little of the matter— is this. There may have been particular questions which have previously been made the subject of reference to arbitration between independent countries of as great consequence as any

* G. & D. 29/124, *Pte Granville Papers*. Gladstone to Granville, Private, 30 August 1881.
† *Hans. Deb.*, 3rd Ser., CCXIV, 103–15, *passim*.

one of the questions which remained unsettled between ourselves and America. But this, I think remains indisputable—
that when so far a step in advance has been made, there has
been no instance in which such a group of controversies,
reaching over so wide a surface, descending so far into detail,
and involving in certain cases such serious issues, have, by the
joint and single act of two great countries, been thus brought
to a peaceful termination.... If a strict doctrine has been laid
down, and if the first consequence of that is that we are called
upon to pay money which under a doctrine more relaxed we
should not have had to pay, the fact of such a strict doctrine
having been laid down is an important fact in the history and
in the gradual formation of international law.... I must say I
think it is a question not of legislating as we legislate here by
an Act of Parliament, which we can pass to-day and undo tomorrow, but we are legislating for the international concerns
of the world, and establishing a general consent of nations,
which no one or no two of them, once they are established,
will be able to undo.... It is not particularly agreeable to
have to pay money to a foreign Power, even though certain
results may be obtained which are not unfavourable to our
own permanent interests. The good sense of the country has,
however, I think, at once passed by all these secondary
matters, some of which are scarcely worthy of consideration;
and, looking to the large interests of humanity and civilization
involved in this mode of dealing with international disputes,
...has arrived at the conclusion that if it be not in every
respect precisely what we could wish, yet it is a thing to be
heartily welcomed and embraced on account of the principle
which it tends to consecrate and establish, and the evils
which it may operate to remove.

49. RUSSIA, THE BLACK SEA CLAUSES AND THE STRAITS

[The British attitude towards the abrogation of the Black Sea clauses of the Treaty of Paris reveals with peculiar clarity a distinctive trait of Gladstone's policy. It was founded on his dominant desire to preserve the rule of law in diplomacy. The actual issue raised by the Russian circular of denunciation seems to have been viewed somewhat differently by Gladstone and by Granville. The latter expressed himself forcibly to his old friend Apponyi, the Austro-Hungarian Ambassador, and roused hopes that Britain would take the lead in opposing Russia. But the final word lay with Gladstone, and when the British reply came— based as we know on a private memorandum drafted by him— Apponyi looked in vain for the "protestation énergique" which Granville's conversation had promised.* Gladstone objected to the form, rather than to the substance, of the Russian action. It is, perhaps, well to remember that Gladstone had opposed the inclusion of the Black Sea clauses in 1856, and he was the more inclined therefore to treat Russia leniently now because he believed these clauses to have been wrong in the first instance. It is not, however, true to say, as Gladstone did, that the Black Sea clauses were not a central feature of the Treaty of 1856.

Granville's dispatch—as he wrote privately to Buchanan—gave "a small hole out of which to creep, if they are not prepared to remain on their high horse".† And Odo Russell was sent on a special mission to the Prussian headquarters at Versailles to try to secure common action between Britain and Prussia. Meanwhile Gladstone and Granville elicited from Russia the assurance that her Ambassador would present Russian views at a Conference "without mentioning the Declaration of His Excellency's Circular of the 31st of October". At the end of November they accepted Bismarck's invitation to a Conference at London, "upon the understanding that it is assembled without any foregone conclusion as to its results". The question of compensation was difficult to settle. Turkey—who had never wanted a Congress—raised diffi- culties when it was proposed that the Sultan should have restored to him his freedom to open or close the Straits at will. Bismarck, who would have agreed to this, refused categorically Granville's second proposal, that Germany, with Italy, should join the Tripartite guarantee of 15 April 1856. In the course of the discussions on this subject Gladstone, in a private letter to Granville, laid down an important principle with reference to

* W.S.A. viii/81, Varia. Apponyi to Beust, Private, 17 November 1870.
† G. & D. 29/114, *Pte Granville Papers*. Granville to Buchanan, Private, 11 November 1870.

guarantees—that they "presuppose the capacity of any guaranteed State to fight for herself" (**Doc. 129**), a point of some interest in view of the later discussions of the guarantee to Belgium.

The final settlement was only reached after much experiment. The Black Sea clauses were abrogated, the Rule of the Straits was modified, and denunciation formally repudiated. The Tripartite Treaty, despite Granville's unwillingness, remained unchanged. Austria-Hungary failed to secure the acceptance of her more vigorous proposals, which would have resulted in the establishment of a port on the Black Sea open to foreign ships of war.

None the less, Gladstone managed to secure the essential point, by the general admission that the rule of law must be strictly preserved in international affairs. Russia, indeed, abrogated a part of the Treaty, and the result of the Conference was to confirm a *fait accompli*. Yet it would be incorrect to describe the Conference as a farce, or to assert that Russia emerged unscathed from the struggle. In return for a particular concession at the moment she promised to support in the future a new and general interpretation of European public law. The pledge was underwritten by all the other Great Powers. A multilateral European treaty was not in future to be abrogated by one power alone; the consent of the other signatory powers was required for either abrogation or revision of such a treaty in whole or in part. It may be said that this principle—embodying the Gladstonian idea that force should be controlled by law—was in substance maintained until the annexation of Bosnia and Herzegovina by Austria-Hungary in 1908.* It represented an important advance in international law and morality.]

Document 127. *Gladstone points out the principles involved in the Russian Circular of 9 November 1870†*

The dispatches of Prince Gortschakoff dated 9th November 1870 declare on the part of Russia that the Treaty of 1856 has been infringed in various respects to the prejudice of Russia and in one case that of the Principalities against the explicit protest of her Representative: and that in consequence of these infractions Russia is entitled to renounce those stipulations of the Treaty which directly touch her interests. It is

* The case of Batoum is not in fact an exception to the rule (*v. infra*, pp. 436–41); Russia here contended, and with some justification, that no violation of the Treaty had taken place.

† G. & D. 29/58, *Pte Granville Papers*. Memorandum by Gladstone. The memorandum is undated, but it is endorsed: "Mr. Gladstone. Rec^d Nov. 10, 1870."

there announced that she will no longer be bound by the covenants which restrict her rights of Sovereignty in the Black Sea.

We have here an allegation that certain facts have occurred which in the judgment of Russia are at variance with certain stipulations of the Treaty: and the assumption is made that Russia, upon the strength of her own judgment as to the character of those facts, is entitled to release herself from certain other stipulations of that instrument.

This assumption is limited in its practical application to some of the provisions of the Treaty: but as every Treaty in point of obligation is one and indivisible, the assumption of a title to renounce any one of its terms is *ipso facto* an assumption of a title to renounce the whole.

The statement which has been made is wholly independent of the reasonableness or unreasonableness on its own merits of the desire of Russia to be released from the observation of the stipulations of the Treaty of 1856 respecting the Black Sea.

But the question now raised is, in whose hands lies the power of giving a release from all or any of these stipulations?

It has commonly been supposed that that Power belongs only to the Powers who have been parties to the original instrument.

The dispatches of Prince Gortschakoff appear to proceed upon a different principle.

They imply that some one of the Powers who have signed the engagement may allege that occurrences have taken place at variance with the provisions of the Treaty, and upon that allegation, although it be one not shared nor admitted, by the Cosignatory Powers, may found not a request to those Powers for the equitable consideration of the case, but an announcement to them that it has emancipated itself or holds itself emancipated from any stipulations of the Treaty which it thinks fit to disapprove.

It is quite evident that the effect of such doctrine and of such proceeding which with or without avowal is founded upon it is to bring the entire authority and efficacy of all

Treaties whatever under the discretionary control of each one of the Powers who may have signed them.

That is to say the result obtained is the entire denunciation of Treaties in their essence. For whereas their whole object is to bind Powers to one another, and for this purpose each one of the parties places a portion of his free agency in abeyance as regards himself and under the control of others, by the doctrine and proceeding now in question one of the Parties in its separate and individual capacity brings back the entire subject into its own control, and remains bound only to itself.

Accordingly Prince Gortschakoff has thought proper to announce in these dispatches the intention of Russia to continue to observe certain of the provisions of the Treaty. However satisfactory this might be in itself it is obviously an expression of the free will of that Power which it might at any time alter or withdraw, and in this which is the true point of view it is equally unsatisfactory with the other portions of his communication because it implies the title of Russia to cancel the treaty on the ground of allegations of which she appoints herself as the only judge.

The question therefore arises not whether any desire expressed by Russia ought to be carefully examined in a friendly spirit by the cosignatory Powers, but whether they are to accept from her an announcement that by her own act, without any consent from them, she has released herself from a solemn covenant.

Document 128. *Granville reflects on the Tripartite Treaty of* 1856, 10 *December* 1870*

I presume a programme to which Russia, Prussia, Italy and Turkey and probably Austria and France would agree would be restoration to the Emperor of Russia of his Sovereign rights in the Black Sea, ditto to the Sultan in the manner most agreable to him and a reaffirmation of all the remainder of the Treaty.

* G. & D. 29/58, *Pte Granville Papers.* Granville to Gladstone, Private, 10 December 1870.

What further can we do. Possibly some declaration of the construction to be put on the clause forbidding Foreign Powers meddling with internal administration of Turkey.

But what sticks in my gizzard is the Tripartite Treaty.* How very foolish it was of us to have concocted it. But there it is, with obligations as binding as were ever contracted. If Prussia who says she was never asked to join it, would consent to do so now, it would rather weaken than strengthen the obligations of England, and would act as a powerful check against Russia trying to put them in force, and be a real equivalent for the concession made to her in the Black Sea. But Prussia is almost certain to decline, and although she will declare as strongly as we like her sense of obligation under the Treaty of March 1856, yet the fact will remain, that while six powers are bound by that Treaty, two of them are not bound by the much stronger Treaty of April.

If Odo [Russell] ascertains that Prussia will not accede to the Tripartite Treaty, how would it do to ask her whether she would do so, if we made the same offer to Russia.

There would be something of the Belgian Treaty of last year in the principle.

It would have a deterring effect upon Russia and yet would rather release us.

If Russia denounced the remainder of the Treaty of 1856, and acted upon the denunciation, England, France, Austria and Prussia would be too strong for her.

If Prussia played false to us, it would diminish the necessity of our putting ourselves forward alone, or with only half the other cosignatories.

What do you think of this.

There is also a question whether when the conference is over we should invite Spain to make a declaration in favour of the Treaty of 1856.

* V. supra, pp. 330–1.

Document 129. *Gladstone defines the implications of a Guarantee, 12 December 1870**

I quite agree that it is difficult to justify the Tripartite Treaty but as a practical question I am inclined to suggest looking at it from another point of view.

I incline to think that any action in regard to it, as for example the asking Prussia to accede, would tend to rivet it upon us, and enhance our obligation.

On the other hand, stringent as it is in its terms, it does not appear to me to have much force as a covenant at present, when Turkey declares her own incapacity to fight except with virtually our money. Guarantees as such seem to me to presuppose the capacity of any guaranteed State to fight for herself; and then to supply a further auxiliary defence. At least I think it must be so in the case where nothing is expressed to give a different construction to the guarantee.

I am not sure that I know what you mean by making the same offer to Russia but I fear it would be futile to ask her to accede to the Tripartite Treaty. For my own part, I do not see that the Straits may not supply a sufficient compensation for the Black Sea changes: but I would urge the Turk to meditate as he smokes his pipe, and let us know what occurs to him in the way of compensations....

I am *rather* against making Spain a party just yet: but things might look different a short time hence.

50. THE NEUTRALITY OF BELGIUM

[It might be argued that Gladstone compromised his general principles in the question of Belgian neutrality at the opening of the Franco-Prussian War, and that he obtained a practical advantage by doing so. A careful study of the whole incident suggests, however, another explanation. Gladstone's private correspondence with Granville shews how greatly he desired to make a special engagement with the belligerent powers to respect Belgian neutrality. It is equally clear that he did not regard his action as injuring the sanctity of the 1839 Treaty. In order to

* G. & D. 29/58, *Pte Granville Papers*. Gladstone to Granville, Private, 12 December 1870.

understand his attitude it is necessary to remember in the first place the publicity attached to the revelation of the Benedetti document in July 1870.* If two of the signatories to the 1839 Treaty could contemplate a secret agreement for a possible violation of Belgium, some immediate action was necessary to make the position clear. Napoleon III wrote a private letter of assurance to the King of the Belgians. But this was not enough in Gladstone's view, and he feared the result of a general declaration by Great Britain. As he said in the House of Commons on 8 August, "much danger might arise from such a declaration... we might inadvertently give utterance to words that might be held to import obligations almost unlimited and almost irrespectively of circumstances". † His private correspondence shews that he still feared that the two belligerents might agree together to disregard Belgian neutrality. He finally decided in favour of two separate treaties between Great Britain and the two belligerents. Each was to be asked separately to sign a treaty guaranteeing Belgian neutrality; each was to undertake to cooperate by force with England in case that neutrality was violated. The treaties were to bind the signatories for the duration of the war and for twelve months longer. The decision was Gladstone's own. On 29 July he was pressing that something should be done "before any great battle takes place to alter the relative position of the two countries". On 2 August he wrote: "I hope you will be able now to prosecute the Treaty with France full gallop." On the following day he supplied Granville with categoric replies to the objections raised by Lyons (**Doc. 130**), while at the same time Granville instituted enquiries of the Law Officers as to the extent of the obligations under the Treaty of 1839. On the 4th Granville urged Lyons to negotiate quickly. The two treaties were signed on the 9th with Prussia and the 11th with France.‡ Ratifications were exchanged before the end of the month.

Two arguments emerge forcibly from these discussions. Gladstone was constantly aware of the interest shewn in the question by Parliament. "We are sure to be pressed again unless we speak", he wrote on the 2nd, "and every time we are pressed the demand for confidence will seem more exacting and supercilious"; and again, "I am very anxious to keep things straight in the H[ouse] of C[ommons]".§ But more compelling even than this motive

* V. *The Times*, 25 July 1870. This document revealed that in 1866 Benedetti had sketched a plan for violating Belgian neutrality. The fact of publication shewed that Prussia did not intend such violation now, and Napoleon on his side issued a hasty disclaimer.

† *Hans. Deb.*, 3rd Ser., CCIII, 1705.

‡ Texts in Hertslet, *Map*, [1875], III, 1886-91.

§ G. & D. 29/58, *Pte Granville Papers*. Gladstone to Granville, Private, 2 August 1870.

was the fear that England might be placed in a position where she would be bound to act alone. The Law Officers justified this fear, for they ruled that, if the failure of other parties to the guarantee to fulfil their obligations destroyed the obligation itself, this "would be opposed to the real meaning of the Treaty on any sound principles of construction" (**Doc. 132**). They recognized, indeed—as did Lord Hardinge in 1908,* also in the case of Belgium—that political considerations differed from legal obligations. But Gladstone did not wish to be faced with the choice of acting alone or not acting at all. On 3 August he wrote of his fear that "our displeasure...might and probably w[oul]d be a sole displeasure". In the House of Commons on 10 August 1870 he stated that the attitude of Austria-Hungary and Russia was "generally favourable"—an entire mis-statement as far as that of Russia was concerned and his object was clearly to stress joint rather than sole action.† From Gladstone's point of view the whole negotiation was an *ad hoc* one, with direct reference to the circumstances of the time and Article III of the treaties was definitely intended from the beginning, privately as well as publicly, to have the effect of "saving all the present obligations so that they might be resumed exactly as they are when they have ceased to be covered by the temporary engagement". Article III of each treaty runs as follows: "This Treaty shall be binding on the High Contracting Parties during the continuance of the present War...and for twelve months after the Ratification of any Treaty of Peace concluded between those Parties [France and Prussia]; and on the expiration of that time the Independence and Neutrality of Belgium will, so far as the High Contracting Parties are respectively concerned, continue to rest, as heretofore, on Article I of the Quintuple Treaty of the 19th April 1839."]

Document 130. *Granville explains to Lyons the urgency of an Anglo-French Treaty, 4 August 1870‡*

There is no time today to argue with you—and it would take some time to do so. As I agree that there are objections to what we are doing. But I believe there are more such to

* *V.* Gooch and Temperley, [*British Documents on the Origins of the War*], [1932], VIII, 377–8, and cp. *supra*, p. 155, note 3.

† On the general bearing of the Treaties and on the attitude of Austria-Hungary and Russia, *v.* Sir E. Hertslet's "Memorandum of the Circumstances which led to the conclusion of separate Conventions with France and Prussia in August 1870, for the Maintenance of the Independence and Neutrality of Belgium", 8 April 1872, printed in Gooch and Temperley, [1932], VIII, 371–4. Russia, in fact, almost repudiated the obligations of the Treaty of 1839, and Austria-Hungary delayed her reply until the end of September.

‡ Granville to Lyons, Private, 4 August 1870. *Pte Granville Papers, F.O.* 362/4. This argument was, in fact, inspired by Gladstone.

any other course. We cannot declare that we are not bound to stir for Belgium. We cannot even say nothing in the present frame of mind of the British Public. If we merely say we will defend Belgium, we incur the same risk as by our proposal, but in a greater degree. For we bind ourselves to do that single handed, which on our plan we shall only do in conjunction with a powerful Nation. I cannot doubt that this alliance will act as a powerful check on either party doing that which we wish to avoid—and makes junction on their part more difficult—there is another argument which cannot be used, but which has its weight. It is more difficult for L[ouis] Nap[oleon] to break his own plighted word, than a Treaty signed by L[ouis] Phillippe.

Be it as it may, the die is cast—and Gramont's reluctance does not make me more averse to it. If both parties agree, the thing will be much criticized, but I suspect will be approved by Public opinion, which is exasperated and alarmed by these revelations and recriminations as to the Draft project —Please hasten the Convention as much as you can.

Bernstorff has no instructions, but I think expects a favorable answer.

Document 131. *Gladstone defends his policy to the House of Commons, 10 August 1870**

...If I may be allowed to speak of the motives which have actuated Her Majesty's Government in the matter, I would say that while we have recognized the interest of England, we have never looked upon it as the sole motive, or even as the greatest of those considerations which have urged us forward. There is, I admit, the obligation of the Treaty. It is not necessary, nor would time permit me, to enter into the complicated question of the nature of the obligations of that Treaty; but I am not able to subscribe to the doctrine of those who have held in this House what plainly amounts to an assertion, that the simple fact of the existence of a guarantee is binding on every party to it irrespectively altogether of the

* *Hans. Deb.*, 3rd Ser., CCIII, 1787–9.

particular position in which it may find itself at the time when the occasion for acting on the guarantee arises. The great authorities upon foreign policy to whom I have been accustomed to listen—such as Lord Aberdeen and Lord Palmerston—never, to my knowledge, took that rigid and, if I may venture to say so, that impracticable view of a guarantee.* The circumstance that there is already an existing guarantee in force is of necessity an important fact, and a weighty element in the case, to which we are bound to give full and ample consideration. There is also this further consideration, the force of which we must all feel most deeply, and that is the common interest against the unmeasured aggrandizement of any Power whatever. . . . It was the combination, and not the opposition, of the two Powers, which we had to fear, and I contend—and we shall be ready on every proper occasion to argue—that there is no measure so well adapted to meet the peculiar character of such an occasion as that which we have proposed. It is said that the Treaty of 1839 would have sufficed, and that we ought to have announced our determination to abide by it. But if we were disposed at once to act upon the guarantee contained in that Treaty, what state of circumstances does it contemplate? It contemplates the invasion of the frontiers of Belgium and the violation of the neutrality of that country by some other Power. That is the only case in which we could have been called upon to act under the Treaty of 1839, and that is the only case in which we can be called upon to act under the Treaty now before the House. But in what, then, lies the difference between the two Treaties? It is in this—that, in accordance with our obligations, we should have had to act under the Treaty of 1839 without any stipulated assurance of being supported from any quarter whatever against any combination, however formidable; whereas by the Treaty now formally before Parliament, under the conditions laid down in it, we secure powerful support in the event of our having to act—a support with respect to which we may well say that it brings the object in view within the sphere of the practicable

* *V. supra*, pp. 156–7.

and attainable, instead of leaving it within the sphere of what might have been desirable, but which might have been most difficult, under all the circumstances, to have realized....

Document 132. *The Law Officers express their opinion on the character of the* 1839 *Treaty,* 6 *August* 1870*

We are honoured with your Lordship's commands signified in Mr. Hammond's letter of the 3rd instant, stating that he was directed by your Lordship to transmit therewith the Treaty concluded on the 19th April, 1839, between Great Britain, Austria, France, Prussia, and Russia, by the 1st Article of which the independence and neutrality of Belgium, as stipulated in the 7th Article of the Treaty signed on the same day between the Netherlands and Belgium, was guaranteed by the five Powers; and he was to request that we would report our opinion at our earliest convenience whether such guarantee is joint or several, and whether the refusal or incapacity of one or more of the guaranteeing Powers to act on their guarantee liberates the remaining Powers from their obligation to do so.

In obedience to your Lordship's commands we have taken the said Treaty into consideration, and have the honour to

Report—

That we are of opinion that, if the Treaty is to be construed by the rules which govern the construction of contracts by the law of this country, the guarantee is a joint one.

We must point out, however, that the only effect of this construction of a guarantee given by several persons is, that the party entitled to enforce it has to sue all the guarantors jointly. He may, however, enforce the whole of the debt or damages against any one guarantor, who in his turn is able to enforce contribution from his co-guarantors. The term joint-guarantee by no means imports that the guarantee of each is conditional on all the others performing their contract, and that upon one or more refusing to do so the others are

* The Law Officers to Granville, 6 August 1870, *F.O.* 83/2234, Gooch and Temperley, [1932], viii, 378–9, No. 311.

released. No such construction would be placed on any guarantee, unless such an intention were clearly expressed in it.

Applying these rules of our municipal law (which we believe to be substantially in accordance in this respect with that of most civilized countries), we reply to Mr. Hammond's second question that the refusal or incapacity of one or more of the guaranteeing Powers to act does not, in our opinion, liberate the remaining Powers from the obligation to do so.

We are quite sensible that other considerations than the strict rules of the municipal law of any country may be applicable to the construction of Treaties. We cannot help thinking, however, that to hold the obligation of each of the five Powers conditional on all the others fulfilling their obligations (a proposition which would lead to the consequence that, if France invaded Belgium, all the other Powers would be thereby released from their obligations to Belgium), would be opposed to the real meaning of the Treaty on any sound principles of construction.

Whether, in the event of none of the co-guaranteeing Powers choosing to co-operate with us, Belgium could reasonably expect Great Britain to undertake single-handed a war against great continental Powers, is a question into which other elements enter than the strict construction of the Treaty, and on which we do not presume to give an opinion.

51. THE DOCTRINE OF ALLIANCES

(a) PORTUGAL

[Under the first Gladstone administration the recognition of British obligations to Portugal called for a new affirmation of old principles; the proposals of Austria-Hungary for an Alliance in 1871–2 raised new issues for the future. Both these questions had to be settled while Europe was disturbed by the shattering results of the Franco-Prussian War.

At the beginning of 1873 Portugal feared, and with some justification, that the Republican party of Spain might attack her independence. On 15 February the Spanish Minister in London raised "a delicate matter" with Granville. He wanted to know what the British attitude would be if an "aggressive movement" against Portugal took place. Granville in reply referred to the Treaty engagements which involved the defence of Portugal "against external aggression"; and said that "the Spaniards could not count upon the indifference of England to an external attack upon Portugal". This reply on the part of Granville is all the more important because, as the Spanish Minister said in comment, "everything depended upon the attitude of England; that if England opposed herself to such a plan, no attempt would be made: otherwise it was sure to happen. That was his personal. opinion." * **Doc. 133** explains Granville's attitude further, and shews that he was careful to safeguard British freedom of action, in communications with Portugal herself.

Granville, it is true, failed to follow up a hint from France that an understanding should be reached for the use of identic language on the subject by the French and British Ministers at Madrid, although according to reports in March both France and Russia were ready to co-operate, at least diplomatically, to protect Portugal. It is clear, however, that Granville was more definite in his recognition of the British obligations to Portugal than his successor, Derby, who, while not denying the existence of the obligations, held that "the less said to the Port[ugue]se the better".† Unfortunately there are no indications available in the archives to shew more precisely the interpretation placed by Granville on the Ancient Treaties, or how far he considered that they were applicable to the "colonial possessions of Portugal". Canning in 1825 had denied any such applicability,‡ and Granville can hardly have been ignorant of this denial. Moreover, the references to Portugal in the debate in the Commons on Guarantees in 1872 ignored the most specific obligation under the Ancient Treaties, that of the Secret Article to the treaty of 1661, and the tenor of the argument used by Gladstone was to emphasize the contemporary setting of that treaty. The position in 1873, therefore, though not wholly clear, contrasts with Lord Salisbury's assertion in 1899 that the British guarantee extended to the colonies, an interpretation generally followed since that date.]

* Granville to Murray, No. 15 Confidential, 19 February 1873, *F.O.* 179/196. Gooch and Temperley, [1927], I, 51, No. 69, *encl.*
† Minutes by Tenterden and Derby on Lytton's dispatch, No. 108, 24 December 1875, *F.O.* 63/1033.
‡ Canning to Chamberlain (Rio de Janeiro), 12 January 1825, *F.O.* 120/68. Cp. Gooch and Temperley, [1927], I, 94.

Document 133. *Granville acknowledges the British obligations to Portugal under the Ancient Treaties, but reserves judgment as to their interpretation,* 27 *February* 1873*

I have received your despatch No. 24 of the 19th Instant reporting the substance of a communication made to you by Senhor Corvo, showing the apprehensions entertained by the Portuguese Government of the effect which the late overthrow of Monarchy in Spain might have on Portugal; and the wish of the Portuguese Government to ascertain whether in the event of the Portuguese Nation remaining loyal to its Sovereign and to its present Constitution, it might expect the effective support of Great Britain against open aggression and invasion on the part of Spain.

You will have seen by my despatch No. 15. Confidential of the 19th instant that I have warned the Spanish Minister that there were Treaty engagements between Portugal and Great Britain to defend Portugal against external aggression; and the Spaniards could not count upon the indifference of England to an external attack upon Portugal.

That statement will have enabled you to reassure the Portuguese Government; but in all your language to Senhor Corvo or others you will be careful to disclaim any disposition or intention on the part of Her Majesty's Government to interfere with the internal affairs of Portugal; and you will make it clear that Her Majesty's Government reserve for themselves to judge of the circumstances under which any appeal is made to them by Portugal for succour.

(b) ANDRÁSSY'S OVERTURE OF 1871–2

[The accession to power of Andrássy in 1871 was the signal for that series of negotiations between the Great Powers of Europe, of which the most tangible result was the nebulous *entente*, the League of the Three Emperors. While, however, Britain remained aloof from these manœuvres she was included in Andrássy's

* Granville to Murray, No. 20, 27 February 1873, *F.O.* 179/196. Gooch and Temperley, [1927], I, 51–2, No. 69, *encl.*

programme, and his first advance to her was in December 1871 when the Three Emperors' League was still in embryo.

The overture elicited from Granville a rather lengthy discourse on British policy, in which after surveying the whole European field he concluded as follows: "Count Andrássy does not appear to ask for any formal agreement. To such, whether of a public or private character it would be difficult for Her Majesty's Government to assent.

"The Policy of successive Governments in this Country has been to avoid prospective understandings to meet contingencies which seldom occur in the way which has been anticipated....

"On the other hand H[er] M[ajesty]'s Gov[ernment]t do not wish to speak in the language of commonplace courtesy....H[er] M[ajesty]'s Gov[ernmen]t will be always ready to communicate with the Austro-Hungarian Gov[ernmen]t in a spirit of perfect openness; and this desire has been much strengthened by the frankness of Count Andrássy's communication to Mr. Lytton." *

The matter was not left here. Further conversations between Andrássy and Lytton and Buchanan resulted in an elaborate instruction from Andrássy to Beust—now Ambassador in London —extracts from which were read to Granville on 11 April.†
Andrássy took his stand on the acceptance of the British policy of non-intervention, and the common object of the two Governments in the maintenance of peace, and proposed as the basis of the understanding that they should "always communicate their views to each other in the first instance. Such co-operation could not be obtained if at one time Russia, at another some other Power, were first consulted." The limit to which Granville would go in committing the Government to co-operation is laid down in the extract given here from his dispatch recording this conversation. Beust's report follows much the same lines but is couched in slightly more specific terms. According to him, Granville, while he refused to bind himself not to consult other Governments on occasions which seemed to him to require it, was prepared to undertake two things:

"1. that she [Great Britain] should inform us [Austria-Hungary] in the event of such a consultation" and

"2. that should England feel constrained to take the initiative in any question not solely affecting herself, she would come to an understanding in the first instance with us and with us alone".‡

* Granville to Buchanan, No. 13 Confidential, 16 January 1872, F.O. 7/796. Andrássy's overture is recorded in Lytton to Granville, No. 108 Most Confidential, 27 December 1871, F.O. 7/791. Cp. E. Wertheimer, Graf Julius Andrássy, [1913], II, 14–18, where the dispatch of 27 December is summarized.

† W.S.A. VIII/83, Depeschen nach England. Andrássy to Beust, Secret, 1 April 1872.

‡ W.S.A. VIII/83, Berichte aus England. Beust to Andrássy, Secret, 11 April 1872.

. These conversations are seen to be the more important since Beust cited them to Derby on the latter's accession to power at the beginning of 1874. But they also reveal an attitude which was highly characteristic of the policy of Gladstone and Granville. Both ministers refused to enter into any new obligations of guarantee or alliance, and indeed, as has been seen, they tended to confine existing obligations within specific limits. With reference to new alliances they formulated a doctrine, very important for the next thirty years, that England should "avoid prospective understandings to meet contingencies" which might not occur.* Their cautious policy in this matter falls into line with their general practice of non-intervention and with Gladstone's initial statement that the fund of the "credit and power" of England "should be thriftily used".† The limits of this somewhat *laissez-faire* attitude are seen in the resolution with which they acted in particular issues, in, for example, the protection of Belgium and the insistence that Russia should obtain leave from a European conference to abrogate the Black Sea clauses of the Treaty of Paris. In all these issues we see their methods in action. In Gladstone's reiterated statements on the rule of law we have the fundamental principles of his policy.]

Document 134. *Granville declines to pledge the British Government, but promises free communication with Austria-Hungary, 15 April 1872‡*

...I replied that, putting aside such questions as our present difference with America, (which H[is] E[xcellency] had quoted as an exceptional case which exclusively concerned one of the Parties to the proposed Agreement), it appeared to me difficult to make a solemn pledge that in all Political questions affecting the East or West of Europe each Gov[ernmen]t should always without exception address itself in the first instance to the other—that I believed our action would be best promoted by the most open communication, and by taking no step without a frank interchange of opinions.

Count Beust considered that without an agreement to communicate with each other in the first instance there could be no practical result.

* Cp. *supra*, p. 344.
† Cp. *supra*, pp. 317–8.
‡ Granville to Buchanan, No. 48 Confidential, 15 April 1872. Endorsed: "Seen by Mr Gladstone and the Queen." *F.O.* 7/796.

He instanced as two of the principal objects to be prevented:—

1. A close alliance between Russia and France;

or, 2ndly. between Russia and Germany.

We both wished Peace to be maintained and Germany to be consolidated, but the first alliance would be a threat against Peace, while the latter would give Encouragement to Russia in a sense unfavourable to our joint interests.

I cited a probable case in which it would be difficult for me to fulfil such a pledge. Supposing Russia were to make some plausible proposition to this Country. I might wish to consult other Countries. I should assuredly consult Austria, but I would not debar myself from consulting Germany at the same time.

Count Beust replied that what he meant was that neither Gov[ernmen]t should take an initiative without consulting the other.

I answered that in regard to the threatening Alliances to which he had referred there would be a wish on our part as well as on the part of Austria-Hungary to address ourselves at once to each other, but without authority from my Colleagues I could not give the formal pledge he desired, but I felt sure that I was only expressing their sentiments when I assured him of our determination to communicate freely and openly at once with the Gov[ernmen]t of Austria-Hungary on the appearance of any European difficulty.

XVIII. DISRAELI AND DERBY, 1874–6

THE CENTRAL POWERS

52. THE OPENING MOVES OF FRIENDSHIP, FEBRUARY 1874

[The advent of the Conservative Government in 1874 was followed by the repetition of the advances made by Austria-Hungary to Granville in 1872 (*v. supra*, pp. 343–6). But in the year 1873 the Three Emperors' League had come into existence, and this gives a special interest to the fact that not only Austria-Hungary, but Germany, made overtures to England in 1874.

In the case of Austria-Hungary, however, both the overture and the response were less formal than before. Derby was right in his conjecture that Beust was speaking without official instructions. "Without being specially authorized to do so," ran Beust's report,* "I nevertheless thought I was in a position to tell him [Derby] that the excellent relations now established between Vienna, Berlin and St. Petersburg—and which could not but be a subject of satisfaction to the cabinet of Britain, desirous as they were to see guarantees of peace—did not prevent my Government from attaching a high price to the friendly relations and to the *entente* existing with England, particularly in the affairs of the East." Beust states further that he drew Derby's attention to the communications of 1871–2. He seems neither to have expected nor received any definite expression of opinion from Derby; but he saw Disraeli at a drawing-room in the afternoon and found him extremely cordial. "It goes without saying that I shall do my best to put this cordiality to good use. Mr. Disraeli is to Lord Derby what Mr. Gladstone was to Lord Granville: only it is to be hoped that the result will be reversed. Mr. Gladstone acted as a check, Mr. Disraeli can if he wishes, act as a spur." It may be noted that, in the German negotiation (**Doc. 136**), Derby for once departed from a non-committal attitude, and pledged Great Britain in strong terms to the defence of Belgium.]

* W.S.A. viii/86, Berichte aus England, 1874. Beust to Andrássy, No. 20 A–C, 26 February 1874.

Document 135. *Derby replies to friendly overtures from Austria-Hungary, 26 February 1874* *

The Austro-Hungarian Ambassador [Beust] called upon me this afternoon by appointment, and in an interview of considerable length expressed his earnest desire that the· Governments of Great Britain and of Austria should maintain a good understanding, and as far as possible act in unison on all questions—especially those connected with the East. He defined the policy of Austria in regard to Turkey, as being one which endeavoured to combine the maintenance of the integrity of the Ottoman Empire with the promotion of all such administrative reforms as might be desirable for the well-being of the Christian populations under Turkish rule. He thought the Austrian Government had in past times looked too exclusively to the maintenance of order, and had ignored the impossibility of maintaining order without conciliating these populations. He knew nothing, he said, of any intention on the part of the Government which he represented to revive the Eastern Question, nor did he believe that such intentions existed. He was anxious that the Government of England should express itself strongly and decidedly on questions of this kind, when they arose; believing that in our so doing lay the best hope of peace being preserved.

Count Beust then referred, but in general terms, to the question of the Suez Canal; and to the financial condition of Turkey. He seemed to wish that Foreign Powers could put some check on the extravagance of the Turkish Authorities, which, if uncontrolled, must shortly end in bankruptcy.

I said in reply that I agreed with him as to the condition of Turkish finance, but I did not see how Foreign Powers could interfere to put it on a better footing. A commission of foreign Representatives, united to give advice on financial questions (which was the remedy I understood him to suggest) appeared to me either useless or dangerous; useless, if, as was probable, its action were to be nullified by the natural

* Derby to Buchanan, No. 22 Most confidential, 26 February 1874. Endorsed: "Seen by Mr. Disraeli and the Queen." *F.O.* 7/825.

jealousy of the Turkish Authorities; dangerous, if it drew to itself the management of the finances of the Empire, and thus virtually obtained a control over every branch of administration. In this view, after a little discussion, Count Beust appeared to concur....

With regard to Eastern matters generally I told Count Beust that I knew as yet but little of the position in which they stood: that I agreed with him in his two leading propositions—first, that the integrity of Turkey should be maintained, and next that no reasonable cause of complaint affecting the Christian populations under Turkish authority should be allowed to subsist; but that on this latter point it was necessary to speak with great reserve, since we both knew that in all countries complaints of political grievances were frequently put forward with objects very different from those which their authors thought fit to avow.

He might be assured, I said, that Her Majesty's Government would at all times be ready to communicate freely with that of which he was the Representative; and that it would give me sincere pleasure to find that we were able to act together. In any case, he might rely on the most entire frankness on my part. England had no object except the maintenance of European peace; and such, as it seemed to me, was also the natural policy of the Austro-Hungarian Empire.

It is only right to add to the above—first that what I have set down is a brief and very imperfect summary of a long conversation; and next, that I did not understand Count Beust to be speaking officially, but rather to be indicating what he personally supposed to be the views of his Government, and endeavouring to elicit mine.

Document 136. *Derby discusses the international situation with Münster, 27 February* 1874*

The German Ambassador [Münster] called upon me this afternoon by appointment, and conveyed to me a message that he had received from Prince Bismarck, expressive of his

* Derby to Odo Russell, No. 93 Confidential, 27 February 1874. Endorsed: "Seen by Mr. Disraeli and the Queen." *F.O.* 64/798.

earnest desire for the maintenance of the most friendly relations with England and of his confidence that a similar feeling was entertained by Her Majesty's Government.

To this communication I made a suitable reply.

Count Münster then proceeded to refer to the recent change of ministry at Constantinople; and observed confidentially that he was aware that an impression existed that this change had been encouraged by the German Minister at that Court. He felt bound to say that he thought the German Minister might have been imprudent in the language used by him and that so far the impression which he had mentioned was not unfounded; but he thought it right to assure me that the language thus used had not had the sanction, nor did it represent the views, of the German Government. Prince Bismarck, he said, was anxious to avoid even the appearance of putting any undue pressure upon, or endeavouring to exert any exclusive influence over, the Government of the Sultan.

The German Ambassador then adverted to the question of the recognition of the Spanish Republic, with regard to which he said there had been an understanding that Her Majesty's Government would not act without previous concert with that of Germany.

I said that I had hardly had time to consider that question, nor in the existing state of Spain did it appear urgent; but I promised him that no step should be taken in the matter without ample notice being given to his Government.

The last question mentioned was that of Belgium. Count Münster informed me in some detail of the strong feeling of irritation that had been produced in the mind of Prince Bismarck by the language of the Belgian Bishops and other ultramontane partisans. The Prince, he said, was convinced that there was, and is, an ultramontane intrigue to bring about the annexation of Belgium to France. He hoped, if any such attempt were made, that Her Majesty's Government would strenuously resist it.

I said that the maintenance of the territorial integrity and independence of Belgium was a principle to which successive Administrations in this Country had again and again pledged themselves; and it seemed to me that the national honour was so bound up with the observance of these promises, that a re-iteration of them could serve no useful purpose. I had no doubt, however, in the event which he anticipated, but which to me did not appear very probable, what our duty would be.

With this assurance the German Ambassador appeared well satisfied.

53. ENGLAND GIVES ADVICE TO BISMARCK IN THE WAR SCARE OF 1875

[Early in April 1875, three days after the famous headline in the Berlin *Post* of the 8th, Bülow, the German Foreign Secretary, informed Münster, his Ambassador at London, that there could no longer be any doubt that French preparations for war went far beyond the needs of a policy of peace. He stated that the Powers, who desired peace, ought to point out at Paris the consequences of these preparations. He instructed Münster, however, not to take the initiative in making a communication to Derby in this sense.*

In fact, on the very day following this instruction Derby assured Münster that it would be a mistake to assume that the increase in French armaments had a threatening aspect, and that an attack by France would only be possible if Germany were already at war with another Power; finally he gave it as his opinion that French fears of a German attack were not unfounded.†

By the first week of May, Derby began to fear that more open intervention would be needed if peace were to be preserved. He enquired of Odo Russell on the 3rd whether any reliance could be placed on the intervention of Russia.‡ Derby was convinced that France had no intention of attacking Germany, but was less convinced of the peaceful character of Bismarck's policy. On 5 May he expressed fears to the Queen to this effect. Already his hope lay in Russia; Disraeli's ideas and those of the Queen even more strongly in that direction.§ On 8 May, official instructions were sent to Odo Russell for combined diplomatic action with Russia—and proposals were made to Italy and Austria-Hungary that they should send similar instructions to their

---

* [*Die*] G[*rosse*] P[*olitik der Europäischen Kabinette, 1871–1914*], [1922], I, 249.
† Derby to Odo Russell, No. 118 Most Confidential, 12 April 1875, *F.O.* 64/822; *G.P.* I, 259–60, Münster to Bismarck, 13 April 1875.
‡ Newton, *Lord Lyons*, [1913], II, 75.
§ *Letters of Queen Victoria*, 2nd Ser., [1926], II, 389–92.

representatives.* On the following day the British Ambassador at St Petersburg was instructed to inform Russia of the steps which were being taken. The idea of adding the pressure of Italy and Austria-Hungary appears to have originated with the Queen. In the whole episode of the war-scare, Bismarck's intentions are still a matter of speculation. But it can hardly be doubted that the combined pressure of Russia and Britain contributed to assure peace, though the former has more usually received the credit than the latter.†]

Document 137. *Derby instructs Odo Russell to support Russian diplomatic action,* 8 May 1875‡

Her Majesty's Government have observed with regret the general apprehension which prevails of a disturbance of European peace. The French Chargé d'Affaires has expressed much uneasiness on the subject of a possible attack, either now or at no distant date, from Germany, the alleged provocation being the rapidity with which the reorganisation of the French Army is proceeding. The German Government is believed to regard these military preparations on the part of France as indicating a design of making war for the recovery of the lost Provinces.

Her Majesty's Government are convinced that no such design is entertained by the Government of France and that such apprehensions, if really felt, are unfounded. They earnestly desire the maintenance of peace and I have to instruct Your Excellency to use all the means in your power to put an end to the misunderstanding which has arisen.

It is believed that the Emperor of Russia will speak in the same sense during his visit to Berlin. Should His Imperial Majesty do so Your Excellency will strongly support his efforts for the preservation of peace.

* Derby to Odo Russell, No. 159, 8 May 1875, *F.O.* 64/822. Derby to Buchanan, No. 100; to Paget, No. 96, 8 May 1875, *F.O.* 7/846. Both documents are marked as having been seen by the Cabinet and the Queen. Cp. also Winifred Taffs, 'The War Scare of 1875', *The Slavonic Review,* IX, [1930–1], 335–49, 632–49.
† For the "war scare" episode generally, *v.* W. L. Langer, *European Alliances and Alignments,* New York, [1931], 41–57.
‡ Derby to Odo Russell, No. 159, 8 May 1875. Endorsed: "Seen by the Cabinet and the Queen." *F.O.* 64/822.

Her Majesty's Representatives at Vienna and Rome have been directed to communicate this Despatch to the Austrian and Italian Gov[ernmen]ts with a suggestion that the Representatives of these Gov[ernmen]ts at Berlin should receive similar instructions.

Document 138. *Derby's interview with Münster,* 9 *June* 1875*

The German Ambassador called upon me on the 9th instant, and in a confidential conversation explained that Prince Bismarck, while appreciating the friendly feeling of England towards Germany, had felt pained by some expressions which he understood to have been used by me and by the representatives of Her Majesty's Gov[ernmen]t at foreign Courts, during the recent communications on the subject of European peace. He appeared, as Count Münster explained it, to have supposed that I had stated in the House of Lords that the German Gov[ernmen]t intended to call on that of France to discontinue its military preparations—and he had authorized Count Münster to deny emphatically that any such intention existed on his part, and to express surprise that it should have been attributed to him. [Explanations given on both sides.] . . .

I reminded Count Münster that neither I, nor anyone speaking by my authority had ascribed aggressive designs of any kind to the German Government. We had from the first treated the difference between Germany and France as one arising out of a simple misunderstanding, capable of being removed by friendly explanation. We might indeed have reminded the Austrian Government that it had probably more to lose by a European war than any other, owing to the peculiar nature of the Austro-Hungarian constitution, but that was a very different thing from warning Austria of a meditated German attack, which I had neither done nor thought of doing. I ended by observing that the wish of this

* Derby to Odo Russell, No. 212 Confidential, 10 June 1875. Endorsed: "Seen by Mr. Disraeli and the Queen." *F.O.* 64/823. Cp. Count Münster's report of 9 June, *G.P.*, [1922], I, 290–2.

Government to maintain friendly relations with that of Germany was undiminished, and that the step taken by us had been taken solely in the interest of peace.

Count Münster promised to report what I had said to Prince Bismarck.

54. BISMARCK'S OVERTURE OF FEBRUARY 1876*

[German overtures to Britain in the Bismarckian period and under Bismarck's successors were generally timed rather to serve the interests of German policy than to fit the possibilities of the English situation. At the beginning of 1876 Bismarck was extremely anxious that the British hesitation to co-operate with the other Powers in the Eastern Crisis should not lead to an open breach in the Concert. Andrássy's note of 30 December 1875—proposing reforms in Turkey to avert war—had been circulated to all the Powers. Bismarck promptly approached Britain for a friendly understanding. At this stage it seems clear that Bismarck was anxious about the results of the Austro-Russian combination, and the maintenance of British co-operation was, therefore, particularly important. On 2 January 1876 Odo Russell called on Bismarck by appointment and was told that "he [Bismarck] thought a frank and frequent exchange of views and wishes on Turkish affairs between us was very desirable at present because England and Germany were the two Powers most earnestly desirous of maintaining the peace of Europe". He even said that he wished to know the British view of the Andrássy proposals before giving his own reply and indicated that he would be willing to delay acceptance of them if Britain desired such a course of action. Further, he elaborated at some length his own policy in connexion with Eastern affairs.†

Derby immediately telegraphed his thanks and promised that he would make a full statement to Münster in reply when his colleagues had been consulted. It was some time, however, before the Cabinet made up its mind. The promised conversation did not take place until 11 February, and it was confined to the Eastern

---

* On this subject cp. David Harris, *A Diplomatic History of the Balkan Crisis, 1875–1878—The First Year*, [1936], 174–8; and the same writer's article, 'Bismarck's Advance to England, January, 1876', *Journal of Modern History*, III, No. 3, [September 1931], 443–56.

† Odo Russell to Derby, No. 8 Secret, 2 January 1876, *F.O.* 64/850. Cp. *G.P.*, [1922], II, 29–31, where the conversation is said to have taken place on the 3rd. In Odo Russell's subsequent dispatch, No. 9 Secret, of 3 January, he said that "The impression left on my mind...is that Prince Bismarck means what he says, and really desires a frank and cordial understanding with England", *F.O.* 64/850.

Question itself.* In a subsequent dispatch to Odo Russell on the 16th, Derby, after some pressure from Disraeli,† explained the British attitude on the more general question of Anglo-German co-operation and instructed him to speak to Bismarck in this sense. This statement gives the keynote to one important aspect of British policy.

Odo Russell acted on his instructions on the 19th, but found Bismarck less anxious to give a general bearing to his overture. "All he had asked for was the faculty of exchanging ideas confidentially with Her Majesty's Government in case of danger. At the present moment, he said, the general aspect of affairs was satisfactory, and if the Insurrection in Bosnia was suppressed before the spring set in, he thought the Eastern Question could be dismissed from our minds for some time to come." And while he expressed his views on the Eastern Crisis at some length, the impression left on Odo Russell's mind was "that Prince Bismarck has no positive or fixed plan of action yet in his mind, but wishes to be prepared for any contingency, as he rather dreads too great an intimacy between Russia and Austria which might isolate Germany in regard to Eastern affairs".‡

The responsibility for the failure of the overture must be evenly divided. By 19 February Bismarck's anxieties were temporarily ended. Britain had acceded to the Andrássy note; the fear of an open Austro-Russian leadership of Europe was lessened. On the other hand the delay of England was an important factor, and Disraeli had some right on his side when he wrote: "It appears to me, that we are hardly taking as much advantage as we might of Bismarck's original overture to us."§ It is significant that the date of this reflection was 8 May—five days before that of the Berlin Memorandum. England, as is well known, rejected the Berlin proposal and thereby launched herself, Turkey, and the Great Powers, on a new and dangerous course.]

* Derby to Odo Russell, No. 115 Confidential, 12 February 1876. Marked: "Seen by Mr. Disraeli and the Queen." F.O. 64/846. Cp. G.P., [1922], IV, 3–4, note. Derby's dispatch has been printed by D. Harris in 'Bismarck's Advance to England, January, 1876', Journal of Modern History, III, No. 3, [September 1931], 450–1.

† Cp. Buckle, Life of Disraeli, [1920], VI, 21–2.

‡ Odo Russell to Derby, No. 76 Most Confidential, 19 February 1876, F.O. 64/850. D. Harris, Diplomatic History of the Balkan Crisis, [1936], 178, gives a different interpretation of Bismarck's reply.

§ Buckle, Life of Disraeli, [1920], VI, 23.

Document 139. *Derby replies to Bismarck,*
16 *February* 1876*

In my Despatch No. 115 marked Confidential, of the 12th instant, I have repeated the principal heads of a conversation between Count Münster and myself on the subject of Prince Bismarck's offer to cooperate with H[er] M[ajesty's] Gov[ernmen]t in regard to Eastern affairs. I have little to add to the statement which I made to Count Münster as to the policy of H[er] M[ajesty's] Gov[ernmen]t, and I would wish Your Excellency to use similar language to Prince Bismarck on any occasion that may arise for discussing the subject.

It is unnecessary to point out to Your Excellency that England desires no exclusive alliances, nor do the principles of English policy admit of such being contracted. The principal object of H[er] M[ajesty's] Gov[ernmen]t is, and must be, the maintenance of European peace. This object may, in certain circumstances, be materially promoted by a cordial understanding, and by concerted action between Germany and England, and the line of policy thus indicated would undoubtedly recommend itself to the sympathies as well as to the judgment of the English people. It is one, however, which, desirable as it may be in principle, cannot be definitely adopted without a clearer knowledge than we now possess of the motives which have led to Prince Bismarck's recent overtures, and of the expectations which he, and the Government which he represents, may have formed of the results of the understanding proposed by him. You will make it your duty to ascertain the truth on these points, and you will lose no opportunity of inviting from Count Bismarck the fullest and most unreserved disclosure of his intentions and ideas.

* Derby to Odo Russell, No. 117 Confidential, 16 February 1876. Marked: "Seen by Mr. Disraeli and the Queen." *F.O.* 64/846. Printed by D. Harris in 'Bismarck's Advance to England, January, 1876', *Journal of Modern History*, III, No. 3, [September 1931], 451–2.

XIX. BEACONSFIELD, DERBY AND SALISBURY, 1876–80

THE EASTERN CRISIS AND ITS AFTERMATH

55. THE POLICY OF DEFENDING BRITISH INTERESTS

(a) DERBY

[British policy in the early stages of the Eastern Crisis was largely negative in character. The instructions to Consul Holmes at the time of the Consular intervention of the Powers in October 1875; the qualified assent given to the Andrássy note; the refusal of the Berlin Memorandum; these well-known episodes reinforced the logic of Derby's lukewarm reply to Bismarck in February 1876 and the inconclusiveness of his conversations with Shuvalov in the autumn of 1875.* The most that can be said of the effectiveness of British action is that it neutralized the efforts of other powers to take the lead in bringing about a solution of the Eastern Question.

The events of May–September 1876 forced the British Cabinet to the consideration of a more positive policy. Servia and Montenegro were at war, Russia was likely to be involved. The private letters and dispatches of the time reveal views ranging from the extreme policy of supporting Turkey, represented by Elliot at Constantinople, to that of "a bold initiative in partition", proposed by Salisbury in the spring of 1877.† Between these extremes there was the attempt to find a peaceful solution in combination with other Powers. This idea is seen in Salisbury's conversations *en route* for the Constantinople Conference; in his cooperation with Ignatiev there; in Beaconsfield's overtures to Shuvalov after the Conference; and in Derby's negotiations with Austria-Hungary. But when on 24 April 1877 Russia declared war on Turkey, Britain hastened to define her position in an intelligible way.

Her policy was then expressed in a series of memoranda communicated to the Russian and Austro-Hungarian Governments.

---

* *V.* Derby to Elliot, No. 326 Confidential, 16 October 1875. Marked: "Seen by Mr. Disraeli; Do. by the Queen." *F.O.* 78/2378. Cp. Shuvalov's account printed by Professor R. W. Seton-Watson in *The Slavonic Review*, III, [1924–5], 426–30.

† *V.* Lady Gwendolen Cecil, *Life of Salisbury*, [1921], II, 134.

Most of those addressed to Russia were laid before Parliament soon after they were written. Thus Derby's note to Shuvalov of 6 May 1877 is a public declaration of policy and must be criticized with that fact in mind. Derby's original draft contained an expression of regret that "the Emperor of Russia should have separated himself from the European Concert and declared war upon the Ottoman Empire". This, however, was deleted before the note was communicated, while the insistence on British warnings to the Porte was retained in the final text. The greater part of the note was concerned with the definition of the limits of the British policy of neutrality. Of the points mentioned one only was of primary importance at the time, since it alone touched on a question of immediate urgency. The original draft ran as follows: "The position of Constantinople is one that confers upon the Government that occupies it certain maritime and political advantages which it is of the highest importance to all Nations, and especially to Great Britain, should be safely guarded.

Her Majesty's Government could not therefore consent to see that City in the occupation of Russia or the existing arrangements, made under the sanction of Europe, for the navigation of the Straits of the Bosphorus and Dardanelles, departed from."

In the final text the wording was changed: "The vast importance of Constantinople, whether in a military, a political or a commercial point of view, is too well understood to require explanation. It is, therefore, scarcely necessary to point out that Her Majesty's Government are not prepared to witness with indifference the passing into other hands than those of its present possessors, of a capital holding so peculiar and commanding a position.

The existing arrangements made under European sanction which regulate the navigation of the Bosphorus and Dardanelles appear to them wise and salutary and there would be, in their judgment, serious objections to their alteration in any material particular." *

Other points made in this communication—the reference for example to the Suez Canal, to Egypt and to the Persian Gulf—have importance for later periods of British policy, but the question of Constantinople was singular at the time because it was a live issue.

The May memorandum was followed by one in July, which in contradistinction to its predecessor was secret and confidential. It is significant that this dealt with one point alone—the possibility of a Russian occupation of Constantinople, "even though temporary". This was the point on which the negotiations between

---

* Derby to Shuvalov, 6 May 1877, *F.O.* 65/986. This volume contains the original draft and its amendments, and a printed copy of the final text. Cp. *A. & P.*, [1877], LXXXIX, [C. 1770], 135-6, and Shuvalov's report, *The Slavonic Review*, v, [1926-7], 421-2.

England and Austria-Hungary broke down. For the latter power, bound by her secret engagements to Russia, was prepared to resist a permanent Russian occupation of Constantinople but not to oppose a temporary one.]

Document 140. *Derby defines the British position in a secret communication to Russia,* 17 *July* 1877*

The Cabinet are deeply impressed with the gravity of the present crisis, and the danger to the general peace which may ensue unless some understanding is arrived at. They have rec[eive]d with sincere satisfaction the assurance given by the Emperor of Russia that, as far as concerns Constantinople, the acquisition of that Capital is excluded from His Majesty's views. But this assurance does not wholly meet the exigencies of the moment, and they have therefore instructed Lord Derby to tell the Russian Ambassador confidentially and secretly that they regard the occupation of Constantinople by Russian troops, even though temporary in duration and dictated by military requirements, as most inexpedient in the interest of the good relations between the two countries.

They therefore express their earnest hope that this step is not contemplated by the Russian Government. Should it unfortunately appear that the occupation is likely to take place, they hold themselves free to adopt any measure, which in their judgment may be required for the protection of British interests.

The Cabinet wish it at the same time to be understood that they will gladly avail themselves of any opportunity that may offer to assist in the restoration of peace on such conditions as may be consistent with the general interests of Europe and with the honour of the Russian Gov[ernmen]t.

This communication is strictly confidential, and the Cabinet are convinced that it will be received by the Russian Gov[ernmen]t in the spirit in which it is intended—not as a menace, but as a friendly warning of danger threatening both Governments which it is most desirable they should avoid.

* Memorandum, Secret and Confidential. Communicated to Count Schouvaloff, 17 July 1877. Marked: "Seen and altered in Cabinet." *F.O.* 65/986.

(b) BEACONSFIELD

[Derby's attitude at the opening of 1877 was one of extreme *laissez-faire*, and involved the narrowest interpretation of international obligations. Russia went to war with Turkey in April 1877. Under the stress of events and the pressure of Beaconsfield, Derby moved slowly towards a more active policy. But by the middle of 1877 Beaconsfield was pursuing a line of policy which might well lead to war and which it was certain that the Foreign Secretary would never sanction. Derby's political influence in the north made his dismissal difficult, but Beaconsfield had replaced Elliot by Layard at Constantinople, and the new ambassador was soon privately informed of the Premier's views.*]

Document 141. *Beaconsfield reasserts his intention to maintain the integrity and independence of the Ottoman Empire, 6 August 1877†*

Many thanks for your letter. I regret the suspicion in the mind of the Sultan as regards our intentions. I admit they are reasonable, but they are not true—at least, so far as I am concerned, being resolved to maintain, if possible, "the integrity and independence" of the Ottoman Empire.

The Turks have proved their independence, for without allies they have gallantly, and, I think, successfully, defended their country, and I still hope to see, at the conclusion of the war, the Porte a recognised power, and no despicable one, in Europe.

If there is "a second campaign", I have the greatest hopes this country will interfere, and pronounce its veto against a war of extermination, and the dark designs of a secret partition, from wh[ich] the spirit of the 19th Century recoils. As we have the command of the sea, why sh[oul]d not a British corps d'armée (viâ Batoum) march into Armenia, and even occupy Tiflis?

We might send another to Varna, and act on the Russian flank.

But all this requires time. The Turks gain victories but don't follow them up. After Plevna, they sh[oul]d have

---

* Cp. Beaconsfield's earlier secret letter to Layard, sent on 6 June 1877, printed in Buckle, *Life of Disraeli*, [1920], VI, 142–3.

† *Pte Layard Papers*, B.M. Add. MSS. 39,136, ff. 72–75. Beaconsfield to Layard, Secret, 6 August 1877.

driven the Russians across the Danube, destroyed the bridge, and taken the Emperor prisoner. Wellesley tells me, that might have been done.

The thing is—to secure another campaign, or rather the necessity for one, for, if Russia is told by England, that "another campaign" will be a casus belli, she may be inclined to make what P.[rince] Gortchakow calls 'une paix boiteuse'.

The danger is, if the Russians rally, again successfully advance, and reach Adrianople this autumn.

What then is to be done? With her suspicions of England, Turkey would be ruined. That is why I sh[oul]d like to see our fleet in her immediate waters, and Gallipoli in our possession as a material guarantee, and with her full sanction. We sh[oul]d then be able to save Turkey.

. . . Parl[iamen]t will be up on the 15th I think tho[ugh] not with[ou]t a foreign debate in the Lords. I shall speak with firmness, whatever others may do, and with every confidence in your efforts, will not despair of the good causes.

[Layard could have no doubt of Beaconsfield's meaning (**Doc. 141**). A system of *double politique* was, in effect, instituted. Derby sent official dispatches of a moderate tone, Beaconsfield wrote private letters of a vehement kind, hinting that vigorous tactics must soon be adopted. In the summer of 1877 he had still hopes of continued resistance by Turkey, if not of her success. But on 10 December Plevna fell, and Turkey's resistance weakened. By the end of the year, his hopes were gone. The third memorandum communicated to Shuvalov—that of 13 December—had therefore different conditions for its setting. Constantinople and the Straits still formed its subject—it did little but repeat the views of July. But by December the Cabinet, however divided, were prepared to state publicly what in July had been private: "The occupation of Constantinople by the Russian forces even though it should be of a temporary character and for military purposes only, would be an event which it would on all accounts be most desirable to avoid."* This, however, represented the limits of Cabinet agreement, even when one member—Carnarvon—had resigned. Beaconsfield thought that this declaration of policy had little meaning, unless it was reinforced by material action, or at least by preparations for material action. Moreover, the Russians

---

* Memorandum endorsed: "Memorandum to be delivered confidentially to Count Schouvaloff. Settled in Cabinet. Seen and approved by the Queen, comm[unicate]d to C[oun]t Schouvaloff—Dec[embe]r 13/77." *F.O.* 65/986. Cp. *A. & P.*, [1878], LXXXI, [C. 1923], 629.

were advancing rapidly and by 19 January 1878 they were threatening Constantinople. Turkey accepted the Russian terms on 27 January, and signed an armistice on the 31st.

Even on 24 January Beaconsfield had been prepared to take action of an extreme kind. He sent telegrams on 24 January 1878, instructing the fleet to move through the Dardanelles, without Derby's consent. They were not (as Tenterden intimated to Layard) "initialled by Lord Derby in the usual way, but were sent under the direct orders of the Cabinet, without his approval of them being signified".* At the last moment the orders were countermanded and Derby, who had offered his resignation, postponed it. But the instructions to the fleet were renewed on 8 February. A protest at once came from the Porte: "The Russian Army is at the gates of Constantinople...the step taken by Her Majesty's Government exposes a million human beings to perish in the midst of a conflict for foreign interests...the Porte protests against it, leaving the responsibility of the frightful catastrophe that may ensue to England." † On the 11th Layard was further instructed that it was "absolutely necessary that British ships should go up to Constantinople".‡ The Porte was much alarmed, and the Turkish Prime Minister expressed the view that it would be necessary to oppose such action by force. The Sultan, equally disturbed, begged that Britain would withdraw her instructions, and telegraphed to the Queen. The Minister for Foreign Affairs, Server Pasha, pressed Layard persistently: "England was pretending to act as the friend of, and in the interests of, Turkey. She was, by the step she was about to take, proving herself Turkey's greatest enemy." Nevertheless, on 14 February Admiral Hornby "passed through the Straits without encountering any other obstacle than the presentation by the Commandant of the Dardanelles of the Porte's protest against his proceedings".§

This occurrence has more importance than has usually been attributed to it. No doubt the reiterated protests of the Porte were largely designed to impress Russia, who was carefully informed of them at the time. No doubt also the outburst of Parliamentary criticism was partly dictated by political exigency. But the incident had two effects of some magnitude. It was one of the reasons which drove Derby to his second and final resignation on 28 March; and it left a deep imprint on Salisbury's mind. It was a powerful factor in inducing him to make that famous declaration on 'the Rule of the Straits' at the Congress of Berlin, whose reverberations continued until the end of the century.]

* *Pte Layard Papers*, B.M. Add. MSS. 39,137, ff. 16–17. Tenterden to Layard, Private, 31 January 1878. There is a copy in the *Pte Tenterden Papers*, F.O. 363/2.
 † Layard to Derby, Tel. No. 186, 9 February 1878, D. 10.15 p.m., *F.O.* 78/4271.
 ‡ Derby to Layard, Tel. 11 February 1878, D. 3.40 p.m., *F.O.* 78/4271.
 § Layard to Derby, No. 223, 14 February 1878, *F.O.* 78/4271.

56. GREAT BRITAIN ASSUMES LEADERSHIP ON THE ADVENT OF SALISBURY TO THE FOREIGN OFFICE

[Salisbury's advent to the Foreign Office came at a critical time. Momentous events had occurred·during the month of March. Turkey had been forced to sign the disadvantageous peace treaty of San Stefano on 3 March and the terms were known unofficially even before that date. On 23 March the exchange of ratifications took place, and the treaty was formally notified to the Powers. Thereafter it became the subject of direct negotiation, and Salisbury and Beaconsfield were determined to upset two of its main provisions. In the first place, they were determined not to allow Russia to create a big Bulgaria, a state with a seaboard on the Black Sea and the Aegean, stretching as far west as Lake Ochrida. So large a state could not be permitted in the interests of the balance of power, for it was expected that it would be a vassal of Russia. Secondly, Beaconsfield and Salisbury, though ready to accept the Russian conquest of Ardahan and Kars, would not allow her to extend as far south as Bayazid and threaten an advance to the Persian Gulf. As Derby was not prepared to take any vigorous action against Russia his resignation followed on 28 March.

The substitution of Salisbury for Derby as Foreign Secretary opened a new era in foreign policy. Vacillation was superseded by vigour and resolution. Salisbury was not always in agreement with Beaconsfield, but circumstances as well as loyalty forced him in the main to conform to his views. The latter was far readier to leave the conduct of affairs to the Foreign Secretary than he had been in the time of Derby.

Salisbury signalized his arrival at the Foreign Office by a public exposition of British policy in the face of the terms of the Treaty of San Stefano. The circular (**Doc. 144**), dated 1 April, was drafted by Salisbury himself during a week-end of seclusion. But a Cabinet Committee (**Doc. 143**) had considered the treaty at the end of March* and Salisbury had already sent his own impressions in a private letter to Beaconsfield on 21 March (**Doc. 142**), while Derby was still hesitating to resign. This frank and decidedly personal exposition of Salisbury's views was made before he was actually Foreign Secretary, so that Beaconsfield knew beforehand that the new minister would have definite opinions of his own.

The first results of Salisbury's advent were these. Great Britain insisted on the submission to a Congress of the whole terms

---

* There were three members of the Committee: Beaconsfield, Salisbury and Cairns. Their report was not, however, signed.

of the preliminaries of peace (i.e. a revision of San Stefano). She was ready to co-operate with other Powers as to the lines of a settlement, which Salisbury desired to be less rigidly conservative than that previously indicated in British official correspondence. Both he and the Cabinet Committee were of opinion that "what would best suit the interests of Great Britain, in the altered state of circumstances, would be that the Straits should be free to ships of war, as well as ships of commerce, and that all forts and batteries should be removed".

Salisbury's appointment was followed by the opening of negotiation, separately, with Austria-Hungary, with Russia, and with Turkey. On 3 April he reminded Beust, the Austro-Hungarian Ambassador, of the point which Derby and Andrássy had reached in their *pourparlers* of 1877, and agreed with him that "some agreement between the two Powers" was desirable.* The conversations were transferred to Vienna, and led to the conclusion of the Convention of 6 June.† This laid down the lines to be followed by the two Powers in connexion with European Turkey, establishing the Balkan range as the limit of direct Turkish rule; providing for concerted opposition to the proposed big Bulgaria; and contemplating the occupation of Bosnia and Herzegovina by Austria-Hungary, and the modification of Servian frontiers.

In the case of Russia, the discussions were in London, and they resulted in the famous Salisbury-Shuvalov memoranda of 30–1 May. These memoranda laid down the concessions which Russia was prepared to make at the Congress as regards both European Turkey and the Russian conquests in Asia: reduction of the limits of the new Bulgarian state, and restriction of Russian influence both in the Balkans and in Asia Minor. On certain points, even where substantial agreement had been reached, there were reservations on one or both sides. Moreover, there was a list of points on which agreement was not reached, on which both Salisbury and Shuvalov reserved to their countries freedom of action at the Congress. This list included "all questions touching the Straits". Thirdly, Shuvalov reinforced his concessions in Asia Minor by a statement that Russia was prepared "to conclude a secret engagement with Britain" that she would not extend her conquests in that region beyond those laid down in this agreement.‡

* Salisbury to Elliot, No. 236 Confidential, 3 April 1878. Marked: "Seen by L[or]d Beaconsfield. The Queen." *F.O.* 7/923.

† Salisbury's instructions to Elliot for the conclusion of this agreement and the text are in *F.O.* 7/924. *V.* Salisbury to Elliot, No. 349, 27 May 1878. Cp. W.S.A., Angleterre I, Memorandum communicated by Sir H. Elliot, 28 May. For modifications of this draft *v.* Salisbury to Elliot, No. 363, 2 June 1878, *F.O.* 7/924. On the conclusion of the agreement generally *v.* W. A. Gauld, 'The Anglo-Austrian Agreement of 1878', *E.H.R.*, XLI, [January 1926], 108–12.

‡ The memoranda are in *F.O.* 65/1022. Cp. B. H. Sumner, *Russia and the Balkans*, [1937], 646–51, Appendix VIII.

Constantinople was the centre of the third negotiation. Layard, the British Ambassador, received his first warning of Salisbury's policy in a private letter of 4 April;* a very frank exposition (**Doc. 145**) on 9 May; and his final instructions in a private telegram of 24 May.† The result was the Cyprus Convention of 4 June. By this arrangement Salisbury, following ideas which he and Beaconsfield had long held in reserve, provided for the British occupation of Cyprus, should Russia secure Kars, Batoum, Ardahan, or any of them, at the Congress. The first Salisbury-Shuvalov memorandum of 30 May provided that Britain would not oppose the cession of Batoum to Russia, and thus the condition was bound to be fulfilled. The Convention embodied also a bilateral engagement between the Sultan and Great Britain for the enforcement of Armenian reform.

These three negotiations all produced definite results. Austria-Hungary gave a large measure of co-operation at the Congress to Britain; Russia explored the most likely subjects of conflict with her, and in some cases found a solution; and the Sultan indicated a basis on which England might work in the future for the preservation of Turkey-in-Asia. To Salisbury—profoundly influenced as he was by his term of office as Secretary of State for India—Asia Minor was undoubtedly more important than the Balkans. His interest in the latter was largely confined to Constantinople, and this interest was due to the fact that the capital commanded the Straits.]

Document 142. *Salisbury defines British policy on the eve of his appointment to the Foreign Office,* 21 *March* 1878‡

I see no difficulty about considering the Treaty§ on Saturday as you say. We ought to prepare ourselves, in case there is *no* Congress, to state which are the articles of the Treaty to which we specially object.

* *Pte Layard Papers*, B.M. Add. MSS. 39,137, ff. 39–40. Cp. Cecil, *Life of Salisbury*, [1921], II, 264–5.

† *Pte Layard Papers*, B.M. Add. MSS. 39,137, ff. 111–12. The formal instructions were given in a dispatch of the same date which was not sent until the 30th. Draft in *F.O.* 78/2768. Marked: "Seen by The Queen and Lord Beaconsfield." Final text in *F.O.* 195/1168. Cp. H. Temperley, 'Disraeli and Cyprus', *E.H.R.* XLVI, [April 1931], 274–9. The dispatch is printed in *A. & P.*, [1878], LXXXII, [C. 2057], 3–4, under date 30 May. Cp. also L. M. Penson, 'The Principles and Methods of Lord Salisbury's Foreign Policy', *Camb. Hist. Journ.* V, [1935], 93.

‡ Cecil, *Life of Salisbury*, [1921], II, 213–14. Salisbury to Beaconsfield, 21 March 1878.

§ Treaty of San Stefano, signed 3 March 1878, in force 23 March. *V. supra*, p. 363. Text in Hertslet, *Map*, [1891], IV, 2672–96.

Of course, we have a right to object to all, as all are contrary to existing Treaties, but it would be doubtful policy to do so in view of English opinion. At all events, I think we should put in the forefront of our objections:

(1) Those articles which menace the balance of power in the Egean.

(2) Those which threaten the Greek race in the Balkan Peninsula with extinction.

And that we should indicate the necessity of either cancelling, *or* meeting with compensatory provisions, the portions of the Treaty which, by reducing Turkey to vassalage, threaten the free passage of the Straits, and also menace English interests in other places where the exercise of Turkish authority affects them.

I am, as you know, not a believer in the possibility of setting the Turkish Government on its legs again, as a genuine reliable Power; and, unless you have a distinct belief the other way, I think you should be cautious about adopting any line of policy which may stake England's security in those seas on Turkish efficiency. I should be disposed to be satisfied with war or negotiations which ended in these results:

(1) Driving back the Slav State to the Balkans—and substituting a Greek province; politically, but not administratively, under the Porte.

(2) Effective securities for the free passage of the Straits at all times, as if they were open sea.

(3) Two naval stations for England—say Lemnos and Cyprus, with an occupation, at least temporary, of some place like Scanderoon; for the sake of moral effect.

(4) Perhaps I would add reduction of indemnity to amount which there would be reasonable prospect of Turkey paying without giving pretext for fresh encroachments.

These are merely suggestions for your consideration—and require no answer.

Document 143. *Report of the Cabinet Committee on the Treaty of San Stefano, 27 March 1878*[*]

The Committee divide their observations on the Treaty into the following heads:

1. Constitution and limits of the New Bulgaria.
2. Position of Thessaly, Epirus, & Crete, and the Greek subjects of Turkey.
3. The Straits.
4. Armenia (the part not included in the indemnity).
5. Bessarabia and the Danube.
6. The indemnity—pecuniary & territorial.
7. General observations.

1. *Constitution and Limits of New Bulgaria.*
Articles VI to XI.

(1) We think objection should be made to the extension of the autonomous province to the Aegean Sea, thereby including large districts where there is an essentially Greek population. The Bulgarian Province should not extend southward beyond the best natural boundary, which can be taken about the parallel of latitude 42°.

(2) The detailed limits, if not definitely arranged at the Congress, should be marked out by a Commission, on which each of the Powers, and Greece should choose one member.

(3) We think objection should be made to the mode of choosing the Governor. A preferable mode would be that during the first ten years he should be chosen by the Signatory Powers, and confirmed by the Porte. After that period, the Prince, on a vacancy, might be chosen by a form of election to be determined on by the Powers. During the ten years the Province should be under the joint Protectorate of the Powers.

(4) We think objection should be made to the period of occupation by Russian troops. We ought, at the Congress, to be ready to support any proposal for a joint occupation by

---

[*] Memorandum, unsigned, printed for the use of the Cabinet, 27 March 1878. *Confidential Print*, No. 3548.

Austrian and Russian troops. In any event, 25,000 at least of the 50,000 Russian troops should leave before the end of one year, and the remainder before the end of two years.

(5) The organization of the administration of the new province, the introduction of the new régime, the surveillance of its "fonctionnement", the number and the formation of the militia, should all be relegated to a Commission chosen by the Powers.

(6) The Tribunal for deciding the rights of Mussulmans to land under Article XI should be constituted and regulated by, and act under the superintendence of, the same Commission, or of a Commission similarly chosen.

(7) Further, every effort should be made with regard to Bulgaria, to obtain stipulations—

(a) For the complete religious toleration & freedom for all sects and denominations; and this should, if possible, be extended to Roumania and Servia.

(b) For the maintenance of a commercial system not less liberal than that which now prevails in Turkey.

(c) That unless and until the consent of the Powers is obtained, foreigners in Bulgaria should have privileges similar to those which they enjoy at present under the Capitulations.

2. *Position of Thessaly, Epirus, Crete, & the Greek subjects of Turkey.*

(1) We think, as already stated, that the southern boundary of the New Bulgaria should run nearly with the 42° parallel of latitude. The territory south of this, down to the Aegean sea-board, and extending from the longitude of Philippopolis on the east, to the Adriatic on the west, would then form a considerable province, in which the Greek element would largely prevail, and we think the welfare and good Government of this Province should be provided for by a Christian Governor, chosen by the Porte from among its Greek subjects, and by institutions similar to those agreed to by the Plenipotentiaries, and proposed to the Porte at the Conference, January 15, 1877. Similar provisions should be made for Thessaly, Epirus, and Crete. The whole to be carried into effect under a Commission,

on which members would be named by the Signatory Powers, and one by Greece.

If this is not assented to, and if the Articles of the Treaty extending Bulgaria to the Aegean are maintained, then we think that it should be proposed by Great Britain to erect the territory already mentioned south of latitude 42°, and also Thessaly, Epirus, & Crete into one or more autonomic tributary province or provinces, with provision for the election of Governors and Joint Protectorate during ten years, similar to Bulgaria; but Greece to be one of the electing and protecting Powers.

3. *The Straits.*

Article XXIV. What would best suit the interests of Great Britain, in the altered state of circumstances, would be that the Straits should be free to ships of war, as well as of commerce, and that all forts and batteries should be removed.

This would be unacceptable to the Porte; but it might possibly be made acceptable by an engagement to maintain the defence and guarantee the safety of Constantinople from the sea with an adequate naval squadron.

If this cannot be done, and if the present rule of the closing of the Straits is continued, we should make it clear, by a statement placed on record at the Congress, that we do not assent to Article XXIV in so far as it would prejudice or limit any right by way of blockade or otherwise which, in the event of war, we, as a belligerent, should be entitled to.

4. *Armenia (the part not included in the Indemnity).*

There is, in Article XVI, a general engagement given by Turkey to Russia as to the future government of the part of Armenia remaining Turkish.

We think that the ameliorations and reforms mentioned in this Article should be secured by an engagement given to all the Powers, and not to Russia alone, and that they should be inaugurated under the superintendence of a Commission of which each Power should appoint a Member.

5. *The Danube & Bessarabia.*

The restoration of Bessarabia to Russia, and the control thus given to Russia over the Danube, are serious departures from the Treaty of Paris, and are in themselves open to grave objection. These matters, however, concern primarily Austria and Roumania, and our policy should be rather to support them in such objections as they will make than to originate objections of our own.

6. *The Indemnity, Pecuniary & Territorial.*

We think that as to the pecuniary indemnity, although we may be able to control the amount which, under duress, Turkey may agree to pay, we ought to place upon record our protest:

(1) Against the extravagance of the amount;

(2) Against the principle of extracting, under pressure, such a sum from a country already insolvent, the effect of which must be to take the indemnity, not from the country, but from its creditors.

We think that we ought further to require, in accordance with the assurance that every part of the agreement between Russia and Turkey should be before the Powers, that the mode of payment and the guarantees referred to in Article XIX, should be now declared; and, if this is not done, that it should, at all events, be stipulated that no guarantee or mode of payment shall be adopted which will interfere with or prejudice any revenue, tax, tribute, or property already specially hypothecated, and that no part of the pecuniary indemnity shall be commuted for any further territorial or other equivalent.

With regard to the territorial indemnity in Armenia, we think that a strenuous effort should be made to throw the western boundary of the proposed annexation so much further to the east as will allow the present commercial route from Trebizond to Persia to continue to run in Turkish territory.

But we think that as to the territorial indemnity also, we should place upon record our dissent from and protest against this annexation, and against the principle on which it is made, and the pretence on which it is justified.

A war carried on until the defeated belligerent engages in form to pay an impossible penalty, which is at once commuted into a large territorial cession, is not the less a war for the acquisition of territory, because it is prefaced by a declaration that the victor "had no desire for conquest or aggrandisement", and had no object but "the amelioration of the Christian population of Turkey".

7. *General Observations.*

It will be necessary that in the following particulars the position of Great Britain should be clearly maintained during the progress of the discussions at the Congress.

(1) There are a number of points in the Treaty with regard to which we have suggested or required alterations. These points must be considered as a whole. We must not, upon any one of the points being conceded or adjusted, be taken as having, in every event, agreed to become bound by, or to have assented to, the Article out of which this point has arisen. When all the points have been gone through, and when all the propositions of Great Britain have been considered, it will be for Her Majesty's Government to judge whether, having regard to the manner in which these points, as a whole, have been dealt with by the Congress, they are willing to be taken as assenting to any part of the Treaty.

(2) The XXIIIrd Article of the Treaty proposes to revive all Treaties between Russia and Turkey, except as altered by the present Treaty. Whether this would or would not extend to the Treaties of 1856, and 1871, the future position of Great Britain as to those Treaties must be safe-guarded. If the arrangements in the present Treaty can be brought into a shape in which they can be accepted by this country, we may be content to revive, along with them, and subject to such new conditions as may be thought necessary, whatever will remain of the Treaties of 1856 and 1871. But if Russia, with the sanction of other Signatories to those Treaties, breaks away from their provisions without our consent, we must be kept free to act

in all respects as if those Treaties were non-existent. They must not be applied to fetter our action in matters as to which we might desire to be free after they have ceased to fetter the action of the other Powers in matters as to which we would wish them to be bound.

Document 144. *The Salisbury Circular to the Powers,* 1 *April* 1878*

I have received the Queen's commands to request your Excellency to explain to the Government to which you are accredited the course which Her Majesty's Government have thought it their duty to pursue in reference to the Preliminaries of Peace concluded between the Ottoman and Russian Governments, and to the European Congress which it has been proposed to hold for the examination of that Treaty.

On the 14th January, in view of the reports which had reached Her Majesty's Government as to the negotiations for peace which were about to be opened between the Russian Government and the Porte, and in order to avoid any possible misconception, Her Majesty's Government instructed Lord A. Loftus to state to Prince Gortchakow that, in the opinion of Her Majesty's Government, any Treaty concluded between the Government of Russia and the Porte affecting the Treaties of 1856 and 1871 must be an European Treaty, and would not be valid without the assent of the Powers who were parties to those Treaties.

On the 25th January the Russian Government replied by the assurance that they did not intend to settle by themselves ("isolément") European questions having reference to the peace which is to be made ("se rattachant à la paix").

Her Majesty's Government, having learnt that the Bases of Peace had been arranged between the Turkish and Russian Delegates at Kyzanlik, instructed Lord A. Loftus, on the 29th January, to state to the Russian Government that Her Majesty's Government, while recognizing any arrangements

* Salisbury to Odo Russell, No. 190, 1 April 1878, *F.O.* 244/314. Printed *A. & P.*, [1878], LXXXI, [C. 1989], 765–72, laid before Parliament on 1 April.

made by the Russian and Turkish Delegates at Kyzanlik for the conclusion of an armistice and for the settlement of Bases of Peace as binding between the two belligerents, declared that in so far as those arrangements were calculated to modify European Treaties and to affect general and British interests, Her Majesty's Government were unable to recognize in them any validity unless they were made the subject of a formal agreement among the parties to the Treaty of Paris.

On the 30th January Lord A. Loftus communicated this declaration to Prince Gortchakow, and his Highness replied that to effect an armistice certain Bases of Peace were necessary, but they were only to be considered as Preliminaries and not definitive as regarded Europe; and stated categorically that questions bearing on European interests would be concerted with European Powers, and that he had given Her Majesty's Government clear and positive assurances to this effect.

On the 4th February the Austrian Ambassador communicated a telegram inviting Her Majesty's Government to a Conference at Vienna, and Her Majesty's Government at once accepted the proposal.

On the 5th February, his Excellency addressed a formal invitation to Lord Derby, stating that:—

"L'Autriche-Hongrie, en sa qualité de Puissance Signataire des actes internationaux qui ont eu pour objet de régler le système politique en Orient, a toujours réservé, en présence de la guerre actuelle, sa part d'influence sur le règlement définitif des conditions de la paix future.

"Le Gouvernement Impérial de la Russie, auquel nous avons fait part de ce point de vue, l'a pleinement apprécié.

"Aujourd'hui que des Préliminaires de Paix viennent d'être signés entre la Russie et la Turquie le moment nous semble venu d'établir l'accord de l'Europe sur les modifications qu'il deviendrait nécessaire d'apporter aux Traités susmentionnés.

"Le mode le plus apte à amener cette entente nous paraît être la réunion d'une Conférence des Puissances Signataires du Traité de Paris de 1856 et du Protocole de Londres de 1871."

On the 9th instant the Austrian Government proposed that instead of the Conference at Baden-Baden as previously con-

templated, a Congress should be assembled at Berlin. Her
Majesty's Government replied that they had no objection
to this change, but that they considered "that it would be
desirable to have it understood in the first place that all
questions dealt with in the Treaty of Peace between Russia
and Turkey should be considered as subject to be discussed
in the Congress; and that no alteration in the condition of
things previously established by Treaty should be acknowledged as valid until it has received the assent of the Powers."

On the 12th March Count Beust was told that Her Majesty's
Government must be perfectly clear on the points mentioned
in the letter to him of the 9th instant before they could
definitively agree to go into Congress.

On the 13th, Her Majesty's Government explained further
the first condition:—

"That they must distinctly understand before they can
enter into Congress that every Article in the Treaty between
Russia and Turkey will be placed before the Congress, not
necessarily for acceptance, but in order that it may be considered what Articles require acceptance or concurrence by
the several Powers, and what do not."

On the 14th the Russian Ambassador communicated the
following telegram from Prince Gortchacow:—

"Toutes les Grandes Puissances savent déjà que le texte
complet du Traité Préliminaire de Paix avec la Porte leur
sera communiqué dès que les ratifications auront été échangées,
ce qui ne saurait tarder. Il sera simultanément publié ici.
Nous n'avons rien à cacher."

On the 17th, Lord A. Loftus reported that he had received
the following Memorandum from Prince Gortchakow:—

"In reply to communication made by Lord A. Loftus of
the despatch by which Lord Derby has replied to the proposal
of Count Beust relating to the meeting of the Congress at
Berlin, I have the honour to repeat the assurance which
Count Schouvaloff has been already charged to give to Her
Majesty's Government, viz., that the Preliminary Treaty of
Peace concluded between Russia and Turkey shall be textually
communicated to the Great Powers before the meeting of the

Congress, and that in the Congress itself each Power will have the full liberty of its appreciations and of its action."

In a despatch received on the 18th, Lord A. Loftus stated that Prince Gortchakow had said to him that of course he could not impose silence on any member of the Congress, but he could only accept a discussion on those portions of the Treaty which affected European interests.

Lord Derby having asked Count Schouvaloff for a reply from Prince Gortchakow, his Excellency informed him on the 19th that he was "charged to represent to Her Majesty's Government that the Treaty of Peace concluded between Russia and Turkey—the only one which existed, for there was no secret engagement—would be communicated to the Government of the Queen in its entirety, and long before ("bien avant") the assembling of the Congress. The Government of the Queen, in like manner as the other Great Powers, reserved to themselves at the Congress their full liberty of appreciation and action. This same liberty, which she did not dispute to others, Russia claimed for herself. Now, it would be to restrict her, if, alone among all the Powers, Russia contracted a preliminary engagement."

On the 21st Lord Derby replied that Her Majesty's Government could not recede from the position already clearly defined by them, that they must distinctly understand, before they could enter into Congress, that every Article in the Treaty between Russia and Turkey would be placed before the Congress, not necessarily for acceptance, but in order that it might be considered what Articles required acceptance or concurrence by the other Powers, and what did not.

Her Majesty's Government were unable to accept the view now put forward by Prince Gortchakow, that the freedom of opinion and action in Congress of Russia, more than of any other Power, would be restricted by this preliminary understanding.

Her Majesty's Government therefore desired to ask whether the Government of Russia were willing that the communication of the Treaty *en entier* to the various Powers should be treated as a placing of the Treaty before the Congress, in order that the whole Treaty, in its relation to existing Treaties, might be examined and considered by the Congress.

On the 26th Count Schouvaloff wrote to Lord Derby that the Imperial Cabinet deemed it its duty to adhere to the declaration which he was ordered to make to the Government of the Queen, and which was stated in the letter which he had the honour to address to him dated the 19th March.

As different interpretations had been given to the "liberty of appreciation and action" which Russia thought it right to reserve to herself at the Congress, the Imperial Cabinet defined the meaning of the term in the following manner:—

"It leaves to the other Powers the liberty of raising such questions at the Congress as they might think it fit to discuss, and reserves to itself the liberty of accepting or not accepting the discussion of these questions."

Her Majesty's Government deeply regret the decision which the Russian Government have thus announced.

How far the stipulations of the Treaty of San Stefano would commend themselves as expedient to the judgment of the European Powers, it is not at present possible to decide. But even if a considerable portion of them were such as were likely to be approved, the reservation of a right, at discretion, to refuse to accept a discussion of them in a Congress of the Powers would not on that account be the less open to the most serious objection. An inspection of the Treaty will sufficiently show that Her Majesty's Government could not, in a European Congress, accept any partial or fragmentary examination of its provisions. Every material stipulation which it contains involves a departure from the Treaty of 1856.

By the Declaration annexed to the first Protocol of the Conference held in London in 1871, the Plenipotentiaries of the Great Powers, including Russia, recognized "that it is an essential principle of the law of nations that no Power can liberate itself from the engagements of a Treaty, nor modify the stipulations thereof, unless with the consent of the Contracting Powers by means of an amicable arrangement".

It is impossible for Her Majesty's Government, without violating the spirit of this Declaration, to acquiesce in the withdrawal from the cognizance of the Powers of Articles in the new Treaty which are modifications of existing Treaty engagements, and inconsistent with them.

The general nature of the Treaty, and the combined effect of its several stipulations upon the interests of the Signatory Powers, furnish another and a conclusive reason against the separate discussion of any one portion of those stipulations apart from the rest.

The most important consequences to which the Treaty practically leads are those which result from its action as a whole upon the nations of South Eastern Europe. By the Articles erecting the New Bulgaria, a strong Slav State will be created under the auspices and control of Russia, possessing important harbours upon the shores of the Black Sea and the Archipelago, and conferring upon that Power a preponderating influence over both political and commercial relations in those seas. It will be so constituted as to merge in the dominant Slav majority a considerable mass of population which is Greek in race and sympathy, and which views with alarm the prospect of absorption into a community alien to it not only in nationality but in political tendency and in religious allegiance. The provisions by which this new State is to be subjected to a ruler whom Russia will practically choose, its Administration framed by a Russian Commissary, and the first working of its institutions commenced under the control of a Russian army, sufficiently indicate the political system of which in future it is to form a part.

Stipulations are added which will extend this influence even beyond the boundaries of the New Bulgaria. The provision, in itself highly commendable, of improved institutions for the populations of Thessaly and Epirus, is accompanied by a condition that the law by which they are to be secured shall be framed under the supervision of the Russian Government. It is followed by engagements for the protection of members of the Russian Church, which are certainly not more limited in their scope than those Articles of the Treaty of Kainardji, upon which the claims were founded which were abrogated in 1856. Such stipulations cannot be viewed with satisfaction either by the Government of Greece, or by the Powers to whom all parts of the Ottoman Empire are a matter of common interest. The general effect of this portion of the Treaty will be to increase the power of the Russian Empire in the countries and on the shores where a Greek population predominates, not only to the prejudice of that nation, but also of every country having interests in the east of the Mediterranean Sea.

The territorial severance from Constantinople of the Greek, Albanian, and Slavonic provinces which are still left under the Government of the Porte will cause their administration to be attended with constant difficulty, and even embarrassment; and will not only deprive the Porte of the political strength which might have arisen from their possession, but will expose the inhabitants to a serious risk of anarchy.

By the other portions of the Treaty analogous results are arrived at upon other frontiers of the Ottoman Empire. The compulsory alienation of Bessarabia from Roumania, the extension of Bulgaria to the shores of the Black Sea, which are principally inhabited by Mussulmans and Greeks, and the acquisition of the important harbour of Batoum, will make the will of the Russian Government dominant over all the vicinity of the Black Sea. The acquisition of the strongholds of Armenia will place the population of that Province under the immediate influence of the Power which holds them; while the extensive European trade which now passes from Trebizond to Persia will, in consequence of the cessions in Kurdistan, be liable to be arrested at the pleasure of the Russian Government by the prohibitory barriers of their commercial system.

Provision is made for an indemnity, of which the amount is obviously beyond the means of Turkey to discharge, even if the fact be left out of account that any surplus of its revenues is already hypothecated to other creditors. The mode of payment of this indemnity is left, in vague language, to ulterior negotiations between Russia and the Porte. Payment may be demanded immediately, or it may be left as an unredeemed and unredeemable obligation to weigh down the independence of the Porte for many years. Its discharge may be commuted into a yet larger cession of territory, or it may take the form of special engagements subordinating in all things the policy of Turkey to that of Russia. It is impossible not to recognize in this provision an instrument of formidable efficacy for the coercion of the Ottoman Government, if the necessity for employing it should arise.

Objections may be urged individually against these various stipulations; and arguments, on the other hand, may possibly be advanced to show that they are not individually inconsistent with the attainment of the lasting peace and stability which it is the highest object of all present negotiations to establish in the provinces of European and Asiatic Turkey. But their separate and individual operation, whether defensible or not, is not that which should engage the most earnest attention of the Signatory Powers. Their combined effect, in addition to the results upon the Greek population and upon the balance of maritime power which have been already pointed out, is to depress, almost to the point of entire subjection, the political independence of the Government of Constantinople. The formal jurisdiction of that Government extends over geographical positions which must, under all circumstances, be of the deepest interest to Great Britain. It is in the power of the Ottoman Government to close or to open the Straits which form the natural highway of nations between the Ægean Sea and the Euxine. Its dominion is recognized at the head of the Persian Gulf, on the shores of the Levant, and in the immediate neighbourhood of the Suez Canal. It cannot be otherwise than a matter of extreme solicitude to this country that the Government to which this jurisdiction belongs should be so closely pressed by the political outposts of a greatly superior Power that its independent action, and even existence, is almost impossible. These results arise, not so much from the language of any single Article in the Treaty, as from the operation of the instrument as a whole. A discussion limited to Articles selected by one Power in the Congress would be an illusory remedy for the dangers to English interests and to the permanent peace of Europe, which would result from the state of things which the Treaty proposes to establish.

The object of Her Majesty's Government at the Constantinople Conference was to give effect to the policy of reforming Turkey under the Ottoman Government, removing well-grounded grievances, and thus preserving the Empire until the time when it might be able to dispense with protective guarantees. It was obvious that this could only be brought about by rendering the different populations so far contented with their position as to inspire them with a spirit of patriotism, and to make them ready to defend the Ottoman Empire as loyal subjects of the Sultan.

This policy was frustrated by the unfortunate resistance of the Ottoman Government itself, and, under the altered circumstances of the present time, the same result cannot be attained to the same extent by the same means. Large changes may, and no doubt will, be requisite in the Treaties by which South-Eastern Europe has hitherto been ruled. But good government, assured peace, and freedom, for populations to whom those blessings have been strange, are still the objects which this country earnestly desires to secure.

In requiring a full consideration of the general interests which the new arrangements threaten to affect, Her Majesty's Government believe that they are taking the surest means of securing those objects. They would willingly have entered a Congress in which the stipulations in question could have been examined as a whole, in their relation to existing Treaties, to the acknowledged rights of Great Britain and of other Powers, and to the beneficent ends which the united action of Europe has always been directed to secure. But neither the interests which Her Majesty's Government are specially bound to guard, nor the well-being of the regions with which the Treaty deals, would be consulted by the assembling of a Congress whose deliberations were to be restricted by such reservations as those which have been laid down by Prince Gortchakow in his most recent communication.

Your Excellency will read this despatch to the Minister for Foreign Affairs, and give him a copy of it.

57. BEACONSFIELD AND SALISBURY DEVELOP BRITISH POLICY AT THE CONGRESS OF BERLIN

[When the Berlin Congress had ended Shuvalov explained the Russian dissatisfaction to Lord Loftus, the British Ambassador at St Petersburg. "It was felt", reported Loftus, "(and he evidently alluded to the Emperor) that the previous arrangements agreed to by England had not been strictly carried out, and he complained that at every step in the Congress he had had to encounter continued opposition on the part of the English Plenipotentiaries. He instanced more especially the strong opposition to the cession to Russia of Batoum, notwithstanding the agreement that England would not oppose it in Congress. Then again he observed the Anglo-Turkish Convention had given great dissatisfaction as proving on the part of England a distrust of the solemn engagement taken by Russia in the Memorandum No. 3." *

The complaint as to Batoum had some justification. Technically, no doubt, the rather obscure wording of the paragraph in which Britain undertook "not to oppose the wish of the Emperor of Russia to obtain the port of Batoum" justified Salisbury in having taken other steps to "protect the Ottoman Empire" from the danger of any future extension of Russian territory. But clearly Shuvalov could have put no such interpretation on the wording used at the time, and, according to Salisbury's own account of his conversation with Shuvalov on 24 May, he went no further than to reinforce the wording of the memorandum by a hint that "other means than...an appeal to arms" would be used for the protection of the Ottoman Empire in Asia.† The British pressure over Batoum at the Congress may, indeed, have been rather the work of Beaconsfield than of Salisbury. This is certainly suggested by the private letter to Tenterden which is printed here (**Doc. 148**).

Salisbury also was dissatisfied. He had proposed, as a *quid pro quo* for the occupation of Batoum, that the Sultan should throw open the Straits to the British Fleet (**Doc. 147**). Philip Currie, who was in attendance as a member of the delegation, attributed this startling proposal to the untimely publication of the first two Salisbury-Shuvalov memoranda. This move, as he described it,

* Loftus to Salisbury, No. 656a Confidential, 20 July 1878, *F.O.* 65/1005. The explanation—in giving which, according to Loftus, Shuvalov appeared 'anxious and dejected'—was the result of a suggestion by Salisbury that the Anglo-Russian memoranda should be laid before Parliament. Russia refused consent, and, in accordance with the special arrangements made at the time, Britain was precluded from publication without her permission.

† Salisbury to Loftus, No. 334, 24 May 1878, *F.O.* 181/567.

was "for a general permission to enter the Straits", an idea, he commented, "which I own rather makes my hair stand on end".*
The paucity of letters and dispatches written by Beaconsfield and Salisbury from Berlin makes it difficult to say whether Salisbury really contemplated a "general permission" of this kind. The Cabinet Memorandum of 27 March (v. **Doc. 143**) rejected this idea because it would be "unpalatable" to Turkey. The memorandum by Tenterden, which Beaconsfield described as his "vade mecum", was rigidly conservative on the point. It quoted the instructions to Odo Russell for the Congress, which said that "Her Majesty's Government will, in preference to the provisions of that Article [XXIV of the Treaty of San Stefano], insist on the maintenance of the regulations which existed before the war".†
Yet Salisbury's private telegraphic communications both with Layard and the Cabinet at home prove that he did contemplate a convention with the Sultan giving special permission for the entry of British ships, and that he intended to use the threat of such an engagement to reinforce the pressure on Russia about Batoum. The Sultan hesitated, and apparently ultimately declined; the British Cabinet was startled, and Salisbury modified his proposal, converting it into the rather obscure declaration which was entered on the protocols of the Conference.‡

The British attitude on these points reinforced the conclusion suggested by earlier British actions. Turkey-in-Asia, the Straits, and in general the maintenance of Mediterranean interests were the keynotes of British policy. In March 1878, just before Derby's fall, a project had been formulated for a Mediterranean League. On 13 March Derby had sent instructions to the Ambassador at Rome to sound the Foreign Minister as to whether he would join with Britain—together with France, Austria-Hungary and Greece—in a League "to consider the maintenance... of their commercial and political interests in the Mediterranean and the Straits and also any act tending to a violation of those interests as questions of general concern" and to "come to an understanding as to the measures which may be necessary for the maintenance of those interests".§ There was some delay, as a change of ministry was in progress in Italy. On 28 March Paget spoke to Corti, who had

* Currie to Tenterden, 17 June 1878, *Pte Tenterden Papers, F.O.* 363/5.
† Notes by Lord Tenterden on the Treaty of San Stefano, *F.O.* 78/2891. Printed for the use of the Cabinet, 8 June 1878. *Confidential Print*, No. 3638.
‡ Salisbury's declaration. Protocol of 11 July 1878. "I declare on behalf of England that the obligations of Her Britannic Majesty relating to the closing of the Straits do not go further than an engagement with the Sultan to respect in this matter His Majesty's independent determinations in conformity with the spirit of existing Treaties." Hertslet, *Map*, [1891], IV, 2727.
§ Derby to Paget, No. 143, 13 March 1878. Endorsed: "Approved by the Cabinet and The Queen." *F.O.* 45/333. Cp. also Memorandum in *Pte Tenterden Papers, F.O.* 363/5, and Dwight E. Lee, 'The Proposed Mediterranean League of 1878', *Journal of Modern History*, III, No. 1, [March 1931], 33–45.

just been appointed, but found him extremely cautious. He was afraid of being drawn into war and certain that "Austria would be gained over by General Ignatieff". On the next day Corti was more specific, for he had consulted his colleagues. Despite their recognition of the identity of British and Italian interests "the Italian Government was not prepared to bind themselves by any engagement by which they might possibly be involved in a policy of action".* The proposal failed, therefore, just before Salisbury assumed office, but it is important both as a precedent for the later agreements—for which Corti himself took the initiative †—and as shewing the trend of British policy at this time.

If further evidence is needed for the concentration of British interests it can be found in two other aspects of policy, both important in this period. Salisbury's correspondence with Layard in 1878–80 proves that his mind was genuinely set on Asiatic reform. The wording of his private letters to Layard in April–June 1878 has sometimes been discounted for the reason that he was here trying to make the acquisition of Cyprus palatable to a Turcophile. In fact, after the Congress as before, his correspondence is full of instructions and suggestions for taking full advantage of the powers gained under the Cyprus Convention for pressing reforms on the Sultan. The methods would seem to have been borrowed from his experience of Indian administration. His success was slight. He was defeated by a combination of causes, some accidental and some inherent in his plans, but the failure does not disprove the reality of his intentions.

The second aspect which is important is the question of Tunis. Again, the policy followed here originated from the Cyprus Convention, and again it may be explained as having been engendered by the desire to make the acquisition of Cyprus palatable, this time to France. But, although Beaconsfield and Salisbury may both have spoken rather freely as well as informally to Waddington at Berlin, it seems probable that to Salisbury at any rate there was some positive attraction in the proposed extension of French influence in the Mediterranean. Viewed in this light, the policy pursued at Berlin may be said to have been in the first place to support Austria-Hungary as far as European Turkey was concerned, with the object of providing what were regarded as reasonable safeguards against misrule. In this policy the Conference of Constantinople had set the standard. Both at the Congress and afterwards it is clear that Salisbury looked to Austria-Hungary to preserve the settlement in the Balkans. Outside that area British interests were greater. The British plenipotentiaries based their action partly on the conception of British interests formulated

* Paget to Derby, Nos. 238 and 240, Most Confidential, 28 and 29 March 1878, *F.O.* 45/337.
† Cp. *infra*, pp. 446–7, **Doc. 175.**

by the divided Cabinet of 1877, and partly on the idea of *sûretés réelles* evolved by Beaconsfield and Salisbury at the time of the Constantinople Conference. Superimposed on these ideas was the vision of a Turkey buttressed by a system of protection—Salisbury's greatest personal contribution to the policy of the time. Turkey, in his view, could no longer stand alone. He hoped that in the most vital spots—at Constantinople itself and in the East Mediterranean—Britain's influence would be predominant.]

Document 145. *Salisbury explains to Layard his views on Turkey-in-Asia, 9 May 1878**

The great problem which the Turk will have to solve, as soon as he has got rid of the Russian army off his soil is—how to keep his Asiatic Empire together. Sooner or later the greater part of his European Empire *must* go. Bosnia and Bulgaria are as good as gone. We may with great efforts give him another lease of Thrace: and he may keep for a considerable time a hold on Macedonia and Albania and possible [*sic*] on Thessaly and Epirus. But he will not get soldiers from them: for the Mussulman population will tend more and more to recede: and it is from them alone that any effective army can be drawn. The European provinces may bring in money: and to some extent, and for some time they may have a strategic value. But if the Turk is to maintain himself at Constantinople it is mainly with Asiatic soldiers that he will do it. The question is how is he to maintain himself in Asia. With the Russians at Kars, the idea of coming change will be rife over all Asia Minor—over Mesopotamia and Syria. If he has his own strength alone to trust to, no one will believe in his power of resistance. He has been beaten too often. The Arabs, and the Asiatics generally will look to the Russian as the coming man. The Turks only chance is to obtain the alliance of a great Power: and the only Power available is England.

Is it possible for England to give that alliance? I cannot speak yet with confidence: but I think so. For England the question of Turkey in Asia is very different from that of

* *Pte Layard Papers*, B.M. Add MSS. 39,137, ff. 82–5. Salisbury to Layard, Private, 9 May 1878. Cp. Cecil, *Life of Salisbury*, [1921], II, 267–8.

Turkey in Europe. The only change possible for the Asiatic Christians would be to come directly under the Government of Russia. There is and can be no question of autonomy—of young and struggling nationalities, and the rest of it. Now the direct Government of Russia is pleasant for nobody: but to Christians of a different rite, it is the most oppressive Government conceivable. Even, therefore, for the sake of the Christians, my hand would not be restrained by any considerations of humanity from engaging to resist the further advance of the Russians. And the vast majority of the populations of Asiatic Turkey are Mahometans: to whom the Turkish Government is congenial and as good as any other Mahometans get except our own. And, while Russian influence over the provinces of European Turkey would be a comparatively distant and indirect evil, her influence over Syria and Mesopotamia would be a very serious embarrassment, and would certainly through the connection of Bagdad with Bombay, make our hold on India more difficult. I do not, therefore, despair of England coming to the conclusion that she can undertake such a defensive alliance. But for that purpose it is, as I said before, absolutely and indispensably necessary that she should be nearer at hand than Malta. I have had ample opportunity during the past year of observing how utterly impossible efficient and prompt military action is from a port that is four days sail from the scene of action. The first blows at least have always to be struck suddenly and secretely: and four days notice—if there is to be a landing at the end of it is almost fatal to military action.

The messenger is waiting. I will not pursue this theme on which my mind dwells constantly. I will only say with respect to the suggested understanding between Greece and Turkey, that it would be far the wisest measure that Turkey could adopt: for it would raise an effective barrier to the Slav. But I fear it could only rest on some alienation of territory.

Document 146. *Greece and the internal Government of Turkey, 30 May 1878**

Your negotiations during the past week have been exceedingly satisfactory, and have very much smoothed our path. We are now at our ease concerning the Turkish Empire in Asia: and I think the negotiations which are now on the point of being concluded will make at least a tolerable situation in Europe. We shall have removed Bulgaria from the Aegean Sea and placed its littoral and the free passage to the other European provinces entirely in the Sultan's hand: and we shall have interposed between him and the tributary state north of the Balkans, a province over which his control will be considerable and sufficient for his own protection. I hope that in Congress we may still further diminish the pressure of Russia on the Bulgarian tributary state, and her temporary power over the Province. If we succeed so far there will only remain two difficulties in his way, though both of them will be formidable. The first is the question of the Greeks. Events have proved that the Greek kingdom possesses very considerable power of exciting to revolt the Greek subjects of the Porte: and that this power is exercised with especial force in the Southern part of Thessaly. The king is well-disposed: but he has no power of restraining his subjects, until he can show them that a policy of conciliation has been as valuable to them as a policy of provocation. If Turkey could give Greece something substantial, and Greece could be brought to accept it of her own free will, the settlement would suffice for half a century. If nothing is given, I cannot doubt that Greece will continue agitating, when the Congress is over and fleets and armies have retired: and the constitution of Turkey is not sufficiently robust to resist many more shocks of this description. It is this consideration which has led me to suggest to you the line of the Calamas and Peneus. It is undoubtedly asking the Turks to give up a good deal: and I should not urge it, if the Greeks were found to be impracticable: but if

* *Pte Layard Papers*, B.M. Add. MSS. 39,137, ff. 138–41. Salisbury to Layard, Private, 30 May 1878.

their consent can be obtained it is well worth the Turks while to buy respite from agitation for a long period at this price. I am very much afraid that the Congress will be too impatient to examine the matter carefully: and that either it will adopt some summary settlement which must be disadvantageous for the Turk: or Germany and Russia will designedly leave the matter open to furnish material for a future conflict. It is therefore a matter of some importance that it should be settled outside Congress if possible.

The other, and far more serious difficulty which besets the Sultan is the condition of his own internal Government. No contrivance will ever make the Central Government anything but a despotism however much it may be fenced in by the local liberties of the various provinces of the Empire. But the despotism is wielded by a monarch who appears to be at the mercy of the fanaticism of his capital, or the teaching of his palace. Nothing but weakness, panics, vacillation, surprises, desperate acts of precaution or of concession can be expected while such a state of things endures. Is it not possible to stop them? Would not Janissaries or Praetorians be better than this? Would it not suit the Sultan better to have some officer of ability—some Western who could be trusted—Baker for instance—attached to his person with a small "Varangian" Guard—either foreigners: or if that was too dangerous—a mixture of Greeks and Arabs who could not be exposed to the contagion of the passions of Stamboul. The present state of the Sultan is really pitiable: and unless we can restore to him some strength, we shall have no fulcrum on which to rest measures either of defence or of reform. We desire to keep the arrangement which you obtained on Sunday last, secret in its details as long as we can: for we cannot expect that France will receive it without a wry face. But if she is not prepared to help us in defending the equilibrium of the Levant, she must let us do it in our own fashion.

I have not answered your telegram from the Sultan asking for money—for as you know we have no power to give it: but to him who does not understand the rigour of Parliamentary precautions the refusal may seem churlish.

Document 147. *Salisbury proposes an agreement with Turkey concerning the Straits*, 16 *June* 1878*

Personal and secret: Would it be possible to obtain from the Porte signature of the following agreement: "In case Russians should seek to acquire or having acquired to retain, Mudanieh Bay [and Batoum],† and England should be of opinion that the presence of a naval force in the Black Sea is expedient with view to protect the Sultans interests in regard to H[is] M[ajesty]'s territories as defined in the preliminary Treaty of San Stefano or in any definite treaty of Peace which shall supersede it, H[is] M[ajesty] will not offer forcible opposition to the passage at any time of the English fleet thro[ugh] the straits of the Dardanelles and Bosphorus for the purpose?" If we had this we should probably prevent Batoum being taken, if it was we should be able to provide security for the Porte without putting upon them the burden and danger of summoning us under the Treaty of 1871.

Document 148. *Beaconsfield comments on the work of the Congress*, 2 *July* 1878‡

We get on here pretty well, the Congress meeting de die in diem, or, at least, five times a week, & the intervals between their assembling, being busily, and efficiently, employed by, what we may call, committees.

I miss you very much, and often want you, but I trust we shall not make any fatal mistakes. Tho' you are not present, you have always a most able and useful representative, in your "Confidential Notes on the Treaty of San Stefano", which is my Vade Mecum, and is of inestimable use to me. It helped me in getting rid of "the three zones", wh[ich] you so clearly described, and, notwithstanding the criticism of the journals, wh[ich] is as much, I believe, the result of ignorance as

* *Pte Layard Papers*, B.M. Add. MSS. 39,137, f. 204. Salisbury to Layard, Tel., 16 June 1878.
    † There is a copy of this telegram in *Pte Tenterden Papers*, *F.O.* 363/4, and this text contains the words "and Batoum" inserted above in square brackets. The copy gives the date of the telegram as 15 June.
    ‡ Beaconsfield to Tenterden, Private, 2 July 1878. *Pte Tenterden Papers*, *F.O.* 363/1.

malignity, I feel confident when the hour arrives, that I shall be able to show, that the establishment of the Balkan frontier, and all its accessories, has materially strengthened the Ottoman Dominion, and was surely no mean diplomatic triumph.

It is a thorough invention, tho' stated in many, & accepted by all, of the papers, that St. Petersburgh sent an ultimatum in answer to our own; and that, among other wonderful things, demanded the possession of Sofia as a sine quâ non. St. Petersburgh sent no ultimation of any kind, but only two humble suggestions, that if the Sultan's troops were admitted, they sh[oul]d at least be limited and that the fortresses sh[oul]d be at once fixed upon & announced. I would not listen to either suggestion, and, of course they were not pressed.

It is thought we shall "finish Europe" on Thursday, and then enter Asia. Here we shall find our greatest difficulty, for something must be done about Batoum, and after that unfortunate Schow[alov]-Sal[isbury] Mem[oran]dum, it is difficult to say what. Tho' not sanguine, I am not absolutely hopeless.

By the bye, I was perfectly aware, that you were completely innocent of any participation, direct or indirect, in that awful bevue of the "Globe" newspaper.* I wish they had not prosecuted the clerk. It is the dirtiest linen, that was ever washed in public by any family.

I never was at this city before. It is a noble one: the streets are well laid out, the public buildings—palaces and hotels, have grandeur, and I never saw so much sculpture, and good sculpture, sub dio. They say the public park is 1500 acres in extent. Hyde and Kensington Gardens together are only half as much.

Gortchakoff is not dying, but very lively and always talking; Schou[valov] has shown considerable abilities in his management of business; Andrassy is an English convert; and P[rince] Bismarck, with one hand full of cherries, and the other of shrimps, eaten alternatively, complains he cannot sleep and must go to Kissingen.

---

* This refers to the publication in the *Globe* of the Salisbury-Shuvalov Memorandum—and the subsequent abortive prosecution of Marvin, the company clerk who had sold the secret. *V.* Buckle, *Life of Disraeli*, [1920], vi, 303.

XX. GLADSTONE AND GRANVILLE, 1880–5

THE OTTOMAN EMPIRE

58. GLADSTONIAN PRINCIPLES AND THEIR APPLICATION

[Gladstone's foreign policy had been successful, both in conception and execution, during his first ministry. France and Germany were induced to acknowledge the inviolability of Belgium; Russia acknowledged the Concert of Europe, and admitted that signatories to a treaty must be summoned to consent to the abrogation of any of its clauses. England and the United States were joined in an experiment in arbitration which inaugurated a new era. Yet in 1880, when Gladstone returned to power with an increased majority, his second premiership was marked by a series of reverses. Granville was outmanœuvred by Bismarck on colonial questions, and British policy towards Germany shewed neither firmness nor discernment. He brought England to the verge of war with Russia over a boundary dispute in Afghanistan, although he, like Gladstone, was opposed to the advance on the North-West frontier of India which in opposition they had both condemned. Gladstone had objected also to the British annexation of the Transvaal and of the Orange Free State. He refused, however, to restore the latter to independence until the former broke out in rebellion, and his policy was to have a tragic aftermath. He had likewise condemned both the purchase of the Suez Canal shares, and the British occupation of Cyprus; yet in both cases he acknowledged the acts of his predecessors and did not surrender the advantages conferred by them. The only case in which he achieved a real success was in securing the execution of the unfulfilled provisions of the Treaty of Berlin by means of the Concert of Europe. The fact seems to be that the period 1868–74 favoured the application of Gladstonian principles in diplomacy, while that of 1880–5 did not. There was revolt and war instead of peace in South Africa and Egypt, and an outburst of international rivalry for dominion in the Pacific and on the African coasts instead of the peaceful maintenance of the *status quo* which he so much desired. Instead of retrenchment, he was forced by public opinion to undertake a series of armed expeditions in Egypt and the Soudan and to increase naval armaments at home. And, in addition, the period saw the revival of the Dreikaiserbund, the "northern conspiracy" as Disraeli had called it, in a sense hostile to Britain. Moreover, Germany joined Italy, as well as Austria-Hungary, in the Triple Alliance. The impression made by the events of this time is that both European and world politics had got out of hand, and Gladstone's principles were not strong enough to hold them. Thus the events of 1880–5 cast an air of irony on the statement of general principles with which Gladstone prefaced his administration in the heat of the Midlothian campaign.*]

Document 149. *Gladstone states his principles of foreign policy, 27 November 1879*†

Gentlemen, I ask you again to go with me beyond the seas. And as I wish to do full justice, I will tell you what I think to be the right principles of foreign policy; and then, as far as your patience and my strength will permit, I will, at any rate for a short time, illustrate those right principles by some of the departures from them that have taken place of late years. I first give you, gentlemen, what I think the right principles of foreign policy. The first thing is to foster the strength of the Empire by just legislation and economy at home, thereby producing two of the great elements of national power—namely, wealth, which is a physical element, and union and contentment, which are moral elements—and to reserve the strength of the Empire, to reserve the expenditure of that strength, for great and worthy occasions abroad. Here is my first principle of foreign policy: good government at home. My second principle of foreign policy is this: that its aim ought to be to preserve to the nations of the world—and especially, were it but for shame, when we recollect the sacred name we bear as Christians, especially to the Christian nations of the world—the blessings of peace. That is my second principle.

My third principle is this. Even, gentlemen, when you do a good thing, you may do it in so bad a way that you may entirely spoil the beneficial effect; and if we were to make ourselves the apostles of peace in the sense of conveying to the

* Cp. Beaconsfield's speech a week earlier at the Guildhall, summarized in R. W. Seton-Watson, *Britain in Europe*, [1937], 544–5.

† Speech at West Calder, Midlothian, 27 November, *v. The Times*, 28 November 1879; cp. E. R. Jones, *Selected Speeches on Foreign Policy*, [1914], 371–4, 382.

minds of other nations that we thought ourselves more entitled
to an opinion on that subject than they are, or to deny their
rights—well, very likely we should destroy the whole value of
our doctrines. In my opinion the third sound principle is
this: to strive to cultivate and maintain, ay, to the very
uttermost, what is called the concert of Europe; to keep the
Powers of Europe in union together. And why? Because by
keeping all in union together you neutralize and fetter and
bind up the selfish aims of each. I am not here to flatter
either England or any of them. They have selfish aims, as,
unfortunately, we in late years have too sadly shown that we,
too, have had selfish aims; but then, common action is fatal
to selfish aims. Common action means common objects; and
the only objects for which you can unite together the Powers
of Europe are objects connected with the common good of
them all. That, gentlemen, is my third principle of foreign
policy.

My fourth principle is—that you should avoid needless and
entangling engagements. You may boast about them; you
may brag about them. You may say you are procuring consideration for the country. You may say that an Englishman
can now hold up his head among the nations. You may say
that he is now not in the hands of a Liberal Ministry, who
thought of nothing but pounds, shillings, and pence. But
what does all this come to, gentlemen? It comes to this, that
you are increasing your engagements without increasing your
strength; and if you increase engagements without increasing
strength, you diminish strength, you abolish strength; you
really reduce the Empire and do not increase it. You render
it less capable of performing its duties; you render it an
inheritance less precious to hand on to future generations.

My fifth principle is this, gentlemen, to acknowledge the
equal rights of all nations. You may sympathize with one
nation more than another. Nay, you must sympathize in
certain circumstances with one nation more than another.
You sympathize most with those nations, as a rule, with
which you have the closest connexion in language, in blood,
and in religion, or whose circumstances at the time seem to

give the strongest claim to sympathy. But in point of right all are equal, and you have no right to set up a system under which one of them is to be placed under moral suspicion or espionage, or to be made the constant subject of invective. If you do that, but especially if you claim for yourself a superiority, a pharisaical superiority over the whole of them, then I say you may talk about your patriotism if you please, but you are a misjudging friend of your country, and in undermining the basis of the esteem and respect of other people for your country you are in reality inflicting the severest injury upon it. I have now given you, gentlemen, five principles of foreign policy. Let me give you a sixth, and then I have done.

And that sixth is, that in my opinion foreign policy, subject to all the limitations that I have described, the foreign policy of England should always be inspired by the love of freedom. There should be a sympathy with freedom, a desire to give it scope, founded not upon visionary ideas, but upon the long experience of many generations within the shores of this happy isle, that in freedom you lay the firmest foundations both of loyalty and order; the firmest foundations for the development of individual character, and the best provision for the happiness of the nation at large. In the foreign policy of this country the name of Canning ever will be honoured. The name of Russell ever will be honoured. The name of Palmerston ever will be honoured by those who recollect the erection of the kingdom of Belgium, and the union of the disjoined provinces of Italy. It is that sympathy, not a sympathy with disorder, but, on the contrary, founded upon the deepest and most profound love of order—it is that sympathy which, in my opinion, ought to be the very atmosphere in which a Foreign Secretary of England ought to live and to move. . . .

Gentlemen, there is only one other point on which I must still say a few words to you. . . . Of all the principles, gentlemen, of foreign policy which I have enumerated, that to which I attach the greatest value is the principle of the equality of nations; because, without recognizing that principle, there is no such thing as public right, and without public international right there is no instrument available for settling the transactions of mankind except material force. Consequently the principle of equality among nations lies, in my opinion, at the very basis and root of a Christian civilization, and when that principle is compromised or abandoned, with it must depart our hopes of tranquillity and of progress for mankind....

59. GLADSTONE AND GRANVILLE MODIFY BRITISH POLICY IN THE NEAR EAST

[The return of the Liberals to power in the spring of 1880 is of the first importance in the history of British policy towards the Ottoman Empire. Both Gladstone and Granville, when in opposition, had severely criticized the settlement of Berlin, and both were determined that they would as far as possible justify their criticism in office. Only a few days, therefore, after their accession to power, Granville issued a circular dispatch to the British representatives at the courts of the other five Great Powers, setting forth the desire of the new British administration that the delay in the execution of the Treaty of Berlin should be ended "by the united efforts of the Powers" (**Doc. 150**). The method proposed was an identic note to the Porte "requiring the Turkish Government to fulfil forthwith its obligations under the Treaty in regard to Greece, Montenegro and Armenia".*

The British circular—which was sent with instructions that a copy should be left with the Ministers for Foreign Affairs at the five courts—gave the keynote to the policy of the Liberal Government by its insistence on joint action by the Powers and its implied disregard of the special claims of Britain. Its importance is enhanced by the private opinions printed here (**Docs. 151–2**), which state in less guarded terms the attitude of Gladstone and Granville. In the first of them Granville defines his policy for the information of the Ambassador at St Petersburg, in the second Gladstone is seen reflecting on the language which he proposed to use at his forthcoming interview with the Ambassador of Turkey.]

* The text of the identic note of 11 June 1880, presented at Constantinople on 12 June, is in A. & P., [1880], LXXXI, [C. 2611], 409–14.

Document 150. *Granville announces to the Powers the attitude of the new administration, 4 May 1880**

H[er] M[ajesty]'s Gov[ernmen]t consider that it is an object of European interest that the delay which has occurred in the execution of certain of the provisions of the Treaty of Berlin should be put an end to, and that this can best be effected by the united efforts of the Powers.

H[er] M[ajesty]'s Gov[ernmen]t are anxious to invite the cooperation of the <u>French</u> Gov[ernmen]t and of the other
                    etc.
Powers to obtain this result, and I have accordingly to request that Y[our] E[xcellency] will propose to <u>M. de Freycinet</u>
                                        etc.
that the <u>French</u> Ambassador at Constantinople should be
              etc.
instructed in concert with the Representatives of the other Powers to address an identic and simultaneous note to the Porte requiring the Turkish Gov[ernmen]t to fulfil forthwith its obligations under the Treaty in regard to Greece, Montenegro and Armenia.

The Porte has for some time had before it a proposal made by the Marquis of Salisbury and which had received the assent of the Powers that an International Commission should proceed to the frontier provinces to determine the rectification of the Greek boundary. The Porte has pointed out the difficulties which might be encountered by such a Commission but has not given any definitive reply. It appears to H[er] M[ajesty's] G[overnment] that it should now be called upon to do so without delay.

The state of things on the Montenegrin frontier requires even more pressing attention. The Turkish Authorities have failed to carry out the agreement entered into with Montenegro and adhered to by the Representatives of the Powers in the protocol of the 18th of April and have allowed the frontier

* Granville to British Representatives at Paris (No. 452), Berlin (No. 183), Vienna (No. 194), Rome (No. 195), St Petersburg (No. 176), 4 May 1880. Endorsed: "Approved by the Cabinet and the Queen." *F.O.* 65/1076. Cp. *A. & P.*, [1880], LXXXI, [C. 2574], 361–2.

positions to be occupied by the Albanians and a collision might at any time occur between the latter and the Montenegrin troops.* The Porte should be required to state specifically its intentions as to the Montenegrin frontier and to bring the arrangement into which it has entered with regard to Kuči Kraina into immediate practical execution.

By the 61st Article of the Treaty of Berlin the Sublime Porte undertook to carry out without further delay, the improvements and reforms demanded by local requirements in the provinces inhabited by the Armenians and to guarantee their security against the Circassians and Kurds and to periodically make known the steps taken to this effect to the Powers who are to superintend their application.

So far as H[er] M[ajesty's] Gov[ernmen]t are aware nothing has been done by the Porte to make known any steps which it may have taken under this Article, nor have any measures been adopted for the Superintendence to be exercised by the Powers. The Reports which H[er] M[ajesty's] G[overnment] have received show that the state of Armenia is deplorable and they cannot think that this Article should be permitted any longer to remain a dead letter. They believe that it is only by the exercise of united pressure that the Porte can be induced to fulfil its duty in this respect and they consider that the due execution of the Article should be at once demanded and the Porte be called upon to state explicitly what the steps are which it has taken in compliance with this provision of the Treaty.

You will read this despatch to M. de Freycinet and leave
etc.
a copy with him requesting to be informed, at his early convenience, whether he is willing to give instructions in a similar sense to the French Ambassador at Constantinople.
etc.

* In the Plava-Gusinje area ceded to Montenegro, the inhabitants were all Albanians and determined to resist annexation by force of arms. As there were no roads, an expedition to this area was difficult, and the Powers finally agreed that Turkey should be asked to cede Dulcigno to Montenegro, leaving Plava and Gusinje untouched. *V. infra*, p. 407.

Document 151. *A private explanation of policy by Granville, 5 May 1880**

There has been a late Cabinet, but I cannot let the Messenger go without one line from me. It is very pleasant to have to work with one whom I know so well and trust so thoroughly as yourself. I hear of nothing but your success at St. Petersburgh. But, although you will not disapprove of Ripon's appointment,† I am afraid you will regret not having a still larger sphere for your work.

I am expecting Lobanoff to talk over the subject of the telegrams from you to me and from his Gov[ernmen]t to himself.

I hope we shall gradually get on a good understanding, but it is not desirable that this should be too ostentatious at first. Our policy as you will guess from the short despatches you have received is to act cordially with Europe and to try to hasten the fulfilment of the conditions of the Treaty of Berlin. I shall allude as little as possible for the present to the Cyprus Convention—we do not wish to give more sanction than necessary to its validity—on the other hand both as regards the Russians and the Turks there would be no advantage in prematurely declaring it to have failed.

The Powers seem inclined at all events to put on a show of concert. The question is if their representations fail, what is to be the next step. We do not shrink from doing what may be judicious, with the other Powers—but we are not inclined for isolated or dual action. Layard will have leave of absence.‡ Goschen will go on a special Embassy to Constantinople for a limited time, without vacating his seat.

* G. & D. 29/209, *Pte Granville Papers*. Granville to Dufferin, Private, 5 May 1880.

† Appointed Viceroy of India, 6 May 1880.

‡ Layard had had a public controversy with Gladstone while the latter was out of office, so that, apart from his Turcophilism, his removal was inevitable. Goschen was appointed 6 May 1880, and Lord Dufferin became Ambassador 26 May 1881.

Document 152. *Gladstone's reflections on British policy,*
23 *May* 1880*

(1) Laud the projects of Constitution for the Provinces
(Vilayet of Salonica, etc.).

(2) Idea that in the last resort the Ottoman power is a
British interest to be sustained by our arms does *not* form the
basis or any part of our policy.

(3) We desire the maintenance of the Turkish Empire
compatibly with the welfare of the people and think that
where autonomy has been or may be granted, the Suzerainty
of the Sultan (which would naturally be associated with
tribute) might still be useful and conducive to the peace of
Europe.

(4) We desire to act in concert with Europe and do not
desire the exercise of separate influence.

(5) If the arrangement as to Cyprus has produced an idea
that we covet Asia Minor or any other territorial acquisition,
we not only disclaim any such idea but should regard the
acquisition as a misfortune.

(6) We view with hope the re-establishment of a Turkish
Parliament but

   (*a*) so that it shall not override any other concessions made
        by the Porte to any of the emancipated Provinces, or
        to be so made under the Treaty of Berlin†

   (*b*) so that the representation be really impartial as between
        the different religions.

(7) That we shall witness with satisfaction any relief which
may be legitimately afforded by improved arrangements fiscal
or political, to the Turkish finances.

* G. & D. 29/123, *Pte Granville Papers.* Memorandum on "proposed language
of Mr. Gladstone to Musurus Pasha", 23 May 1880.
† But see as to this H. Temperley, 'British policy towards Parliamentary rule
in Turkey', *Camb. Hist. Journ.*, iv, No. 2, [1933], 183–4, 185 n., and Lord
Fitzmaurice's comments, 191 n.

60. GLADSTONE AND GRANVILLE CONTEMPLATE THE CANCELLATION OF THE CYPRUS CONVENTION BUT DO NOT ACHIEVE IT

[The reference to Armenian reform in Granville's circular dispatch of 4 May 1880 (*supra*, pp. 395–6) indicated clearly that under the new administration Asiatic reform was to be based on the Treaty of Berlin and not on the Cyprus Convention. On this subject both Gladstone and Granville felt a certain delicacy. The Cyprus Convention was objectionable to them both, and from the beginning they were feeling their way towards its cancellation. Early in June Granville prepared a dispatch (**Doc. 153**) which explained their attitude at length to Goschen. The private correspondence of this time shews that Gladstone wholly approved the policy, but that the Queen gravely doubted its wisdom. Yet the Cyprus Convention was not in fact cancelled, in spite of the views of Gladstone and Granville. Thus Salisbury's prophecy of 18 April 1878 was fulfilled: "This country, which is popularly governed...would probably abandon the task of resisting any further Russian advance...if no other but speculative arguments can be advanced in favour of action. But it will cling to any military post occupied by England as tenaciously as it has clung to Gibraltar." * The Queen's doubts of the new policy are shewn in correspondence published in her *Letters*† and by her vigorous minute on the draft. Against the statement that "The acquisition of Cyprus is in their view of no advantage to the country either in a military or political sense", the Queen wrote "I do not the least agree in this. V.R.I." The Queen's approval was therefore merely formal.]

Document 153. *Gladstone's comments on the draft dispatch to Goschen, 9 June 1880‡*

Besides a couple of merely verbal notes in pencil on the Convention draft, there is a serious point on which I am anxious to be quite safe.

Can we safely give up the stipulations on behalf of the

---

* *Pte Layard Papers*, B.M. Add. MSS. 39,137, f. 62. Salisbury to Layard, 18 April 1878. Cited H. Temperley, 'Disraeli and Cyprus', *E.H.R.* XLVI, [April 1931], 276–7.

† *Letters of Queen Victoria*, 2nd Ser., [1928], III, 111–13. In a letter to Goschen of 17 June 1880 Granville wrote: "The Queen is rather unhappy at our anti-Turkish proceedings. She gave a grudging assent to the Anglo-Turkish Convention draft." G. & D. 29/210.

‡ G. & D. 29/123. *Pte Granville Papers*. Gladstone to Granville, 9 June 1880.

subjects of the Porte *throughout Asia* upon consideration of Art. 61 Berlin for Armenia and the Sultan's will and intention for reform?

Ought not this to be covered by some reference however general to the concern which we felt after the Treaty of Paris for all the subjects of the Ottoman Empire, so as not to renounce such general rights as belong to civilized Powers to take cognisance in extreme cases of misgovernment and misery?

This is a matter of delicacy as well as weight and I am not suggesting any particular form of expression. This is the only point I have to raise—the letter to the Q[ueen] I think excellent.*

Document 154. *Granville expounds the attitude of the Liberal Government to the Cyprus Convention and earns the disapproval of the Queen, 10 June 1880†*

The Turkish Ambassador let drop some remarks in conversation with me a few days ago on the subject of the Convention of the 4th of June, 1878. He said that the Sultan's assent had been given to its provisions under a false impression; that H.M. had not at the time been aware that a portion of his European dominions would be given over to Austrian occupation under the sanction of the Powers at Berlin—an alienation of territory which had not been contemplated by the Treaty of San Stefano. H[is] Exc[ellen]cy said that the Turkish Gov[ernmen]t would be glad if an arrangement could be made to cancel the Convention.

Musurus Pasha observed that it was not to the occupation of Cyprus that the Sultan and his Gov[ernmen]t objected. He even hinted that the Porte would be glad to come to an arrangement for commuting the annual revenue to which the Porte is entitled under Art. III of the annex to the Convention, for the payment of a lump sum.

But he said that the condition that was felt to be most

* I.e. of 9 June 1880, *v. Letters of Queen Victoria*, 2nd Ser., [1928], III, 111–12.
† Granville to Goschen, No. 71, Very Confidential, 10 June 1880. Endorsed: "Seen by Mr. Gladstone, the Cabinet and the Queen." *F.O.* 78/3074.

galling at Constantinople was the right of local interference with the internal administration of the Sultan's Asiatic dominions which was claimed by the British Consular Authorities in virtue of the Sultan's engagement to introduce reforms in the G[overnmen]t. He added that this condition had created an aversion to employ Englishmen in the Ottoman public service which had not previously existed.

I answered that I had no knowledge of the exact circumstances or impressions under which the Convention had been concluded, and could not enter into that part of the subject; that I had not concealed in Parliament at the time of its announcement my opinion as to the impolicy of the Convention, but I added that to dissent from the expediency of an international arrangement was a very different thing from reversing it after it had been concluded.

On a subsequent occasion H[is] Ex[cellenc]y reverted to the subject and developed further the ideas he had thrown out. He spoke again of the probable willingness of the Porte to leave Cyprus in English possession and to accept the payment of a lump sum in lieu of the annual income stipulated by the Convention. On the other hand he said that his Gov[ernmen]t would be ready to release England from the obligation under the Convention to defend the Asiatic Provinces of Turkey from attack by Russia, provided we would consent to forego the special powers of interference in the administration of the Country which were claimed by our Consular Officers in Asia Minor in virtue of its provisions.

I asked His Exc[ellenc]y to give me confidentially his views on paper pro-memoriâ which he promised at once to do; but on the 20th, when taking leave of me for Const[antino]ple, he said he preferred renewing the subject at Const[antino]ple.

I think it desirable that Y[our] Exc[ellenc]y should be made acquainted with the above, not with a view to your making any direct overtures to the Turkish Gov[ernmen]t, but in order that you may be prepared for those which seem likely to be addressed to you and which should be rather invited than discouraged by you.

Y[our] Exc[ellenc]y I have reason to know, shares the opinion of the members of H.M. Gov[ernmen]t that grave objections exist to the Anglo-Turkish Convention.

The acquisition of Cyprus is in their view of no advantage to the Country either in a military or political sense,* while the mode of acquiring the Island was calculated to destroy the opinion of Europe that England was entirely without a wish for territorial aggrandisement at the expense of Turkey. It has undoubtedly inspired the Sultan with fears on this point.

The Convention is an isolated arrangement concluded between Great Britain and Turkey without the participation, consent or knowledge of the other Powers. Though tacitly recognized by them it remains to this day without any explicit sanction on their part, and whether its provisions do or do not involve a direct infraction of the Treaties of Paris 1856, and London 1871, yet it is manifestly in spirit a departure from the general principle of concerted interest in regard to Turkish Affairs which the Treaty of Paris in particular was, in our opinion, designed to establish.

The tenure of the Island is uncertain and anomalous, creating difficulties with regard to its permanent administration and raising questions, both with the Porte and with other foreign Powers which have not yet been solved.

The guarantee of the Sultan's territories in Asia, as fixed by the Treaty of Berlin was described by Lord Salisbury in his letter to M. Waddington communicating the Convention as an "onerous obligation". It is in fact a heavy responsibility, which while it gives no additional power to effect the object, may at times and under circumstances which it is impossible to forsee, offer to this country the alternative of either doing that which may be most inconvenient and even dangerous, or of failing to meet our Treaty obligations—unless indeed the Treaty be denounced in consequence of the Porte having entirely failed to carry out the reforms in the Sultan's Asiatic dominions which they bound themselves to do.

I do not find any proof that the denunciation of the Treaty on such grounds has been contemplated by our predecessors

* Marginal note in pencil: "I do not the least agree in this. V.R.I."

in office, and it would of course require much consideration before doing so.

The matter would however be facilitated if the first advance were to be made from the side of the Turkish Government, and it is in view of the possibility of such an advance that I offer the following further observations.

One great difficulty in the way of abrogating the Convention would be the question how to deal with Cyprus. We do not, as I have already stated, consider its retention to be of importance to Great Britain. But there can be no doubt that any return to Turkish administration would be viewed with great disfavour by the inhabitants and it does not appear that it is desired by the Porte.

It is a question whether, if we are to retain possession of the Island, it should not be on a more definite tenure than now exists, and one which would release the administration of it from many of the difficulties by which it is now surrounded, or whether we should proceed on the basis of a negotiation which took place on this subject in April 1879 but which was not brought to a successful issue. Your Excellency will find the record of this negotiation in the archives of Her Majesty's Embassy.

In either case it would probably be easy to raise a loan on the security of the Cyprus Revenue sufficient to furnish the capital sum required by the Porte and possibly a surplus which might be applied to necessary public works in the Island.

I pass to the question of the Sultan's engagement under the Convention "to introduce necessary reforms, to be agreed upon later between the two Powers, into the Government and for the protection of the Christian and other subjects of the Porte in his Asiatic Territories". For the proper consideration of this point it is necessary to examine how far the engagement is or promises to be of practical benefit under existing circ[umstanc]es.

Y[our] Exc[ellenc]y is aware that as a matter of fact no substantial progress has been made towards the introduction of the reforms specified as necessary by my predecessor, and accepted with some qualifications by the Porte. The representations of H[er] M[ajesty's] Gov[ernmen]t on this head have been continually met by the statement that in the exhausted state of the Ottoman Exchequer nothing could be done. It is true that the presence of British Consular Officers in Asia Minor has been useful to bring to light many abuses, to procure the redress of some of them by the Turkish Authorities and to distribute relief from funds collected by voluntary subscription in England to the population which has been suffering from the recent scarcity of provisions. It is easy, however, to understand the jealousy with which the Turkish Authorities would be inclined to regard anything bearing the appearance of a special protectorate of Ottoman subjects by the officers of a Foreign Power, and it is at least open to question whether acts of individual intervention of this nature, however useful and even necessary at the moment, offer the best method of securing real and lasting reforms in the administration of a Country.

Her Majesty's advisers are no less anxious than were their predecessors for the good government of the Sultan's subjects. They can never renounce the concern which they felt after the Treaty of Paris for all the subjects of the Ottoman Empire, and whether England remains bound by the terms of the Convention or no, it would still continue to be an object of solicitude to her that such ameliorations should take place in the condition and administration of the Asiatic Provinces of Turkey as are requisite for the welfare of their inhabitants and creeds, without bringing them under subjection to any foreign Power. It may, however, be matter for serious consideration whether for the present prosecution of this object H[er] M[ajesty's] Gov[ernmen]t might not be content with the engagements of all the Powers contained in the 61st Article of the Treaty of Berlin, and the right of supervision conferred by that Article, provided they could have a practical assurance that the Sultan had both the means and the intention of proceeding at once with the work of reform.

For this purpose it might be stipulated that a certain proportion of any moneys to be paid over to the Porte in commutation of the Cyprus revenue should be devoted to the furtherance of Reforms in Asiatic Turkey, for the delay of which the want of Funds has been pleaded.

Finally, as regards the obligation to defend the Asiatic possessions of the Sultan from attack by Russia. Supposing ourselves to be freed from that obligation Great Britain must still reserve to herself full liberty of action if events should at any time occur, calculated to place in peril interests which she might think it necessary or right to defend.

You will consider this Despatch as written to guide Your Excellency in any conversation which may be initiated by the Turkish Government on this subject; and to elicit Your Excellency's opinion on so important a transaction.

But you will not consider it as giving you authority to act without further communication with Her Majesty's Government.

[The dispatch of 10 June (**Doc. 154**) was a preliminary exposition of policy, and the Ambassador, Goschen, was specifically prohibited from acting on it. In fact, the policy was to a large extent enforced. The special powers of the Consuls in Asia Minor were withdrawn, claims of interference based on the Cyprus Convention ceased, and the principle that all pressure for reform should be by the Powers jointly, and not by England alone, became part of the permanent policy followed by Britain in the Ottoman Empire. From this time, therefore, the brief interlude of the exercise of special British responsibility may be regarded as ended. It is to be noted that even Gladstone at this time did not contemplate the surrender of Cyprus itself. Six months later, it is true, he was thinking of handing it over to Greece "in sovereignty not in mere occupation", finding an additional motive for his proposal in the "strong challenge" that it would imply to the late Government. But even at this period he answered Granville's doubts with an explanation that he had not intended any immediate action. It was only an "idea for the future".* On the strength of this (*v. infra*, p. 406) he wrote in June 1881, with regard to the cession of Cyprus, "The Government have not advised anything of the kind".]

* G. & D. 29/123, *Pte Granville Papers*. Gladstone to Granville, 20 December 1880.

Document 155. *Gladstone suggests handing over Cyprus to Greece,* 17 *December* 1880*

[After mentioning a suggestion that Bismarck wished to cede Crete to Greece, instead of Thessaly or Epirus as proposed Gladstone adds:]

. . . If this is to happen and Crete to be Greek, it seems to be not wholly unworthy of consideration whether Cyprus might not be handed over by the Porte and us, in sovereignty not in mere occupation. This would incidentally be a strong challenge to the late [Disraeli] Government, but I do not know that it would be an unsafe one. Of course it should not be thought of unless desired by the [Cypriot] people. At present they can hardly have dreamt of it.

[There was, however, an amusing sequel. The Queen seems again to have pressed hard in the matter in June 1881. At any rate Gladstone wrote to Granville: "It is announced that the Queen will not consent to a cession of Cyprus; but as the Government have *not* advised anything of the kind (nor indeed *entertained* the subject) it is difficult to understand this intimation otherwise than [as] a notice. Again neither is a notice intelligible otherwise than as a virtual prohibition. But it is totally incompatible with Ministers under the British Constitution, as I need hardly say, indeed I do not see *how it would be admissible under any form of government*—to acquiesce in any limitation of their duty to advise on any subject from time to time as the honour and interests of the Crown appear to require."† Gladstone's doctrine is the legal one that you "cannot bind the future", but it is rather piquant to find Gladstone saying that even the Ministers of a despotic Sovereign could not bind the future about Cyprus. He added, however, the prudent postscript "I do not urge this as a matter which need now be discussed".

The last reference to Cyprus from Gladstone is in a letter to Madame Novikov in 1896. "Bad as the Cyprus Treaty is, it contains no obligation to aid the Assassin‡ in Armenia, except *on condition of Reforms.* And he has been informed long ago that the Covenant fell to the ground by his Breach of faith in not giving

---

* *Pte Gladstone Papers.* Gladstone to Granville, 17 December 1880.

† *Pte Gladstone Papers.* Gladstone to Granville, 15 June 1881; italics are the Editors', here and in preceding passages.

‡ Sultan Abdul Hamid, so denounced by Gladstone in 1896 because of the recent massacres in Armenia.

the reforms."* It is important to note that, while there were certainly occasions when Salisbury thought that the state of public opinion would not allow him to defend the Sultan, he never admitted that the obligation had lapsed. A Blue Book in 1899, which bears the title of *Guarantees or Engagements by Great Britain,* reproduces the Cyprus Convention, and even in 1913 Sir Edward Grey negotiated about Armenian reforms on the assumption that the Cyprus Convention was still in force†.]

61. THE ENFORCEMENT OF THE TREATY OF BERLIN

[The decision of the Cabinet that the special claims of Britain to interfere in Turkey-in-Asia should be allowed to fall into abeyance coincided with a crisis in another aspect of the problems left over by the Berlin settlement. Article XXIX of the Treaty of Berlin had provided for the cession of Antivari to Montenegro, but had left other details of her territorial limits to be settled by a frontier commission, while in the case of Greece the Powers had done no more than suggest the line of the new frontier in a Protocol, and left   to be decided as the result of direct Turco-Greek negotiations. A conference in Berlin in June 1880, necessitated by the failure of these negotiations, produced a decision which Turkey refused to execute. In the case of Montenegro a naval demonstration off the Albanian coast enforced the terms of the Treaty.‡

Britain took the lead in demanding forcible measures, as the letters of 16–19 September shew. On 30 September Gladstone laid before the Cabinet proposals for action on the basis of the *protocole de désintéressement* to which the Powers had already agreed. A comparison of Gladstone's plan with his report to the Queen of the decisions of the Cabinet§ reveals the fact that they held more firmly than he to the principle of the co-operation of all the Powers.]

Document 156. *Gladstone contemplates the use of force,* 16–19 *September* 1880||

Our ideas are not recondite, nor are they developed except in proportion to what is immediate or at least not remote.

We are for the concert of Europe—we hope it will continue

---

* *Pte Gladstone Papers.* Gladstone to Mme Novikoff, 13 September 1896; italics are Gladstone's.

† *V.* Temperley and Penson, *Century of Diplomatic Blue Books,* No. 1530; Gooch and Temperley, [1936], x (1), Ch. LXXXVIII, *passim.* It should be remembered that the Asquith Government, in the year 1915, offered Cyprus to Greece if she would assist England in the War.

‡ *V. supra,* p. 396.   § *V. infra,* pp. 409–10.

|| *Pte Gladstone Papers.*

to subsist, we think that then it will prevail—for surely Europe will not run away from the Turk with its tail between its legs.

But it will be too bold to say positively [that] it will be so maintained as to prevail—for we must remember that it united in 1853 and 1854, but not in 1855. Should it be broken up in its entirety, two duties will remain, one to let it be known who has broken it, the other to see whether enough remains to be sufficient for the end in view.

What I have said in these last lines is the part of our creed which has as yet been least opened out, and which perhaps might be developed with great utility from time to time.*

The mind of the Sultan, who *is* the Turkish Government, is a bottomless pit of fraud and falsehood, and he will fulfil *nothing* except under force or the proximate fear of *force*.†

As to sole action with Russia, or rather dual action, I have never (in 1876 or now) said a word for it, or such action with any other power. But it would be unwarrantable to ask any abstract pledge of us on the subject.‡

[It appears from a letter written to Granville on the 20th that Gladstone anticipated strong opposition from the Queen.]

Document 157. *Gladstone explains his policy to the Cabinet, 30 September* 1880§

In pursuit of the common object, and subject to the self-denying engagement, and after we have concerted with the Prince of Montenegro the means of applying force to drive the Albanian invaders from the district of Dulcigno, I am of opinion that we ought not to refuse his application.

And that if we can arrange for an active concert of at least *three* of the Powers, together with the approval or acquiescence of the rest, we ought to prepare for proceeding, either locally

---

* Gladstone to Lord Reay, 16 September 1880.
† Gladstone to Lord Acton, 19 September 1880. Italics are Gladstone's.
‡ Gladstone to Granville, 19 September 1880.
§ G. & D. 29/123, *Pte Granville Papers*. Memorandum by Gladstone for the Cabinet, 30 September 1880.

or otherwise, with the limited object at present of fulfilling the Treaty of Berlin on the Montenegrin frontier, and subject to the self-denying engagement already entered into.

Should there be further contumacy it might be right to consider how far the settlement of the Greek frontier should be combined in the same arrangement.

1. The Cabinet has to consider whether it will endeavour to make arrangements for concerted military action (local or otherwise) in support of the obligations imposed by the Treaty of Berlin as to the frontier of Montenegro.

2. Assuming (a) that the decision is affirmative

(b) that the self-denying engagement remains in force.

Query whether to proceed as follows:

1. *Acquaint Austria*, and inquire whether she would so far enter into it as to put forward a force for the *defence* of the S. and S.E. frontier of Montenegro (so as to liberate the whole Montenegrin army: N.B. the occupation of the Principalities during the Crimean War).

2. *Acquaint Italy*, and ask whether she will at once endeavour, with England and any other Power which may concur, to agree upon the best means of repelling any military action of the Sultan directed against the Prince of Montenegro to prevent his occupation of the territory due to him under the Treaty of Berlin.

(Acquaint Italy confidentially that if she agrees to the use of ships, and of the ship-force by land under proper conditions, we should not understand her as binding herself to send a land-force.)

3. Collect the fleet at Malta and announce it.

[A telegram was then sent to Goschen at Constantinople instructing him (1) to grant or to recognize the delay afforded until Sunday the 3rd, (2) to put forward the demand suggested by Austria-Hungary respecting the action of the local Turkish force, (3) to signify that, if this delay did not suffice or procure an advantageous arrangement, the matter could not end there. The Queen was informed at the same time that the Cabinet would "strongly repudiate the idea of the sole action of England. They do not think that England should undertake action...with Russia or with any single Power", and "earnestly seek to maintain the European concert entire and to encourage its cautious but decided action". This was on the 30th, and the Queen replied on 2 October in a style which shewed that she wished for caution, and it is doubtful whether she approved of decided coercion, or, in fact, of what followed.*]

Document 158. *Turkey collapses and Gladstone rejoices, 4–12 October 1880*

[The Great Powers had each sent a man-of-war to the naval demonstration off the coast of Albania in favour of Montenegro. But Austria-Hungary and Germany refused to do anything "leading to a war with Turkey", and France was dubious. Russia and Italy were, however, favourable. On Monday, 4 October, the Sultan formally refused to cede Dulcigno. But he did not then know that any Power was ready to coerce him. Britain then proposed to send the united fleet to Smyrna to seize the rich Turkish customs house there and sequestrate the dues. England and Russia were actually prepared to use force, and the Sultan learned of this fact on 9 October, without hearing that Germany and Austria-Hungary had refused to act. He decided therefore to cede Dulcigno and make concessions as to Greece. Granville and Gladstone received the news of the Sultan's surrender "with as much surprise as delight" on Sunday, 10 October. On the 12th the news was formally confirmed and the crisis was over. Gladstone's private letters tell the story, and lay bare his profound emotion at his success.]

"Praise to the Holiest in the Height."

It is the working of the European Concert for purposes of justice, peace and liberty, with efficiency and success, which is the great matter at issue. This has always been the ideal of my life in Foreign Policy; and if this goes forward rightly to the end, it will be the most conspicuous instance yet recorded, the best case of success achieved.†

It demonstrates the power of a real concert believed to exist. And makes it more difficult for the shabbier Powers not to join us or give us countenance which is aid of a certain kind.‡

---

* G. & D. 29/123, *Pte Granville Papers.* "Memorandum communicated by Mr. Gladstone to the Queen", 30 September 1880. The Queen's reply of 2 October 1880 is in *Letters of Queen Victoria*, 2nd Ser., [1928], III, 147.

† *Pte Gladstone Papers.* Gladstone to Mrs Gladstone, 10 October 1880.

‡ *Pte Gladstone Papers.* Gladstone to Mrs Gladstone, 11 October 1880. Italics are Gladstone's.

In one thing only the Sultan is quite consistent. He never speaks a word of truth.*

One thing only was new on Saturday [the 9th] in the situation at Constantinople. On that day he [the Sultan] learned that the English Government had proposed to the Powers the occupation of Smyrna, and on that night he sent his solemn promise to *hand over* Dulcigno.†

62. GLADSTONE'S PYRRHIC VICTORY AND THE DREIKAISERBUND

[Gladstone appeared definitely to have triumphed. Europe had coerced the Sultan but that coercion was disapproved by two out of the three great military Powers in Eastern and Central Europe. The partial surrender of Turkey saved Gladstone from the logical results of his policy, and made possible a provisional settlement of the frontier question. But these results were small indeed in comparison with the effect produced on the balance of power in the Near East. Gladstone had won success by a lucky accident, and he paid for it at a heavy price. His Cabinet did not want any more adventures. All the Powers except Russia had been conspicuously timid, and Gladstone was not prepared for a close union with Russia, or indeed for anything except the Concert of Europe. But the Concert had really failed even in this instance, though accident had converted failure into success. It was not likely to succeed another time. The initiative was now in the hands of Bismarck who did not believe in the vague concert of many, but in the close union of a few Powers, and who called Europe "a geographical expression".

Bismarck seems to have abstained from co-operation because he feared that war in the Near East might result from the use of force, and because he feared to separate the action of Russia from that of Austria-Hungary. He also greatly feared concerted action against Turkey by Russia and Great Britain.‡ Hence, immediately after this Gladstonian success, he sought to reconstitute the Dreikaiserbund.

Granville contributed to the change innocently enough in March 1881, when he commended Goschen on his return from visiting Bismarck. It has been "my object", wrote Granville, "to show B[ismarck] that he has our earnest support, and that

---

* *Pte Gladstone Papers*. Gladstone to Mr Speaker, 12 October 1880.

† *Pte Gladstone Papers*. Gladstone to John Morley, 12 October 1880. Italics are Gladstone's.

‡ *V.* Bismarck's general instruction on Eastern policy of 7 November 1880, G.P., [1922], IV, 17–20, and the notes of the German Editors.

I do not wish to put my finger in the pie, excepting when and as much as he desires it".* Bismarck's real desire was to destroy the Concert of Europe in Eastern affairs, by substituting for it the predominance of Austria-Hungary, Germany and Russia in that area. England, Italy and France were to be excluded. And he accomplished his object on 18 June 1881, when representatives of the Three Emperors signed a convention at Berlin. Article III provided for the closing of the Bosphorus and the Dardanelles, as "summed up in the declaration of the second Plenipotentiary of Russia at the session of July 12 of the Congress of Berlin (Protocol 19)".† The Dreikaiserbund was therefore meant to destroy the English doctrine of permission to enter the Straits at the Sultan's call, and also to exclude English influence from the Near East. This seems to have been the ultimate result of Gladstone's coercion of the Sultan, of his refusal to act alone, and of his adherence to the European Concert.]

Document 159. *Gladstone proposes a warning to Austria-Hungary*, 13–28 December 1881‡

...We have not I think heard anything from Vienna of the Austrian conscription in Bosnia and Hercegovina. I hope there may be no such thing. But if there is, it seems to me impolitic, cruel, and of most doubtful title.

(We seem however to hear very little from Vienna.)

I am afraid that Austria is egged on by Bismarck and if she provokes a conflict with Russia in the Balkan Peninsula she will probably come to grief. She will never as against Russia commend herself to an Orthodox or even a Slav population: and Russia has much more to offer Turkey than she has....

...I hope there is nothing in the rumour reported now by Dufferin of an arrangement between Russia and Austria as to the Balkans. As to partition it can hardly be true. But neither the one nor the other is trustworthy as a nurse of that which alone I presume we desire namely the free peaceful growth and development of local liberties. Would you be prepared

* G. & D. 29/210, *Pte Granville Papers*. Granville to Goschen, Private, 14 March 1881.
† A. F. Pribram, *Secret Treaties of Austria-Hungary*, [1920], I, 39; for Salisbury's declaration *v. supra*, p. 382, and n. 3.
‡ G. & D. 29/124, *Pte Granville Papers*. Gladstone to Granville, 13 and 28 December 1881.

under the circ[umstance]s to put it upon record that we would not view with approval any arrangement between foreign Powers which either directly or indirectly tended to invade or undermine their liberties....

63. GLADSTONE AND GRANVILLE UNWILLINGLY ACKNOWLEDGE THE OBLIGATIONS INCURRED BY SALISBURY AS TO TUNIS*

[In 1880–1 the Liberal Government might well have felt, as Salisbury had felt three years earlier, that their chief task was to pick up china which someone else had broken. At the very time when they were launching a new policy in Turkey-in-Asia and carrying out the Berlin settlement in the Balkans, they were forced to consider Turkey-in-Africa. On 9 June 1880 the French Ambassador reminded Granville of the "very friendly language" used as to Tunis by Beaconsfield and Salisbury at Berlin. The French Government "would be glad to know as early as convenient whether the present Government shared the views of their Predecessors". Granville, after a few days' consideration in which he read the archives, gave his reply on 12 June. He referred to the "discrepancy between what was originally mentioned in private conversation and what was afterwards recorded officially"; he cited Salisbury's safeguarding phrase about the position of Italy; he said that "in the view of Her Majesty's Government Tunis was a portion of the Ottoman Empire, to dispose of which Great Britain had no moral or international right"; and he repeated Salisbury's denial of any "jealousy of the influence which France ..exercizes and is likely to exercize over Tunis". Finally, by specifically endorsing the attitude of the Conservatives as far as the question of Italy was concerned, he made it clear that he was neither cancelling nor confirming their assurances on the main question.

Nine months passed before France was ready for action, and when the time came Granville was powerless. His letter to Gladstone on 21 April 1881 shews him ready to contemplate even the "appalling" risk of a war with France rather than allow her to continue without protest. He foresaw the fortification of Biserta, with its consequence in the "neutralizing" of Malta, and he strengthened himself by remembering the effect of the decided language of successive Foreign Secretaries in the time of Louis Philippe and Napoleon III. He reiterated the Liberal doctrine

* Cp. W. L. Langer, *European Alliances and Alignments*, [1931], 217–50, Chapter VII, *passim*.

that Tunis was part of the Ottoman Empire.* He was prepared
—as Gladstone was not—to try to rouse Europe to assist him in
his opposition.

In the event Gladstone's view prevailed. "Pray remember our
second Malta", he wired in reply, and his arguments completed
Granville's conversion to a policy of unwilling acceptance (v.
Doc. 160). The laying of the Conservative pledges before Parliament was the only solace for defeat.†]

Document 160. *Granville explains the limits imposed upon his policy, 22 April* 1881‡

You will not like a Despatch I send you, and I am rather
sorry to send it. But I do not see how we are to give France
carte blanche.

I dislike barking without biting, but if the result of not
barking (in contradistinction to all that was done under Louis
Philippe and Napoleon, when English remonstrances certainly
stopped the French) is the annexation of Tunis, or the creation
of the great port of Biserta, impregnable by a naval force and
neutralizing Malta, we should look rather foolish.

Notwithstanding the present Chauvinism about Tunis, it
would not be a sweetmeat for the French to have England,
Italy and the Arabs inside and outside Algeria against her.

It is well that she should imagine that this is not perfectly
impossible.

But of course I wish to ruffle her as little as possible, and
nobody will wrap up the warning of our doctrine as to
Ottoman Empire better than you will.

Document 161. *Gladstone recognizes that his hands are tied,* 22 *April* 1881§

As to Tunis I hope my telegram has been intelligible to you,
and to you only.

* G. & D. 29/124, *Pte Granville Papers*. Granville to Gladstone, 21 April 1881.
† *V. A. & P.*, [1881], xcix, [C. 2886], 501–7. Cp. Temperley and Penson,
Century of Diplomatic Blue Books, 295, No. 1061.
‡ G. & D. 29/202, *Pte Granville Papers*. Granville to Lyons, Private, 22 April
1881.
§ G. & D. 29/124, *Pte Granville Papers*. Gladstone to Granville, 22 April 1881;
published in Fitzmaurice's *Life of Granville*, [1905], ii, 236.

The 'second Malta' you will recollect was the character given to Cyprus, as it was to be, by Disraeli.

It appears to me that our position for resisting the French intrigues in Tunis—which are but too palpable—has been frightfully weakened: *first* by the acquisition of Cyprus in utter defiance of the Treaty of Paris, *secondly*, to a degree not yet quite cleared up, by Salisbury's declaration: which, whatever it may have been, I suppose binds us.

The first point I think most grave, and in fact the position seems to me not tenable beyond the point of friendly remonstrance in case of need.

Nothing could I think possibly be better than your letter to Menabrea.

You will have understood that I do not retract my approval as to sending ships, and if the occasion arise I would send a sufficiency.

The possible harbour is a grave fact but I do not see that it neutralises Malta more than it is neutralised by Malta. The other side is in other hands: and there is another access by Tacursia say 20 to 100 miles round.

XXI. GLADSTONE AND GRANVILLE, 1882–5

THE EGYPTIAN QUESTION

64. GLADSTONE AND GRANVILLE ENTER ON THE EGYPTIAN ADVENTURE

[Gladstone's action in Egypt is the most puzzling aspect of his policy. For the occupation and ultimate annexation of Egypt were contrary to his intention as well as contradictory of his principles. He wished to restrict, rather than to increase, responsibilities and territorial obligations; he was anxious not to come into conflict with foreign Powers; he desired to encourage and not to repress national movements wherever they manifested themselves. The Egyptian adventure, therefore, violated the fundamental principles of his policy.

Gladstone and Granville were at pains to shew that their hands had been tied by the commitments of Disraeli. They had some justification for this claim. For joint Anglo-French intervention in financial affairs had been established in 1876–9, and in 1879 the Khedive Ismail had been deposed, and replaced by Tewfik, by joint action of the two Powers. Yet a wholly new feature in the position developed, during the years 1880–2, when an Egyptian national movement, disguised under the colour of a military revolt, endangered the continuance of the Khedive's rule. In the face of this threat to the peaceful development of Anglo-French financial policy Granville addressed to Malet on 4 November 1881 a "clear exposition of our views and objects".* This consisted in part of a series of general statements of Liberal principles as applied to Egypt—"The Gov[ernmen]t of England would run counter to the most cherished traditions of national history, were it to entertain a desire to diminish that liberty [i.e. a 'measure of administrative independence'] or to tamper with the institutions to which it has given birth." In part it expressed the British insistence on the "tie which unites Egypt to the Porte", and on the fact that "the only circumstance which could force us to depart from the course of conduct which I have above indicated [i.e. non-interference] would be the occurrence in Egypt of a state of anarchy".

But it is necessary to look further for a full explanation. Gladstone held as sacred the obligations of Governments to their

---

* Granville to Malet, No. 216, 4 November 1881, *F.O.* 78/3320. Cp. *A. & P.*, [1882], LXXXII, [C. 3105], 1–4.

debtors and the duty of Governments to practise financial probity. Thus the Turkish repudiation of debts in 1875 was described by him as "the greatest of *political* crimes".* The position of Egypt differed only because England could coerce Turkey but had no weapon with which to discipline Egypt. Years before, Canning had laid it down as a principle—which Palmerston later had recognized—that the contraction of a loan by a British Government with an undeveloped Power was undesirable because it ultimately involved interference with internal affairs. British financial interests in Egypt were so great and the financial situation of Egypt so unsatisfactory that interference was the natural sequel. Gladstone's intense enthusiasm for orthodox financial methods thus led him on to adopt unorthodox political measures in Egypt.

Yet it must be remembered that the independence of Britain's action was ultimately due as much to France as to herself. Gladstone and Granville co-operated freely in the vigorous policy of France which characterized the period of the Gambetta administration (November 1881–January 1882). But the fall of Gambetta and the interposition of Bismarck ended this attempt to extend the sphere of Anglo-French co-operation. Dissatisfaction with the working of the new ministry appointed by the Khedive in February prepared the way for the adoption of a bolder policy on the part of Britain. The crisis produced by Arabi Pasha's national movement during April to May called for a definite decision. Britain and France disagreed as to the desirability of invoking Turkish aid, but both sent squadrons to Alexandria (**Doc. 162**) and Britain also acquiesced in, if she did not approve, the reference of the whole question to an ambassadorial conference at Constantinople (**Doc. 163**).]

Document 162. *Granville explains the dispatch of ships to Alexandria,* 23 *May* 1882†

In sending ships to Alexandria, H[er] M[ajesty's] G[overnment] had no intention of interfering with the Sultan's rights by carrying on military operations in Egypt or occupying the country, nor any idea of altering the constitutional status quo.

If the exercise of the Sovereign's authority should become necessary, the two Powers would naturally have recourse to the Sultan, and ask him to join with them in settling the difficulty by a common agreement.

England and France have acted alone because only their

---

* Italics are the Editors'.

† Granville to Dufferin, Tel. No. 166, 23 May 1882, *F.O.* 78/3395.

interests and those of Europeans were in danger. Neither Mussulman interests nor the rights of the Sultan were threatened, and there seemed therefore to be no reason for Porte to take steps to protect them.

If we had to carry our action beyond the protection of Europeans and the maintenance of our special interests we sh[oul]d necessarily resort to co-operation of the Sultan.

I hope this explanation will calm Porte's susceptibilities aroused by a misunderstanding of our motives.

Speak to Turkish Min[ister] for F[oreign] A[ffairs] in this sense. French Ambassador has had similar instruction.

Document 163. *Granville issues instructions for the Conference of Constantinople,* 21 *June* 1882*

Y[our] E[xcellency] has already rec[eive]d instructions with regard to the meeting of the Conference and you are fully informed of all that has passed between H[er] M[ajesty's] Gov[ernmen]t and the other Powers.

Y[our] E[xcellency] is acquainted with the reasons which have made the consideration of Egypt[ia]n Affairs by a Conference necessary.

The essential feature is that repeated military demonstrations have destroyed the authority of the Khedive and removed all security for the engagements entered into and rights assured by Firmans and Treaties. The authority of the Khedive should be supported and relieved from the dictation of the military party.

For these reasons the temporary arrangement which exists cannot be accepted as a solution. It furnishes no guarantee that the power which has been already exerted will not be exerted again to the destruction of the order of things established by law and of the rights guaranteed to Europeans.

The Sultan has taken upon himself the responsibility attaching to his position by sending an Imperial Comm[issione]r to Egypt. His Majesty must feel that further measures are necessary to enforce his authority.

* Granville to Dufferin, Tel. No. 290, 21 June 1882, Endorsed: "Seen by Lord Hartington." *F.O.* 78/3395.

You will join with your French Colleague in proposing at the outset of the Conference the signature of the Self-Denying Protocol upon the terms of which the several Gov[ernmen]ts are already agreed.

You will also join with him in proposing that a request should be addressed to the Sultan to send an adequate Turkish force to Egypt for the restoration of order.

You are aware of the conditions on which it is desired that these troops sh[oul]d be sent. In these conditions the French Gov[ernmen]t have concurred, but some objections have been raised by other Gov[ernmen]ts as to their being too stringent, which do not appear to be wholly without foundation. H[er] M[ajesty's] Gov[ernmen]t are quite ready that you should concert with your Colleagues upon these conditions always providing that they are sufficient to ensure that satisfactory engagements should be entered into by the Porte to secure the due limitation of the object for which the troops are employed.

If the Sultan should decline, the Conference will be invited to concert effective means for the re-establishment of legality and security in Egypt. So far as H[er] M[ajesty's] Gov[ernmen]t can at present judge, this invitation will be to ask the Powers to provide or sanction a military intervention other than Turkish under their authority.

Y[our] E[xcellency] will also take an opportunity of intimating to the Conference, but without asking for any action on their part, that H[er] M[ajesty's] Gov[ernmen]t intend to require full reparation and satisfaction for the outrages on British Subjects during the late disorders in Alexandria and the insults offered to H[er] M[ajesty's] Consul and to officers in H[er] M[ajesty's] service.

H[er] M[ajesty's] Gov[ernmen]t have full confidence in Y[our] E[xcellency]'s energy and discretion to carry out their views. They do not attach importance to particular forms, and are anxious, as much as possible, to consult the dignity and wishes of the Sultan, but their desires are concentrated on the necessity of obtaining the practical objects which they have in view.

65. THE BOMBARDMENT OF ALEXANDRIA

[The responsibility for the conversion of the joint Anglo-French naval demonstration at Alexandria into the sole action of Britain in the bombardment of the forts lies partly in the changes in French policy and partly in misunderstandings on the British side. The ministry of M. Freycinet, itself uncertain and short-lived, was undoubtedly influenced by reaction from the forward policy of Gambetta. On the other hand it is impossible to acquit Britain altogether of responsibility, or to find other justification than that of Lord Cromer, who favoured any measure which increased British activity in Egypt.* In the first days of July Admiral Seymour had received orders to "destroy earthworks and silence batteries" if he could not otherwise prevent work on the fortifications, and on the 4th, while he was instructed to invite the co-operation of the French admiral, he was also told: "We do not know the orders given by the French Government to their Admiral but you are not to postpone acting on your instructions because French decline to join you." † On the 5th the Cabinet decided that British troops should be sent to Egypt in "certain eventualities".‡ The British bombardment of Alexandria began on 11 July 1882. Granville did not wholly share Gladstone's hesitations§ (**Doc. 164**), but rather welcomed the incursion of decisive force into the slow movement of the Conference at Constantinople, and hardly regretted the abstention of France.]

Document 164. *Granville explains his attitude to the bombardment,* 12 *July* 1882‖

I have asked Münster to obtain the Chancellor's views as to what means are to be used if the Sultan refuses or delays.

Münster feels sure that his chief will be reticent.

A bombardment is a horrible thing, but it will clear the air and accelerate a solution of some sort or other.

---

* Cp. Cromer, *Modern Egypt*, [1908], I, 323–30. Cp. also the dispatch explaining British action, Granville to Dufferin, No. 389A, 11 July 1882, *F.O.* 78/3378. *V. A. & P.*, [1882], LXXXII, [C. 3258], 439–54. The dispatch was laid as a separate paper on 20 July.

† Admiralty to Admiral Seymour, Tels. 3 and 4 July 1882, *F.O.* 78/3471.

‡ *V.* Fitzmaurice, *Life of Granville*, [1905], II, 266.

§ Cp. Morley, *Life of Gladstone*, [1903], III, Bk. VIII, Chap. v, 80–6.

‖ G. & D. 29/206, *Pte Granville Papers.* Granville to Ampthill, Private, 12 July 1882. Part printed in Fitzmaurice, *Life of Granville*, [1905], II, 267.

It is well also for a country whose strength is maritime, that naval demonstrations sh[oul]d not be thought to be absolutely without a sting.

I am as decided as ever against a dual armed and political intervention of the English and French. One great objection is that if you differ you immediately come to a deadlock.

66. OPERATIONS IN THE SOUDAN

[The first step towards British intervention by force in Egypt roused less opposition among the Powers than those that succeeded it. Undoubtedly neither Gladstone nor Granville wished for an occupation of Egypt that should last longer than was essential for the re-establishment of the Khedive's government on the old footing. Both were sincere in preferring indirect to direct responsibility. When Tel-el-Kebir had established the success of the English troops in the autumn of 1882, Granville issued a circular to the Powers explaining his attitude to continued intervention.* The Queen alone professed anxiety lest the results of success should be thrown away. Gladstone and Granville, hard put to it to defend their policy in Parliament,† tried in vain to put responsibility on their predecessors,‡ and thought of confining their obligation within narrow geographical limits. But a new fanatic, the Mahdi, revolted in the Soudan, defeated the Egyptian troops, and at the same time destroyed Gladstone's policy. In November 1883, when the Mahdi had again routed Egyptian forces, Chérif Pasha sounded Baring (Cromer) as to whether Britain would send English or Indian troops, hinting that the alternative was to ask help of Turkey. Baring asked Granville for instructions, giving as his own view that "the wisest course for the Egyptian Gov[ernmen]t to adopt is to accept defeat and fall back on whatever point on the Nile they can hold with confidence".§ Granville telegraphed back, "We cannot send English or Indian Troops. Do not encourage British officers to volunteer. It could not be for the advantage of Egypt to invite Turkish Troops into the Soudan." And then came the logical conclusion from all this. "If consulted recommend abandonment of the Soudan within certain limits",‖ and a few days later, "We

---

* Granville's circular dispatch, 3 January 1883, *F.O.* 244/365. *V. A. & P.*, [1883], LXXXIII, [C. 3462], 38–40. Communication to the Powers was delayed until the 13th. Cp. Fitzmaurice, *Life of Granville*, [1905], II, 306 sqq.

† *Hans. Deb.*, 3rd Ser., CCLXXVI, 1300–22, 2 March 1883.

‡ *V.* Temperley and Penson, *Century of Diplomatic Blue Books*, 299–301.

§ Baring to Granville, Tel. No. 163 Confidential, 19 November 1883, *F.O.* 78/3562.

‖ Granville to Baring, Tel. No. 99, 20 November 1883, *F.O.* 78/3561.

can take no steps which will throw upon us the responsibility of operations in the Soudan which must rest with the Egyptian Gov[ernmen]t relying on their own resources". On this occasion, in order, as he explained to Gladstone, "not to leave Baring quite en l'air", Granville added: "We think that the restricting the operations as proposed by the Egyptian Gov[ernmen]t to defensive operations seems to be, reasonable."* In December the same policy was reiterated even more definitively. It was unfortunate for Gladstone and Granville that their policy involved the holding of Khartoum "if possible sufficiently long to allow advanced posts of Soudan to rejoin... [and then] to fall back from Khartoum on to Egypt proper",† and that this proved difficult of achievement and disastrous in result.]

Document 165. *Granville defines the attitude of the Government,* 13 *December* 1883‡

H[er] M[ajesty's] Gov[ernmen]t have had under their consideration your recent telegrams on the subject of the Soudan.

H[er] M[ajesty's] Gov[ernmen]t have no intention of employing British or Indian troops in that province.

H[er] M[ajesty's] Gov[ernmen]t have no objection to offer to the employment of Turkish troops provided they are paid by the Turkish Gov[ernmen]t and that such employment be restricted exclusively to the Soudan, with their base at Suakim.

Except for securing the safe retreat of the garrisons still holding positions in the Soudan H[er] M[ajesty's] Gov[ernmen]t cannot agree to increasing the burden on the Egyptian revenue by expenditure for operations which even if successful and this is not probable, would be of doubtful advantage to Egypt.

H[er] M[ajesty's] Gov[ernmen]t recommend the Ministers of the Khedive to come to an early decision to abandon all territory South of Assouan, or at least of Wadi Halfa.

They will be prepared to assist in maintaining order in

* Granville to Baring, Tel. No. 105, 25 November 1883, *F.O.* 78/3561.
† Baring to Granville, Tel. No. 181 Confidential, 25 November 1883, *F.O.* 78/3562.
‡ Granville to Baring, Extender of Tel. No. 128A, 13 December 1883, *F.O.* 78/3551.

Egypt proper and in defending it as well as the ports in the Red Sea.

The proposed employment of Sebehr Pasha appears to H[er] M[ajesty's] Gov[ernmen]t inexpedient both politically and as regards the Slave Trade.

[On 4 January 1884 Granville urged that the defence of Khartoum should not be attempted: "All military operations excepting those for the rescue of outlying garrisons should cease in the Soudan, excepting in the ports of the Red Sea where assistance can be afforded by Her Majesty's Naval forces;... Her Majesty's Gov[ernmen]t", he added, "will on their part be prepared to assist in maintaining order in Egypt proper and in defending it as well as the Ports in the Red Sea."* The work of evacuation entailed Gordon's expedition. In July, when Granville was drafting a dispatch to Egerton prescribing the methods to be adopted in certain questions of internal reform,† Gordon was besieged in Khartoum. His danger was not realized; the decision to send an expedition to his relief was delayed until August; the Egyptian policy of the Liberal administration closed amidst storms of criticism roused by the disaster of Gordon's death.]

67. THE EGYPTIAN CONFERENCE AND THE COLONIAL QUESTION

[The significance of the Egyptian adventure can hardly be exaggerated. Liberal discredit, important as it seemed at the time, was one of the least far-reaching of its effects. Egypt remained a constant factor in British policy until 1914. It inflamed or at least affected almost every international transaction. After producing intense irritation in France for a score of years, it led to the Anglo-French *entente*. It helped much to irritate and to disturb Anglo-German relations. Salisbury's plaint in 1887—"I heartily wish we had never gone into Egypt. Had we not done so, we could snap our fingers at all the world"‡— was no idle reflection. So long as Anglo-French rivalries in Egypt were unsolved, and the British position in the country was undefined and unrecognized, the rest of Europe was in a position to bargain with Britain, to put pressure on her, or to force her hand. And, as might have been expected, the first person to recognize this fact was Bismarck.

The financial situation in Egypt, always bad during this period, was critical in 1883–4, when the expenses of the Soudan campaign

* Granville to Baring, No. 5 Secret, 4 January 1884, *F.O.* 78/3662.
† Granville to Egerton, No. 357, 25 July 1884, *F.O.* 78/3664.
‡ *V.* Cecil, *Life of Salisbury*, [1932], IV, 42.

were added to the other factors in financial insolvency. In the face of this crisis Granville issued invitations in April 1884 for a Conference of the Powers. France, under the guidance of Ferry, accepted unwillingly and on conditions.* Everything depended on the attitude of Bismarck, with whose representative the agents of the other Triple Alliance Powers could be depended upon to vote. It was between the invitation of April and the meeting of the Conference at the end of June that the colonial question first became an important issue in Anglo-German relations.†

Granville's dispatch (**Doc. 166**) records his first conversation with Bismarck's son on the occasion of the latter's special mission to England in June 1884.‡ The date, 14 June, is important. Fourteen days before the meeting of the Egyptian Conference Granville learnt for the first time of the strength of German feeling on the colonial question. Bismarck indeed was under the impression that his dispatch to Münster of 5 May§ had cleared away any British misapprehensions on this score, although by the beginning of June he was doubtful of the effectiveness of Münster's explanations.‖ It is not necessary to enter here into the merits of the colonial dispute of the moment—that relating to Angra Pequeña. The responsibility for the misunderstanding must be divided between Münster, whose Anglophile tendencies led him to minimize the strength of Bismarck's feeling, and Ampthill, whose failing health caused him to miss the significance of Bismarck's hints. Perhaps even more blame must be assigned to the British administrative system. The Foreign Office consulted the Colonial Office; the Colonial Office, under Derby, was itself dilatory and was made more so by the need for consulting the Government of the Cape. But, wherever the chief responsibility may lie, the fact remains that during the sessions of the Egyptian Conference Bismarck was in a state of extreme irritation with England, from which he never fully recovered during the period of the Gladstone administration. His fitful complaints of the numberless written communications made to him on the colonial question, his outburst to the new British Ambassador, Malet, about the deficiencies of Münster, the bitterness of his objection to

* Cp. D[ocuments] D[iplomatiques] F[rançais], [1933], 1re Sér., v, 274–5, No. 254, Ferry to d'Aubigny, 29 April 1884; 306, No. 286, Waddington to Ferry, 30 May 1884; 325–8, No. 311, 17 June 1884, enclosing copies of Anglo-French notes exchanged on 16–17 June.

† Cp. W. O. Aydelotte, 'The first German Colony and its diplomatic consequences', Camb. Hist. Journ., v, No. 3, [1937], 291–313. Cp. also A. J. P. Taylor, Germany's First Bid for Colonies, [1938], passim.

‡ Cp. G.P., [1922], iv, 64–76.   § V. G.P., [1922], iv, 50–2.

‖ V. G.P., iv, 59–62. On the question of the non-communication of Bismarck's dispatch, cp. Waddington's report of a conversation with Münster on 9 March 1885, in which the latter said that Bismarck owned that he had been mistaken about the communication of this dispatch, D.D.F., [1933], 1re Sér., v, 642, No. 618; cp. also Fitzmaurice, Life of Granville, [1905], ii, 427–8.

publication in British Blue Books, regardless of the fact that on colonial questions he published White Books himself—all these signs point convincingly to the seriousness of Anglo-German tension. It was not until March 1885 that any solution was found for the various colonial problems under dispute.* It is little wonder, therefore, that Bismarck supported France at the Egyptian Conference, and at the critical moment left Britain completely isolated among the Powers.]

Document 166. *Bismarck uses the Egyptian Conference to bargain with Granville on Colonial Questions,* 14 *June* 1884†

In the course of the Conversation reported in my previous despatch of this day's date, Count Herbert Bismarck observed that while Prince Bismarck still entertained the same friendly feelings towards Her Majesty's Gov[ernmen]t, and was desirous of supporting their policy in Egypt, His Highness thought it right that I should be warned that the feeling in Germany as regards these Colonial questions was so strong that with the best wishes he felt he should be unable to afford us the same friendly assistance as hitherto, unless he could give some satisfaction to public opinion on the subject.

I said that I objected to anything in the nature of a bargain between us. Each question ought to be discussed on its own merits.

As regards Egypt, I relied upon the support of the Chancellor. My reliance was based on two grounds; firstly the very friendly attitude which His Highness had invariably maintained towards us, both in words and deeds; and secondly the general policy which during the four years I had been in office, His Highness had consistently and successfully pursued with a view to maintaining the peace of Europe.

The failure of the Conference I observed, would be a great disaster, and might lead to very serious complications.

* Cp. *G.P.*, [1922], IV, 100–7. Report of Count Herbert Bismarck, 7 March 1885. *V.* also *A. & P.*, [1884–5], LV, [C. 4442], 551–8; exchanges of notes took place between 29 April and 16 June.

† Granville to Ampthill, No. 169B Confidential, 14 June 1884. Endorsed: "Seen by Mr. Gladstone and by the Queen." *F.O.* 64/1102.

Count H. Bismarck said that he did not raise any question of bargain, but the German Gov[ernmen]t expected their rights to be respected.

I replied that if the German Gov[ernmen]t had rights, which we, on examination could admit, Count H. Bismarck might be sure that we should not only do so, but be ready to meet the German Gov[ernmen]t with great cordiality in the matter.

68. THE BRITISH OCCUPATION OF EGYPT

[The echoes of the Soudan tragedy were still sounding when Granville became involved in a further crisis. In the spring of 1885 England came to the brink of war with Russia. The repercussions of the so-called Penjdeh incident were widespread. It originated in the policy of the two Powers for developing and protecting their Central Asiatic interests;* but the fear of conflict reacted on the position of Britain in all directions. It interrupted her pursuance of the Soudan campaign. It strengthened the bonds that linked the Three Emperors in an *entente* hostile to Britain, and gave a practical example of the differences of principle as to the reading of the Rule of the Straits† which Salisbury and Shuvalov had exhibited at Berlin. Finally, it gave a new significance to the attitude of Turkey.

Though Turkish support was important at this moment, Granville refused to abandon his Egyptian policy to gain it (**Doc. 167**). In spite of the warning in September 1884 that the Three Emperors were about to discuss the Egyptian question "in a sense hostile to England and favourable to France",‡ and in spite of evidence that France, Austria-Hungary and Germany were supporting Russia in her representations to Turkey, Granville maintained unaltered his determination not to give way to Turkish protests.

In view of these circumstances particular interest attaches to the Turkish views expressed in June 1885 to Salisbury, and to Salisbury's comments on the situation bequeathed to him by his predecessors (**Doc. 168**).]

* Cp. *Cambridge History of India*, [1932], VI, 423–5, for an outline of the incident.
† Cp. *supra*, pp. 382, 412.
‡ Dufferin to Granville, Tel. No. 42 Secret, 2 September 1884, *F.O.* 78/3629.

Document 167. *Granville explains the impossibility of fixing a date for the evacuation of Egypt, 28 April 1885**

Since date of despatches by Last messenger I have had several interviews with Hassan Fehmi Pasha. I have told him that we could not fix a date for evacuation of Egypt. I have agreed to Turkish Commissioner going to Cairo to discuss with Government and our officials future organization of army.

I have pressed for views of the Porte as to sending Turkish troops to Suakin and Zeila. When we occupied latter we had promised to hand it over to Sultan if desired. There was now a question of other foreign nations going there. We could not remain indefinitely and wanted early answer.

With regard to Soudan I mentioned our wish to curtail our operations, and in answer to a question from him as to Government reverting to Sultan said we should be glad to have his opinion or that of the Porte as to future form of Government.

I have arranged with Hassan Fehmi the terms of an Iradé to be issued by the Sultan sanctioning Egyptian laws and confirming legislative rights of Khedive and also a draft of an Act for the neutralization of Egypt to be presented to the Powers by England and Turkey.

Secret. With regard to the attitude of Turkey in the event of a war between England and Russia I have abstained from putting any pressure on the Sultan and have confined myself to urging upon Fehmi Pasha and Musurus the importance in the interests of Turkey of his not fettering his liberty of action by any hasty engagements.

Document 168. *Turkey complains to Salisbury of the policy of the Liberal Administration, 30 June 1885*†

The Turkish Ambassador called to-day and expressed to me the discontent of the Sultan with the events that had taken place in Egypt, especially with the invasion of Egypt by England. H[is] E[xcellency] said that the Sultan's desire was that while recognising the position of England in respect

---

* Granville to White, Tel. No. 46 Confidential, 28 April 1885, *F.O.* 195/1504.
† Salisbury to White, No. 238, 30 June 1885, *F.O.* 78/3746.

to Egypt, and her claim to a preferential influence, the authority of H[is] M[ajesty] over that part of his dominions should be established. In doing so he guarded himself specially against being supposed to wish to interfere with any of the existing rights of the Khedive of Egypt under the firmans. He was of opinion that England had no right to alienate the whole of the Soudan from Egypt, because it was an integral part of theOttoman dominions, and that Khartoum was absolutely necessary to the good order of Egypt. He thought that by a good understanding with the Sultan, the Turkish army, or an army raised with the consent of the Sultan, might be used in place of the Egyptian army that had been destroyed, both to maintain the Egyptian power in Khartoum and Dongola, and also to uphold the Khedive's authority at Cairo.

I told H[is] E[xcellency] that I was well aware of all the difficulties of the present situation, that I quite recognised the fact that an attempt on the part of a Christian power to assume the government over a purely Mussulman population would be very arduous, and that, as far as it was practicable, Mussulmans were better under the dominion of a Mussulman government. I also said that I recognised that for many purposes a Turkish army would be far more effective in the provinces of Upper Egypt and the Lower Soudan than British troops could be, because the latter were little able to bear the influences of the climate, and had to struggle with the religious prejudices of the people. But at the same time I said that no step of immediate retreat was possible: that though we were very anxious to maintain the rights of the Sultan and the provisions of treaties, we were responsible for the condition of Egypt at the present moment, and we could not abandon it hastily; and that even such a measure as the introduction of Turkish troops could not be contemplated until we had dealt in the first place with the financial difficulty, and in the second had satisfied ourselves that such a measure would meet with the concurrence of other powers. I looked however for the ultimate solution of the Egyptian question more to a good understanding between England and the Porte than to any other mode of dealing with it.

XXII. SALISBURY, ROSEBERY, IDDESLEIGH, 1885–6

BULGARIA AND BATOUM

69. SALISBURY ADAPTS HIS NEAR EASTERN POLICY TO THE CIRCUMSTANCES OF THE TIMES

[After the Penjdeh question had been settled, a serious crisis arose over Bulgaria. It began in September 1885 with the rebellion in Eastern Roumelia, and the decision of Prince Alexander of Battenberg to reunite the Bulgarias by adding Eastern Roumelia to his dominion. Salisbury had then been in power for three months, and had already shewn friendliness to the Central Powers. His private letter to Bismarck of 2 July expressed his wish to recover "the good understanding between the two countries which we value as of supreme importance, but which in recent times has been slightly clouded"; and although Bismarck's reply was cautious and even cool,* Salisbury persisted in his policy of co-operation. His first instruction to Constantinople now was: "As a general rule you may associate yourself with any advice in which your Austrian and German colleagues join." †

But if the first principle on which Salisbury acted was that of co-operation with Germany, there was another of equal importance in his view. In the telegram to Constantinople which has already been quoted, he emphasized the fact that his policy was "to act with the other Powers in upholding [the] Treaty of Berlin...our interests are not sufficient to justify our acting alone". In this respect, he took his stand on the policy, which had been maintained so strongly by his predecessors in office, that in Near Eastern affairs it was the Concert of Europe that must act, and on the lines of the Treaty settlement. On the plea that "isolated action" was undesirable, Salisbury refused, on 23 September, Bismarck's suggestion that he should send "the Mediterranean fleet eastward, not to Besika Bay, but perhaps to the Piraeus" in order to "give the Sultan moral support".‡ He was prepared—in his own words —"in concert with other Powers, to move diplomatically", and to suggest to the Cabinet "any proposals for more energetic action of a conjoint character".

---

* *G.P.*, [1922], IV, 132–4. Both Salisbury's letter and Bismarck's reply are given there.

† Salisbury to White, Tel. No. 85A, 22 September 1885, *F.O.* 78/3757.

‡ Malet to Salisbury, Tel. No. 74, 22 September 1885; Salisbury to Malet, Tel. No. 90, 23 September 1885, *F.O.* 64/1081.

Unfortunately for the success of this plan, the members of the Dreikaiserbund were bound to one another by secret understandings of which Salisbury knew little,* and Austria-Hungary was tied by her Treaty with Servia of 1881. Faced by his growing realization of these factors, Salisbury accepted the proposal for a Conference at Constantinople, supported as it was by Bismarck. His telegraphic instructions to the British representative shew that he had considerable doubt as to the result (**Doc. 169**).

Both to France and to Austria-Hungary Salisbury reiterated his view that he was "opposed to the deposition of Prince Alexander", and he made no attempt to conceal his motive that "any successor would certainly be more Russian than he is".† In his first reply to the proposal for a Conference he insisted that it was "impossible for Her Majesty's Government to give their adherence to a proposal" which "would involve a Turkish military execution conducted in Eastern Roumelia with the Sanction of Europe"; a possibility which he characterized as "at variance with the principles on which in recent times the policy of England has been conducted".‡ Finally, after some pressure by Bismarck, Salisbury accepted the invitation to enter the Conference, although on condition that he reserved "full Liberty" if coercive measures were proposed. In fact his delay had made possible the victory of Alexander. When consent was given to the Conference Salisbury telegraphed instructions, cautioning his representative against going too far in agreement with the other Powers. "No kind of sanction", he said, "is to be given by you to any declaration in favour of the *status quo ante* without reference to me"; and again: "If any Member of the Conference proposes any step which under Treaty is now in the power of the Porte, it should be objected to as not within the competence of the Conference.... The business of a Conference is with international relations, and European Law, not with the acts of internal administration to be taken in the dominions of one of its Members under existing Treaty rights."§ He himself prescribed a formula forthwith (**Doc. 170**).

Some important consequences followed from these principles. From France, and from France alone, could the British representative at the Conference find any support. There was an essential antagonism between the views on which Austria-Hungary and Russia had agreed and those which the British representative was instructed to maintain. Moreover, the British position was

---

* Cp. however Paget's report on the subject, Paget to Salisbury, No. 267, 24 September 1885, *F.O.* 7/1079.

† Salisbury to Paget, Tel. No. 48, 28 September 1885; Salisbury to Walsham, No. 781 A, 28 September 1885, *F.O.* 27/2727.

‡ Salisbury to Malet, No. 453, 16 October 1885, *F.O.* 64/1075. This is an extender of Tel. No. 128, 16 October 1885, *F.O.* 64/1081.

§ Salisbury to White, Tels. Nos. 192 and 193, 11 November 1885, *F.O.* 78/3757.

made more difficult by the fact that Salisbury was "taking a new departure" in the Bulgarian question.* He was, indeed, resisting Europe, while ostensibly acting in concert with her. He was following a policy which implied a modification of the Treaty of Berlin, while preserving its sanctity by an "act of veneration" (**Doc. 171**). Salisbury published his defence in a long Blue-Book dispatch, and gave further explanations in Parliament.† He was silent, however, on three points. He had pinned his faith to Austria-Hungary, and her secret understandings with Russia and Servia destroyed his plan; he was subject to constant pressure from the Queen, who was strongly in favour of Prince Alexander; he was determined that Russian influence should not prevail. In such circumstances his ability to impose his terms was the result rather of the victory of Slivnitsa and the hastiness of the Sultan than of any inherent strength in his attitude. Yet the effect in the eyes of Europe was important. He had re-asserted English influence in continental affairs—Bismarck's cordiality grew substantially as a result—and he had prepared the way for the work of Rosebery in freeing foreign policy from the domination of party politics.‡]

Document 169. *Salisbury gives instructions for the Conference at Constantinople,* 28 September 1885§

It seems doubtful whether Austria is in favour of maintaining the Prince of Bulgaria; but there is a strong vein of Russian influence just now at Vienna. Andrassy denounces Kalnoky as the dupe of Russia. Germany and France have shown no inclination to get rid of Prince of Bulgaria. French Amb[assado]r's language was favourable to the idea of personal union in the Prince. There is no doubt that any successor would be much more Russian. You should therefore not admit that suggestion at all.

The Powers seem inclined to do their best to keep Greece and Servia from acting. But Austria is the only Power who has any hold in Servia, and her policy is obscure just now.

It would be desirable to keep up all the Sultan's rights as to Eastern Roumelia, except the nomination of the Governor

---

* Sir William White's idea of "the Balkans for the Balkan peoples" was substantially that of Salisbury, and he applied it to Bulgaria at this time.

† A. & P., [1886], LXXV, [C. 4612], 221–3. The original draft in *F.O.* 78/3747 shews that the dispatch (dated 2 November) was printed unaltered.

‡ Cp. however *infra*, p. 512 n.

§ Salisbury to White, Tel. No. 101, 28 September 1885, *F.O.* 78/3757.

General. Special security should if possible be provided for the tribute.

Sultan should be pressed to keep as much force as he can in Macedonia, especially on the Bulgarian and Servian frontiers.

French Gov[ernmen]t profess to be very anxious to act with us in this matter.

I have instructed Rumbold to urge inaction on the Greek Gov[ernmen]t. Let me know if you hear of any Greek intrigues either in Crete or Macedonia or Albania.

Document 170. *Salisbury finds a formula for the Bulgarian situation, 19 November 1885**

...I subjoin the text of resolutions as I should prefer them to stand....

Considering that the order of things legally established by the Treaty of Berlin was set aside by a popular movement; and that the Prince of Bulgaria who had subsequently occupied the province, has now withdrawn himself and his troops from it:

1. The Sublime Porte with the sanction of the Powers will appoint a special Commissioner ad hoc for the maintenance of order in Eastern Roumelia and invites the inhabitants thereof to submit themselves to his authority during the continuance of his office.

2. The Sublime Porte in its solicitude for the well-being of the populations proposes at the same time to the Conference to nominate a sub-commission, which will enter immediately on its duties, and which will take into consideration the condition of the people in Eastern Roumelia, and the wishes they may express through their Legislative Assemblies, and will report to the Conference its advice as to the order of things to be definitively sanctioned by the Sublime Porte and the Powers.

These resolutions shall be simultaneously intimated to the authorities in Eastern Roumelia.

* Salisbury to White, Tel. No. 204, 19 November 1885, *F.O.* 78/3757.

Document 171. *Salisbury defines the British attitude to the Treaty of Berlin, 4 December 1885**

Count Hatzfeldt has I think forgotten one essential point on which we talked a good deal, namely that the words "within the limits of the Treaty of Berlin" must be left out of the second resolution, where they occur twice. We agreed to substitute an "act of veneration" for the Treaty of Berlin: and this if it had been proposed Sir W. White would have accepted. I have read the Protocols of the seventh sitting† and M. de Relichoff (followed by the R.R. of Austria Germany and Italy) expressed himself emphatically against any language that would leave it open to the populations to hope for a change in the Treaty of Berlin.

The rash act of the Sultan in dispensing with the assent of the Conference and doing that, of his own authority, which he had asked the Conference leave to do, makes our position one of extreme difficulty. He has in so doing broken the Treaty of Berlin in two points: he has appointed a Governor-General without the consent of the Powers: and he has appointed a Moslem instead of a Christian. It is impossible *now* for the Conference to pass the first resolution without, in the first instance, passing a censure on the Porte for having broken the Treaty of Berlin, just as was done a month ago in reference to Prince Alexander.

The Conference—and especially England—has been treated with so much disrespect by the Porte, that I hardly like to give any instructions of a conceding character to Sir W. White, until we have some very distinct assurances as to the course which will be taken. . . .

70. ROSEBERY AND THE CONTINUITY OF BRITISH FOREIGN POLICY

[The few months of Liberal administration between 3 February and 20 July 1886 are mainly important because they initiated Rosebery into the work of the Foreign Office.

The political situation in England made it likely that the administration would be short-lived. Gladstone was almost wholly

* Salisbury to Pauncefote, 4 December 1885, *F.O.* 64/1075.
† *V. A. & P.*, [1886], LXXV, [C. 4612], 372–83.

occupied with the Irish problem. The European crisis over Bulgaria was still unsettled. For all these reasons it was urgent to avoid a breach in the foreign policy of Britain, and Rosebery was clearly at some pains to emphasize its continuity. In his first conversation with the Austro-Hungarian Ambassador he expressed his resolve to continue Salisbury's policy of co-operation with Germany in questions of the Near East, and Hatzfeldt said that similar assurances had been given to him.* Two days after his advent to power Rosebery instructed Rumbold, then British minister at Athens, that the new Government proposed to maintain to the fullest extent the policy of its predecessors in relation to Greece.† He reiterated to Waddington Salisbury's wish that France should co-operate in the naval demonstration at the Piræus. In fact, he went a step in advance of Salisbury in co-operation with the Powers. The French *Chargé d'affaires* at Constantinople reported on 17 February that an important change had taken place in the diplomatic situation. Formerly, he said, "Russia, supported by Germany, had led a diplomatic campaign against an isolated England". Now it was Russia who stood alone; and Germany and England who took the initiative.‡ By the end of the month terms had been arranged for a settlement between Turkey and Bulgaria and for peace between Bulgaria and Servia, and if the position of Prince Alexander was weaker under this settlement than it might have been had Salisbury been in power, in principle at least Rosebery had followed his predecessor. In respect of Greece he carried Salisbury's policy to its logical conclusion, taking the lead among the Powers in the movement which ultimately forced her to disarm. As he wrote to Malet on 24 February, he preferred pressure without force. "It would be an excellent thing if we could get Greece to give way without the portentous machinery of a blockade." But he added at the end of the same letter: "Do not mistake me. I am as determined as ever to proceed with the blockade should the Greeks not give way."§ Probably nothing could have achieved more in the direction of disabusing the minds of foreign statesmen of the idea that changes in Government in England brought changes in foreign policy than this action in the matter of Greece. It is interesting to note that the Queen appears to have exerted her influence on Rosebery in the direction maintaining continuity of policy.‖]

* W.S.A. VIII/103, Berichte aus England. Károlyi to Kálnoky, No. 83 Confidential, 17 February 1886.
† Rosebery to Rumbold, No. 25A, 8 February 1886, *F.O.* 32/571. Cp. *A. & P.*, [1886], LXXIV, [C. 4765], 574.
‡ Hanotaux to Freycinet, 17 February 1886, *D.D.F.*, [1934], 1re Sér., VI, 203–6, No. 191.
§ Lord Crewe, *Lord Rosebery*, [1931], I, 263–4. Rosebery to Malet, Private, 24 February 1886.
‖ Cp. *Letters of Queen Victoria*, [1930], 3rd Ser., I, 47–8. Cp. also *infra*, p. 512 n.

Document 172. *Rosebery maintains the policy of his predecessors in relation to Greece, 8 February* 1886*

The Greek Minister called upon me here today by appointment.

In reply to an enquiry from me, he stated that he had received and communicated to his Government a letter which the Prime Minister, as the only Minister actually appointed of the new Government, had addressed to him on the 2nd instant.

In that letter Mr. Gladstone informed him that he had thought it right to ascertain from the most trustworthy sources what were the engagements with respect to the peace of the East into which this country had already entered under the auspices of Her Majesty's late Government. As the result of his enquiries, he could not doubt that Her Majesty is engaged to the other Powers in the terms of the recent note, which conveyed an intimation to Greece as to the course to be pursued by the Powers in the event of an attack by Greece upon Turkey, in the absence of a just cause of war.

In making this communication, Mr. Gladstone stated that he was far from signifying any change of views or of his good wishes for the prosperity of Greece, practical evidence of which would not be wanting should he at any time be able to give it compatibly with the interests of peace and of justice to others.

M. Gennadius said that M. Delyannis had sent an answer which he thought must have already reached Mr. Gladstone. This answer contained a statement respecting the present state of affairs in Greece, which M. Gennadius repeated to me, adding that, in his opinion, no Government could exist in Greece which did not pursue the present warlike course.

I then informed M. Gennadius that on Her Majesty's Government acceding to office they had found engagements entered into with regard to Greece from which they could not recede, and that I was bound to say I considered their

* Rosebery to Rumbold, No. 25A, 8 February 1886. Endorsed: "Mr. Gladstone, The Queen." *F.O.* 32/571. *A. & P.,* [1886], LXXIV, [C. 4765], 574.

fulfilment to be for the best interests of peace and of Greece herself. The instructions therefore to our fleet and to our Minister at Athens remained in force.

I was happy, however, to think that Mr. Gladstone's letter furnished a bridge of honour for Greece, as it could be no discredit to her to yield to the advice of so old and approved a friend.

After some further conversation, in which he alluded to the provisions of the Treaty of Berlin, M. Gennadius asked me whether there were no hope of Her Majesty's Government prevailing upon Turkey to concede the remaining portion of that accession of territory which had been suggested by that instrument.

I replied that we had only to deal with the present condition of affairs, and that in any case it would be impossible to make any application on behalf of Greece while she continued in her present armed and threatening attitude, and therefore on that subject I could say nothing.

M. Gennadius promised to telegraph to M. Delyannis the substance of what I had said to him.

71. BATOUM AND THE STRAITS

[The Russian decision to alter the status of Batoum was made known to Rosebery on 3 July 1886. The Russian Ambassador, Baron de Staal, was carefully instructed by M. de Giers as to the explanations which he should make, and every effort was used to persuade Rosebery that the change was in no way a breach of the Treaty of Berlin, and that its motives were purely economic. The port was to remain "essentially commercial", in accordance with the requirements of the Treaty of Berlin, and the withdrawal of the privileges of "free port" status was the result merely of the necessity for removing the hardships on the inhabitants which the existing *régime* entailed.*

Rosebery's response was vigorous, although he was careful to safeguard himself against the implication that he might follow words by action. The dispatch recording his views was described by Giers as "the most wounding [blessante] communication that one Power could address to another", and Giers rightly termed it a "Blue-Book Dispatch", for it was laid before Parliament on

* Cp. A. Meyendorff, *Correspondance diplomatique du Baron de Staal*, [1929], I, 299–300.

19 August. It is difficult at first sight to justify Rosebery's indignation or to explain his insistence on the connexion between the "free port" status of Batoum and Salisbury's declaration at Berlin concerning the Rule of the Straits. But two facts throw light on his attitude. The Russian communication followed closely in point of time the crisis over Penjdeh, when the question of the Straits was of first importance, and the Bulgarian crisis, when Russian policy in the Balkans roused considerable suspicion. Further, Rosebery clearly disbelieved the explanation of de Giers. He wrote a minute on the margin of one of Morier's dispatches reporting the assurances of de Giers as to the future status of Batoum: "This is strange when we know that Batoum is being strongly fortified."

Whatever the reasons for Rosebery's attitude, the language used in his dispatch was too severe. He over-emphasized the binding nature of the obligation, and he assumed that Russia was violating the Treaty when she was, in fact, interpreting a dubious clause to her advantage. Moreover, his statements invite comparison with his own attitude later to the Mediterranean Agreement of December 1887. He speaks of the "direct, supreme and perpetual interest" of maintaining "the binding force and sanctity of international engagements"—a principle which "Great Britain is ready at all times and in all seasons to uphold". These are very comprehensive terms; they were enunciated to Russia and published in a Blue Book. Yet when faced by the dilemma of 1892–4, Rosebery acknowledged his reluctance to take cognisance of an understanding which his predecessors had concluded, and belittled the binding character of their assurances to a foreign Power. He expressed these sentiments to a foreign ambassador, by his own admission, before he had read the terms of the understanding in question, and took refuge in complicated distinctions between arrangements which had the sanction of Parliament and those which had not.* This was hardly the best way of impressing upon foreign Powers the "binding force and sanctity of international engagements" or Britain's interest in upholding them.]

Document 173. *Rosebery writes a "Blue-Book" dispatch on Batoum*, 13 July 1886†

On the 3rd instant the Russian Ambassador delivered to me a copy of a Circular despatch from his Government announcing the determination of the Emperor of Russia to abrogate the clause of the LIXth Article of the Treaty of

* *V. infra*, pp. 475–6.
† Rosebery to Morier, No. 157, 13 July 1886, *F.O.* 65/1255. *A. & P.*, [1886], LXXIII, [C. 4857], 158–60.

Berlin, which declares His Majesty's intention to constitute Batoum a free port. It is argued in the Circular and the Memorandum annexed to it that this step is no infraction of the Treaty, as the Article is not an ordinary one, but rests on a spontaneous declaration of the late Emperor.

The Circular further explains that the inconvenience arising from the status of Batoum under the Treaty renders an alteration of that status necessary.

And lastly, it announces that as Batoum would remain essentially a commercial port, the situation would not be changed.

As regards the last point, I need only say that Her Majesty's Government fully appreciate this declaration.

I took the opportunity of at once pointing out to M. de Staal some of the considerations which occurred to me at first sight. These observations I have already recorded in my despatch No. 153 of the 3rd instant to your Excellency.

But it is necessary, without loss of time, to define the attitude of Her Majesty's Government in face of this proceeding.

In the first place, it must be understood that Her Majesty's Government cannot accept the view that this step on the part of Russia does not constitute an infraction of the Treaty of Berlin, of which, indeed, it obliterates a distinct stipulation. Granting the doctrine, which as far as Her Majesty's Government are aware is an entirely novel one, that the spontaneous declaration of His Majesty the late Emperor is not to be considered as binding because it was spontaneous, it cannot be denied that its embodiment in the Treaty placed it on the same footing as any other part of that instrument. If this be not so, for what reason was it inserted? Had it merely been desired to place an intention on record, the statements in the Protocol were more than sufficient. But there are further circumstances which are conclusive on this point.

I have already cited both to Your Excellency and to M. de Staal the passages from the Protocols to the Congress of Berlin, which show that Prince Bismarck and Count Andrássy on the part of Germany and Austria-Hungary, and Count Schouvaloff on the part of Russia, recognized the action of

Russia as 'constituting' Batoum a free port, not at the will and pleasure of the Russian Government, but as a definitive act, endorsed by Europe, and international in its character; while the British Plenipotentiaries stated that it was the condition on which they assented to the acquisition of Batoum by Russia. The declaration, accepted in this spirit and on this understanding, was embodied in an integral clause of the Treaty. It is, therefore, impossible to contend that this provision stands on a different footing from the other stipulations of that instrument. This being so, the terms of the Protocol of London of the 17th January, 1871, are applicable in all their force.* I have already cited it to your Excellency, and I need hardly repeat that the Great Powers on that occasion recognized by a solemn act "that it is an essential principle of the law of nations that no Power can liberate itself from the engagements of a Treaty, nor modify the stipulations thereof, unless with the consent of the Contracting Powers by means of an amicable arrangement". That consent Russia does not even seek on the present occasion. But it is scarcely possible that her Government should consider this international Act as having become obsolete, for it was appealed to by the Russian Plenipotentiary in the recent Conference at Constantinople. In the seventh sitting of that Conference, on the 25th November last, M. de Nélidoff remarked: "A un point de vue plus général, le maintien du Traité du Berlin était en accord avec les termes du Protocole signé à Londres le 17 Janvier, 1871, Protocole qui établit comme un principe essentiel du droit des gens", etc.

"Ce principe nous paraissait particulièrement applicable à la situation diplomatique produite par les récents engagements, et aucune Puissance n'ayant exprimé l'intention de s'écarter du Traité de Berlin, nous avions des raisons de croire à son maintien intégral."

To these observations the British Plenipotentiary replied: "Le fait de viser dans la Conférence l'un des Articles du Traité ne peut conduire à cette conclusion qu'on désire toucher à la validité du Traité lui-même; bien au contraire,

* Cp. *supra*, p. 331, and n.

le Gouvernement Anglais y tient tout autant que les autres Puissances."..."Aucune modification au texte d'un Article du Traité de Berlin ne peut évidemment être faite que du consentement unanime des Puissances, et c'est justement le terrain sur lequel le Gouvernement Britannique s'est toujours placé, et sur lequel il se maintient aujourd'hui."

Under these circumstances, Her Majesty's Government cannot recognize any amount of commercial inconvenience as furnishing a justification for a peremptory declaration of the Russian Government on its own sole authority that this portion of the Treaty is to be regarded as no longer valid. The question, from this point of view, is one which concerns all the Powers parties to the Declaration of the 19th January, 1871, and to the Treaty of Berlin.

Apart from the position of Great Britain as one of those Powers, Her Majesty's Government have little or no material interest in the question. As a matter of commerce, it may be remarked that the trade of France with Batoum is much the most considerable, that of Turkey comes next, and that of Great Britain is relatively small. Nor are there any further interests involved which mainly concern this country. Other Powers are, no doubt, directly or indirectly affected by the alteration of the commercial status of Batoum, but Her Majesty's Government do not feel that this is sensibly the case so far as Great Britain is concerned.

One direct, supreme, and perpetual interest, however, is no doubt at stake in this transaction—that of the binding force and sanctity of international engagements. Great Britain is ready at all times and in all seasons to uphold that principle, and she cannot palter with it in the present instance.

Her Majesty's Government cannot, therefore, consent to recognize or associate themselves in any shape or form with this proceeding of the Russian Government. They are compelled to place on record their view that it constitutes a violation of the Treaty of Berlin, unsanctioned by the signatory Powers, that it tends to make future Conventions of the kind difficult, if not impossible; and to cast doubt at least on those already concluded.

It must be for the other Powers to judge how far they can acquiesce in this breach of an international engagement. But in no case can Her Majesty's Government have any share in it. It must rest upon the sole responsibility of its authors.

Your Excellency will read and give a copy of this despatch to M. de Giers.

72. SALISBURY'S ATTITUDE TO THE BULGARIAN QUESTION, 1886

[On Salisbury's return to power in August 1886, he was faced by certain features in the foreign situation which vitally affected the policy of his administration. In the first place, while the Liberal Government had successfully maintained and developed good relations with Germany, its brief period of power had increased the alienation of France. The French Ambassador complained to Salisbury on 12 August of the *non possumus* attitude of Rosebery in colonial differences.* And in regard both to colonial questions and to those relating to the Suez Canal, Waddington had found Rosebery difficult of access and Gladstone distracted by Irish affairs. The second problem which immediately confronted Salisbury could not brook delay. On 21 August Prince Alexander made his first abdication at the pistol point, and on 7 September his abdication was made formal. A third problem was closely connected with this. The Russian alteration in the status of Batoum was looked upon, in some quarters of England at least, as the prelude to an aggressive Russian policy in the Balkans. Unfortunately for Salisbury, his Cabinet was divided as to the attitude to be taken. He was indeed supported by Iddesleigh, who was then Foreign Secretary; but as he reported to the Queen on 7 September: "A section of the Cabinet showed a strong inclination to depart from the traditional policy of this country of resisting the designs of Russia upon the Balkan Peninsula."† The leader of this section was the Chancellor of the Exchequer, Lord Randolph Churchill. The position was made more difficult by the fact that Churchill held long conversations with the ambassadors of foreign Powers, and by the growing differences, albeit on matters of detail, between Salisbury and the Foreign Secretary. The press was for the most part on Churchill's side. His resignation in December and the death of Iddesleigh in the following month ended a period in which Cabinet differences hampered, if they did not seriously damage, the conduct of foreign

* *D.D.F.*, [1934], 1re Sér., VI, 288–90, No. 284.
† Cecil, *Life of Salisbury*, [1931], III, 319.

relations. Salisbury was now able to resume his personal control of foreign affairs.

In the interval, Britain was compelled by force of circumstances to declare her hand on Near Eastern questions. The most hopeful ally for a policy of maintaining the *status quo* in the Balkans was Austria-Hungary, and at the end of September Paget, then British Ambassador at Vienna, was instructed to communicate a confidential memorandum to Kálnoky setting forth the British position (**Doc. 174**). The memorandum, as the German Ambassador at Vienna rightly commented,* made no specific proposals. It was clearly, however, a preliminary sounding as to the possibility of Anglo-Austrian co-operation and has, therefore, an important place in the moves for an Anglo-Austrian *entente* which preceded the conclusion of the Mediterranean Agreement at the beginning of the following year. It is important also because, at the time at which it was presented, Austria-Hungary was developing her policy in the direction of the complete break-up of the Dreikaiserbund. Finally, it contained a specific statement of the fact that for Constantinople at least England would fight.]

Document 174. *Confidential Memorandum communicated to Austria-Hungary on 2 October* 1886†

Whatever some newspapers may say it is certain that English interests must be largely affected by any important changes at Constantinople, or in the Balkan Peninsula. The physical, and perhaps still more the moral advance of Russia threatens our communications with our Eastern possessions, and may directly and indirectly shake our power over our Mahometan subjects. We may not be primarily so much interested in the independence of Bulgaria and the smaller Balkan States as Austria-Hungary; but the growing power of Russia in those countries is of nearly as much consequence to us, and threatens us with almost as serious changes as Austria-Hungary can herself apprehend. I cannot doubt that the Austrian statesmen realise these dangers, and I should hope that they see that what is now going on in Bulgaria cannot be neglected either by themselves or by England.

---

* *G.P.*, [1922], IV, 277, Prince Henry of Reuss to Bismarck, 4 October 1886.
† W.S.A. VIII/105, ff. 99–103. Communication by the British Ambassador at Vienna. It is dated 'September 1886', but is endorsed as communicated on 2 October. The draft is in F.O. 7/1092.

The question is, at what point, and in what manner, can a stand be made to avert this mischief.

At the present moment it seems as if one of two things must happen in Bulgaria. Either the Russians will quietly monopolise all influence there, in which case they will be in no hurry to take any alarming step such as the occupation of the country; or the Bulgarians will resist, will stand up for their independence, and will so give the Russians a pretext for coming in with a corps d'armée to preserve order.

I hope that, in the second of these supposed cases, Europe would take care to interpose, and would protest against Russia's assuming alone to deal with a matter of general European concern: and, if such should be the feeling of other Powers, I am confident that England would take an active part in insisting on proper measures being adopted to secure the rights of Europe, and the independence of the Bulgarians. In such a cause I feel sure that an English Government of whatever shade of politics, might count on the hearty support of the people.

The more dangerous of the two alternatives which I have suggested is undoubtedly the first. It is to be feared that Russia may so influence the Bulgarian people that, partly by cajolery, partly by fear, and partly by corruption, they may practically give themselves up to her. In that case the influence would be exerted not only over the Balkan States, but over Constantinople itself. The Sultan in the hands of Russia would be a very formidable power; and it could not be long before England would find herself in a position from which she would hardly be able to extricate herself without a serious war, which might lead to consequences at present beyond calculation.

It might seem a matter of course that we should take early steps to anticipate and prevent these dangers. But the Constitution of this Country and the play of Party, place great obstacles in the way of adopting a far seeing policy, especially if it is a policy in which we seem to stand alone. For a clearly defined object such as the defence of Constantinople, England no doubt would fight. Whether she would do so to obviate the danger of an attack is very questionable, unless she had the full support of some other Powers.

The circumstances of this Autumn have been very disquieting. The outrage on the Prince of Bulgaria was a serious matter, and it was rendered more grave by the part played in it by Russia. But these are not the only alarming symptoms. The unwillingness of the Porte to take any step, although one was recommended to them, the unwillingness of the German Powers to join in any attempt to maintain Prince Alexander, even after his reception by the Bulgarians had demonstrated his popularity among his subjects, and the language which the Prince himself thought it necessary to adopt and which appeared to imply that he was under special obligations to Russia have all combined to show with what impunity Russia may carry on whatever designs she has formed.

What is to be done? It is difficult to say; but I think it quite clear that we must prepare for a long and difficult diplomatic struggle. We cannot work at once at Constantinople and in Bulgaria. We must endeavour to encourage the Porte to resist the blandishments and the menaces to which they will be exposed. I hope Sir William White will prove equal to the difficult task he will have to perform. But he will not succeed unless he knows, and unless the world knows that in the event of a crisis England will not stand alone but will have the active support of other Powers.

XXIII. SALISBURY, PRIME MINISTER AND FOREIGN SECRETARY, 1887–92

73. WAR CLOUDS IN THE SPRING OF 1887, AND THE FIRST MEDITERRANEAN AGREEMENT

[In the spring of 1887 there were two centres of anxiety in Europe. The Bulgarian throne was still vacant, for Ferdinand of Coburg's refusal in the winter of 1886 had not yet been transformed into his acceptance of the following August. And just at this time, when any settlement of this question might bring to a head the latent antagonisms among the Powers, one of the periodic Franco-German war scares was agitating Europe. There were rumours of a Franco-Russian understanding, and General Boulanger's ambitions gave to French policy a dangerous flavour of aggression. The fears of the neighbours of France—both Belgium and Italy—also contributed to lend a special importance to British policy in the early months of 1887.

At this time Anglo-Russian relations over the Bulgarian question improved. Salisbury laid down three points as the basis of his policy—clearly with a conciliatory intention. He recognized, first, British obligations under the Berlin Treaty; secondly, the legitimate desires of Russia; thirdly, he said that he would take into consideration "as far as possible" the national aspirations of Bulgaria.* The very vagueness of these principles added to their air of conciliation.

As the Bulgarian crisis became less acute Franco-German relations caused anxieties to Europe. "Waddington", wrote Salisbury on 24 January, "was...very uneasy." Hatzfeldt, the German Ambassador, was equally fearful of war. At the end of January the Belgian Prime Minister reminded Lord Vivian, the British Minister at Brussels, of the special engagements entered into by Britain in 1870, and enquired whether a similar undertaking would be given now. No reply was made to this enquiry by Salisbury. Then on 4 February appeared the famous letter signed "Diplomaticus" in the *Standard*, throwing doubt on the readiness of Britain to act in accordance with her obligations. The genesis of the article is discussed by Lady Gwendolen Cecil in her *Life of*

* Cp. the reports of Károlyi, Austro-Hungarian Ambassador in London, on 24 January and 2 February 1887. W.S.A. viii/105, Varia NB. 1888.

Robert, Marquis of Salisbury, and her conclusion is that her father probably had previous knowledge of it, although the arguments which it contained were not in accordance with his views.* Salisbury himself approved Vivian's advice to the Prince de Chimay: "not to attach any importance to a Newspaper Article as it was a mistake to suppose that the 'Standard' or any other paper was the official or even inspired organ of Her Majesty's Government". This approval was later described by Vivian as "the only crumb of comfort" he had been able to give the Prince de Chimay. The leader of the opposition in the Belgian Chamber found further reassurance in the record of Britain's earlier attitude. On 4 March he quoted speeches made in 1867 by Derby and Clarendon, defining the Belgian Guarantee as both collective and individual—unlike that of Luxemburg—and referred to the British declarations in 1870 by Granville, Cairns, Stratford de Redcliffe and Gladstone. On the basis of these precedents the leader of the opposition reproached the Government for having doubted "that the honour and interest of England were alike engaged in the guarantee of the neutrality and independence of Belgium". Vivian himself, meanwhile, had despaired of specific instructions, understanding from Salisbury's silence "that her Majesty's Government consider it inopportune or inexpedient to express any opinion on the validity of the Treaty guarantees of the neutrality of Belgium, or to commit themselves in any way as to their future policy" **(Doc. 177)**.† The attitude of Salisbury at this time was not heroic, but it was intelligible. Feeling in England, and still more in Canada, was hostile to France, and he clearly feared that public opinion might prevent him from fulfilling even so longstanding a national engagement. He was doubtless confirmed in the idea that it was unwise to undertake new obligations, if old ones could not be certain of fulfilment.

Salisbury kept silence towards Belgium but responded favourably to the overtures of Italy, which were, significantly and openly, supported by Germany.‡ They were at first concealed from Austria-Hungary at the express wish of Italy. Bismarck appeared, indeed, as the force behind the whole negotiation. He instructed Hatzfeldt to use encouraging terms in speaking to Salisbury about Egypt—a marked contrast to his attitude during 1884–5.

While, however, Britain and Italy reached the first understanding alone, conversations with Austria-Hungary were proceeding at the same time. In the discussion between Kálnoky and Paget on 8 February, the latter even went so far as to ask what, in Kálnoky's view, England could do in the event of an

---

* Cecil, *Life of Salisbury*, [1932], IV, 57–62.
† *V.* Gooch and Temperley, [1932], VIII, 374–5, and Vivian to Salisbury, No. 74, 5 March 1887, *F.O.* 10/498.
‡ *G.P.*, [1922], IV, 297 sqq.

Austro-Russian war to help Austria-Hungary and to give her material support. It is true that he gave to this enquiry a personal guise, insisting that he was without instructions on the subject. But although Károlyi a month later characterized Paget as "a true Hotspur" and doubted his authority for some of his remarks, his comment on this conversation was that Salisbury's own language led him to doubt whether Paget was really acting on his own initiative.* Paget's question to Kálnoky was put four days before the exchange of notes between Salisbury and Corti.† On the 19th Paget saw Kálnoky again and informed him of the Anglo-Italian notes, saying specifically on this occasion that he was acting on Salisbury's instructions. He communicated the text of the notes expressing Salisbury's hope that Kálnoky might find in them a basis of co-operation.‡ Similar action on this date by the Italian Ambassador at Vienna emphasized the significance of Paget's communication; for both in Italy and in England the notes were regarded as strictly secret.

Conversations continued at London and Vienna on the dual basis of the Anglo-Italian notes and the common interests of Britain and Austria-Hungary in the Near East. On 3 March Károlyi reported that he had emphasized three points to Salisbury: the permanent interest of Austria-Hungary in the maintenance of peace; her determination to act decisively if Russia made the preservation of peace impossible; and her confidence in the ultimate co-operation of Britain in such a war, a confidence that was not limited to the duration of the present ministry, for Britain's own interests would compel her to participate when once the war had broken out. Salisbury's language, as Károlyi reported it, indicated that he too was considering the ultimate possibilities of material action. "Naturally", Salisbury said, "we could give you no help in the Carpathians, and in order to co-operate with you against Russia in the Black Sea, we must first be able to get there." Károlyi added that the attitude of Turkey must necessarily exercise a great influence, though not perhaps a controlling one, on the decision of England.§ At the same time Salisbury consistently maintained that it was impossible for him to give any definite pledge as to British action. He explained carefully to Károlyi that in his negotiations with Italy "material support" had in no way been promised on the English side. No British ministry could bind itself in advance to co-operate in war. "The

* W.S.A. Pol. A. Rot. 465, Geheim xiv. Memorandum of conversation with Paget, 8 February, Kálnoky to Széchényi, 19 February, and Károlyi to Kálnoky, Private, 3 March 1887.

† Gooch and Temperley, [1932], viii, 1–2.

‡ W.S.A. Pol. A. Rot. 465, Geheim xiv. Memorandum of a very secret conversation with Paget, 19 February 1887.

§ W.S.A. Pol. A. Rot. 465, Geheim xiv. Károlyi to Kálnoky, Private, 3 March 1887.

last occasion on which England had promised alliance in the event
of war, was the Anglo-Turkish Convention concerning Cyprus.
But this undertaking was also not unconditional but limited, since
the guarantee of Turkey's Asiatic possessions was made dependent
on the reforms which were to be introduced in them."* The
results of these pourparlers were two exchanges of notes between
Károlyi and Salisbury and between Károlyi and Corti, dated
24 March, by which Austria-Hungary acceded to the Anglo-
Italian understanding.†

The first Mediterranean Agreement of 1887 was thus a series
of notes. It is true that it was engineered by Bismarck and
that it brought England into Germany's orbit. But it had moral
value only and contained no pledge that England would support
her obligations with material force. Both with Italy and Austria-
Hungary the expressions used by Salisbury were carefully worded
to exclude a determination beforehand of the action which Britain
would take, and Salisbury maintained the position that his
obligations went no further than those directly expressed by
himself.]

Document 175. *Salisbury's reaction to the Italian overture, 2 February* 1887‡

Lord Salisbury with his humble duty respectfully submits
the following.

Yesterday Count Corti came to see Lord Salisbury. He
was the bearer of propositions from the Italian Government
for a closer understanding between Italy and England. He
left a memorandum with Lord Salisbury of which the effect
was to offer an alliance in case of war against France. There
were other propositions of co-operation which were more
acceptable, such as common efforts for maintaining the *status
quo* in the Ægean, the Adriatic, the Black Sea, and on the
African Coast. But the paper ended with a proposal that,
in case either Power was at war with France, the other Power
would give it naval assistance. Lord Salisbury promised to
bring the matter before his colleagues; but told Count Corti,

---

* W.S.A. Pol. A. Rot. 465, Geheim xiv. Károlyi to Kálnoky, No. 12 B
Secret, 3 March 1887. Cp. Salisbury's report to the Queen on 10 February,
Letters of Queen Victoria, 3rd Ser., [1930], I, 272.

† Texts in Gooch and Temperley, [1932], viii, 3–4, 6–7. For the Second
Mediterranean Agreement *v. infra*, pp. 454–62.

‡ Salisbury to the Queen, 2 February 1887, *Letters of Queen Victoria*, 3rd Ser.,
[1930], I, 268–70.

first, that England never promised material assistance in view of an uncertain war, of which the object and cause were unknown; secondly, that any promise even of diplomatic co-operation could not be directed against any single Power such as France. But that, on the other hand, the policy of Italy and Great Britain was very similar; and that, within the limit of the principles mentioned by Lord Salisbury, we should be glad to co-operate with them; especially in the maintenance of the *status quo*.

To-day the matter was discussed at length in the Cabinet; and it was resolved Lord Salisbury should draw up a reply in the above sense. This afternoon he saw Count Hatzfeldt, who brought a message from Prince Bismarck, earnestly recommending an understanding of this kind as a means of preserving peace. A similar message had been sent by Sir E. Malet in a private and secret telegram. Lord Salisbury discussed the matter at length with the German Ambassador in the same tone. He impressed upon the latter that, though the assistance of England might be confidently looked for to maintain the *status quo* in the Mediterranean, and might be very probably looked for if France were to attack Italy, and Italy found herself in any danger, it was very unlikely to be given if Italy made an aggressive war on France. Count Hatzfeldt pressed the case of a war in which Italy should be the nominal assailant, having attacked merely to anticipate a certain attack from France. In this case, Lord Salisbury did not hold out any hope of English sympathy and aid. It was arranged that Lord Salisbury should see Count Corti again, and discuss the matter, before answering Count Robilant's memorandum. Lord Salisbury then represented to Count Hatzfeldt your Majesty's earnest horror of the possible calamities of an impending war, and impressed considerations of that kind as strongly as possible. He only replied, as Lord Salisbury expected, by the most earnest asseverations of the pacific intentions of the German Government. Nevertheless, Lord Salisbury thought he traced in a very long conversation, indications of great anxiety; and a disposition to press the idea that the beginner of actual operations was not necessarily the aggressor, but might be forced into war by the preparations of his opponent.

This matter is to be treated with the utmost secrecy. Lord Salisbury is forbidden to say anything to the Austrian Ambassador about it, a suspicious circumstance which Hatzfeldt attempts to explain by a reference to Karolyi's individual character and modes of proceeding. Lord Salisbury greatly fears that the Trentino is in issue.

Lord Salisbury prays your Majesty to let him have this letter back to copy, as it is the sole record he has kept of their conversation. At present he is keeping the matter secret even from the Foreign Office, and has told no soul except his colleagues.

Document 176. *Salisbury defines the limits of co-operation with Italy, 12 February 1887**

The statement of Italian policy which is contained in Your Excellency's despatch of the 12th inst[ant] has been received by Her Majesty's Government with great satisfaction, as it enables them to reciprocate cordially Count Robilant's friendly sentiments, and to express their own desire to co-operate heartily with the Government of Italy in matters of common interest to the two countries. The character of that co-operation must be decided by them, when the occasion for it arises, according to the circumstances of the case. In the interest of peace, and of the independence of the territories adjacent to the Mediterranean Sea, Her Majesty's Gov[ernmen]t wish to act in the closest concert and agreement with that of Italy. Both Powers desire that the shores of the Euxine, the Ægean and the Adriatic, and the Northern Coast of Africa shall remain in the same hands as now. If, owing to some calamitous event, it becomes impossible to maintain the absolute *status quo*, both Powers desire that there shall be no extension of the domination of any other Great Power over any portion of those coasts.

* Salisbury to Corti, 12 February 1887, *F.O.* Original Treaties, General No. 1; printed in Gooch and Temperley, [1932], VIII, 2.

It will be the earnest desire of Her Majesty's Gov[ernmen]t to give their best co-operation, as herein-before expressed, to the Government of Italy in maintaining these cardinal principles of policy.

Document 177. *Salisbury's silence on British obligations to Belgium, 26 February* 1887*

Although I understand from Your Lordship's silence that Her Majesty's Government consider it inopportune or inexpedient to express any opinion on the validity of the Treaty Guarantee of the neutrality of Belgium, or to commit themselves in any way as to their future policy, I believe that Your Lordship would wish to be kept well informed of the position of affairs here.

A report, to which the Articles in the "Standard" have lent some colour, has been eagerly propagated by the Radical press, that an understanding has been come to with Germany, either with the connivance of the Belgian Government, or behind its back, by which Germany would secure a right of passage for her troops through Belgium in return for an undertaking to restore her independence at the conclusion of the war and perhaps to compensate her for her complaisance at the expence of France.

This report, whether manufactured here or at Paris, has appeared in the Newspapers and has been strongly commented on by the Radical press which has not hesitated to impute complicity in the scheme to The King, whom it suspects of German proclivities. The inherent improbability and absurdity of this rumour is apparent. No Government in Belgium would ever dare to lend itself to a scheme which, while certainly ensuring its own immediate and ignominious downfall, would seriously compromise the position of the King and probably provoke a revolution....

* Vivian to Salisbury, No. 60, 26 February 1887, *F.O.* 10/498. Cp. Gooch and Temperley, [1932], VIII, 375.

74. THE WOLFF CONVENTION

[Reference has already been made to Salisbury's policy of a *détente* with Russia, which accompanied the discussions leading to the first Mediterranean Agreement. At the same time, also, he was seeking to diminish his dependence on the Central Powers by clearing away the difficulties between Britain and France.

Here the chief problem was Egypt. In 1887 Salisbury made his second attempt to put the British position in Egypt on a more satisfactory footing by the negotiation of the Wolff Convention. His return to power in 1885 had been followed by the dispatch of Sir H. Drummond Wolff on a special mission to Constantinople. "The end to which I would work", Salisbury instructed Wolff, "is evacuation, but with certain privileges reserved for England";* the method which he desired to use was Anglo-Turkish co-operation. The negotiation failed in its immediate object, for Turkey was not ready to take part in any effective garrisoning of the Egyptian frontiers. But Salisbury, though he recognized the failure, did not understand the essential defects of the policy; he overlooked, as Cromer pointed out later, the antagonism of Egyptian nationalists to Turkey. His failure to grasp this factor laid him open to further disappointment, for his negotiations of 1887 were again on the basis of an Anglo-Turkish understanding. Wolff was once more sent to Constantinople; and on 22 May the Convention was signed. The date for British evacuation was fixed at three years from this time, but it was provided that "if, at that time, the appearance of danger in the interior or from without should necessitate the adjournment of the evacuation, the English troops will retire from Egypt immediately after the disappearance of this danger". Ratifications were to be exchanged within a month. On 29 May the text was communicated by the Grand Vizier and the Minister for Foreign Affairs to the French Ambassador. A summary was sent home by telegraph, and without waiting for the full text M. Flourens, the French Minister for Foreign Affairs, instructed his Ambassador that he would not be able to give his adhesion to the project, as he at present understood it, and he communicated this instruction to Russia.† The Central Powers remained true to their *entente* with England. Only once during the negotiations did Bismarck jerk the reins by which he held control, and then when Britain responded, he returned to her support (**Doc. 179**). After the signature, as before, the ministers at Berlin, Vienna and Rome spoke in defence of British action. But there was one court where Franco-Russian protests meant much. Turkey first hesitated, and then refused ratification. Salisbury thus failed for a second time to settle the Egyptian question on the basis of Anglo-Turkish co-operation.]

* Cecil, *Life of Salisbury*, [1931], III, 235.
† *D.D.F.*, [1934], 1re Sér., VI, 542-4, Nos. 534 and 535.

Document 178. *Salisbury defines his attitude to the evacuation of Egypt,* 27 *April and* 3 *May* 1887*

Your No. 76. The proposed draft is unsatisfactory especially on two points. It makes our independent right of reentry contingent on some action or inaction at Constantinople: and as dependent in some form on the authorization of the Sultan.

Secondly. It makes our evacuation certain: while the inviolability of Egypt to other Powers is to depend on their signing an agreement to that effect after we are gone. Pray make it clear either in the Convention or some document annexed to it, that we do not leave until the other Powers have assented to the stipulations which bind them not to enter, and enable us to do so under specified conditions.

Your declaration that the failure of any of the Powers to assent to the Convention will contribute an external danger under the sixth line of eighth clause should be recorded by you and accepted by the Turks either before you sign Convention or at the same time. This is very important.

Document 179. *Britain obtains the support of the Central Powers and pays the price demanded by Bismarck,* 17 *February,* 14 *April and* 4 *May* 1887

Yours 14. I have received strong assurances from C[oun]t Hatzfeldt of Bismarck's general support of our Egyptian policy: but he has said nothing about Radowitz. I will enquire the first time I see him.†

Your tel. No. 56 of yesterday. I think you may treat Italian [sic] as frankly as before as the policy seems unchanged.‡ Though we have no alliances our relations with Austria and Italy are singularly cordial: and you may act on that assump-

---

* Salisbury to Wolff, Tel. No. 35 Secret, 27 April, 1887; Tel. No. 38 Secret, 3 May 1887, *F.O.* 78/4060.
 † Salisbury to Wolff, Tel. No. 11, 17 February 1887, *F.O.* 78/4060.
 ‡ Depretis reconstituted his Cabinet on 4 April 1887, and took over the Ministry of Foreign Affairs from Robilant. Crispi became President of the Council and Minister for Foreign Affairs on 8 August.

tion. As regards Egypt also, though not as regards Bulgaria, Germany appears to be entirely with us. It is not worth while estranging any of these for the sake of conciliating France.*

It is not worth quarrelling with Bismarck at this juncture for the sake of maintaining H. at Zanzibar where he is not a success..., so, on the understanding that I could do it without injury to him, I thought the balance of advantages was in favour of consent. But that circumstance does not affect the monstrousness of the demand or the danger we shall incur if we remain exposed to sallies of temper of this kind. It is only Egypt that puts us in this difficulty, for otherwise Bismarck's wrath would be of little moment to us. It is heartily to be wished we were delivered from this very inconvenient and somewhat humiliating relation.†

Document 180. *Salisbury recognizes the need for acknowledging the existence of the Mediterranean declaration,* 26 *May* 1887‡

Your 117. I am afraid it is impossible to conceal existence of Mediterranean declaration: though I might perhaps give its general purport without laying it on table.

75. THE SECOND MEDITERRANEAN AGREEMENT, DECEMBER 1887

[The second Mediterranean Agreement of December 1887 is extremely important. It was signed six months after the "Reinsurance Treaty", to the negotiation of which Bismarck had turned after launching the *entente* between Britain and his two allies in the spring. It was even more important than the "Reinsurance Treaty" in marking the decay of the Bismarckian system. By the "Reinsurance Treaty" Bismarck's attitude in the Near East was defined. It contained, as an "additional and very secret protocol", two promises to Russia, one to aid her "to re-establish a regular and legal Government in Bulgaria"—the restoration of Alexander of Battenberg being expressly excluded— and the other to give "benevolent neutrality" and "moral and diplomatic support" to Russia should the Emperor "find himself under the necessity of assuming the task of defending the entrance

* Salisbury to Wolff, Tel. No. 26 Secret, 14 April 1887, *F.O.* 78/4060.
† Salisbury to Scott, 4 May 1887, Cecil, *Life of Salisbury*, [1932], IV, 43.
‡ Salisbury to Wolff, Tel. No. 67, 26 May 1887, *F.O.* 78/4060.

of the Black Sea in order to safeguard the interests of Russia".* The wording of these two promises should be compared carefully with that of clauses 4 and 5 of the December Mediterranean Agreement. Salisbury indeed by his insistence on Bismarck's support before he accepted this agreement established a claim to take an important share in accelerating the decay of the system which Bismarck had built. For while the first Mediterranean Agreement was a successful attempt on the part of Bismarck to bring England into his orbit, the second Agreement was an equally successful retaliation by Salisbury. In effect it is an anti-Russian document, and it did much to counteract the significance of the Russo-German "Reinsurance Treaty". It must always be doubtful whether Bismarck could have preserved his connexion with Russia beyond the year 1890 in anything but form. Salisbury undoubtedly made it more difficult for him to maintain the relationship. Enough stress has not been laid hitherto on the importance of the second Mediterranean Agreement from this standpoint nor on Salisbury's share in undermining the Alliance system.† The occasion of the December Agreement was provided by Bulgaria. For in July, three weeks after the signature of the "Reinsurance Treaty", the Bulgarian crisis entered on a new phase. Ferdinand of Saxe-Coburg was again, and this time more formally, invited to assume the Bulgarian throne; he accepted and set out for the Principality, over which he was to rule for some time unrecognized by a single European Power. Interest was thus again concentrated on Bulgarian affairs. Rumours of overt action on the part of Russia stimulated anxiety even in Germany and more seriously in Austria-Hungary and Italy. The idea that the *entente* between these two Powers and Britain should be developed to meet the situation appears to have arisen first in August.‡

In a dispatch of 23 August Calice, the Austro-Hungarian Ambassador to the Porte, said that he and his colleagues— Baron Blanc and Sir William White—had frequently discussed in an academic fashion "the idea of consolidating and developing our Group" in order to increase its effectiveness in Near Eastern affairs. He referred also to the influence, which both White and Baron Blanc exercised over their respective Governments, and commented on the importance of this personal factor "for the consolidation of our group"; the moving spirit in these discussions was, he said, Baron Blanc. It was from this "academic" beginning that the second Mediterranean Agreement evolved. Salisbury knew of the "meditations and consultations" but apparently did not receive the text of the *Bases* of the proposed agreement until the end of October, when Bismarck, acting his usual part

* A. F. Pribram, *The Secret Treaties of Austria-Hungary*, [1920], I, 278–81.
† Cp. however W. L. Langer, *European Alliances and Alignments*, [1931], 423–4.
‡ W.S.A. VIII/460b, Accord à Trois 1887. Kálnoky to Calice, 18 August; Calice to Kálnoky, 23 August 1887. Cp. W. N. Medlicott, 'The Mediterranean Agreements of 1887', *The Slavonic Review*, v, [1926–7], 66–88.

of European stage-manager, communicated them to Malet.*
Actually the terms had long since been drafted. For while Crispi,
the new Italian Minister for Foreign Affairs, was recalling Corti
from London with rebukes and was pressing the *Chargé d'affaires*
Catalani to strengthen the bond with England,† Calice and his
two colleagues at Constantinople produced a workable "sketch".

The eight points which became the formula of the second (or
December) Mediterranean Agreement were sent to Kálnoky by
Calice in a private letter of 17 September. In forwarding them
Calice explained the objects which he and his two colleagues had
in mind. They were of opinion, he said, that such an arrangement
would "give Turkey a power of resistance—at least a moral one".
Moreover, it would restrain Russia. And if it failed in the second
object, Calice foreshadowed possible action by the three Powers:
the occupation of suitable parts of the Balkan Peninsula and the
stationing of a fleet before the Dardanelles. Thus Russian action
would be stemmed, Turkey would be shaken from her lethargy
and the way would be prepared for the co-operation of the four
Powers in the event of a conflict with Russia. Meanwhile Baron
Blanc had also reported the substance of the proposals and Crispi
had expressed approval: the principles they embodied had been
those of Italy from the outset; Kálnoky approved them; they were
in accord with the "secret wishes" of Germany; all that remained,
said Crispi, was "to overcome the reluctance which the Cabinet
of St James persistently showed".

Crispi's suspicions of Salisbury, however, were probably based
more on the experiences of the past few months than on immediate
difficulties, although Salisbury's language was deliberately guarded.
According to a telegram from Rome of 22 September he had
written that he entirely shared Crispi's views as to the advantage
of a full exchange of ideas between the Ambassadors at Constantinople; that he would be very pleased to hear of any suggestion
which Calice should put forward with a view to "concerted and
co-operative action by the three Powers"; but that he was naturally
unable "to give an opinion on a projected agreement before its
text had been submitted".‡ Salisbury's hesitations were noted,

---

* Gooch and Temperley, [1932], VIII, 14–15, Malet to Salisbury, 25 October
1887. Cp. also Cecil, *Life of Salisbury*, [1932], IV, 69.

† W.S.A. VIII/104, Berichte aus England, August–December 1887. Biegeleben
to Kálnoky, Tel. No. 45, 3 November 1887. This quotes a telegram from Crispi
to Corti: "Vous ne me comprenez pas ou ne voulez pas me comprendre et je
suis forcé de vous mettre en disponibilité." Catalani had just returned from
Turin, to which he had been summoned by Crispi to receive instructions. In
the "Memorandum on the Anglo-Italian and Anglo-Austrian Agreements of
1887" written by Sir T. (Lord) Sanderson on 1 July 1902, Corti's recall is dated
13 February. Cp. Gooch and Temperley, [1932], VIII, 2.

‡ W.S.A. VIII/460b, Accord à Trois 1887. Calice to Kálnoky, Secret,
20 September. Crispi did not know of the actual text of the *Bases* until October;
Bruck to Kálnoky, No. 59 Secret, 15 October; Enclosure in Calice to Kálnoky,
24 September 1887.

but with greater sympathy, by Austria-Hungary and Germany.* Crispi discussed the proposals with Bismarck when visiting him at the beginning of October,† and according to his own account gained Bismarck's approval for the *Bases* on which Italy and Austria-Hungary were working. Crispi seems, however, to have overstated Bismarck's support. He urged Bruck, the Austro-Hungarian Ambassador at Rome, to suggest to Kálnoky a secret Austro-Italian arrangement extending Article 8 of the *Bases* by prescribing the action to be taken should action become necessary, and he implied Bismarck's approval. Bismarck's comment shows that he thought this "premature and, on account of the possibility of its becoming known, dangerous"; if Turkey heard of it she might be influenced in the direction of an arrangement with Russia. And in his view the attitude of Turkey was more valuable to Austria-Hungary and Italy even than that of Britain. It is clear that in giving this advice he had the Penjdeh crisis in mind.‡ It is clear too that Bismarck was in a position awkward even for him, for he was being asked to favour an arrangement whose objects were directly opposed to his secret understanding with Russia in the "Reinsurance Treaty". While, therefore, he did not wholly trust Salisbury, and scoffed at the idea of secrecy in a Cabinet of sixteen members, he had interests of his own to serve in limiting the proposed arrangement to the *Bases* which Salisbury might accept.

On 22 October the Austro-Hungarian *Chargé d'affaires* at Berlin reported that Bismarck was prepared to support the project strongly in London, that a communication had been made privately to Malet, and that Hatzfeldt had been directed to bring all his influence to bear to secure this end.§ On the same day Kálnoky spoke to Paget about the proposals in some detail.‖ Instructions for a concerted representation to Salisbury were sent by Kálnoky on 24 October, and these were followed on the next day by two secret dispatches explaining the purpose of the arrangement and by a private letter detailing the arguments which were to be used.¶ In the latter he asserted that the time was peculiarly opportune for the move, particularly because Bismarck was irritated with Russia—an irritation which was "un atout très important dans

* Cp. the language used by Count Herbert Bismarck to Malet on 25 October 1887, Gooch and Temperley, [1932], VIII, 14–15.
† *G.P.*, [1922], IV, 351 n.
‡ *G.P.*, [1922], IV, 358–62; Count H. Bismarck to the *Chargé d'affaires* in Vienna, 4 November 1887, enclosing copy of Bruck's dispatch to Kálnoky of 15 October 1887. For the latter, which cites Crispi's account of his interview, cp. W.S.A. VIII/460b, Accord à Trois 1887.
§ W.S.A. VIII/460b, Accord à Trois 1887. Eissenstein to Kálnoky, No. 98 Secret, 22 October 1887.
‖ *V.* Gooch and Temperley, [1932], VIII, 16–17.
¶ W.S.A. VIII/460b, Accord à Trois 1887. Kálnoky to Biegeleben, Tel. No. 81 Secret, 24 October 1887; No. 1 Secret, No. 2 Secret, and Private letter, 25 October 1887.

notre jeu".* On the 29th Biegeleben telegraphed Salisbury's thanks, and said that the Cabinet would be consulted on the following Thursday.

According to Biegeleben's account of the 31st, Salisbury was much struck by Kálnoky's trenchant logic, but Biegeleben owned that as he had not been able to secure an interview until just before the train left for Hatfield there had not been time for much discussion.† There appears to have been more than one Cabinet meeting on the subject. Salisbury is reported as having told Catalani after a meeting on the 8th that the Cabinet was favourable, but that there could be no definitive reply until "Friday". On the 14th he was "very well disposed" to the proposals but was still expressing doubts. Eight days later Bismarck, responding to a hint from London, wrote a long letter to Salisbury setting forth the attitude of Germany and supporting the proposals.‡ He had already communicated secretly the text of the Austro-German Treaty; and this was in itself an assurance, since Germany's obligations to Austria-Hungary were thereby made clear.§ Armed with these evidences of Germany's moral support, Salisbury prepared to accede to the *Bases*. He made, it is true, certain comments and qualifications, and ultimately couched his assent in separate replies to the Austro-Hungarian and Italian Ambassadors. He stipulated in particular that the notes should remain secret, and took special care that secrecy should be preserved in England.‖ His insistence on a separate reply caused some apprehension to Austria-Hungary and Italy, as did also his reiteration of the view that England's interests in Near Eastern affairs were not so great as those of Austria-Hungary. "We leave to you", he said, "le beau rôle; you lead, we follow you." But the assurance that he would work with Austria-Hungary and Italy was a substantial gain; as Crispi said, "the principal thing is to bring the negotiation to an end, so that Salisbury does not escape us".¶ Salisbury's own comments suggest that he had a very shrewd idea of the position (**Docs. 181, 182**).]

* The texts of Kálnoky's dispatch No. 2 and of his private letter of 25 October were communicated to Salisbury and are printed in Gooch and Temperley, [1932], VIII, 9–10, 15–16. The drafts are in W.S.A. VIII/460b, Accord à Trois 1887. The phrase quoted above is given thus in the draft. The copy communicated to Salisbury has "dans notre partie".

† W.S.A. VIII/460b, Accord à Trois 1887. Biegeleben to Kálnoky, Secret 31 October 1887.

‡ *G.P.*, [1922], IV, 376–80; cp. Cecil, *Life of Salisbury*, [1932], IV, 72–5.

§ Cecil, *Life of Salisbury*, [1932], IV, 72.

‖ Gooch and Temperley, [1932], VIII, 11, 13.

¶ W.S.A. VIII/460b, Accord à Trois 1887. Károlyi to Kálnoky, No. 47B Secret, 7 December; Bruck to Kálnoky, No. 79 A–B Secret, 10 December 1887; cp. Cecil, *Life of Salisbury*, [1932], IV, 78–9.

Document 181. *Salisbury agrees, unwillingly, to strengthen the Accord à Trois, 2 November 1887**

The result of your meditations and consultations at Constantinople with your two colleagues has come to the birth. Germany, Austria and Italy have each communicated to us your eight bases with an earnest recommendation that we should accept them. They are all struck with the opportuneness of the moment for such an agreement, in view especially of the failings of their intended partners. Austria presses on us to take advantage of the Chancellor's ill-temper with Russia, which Kalnoky says is an *atout* in our game. Germany urges us not to let slip the happy moment when Italy promises active assistance and yet repudiates the idea of compensation. Italy is especially struck by the phenomenal courage and decision of Austria and I have no doubt some equally complimentary reason founded on England's present condition has been a powerful argument for mutual co-operation among the trio. We submit the matter to the Cabinet tomorrow and on so difficult a question I cannot forecast the result. My own impression is that we must join, but I say it with regret. I think the time inopportune and we are merely rescuing Bismarck's somewhat endangered chestnuts. If he can establish a South-Eastern raw, the Russian bear must perforce forget the Western raw on his huge carcase. If he can get up a nice little fight between Russia and the three Powers, he will have leisure to make France a harmless neighbour for some time to come. It goes against me to be one of the Powers in that unscrupulous game. But a thorough understanding with Austria and Italy is so important to us that I do not like the idea of breaking it up on account of risks which *may* turn out to be imaginary.

The Suez Canal Convention has had the effect for the moment of improving our relations with France. After the experience I got of the Chancellor's pretty ways during Wolff's negotiations, I do not wish to depend upon his good

---

* Salisbury to White, 2 November 1887, Cecil, *Life of Salisbury*, [1932], IV, 70–1.

will, and therefore shall keep friends with France as far as we can do it without paying too dear for it. The threat of making us uneasy in Egypt through the action of France is the only weapon he has against us, and we are free of him in proportion as we can blunt it.

Document 182. *Salisbury communicates his adherence on nine points,* 12 *December* 1887*

Most Secret.

Her Majesty's Government have considered the points commended to their acceptance by the identic note of the Austro-Hungarian and Italian Governments.

The three Powers have already communicated to each other their conviction that it is their common interest to uphold the existing state of things upon the shores of the Mediterranean and the adjoining seas. The four first points recited in the note are in strict conformity with this understanding, as well as with the policy which has always been pursued by the Government of Great Britain.

The fifth, sixth, and seventh points refer to certain special dangers by which the state of things established by Treaties, and the interests of the three Powers in the East, may be menaced; and to the course which should be pursued if those dangers should arise. The illegal enterprises anticipated by the fifth Article would affect, especially, the preservation of the Straits from the domination of any other Power but Turkey, and the independent liberties of the Christian communities on the northern border of the Turkish Empire, established by the Treaty of Berlin. Her Majesty's Government recognize that the protection of the Straits and the liberties of these communities are objects of supreme importance, and are to Europe among the most valuable results of the Treaty; and they cordially concur with the Austro-Hungarian and Italian Governments in taking special precautions to secure them.

* Salisbury to the Austro-Hungarian and Italian Ambassadors, 12 December 1887, *F.O.* Original Treaties, General No. 1; printed in Gooch and Temperley, [1932], VIII, 12-13.

The eighth point provides against a contingency which, without technical illegality, may frustrate the object of the Treaties altogether. It is necessary, however, to avoid a premature publicity which might precipitate the lapse of Turkey into that state of vassalage from which it is the aim of the three Powers to protect her.

In view of these considerations, the Undersigned, Her Majesty's Sec[retar]y of State for F[oreign] A[ffairs], etc: is charged by Her Majesty's Government to communicate to the Austro-Hungarian and Italian Governments their entire adhesion to the nine points recited in the identic note of the two Powers, that is to say:

1. The maintenance of peace, to the exclusion of all policy of aggression.

2. The maintenance of the *status quo* in the East based on the Treaties, to the exclusion of all policy of compensation.

3. The maintenance of the local autonomies established by those same Treaties.

4. The independence of Turkey, as guardian of important European interests; the Caliphate, the freedom of the Straits, &c., to be independent of all foreign preponderating influence.

5. Consequently, Turkey can neither cede nor delegate her rights over Bulgaria to any other Power, nor intervene in order to establish a foreign Administration there, nor tolerate acts of coercion undertaken with this latter object, under the form either of a military occupation or of the dispatch of volunteers. Neither will Turkey, who has by the Treaties been constituted guardian of the Straits, be able to cede any portion of her sovereign rights, nor delegate her authority to any other Power in Asia Minor.

6. The desire of the three Powers to be associated with Turkey for the common defence of these principles.

7. In case of Turkey resisting any illegal enterprises such as are indicated in Article V, the three Powers will immediately come to an agreement as to the measures to be taken for causing to be respected the independence of the Ottoman Empire and the integrity of its territory as secured by previous Treaties.

8. Should the conduct of the Porte, however, in the opinion of the three Powers, assume the character of complicity with or connivance at any such illegal enterprise, the three Powers will consider themselves justified by existing Treaties in proceeding either jointly or separately to the provisional occupation by their forces, military or naval, of such points of Ottoman territory as they may agree to consider it necessary to occupy in order to secure the objects determined by previous Treaties.

9. The existence and the contents of the present Agreement between the three Powers shall not be revealed either to Turkey or to any other Powers who have not yet been informed of it without the previous consent of all and each of the three Powers aforesaid.

76. THE FALL OF BISMARCK

[The years 1887–90 may be regarded as the peak period of Anglo-German co-operation, although the friendship was always intermittent. At the end of 1887 rumours were prevalent in Europe that England had joined the Triple Alliance. An article in *The Times* of 22 December gave currency to this view. Salisbury however specifically denied to Waddington on 14 December that any "proposal to join it [the Triple Alliance] had ever been made to H[er] M[ajesty's] Gov[ernmen]t" and pointed out that he was in fact "entirely unaware of the covenants which constituted the Triple Alliance". His assurance seems to have been imperfectly accepted, and on the 19th he repeated his disclaimer in response to a specific question as to whether he was "prepared formally to deny the existence of an agreement between Germany and England as to the course to be pursued by England in the event of a Franco-German War". But he refused to allow Waddington to communicate that answer officially to his Government "as I was not prepared to admit that the question was one which I ought, as a matter of strict rule to answer".* Waddington seems to have observed this injunction, for no report of the conversation appears among his dispatches of the time.†

The *rapprochement* of the winter of 1887 was followed by a series of attempts to solve Anglo-German colonial differences. The

* Salisbury to Egerton, Nos. 657 and 675, 14 and 19 November 1887, *F.O.* 27/2853.

† I.e. there is no such report included in *D.D.F.*, 1re Sér., vi. Cp. on this subject Herbette's report of a conversation with Malet on 18 December 1887, *D.D.F.*, [1934], 1re Sér., vi, 661–2, No. 663.

Samoa Agreement of 1889 and the Brussels Conference on the Slave Trade in the same year both bore witness to the determined effort to make Anglo-German co-operation a reality. "I am very much pleased with Lord Salisbury," the German Ambassador said to his Austro-Hungarian colleague at the end of 1888; "he has done what he could."* Salisbury's efforts in the colonial question were remarkably successful, if we compare them with the course of similar negotiations at other periods. The difficulties were greatest in Zanzibar, for, as Salisbury said in 1888: "We have left Prince Bismarck [a] free hand in Samoa (and a pretty mess he has made of it!), but we can not do so in Zanzibar. The English and Indian interests are both too strong."† Yet even here a solution was ultimately found in the Anglo-German agreement of 1890.‡ Throughout these years, it is true, Salisbury found the effort of co-operation uncongenial. He never wholly trusted Bismarck. "The Chancellor's humours", he wrote to Malet, "are as changeable as those of the French Assembly, and you never can be certain that he will not try to levy a sort of diplomatic blackmail by putting himself against you on some matter in which you are interested, unless you will do something to gratify some one of his unreasonable personal antipathies."§ It is easy therefore to understand Salisbury's failure to respond more definitely to Bismarck's overture of 1889.‖ This overture came, indeed, at a very inopportune moment. The incidents involved in the visit of the Prince of Wales to Vienna had left a very strong feeling at the British court, while Salisbury was irritated by the results of his conciliatory action over Samoa. "Prince Bismarck", he said to Deym, "has succeeded once in attaining great results with Blood and Iron, and he believes that these means must always bring assured success. The conditions of the colonial situation are not sufficiently known to him, and the manner in which he has inaugurated the colonial policy of Germany will cost her many sacrifices and will lead nowhere."¶

A discussion of colonial questions was one of the objects of Count Herbert Bismarck's visit to England in March 1889, but the final settlement of the Zanzibar-Heligoland bargain was not made until after Bismarck's fall.

* W.S.A. VIII/105, Berichte aus England. Heidler to Kálnoky, No. 42 A–F, Very Confidential, 7 November 1888.
† Cecil, Life of Salisbury, [1932], IV, 234–5.
‡ Hertslet, Map, [1891], IV, 3286–7.
§ Cecil, Life of Salisbury, [1932], IV, 100: Salisbury to Malet, 11 April 1888.
‖ Cp. Cecil, Life of Salisbury, [1932], IV, 110 ff. G.P., [1922], IV, 400 ff. Salisbury's assurance to Count Hatzfeldt that he would treat the matter as secret has unfortunately deprived us of any British records. Cp. Gooch and Temperley, [1928], III, 409, where Sir Eyre Crowe comments on the insufficiency of the British archives for the study of Anglo-German relations in the time of Salisbury.
¶ W.S.A. VIII/107, Berichte aus England. Deym to Kálnoky, No. 3 F Confidential, 25 January 1889.

"Lord Salisbury", telegraphed Deym on 20 March 1890, "deplores the resignation of Prince Bismarck. He is not afraid that it will immediately involve changes in the relations of Germany with the other Powers, but the Emperor's views being yet unformed, the future seems to him to have become uncertain." Caprivi, it is true, assured him in a private letter that he could fully depend on the continuity of German policy;* but Salisbury was not sanguine of the permanence of this intention (**Doc. 183**). The fall of Bismarck thus reacted unfavourably on Anglo-German relations, and was partly responsible for Salisbury's later unwillingness to renew to the full his association of 1887 with the Triple Alliance although no doubt he was also influenced by the criticism which this association had aroused in Parliament. For the next three years the main link which bound Britain to the Central Powers was her connexion with Italy.]

Document 183. *Salisbury on the results of Bismarck's fall,*
9 April 1890†

Your private letter of the 3rd, which I received by courier and for which I thank you very much, was of great interest to me because I gather from it to my relief that the retirement of Prince Bismarck causes you no anxieties, and that both the character and the other qualities of the Emperor William II warrant your assured expectation that the confidential relations between us and Berlin will continue entirely unchanged and that you look forward with confidence to the future.

As I have already had the honour to report, Lord Salisbury does not share your confidence, even if the official language of the English Cabinet is in complete agreement with that of our own in the view that there is no fear of a change in the foreign policy of Germany.

But Lord Salisbury is less convinced of the fact that the Emperor William "acts with much more reflection than is generally believed", and seems to fear that he might allow himself to be carried away by temporary impressions to abandon the paths which German policy has hitherto pursued.

* W.S.A. VIII/108, Berichte aus England. Deym to Kálnoky, Tel. No. 25 Secret, 20 March, and No. 28 A–G Very Confidential, 23 April 1890.
† W.S.A. VIII/109, Varia. Deym to Kálnoky, Private and Confidential, 9 April 1890. Throughout this letter the form of the second person singular is used in the original.

He does not doubt the sincerity of the assurances which the German Emperor has given to the representatives of the friendly Powers, but adds: "Even if he thinks thus today, what guarantee have we that he will not change his mind overnight?"

But what he seems to fear most is that as a result of the change in leadership in foreign affairs it is in the manner of treatment accorded to any new question which may arise that the absence of Prince Bismarck will make itself felt.

Concerning General Caprivi Lord Salisbury has up to now expressed his opinion very little. The former is an entirely unknown personality to him and the figure of the Chancellor has receded into the background in his mind because he assumes that the Emperor intends to direct foreign policy himself.

There is no doubt that a suggestion or a friendly piece of advice from General Caprivi today will not carry the same weight as an expression of opinion from Prince Bismarck carried formerly, and I am convinced that here in particular Count Hatzfeldt will soon become aware that the German Cabinet—in spite of the position of the German Empire as a Power, which has certainly suffered no diminution—no longer enjoys the same prestige as hitherto.

The article from the Times which I ventured to lay before you recently was certainly written by their permanent correspondent in Vienna; it displays a tone antagonistic to yourself, as indeed is to be expected from the antecedents of the writer; but the rightness of one idea underlying the article cannot be denied, namely that as a result of Prince Bismarck's retirement the Austro-Hungarian Cabinet will take the foremost place in the Triple Alliance and on many occasions it will prove necessary for you to take over the rôle of leader which you might have left to Prince Bismarck had he still been at the helm.

This seems to me to be the bright side for us in the question of the change of Chancellors, and in this respect the retirement of Prince Bismarck may still prove of advantage, even though in many other respects I deplore it.

It is particularly to be deplored with reference to the internal condition of Germany which will, I fear, be exposed to the dangers of experimentation. . . .

Minute by the Emperor Franz Joseph

This letter seems to me to contain much that is right.

Franz Joseph.

77. THE RUSSIAN VOLUNTEER FLEET AND THE RULE OF THE STRAITS

[The enforcement of the rule of the Straits forbidding the passage of foreign warships had been subject to certain exceptions from 1856 onwards. Applications for special privilege were so frequent in the years 1856–68 that in the latter year the Porte issued a circular to the effect that henceforth there was to be absolutely no exception save for ships by which the ruler of an independent state was being conveyed. In fact, however, the rule was relaxed after this date as before for "visits of Princes and other distinguished persons". Any other relaxation always produced a British remonstrance to the Porte. In the summer of 1890 vessels of the Russian Volunteer Fleet obtained permission to pass, and Salisbury instructed the British Ambassador to protest. At the same time, however, he contemplated a joint protest by the Powers, and drafted a circular dispatch for this purpose. Before issuing it, he consulted Hatzfeldt, who advised against it, and Hatzfeldt's discouragement was reinforced by advice given by Kálnoky to the British Ambassador at Vienna. In the following year Kálnoky informed Sir William White, while he was at Vienna, that, in his opinion, "Russia's attention was not attracted so much to Bulgaria as to the question of the Straits". White entirely concurred in this view. Shortly after this, on 19 September 1891, the Porte issued a circular to the signatory powers referring to the arrangements made for the passage of transports belonging to the Russian Volunteer Fleet. In this circular a distinction was drawn between vessels carrying a merchant flag, which were to be allowed to pass freely as commercial ships, and ships carrying soldiers, for whose passage a special *Iradé* would be needed. Salisbury consulted Kálnoky on the terms of a reply (**Doc. 184**). They were in general agreement, but the passage, "indicating that any privilege in respect of the Straits granted to any one Power is *ipso facto* granted to all", clearly originated with Salisbury.* The dispatch is im-

* W.S.A. VIII/111, Varia d'Angleterre 1891. Paget to Kálnoky, 1 October 1891.

portant because it was the foundation of a new policy. It was quoted later both by the British Government and by foreign representatives as the expression of Salisbury's doctrine. "Lord Salisbury", Count Metternich stated in 1911, "had laid it down that, if the Straits were opened at all, they must be opened equally for every one." *]

Document 184. *Salisbury consults with Austria-Hungary as to the reply to Turkey*, 1 October 1891†

Having made Lord Salisbury acquainted, by a Telegram dated the 24th of September, with the tenor of the answer which you proposed to make to the Turkish Circular respecting the arrangements for the passage of the Transports belonging to the Russian Volunteer Fleet through the Straits, I received from him last night a Telegram in which he desires me to thank you for your communication, and to say that he agrees in the proposed answer, but that he proposes to insert some words indicating that any privilege in respect of the Straits granted to any one Power is ipso facto granted to all. He adds that his intention would be to make the communication in a despatch to Sir William White, but that if you think the form of a note to the Turkish Ambassador or Chargé d'Affaires preferable he is quite ready to adopt it.

By a despatch which I sent home by our Messenger yesterday I informed Lord Salisbury that you had decided on making your reply in a despatch which you would address to Baron Calice of which he would be instructed to leave a copy with the Porte, and I gave its purport as follows:

"After expressing thanks for the communication of the Turkish Gov[ernmen]t and taking act of the declaration that the instructions to the Commandant of the Straits do not carry with them any alteration or modification of existing Regulations, but are simply intended to make those Regulations clear so as to prevent the recurrence of misunderstandings in future,—the despatch will state that the Imperial Gov[ernmen]t have learnt with satisfaction that H[is] M[ajesty] the

* Gooch and Temperley, [1933], IX (I), 321, No. 304.
† W.S.A. VIII/III, Varia d'Angleterre 1891. Paget to Kálnoky, 1 October 1891.

Sultan has not divested Himself of any of the rights conferred on Him by Treaties, to which the other Great Powers are also parties, for closing the passage of the Straits to the Ships of War of all Nations, rights which the Imperial Gov[ernmen]t is happy to infer it is H[is] M[ajesty]'s intention to continue to uphold."

This is a slightly different wording from my Telegram of the 24th of September, but the sense is precisely the same. Please recollect that I only reported what I understood it to be your intention (in both cases) to answer, and that I had no pretension to give the exact wording. I can shew you the original Telegram if you like, but I do not bring it at once in case it should not be convenient to you to receive me. I am at your orders of course at any time you may please to name. . . .

Document 185. *Salisbury lays down his own principles regarding the Rule of the Straits, 2 October 1891**

The Turkish Ambassador called at the F[oreign] O[ffice] on the 24th ult[imo] and communicated a circular desp[atch] from his Gov[ernmen]t, of which a copy is enclosed, describing the arrangement recently arrived at between the Sublime Porte and the Russian Embassy with regard to the passage of the Straits of the Bosphorus and the Dardanelles by vessels of the Russian Volunteer fleet, carrying the merchant flag, and conveying convicts or soldiers on their way to or from the Russian possessions in the far East.

H[er] M[ajesty's] Gov[ernmen]t desire to express their thanks to the Porte for the explanations offered in this paper. They take note of the declaration that there has been no infringement of the Treaty stipulations by which the Sultan pledges himself not to permit the passage of the Straits by ships of war in time of peace, and they are glad that the well known intention of the Porte to maintain those stipulations has received a fresh confirmation.

The agreement of the Powers on this subject is recorded

* Salisbury to White, No. 214, 2 October 1891, *F.O.* 78/4473. Cp. Gooch and Temperley, [1933], IX (1), 774–5, App. II.

in a series of international instruments: in the Convention of London of July 13, 1841, in the Convention annexed to the Treaty of Paris of March 30, 1856, again (with certain modifications required by the altered circumstances of the case) in the Treaty of London of March 13, 1871, and once more by Article 63 of the Treaty of Berlin of July 13, 1878.

In the opinion of H[er] M[ajesty's] Gov[ernmen]t it is of the essence of the rule thus sanctioned by the European Powers that it is applicable to all countries alike: and that any right in respect to the passage of the Straits which is a departure from the provisions of the existing treaties, will, if granted by the Sultan to one Power be, as a matter of course and *ipso facto*, equally granted to all.

[I think this will do very well. I have modified it to prevent our appearing to claim that an exceptional admission—e.g. of a Grand Duke—must necessarily involve the passage of five other Grand Dukes.*]

The arrangement made with the Russian Gov[ernmen]t on the present occasion does not appear to H[er] M[ajesty's] Gov[ernmen]t to be of a kind to call for further observation on their part.

Your Excellency will read this despatch to the Min[iste]r for F[oreign] A[ffairs] and give him a copy of it.

* Marginal note by Salisbury.

XXIV. ROSEBERY AND KIMBERLEY, 1892–5

78. THE LIBERAL ADMINISTRATION AND THE ACCORD À TROIS

[The assumption of power by a Liberal Government in England was watched with some anxiety by the Central Powers. Salisbury's policy of co-operation with Germany had been, in reality, forced upon him by the circumstances of the time. The colonial aspects of his policy shew that he found the bond an irksome one. But this fact only affected Anglo-German relations, so that the British connexion with the other two members of the Triple Alliance rested more firmly on common interests. The link was strongest with Italy. In the few years which followed the conclusion of the Mediterranean Agreements of 1887, Anglo-Italian friendship was deepened by the growing anxiety in both countries concerning the Franco-Russian *rapprochement*. When Salisbury fell in August 1892 he felt considerable anxiety about the future—an anxiety fully shared by the Queen.* The best reply to those who describe him as an "isolationist" is to be found in the letter he wrote on quitting office to the Permanent Under-Secretary at the Foreign Office, Sir Philip Currie. His biographer says that it was intended for Rosebery's perusal, and this statement is confirmed by internal evidence. Currie, alone among the permanent officials, knew the text of the December Mediterranean Agreement,† it was the new Foreign Minister whom Salisbury wished to impress. "The key of the present situation in Europe", he said, "is our position towards Italy, and through Italy to the Triple Alliance." He had always abstained, as every English minister must, from giving "any assurance of material assistance", but, he said, in this abstention "I have gone as far in the direction of pure neutrality as I think I could safely go". The tenor of his letter is unmistakably a plea for the continuance of the policy of the Anglo-Italian *entente*. He even suggested that any change would entail "very serious risks to European peace...as well as to the interests of this country".‡

* Cp. Lord Newton, *Lord Lansdowne*, [1929], 100.
† Cp. Gooch and Temperley, [1932], VIII, 13; W.S.A. Geheim xxv, Deym to Kálnoky, Tel. No. 20 Secret, 20 March 1890. Deym reports Salisbury's statement that "besides himself and the Queen only Sir Philip Currie knew the text"; he said also that no ambassador except Paget had been informed of the Agreement.
‡ Cecil, *Life of Salisbury*, [1932], IV, 404–5: Salisbury to Currie, 18 August 1892.

The absence of any reference to Austria-Hungary can be explained in several ways. In the first place the whole record of the negotiations from 1887 to this date shews that Italy had taken the lead in the conversations with Britain, just as Austria-Hungary had been mainly responsible for keeping Germany informed. Secondly, the anxiety of 1892 was centred on Italy; both because of her tension with France over the fortification of Biserta, and because it was feared that, in reaction, she might join the nascent Franco-Russian connexion. Thirdly, and this fact may well have weighed heavily with Salisbury, an *entente* with Italy—despite Parliamentary criticism in 1888–90—would be less uncongenial to a Liberal Administration than one with Austria-Hungary.

Rosebery, the new Liberal Foreign Minister, was strikingly frank to the Austro-Hungarian Ambassador. He would not disguise from him, he said, that Gladstone had been little inclined in the past to an Anglo-Austrian friendship, but Gladstone was preoccupied with the Irish question. Rosebery was not at this time prepared, however, to give any assurances even to Italy. His statement to Hatzfeldt on 5 September was extremely cautious, and he refused to alter its wording in any way.*

A few months later, however, the situation changed. British relations with France became more unfriendly. The most acute phase in this antagonism began in July 1893, when the sending of two French gun-boats up the river Mekong caused the smouldering Anglo-French rivalry over Siam to burst into flame. At that time there was a fierce press controversy in both England and France, which kept the tension unabated throughout the summer and autumn. A second factor increased the significance of this estrangement. As the year 1893 advanced it became clear to all the Powers that the long feared Franco-Russian understanding was developing. The visit of the Russian squadrons to Toulon in October attracted widespread attention, and although the exchange of letters which confirmed the Franco-Russian military convention did not in fact take place until the turn of the year, the effect of the *rapprochement* on the international situation preceded it. And at this very time rumours were rife of a projected Russian move in the Straits. These rumours had some justification in two actions taken by Russia at this time. In the first place she decided to maintain a Mediterranean squadron; and secondly, she was negotiating a commercial treaty with Turkey. Article 17 of the proposed treaty permitted the transport of war materials through the Straits. This was a concession which must in the nature of things be peculiar to Russia, for a similar privilege would serve no interest of any other Power. The Austro-Hungarian Ambassador at the Porte pointed this out to Sir A. Nicolson; Currie reinforced the argument by a minute, and Rosebery was clearly much disturbed. "Sir

* Gooch and Temperley, [1932], VIII, 4, 7; *G.P.*, [1927], VIII, 82–9.

A. Nicolson tells me privately", he wrote, "that the Porte pretends to think, or thinks, that the Russian Mediterranean fleet is directed against us. I think he had better say that any such concessions will reopen the Eastern question and compel us to review our position." *

These were the circumstances in which Rosebery opened his famous conversations with the Austro-Hungarian Ambassador in the summer of 1893. He was still not prepared to give binding assurances; but Salisbury too had refused these. He was, to all intents and purposes, prepared to revive the *entente* established in December 1887, although Sir Charles [Lord] Hardinge, writing many years later, said that the "Anglo-Italian agreement practically terminated in 1892, when L[or]d Rosebery came into office".† This was not the case as **Docs. 187–9** clearly shew. But the reasons for Lord Hardinge's statement are clear. The agreements were never formally renewed. There is no record of Rosebery's conversations of 1893–4 in the Foreign Office archives, though they are to be found in Austro-Hungarian and German sources. Despite Rosebery's coldness in 1892, there was a hint of greater readiness on his part to negotiate in a farewell speech by Paget at Vienna in May 1893 which he emphasized in a letter to Kálnoky.‡ The speech was commented on favourably in the English press, and Rosebery expressed his approval to Deym of what had been said (**Doc. 186**). Kálnoky, on hearing of this, suggested that Deym should draw Rosebery's attention to the exchange of notes in 1887, "of which Sir Ph. Currie as Permanent Under-Secretary must certainly have knowledge". When he had informed himself of the tenor of these notes he might be prepared to ratify them.§ The Austro-Hungarian Ambassador acted on these instructions on 27 June.

Conversations continued during the autumn, but on no occasion did Rosebery go beyond the statements which he had made in June (**Doc. 187**). His position was in fact made more difficult by differences of opinion with Gladstone on the desirability of strengthening the fleet. An important conversation took place on 28 December (**Doc. 188**).|| It was held on Rosebery's initiative, and it indicated that he meant to develop a naval strength great enough for the defence of British interests, and to maintain, at the same time, an understanding with the Central Powers. But he was not prepared to turn this into an alliance.

* Nicolson to Rosebery, No. 414 Confidential, 29 August 1893. *Minute* by Rosebery dated 23 September, *F.O.* 78/4592.
† Gooch and Temperley, VIII, [1932], 32, No. 17, *min.* The minute is written on a dispatch dated 11 March 1907.
‡ W.S.A. VIII/113, Varia d'Angleterre 1893. Paget to Kálnoky, 13 May 1893.
§ W.S.A. Geheim xxv/b. Kálnoky to Deym, Private letter, Secret, 22 June 1893.
|| W.S.A. VIII/172, England III. Deym to Kálnoky, Secret, 29 December 1893. Cp. Hatzfeldt's report, *G.P.*, [1927], VIII, 127–8.

This attitude he continued to maintain in the winter of 1893–4, when Austria-Hungary feared a Russian move in the Near East, and was not quite sure of Germany. She therefore turned to Great Britain. Would Rosebery fight for Constantinople? That was one of the two "questions", said Sir Philip Currie in 1885, on which it had been assumed, "ever since I came to the Foreign Office" that England would fight. * On 25 January 1894 Kálnoky instructed Deym to raise this question with Rosebery. Deym saw Rosebery on the 31st, and found that he had prepared a statement shewing the lengths to which he would go (**Doc. 189**). Rosebery was partly influenced by Germany's aloofness in the Near East, but mainly by his unwillingness to give binding assurances. He refused, in spite of pressure, to bring the matter before the Cabinet. But as will be seen (*infra*, p. 487) he made an important statement four weeks later.]

Document 186. *Rosebery assures Austria-Hungary of his recognition of Near Eastern interests, and of his control of foreign policy, 14 June 1893*†

When I [Deym] saw Lord Rosebery again for the first time after a considerable interval, he asked me at once, whether I was satisfied with Sir Augustus Paget's speech, and said that he considered the speech a very good one and was in agreement with all that had been said.

I replied that I was very glad to learn that he welcomed the views expressed by Sir Augustus Paget on the relations between England and Austria-Hungary, but that it had given me no less pleasure to observe that the English Press, almost with one voice, had expressed agreement with the English Ambassador's speech, in some cases in very cordial terms, and that I had found no protest in any paper against the cooperation of England and Austria-Hungary. To this Lord Rosebery replied that at present those who disapproved of his policy formed a small minority, and that it was generally recognised, both in the Liberal and the Conservative party, that England's interests in the Balkan Peninsula were identical with those of Austria-Hungary, and that outside these there was no question on which the interests of the two States were divergent. This statement of Lord Rosebery's gave me a

---

* Cecil, *Life of Salisbury*, [1931], III, 259. Belgium was the other "question" on which England would fight—"if she had an ally".

† W.S.A. Geheim xxv/b. Deym to Kálnoky, Secret, 14 June 1893.

welcome opportunity to sound him further concerning the attitude of England in certain eventualities. I told him that I was glad to hear this from him, but that I must assume that if our interests in the Balkan Peninsula were identical, England must have the same interest as ourselves in seeing that Constantinople should not fall into the hands of the Russians, and I put to him the direct question: "If Russia threatens Constantinople, will England give support to the Sultan in order to ward off a Russian attack?" To this Lord Rosebery replied: "I should not venture to undertake an obligation in this matter; but there is no doubt that the first news of a Russian attack on Constantinople would raise a general cry of war* in England, and that if the same mood prevailed in England as is prevalent now, the cry of war would be so loud that the voice of those who are against any intervention in continental policy and are in favour of peace à tout prix would be drowned and overwhelmed. But, as I said, I could not undertake an obligation of immediate action on the part of England."

Lord Rosebery went on to discuss the views on foreign policy prevailing in the Cabinet; he admitted that the Prime Minister inclined to the policy of non-intervention—or rather, had formerly inclined to it, for now, he said, he could not complain of any difficulties with the Prime Minister: on the contrary, the Prime Minister gave him quite a free hand, and on the part of his other colleagues also he found complete agreement with the policy on which he had embarked.

In the course of further conversation I remarked that a close association of England with the Triple Alliance could only ensure all the more the preservation of peace, and that in view of the attitude of France, a *rapprochement* with the Triple Alliance could certainly only be advantageous to England. On this Lord Rosebery let fall the remark that certainly England's relations with France left much to be desired, and the French Government was acting in every way as if its aim were to drive England into the arms of the Triple Alliance.†

* "Ein allgemeines Kriegsgeschrei hervorrufen würde."
† Cp. Rosebery's report to the Queen on 26 July 1893, Crewe, *Lord Rosebery*, [1931], II, 425–7, where a similar expression is used. Cp. also *Letters of Queen Victoria*, 3rd Ser., II, [1931], 284–5.

Document 187. *Rosebery explains his attitude to the*
Mediterranean Agreements, 27 June 1893*

In accordance with the commission with which you
honoured me in your private letter of the 22nd, I [Deym] took
yesterday the first opportunity which presented itself, in
order to sound Lord Rosebery as to whether he would be
inclined for his part to ratify the consent given by the English
Cabinet to the Punctations arranged in the year 1887 on the
basis of our common interests in the East.

I referred to my conversation with him concerning the
speech of Sir Augustus Paget, and informed Lord Rosebery
that Your Excellency had intimated your lively satisfaction
that in the important questions of the Balkans he had also
expressed himself as being in such full accord with our policy.
He thereupon interrupted me with the remark that this
complete accord actually existed, and that the political views
developed by Sir Augustus Paget in his speech were bound
to have his full approval, because he was convinced that the
foreign policy pursued by England in recent years was the
only right one and could only be to her advantage.

Continuing, I then referred to the exchange of communications which had taken place on Your Excellency's instructions,
and drew Lord Rosebery's attention to the practical advantage
which this general understanding between us, England and
Italy had had, in that we had remained in constant touch and
were able to regard and to deal with the questions which arose
from a similar standpoint.

To this Lord Rosebery only replied: "I must explain to
you first of all quite frankly, that I have never taken cognizance of the letters exchanged and the Punctations to
which you refer, although the fact of their existence is known
to me. My reason was this: if a Parliamentary question on
this matter were to be addressed to me, I wished to be in a
position to answer with a good conscience that these letters
were unknown to me. For the rest, such an exchange of
notes has no great value in my eyes, since without the

* W.S.A. Geheim xxv/b. Deym to Kálnoky, Secret, 28 June 1893.

ratification of Parliament the consent of the Cabinet has no binding force; in spite of all the identity of views existing between Count Kálnoky and myself, I should not feel myself impelled, therefore, to confirm this identity of views by an exchange of notes."

I then observed to the Secretary of State that it was not a question of devising a new exchange of notes, but rather of subjecting to discussion the separate points concerning which agreement had been reached with his predecessor, in order to establish how far he himself was in agreement with these.

Lord Rosebery replied that he would also have scruples in doing this, since such an exchange of ideas and a ratification on his part of the consent of the former Cabinet to the Puncta-tions would only have any value if this ratification were made in consultation with the Cabinet. But he could not conceal from me the fact that in respect of foreign policy very divergent views existed in the Cabinet. It could not be unknown to me that Mr. Gladstone, especially in earlier days, was by no means kindly disposed to Austria-Hungary.

It was to be feared, therefore, that whereas to-day identity of interests between England and Austria-Hungary exists in actual fact, is recognised, and is not seriously controverted in any quarter, such a discussion and definition of concordant views might lead to the recording of a divergence in view.

"If, however," Lord Rosebery continued, "I were to come to an understanding on individual concrete questions without the knowledge of the Cabinet, I should be in danger of someone's getting wind of it and I should be asked about it in the Cabinet. In that case no alternative would remain to me but to retire, a course which I flatter myself I may assume would be regarded by you with regret. In any case it is very doubtful whether after my retirement anyone would take over the conduct of foreign affairs whose ideas would be so much in accord with those of your Cabinet. To-day I can say that in the conduct of foreign affairs no obstacles are placed in my way by the Prime Minister, nor by my colleagues in the Cabinet. But if I were to allow myself to be persuaded to agree in advance that England would take up a definite attitude in certain cases, my position would become quite untenable."

Lord Rosebery said further that he personally was in complete agreement with Your Excellency's ideas, that I had had opportunity repeatedly of getting to know his mind, and that he also cherished the hope that Your Excellency would give him your whole confidence; but that this agreement of views was a purely personal one, and that our intimate reciprocal relations must rest exclusively on reciprocal confidence.

Lord Rosebery mentioned also that during his period of office my Italian colleague had likewise brought up the question of an exchange of notes between Lord Salisbury and the Italian Ambassador, and that he had been precluded, for the same reasons that he had explained to me, from entering into discussion of these documents, although he had assured my colleague that he was as deeply concerned as his predecessor in the maintenance of the *status quo* in the Mediterranean.

Finally Lord Rosebery repeated a remark which I have already had the honour to report to you in a private letter—namely, that the French Government was acting in every way as if it aimed at alienating the few friends which still remained to it in the English Cabinet and at driving England into the arms of the Triple Alliance.

After the foregoing explanation of Lord Rosebery, I did not think it opportune to insist further on a discussion of this question, and confined myself to telling him that I could fully appreciate the difficulties of his position, and that I could assure him that Your Excellency's attitude to him was one of entire confidence.

Document 188. *Rosebery relies on the strength of the British fleet, 28 December* 1893*

Lord Rosebery let me know yesterday that he would come to the Foreign Office and would receive me.

I apologised to him in case he should have come on my account, saying that I had no communication to make to

* W.S.A. vIII/172, England III. Deym to Kálnoky, Secret, 29 December 1893.

him, but had only enquired whether he would be coming to
the Foreign Office so that I might take leave of him. He
assured me that it had in no way inconvenienced him to
come, that on the contrary he was anxious to speak to me
before my departure, because he wished to express his views
further on the questions to which we had recently referred.

This opening gave me a welcome opportunity to return to
the subject, and I repeated as exactly as possible the explanation contained in your despatch of the 20th.

The Secretary of State made clear to me first of all that he
was deeply concerned in the preservation of England's position
in the Mediterranean, and that he was not blind to the fact
that the present political situation held dangers for the
English. He had indeed insisted in the Cabinet that a
decision should be made for a sufficient increase in the fleet
and he asked me to inform Your Excellency in strict confidence
that this was now assured. He added: "If the Cabinet had
refused to order this, I should have handed in my resignation.
This increase will be such that there can no longer be doubt
in any quarter that we are determined to maintain our
supremacy at sea undiminished, and I anticipate that this
measure, which for the present it is true, I must treat as
secret and only communicate to you for Count Kálnoky—
and I ask you not to mention it in an official despatch—will
suffice to remove completely the uneasiness of Italy concerning
her own position in the Mediterranean."

Lord Rosebery then explained that the English war fleet
today was far superior to the French and Russian fleets
combined, but that it was a question of continuing to have
a stronger fleet even after the equipment of all the warships
now being built in Russia and France, and that measures had
been taken to secure this.

Passing to my explanations, the Secretary of State said
that he would not deny the danger that there might be a
rapprochement between France and Italy, and that Italy might
allow herself to be persuaded to undertake to remain neutral
in the case of a war between England and France; he would
moreover admit that it would be in the interests of England

to come to an understanding with Italy to ensure for herself the co-operation of the Italian fleet; but for this England, on her side, would have to take over definite obligations, a course which was entirely opposed to English policy.

No one in England would be ready to see the country committed for the future, and he could not embark on a policy of alliances.

He observed further: "You were kind enough to lay stress on my position in the country and in the Cabinet, and on the esteem which I enjoy with both parties; but I must frankly acknowledge to you, that my position is not so strong that I should venture today to confront the Cabinet with such a proposal."

As far as the danger of an understanding between France and Italy is concerned, Lord Rosebery is of opinion that it is not so threatening at the moment. Above all, he said, Italian interests in the Mediterranean are so identical with those of England that co-operation between her and Italy is clearly indicated, and only if England had shown herself unsympathetic on the question of the position in the Mediterranean might Italy have thought herself obliged to make a pact with France. As things are, however, it would take a good deal to make the Italian Government come to such a decision. With regard to the advantages which France might offer to Italy, the Secretary of State believes above all that the present French Chamber is just as much inclined to protective tariffs as the previous one, and would never be persuaded to make any substantial commercial concessions to Italy. Certainly France could aid Italy by supporting the issue of a loan in France. But England also would be in a position to help Italy in this way, said Lord Rosebery, adding however immediately: "It is true that the present moment would be highly unfavourable to the issue of a loan in England, since people have burnt their fingers so severely with foreign securities that it is difficult to place any foreign loans."

But as far as an understanding on their respective territorial situations is concerned, Lord Rosebery thinks that the chauvinistic spirit of the French is too strong for any concession in this matter to be made to Italy, and therefore has little apprehension of an understanding. But what he chiefly relies on, he said, is the maladroitness of French statesmen, who have recently done everything to make enemies of the whole world. Not only did they make themselves as disagreeable as possible to England and Italy but also to Spain.

Lord Rosebery ended with the remark that England must see that she had a fleet so powerful that France could not venture to attack her, even with the help of an ally.

I repeated to Lord Rosebery in conclusion that Your Excellency had only wished him to know your conception of the political situation, but that you had in no way intended to offer him any counsel.

Document 189. *Rosebery refuses to give binding assurances concerning Constantinople, 31 January 1894**

As I [Deym] have already ventured to report to Your Excellency by telegraph, I have mentioned the content of the secret communication of January 25th, No. 1. to Lord Rosebery, and have utilised all the arguments contained in the communication in order to convince Lord Rosebery that, even if there is no imminent danger, it is still imperative that the English cabinet should come to a decision now, as to whether, in the event of Russia's bringing up the question of the passage through the Dardanelles and the Bosphorus, they are prepared to adhere firmly to the traditional English policy and to oppose by every possible means any alteration of the status quo with regard to the closing of the Straits,—or whether they will abandon the Straits, and with them Constantinople, to Russia.

Sir Edmund Monson's report had already prepared Lord Rosebery for my broaching the question, and he was ready with a reply in fairly general terms. What he did not seem to have reckoned with, however, were the conclusions which Your Excellency explained that you would be obliged to

* W.S.A. viii/172, England iii. Deym to Kálnoky, No. 7A–E Secret, 7 February 1894. A short telegraphic report of the interview was sent on 31 January.

draw, should the English cabinet resolve to abandon the Straits to Russia.

I explained to him that the Royal and Imperial Government could not expose itself to the danger of being unable to count with certainty on England's protection of Constantinople, should the case in point arise, and that, if England for any reason had to abandon her traditional policy in the question of the Straits, the Royal and Imperial government would find itself compelled to confine its activities to the maintenance and safeguarding of Austro-Hungarian interests in the Balkans, and to leave the Straits to their fate, i.e. to Russia.

The Secretary of State agreed entirely that, if Russia were to gain free passage for warships through the Bosphorus, this would mean that Constantinople was handed over to Russia. He objected, however, that, even if Russia came to an agreement with the Sultan, she could not gain the free passage through the Straits without the concurrence of the Guaranteeing Powers, and that she would never obtain this concurrence from England. I admitted this, provided that the possibility of a coup de main were completely disregarded. Yet even if Russia should first attempt to attain the desired end by diplomatic means, a great deal would depend on the way in which the Powers protested against such a demand. I explained that, for us it was a question of finding out, whether England is determined even to go as far as war in the event of an attempt on the part of Russia, to override the opposition of the Powers. The resoluteness with which such a project was opposed from the very beginning, might well determine, whether Russia will attempt to gain the free passage by force. I pointed out that the attitude of Austria-Hungary towards such a question, would naturally depend on the way in which England was determined to proceed, and hence Lord Rosebery must find it quite comprehensible, that Your Excellency believed it essential to insist, that the English cabinet should deal with this question and reveal to us in strict confidence, what attitude they intend to assume in such an eventuality.

I added that I was not instructed to make any positive proposals to him, and that for us it was in the first instance a question of finding out exactly how far we could rely on England.

Although Lord Rosebery assured me that Sir Philip Currie had received from him the most comprehensive instructions, and would repeat to Your Excellency, what he had told me, I will nevertheless not neglect to reproduce the utterances of the Secretary of State as accurately as I can.

As regards England's attitude in the event of a Russian attempt to force the free passage through the Straits, Lord Rosebery obviously did not originally intend to give me such precise assurances as he ultimately did; for only when he perceived that his asseverations in quite general terms of adherence to the English policy did not satisfy me, did he take another tone and say: "Je vous donne l'assurance que je suis parfaitement décidé à maintenir le status quo actuel dans la question des détroits et que je ne reculerais pas devant le danger d'entraîner l'Angleterre dans une guerre avec la Russie; mais je dois vous dire franchement que si la France se trouvait à côté de la Russie, il ne serait pas possible à l'Angleterre de défendre Constantinople contre les deux puissances, en tout cas nous ne pourrions laisser notre flotte dans la Méditerranée courir le risque d'une catastrophe, se trouvant entre la flotte russe et la flotte française. Dans ce cas il nous faudrait l'assistance de la triple alliance pour tenir la France en échec. C'est moi et non le cabinet anglais qui vous donne ces assurances et vous pouvez compter sur ma parole."* Here he also let fall the remark that, even if we had a powerful army, our fleet could not come into question on this matter; and that the help of the Italian fleet could hardly suffice England in such a case, since, although Italy possessed a number of very good ships, yet complete ignorance prevailed as to the value of the Italian fleet in case of war.

I raised the objection that, while indeed we placed unbounded confidence in him, I still feared that Your Excellency

* Quoted in translation in W. L. Langer, *The Franco-Russian Alliance, 1890–1894*, [1929], 379. The date of the report is given there as 31 January 1894.

could hardly base Austro-Hungarian policy on his personal assurances, since, if the case in point arose, the cabinet might decide in a contrary sense. To this he replied: "C'est moi le ministre des Affaires étrangères qui vous donne ces assurances, c'est moi qui dirige la politique étrangère et je suis sûr, le cas échéant, d'être soutenu par l'opinion publique en Angleterre." Thereupon I remarked that Your Excellency had considered it especially important, that the English cabinet should be consulted on this question, and Lord Rosebery answered: "Ce que vous me demandez il m'est impossible de le faire et ce n'est pas dans votre intérêt que je le fasse." Thereupon I asked him whether I was to take these words to imply that, if he were to bring the question before the English cabinet to-day, the latter would perhaps adopt a decision counter to the principle of adherence to the traditional English policy. The minister interrupted me: "By no means, even if Mr. Gladstone himself is no friend of Turkey, and the party that will not hear of active participation of England in European policy in the East is also represented in the cabinet, I am yet absolutely convinced that the Cabinet would never adopt a decision to the contrary effect, but would entirely approve of my policy. One thing, however, which I should not only have to fear, but of which I am quite certain, is, that the cabinet would declare itself obliged to decline to form binding resolutions to-day for an eventuality that is still far distant. If therefore I were forced to give you an answer of this kind from the English cabinet, the situation would be much more unfavourable for you. To-day you have my word, and on this you can rely with certainty as long as I am minister."

When, in spite of this, I endeavoured to persuade him of the advantage of securing the agreement of the cabinet, Lord Rosebery said: "Franchement je trouve que vous êtes un peu trop exigeant de vouloir que je soumette déjà aujourd'hui à la délibération du Cabinet une question qui ne surgira probablement pas de si tôt et en tout cas dans un temps tout-à-fait indéterminé.—Et après tout si la Russie avait réellement l'intention de mettre cette question sur le tapis un de ces jours, elle ne pourra trouver une solution sans le concours des Puissances. Il sera bien encore temps lorsque la Russie s'adressera aux Puissances de demander au Cabinet de sanctionner ma politique au sujet des mesures à prendre. En présence d'un danger imminent, le Cabinet anglais, soutenu par le sentiment du pays, sera unanime à maintenir le prestige de l'Angleterre, je n'ai pas le moindre doute à ce sujet."

Lord Rosebery then added in explanation, that he was not of opinion that the English fleet was no match for the combined Franco-Russian fleet, but here the special point in question was the critical situation in which the English fleet would be placed, between the French fleet in the Mediterranean and the Russian fleet in the Black Sea. If France were not kept in check at all, he thinks that, in the event of England's having to take up the struggle against both Powers, there would remain no alternative for her, but to withdraw from the Mediterranean, as long as her fleet had not achieved a success.

Lord Rosebery expressed his regret concerning Germany's complete lack of interest in the question and especially deplored her emphatic assertion, that her interests were not involved in the Eastern question. He considered that this attitude on Germany's part greatly aggravated the danger. The Secretary of State also spoke of the possibility of the Powers being unable to agree to use their combined forces, to prevent Russia from gaining free passage through the Bosphorus. He considered that in this case Constantinople must be placed under international protection, to avoid its being abandoned to the Russians. However, I refrained from following up the minister's discussion of such an eventuality, because it lay outside the scope of my instructions.

Lord Rosebery moreover remarked that he questioned the perfect entente between France and Russia, and that it was still doubtful how far this extended.

It could not escape my notice that my statements about a possible change of Austro-Hungarian policy in the question of the Straits, in the event of our being unable to rely with certainty on the English fleet, had made a deep impression on the Secretary of State. I therefore read him the extract from Your Excellency's private letter of October 25th, 1887, to Baron Biegeleben. I had taken a copy of this with me, with the omission of the last section, which states that Russia possesses neither a fleet nor an ally. I told him that this extract from a private letter of an earlier date had been sent to me by Your Excellency for my personal information, because Your Excellency would be obliged to assume the same attitude to-day, if England were inclined to abandon her traditional policy in this matter. I omitted the aforesaid passage deliberately, because I did not consider it expedient to draw his special attention to the fact, that the present situation is considerably less favourable for England, as he must surely realize this in any case.

At Lord Rosebery's request, I then let him read the extract again himself; he expressed his astonishment, that Austria-Hungary might perhaps rest content with the exclusion of Russian influence merely from that part of the Balkan states adjoining our frontier and stretching to the Aegean Sea on the other, without extending this exclusion of Russian influence to the countries bordering the Black Sea.

I answered the Secretary of State, that such a state of affairs would indeed be extremely unfavourable, and that we could only be reconciled to it if England's attitude placed us in the unfortunate position of having no alternative. I bade him consider how long it would be possible to exclude Russian influence from Bulgaria, if Russia were to gain a firm footing in Constantinople. In the course of our conversation, I also referred to the telegram, which Lord Derby had addressed to Sir Andrew Buchanan on August 14th, 1877,* and of which Lord Rosebery was hitherto ignorant. However, he made a note of the date, and said he would have it brought to him, and take cognisance of it.

The Secretary of State repeatedly requested me to regard his assurances as strictly confidential, and added jestingly: "C'est qu'il y va de ma tête si on apprenait ici que je vous ai donné ces assurances." I therefore considered it expedient to call on him again the next day and ask him whether Sir

* Cp. Derby to Buchanan, No. 284, 24 August 1877, *F.O.* 7/894; printed by Dwight E. Lee in *Slavonic Review*, x, [1931–2], 463–5.

Philip Currie was aware, how far he [Lord Rosebery] was resolved to adhere to the traditional English policy,—and that, if need be, he would not shrink from war,—and whether therefore, Your Excellency might speak openly with Sir Philip Currie and Sir Edmund Monson about the assurances which I had received. Lord Rosebery replied that Sir Philip Currie enjoys his complete confidence, and possesses accurate knowledge of his intentions, and that it could therefore only be agreeable to him if Your Excellency would speak unreservedly with Sir Philip Currie. As far as Sir Edmund Monson is concerned, Lord Rosebery said that he had indeed no reason to fear that he might commit any indiscretion, but as he had expressed himself so candidly to me, he would be pleased if Your Excellency were somewhat reserved towards the ambassador with reference to his statements;—the more so as he had as yet committed nothing to writing concerning our conversation, and had not yet informed the ambassador about it.

I took advantage of this opportunity to inform the Secretary of State what I had reported to Your Excellency by telegraph, because I wanted to make sure that I had reproduced the substance of his statements accurately. Thereupon he remarked, that he had given the matter deep consideration since the previous day, and was confirmed in his conviction, that it would on no account be advisable to bring the question up for discussion in the Cabinet at present.

The task imposed upon me by Your Excellency,—that of prevailing upon Lord Rosebery to look more closely into the question of the Straits, and of convincing him that it was essential that the English cabinet should define their attitude to this question,—was no easy one, and I admit that I did not entertain very sanguine hopes as to the success of this confidential démarche. At the same time I could not help realizing that it was essential, in the present political situation, that Lord Rosebery should be persuaded to declare his hand, —for as far as we knew he had not gone into the question thoroughly as yet, and his intimations to me on various occasions were of such a general character that it was impossible to deduce from them with any certainty, how far he is determined to adhere to the traditional English policy in the East.

Even if I have unfortunately not succeeded in persuading Lord Rosebery of the necessity of bringing this extremely important question before the cabinet—and I must venture to observe with all respect, that my last interview with the Secretary of State left me no hope whatever, of his being prevailed upon to do this before the question is broached by Russia,—yet I believe none the less, that this démarche has brought about a certain clarification of ideas, and that Lord Rosebery's statements, which are as straightforward and definite as could be desired, can by no means be regarded as valueless. For even if he has bound himself by no protocol, he has committed himself personally, and, at least as long as he is in charge of English policy, we know how far we can rely on England,—and this confidential discussion would always offer a starting-point, from which to come to an agreement on a concrete question.

[On 26 February Rosebery followed up this inconclusive interview by an important specific pronouncement. England could defend the Straits alone against Russia. He would indeed prefer not to have Austria-Hungary or Italy with him, because he did not want a European war on the question of the Straits. What he did ask was that he might "count on the Triple Alliance to prevent France from taking part in the struggle". Rosebery ended: "Maintenant vous connaissez le fond du sac." *

Kimberley, who succeeded Rosebery at the Foreign Office, confirmed his assurances. On 13 March 1894 he told Deym that Rosebery had informed him of the *pourparlers*, and that "he associated himself entirely with the declaration of Lord Rosebery, only personally of course, for the moment did not seem to him any more suitable for submitting the matter to the Cabinet. He could only approve the reservation which Rosebery had made for the case in which France should make common cause with Russia, for, in consideration of the scant friendship which France was shewing for England, this did not seem to him an impossibility." †]

* W.S.A. VIII/172, England III. Deym to Kálnoky, Tel. No. 14, 26 February 1894. There does not seem any reason to doubt the authenticity of this conversation or of the next one.

† W.S.A. VIII/172, England III. Deym to Kálnoky, Tel. No. 22 Secret, 14 March 1894.

79. THE BASIN OF THE NIGER

[The three main colonial issues in the time of the Gladstone-Rosebery administration concerned three river valleys in Africa, the Niger, the Nile, and the Congo. The Royal Niger Company, whose charter dated from 1886, was operating in the lower reaches of the river, while the French were active on its upper course. During 1894 the question became acute, for Germany concluded agreements with both Britain and France concerning the hinterland of the Cameroons. Kimberley, when he heard of the Franco-German negotiations, protested that they affected the British position on the Benue river (a confluent of the Niger). Despite this, however, the agreement was concluded unchanged, and Kimberley heard that in the course of the discussions the German negotiator had used language indicating that common antagonism to the Royal Niger Company was a factor in the settlement (**Doc. 191**). The wording of the Preamble to the Agreement contained, moreover, specific criticisms of the Company. The incident is significant because it led Kimberley to adopt an attitude of watchfulness to Germany in African questions more than two months before the German protest against the Congo Treaty.]

Document 190. *Kimberley adopts an attitude of watchfulness towards Germany in African questions,* 31 *March* 1894*

Say to Sir E. Malet that this whole proceeding shows how little reliance can be placed in the assurance of the German Government that they desire to co-operate with us in Africa, assurances repeated to me by C[ount] Hatzfeldt at an interview which I had with him on the 28th inst[ant].

It appears from the memo[randum] that the German G[overnment] contemplate joining the French and putting pressure on the Niger Company.

It will be necessary for us now to be strictly on the guard against this possible combination with our rivals there and elsewhere in Africa, and to be cautious in making any concession to them in relation to African questions.

Point out that Berlin Act is wrongly quoted.

K[IMBERLEY]

March 31/94.

* Minute by Kimberley, 31 March 1894, *F.O.* 64/1332.

Document 191. *Kimberley maintains British interests in the Niger Valley, 11 April 1894**

...I subsequently in the course of conversation [with Count Hatzfeldt] referred generally to our relations with Germany in Africa, and said I could not conceal from him that the conclusion of the Treaty by which the French were given access to the Niger had made a disagreeable impression upon us more especially as it appeared from the statement which accompanied the publication of the Treaty that this stipulation was conceived in a spirit of hostility to the Niger Company.

Count H[atzfeldt] said that all this difficulty had arisen from our not having acted in concert with Germany when we entered into the agreement with France as to our mutual spheres of influence in the vicinity of Lake Tchad.

I said however this might be, bygones were bygones and what was of importance now was that we should act in concert in questions which still remained to be settled and I instanced the country in the vicinity of Togoland. The French were pressing forward from Dahomey in that direction and it would be very desirable that we should have an understanding with Germany in order to counteract their designs in that quarter.

K[IMBERLEY]. Apr. 11.

80. ROSEBERY, KIMBERLEY, AND THE POLICY OF THE FREE HAND

[The attitude of Germany was decisive in the summer of 1894 in lessening English friendship for the Triple Alliance.† The spring opened with renewed assurances of Anglo-Austro-Hungarian co-operation in the Near East. The dissociation of Germany from an active policy at Constantinople was a fact which both Britain and Austria-Hungary had to recognize, and on them fell the duty

* Minute by Kimberley, 11 April 1894, *F.O.* 64/1332. This minute, written in Kimberley's own hand, became the basis of his dispatch to Malet, No. 41 Africa, 17 April 1894.
† Cp. W. L. Langer, *The Franco-Russian Alliance, 1890–1894*, [1929], 350-91; *The Diplomacy of Imperialism*, [1935], I, 48-56, 132-41.

of opposing Russia's designs. Monson, who had succeeded Paget at Vienna, reported that Kálnoky was "evidently much relieved by the knowledge that his Ambassador at the Porte no longer stands alone but is supported by the courage and firmness of a really strong British colleague [Currie] holding views and assuming an attitude identical with his own".*

This was the situation when British activities in a wholly different sphere brought about a serious change. On 12 May 1894 the Congo Treaty was signed between England and the King of the Belgians. The circumstances of the case and the general state of Anglo-French relations made it inevitable that France would object, but it was not expected that Germany would do so. But in fact Germany protested vigorously, fastening upon Article III, and pointing out that this gave to Britain a strip of territory running from the north of Lake Tanganyika to the south of Lake Albert Edward, which had already been the subject of Anglo-German controversy in 1890.† The official protest was made on 11 June. The Kaiser raised the question informally with Malet on the 9th. "He said", Malet reported, "that leasing of the strip was fatal to future of German East Africa.... It is above all things your interest to avoid a Conference and how can you prevent a Conference if there is a general demand for it?"‡ Four days later Rosebery sent for the Austro-Hungarian Ambassador and warned him in forceful terms of the possible results of the German attitude,§ emphasizing his views in a second conversation of the 14th (**Doc. 192**). Kálnoky telegraphed in reply that he was communicating Rosebery's views to Germany,‖ but that he hoped they were the result of a temporary irritation. He was to some extent justified by events. On the 16th Deym was again asked to call on Rosebery and was told that the latter, after reflecting on their previous conversation, "had come to the conclusion that he [Deym] was right. That a strip of territory 25 kilometres in extent, in Africa, part of it desert, was not important enough to England to warrant a complete change in her foreign policy. Moreover, he had studied the text of the German note and that had also convinced him that he had been mistaken in thinking it wounding." Rosebery also asked him to say that he withdrew the communications he had made on the earlier occasions. He added a request that Kálnoky, if he had not already mentioned the matter to Berlin, should state to the Berlin Cabinet that "in the interests of the maintenance of

---

* Monson to Kimberley, No. 82 Secret, 31 March 1894, *F.O.* 7/1213. Sir Philip Currie succeeded Sir Clare Ford at Constantinople in March 1894.
† Cp. *Letters of Queen Victoria*, 3rd Ser., [1931], ii, 405–7.
‡ Malet to Kimberley, Tel. No. 9 Africa Secret, 11 June 1894, *F.O.* 64/1375. Cp. the Emperor William's account of this conversation, *G.P.*, [1927], viii, 446–8.
§ Cp. Rosebery's report of this conversation to the Queen, Crewe, *Lord Rosebery*, [1931], ii, 448–9.
‖ Cp. *G.P.*, [1927], viii, 455, 456–7.

the *entente* which exists between the Cabinet of London and the Triple Alliance in those questions of European policy where they had common concern, it would be desirable to consider English susceptibilities in Colonial matters".* Conversations followed both with Hatzfeldt in London and through Malet at Berlin. King Leopold was terrified at Germany's intervention and Rosebery did not feel he could resist. He had a wholesome respect for the German army and therefore withdrew Article III of the Congo Treaty. When a Blue Book was laid on the negotiations, the incident could be regarded as closed.† In fact, however, the feeling it engendered on Rosebery's side was sufficient to prevent any further development of the *entente* in his period. Germany had proved, at once, objectionable and formidable and had spoiled his plan. Once again, as in the days of Salisbury, the colonial question had disturbed the general tenor of European policy.]

Document 192. *Rosebery threatens to return to a policy of the Free Hand,* 13 *June,* 14 *June* 1894‡

Lord Rosebery asked me to come to see him this afternoon§ and to bring to Your Excellency's knowledge what follows:

The Prime Minister is very uneasy about the political situation in Europe and considers the death of the Emperor of Morocco as a new danger to European peace. Up to the present since he has been in power, the English Government has always supported fully the policy of the Triple Alliance. The attitude of Germany in Colonial questions causes him to reflect and he asks himself whether England would not do better to alter her policy and to recover complete freedom of action. Germany was a party to the Triple Alliance and if she follows in Africa a policy hostile to England and makes common cause with France, it will become impossible for the Cabinet of St. James to maintain her *entente* with the Triple Alliance in European questions.

* W.S.A. viii/172, England iii. Deym to Kálnoky, Tel. No. 32 Secret, 16 June 1894; Hatzfeldt reported the gist of this conversation, as it had been given to him by Deym, on the same day. *G.P.*, [1927], viii, 456–7.
† Cp. Temperley and Penson, *Century of Diplomatic Blue Books*, No. 1404a.
‡ W.S.A. viii/172, England iii. Deym to Kálnoky, Tels. Nos. 29 and 31 Secret, 13 and 14 June 1894.
§ Cp. *Letters of Queen Victoria*, 3rd Ser., [1931], ii, 404–5.

"Today, my hands are tied," said Lord Rosebery, "for I have taken engagements for certain eventualities and what I have promised I hold to loyally, but I consider myself entitled to expect in return better treatment on the part of Germany. In short if Germany continues to show herself so hostile to the Cabinet of St. James I shall feel obliged to take back the assurances which I have given on the subject of Constantinople."

Lord Rosebery called on me to add to the communication which he made to me yesterday. He meant not only that he would take back his assurances on the subject of Constantinople but also the undertakings he had given to the Triple Alliance on the question of Italy and other matters if Germany continues to place herself on the side of France in Colonial questions; for it would not be possible for him to remain the friend of Germany in Europe if she shows herself hostile to England in Africa.

Document 193. *Kimberley defines his position in relation to Germany and Russia, 21 November 1894**

I had to-day some conversation with Count Deym on the subject of our relations with Germany and the Triple Alliance.

I told H[is] Ex[cellency] that in a recent discussion with the German Ambassador I had expressed to him my regret that it should be supposed that the closer relations between us and Russia, would prejudicially affect our relations with Germany. I had assured him that a good understanding between us and Russia in no way implied that we had become insensible to the importance of friendship with Germany.

I alluded to the German complaints of our conduct with respect to Colonial questions, and said that I could not see why even if we were not always able to meet the wishes of the German Gov[ernmen]t on such matters this should imply

* Kimberley to Monson, No. 147 Secret, 21 November 1894, *F.O.* 7/1212. This dispatch is endorsed as having been seen by the Queen, Lord Rosebery, Chancellor of the Exchequer. The first draft bears corrections in Lord Kimberley's hand.

an estrangement from Germany and the Triple Alliance. I added that I had learned confidentially that the German Emperor appeared to expect that Russia would before long raise the question of the free passage for her ships of war through the Dardanelles, and I asked His Ex[cellency] whether he had heard anything which confirmed this belief.

Count Dehen [sic: Deym] said he had observed, as we had, with much regret the symptoms in Germany, and especially in the German Press, of suspicion of England and of a belief that we were insensible to German wishes and interests.

He did not himself see any special reason to infer from the present political situation that the Russian Government would shortly raise the question of the passage of the Russian ships of war through the Bosphorus and Dardanelles. His Ex[cellency] concurred with me in thinking that, although it was the settled policy of this country not to enter any close engagements with the Triple Alliance, that was no reason why we should cease to have cordial relations with Germany and the other parties to that alliance.

I assured His Excellency that we warmly appreciated the very friendly relations which happily existed between us and Austria and also with Italy, and I trusted that the signs of irritation on the part of Germany would pass away when it was seen that there was really nothing in our policy which could be injurious to any vital German interest.

[Editors' Note. The policy of Rosebery in connexion with the control of the Nile Valley, and the utterances thereon both of Kimberley and Sir Edward Grey in 1895, have been included in chapter xxv, infra, pp. 501–5.]

XXV. SALISBURY, 1895–1900

81. THE "INTEGRITY OF TURKEY"—
BRITAIN, RUSSIA AND GERMANY, 1895

[By the end of the Rosebery administration colonial difficulties had endangered the policy of co-operation with the Central Powers. The Armenian massacres had proved a problem too difficult for the Liberal Government, and was to prove by no means easy for their successors. For the last months of Rosebery's administration, Britain, France and Russia had been working in an uneasy combination to introduce reform into the Asiatic provinces of Turkey. Salisbury on his accession to power had immediately to formulate his views on the Eastern Question, but did not find it much easier than his predecessors to follow a consistent policy. Hence the conversations with Hatzfeldt of July–August 1895;* the perplexing incidents of the Emperor William's visit to Cowes; and the belief in Germany and Austria-Hungary that Britain was abandoning her traditional policy of supporting the Turk and resisting the Slav.

There is little evidence to be found for Salisbury's attitude in 1895, other than that provided in the *Grosse Politik*; unfortunately his private papers are not yet published for this year. The British archives give some help, however, in elucidating it. It appears from them that in August 1895 the Emperor William talked to the British military attaché at Berlin about his uncertainty with regard to Salisbury's policy in the Near East. The Kaiser himself was convinced "that nothing will result until a British Man of War appears in the Golden Horn with an ultimatum....I shall warmly support this action under one condition, namely that you do not spring this upon us like a thunder clap out of a blue sky." It appears also that in November a proposal originated from Austria-Hungary for combined naval action at Constantinople. At that time each of the Powers had one *stationnaire* ship in the Straits, and it was proposed that a second should be called up. Russia agreed to this, but Monson reported that Russia "objects to all idea of passage of Dardanelles by other foreign ships of war, founding her objection on the Treaty of Paris". Prince Lobanov maintained his objection, and France supported him. The Sultan gave way in December to the extent of allowing the second *stationnaires* to be summoned.

* V. *G.P.*, [1927], x, 3–35; cp. also pp. 39–63, *passim*; there is a useful monograph by Hugo Preller, *Salisbury und die türkische Frage im Jahre 1895*, [Stuttgart, 1930]. Cp. also W. N. Medlicott, 'Lord Salisbury and Turkey', *History*, xii, No. 47, [October 1927], 244–7; W. L. Langer, *The Diplomacy of Imperialism*, [1935], i, 195–210.

In October and December 1895 two further conversations took place between the Emperor William and the military attaché at Berlin.* After the second of these interviews Sir Frank Lascelles, now British Ambassador at Berlin, questioned the statement that England and Russia had been discussing the possibility of a "Condominium" of the two Powers at Constantinople. On the receipt of Lascelles's enquiry Salisbury telegraphed "Deny most categorically that H[er] M[ajesty's] G[overnme]nt have ever even mentioned to Russia the idea of a condominium between England and Russia at Constantinople".†

It seems probable that what happened in 1895 was that Salisbury, in reaction from the Armenian massacres and in anticipation oɩ growing unrest at Constantinople, spoke his doubts freely to Hatzfeldt—and perhaps also to the Russian Ambassador—about the continuance of Turkey's rule. He may have been partly influenced by Germany's persistent disassociation of herself from the policy of Austria-Hungary in the Near East.‡ But it seems unlikely that Salisbury made any proposals as specific as those attributed to him in Germany, and it is certain that he was in fact prepared to co-operate fully with Austria-Hungary in the immediate issue. None the less, the incident left a bad impression on the Kaiser, and tended to exacerbate Germany's relations with Britain.]

82. AUSTRIA-HUNGARY'S OVERTURE TO BRITAIN, 1896-7

[At the beginning of 1896 Austria-Hungary made a new overture to Britain for co-operation in the Near East. Her Ambassador, Count Deym, approached Salisbury on the question of the Mediterranean Agreements, thus renewing the proposals which he had made to Rosebery in 1893. Salisbury's reply on this occasion was, in effect, that while he would not again pledge himself to so great an extent as he had in the Agreement of December 1887, he would be prepared to renew that of March.§ The distinction is an important one. The March notes expressed merely the general desire for co-operation, whereas the *Bases* of December had included a determination to support the "independence of Turkey as guardian of important European interests", and had laid stress on Turkish independence in connexion with

* *V. G.P.*, [1927], XI, 8-11; X, 251-5.
† Lascelles to Salisbury, No. 17 Secret, 21 December 1895, *F.O.* 64/1351; Lascelles to Salisbury, Tel. No. 37, Salisbury to Lascelles, Tel. No. 141, 21 December 1895, *F.O.* 64/1352.
‡ Even in 1895, while Germany had agreed in principle to the summons of a second *stationnaire*, she said that she could not spare a vessel for the purpose.
§ Gooch and Temperley, [1932], VIII, 13.

the "freedom of the Straits". In the nine years that had passed since he signed this Agreement, Salisbury's ideas on the Straits had developed, although there had been no radical alteration. In August 1896 he expressed his views on the subject to Lascelles, commenting on a conversation which the latter had held with the Emperor William: "Express my gratification at H[is] I[mperial] M[ajesty] having done me the honour to consult us. Our view is, and has been for some time past, in favour of opening the Straits to all nations.

"The opening of the Dardanelles alone would be a less complete and satisfactory arrangement: but it would be acceptable to H[er] M[ajesty's] G[overnment].

"The strongest objection will be found with Austria."*

Salisbury was right on the last point. In 1897 Austria-Hungary made yet another attempt to secure British co-operation, thus eliciting from Salisbury a detailed exposition of his views. They made an unfavourable impression on Count Goluchowski. The British Ambassador at Vienna reported his comment that Salisbury's language "unfortunately confirmed the doubts he had found to exist at Berlin and which he had done his best to combat regarding the value now attached by us to what had hitherto been held to be the cardinal principle of British policy in regard to Constantinople and the Dardanelles". Sir Horace Rumbold added: "He [Count Goluchowski] is very anxious that the change of attitude indicated should be kept entirely secret. If known it might possibly encourage Russia to attempt a *coup de main* which at present that Power does not, in his opinion, contemplate."†]

Document 194. *Salisbury refuses to pledge himself to action,* 20 *January* 1897‡

The Austrian Ambassador to day renewed a proposal which he had made to me in the spring of last year, with respect to the protection of the Straits of the Bosphorus and Dardanelles from any possible enterprise on the part of Russia. He stated, as he had stated on the former occasion, that in the view of the Austrian Gov[ernmen]t it was England that was more interested than any other Power in preventing the acquisition of dominion over the Straits by Russia; and that therefore it should be England that should take the lead

* Salisbury to Lascelles, Tel., 28 August 1896, *F.O.* 78/4884.
† Rumbold to Salisbury, Tel. No 3 Secret, 27 January 1897, *F.O.* 78/4884.
‡ Salisbury to Rumbold, No. 6 Very Confidential, 20 January 1897, *F.O.* 78/4884. Printed in Gooch and Temperley, [1933], IX (I), 775–6.

in defending them against any attempt to establish that dominion. If England would undertake the maritime portion of the task, and would send up a fleet into the Bosphorus to resist any such attack on the side of Russia, the Austrian Gov[ernmen]t would not refuse on its part to undertake the military measures which would be necessary for preventing Russia, with the help of any of the Balkan States, from establishing itself in a position to command the Straits.

I replied that I did not think that my answer to him on the present occasion could differ substantially from that which I had given to him 12 months ago. I admitted the interest of England in the case, though I could not admit that England had an interest more vital than that of Austria and France. But I said it was quite impossible for England to make any such engagement as that which he desired. The institutions under which we lived entirely prevented H[er] M[ajesty's] Gov[ernmen]t from making any engagement with respect to the military or naval action of England upon contingencies which had not yet arisen. When these contingencies arose, they would be fully considered by the Parliament and public opinion of this country, and no influence of any Government, and probably no promise into which any Government might have entered, would in such a case avail to prevent the country from acting upon its own views of what was right and expedient in such a matter. There were three considerations which altered the conditions of the problem, and which therefore made it more difficult to predict beforehand the course which England would think it right to take. In the first place, as His Excellency might have observed, the sympathies of England in respect to the Ottoman dominion had undergone an entire transformation from the complexion which they presented 40 years ago. The process had been to a certain extent gradual, that is to say it was the result of a series of agitations produced by the ruthless and unpopular conduct of the Ottoman Gov[ernmen]t in various parts of its dominions. But the change was now complete. The antipathy to assisting the Sultan would be extreme, and I could not answer for it that considerations of a higher policy would be sufficiently clear or sufficiently powerful to induce the English people to make great sacrifices of blood and treasure in support of a Gov[ernmen]t which they so thoroughly detested. The second consideration was that on all former occasions when the policy of England was spoken of as binding her to maintain the Sultan's independence in the Straits, it was always assumed, and followed necessarily from the facts of the time, that such efforts would be made with the sanction and support of the Sultan, and not in spite of him. Such a view of the case could not be confidently held now. By the elaborate fortification of the Dardanelles, and the utter neglect of the Bosphorus, the Sultan had stated as clearly as if it had been written down in a proclamation, that he preferred the probability of being invaded by the Russians to the chance of being assisted by the Western Powers. I knew no declaration of English policy which had ever pointed in the direction of assisting the Sultan to an independence which he did not desire, against an invader whom he himself had welcomed.

The third consideration depended very much upon the second, namely that the forcing of the Dardanelles had become in later years a much more arduous task than it was 20, or even 10 years ago. I could not form a judgment myself on a matter which is not within my competence; but I had told His Excellency last year that the balance of opinion among our nautical experts was strongly unfavourable to any attempt to force the Dardanelles by the action of the fleet, without accompanying it with military measures against the forts by land. If this was true it seemed to me to dispose of the idea that England could alone force her way through the Dardanelles. At the same time I was careful, while pointing out to His Excellency that this statement had been made to him before, to guard myself from any kind of intimation that England renounced the right of taking those measures, if, when the contingency arose, it was thought desirable. I made no kind of pledge one way or the other. I merely reserved our full liberty of action. His Excellency replied that in that case Austria must reserve her full liberty of action also, and that she could not come under any engagement, expressed or implied, with respect to the Straits. It was the strong belief of her Gov[ernmen]t that whatever policy France might nominally pursue, the necessity of her position would drive her into alliance with Russia, even in such a contingency; and he further stated that unless Austria was backed by the naval force of Great Britain, she could not count, in any action that she might be disposed to take upon Russia, upon the co-operation of Germany.

I stated to His Excellency the apprehensions which I constantly entertained, and which I had mentioned to other Ambassadors, that our hands might be forced by some movement at Constantinople which might threaten the lives of our own nationals. It was very difficult to foresee to what extent we should be placed under compulsion to disregard all other considerations in providing for their security. I hoped that sufficient pressure might be put upon the Sultan to insure his taking the precautions that were necessary against such an emergency. I did not however dwell upon these considerations, because the point of view from which I spoke was almost exactly that of the Austrian Foreign Minister in speaking to your Excellency about a fortnight ago.

83. BRITAIN'S OVERTURE TO RUSSIA, 1898

[Salisbury's negotiation with Russia in January 1898 was hardly known until it was disclosed in full in *British Documents on the Origins of the War*. It is one of the rare instances in which Salisbury shewed daring. The origin is to be found in the situation in China. On 14 November 1897 a German squadron occupied Kiao-chao; a month later Russia occupied Port Arthur. Salisbury took a bold initiative to avert the break-up of China and made his final—and most important—overture to Russia. He was anxious to preserve the *status quo* in Europe as well as in Asia, and linked Turkey with China in his offer. In the twelve months that had elapsed since Salisbury's exposition of his policy to Austria-Hungary in January 1897, two movements had taken place. Austria-Hungary and Russia had reached a *rapprochement* in Balkan affairs, through the conclusion of the Balkan Agreement of 8 May 1897;* and at the very end of the year, on 14–17 December, Russia and Germany had expressed to one another their readiness to work together in the Far East. It was this last fact which doomed the

* A. F. Pribram, *The Secret Treaties of Austria-Hungary*, [1920], 1, 184–95.

overture to failure. The Tsar's reception of the overture was apparently cordial. But, while he professed to be considering it, his ministers were in reality arranging to imitate Germany and to occupy more Chinese territory.* By mid-March it was seen that the negotiations would fail, and on the 16th Russian forces actually occupied Port Arthur. Salisbury was deeply humiliated and the breach with Russia was not fully healed until 1907.]

Document 195. *Salisbury makes an overture to Russia, 25 January* 1898†

Our idea was this. The two Empires of China and Turkey are so weak that in all important matters they are constantly guided by the advice of Foreign Powers. In giving this advice Russia and England are constantly opposed, neutralizing each other's efforts much more frequently than the real antagonism of their interests would justify; and this condition of things is not likely to diminish, but to increase. It is to remove or lessen this evil that we have thought that an understanding with Russia might benefit both nations.

We contemplate no infraction of existing rights. We would not admit the violation of any existing treaties, or impair the integrity of the present empires of either China or Turkey. These two conditions are vital. We aim at no partition of territory, but only a partition of preponderance. It is evident that both in respect to Turkey and China there are large portions which interest Russia much more than England and *vice versa*. Merely as an illustration, and binding myself to nothing, I would say that the portion of Turkey which drains into the Black Sea, together with the drainage valley of the Euphrates as far as Bagdad, interest Russia much more than England: whereas Turkish Africa, Arabia, and the Valley of the Euphrates below Bagdad interest England much more than Russia. A similar distinction exists in China between the Valley of the Hoango with the territory north of it and the Valley of the Yangtze.

* For the incident as a whole *v.* Gooch and Temperley, [1927], I, 1–18; for the Tsar's later and inaccurate description of it *v.* ibid. I, 5, *Ed. Note.* Cp. also the views attributed to Chamberlain by the Russian Ambassador in December 1897, A. Meyendorff, *Correspondance diplomatique de Baron de Staal,* [1929], II, 357–8.

† Salisbury to O'Conor, Tel. No. 22 Secret, 25 January 1898, *F.O.* 65/1557. Printed in Gooch and Temperley, [1927], I, 8, No. 9.

Would it be possible to arrange that where, in regard to these territories our counsels differ, the Power least interested should give way to and assist the other? I do not disguise from myself that the difficulty would be great. Is it insuperable? I have designedly omitted to deal with large tracts in each Empire, because neither Power has shown any keen interest in them.

84. THE CONTROL OF THE NILE VALLEY

(i) GREY AND KIMBERLEY

[In his *Twenty-Five Years* Sir Edward Grey, writing long after the event, tells a curious story about his famous declaration on the subject of the Nile Valley. He says that it was on the Niger problem that Parliamentary questions had been expected and that he "transferred to the subject of the Nile the firmness I had been authorized to show...about West Africa". A study of the archives suggests that his memory failed him on this point.*

On 28 March 1895, the day of the speech, Kimberley and the French Ambassador, Baron de Courcel, discussed both the Niger and the Nile Valley questions. The Niger part of the conversation was recorded in a dispatch to Lord Dufferin;† Kimberley referred to reports of French expeditions to Bajibo and Boussa on the Upper Niger: "I said I could not conceal from him that the news was of a very serious character.... I earnestly hoped that if the news was true prompt orders would be given for the withdrawal of these expeditions." There had already been one dispatch from which the Cabinet had removed all expressions offensive to France. But Kimberley did not say on the 28th that he expected questions in Parliament that evening on the Niger.

A second dispatch dealt with the Nile Valley, about which Kimberley did say that he expected questions.‡ "I said that they [i.e. the rumours of a French expedition towards the basin of the Nile] had caused some disquiet here, as His Excellency would have seen from the remarks on the subject in the public press, and it was probable that they would be referred to in the House of Commons tonight [28th].... I understood that the main objection put forward by the French Government to our sphere of influence over the Nile basin was that the territories over which it extended pertain to Egypt. We had, however, on our part fully admitted

* *Twenty-Five Years*, [1925], 1, 18–20. Grey's assertion has been ably questioned by W. L. Langer, *The Diplomacy of Imperialism*, [1935], 1, 265–6, and these conclusions seem to be borne out by the unpublished evidence quoted here.

† Kimberley to Dufferin, No. 111A Africa, 28 March 1895, *F.O.* 27/3229.

‡ Kimberley to Dufferin, No. 111 Africa, 28 March 1895, *F.O.* 27/3229.

that Egypt had a dormant claim to these territories and had declared our readiness if Egypt should be hereafter in a position to re-occupy them, to recognise her right to their possession."

The above evidence makes it improbable that Sir Edward Grey did not know his chief's views on the 28th, or that his own utterance on the same day (**Doc. 196**) was unforeseen or unpremeditated. Rosebery's private secretary, writing on 29 March, seems to confirm this view. On the 31st Rosebery himself reported to the Queen that the Cabinet, with one dissentient, "adhered to Sir Edward Grey's declaration".* It is in this light that we must read Kimberley's interview of 1 April with Baron de Courcel (**Doc. 197**). Some French authorities have argued that Kimberley then admitted that the question of the Nile "remained open to debate".† This assertion is contradicted by the British version of the interview, and is also inconsistent with the decision of the Cabinet which had endorsed the utterance of Sir Edward Grey.‡]

Document 196. *Sir Edward Grey's warning to France against penetration to the Nile*, 28 March 1895§

. . . Towards Egypt this country stands in a special position of trust, as regards the maintenance of the interests of Egypt, and the claims of Egypt have not only been admitted by us, but they have been admitted and emphasized lately by the Government of France. I stated the other day‖ that, in consequence of these claims of ours, and in consequence of the claims of Egypt in the Nile Valley, the British and Egyptian spheres of influence covered the whole of the Nile waterway. That is a statement following logically upon what has happened in past years, and of what has been in the knowledge of the world for the last two years. I am asked whether or not it is the case that a French expedition is coming from the West of Africa with the intention of entering the Nile Valley and occupying up to the Nile.¶ I will ask the Committee to be careful in giving credence

* *Letters of Queen Victoria*, [1931], 3rd Ser., II, 490–2.

† *V.* evidence quoted by W. L. Langer, *The Diplomacy of Imperialism*, [1935], I, 266, n. 12.

‡ Grey's speech and Kimberley's dispatch, giving the interview of 1 April, were published in the Fashoda Blue Book, *A. & P.*, [1899], CXII, [C. 9054], 883–4.

§ Speech by Sir E. Grey in the House of Commons, 28 March 1895. *Hans. Deb.*, 4th Ser., XXXII, 405–7.

‖ 11 March 1895. *V. Hans. Deb.*, 4th Ser., XXXI, 782.

¶ There was at this time no question of a French expedition led by Marchand. That of Monteil was actually in suspense, but one led by Liotard was active.

to the rumours of the movement of expeditions in Africa. Even places in Africa are apt to shift about, and it is sometimes found that some place supposed to occupy a particular position does not, in fact, occupy that position. Rumours have come with greater or less freedom with regard to the movements of expeditions in various parts of Africa, but at the Foreign Office we have no reason to suppose that any French Expedition has instructions to enter, or the intention of entering, the Nile Valley; and I will go further and say that, after all I have explained about the claims we consider we have under past Agreements, and the claims which we consider Egypt may have in the Nile Valley, and adding to that the fact that our claims and the view of the Government with regard to them are fully and clearly known to the French Government—I cannot think it is possible that these rumours deserve credence, because the advance of a French Expedition under secret instructions right from the other side of Africa, into a territory over which our claims have been known for so long, would be not merely an inconsistent and unexpected act, but it must be perfectly well known to the French Government that it would be an *unfriendly act*,* and would be so viewed by England.... [After referring to two French expeditions reported on the Niger.]...It would be idle to deny that there is some importance to be attached to the fact that, during the whole of the Debate no foreign Power has been alluded to except the French Government. Why has that been so? I think it has been so because events in Siam and in Africa have created an unfavourable effect on public opinion in this country, not an anxiety about what has happened—at the proper time I shall be able to defend Her Majesty's Government and to maintain that British interests have not been sacrificed—I say I do not think the anxiety is as to what has happened, but as to what may happen, in the future. During the last two years no provocation whatever as regards the French has come from our side. We have striven to our utmost to reconcile the conflicting interests of

* Italics the Editors'. Henry Labouchere, M.P. and Editor of *Truth*, described this utterance as "a quasi-declaration of war against France".

the two countries and to promote the maintenance of good relations between the two countries, and we shall omit nothing consistently with the preservation of important and undoubted British claims still to maintain those good relations. But something else besides our own effort is necessary, and that is the co-operation of the French Government and the French public. With that co-operation the task we have fulfilled with success hitherto, of preventing these local differences in different parts of the world from causing any serious disturbance of the relations of two great Powers, ought to be an easy one. We rely now, as we have relied not unsuccessfully hitherto, on the sense of justice and fairness of the French Government and the French people, to reconcile what conflicting interests there may be in different parts of the world, with the maintenance of close and good relations between the two countries.

Document 197. *Kimberley reinforces Grey's warning,* 1 *April* 1895*

Our conversation then turned upon the declaration made by Sir E. Grey on the 28th ultimo in the House of Commons in respect to the British sphere of influence in the Nile basin.

Baron de Courcel said that he had no instructions from M. Hanotaux to speak to me on that subject, he had only heard from him privately, but he could not conceal from me the painful impression which would be created in France by Sir E. Grey's speech, and he feared it would have a prejudicial effect upon the relations between the two countries. It amounted to this, that whilst the negotiation was still pending between the two Governments, we had declared that we could admit no question as to our rights in the territory which was the subject of the negotiation.

I replied that, looking at the matter from our point of view, it seemed to me that for this very reason we should have just ground for complaint if, whilst the negotiation was still pending, a French expedition entered the territory, which was the subject in discussion. I hoped, however, that we

* Kimberley to Dufferin, No. 112A, 1 April, 1895, *F.O.* 27/3229. *A. & P.,* [1899], cxii, [C. 9054], 884.

should receive from the French Government an assurance that these rumours were unfounded.

His Excellency said that no news had been received of the expedition in those parts, with which communication was extremely tardy and difficult and that he did not, therefore, see how it would be possible for the French Government to give assurances while they were in ignorance of the actual facts.

I said that no advance had taken place on our part beyond Unyoro, where, as he was aware, we had been engaged in a war with the natives, which was necessary for the protection of Uganda; nor had any instructions been given which would authorize any such advance. In point of fact, the *status quo* had not been disturbed by us.

I attached much more importance to action than to words, and I hoped that the French Government would be guided by the same principle.

Baron de Courcel said he could not but regard the declaration made in the House of Commons as amounting to a "prise en possession" on our part of the whole basin of the Upper Nile.

I replied that I could not see that the reiteration of a claim to a sphere of influence over the Nile Basin, which we had already made fully known to the French Government, could be regarded as a "prise en possession".

I would remind him also, that we had stated in explicit terms that we did not ignore the claims of Egypt, and had assured the French Government that, if Egypt should hereafter be able to reoccupy the territories in the Soudan formerly under her rule, we should recognize her right to their possession.*

(ii) SALISBURY AND THE FASHODA CRISIS

[Sir Edward Grey's declaration did not deter the French from pushing towards the Nile. And they pushed towards it in two directions; from Jibuti and from Abyssinia in the East; and from the Congo and the Niger in the West. As regards Abyssinia it is sufficient to say that a British Mission under Mr (later Sir) Rennell Rodd was sent out in 1897 to Addis Ababa, and found disquieting symptoms of French activity. A Mission under Colonel James Macdonald also went up from Uganda in 1897 but failed to

* Cp. *infra*, pp. 507–9, 511.

reach the Nile. The French were not only active in Abyssinia but were striving to reach the Nile from the West. Captain Marchand, who had been associated with Monteil, finally left Brazzaville in March 1897 and reached the Bahr-el-Ghazal. There he co-operated with Liotard in establishing French posts in that area.

He did not, however (and the fact is important), make any contact with the French expeditions from Abyssinia or the East. But on 10 July 1898 he reached Fashoda, with half a dozen Frenchmen and over a hundred Senegalese, and hoisted the French flag on the old Egyptian fort there. It looked as if he intended to claim the whole Bahr-el-Ghazal province for France. At any rate that area was to be the bone of contention.

Salisbury, for reasons that it is impossible to give fully here,* had ordered a British advance to Dongola. Kitchener received the telegram at 3 A.M. on 13 March 1896. He woke up Sir Reginald Wingate by throwing stones at his window, secured the Khedive's assent and ordered his troops to march by 10 A.M. He thus took the first step on the road to Khartoum and to the conquest of the Soudan. He began building a railway and pushed relentlessly southwards. Kitchener took care to occupy Berber, and thereby brought the whole force of the Khalifa against him. Salisbury and the Cabinet, mindful of the fate of Gordon, could not leave his successor in the lurch, and promised British troops, and early in 1898 an expedition on the grand scale was ready. On 8 April Kitchener defeated the advance guard of the Khalifa's host, capturing its commander at the Atbara. He moved steadily onwards to Khartoum and on 2 September defeated the army commanded by the Khalifa himself. The result, as stated by himself, "is the practical annihilation of the Khalifa's army, the consequent extinction of Mahdiism in the Soudan, and the submission of the whole country formerly ruled under Egyptian authority".†

It was on 2 August that Salisbury, with a clear anticipation of coming events, sent Kitchener definite instructions (**Doc. 198**). It will be observed that they clearly contemplate a possible claim to some part of the Nile Valley by France or by Abyssinia, that Sir Edward Grey's declaration had been endorsed by Salisbury at the end of 1897, and that Kitchener was to use his discretion in dealing with "a French force...found in occupation of some portion of the Nile Valley", and to proceed in person in a flotilla up the White Nile as far as Fashoda.]

* Cp. W. L. Langer, *The Diplomacy of Imperialism*, [1935], I, chap. IX *passim*. The main reason was the defeat of Italian troops by the Abyssinians at Adowa, the news of which was known in Europe on 3 March 1896. Salisbury had the double object of relieving the Italians at Kassala, and "to use the same military effort to plant the foot of Egypt rather farther up the Nile". Zetland, *Lord Cromer*, [1932], 223.

† Dispatch of Kitchener, 5 September 1898, *London Gazette* of 30 September 1898.

Document 198. *Salisbury asserts British interests,*
2 *August* 1898*

It is desirable that you should be placed in possession of the views of Her Majesty's Government in respect to the line of action to be followed in the event of Kartoum being occupied at an early date by the forces now operating in the Soudan under the command of Sir Herbert Kitchener.

In view of the substantial military and financial co-operation which has recently been afforded by Her Majesty's Government to the Government of the Khedive, Her Majesty's Government have decided that at Khartoum the British and Egyptian flags should be hoisted side by side. This decision will have no reference to the manner in which the occupied countries are to be administered in the future. It is not necessary at present to define their political status with any great precision. These matters can be considered at a later period. You will, however, explain to the Khedive and to his Ministers that the procedure I have indicated is intended to emphasise the fact that Her Majesty's Government consider that they have a predominant voice in all matters connected with the Soudan, and that they expect that any advice which they may think fit to tender to the Egyptian Government, in respect to Soudan affairs, will be followed.

Her Majesty's Government do not contemplate that after the occupation of Khartoum any further military operations on a large scale, or involving any considerable expense, will be undertaken for the occupation of the provinces to the south; but the Sirdar is authorised to send two flotillas, one up the White and the other up the Blue Nile.

You are authorised to settle the composition of these two forces in consultation with the Sirdar.

Sir Herbert Kitchener should in person command the White Nile Flotilla as far as Fashoda, and may take with him a small body of British troops, should you concur with him in thinking such a course desirable.

* Salisbury to Cromer, No. 109 Secret, 2 August 1898, *F.O.* 78/5050, printed in Gooch and Temperley, [1927], I, 159–60, No. 185.

The officer in command of the Blue Nile Flotilla is authorised to go as far as the foot of the cataract, which is believed to commence about Roseires. He is not to land troops with a view to marching beyond the point on the river navigable for steamers. Should he, before reaching Roseires, encounter any Abyssinian outposts, he is to halt, report the circumstances, and wait for further instructions.

There are two points to which Sir Herbert Kitchener's attention should be specially directed.

The first of these is that in dealing with any French or Abyssinian authorities who may be encountered, nothing should be said or done which would in any way imply a recognition on behalf of Her Majesty's Government of a title to possession on behalf of France or Abyssinia to any portion of the Nile Valley.

As regards France, the following extract from a note addressed by Sir Edmund Monson to M. Hanotaux on the 10th December, 1897, sets forth the view held by Her Majesty's Government on this subject—

"Her Majesty's Government", Sir Edmund Monson said, "must not be understood to admit that any other European Power than Great Britain has any claim to occupy any part of the Valley of the Nile. The views of the British Government upon this matter were plainly stated in Parliament by Sir Edward Grey some years ago,[*] during the administration of the Earl of Rosebery, and were formally communicated to the French Government at the time. Her Majesty's present Government entirely adhere to the language that was on this occasion employed by their predecessors."

The second point, which you should press strongly on the attention of Sir Herbert Kitchener, is the necessity of avoiding, by all possible means, any collision with the forces of the Emperor Menelek.

It is possible that a French force may be found in occupation of some portion of the Nile Valley. Should this contingency

---

[*] *V. supra*, pp. 502–4.

arise, the course of action to be pursued must depend so much on local circumstances that it is neither necessary nor desirable to furnish Sir Herbert Kitchener with detailed instructions. Her Majesty's Government entertain full confidence in Sir Herbert Kitchener's judgment and discretion. They feel assured that he will endeavour to convince the Commander of any French force with which he may come in contact that the presence of the latter in the Nile Valley is an infringement of the rights both of Great Britain and of the Khedive.

Sir Herbert Kitchener is authorised, should he think such a course desirable and practicable, to send a small force up the White Nile beyond its junction with the Sobat. The Officer Commanding this force should endeavour to open up communication with the troops of the Congo State, who, it is known, are in occupation of some portion of the Nile Valley above Lado. I enclose three copies of the Agreement, signed on the 12th May, 1894, between Her Majesty's Government and the King of the Belgians.* The officer in command of the Upper Nile Expedition, who should be furnished with a copy of this Agreement, must be careful to explain to any Belgian authorities with whom he may come in contact that, under Article II of this Convention, Her Majesty's Government do not recognise that the King of the Belgians has any right of permanent possession to any part of the Nile Valley, but, on the other hand, that there is no intention of interfering with the arrangement under which certain territories are temporarily leased to the Congo State.

It is scarcely necessary for me to add that, in the execution of the difficult and important work which now lies before him, Sir Herbert Kitchener may rely on the full and cordial support of Her Majesty's Government.

COMMENT ON FASHODA BY THE EDITORS

[The Fashoda incident, though reported in *British Documents on the Origins of the War*, is not yet treated in the *Documents Diplomatiques* of France. It is difficult to reconstruct the evidence, as Marchand produced an obviously biassed account in *Le Figaro* of

* Cp. *supra* p. 490.

26 August 1904, and General Mangin's account in the *Revue des Deux Mondes* of 15 September 1931, like M. Hanotaux's *Fachoda*, Paris, [1909], are also partisan. What follows is an attempt to reconcile the evidence by comparing the various accounts and by consultation with two living witnesses of the scenes described.

On 7 September a Mahdiist steamer coming from the South, was stopped near Khartoum. It reported that it had been fired on by white men ("Turks") at Fashoda. Marchand says that Kitchener thought that these white men were a Belgian Mission but this is one of his many mistakes. Kitchener's instructions (**Doc. 198**) gave him a strong hint that the expedition would be French and an English eyewitness reports that one of the men, when asked about the flag, drew a tricolor in the sand with his stick. Kitchener decided to go down to meet them. He was authorized in his instructions to take a small body of British troops. But he was already sending home white soldiers by every boat downstream. He took only one white company and two black Soudanese battalions on his voyage. It is, therefore, clear that he did not expect any serious resistance, and had absolute confidence in his Sudanese. Mangin's suggestion that "the Sudanese troops in the Sirdar's forces were disposed to side with the French" is stated by British eyewitnesses to be ridiculous. It is not indeed the way of orientals to rebel against a white commander who has just won a colossal victory. Equally absurd is the suggestion of Marchand that the fort could have been defended. According to an eyewitness its two guns could have been silenced and the fort destroyed in a few minutes by the flotilla which already had its guns trained on it. On the other hand, Kitchener's assertion that Marchand's position was untenable and dangerous, and that he really needed British help, may be an exaggeration. But there is an important qualification to this. Even if the local tribes had intimated loyalty to Marchand, there is evidence that they at once made overtures to Kitchener, and the sheikh of Sobat was particularly friendly to Britain. Thus resistance, in any serious sense, was impossible, despite Marchand's disclaimers.* According to Kitchener, Marchand himself said at the interview, "resistance was impossible".

It is historically of some importance to ascertain what passed at the interview between Kitchener and Marchand at Fashoda.

---

* Some of Marchand's assertions, in points of detail, are certainly inaccurate. He states he was "alone" with Kitchener, but one, who saw the interview, says that Wingate and a French officer were both present at it the whole time. Again he makes fun of Kitchener's French and of his accent, but Kitchener had been educated in France and, according to Sir George Arthur a noted French scholar, "he spoke French well". He states also that Kitchener, when he left, turned back to Khartoum. On the contrary he went upstream to Sobat. On returning he did not see Marchand again, but sent him a letter. All this makes one somewhat sceptical as to Marchand's accuracy.

There is obvious restraint in Kitchener's telegram on the affair, and there is not only restraint but omission in Wingate's letter to the Queen's private secretary.* Marchand says boldly in *Le Figaro* that when Kitchener prepared to haul down the French flag, he intimated that he would resist that measure by force. Kitchener says Marchand admitted "resistance was impossible", but this phrase may apply to effective resistance and not to a gallant but hopeless struggle for French honour. In any case, and there are several witnesses to this fact, Kitchener terminated the proceedings by inviting Marchand to a whisky and soda.

Marchand asserts that he was "ready himself to hoist the Egyptian flag south of the fort, on the village". But Kitchener asserts that he made difficulties as to this, and ultimately gave way only to a threat of force. "[Kitchener]...caused the [Egyptian] flag to be hoisted on a ruined bastion of the old Egyptian fortifications about 500 yards south of the French flag, and on the only road which leads to the interior from the French position, which is surrounded by impassable marshes on all sides." What is really significant is that the British and Egyptian flags were hoisted together over Khartoum, the Egyptian alone over Fashoda. The fact is that the Congo Treaty of 1894 (*v. supra*, p. 490), which transferred Bahr-el-Ghazal to King Leopold, weakened the British claim; it did not, however, affect the Egyptian claim of previous possession, which could therefore still be asserted. This claim had been put forward by Sir Edward Grey (*supra*, p. 502), and also by Kimberley (*supra*, p. 505). In his instruction of 2 August 1898 (**Doc. 198**) Salisbury ordered the British as well as Egyptian flags to be hoisted at Khartoum, and suggested that the presence of a French force in the Nile Valley was "an infringement of the rights both of Great Britain and of the Khedive" (*supra*, p. 509). But south of Khartoum England had signed away her rights at least once. It was obviously safer to rely on the rights of the Khedive alone at Fashoda, and to hoist the Egyptian flag.† And this was accordingly done.

The actual struggle over Fashoda was a severe one. It brought England and France to the brink of war and this eventuality had been clearly envisaged by Salisbury beforehand. It has been suggested, in influential quarters, that his Government had no policy and got into the scrape without reflection. It has been added that they were pulled out of it by Rosebery, who intervened with a speech at Epsom on 12 October.‡ In this speech he suggested, referring to Grey's utterance, that foreign policy

* Kitchener's report in Rodd to Salisbury, Tel. No. 244, 25 September 1898, *v.* Gooch and Temperley, [1927], I, 167–8, No. 193; Wingate to Bigge, 23 September 1898, *v. Letters of Queen Victoria*, 3rd Ser., [1932], III, 285–7.
† The whole matter is ably discussed in W. L. Langer, *The Diplomacy of Imperialism*, [1935], II, chap. XVI.
‡ *V. The Times*, 13 October 1898.

should have continuity* and emphasized that the whole nation
was behind Salisbury.

The British documents do not, however, suggest that Salisbury
had any doubt as to his policy or was prepared to falter in carrying
it out on this occasion. By 4 November Salisbury was informed
by the French Ambassador that "the decision had been taken
by his Government to withdraw M. Marchand's party from
Fashoda"; while M. Delcassé, in giving the same information at
Paris the day before, "showed considerable emotion".† The
Fashoda crisis was over.]

85. THE PROBLEM OF AFRICA

[British relations with Portugal had been by no means free
from fluctuations since Granville acknowledged in 1873 the
existence of British obligations. Within two years of that date
Portugal was once more apprehensive of attack, and the Minister
for Foreign Affairs again sounded the British Ambassador, Lord
Lytton, as to the attitude of Britain. The reply was cautiously
worded and in general terms: "I did not think His Excellency
could expect from Her Majesty's Government definite answers
to indefinite questions....I felt authorized to give him every
assurance of unabated cordiality in the sincere interest which
England had so long felt, and so signally proved, in the preservation of Portuguese independence." In a minute written on this
dispatch, Tenterden commented that Lytton's "language might
be approved but the less said to the Port[ugue]se the better. It is
always dangerous to answer hypothetical questions and particularly
so when we know that the answer will be repeated all over
Europe." Derby added that he agreed.‡

In 1875, as in 1873, Portugal feared attack on her own territory;
at neither date was the colonial question directly involved. Moreover, in 1876–7, when the Portuguese colony of Goa was under
discussion, Derby supported the view of Hertslet and Pauncefote
that it would be better to avoid reference to the Ancient Treaties,
for the very reason that they involved a colonial guarantee.§ It is

---

* Rosebery is usually claimed as the first advocate of continuity, but he
himself qualified his doctrine in an important particular. In January 1886 he
was reproached by Count Hatzfeldt with the fact that "the foreign policy of
one British Ministry was overturned by the other". Rosebery replied that "this
was true, but a successful foreign policy would not be". The condition of continuity
was success. Crewe, *Lord Rosebery*, [1931], I, 262, *v. supra*, pp. 431, 434.

† *V.* Gooch and Temperley, [1927], I, 188–9, Nos. 226–8. For the final steps *v.*
ibid. I, 193, *Ed. Note.*

‡ Lytton to Derby, No. 108 Confidential, 24 December 1875, *F.O.* 63/1024,
and Minutes by Tenterden and Derby, 4 January 1876, *F.O.* 63/1033.

§ *F.O.* 63/1082. Minutes by Hertslet, Pauncefote and Derby, 17–18 January
1877.

interesting that just before this, in 1875, Portugal in the interests of another of her colonial dependencies took the step which was to bring more than twenty years later the very confirmation of the Ancient Treaties which Derby deprecated. In that year she concluded a treaty with the Transvaal State providing for railway communication with Lourenço Marques on Delagoa Bay. From the Portuguese standpoint the treaty was part of a general policy, fitfully pursued, for the development of the vast area in East Africa over which she claimed sovereignty.

Salisbury conducted long negotiations on these East African claims during his administration of 1886–92. The lease of territory by the Sultan of Zanzibar to the British East African Company in May 1887 was only one move towards the realization of the extensive projects which were being formed in several parts of Africa at this time. In 1889 Sir Harry Johnston became Consul-General in Portuguese East Africa. He has given his own account in his autobiography of the plans which he developed at this period for the extension of British influence north of the Limpopo River, between that region and Lake Nyassa.* The Nyassaland Protectorate was formed shortly afterwards, and in the meantime the activities of Cecil Rhodes had led to the formation of the British South Africa Company, whose operations lay in the first instance between the Limpopo River and the Zambesi.†

The most difficult of the international negotiations which resulted from this forward movement in the sub-continent was that with Portugal, who claimed huge stretches of territory on the ground of prior discovery. At the end of 1889 Salisbury wrote to the Queen that he utterly rejected "the archaeological arguments of the Portuguese who claim half Africa on the supposed cession to them in 1630 of the Empire of Monomotapa, of which event Lord Salisbury can find no account whatever in this country".‡ The controversy was so acute that on 11 January 1890 an ultimatum was sent to Portugal by Britain, reinforced by the dispatch of British warships to the coasts of Mozambique and the sailing of the Channel fleet under sealed orders. In March 1890 Salisbury refused to refer the dispute either to a conference or to arbitration. On 20 August a settlement was reached by negotiation. But the Cortes refused to ratify it, and a new Convention was not concluded until May 1891.

From this date discussion about the Portuguese colonies took a new turn. Among the several European Powers who were stabilizing or extending their influence in Africa at this period Portugal was remarkable in that she shewed little capacity for

* Cp. Sir Harry Johnston, *The Story of My Life*, [1923], 226–42, *passim*.
† Cp. Basil Williams, *Cecil Rhodes*, [1921], 130–9; Eric Walker, *History of South Africa*, [1935], 417–21.
‡ Cecil, *Life of Salisbury*, [1932], IV, 263, Memorandum for the Queen, 27 December 1889.

developing the material resources of the regions under her control. Her governments at home were too unstable and her financial resources were inadequate for this purpose. As early as 1895 Germany began to mention in conversations with Great Britain the possibility of a decline of the Portuguese Colonial Empire—at the very period when Britain, according to Germany, was contemplating the disruption of the European Empire of Turkey. In 1898 the currency of more definite rumours led to the conclusion of the ill-fated Anglo-German Agreement, which provided for a new form of partition—the apportioning to each of the two Powers of colonial areas whose revenues might be the securities for loans.* The secret part of the convention contemplated a period when the integrity of Portuguese colonial possessions could no longer be maintained, and a secret note established the principle that any concessions by Portugal to one Power should not become valid until an equivalent grant had been made to the other.†

When these negotiations opened Salisbury "took occasion to intimate to Count Hatzfeldt that the Cabinet were fully alive to the importance of the Ancient Treaties between Portugal and Great Britain, which had been confirmed by Lord Granville in 1873, and in some degree by Lord Derby in 1876. Without binding ourselves", he added, "to details which might have become antiquated, we held, as Lord Granville did, that the Treaties contained stipulations which, in substance, were still binding upon Great Britain."‡ In fact there could be little doubt of their binding character. In 1859, in 1871 and in 1899 the return of *Treaties of Guarantee* laid before Parliament§ gave the texts of the most important sections of the Ancient Treaties, including those of 1642 and 1661. The treaty of 1661 specifically extended the guarantee to the colonies of Portugal.

In 1899, when the obligations to Portugal were thus printed for the third time within a period of forty years, both Portugal and Britain were facing grave difficulties. In the case of Portugal the old dangers of political uncertainty and financial stringency prevailed; and to these were added new fears roused by the rumours of the Anglo-German secret convention of 1898. Britain, on the other hand, was faced with the imminence of the Boer War. In these circumstances, Delagoa Bay became a vital interest to Britain, for it provided the only line of communication, not in British territory, between the Transvaal and the outer world. In September 1899 the Portuguese Ambassador in London, Senhor

---

* Cp. Dugdale, *Arthur James Balfour*, [1936], I, 266–72. Mr Balfour was in charge of the Foreign Office at the time.

† Gooch and Temperley, [1927], I, 71–5, Nos. 90–2, *encls*.

‡ Gooch and Temperley, [1927], I, 49, No. 67. Salisbury to Gough, No. 101 Africa Confidential, 21 June 1898. Cp. *G.P.*, [1924], XIV (I), 261.

§ *A. & P.*, [1859], XXXII, [2574], 619–30; *A. & P.*, [1871], LXXII, 275, pp. 512–23; *A. & P.*, [1899], CIX, [C. 9088], 73–85.

de Soveral, made proposals to Salisbury for an Anglo-Portuguese alliance. On 14 October the Anglo-Portuguese declaration was signed at London.* It blocked the line to the Transvaal and renewed the Ancient Treaties, citing in particular those of 1642 and 1661, including the guarantee of the colonial possessions of Portugal.† Salisbury, like Granville, thus recognized the obligations to Portugal. But in this case it was done by a written declaration; the colonies were specifically included, and a price was paid by Portugal in return.]

Document 199. *Salisbury confirms British obligations to Portugal under the Ancient Treaties, October* 1899‡

I am much obliged to you for your letter, and for the proposed formula of Agreement which you enclose.

If we sign it it will be very carefully scrutinised, and therefore I have considered your words in conjunction with the ancient treaties to which you refer.

The obligation upon Portugal "to maintain and defend the integrity and sovereignty of the British territories" can only be deduced from the treaties of the fourteenth century, which is going very far back. The word "sovereignty" is hardly applicable to present circumstances; for we have again and again stated that we do not claim, and are not seeking to establish, our sovereignty over the Transvaal; and, therefore, I could hardly sign a Treaty with Portugal implying the contrary assertion. But my strongest objection to the proposed statement of the obligations of *Portugal* is that it does not offer to Great Britain what Great Britain desires to have. We desire an engagement that, if we are at war with the Transvaal, the Portuguese Government will, on our invitation, declare war with the Transvaal also. This is of importance to us because if we are fighting the Transvaal it is essential that we should stop the supply of arms through Lourenço Marques; and for this purpose it is necessary that Portugal should free herself from the Treaty of 1875 with the Transvaal. A state

* On the inaccurate use of the term "Windsor Treaty" *v.* Gooch and Temperley, I, 99, *Ed. Note*; VIII, 49, *Ed. Note*; X (II), 483-4, *Ed. Note*.
† Gooch and Temperley, [1927], I, 93-4, No. 118.
‡ Salisbury to Soveral, Private, Enclosure 3 in Salisbury to MacDonell, 7 October 1899. Printed in Gooch and Temperley, [1927], I, 92-3, No. 117.

of war between Portugal and the Transvaal will cancel the Treaty at once. If Portugal does not adopt this, or some other mode of putting an end to the obligation to allow arms to pass through Lourenço Marques, the situation will become very grave, for Great Britain will have no other means of attaining an end which is essential to her except by a blockade.

For these reasons I do not think that the reciprocal form of obligation proposed in your formula is admissible. I have no objection to the obligations *of England* as stated in it except that I prefer the *ipsissima verba* of the "ancient treaties."

They run thus in the Secret Article of the Treaty of 1661:

"The King of Great Britain...doth promise and oblige himself <u>to defend and protect all conquests or Colonies belonging to the Crown of Portugal against all his enemies as well future</u> as present."

The words I have underlined are the best expression of the Conventional obligation of England towards Portugal, arising out of the Treaty of 1661. But, of course, they are associated with and dependent upon the closing words of the first Article of the Treaty of 1642, which is re-enacted by the Treaty of 1661.

86. THE END OF "ISOLATION"

[Even in 1871 Salisbury had drawn attention in a famous speech in the Lords to the magnitude of British obligations under treaty engagements.* At the time of the Eastern Crisis of 1875–8 his impressions were strengthened by the difficulty of reconciling the policy of the moment with the undertakings of the Tripartite Treaty of 1856. He had thus become reluctant to conclude alliances. In 1887 he laid down principles in his negotiations with the Central Powers † which were maintained unaltered by his Liberal successors in office. From that time they were an accepted factor in British relations with the Powers of Europe.

Dislike of binding alliances did not prevent Salisbury from establishing, and Rosebery and Kimberley from maintaining, *entente* relationships. All were prepared to admit that an *entente* might have to be reinforced by practical co-operation. Throughout this period, therefore, "isolation" is too strong a term to apply to British policy.

* *Hans. Deb.*, 3rd Ser., ccIV, 1366–7, 6 March 1871. Cp. Temperley and Penson, *Century of Diplomatic Blue Books*, 220.

† *V. supra*, pp. 447–8, 449, 450.

In Salisbury's last ministry, however, the position became less easy to define. He had failed to respond to the overtures of Austria-Hungary, he had watched the decline in the strength of the bond between Italy and Britain; he had seen the cumulative effect of the irritation caused by Anglo-German colonial controversy. All these contributed to a greater separation of England from the Central Powers. The fundamental factor in the situation was that Salisbury attached less importance to the Near East and more to European interference in the Far East and in Africa. In 1897 England was isolated in a far more literal sense than she had been for many years. And in close succession there came a series of crises. In the Far East Anglo-German co-operation had just broken down. Germany had turned a deaf ear to British proposals in 1894; in 1895 she had acted with France and Russia in presenting an ultimatum to Japan, while England stood aloof. In the same year England threw cold water on Germany's desire for a port in the Far East. In 1897 Germany took the port without consulting Britain, when she seized Kiao-Chao. In Africa Anglo-German co-operation was even more difficult. Germany used Britain's need for support in Egypt to secure compliance with her own demands elsewhere. Her protest against the Congo Treaty of 1894 impressed Britain—however unintentionally—with the unreality of Anglo-German friendship.* Meanwhile Anglo-French friction, continuous over Egypt, had occurred in several parts of the African continent, and was still present in 1898 on the Niger and the Nile. The most patient negotiation of boundary treaties could not solve all the irritations of colonial competition.

In 1897–8, therefore, the isolation of Britain was fairly complete. She was saved in the Fashoda crisis by the very diversity of her interests; Russia would not run the risk of being embroiled in Asia on account of French activities on the Nile. She was saved again in the Boer War by that bulwark on which Rosebery had been prepared to rely in 1894—the superiority of the British fleet. This at least was the British view. The Kaiser has claimed that it was he who prevented a combination of the Powers against Britain. But, if so, it was because he understood that superiority better than other Continental rulers.

Some such considerations were passing through the mind of Salisbury when he wrote his famous memorandum in 1901 (**Doc. 200**). Its immediate purpose was to shew to Lansdowne, who had recently succeeded him as Foreign Secretary, the reasons for his failure to respond to the German overtures for an alliance. This time Salisbury could not avoid shewing his hand, as he had

---

* In this respect it is an important anticipation of the feeling aroused by the Kaiser's telegram to Kruger. But there is this difference. German action in 1894 was resented mainly by the British Foreign Office; in 1896 it was even more resented by the public.

succeeded in doing to a large extent in former years. On the last occasion, in 1898, he had avoided a definition of his attitude by leaving it to Chamberlain to make unofficial soundings.* Now at last he was forced into the open, and in this memorandum, preserved with the greatest secrecy by Lansdowne, he placed on record the conclusions to which he had been brought by his long years of experience. It is the creed of a statesman who had indeed constantly shewn his readiness to co-operate, but who in the last resort was always prepared to stand alone.]

Document 200. *Memorandum by the Marquess of Salisbury,* 29 *May* 1901†

This is a proposal for including England within the bounds of the Triple Alliance. I understand its practical effect to be:—

1. If England were attacked by two Powers—say France and Russia—Germany, Austria, and Italy would come to her assistance.

2. Conversely, if either Austria, Germany, or Italy were attacked by France and Russia, or, if Italy were attacked by France and Spain, England must come to the rescue.

Even assuming that the Powers concerned were all despotic, and could promise anything they pleased, with a full confidence that they would be able to perform the promise, I think it is open to much question whether the bargain would be for our advantage. The liability of having to defend the German and Austrian frontiers against Russia is heavier than that of *having to defend the British Isles against France*. Even, therefore, in its most naked aspect the bargain would be a bad one for this country. Count Hatzfeldt speaks of our "*isolation*" as constituting a serious danger for us. *Have we ever felt that danger practically?* If we had succumbed in the revolutionary war, our fall would not have been due to our isolation. We had many allies, but they would not have saved us if the French Emperor had been able to command the Channel. Except during his reign we have never even been in danger; and, therefore, it is impossible for us to judge whether the

---

* *V.* J. L. Garvin, *The Life of Joseph Chamberlain*, [1934], III, 254–77.
† Gooch and Temperley, [1927], II, 68–9, No. 86.

"isolation" under which we are supposed to suffer, does or does not contain in it any elements of peril. It would hardly be wise to incur novel and most onerous obligations, in order to guard against *a danger in whose existence we have no historical reason for believing*.

But though the proposed arrangement, even from this point of view, does not seem to me admissible, these are not by any means the weightiest objections that can be urged against it. The fatal circumstance is that *neither we nor the Germans are competent to make the suggested promises*. The British Government cannot undertake to declare war, for any purpose, unless it is a purpose of which the electors of this country would approve. If the Government promised to declare war for an object which did not commend itself to public opinion, the promise would be repudiated, and the Government would be turned out. I do not see how, in common honesty, we could invite other nations to rely upon our aids in a struggle, which must be formidable and probably supreme, when we have no means whatever of knowing what may be the humour of our people in circumstances which cannot be foreseen. We might, to some extent, divest ourselves of the full responsibility of such a step, *by laying our Agreement with the Triple Alliance before Parliament* as soon as it is concluded. But there are very grave objections to such a course, and I do not understand it to be recommended by the German Ambassador.

The impropriety of attempting to determine by a *secret contract* the future conduct of a Representative Assembly upon an issue of peace or war would apply to German policy as much as to English, only that the German Parliament would probably pay more deference to the opinion of their Executive than would be done by the English Parliament. But a *promise of defensive alliance with England would excite bitter murmurs in every rank of German society*—if we may trust the indications of German sentiment, which we have had an opportunity of witnessing during the last two years.

It would not be safe to stake any important national interest upon the fidelity with which, in case of national exigency, either country could be trusted to fulfil the obligations of the

Alliance, if the Agreement had been concluded without the assent of its Parliament.

Several times during the last sixteen years Count Hatzfeldt has tried to elicit from me, in conversation, some opinion as to the probable conduct of England, if Germany or Italy were involved in war with France. I have always replied that no English Minister could venture on such a forecast. The course of the English Government in such a crisis must depend on the view taken by public opinion in this country, and public opinion would be largely, if not exclusively, governed by the nature of the *casus belli*.

EPILOGUE BY THE EDITORS

[The long period of Salisbury's connexion with the conduct of foreign affairs had seen many phases of co-operation; generally with the Central Powers, sometimes with France and Russia. To the latter, moreover, he had from time to time made overtures —the most important of them in 1898 (**Doc. 195**). Though these overtures had failed, they must be taken into account in judging the principles on which he acted. But frequent though his co-operation was—and still more frequent his readiness to co-operate—he had been consistent in refusing to pledge the country in advance to action in circumstances which had not yet arisen. His retirement from the Foreign Office was followed within a short time by the conclusion of the Anglo-Japanese Alliance and later by the founding of the Anglo-French *entente*. At the time of the negotiation of the former he was still Prime Minister of Britain. There is little evidence of his attitude towards it, yet enough to reveal an important cleavage between him and Lansdowne, a difference · that was soon to be far-reaching. While admitting Salisbury's argument that England might not have felt the danger of isolation "practically" in the past, Lansdowne added: "I think, however, that we may push too far the argument that, because we have *in the past* survived in spite of our isolation, we need have no misgivings as to the effect of that isolation *in the future*. In approaching the Japanese we have, indeed, virtually admitted that we do not wish to continue to stand alone."* And it is evident that the Cabinet was with Lansdowne in fearing the practical effects of that isolation of which Salisbury made light.

The departure from isolation was signalized by a Treaty of Alliance with Japan, which bound England in advance to potential action in the Far East. The Treaty was thus revolutionary, a departure not only from the principles of Salisbury but even from those of Canning, which deprecated increase of obligations by guarantees or alliances (*v. supra*, pp. 81–4). Salisbury was thus faced with an innovation. He may have consoled himself by the reflection that the Treaty restricted its action to one part of the Far East; but this was not, in fact, a real consolation any more than it was a real restriction. England could not remain friendly to or co-operate with Russia in Europe, if she was bound by an alliance to restrain her aggression in Asia. An alliance, even if confined to a limited sphere, was in the end bound to cause a departure from Salisbury's principles and to inaugurate a new age. The Anglo-

---

* Memorandum of Lord Lansdowne, 22 November 1901. Gooch and Temperley, [1927], II, 77, No. 92. Italics are the Editors'.

French arrangement, which was an *entente* not an alliance, might be claimed more plausibly for the Salisbury tradition. For his tenure of office had seen many examples of colonial agreements, and of co-operative action within limited areas. None the less, the Anglo-French *entente*, like the Anglo-Japanese Alliance, contemplated potentialities, and belonged therefore to the species of commitment which Salisbury had always avoided. His utterance in November 1901 really marks the end of an epoch, and the series of agreements which followed introduces us to a new age.]

HAROLD TEMPERLEY
LILLIAN PENSON

NOTE BY THE EDITORS

CANNING, SPAIN AND BRITISH TRADE WITH THE SPANISH COLONIES 1810–24

In the *American Historical Review*, XLIII, No. 2, January 1938, 288–9, Miss Goebel challenges Canning's statement, given in the text (*supra*, p. 72): "That permission to trade with the Spanish Colonies had been conceded to Great Britain in the Year 1810... [when Spain asked Great Britain to mediate between her and her colonies] That this Mediation indeed was afterwards not employed, because Spain changed her Counsel;—but that it was not therefore practicable for Great Britain to withdraw Commercial Capital once embarked in Spanish America, and to desist from Commercial intercourse once established.—

That it had been ever since distinctly understood, that the Trade was open to British Subjects, and that the ancient Coast Laws of Spain were, so far as regarded them at least, tacitly repealed."

This was published on 4 March 1824 (*v. supra*, p. 70 and n.) and Sir James Mackintosh the next day (the 5th) asked Canning if the Treaty, embodying this agreement, had been printed, and, if not, asked, that it should be laid. Canning answered: "No such treaty was in existence to the best of his knowledge. In the year 1810, when this country proposed to interpose her mediation between Spain and her colonies in America, it was merely upon an understanding between the two governments, that the coast law of Spain should be suspended, as between the subjects of the two nations. No instrument, as far as he had ascertained, was in existence, in which this agreement was recorded." *

Mackintosh asked a second question as to whether a copy of a decree of Ferdinand VII, authorizing this trade, existed. Canning replied to this that he knew of that "only as a matter of public notoriety", and could not say whether His Majesty's Government had it in a shape "that would entitle it to be considered as a document in their possession". As Mackintosh was a friend of Canning's, he in all probability gave notice of his question beforehand, so that Canning had time to look the matter up.

Miss Goebel comments that hitherto "Canning's claim has been accepted at its face value", but that "any such statement is false. That Canning was misinformed in this matter seems improbable" (*Am. Hist. Rev.*, XLIII, No. 2, January 1938, 288). She adds that the statement "falls to the ground under the weight of the evidence of earlier years" etc. The matter is of some interest because

---

* *Hans. Deb.*, New Ser., X, 753–4.

Canning was a disciple of publicity, and would have been unwise to make any statement in public which either Spain or France could refute. It is singular, at least, that Spain did not, in her heated and abundant correspondence with him, ever try to refute this statement of fact. Indeed she had admitted the principle by 1822. For in that year, as Canning pointed out (*supra*, p. 73), the Spanish Government signed a convention to give redress for seizures of certain British vessels engaged in this Spanish colonial trade. By doing that she certainly gave not a "tacit", but an official and open, permission to England for this trade. Canning need not have gone back further than this year (1822) if he wished to establish the formal right. But he evidently thought the "tacit" right went back to 1810.

What is the explanation, and at what period, did Spain admit British trade with her colonies? Miss Frances Horsfall, who has made some researches on the subject, found in *F.O.* 72/96 a document shewing that in July 1810 an edict was printed in Cadiz under the signature of the Minister of Finance, throwing open a direct trade between the Spanish colonies and the nations of Europe and America not at war with Spain. But this edict apparently was due to the signature of the Minister being obtained under false pretences by an under-secretary, who was in fact an American. It was subsequently disavowed by the Junta and the under-secretary dismissed. It may be that Canning quoted this edict originally, believing it to be genuine. On being questioned by Mackintosh, he may have gone into the matter and found out his mistake. His reply proves that he was not prepared to quote or to defend the edict as a document in British possession.

On 25 January 1810 Henry Wellesley wrote to the Marquess Wellesley that there had been much agitation among British merchants for placing the Spanish American trade on a proper footing.* Repeated demands on the Spanish Government were made by the Marquess Wellesley for a British share in the Spanish colonial trade during this year (*F.O.* 185/18, No. 21; *F.O.* 72/93, No. 24; *F.O.* 72/96, No. 58; *F.O.* 72/97, Nos. 81, 83). But nothing came of these demands. The Spanish Foreign Minister said they could never be granted. He meant, at least, openly. A third effort was made by the Cortes in December 1811, when it discussed opening Spanish colonial trade with England in return for a loan. But Castlereagh ultimately rejected this (*F.O.* 72/115, No. 130; *F.O.* 72/134, 1 May 1812).

Miss Horsfall points out that none of these cases provide sufficient ground for Canning's direct statement, though the bogus edict may afford some explanation of it.

The Editors think, however, that another interpretation of Canning's statement is possible. He says in the original document

* *Wellesley Papers*, [1914], I, 298.

"That permission to trade with the Spanish Colonies had been conceded to Great Britain in the Year 1810". When pressed in the Commons he said there was "no instrument" or treaty, "merely ...an *understanding*".* This is surely plain enough, it means that there was a "gentleman's agreement" that England could so trade without official permission. The same meaning is further implied in Canning's original statement: "it had been ever since [1810] distinctly *understood*...that the ancient Coast Laws of Spain were, so far as regarded them at least, *tacitly* repealed".* The trade of Buenos Aires was closed by order of the Spanish Home Government at the end of 1809 (*Am. Hist. Rev.*, XLIII, No. 2, 312) but thrown open by the revolutionary leaders in May 1810. This appears to be just about the time that the Spanish Home Government may have admitted by an informal understanding that they would tolerate, or tacitly wink at, the throwing open of such trade, in return for British mediation. But neither suggestion ever seems to have got into official documents. There is also very little trace even in private papers.†

Spain was at this time both a weak and a proud nation, and such governments can seldom agree to make a concession involving loss of prestige in the eyes of their own subjects. Their face was entirely saved if they refused to make this concession officially, but did so unofficially. A similar illustration can be taken from Greece during the late war. In 1915 Venizelos, when Premier, privately invited England and France to occupy Salonica. But, when they actually landed, he took care to make an official protest, thereby saving his face and safeguarding Greece's sovereignty. Devices of this kind are much commoner with weak and proud states than is generally known. A tacit winking at the throwing open of Spanish colonial trade, entirely protected the Spanish Government from criticism at home, while entirely satisfying the British traders abroad. Miss J. O. McLachlan states, on the evidence of researches in British and Spanish Archives in the eighteenth century, that similar devices were more than once adopted, at least temporarily, by the Spanish Home Government in dealing with England in that period. The Anglo-Spanish Convention of 1822 afforded redress to British vessels seized by Spanish ones, and was thus a formal and official confirmation of the "tacit" permission already accorded to British trade with the Spanish colonies. It seems strange that Canning should have risked a rebuff by making an obviously untrue statement as to 1810 and then publishing it, for it would thus have given Spain,

* Italics the Editors'.

† It is, however, interesting that Sir Arthur Wellesley in a private letter to Henry Wellesley of 10 August 1810 shews that he disapproved of the British demand for "free trade with the [Spanish] colonies". He fears, evidently, that the Spanish Government would yield, or had yielded, to the demand. *Dispatches of the Duke of Wellington*, 1st Ser., [1844], IV, 221.

and perhaps France also, a weapon in the paper warfare that followed. It seems still more strange that Spain never contested his statement.

The obvious explanation seems to be that Spain did not wish to raise the question of "tacit" consent to trade, because she would then have had to admit her earlier readiness to accept England's "mediation" between her rebel colonies and herself.* Spain could not afford to do this in 1823 as Canning, of course, very well knew. But it seems very unsatisfactory that there is no evidence, even in private papers, extant on the subject. The only explanation is that the Marquess Wellesley was the most otiose of British Foreign Secretaries during his term of office from 1809 to 1812. He was a close friend of Canning's and was actually consulted by him on various points of his Spanish American policy in 1824. It is possible therefore that Wellesley in 1823 supplied him with the information about the Spanish decree of 1810 without realizing that it was bogus; and gave the information about mediation and "tacit" consent to trade which he, *more suo*, failed subsequently to support by documents. This explanation is at least more satisfactory than the suggestion of Miss Goebel that Canning published a statement which could not be substantiated and which, in the controversy that was bound to follow, would have put him at a disadvantage both with France and with Spain. That was an unlikely step for him to take in developing his new policy of publicity. Canning had reproved Strangford in September 1823 for making a statement in an official dispatch, which "was not the fact".† He added that there was always the possibility of an official dispatch being published and the inaccuracy revealed. Less than a month later Canning prepared the Polignac Memorandum, which from the start he had designed to publish. It seems improbable that he would have made a statement in it which he knew "was not the fact", when he had just rebuked a subordinate for doing this very thing. The subject is of some interest as it affects Canning's Blue-Book policy, which is more fully described in Temperley and Penson, *A Century of Diplomatic Blue Books*, 30–7.

* Miss Horsfall points out that mediation was actually offered to, and formally accepted by, Spain in 1811, *F.O.* 72/112, H. Wellesley to Marquess Wellesley. Cadiz, 30 June 1811. It was never actually acted on. Canning was in very close touch with the Marquess Wellesley in 1810 (Add. MSS. 37,295, ff. 288–9, 298–9. Canning to Wellesley, 9 May and 30 May 1810), and probably also in 1811.

† The dispatch to Strangford is of 16 September 1823, *F.O.* 78/113; *v.* Temperley, *Life of Canning*, [1905], 208.

INDEX

References in Arabic *lettering are to pages.* **Clarendon** *type is used for Document numbers, and italic type for dates.*

ABERDEEN, GEORGE HAMILTON GORDON, 4TH EARL OF, SECRETARY OF STATE FOR FOREIGN AFFAIRS, 1828–30, 1841–6; PRIME MINISTER, 1852–5
   first diplomatic experience of (*1814*) 190; failures of (*1828–30*) 190; comparative success of second period of office in United States, and policy towards Europe (*1841–6*) 190–1
   and Austria (*1853*) 190, **Doc. 53**
   and Derby's policy (*1852*) 188
   and France 190
   and Greece 190
   and Naples 190–2, **Doc. 51**; Palmerston on 191
   and Napoleon I (*1814*) 190
   and Portugal 190
   and Russia, conversations with Nicholas (*1844*) 134–5, 138 n., 190; (*1853*) 138, 145
   and Spanish Marriage Question 190
   and the Straits (*1853*) 145
   and the United States (*1846*) 190
ABERDEEN ACT, 1845
   re Slave Trade **Docs. 114, 115**
ABYSSINIA
   Sir R. Rodd's mission to (*1897*) 505; French activities in 505–6; defeat of Italy in 506 n.
ADEN
   British occupation of (*1839*) 124, 126 n.
ADRIATIC AND AEGEAN COASTS
   Austria and, Russian proposal that they should go to (*1853*) ,135
   Malmesbury's proposal for neutrality of (*1859*) 202
   Mediterranean Agreement (*Feb., Mar. 1887*) **Docs. 175, 176**
ALABAMA ARBITRATION *v. sub* ARBITRATION
H.R.H. ALBERT, PRINCE CONSORT
   227
ALEXANDER I, TSAR OF RUSSIA, 1801–25
   and Pitt (*1805*) 9–10, **Doc. 2**
   and Holy Alliance 36–7
   and Quadruple Alliance 38, 45–6, 51
   and Poland 232–3, 234–5, 242
ALEXANDER II, TSAR OF RUSSIA, 1855–81
   and Poland 236, 242
ALEXANDER OF BATTENBERG, PRINCE OF THE BULGARIANS, 1879–86
   429, 430, 441, 444, 454
ALEXANDRIA
   bombardment of (*1882*) 417, 420, **Doc. 164**

ALLIANCES, BRITISH POLICY IN (*v.* also *sub* TREATIES)
Castlereagh on (*1820*) 63
Derby on (*1876*) **Doc. 139**
Gladstone on (*1869*) **Doc. 123**; (*1879*) 392
Granville on (*1872*) 344–5, **Doc. 134**
Palmerston on (*1841*) 137
Rosebery on (*1893*) **Doc. 187**
Salisbury on 447–8, 516–17, **Doc. 200**, 521–2

ALSACE-LORRAINE
French retention of (*1815*) 28
Prussian annexation of (*1870*) 323–4; Gladstone on 323–4, **Doc. 125**;
    Granville on 323–4

AMERICA, LATIN (*v.* also *sub* BRAZIL)
68

AMERICA, SPANISH
British trade with 69, 72–3, 523–6
recognition of 65, 68, 69, **Doc. 8**, 76, **Doc. 9**

AMERICA, UNITED STATES OF
and Great Britain, Peace of Ghent 33; Oregon boundary treaty 190
and Spanish America 70; Canning's wish to consult *re* 75 n.
Civil War in 294, **Docs. 105–7**, 296–8, **Docs. 108, 109**
    Gladstone and, his desire for continuance of Union **Doc. 107**; his
        speech on "making a nation" (*Oct. 1862*) 296–7; his belief that
        recognition must come soon 299
    Napoleon III and, project for joint intervention 298, **Doc. 108**
    Palmerston and, advantages of an independent South (*1862*) **Doc.
        105**, 296; his belief in success of South 297; discussions on
        recognition 297–8; belief in possibility of Anglo-American war
        (*1863*) **Doc. 109**
    Russell, Palmerston and, belief in possibility of Anglo-American war
        Doc. 109
    v. also *sub* GLADSTONE

ANDRÁSSY, COUNT JULIUS, AUSTRO-HUNGARIAN MINISTER FOR FOREIGN
    AFFAIRS, 1871–9
and Eastern Crisis, Andrássy note (*30 Dec. 1875*) 354, 357
Disraeli on 389
overture to Granville (*1872–3*) 343–5, **Doc. 134**

APPONYI, COUNT RUDOLF, AUSTRO-HUNGARIAN AMBASSADOR AT LONDON,
    1856–71
on Palmerston and Russell 281; on danger of war between France,
    Russia and Prussia (*1866*) 307; on Stanley **Doc. 117**, 308; on
    Granville and the Black Sea question (*1870*) 330

ARBITRATION
Brazil and (*1863*) 300, **Docs. 110–13**
Gladstone and Alabama case (*1871–3*) 300, 327–8, **Doc. 126**, 390
Malmesbury and 198, **Doc. 55**
Palmerston and 284, (*1849*) 301; proposal to America for (*1848*) 300
Russell and 284, 300
Salisbury and 513

ARGENTINE REPUBLIC
  liberation of 68; Spain and 68, 75–6; recognition by Britain of 69, 76;
    refusal of Canning's offer to guarantee Delta of la Plata 82
  ports opened 525

ARGYLL, GEORGE DOUGLAS CAMPBELL, 8TH DUKE OF
  and American Civil War Doc. 108

ARMENIA
  administration and reforms in (1878) 365, 369, 370, 384–5; (1880) 396,
    Docs. 153, 154, 405, 407; (1896) 406; (1913) 407
  massacres in (1894–5) 494

ASSAB BAY
  Franco-Italian dispute re 328

AUGUSTENBURG, FREDERIC, PRINCE, DUKE OF
  261, 264, 266, 278

AUSTRIA (AUSTRIA-HUNGARY)
  constitutions in (1848) 153; Constitution of, Derby on (1875) 353;
    revolutions of (1848–9) and 153–5, 158–9, 162–5, Docs. 41,
    42, 169–72; importance of, for balance of power Doc. 44, as a
    counterpoise to Russia and France Doc. 100; increased importance
    of, in Triple Alliance as result of Bismarck's fall (1890) 465; military
    strength of (1870) 320
  and Belgium (1831–9) 89, 95, 97, 101, Doc. 17, 132; (1870) 337
  and Bosnia and Herzegovina (1878) 364; (1881) 412; (1908) 331
  and Egypt (1839–41) 122, 132–3; (1884) 426; (1887) 452, Doc. 179
  and France (1792) 2; (1805) 10; (1831) 93; (1859) 203–5, Docs. 61, 62,
    291, Doc. 100
  and Germany (1871–3) 343–4, 347; (1875) 352, 353; (1881, 1882) 390–1,
    412; (1890) 465
  and Great Britain (1791), Pitt's negotiations between Russia and Austria
    and Turkey 1; (1805) Pitt's proposals re 10, 14, 16, 17; (1807)
    Canning on Austrian supremacy in Germany 26; (1813) Castle-
    reagh's proposals re 32, 33; (1818) differences in interpretation
    of the alliance 38–9; (1824) Canning on 87; (1832) cooperation
    between, against Mehemet Ali 118, (1839) 122; (1849) Palmerston
    on Doc. 44; (1852) Malmesbury on Doc. 50; (1853) Aberdeen
    on 190, Doc. 53; (1859) Rechberg on Doc. 100; (1871–2)
    Granville and 343–4, Doc. 134; (1874) Derby and 345, 347,
    Doc. 135, (1877) 357–9, 364; (1878) Salisbury and 364, 365,
    373–4, 383; (1880–1) Gladstone and Doc. 159, 471, 476; (1886)
    Rosebery and 434; (1886) Salisbury and 442, Doc. 174, (1887)
    446–8, 450, 453, 454–8, Docs. 181, 182, (1891) Doc. 191;
    (1893–4) Rosebery and 472–3, Docs. 186–9, 487, 489–90; (1896–
    7) Salisbury and 495–6, Doc. 194, 517
  and Greece (1841) 107, Doc. 22
  and Hungarian refugees in Turkey (1849) 177–81
  and Italy (1805) 10, 15–16, 17; (1813) 33; (1821) 64; (1848–9) 162–5,
    Docs. 42, 44; (1860) 218–19, 225, 226–7, 229; (1867) 308; (1919)
    234

AUSTRIA (AUSTRIA-HUNGARY) *continued*
  and Near East (*1791*) 1; (*1832*) 118; (*1839*) 122–3; (*1841*) 124, **Docs.
    31–2**; (*1853*) 139, 142, 145; (*1875–8*) 354, 357–8, 359, 364–5;
    (*1880–1*) 409–10; (*1885–6*) 430, **Doc. 169**, 442, **Doc. 174**; (*1887*)
    446–8, 455–8, **Docs. 181, 182**; (*1893–7*) 471–3, **Docs. 186–9,**
    494, 495–6, **Doc. 194**
  and Netherlands (*1805*) 14; (*1813*) 32; (*1833*) 89
  and Poland (*1863*) 237–9, **Docs. 73, 75, 76, 78**
  and Prussia (*1805*) 17; (*1815*) 35; (*1860*) 226–7; (*1863*) **Docs. 82, 83**;
    (*1866*) 305, **Doc. 118**; (*1870*) 320
  and Russia (*1790–1*) 1; (*1814–15*) 34–5; (*1815*) 37; (*1824*) 87; (*1831–9*)
    101; (*1832*) 118; (*1848–9*) 158–9, 170–1, **Doc. 43**, 178–9, **Doc. 45**;
    (*1853*) 135, 145; (*1856*) 287; (*1859*) **Doc. 100**; (*1860*) 226–7; (*1863*)
    236–9, **Doc. 73**, 241, **Docs. 75–8**; (*1870*) 330; (*1872*) 346; (*1876*)
    355; (*1881*) 390, 411, 412; (*1884*) 426; (*1885*) 430, 431; (*1886*) 442,
    Doc. 174; (*1887*) 446–7, 455–7; (*1891*) 466–8; (*1893–4*) 472–3,
    474, **Doc. 189**, 489; (*1895*) 494; (*1897*) 496, 499
  and Sardinia (*1859*) 197–8, **Docs. 54, 55**; war with (*1859*) 203–5, **Docs.
    61, 62**
  and Schleswig-Holstein (*1852, 1863–4*) 260–2, **Docs. 88, 92**; ultimatum
    to Denmark 262, 264; reluctant assent to invasion of Jutland 267;
    establishment of condominium with Prussia in Duchies 278
  and Servia (*1878*) 364; (*1881*) 430; (*1885*) 431
  and Spain (*1821*) 64; (*1834*) 103
  and Venetia 218–19, **Docs. 70, 71**

BALANCE OF POWER
  disturbance of, by union of Naples and Sicily to Piedmont 228; by
    creation of a big Bulgaria 363
  importance to, of Austria **Docs. 44, 100**; of Danish monarchy (*1852*) 260
  Vienna and settlement of (*1814–15*) 34–5
  Palmerston and, as a principle of British policy (*1841*) 138; *re* Austria
    and Hungary (*1849*) 170, 171, **Doc. 44**; *re* Austrian rule in Italy
    (*1848–9*) 164–5; *re* Prussia (*1865*) **Doc. 97**; Rechberg's views on
    (*1859*) **Doc. 100**
  Pitt and (*1805*) 10
  Russell and (*1859*) **Doc. 58**; (*1860*) 214, **Doc. 67**

BALTIC
  Malmesbury's proposal for neutrality of (*1859*) 202

BARING, EVELYN (LORD CROMER), BRITISH AGENT AND CONSUL-GENERAL
    IN EGYPT, 1883, 1885–1907
  and Egypt (*1883*) 421

BARRIER TREATY
  19

BATOUM
  acquisition of, by Russia (*1877–8*) 360, 365, 378, 381, 382, 388, 389;
    alteration in status of (*1886*) 436–7, **Doc. 173**, 441

BELGIUM
  guarantee of
    Austria and, Metternich's interpretation of (*1837*) **Doc. 17**, Palmer-
      ston on (*1841*) 132; attitude of (*1870*) 337

France and (*1870*) 336–8

Great Britain and, not ready to defend alone if violated, Gladstone's anxieties *re* (*1870*) 336–7, 338–9, Law Officers on 341; Currie on (*1885*) 473 n.; Hardinge on (*1908*) 155 n., 337

statements *re* character of, by Palmerston (*1837*) **Doc. 16,** (*1841*) **Doc. 32;** contrast with guarantee to Luxemburg, by Stanley (*1867*) 309, 310, 312; Derby and Clarendon cited as regarding it as "both collective and individual" 446; Gladstone's policy in concluding treaties of (*1870*) 335–7, **Docs. 130, 131,** 445, 446; Law Officers' interpretation of (*1870*) **Doc. 132;** memorandum by Hertslet on (*1872*) 337 n.; Currie on fighting for Belgium "if she had an ally" 473 n.; Salisbury's silence *re* (*1887*) 445–6, **Doc. 177;** Hardinge's comment on (*1908*) 155 n., 337; Sir Edward Grey and (*1914*) 316

Prussia and (*1870*) 336–7

Russia and (*1870*) 337

independence of 89–90, **Docs. 12–17,** 101, 206, 254; Palmerston and 88–90, **Docs. 12–16,** 100, 101, 104

and Austria (*1831–9*) 89, 95, 97, 101, **Doc. 17,** 132

and France, invasion of (*1792*) 2, (*1831*) 89; French designs on (*1831*) **Docs. 12, 14**

and Germany (*1874*) **Doc. 136**

and Luxemburg (*1831*) 89, 90–1

and Prussia (*1831–9*) 89, 95; (*1870*) 336–7

and Russia (*1831–9*) 89, 95; (*1870*) 337

and settlement after Napoleonic wars, Pitt and (*1793*) 89, (*1805*) 9–10; Castlereagh and (*1813*) 28, 32; union with Holland 9–10, 28, 32, 35, 89

BENEDETTI, COUNT, FRENCH AMBASSADOR AT BERLIN, 1864–70

and Belgium 336

BERLIN MEMORANDUM, 13 MAY 1876

355, 357

BERLIN, TREATY OF *v. sub* TREATIES

BERNSTORFF, COUNT VON, PRUSSIAN MINISTER FOR FOREIGN AFFAIRS, 1818–32

and Luxemburg 311–12, 313, **Doc. 122**

BEUST, COUNT VON, AUSTRO-HUNGARIAN CHANCELLOR AND MINISTER FOR FOREIGN AFFAIRS, 1867–71; AMBASSADOR AT LONDON, 1871–8, AT PARIS, 1878–82

Derby and 345, 347, **Doc. 135**

Granville and 344, **Doc. 134**

on Derby and Granville (*1874*) 347

BISMARCK, COUNT HERBERT

visit to England (*1889*) 463

BISMARCK, PRINCE OTTO VON, MINISTER-PRESIDENT OF PRUSSIA, 1862–71; CHANCELLOR OF THE NORTH GERMAN CONFEDERATION, 1867–71; IMPERIAL CHANCELLOR, 1871–90

effect of his policy on constitutionalism **Doc. 82,** 284; fall of 463–4, **Doc. 183**

and armaments (*1870*) 318–19, **Doc. 124**

and colonial questions (*1884–5*) 424–5, **Doc. 166;** (*1887–90*) 462–3

BISMARCK, PRINCE OTTO VON *continued*
  and Egypt (*1884*) 423–4, **Doc. 166**
  and Great Britain, Disraeli's conversation with (*1862*) **Doc. 80**; overture
    to Derby (*1874*) **Doc. 136**; and War Scare (*1875*) 351–2, **Doc.
    138**; renewed overture (*1876*) 354–5, **Doc. 139**; communications
    with Salisbury (*1885*) 429, (*1887*) 455, 458, (*1889*) 463
      Clarendon on (*1869*) 322
      Derby on (*1875*) 351
      Disraeli on (*1878*) 389
      Gladstone on (*1870*) 324–5
      Palmerston on (*1860–3*) **Docs. 81, 82**
      Russell on (*1863*) **Doc. 82**
      Salisbury on (*1888*) 463, 464; (*1890*) **Doc. 183**
  and Luxemburg (*1867*) 309–10, 311, 315–16
  and Near East (*1876*) 354–5, **Doc. 139**; (*1881*) 411–12, **Doc. 159**;
    (*1887*) definition of policy in Reinsurance Treaty 454–5; encourage-
    ment of Mediterranean Agreements 446, 448, 449, 455–8; Salis-
    bury's suspicions of **Doc. 181**
  and Schleswig-Holstein question 248–9, 261–2

BLACK SEA
  Russia and, Pitt's attempt to stop further advance (*1791*) 1; cancellation
    of Black Sea clauses of Treaty of Paris (*1870–1*) 328, 330–1,
    Doc. 127, 345
  status quo in, Mediterranean Agreement (*Feb., Mar. 1887*) and 448, 450

BOER WAR
  and British isolation 517
  and negotiations with Portugal (*1899*) 514–15, **Doc. 199**

BOSNIA AND HERZEGOVINA
  Austria-Hungary and, occupation of (*1878*) 364, conscription in (*1881*)
    412; annexation of (*1908*) 331

BRAZIL
  blockade of Rio (*1862*) 300
  compared by Palmerston to a Billingsgate Fishwoman, **Doc. 111**
  disputes *re* (*1862*) 300, **Docs. 111–13**; Palmerston on **Docs. 111–12**,
    Salisbury on 300
  recognition of, by Canning 68; refusal of guarantee of navigation of
    Rio de la Plata 82
  slave trade in 302, 303, **Doc. 116**

BULGARIA
  independence of, proposed by Nicholas I (*1853*) 135
  settlement of, Berlin and (*1878*) 363, 366, 367–8, 369, 377, 388
  union of two Bulgarias (*1885–7*) 429–31, **Docs. 169, 170**, 434, 441–2,
    Doc. 174, 445

BÜLOW, BERNHARD ERNST VON, GERMAN SECRETARY OF STATE, 1873–9
  and War scare (*1875*) 351

CAMBON, PAUL, FRENCH AMBASSADOR AT LONDON, 1898–1920
  and guarantee to Luxemburg 316

CANNING, GEORGE, SECRETARY OF STATE FOR FOREIGN AFFAIRS, 1807–9, 1822–7; PRIME MINISTER, 1827

George IV and, gets him to amend a speech (*1826*) 67 n.

Burke, connexion with 24

Canning, Stratford Viscount de Redcliffe, and 86 n.

Castlereagh, relation to 22, 64–5; connexion with State Paper of (*5 May 1820*) 47–8

Palmerston, disciple of Canning, and difference from 84, 88, 90

Pitt, relation to, and difference from 22

Salisbury, erroneous interpretation of policy of (*1896*) 84

and the Congress System 65–6; his acceptance of Castlereagh's State Paper of (*5 May 1820*) (*14 Ap. 1823*) 48; his influence upon it 47 n., 48 n.; quotes from it 65–6; objection to interference in Spain and Naples 86; his instruction to Wellington at Verona 64; his break up of the Congress System 65; his demand that no European Congress should discuss Spanish America without the United States 70, 75

and constitutions and constitutionalism, general attitude towards (*4 Dec. 1824*) **Doc. 11**; not friendly to constitutions as such 85–6, nor to revolution (*28 Ap. 1823*) 87 n.; error of Portuguese historians in supposing that he sent troops to Portugal to defend constitution not frontier (*1826*) 85 and n., 86 and n.; Peel on (*1829*) 85 n.; Salisbury in error *re* 84 and n.

and despotisms and democracies, not friendly to the first 65; nor to the second 85–6; desire to hold the balance between the two 84–5, 87 and n.

and guarantees, general reluctance to give 82; his classic despatch on **Doc. 10**; his offer to give naval guarantee of Cuba to Spain 81–2; to guarantee free navigation of the Rio de la Plata 82; his agreement to respect guarantee to Portugal 82, 85, 86 and n.; his refusal to extend it to her colonies 82, 342; considers, but declines, a guarantee to Greece 82

and nationality, connexion with Burke over nationality in Poland 24; difference from Pitt over Spanish nationality 22; speech on recognition of Spanish nationality (*28 Ap. 1823*) 24 and n.; effort to unite nations and governments against Napoleon (*1807–9*) 23–4

and public opinion, belief in, as the source of England's power 65–6; speech (*12 Dec. 1826*) 66–7; policy of publicity unusual 65 and n.; Blue-Book publication 65 and n.

and recognition of new or revolted states, his general theory of (*25 Mar. 1825*) **Doc. 9**; his insistence on stability and not legitimacy as the test 77; his error in supposing that accrediting of consuls did not imply political recognition 69 and n.; his insistence on importance of protecting British trade with *de facto* independent states, and particularly with Spanish America 68–9, 72–3; his inaccuracy as to (*1810*) 72, 523–6

and America, Latin (*v.* also *sub* United States)

Brazil, recognized as independent by Canning (*1825*) 68; refuses Canning's offer to guarantee Delta of la Plata 82

and America, Spanish (*v.* also *sub* United States)

refusal of Canning to enter a Congress *re* with Spain 69, unless United States invited 69–70, 75 and n.

CANNING, GEORGE *continued*

> *recognition* of, by, anticipation by Castlereagh (*1822*) 68; Canning and 68, accrediting of consuls (*1823*) 69 and n., 72; induces France to abjure project of recovering colonies by force **Doc. 8**; full political recognition accorded (*1825*) 65, 76; recognition not dependent on monarchical form of government 75 and n., a question of stability and fact 77, full theory stated **Doc. 9**; distinction between *de facto* and *de jure* recognition 77, 78 and n., 80; difference between, and modern international law theory 69 n.

> *trade*, Spanish colonial, situation between Spain, her revolted colonies and England (*1810*) 69; Canning's inaccuracy *re* 72, 523–6; situation (*1822*) 73; England no desire for separate right 73; but interdiction of by Spain would be followed by political recognition (*1823*) 73; consuls accredited to various colonies (*1823*) 69, 72

French designs on (*1823*) 68–70, solemnly abjured by Polignac **Doc. 8**

Individual States

> *Argentine Republic* (Buenos Ayres and Rio de la Plata), negotiations between Spain and (*1823*) 68, 75–6; territory entirely liberated (*1823*) 68; consuls accredited (*1823*) 69; full political recognition (*1825*) 76; Canning's offer to guarantee Delta of la Plata refused by 82

> *Chile*, situation in (*1823*) 68

> *Columbia* (including Venezuela), territory entirely liberated (*1823*) 68; France and (*1823*) 74; full political recognition (*1825*) 76

> *Cuba*, Canning's offer to guarantee to Spain (*1825*) 81

> *Mexico*, one castle held by Spain (*1823*) 68; consuls accredited by, to (*1823*) 69; full political recognition (*1825*) 76

> *Peru*, situation in (*1823*) 68

and Austria, Canning's objections to Metternich (*1824*) 87; theory of *de jure* recognition 76

and France, on Louis XVIII and his restoration 79; forcible intervention in Spain (*1823*) 64, 68, Canning's three conditions *re* 68; references to 66, 81; fear as to French designs on Spanish America 68–9, the cause of commercial recognition (*1823*) 69; Polignac abjures attempt to reconquer Spanish colonies by French arms (*1823*) 69, **Doc. 8**; associated with Russia and England in treaty over Greece (*1827*) 85

and Germany, Canning on its future and the danger from Prussia (*16 May 1807*) **Doc. 3**

and Norway, coercion of (*1814*) 25

and Poland 25

and Portugal (*1807–9*) 22; her possession of by Spain (*1580–1640*) 78 and n.; House of Braganza guaranteed their throne when driven to Brazil 81; Canning denies applicability of British engagements to colonies (*1825*) 82, 342; Canning's condition to France *re* integrity of (*1823*) 68; danger of aggression from Spain, the *casus foederis* invoked and recognized by Canning (*1826*) 85; his dislike

INDEX

of constitution of 85 and n., error of Portuguese historians *re* 86 and n.; Canning's speech on (*12 Dec. 1826*) 67; proposals *re* Dom Miguel 85–6, Peel on 85 n.

and Prussia, Canning on danger to Germany from (*1807*) **Doc. 3**; theory of *de jure* recognition refuted by Canning 76

and Russia, to be used to check Prussia (*1807*) 27; Canning refuses to attend Congress *re* Turkey, summoned by (*1824*) 65; associated with France and England in treaty over Greece (*1827*) 85; theory of *de jure* recognition refuted by Canning 76

and Spain, policy in regard to war in (*1807–9*) 22–3; his doctrine as to Spain at first sight revolutionary, tries to unite nations and governments against Napoleon 23–4; speech on recognition of Spanish nationality (*28 Ap. 1823*) 24 and n.; Dutch and Portuguese revolts from 78; Canning's desire to avert forcible interference in (*1822*) 64; French invasion, Canning's three conditions *re* 68, his fear of French invasion 69, his refusal to guarantee territory or institutions of 81–2, **Doc. 10**

Spanish American Colonies in relation to, situation in (*1810*) Canning incorrect in regard to 72, 523–6; Spain's redress in regard to (*1822*) 73; England no desire for separate right to 73, but a Spanish interdiction would produce political recognition of 73; Polignac and Canning on inability of Spain to recover (*1823*) 71, 73; design of France to recover 68–9; Polignac disclaims use of force 73–4

Spain's desire for a Congress refused by Canning (*Dec. 1823*) 65, who demands admission of the United States 69, 75 and n.; he denies that separation is England's work or wish (*1825*) 78; Spanish separate negotiation with Argentine 68, Canning on 75; Spanish theory of *de jure* recognition 76, 80; Canning's *de facto* theory and general doctrine of **Doc. 9**

and United States, theory of recognition 76; Canning and Monroe Doctrine (*1823*) 69–70; claim to invite to Congress on Spanish America, horrifying to Europe (*1823*) 70, 75 and n.

CANNING, STRATFORD (VISCOUNT STRATFORD DE REDCLIFFE), BRITISH AMBASSADOR AT CONSTANTINOPLE, 1832, 1842–52, 1853–8
and Crimean war 138, **Doc. 34**, 144–5
and the fleet (*1832*) 118; (*1853*) 145
and Mehemet Ali 118
and refugees in Turkey (*1849*) 178
and revolution (*1848*) 154–5

CAPRIVI, GENERAL, GERMAN CHANCELLOR, 1890–4
465

CASTLEREAGH, ROBERT STEWART, VISCOUNT, LATER 2ND MARQUIS OF LONDONDERRY, SECRETARY OF STATE FOR FOREIGN AFFAIRS, 1812–22
relation to Pitt 9, 22, 28 and n.; and to Canning 47–8, 65
and alliances 37–9, **Docs. 5–6**
and guarantees for Europe 28; Prussia's scheme of territorial guarantee (*1815*) 38
and Holy Alliance (*26 Sept. 1815*) 36–7, 39 and n.
and nationality 22

CASTLEREAGH, ROBERT STEWART, VISCOUNT *continued*

and non-intervention, *positive* (*1818*) 37; State Paper of (*5 May 1820*), foundation of British foreign policy 47–8, **Doc. 6**; *negative* (*1820*) 64

definition of Alliance as not intended to interfere in internal affairs 54, quoted by Canning (*30 Ap. 1823*) 54 n., 65–6; Castlereagh's further explanation 61

Canning on State Paper of (*5 May 1820*) and non-intervention (*14 Ap. 1823*) 48, his connexion with 47–8 and n.

Circular of (*19 Jan. 1821*) 48 and n., 64

and parliamentary criticism and public opinion, Professor Webster on his impatience of 65

peace-making, instructions for (*Dec. 1813*) 29, **Doc. 4**

and Treaty of Chaumont, meaning of 41–2

and 1st Treaty of Paris (*30 May 1814*) 36 and n., 39

and 2nd Treaty of Paris (*20 Nov. 1815*) 36 and n., 39, 40–1; Arts. II and III 42 and n., 43; Art. V 43 and n.

and Treaty against Napoleon, Vienna (*25 Mar. 1815*) 45 and n.

and Treaty of Vienna (*9 June 1815*) 36, 39, 40–1

on these treaties as foundations of peace **Doc. 5**

and Austria, proposals *re* Italy (*1813*) 32, 33

and Denmark, to be discussed with Sweden 31, 33; Heligoland to be ceded to Britain 31

and France, naval power of, to be restricted (*1813*) 30; military power reduced (*1820*) 60

and French Colonies and oversea possessions (*1813*) 31; Mauritius to be British 31; Malta to remain British (*1813*) 31; (*1815*) 28

and Germany (*1813*) 33; (*1820*) 59, 62; on Prussia (*1814*), views to Wellington 25 n.; Prussia and territorial guarantee (*1818*) 38; Rhine, Left Bank of (*1813*) 32; *re* Spain (*1820*) 49, 59

and Holland, proposals *re* Archduke Charles 32; prefers restoration to *1792* limits (*1812*) with Barrier 30–1; Barrier deeply interesting to Allies 32; Holland to be party to guarantee of settlement 34; House of Orange 30, 32

and Dutch colonies, Britain to retain Cape (*1813*) but give compensation 31; to retain conquests if Barrier not erected 32; (*1815*) 28

and Italy (*1813*) 33; attempt of Austria, Prussia and Russia to intervene in Naples (*1821*) 64

and Portugal (*1813*), to be guaranteed against France 30

and Russia, Castlereagh's difficulties with, at Paris 35, 37, at Aix-la-Chapelle (*1818*) 37–9, **Doc. 5**; Tsar's attempt to intervene in Spain (*1820*) 51, 55–6, 59; difficulties with (*1821–2*) 64

and Spain (*1813*) to be guaranteed against France 30; to be party to guarantee of settlement 34; refusal to coerce (*1820–1*) 48–9; Wellington on 50; Spain's objection to interference 52–3; military power reduced 60–1; views on revolution in (*5 May 1820*) 50–3, *re* Wellington and 53

and Sweden (*1813*) 31

and Turkey, attempts to restrain Alexander from going to war with, over Greece (*1822*) 64

and United States (*1813*) 33

CAVOUR, COUNT DI, SARDINIAN PRIME MINISTER, 1852–61
  Malmesbury's remonstrance with (*1859*) **Doc. 54**
  Palmerston and 283
  and Garibaldi's expedition 215

CHARLES ALBERT, KING OF SARDINIA, 1831–48
  grant of constitution by 162, 166
  and revolution of (*1848–9*) 162–5, 223

CHARTIST MOVEMENT
  154

CHAUVELIN, MARQUIS DE, FRENCH AMBASSADOR AT LONDON, 1792–3
  dismissal of 2

CHILE
  situation in (*1823*) 68

CHINA
  Palmerston's treatment of, judged indefensible by Satow 284
  position in (*1897–8*) 499
  Salisbury's overture to Russia *re* (*1898*) **Doc. 195**

CHRISTIAN IX, KING OF DENMARK, 1863–1906
  acknowledgement of, as heir to Frederick VII 260
  accession of (*1863*) 261; attitude of Austria and Prussia to 261; issue of
    constitution by 261; revocation of March patent 261

CHURCHILL, LORD RANDOLPH
  441

CLARENDON, GEORGE WILLIAM FREDERIC VILLIERS, 4TH EARL OF, SECRE-
  TARY OF STATE FOR FOREIGN AFFAIRS, 1853–8, 1865–6, 1868–70
  appointment of, as foreign secretary (*3 Nov. 1865*) 305; Gladstone on
    his principles of policy (*1869*) **Doc. 123**
  and Austro-Prussian war (*1866*) 305
  and Crimean war 138 n., **Doc. 34**, 145–6, **Doc. 35**
  and mediation clause of Treaty of Paris (*1856*) 198
  and reduction of armaments (*1870*) 318–19, **Doc. 124**
  and Schleswig-Holstein, mission to Paris 268; comment on Russell's
    plan (*May 1864*) **Doc. 94**
  on Derby (*1857*) 309
  on Ferdinand II, King of the Two Sicilies (*1858*) **Doc. 64**
  on Palmerston, and constitutionalism as a panacea 283

COBDEN, RICHARD
  and Anglo-French naval agreement (*1861*) 291
  and non-intervention 305–6

COLUMBIA
  liberation of (*1823*) 68; and France (*1823*) 74; full recognition of
    (*1829*) 70

COLONIES
  restoration of, after Napoleonic wars 28, 29–30, 31, 32–3, 35
  Stanley's view of their importance (*1866*) 306
  France and (*1886*), complaint against Rosebery 441; (*1894*) African
    problems 488, **Docs. 190, 191**; (*1895*) Niger and Nile Valleys 501–2,
    Docs. 196, 197; (*1897–8*) Nile Valley 505–6, **Doc. 198**, 509–12

538   INDEX

COLONIES *continued*
  Germany and (*1884–5*) 424–5, **Doc. 166**; (*1887–90*) 462–3; (*1894*) 488, **Docs. 190–2,** 494
  Portugal and, Ancient Treaties, applicability to, Canning on 82, 342, Granville on 342–3, 512–13, 514, Derby on 342, 512–13, Salisbury on 342, 514–15, **Doc. 199**; British negotiations with Portugal *re* Goa (*1876–7*) 512, *re* East Africa (*1887–91*) 513; with Germany *re* Portuguese colonies (*1898*) 514; conditions in 514–15; slave trade in 303–4
  Spanish colonies, Canning and trade to 69, 70, 72–3, 523–6; recognition of independence of 68–70, **Doc. 8,** 76–7, **Doc. 9**

CONCERT OF EUROPE
  Gladstone, Granville and (*1880*) 390, 392, 394, **Docs. 150–1,** 407, 408, 410, 411–12
  Palmerston and, against Mehemet Ali 122, 129; *re* Straits' Convention 131
  Pitt and 9, 12–13, 20
  Salisbury and 429

CONFERENCES AND CONGRESSES
  Canning and, general 65–6; *re* Conference of Verona (*1822*) 64–5; *re* Spanish colonies (*1823*) 65, 69, 70, 75; *re* Turkey (*1824*) 65
  Castlereagh and, general 28–9, 38, **Docs. 5, 6**; *re* Conference of Verona 64; *re* war between Russia and Turkey 64
  Palmerston and, proposes Conference *re* Poland (*1863*) 241; refuses *re* Spain (*1837*) **Doc. 20**; (*1849*) **Doc. 60**; (*1862*) 205; refuses invitation of Napoleon III to (*1863*) 249, 253, **Docs. 85–7,** 259
  Russell and (*1859*) 203, **Doc. 59**; (*1863*) **Doc. 71,** 238–9, 256, **Doc. 87**
  Salisbury and, general (*1885*) 430; refuses conference or arbitration on Portuguese colonial question (*1890*) 513
  proposals for (*1859–63*) 203, **Doc. 71**; (*1863*) *re* Poland 238, 241
  Aix-la-Chapelle, Conference of 37, 206
  Berlin, Conference of, *re* Greece (*1880*) 407
  Berlin, Congress of 363, 364, 365, **Doc. 144,** 381–4, **Doc. 148**
  Constantinople, Conference of (*1876–7*) 357, 383, 384
    re Egypt (*1882*) 417, **Doc. 163,** 420
    re Bulgaria (*1885*) 430, **Docs. 169–71**
  London, Conference of, *re* Belgium (*1831–9*) 89, 96
    re Schleswig-Holstein (*1864*) 268, 271, 272, 277
    re Luxemburg (*1867*) 309, 311–12
    re Black Sea clauses (*1871*) 328, 330–1
    re Egypt (*1884*) 424, 425
  Paris, Congress of, and Polish question 235
  Troppau and Laibach, Conferences of 206
  Verona, Conference of 64–5, 206
  Vienna, Conference of (*1853*) 145, 149
  Vienna, Congress of 28–9, 34–6, 207

CONGO
  negotiations *re* (*1894*) 488, 490–1, 509, 511, 517

CONSERVATISM
  Gladstone on **Doc. 52**

CONSTANTINOPLE
Conference of (*1876–7*) 357, 383, 384
Derby on importance of (*1877*) 358–9, **Doc. 140,** 361
Menšikov mission to (*1853*) 144–5, 149
Palmerston's failure to send the fleet to (*1832*) 118; the discretionary order (*1834*) 119; revoked by Wellington 117, 120, **Doc. 25**
Russian fleet before (*1833*) 118, 119; Russia renounces desire to annex (*1853*) 134, 138, 140
Rosebery and (*1893–4*) 473, 474, **Doc. 189,** 492
Salisbury and (*1878*) 383–4; (*1886*) 442, 443; (*1895*) 495
Stratford de Redcliffe and (*1832*) 118; Clarendon's instructions *re* (*1853*) 140, 145–6

CONSTITUTIONS AND CONSTITUTIONALISM
Austria (*1848*) 153, 154; German confederation (*1807*) 25, **Doc. 3,** (*1815*) 35, (*1848*) 153–4; Greece (*1832, 1841*) 107–8, **Docs. 22, 23**; Hungary, concessions in (*1848*) 169, Schwarzenberg's *constitution octroyée* (*1849*) 170; Naples 191–2, **Doc. 51**; Poland (*1815*) 232–3, 234, 242, (*1831*) 233, 234–5, (*1848*) 161, 235, (*1863*) 233; Spain and Portugal 81, 83, 102–4, 105, **Doc. 21**; Prussia (*1848*) 153, 154; Sardinia (*1848*) 162, 166
Canning and 81, 84–6, **Doc. 11,** 104, 107
Clarendon and 283
Gladstone and 393; *re* Turkey 398
Granville and **Doc. 47,** 186, **Doc. 48**
Malmesbury and 197; *re* Sardinia **Doc. 54**
Palmerston and 84, 100–1, **Docs. 19, 21,** 107, 108, **Docs. 22, 23,** 162, 176, 233–4, 283–4; *re* Belgium 104; Greece 107–8, **Docs. 22, 23**; Hungary 169–71, **Doc. 44**; Italy 164–5, **Doc. 41,** 228; Poland 159, **Doc. 39,** 233–4, 235; Portugal and Spain 102–3, 104; Prussia 248–9, **Doc. 82**
Russell and 283–4; *re* Italy 203, 228; Poland 235–6, **Doc. 76**

CORTI, COUNT, ITALIAN MINISTER FOR FOREIGN AFFAIRS, 1878; AMBASSADOR AT LONDON, 1885–8
recall of 456 and n.
and Mediterranean Agreements (*1878*) 382–3; (*1887*) 447–8, **Docs. 175, 176**

COUZA, PRINCE
257

CRACOW
157, 158, 164, 208, 243

CRETE
proposals *re* (*1853*) 135; (*1880*) 406
revolt in (*1867*) 306

CRIMEAN WAR
origins of 134–52; Holy Places dispute, British attitude *re* 138, 149, instructions to Stratford de Redcliffe *re* **Doc. 34,** his settlement of 144; Menšikov mission 144–5, 149; British and French squadrons sent to Besika Bay 145; Russian occupation of the Principalities 145; negotiations at Vienna and Constantinople 145, 146–8;

CRIMEAN WAR *continued*
> Vienna Note 145, 146–51, Russian objections to 148–51; British fleet called up to Constantinople, violation of the Straits' Convention 145–6, **Doc. 35**; British attitude *re* Turkish integrity 146, 151–2; Turkish declaration of war (*4 Oct. 1853*) 146; Russian destruction of Turkish squadron at Sinope 146, final cause of war 146; treatment of Russia after 209
>
> Treaty of Paris *v. sub* TREATIES

CRISPI, COUNT, ITALIAN MINISTER FOR FOREIGN AFFAIRS, 1887–91; PRIME MINISTER, 1893–6
> *and* Mediterranean Agreements (*1887*) 456–7

CUBA
> Canning offers to guarantee to Spain (*1823*) 81

CURRIE, SIR PHILIP, LATER 1ST BARON, UNDER-SECRETARY OF STATE FOR FOREIGN AFFAIRS, 1888–93
> *and* Belgium 473 n.
> *and* British interests (*1885*) 473
> *and* Mediterranean Agreements 470 and n., 472, 486
> *and* Near East 490
> Rosebery's confidence in 486
> Salisbury's letter to (*1892*) 470

CUSTOZZA, BATTLE OF, 25 JULY 1848
> 163, 165

CYPRUS
> British occupation of (*1878*) 365, 383; Gladstone and 390, (*1880*) 397, 398, 399, **Doc. 155**; Granville and (*1880*) **Doc. 154**, 405; Gladstone and Granville and (*1881*) 406–7, 414; Queen Victoria and (*1880–1*) 399 and n., 402 n., 406; Sir E. Grey and (*1913*) 407

CYPRUS CONVENTION *v. sub* TREATIES

DE COURCEL, BARON, FRENCH AMBASSADOR AT LONDON, 1894–8
> *and* Nile Valley 501–2

DEFENCE, NAVAL AND MILITARY
> Gladstone and 289 n., 290, 472
> Palmerston and 284, 288–91, **Docs. 102–3**
> Rosebery and strengthening of fleet 472, **Doc. 188**
> Russell and 284, **Doc. 101**

DENMARK (*v. also sub* SCHLESWIG-HOLSTEIN QUESTION)
> Castlereagh's proposals *re* (*1813*) 31, 33
> integrity of, Treaty of London (*1852*) and 260; obligations of Powers to maintain 276; preservation of (*1864*) apart from Schleswig, Holstein and Lauenburg 277–8
> Palmerston's warning to those who wish to attack (*1863*) **Doc. 84**
> *and* Schleswig-Holstein 228; treatment of by 260–2, **Docs. 88–90**

DERBY, EDWARD GEORGE GEOFFREY SMITH STANLEY, 14TH EARL OF, PRIME MINISTER, 1852, 1858–9, 1866–8
> Clarendon on 309
> speech by, on Schleswig-Holstein (*2 Feb. 1864*) 267; on Luxemburg guarantee (*13 May 1867*) **Doc. 120**
> Stanley and 313, 315–16

DERBY, 15TH EARL OF, *v. sub* STANLEY

DEYM, COUNT, AUSTRO-HUNGARIAN AMBASSADOR AT LONDON, 1888–1903
   463, 464, **Doc. 183**, 472, 473, **Docs. 186–9**, 490, **Docs. 192, 193**

DISARMAMENT
   Clarendon's proposals *re* (*1870*) 318–19, **Doc. 124**
   Cobden's scheme for Anglo-French naval treaty (*1861*) 291
   Malmesbury's suggestions for (*1859*) 197–8
   Stanley's attitude to (*1868*) 318
   Austria and (*1859*) 197–8, 201
   France and (*1870*) 318–19
   Prussia and (*1870*) 318–19, **Doc. 124**

DISRAELI, BENJAMIN (EARL BEACONSFIELD), PRIME MINISTER, 1874–80
   Beust on 347
   conversation with Bismarck (*1862*) **Doc. 80** and n.
   and Austria-Hungary (*1874*) 347
   and Egypt 416
   and Germany (*1875*) 351–2; (*1876*) 355
   and Near East (*1875–8*) 357–9, 360, **Doc. 141**, 361–2, 363, 381–4,
      Doc. 148
   and Russia (*1875*) 351–2; (*1877*) 357
   and Tunis (*1878*) 383, 413

DON PACIFICO CASE
   183

EASTERN CRISIS, 1875–8
   British policy in, consular intervention 357; Andrássy Note 354, 357;
      Berlin Memorandum 355, 357; Constantinople Conference 357,
      383, 384; negotiations with Russia and Austria-Hungary (*1877*) 357–
      9, **Doc. 140**, (*1877–8*) **Doc. 141**, 361–2; Treaty of San Stefano
      363–4, **Doc. 143**; Salisbury circular (*1 Ap. 1878*) 363, **Doc. 144**;
      Salisbury's private views 363–4, **Doc. 142**; negotiations with
      Austria-Hungary, Russia and Turkey (*1878*) 364–5; British con-
      ditions of entering Berlin Congress **Doc. 144**; Cyprus Convention
      policy 365, 366, 381, 383; importance of Asiatic reform **Doc.
      145**
   Germany and 354–5, **Doc. 139**

EDINBURGH REVIEW
   article by Gladstone in 323–4

H.M. KING EDWARD VII, 1901–10
   marriage of (*1863*) 261
   and seizure of Düppel 277
   visit to Vienna (*1889*) 463

EGYPT
   firmans granted to (*1841*) 123
   Mehemet Ali and Turkey 117–20, 121–4, **Docs. 26–32**
   Tewfik, establishment of (*1879*) 416; policy of 417, 418
   revolt in, under Arabi Pasha 416, 417, 418; revolt of Mahdi 421
   Austria and (*1839–41*) 122, 132–3; (*1884*) 426; (*1887*) 452, **Doc. 179**

EGYPT *continued*

France and, Mehemet Ali (*1839–41*) 122–4, **Doc. 30,** Anglo-French financial policy (*1876–82*) 416–17; French attitude **Docs. 162, 163,** 420, **Doc. 164;** (*1884–7*) 423–4; (*1887*) protests against Wolff Convention 452; (*1895*) and Nile Valley 501–2, **Doc. 196,** *v.* also *sub* FASHODA INCIDENT

Germany and (*1884–7*) 423–4, **Doc. 166,** 426, 452; support of Wolff Convention at a price **Doc. 179**

Great Britain and (*1876–80*) 416; Granville on British policy (*1881*) 416; cooperation with Gambetta (*1881–2*) 417; dispatch of ships to Alexandria 417, **Doc. 162;** Conference of Constantinople and (*1882*) 417, **Doc. 163;** Battle of Tel-el Kebir 421; operations in Soudan (*1883–4*) 421–2, **Doc. 165;** fall of Khartoum 423; Conference of London (*1884*) 424, **Doc. 166;** Granville's refusal to fix a date for evacuation (*1885*) **Doc. 167;** Turkey complains to Salisbury of Liberal policy **Doc. 168;** Salisbury attempts to find a solution in the Wolff Conventions (*1885, 1887*) 452; effect on evacuation policy **Doc. 178;** Bismarck supports Britain but demands colonial concessions **Doc. 179**

Prussia and (*1839–40*) 122

Russia and (*1832–3*) 118–20; (*1839–40*) 122; (*1853*) 135; Dreikaiserbund and (*1884–5*) 426; (*1887*) 452

Turkey and *v. sub* TURKEY

ELLIOT, SIR HENRY, BRITISH AMBASSADOR AT CONSTANTINOPLE, 1867–77

policy at Constantinople 357; recall of 360

FASHODA INCIDENT

505–6, **Doc. 198,** 509–12, 517

FERDINAND I, EMPEROR OF AUSTRIA, 1835–48

grant of liberal constitutions (*1848*) 154, 170; abdication of (*1848*) 154, 170

FERDINAND I, KING OF THE TWO SICILIES, 1815–25

restoration of (*1815*) 35; revolution against (*1820*) 47

FERDINAND II, KING OF THE TWO SICILIES, 1830–59

misgovernment of, after *1848*, 190–2, **Doc. 51,** 212

revolution against (*1848*) 163

Aberdeen, Gladstone and 191–2, **Doc. 51**

Palmerston on (*1848*) **Doc. 41;** Palmerston and Clarendon on (*1857–8*) **Docs. 63, 64**

Russia and 212

Schwarzenberg and 192, 193

FERDINAND VII, KING OF SPAIN, 1808, 1814–33

and Spanish colonial trade 523

FERDINAND OF COBURG, PRINCE OF THE BULGARIANS, 1887–1909; TSAR OF THE BULGARIANS, 1909–18

accession of 445, 455

FRANCE

barrier against (*1805*) 16–17, 18; (*1813*) 30, 31, 32–3

colonies ceded to Britain (*1815*) 28, 31

conditions in (*1820*) 59–60

constitution of (*1814*) 43

military strength of (*1820*) 60; (*1870*) 320–1; (*1875*) 351

revolution in, Castlereagh on conditions of interference (*1818*) 37, 41–3, 44; (*1830*) 89

and Austria (*1792*) 2; (*1805*) 10; (*1831*) 93; (*1859*) 203–5, **Docs. 61, 62,** 291, **Doc. 100**

and Belgium (*1792*) 2; (*1830–9*) 89–90, **Docs. 12, 14**; (*1870*) 336–7

and Egypt (*1839–41*) 122–4, **Doc. 30**; (*1876–82*) 416–17, **Docs. 162, 163,** 420, **Doc. 164**; (*1884–7*) 423–4; (*1887*) 452; (*1895*) 502–3, **Doc. 196**

and Germany, war scare (*1875*) 351–2, **Docs. 137, 138**; (*1887*) 445–6

and Great Britain (*1786, 1788*) Pitt and 1; (*1792–3*) attitude to French Revolution 2–3, **Doc. 1,** 8, 9; (*1805*) Pitt's proposals *re* 10, **Doc. 2**; (*1813*) restriction of naval power 30; (*1813–15*) question of French colonies 28, 31; (*1814*) restoration of Louis XVIII 79; (*1822–3*) intervention in Spain 64, 66, 68, 81, *re* Spanish America 68–9, **Doc. 8**; (*1827*) Greek question 85; (*1830*) July Revolution 89; (*1831–2*) *re* Poland 233, 235; (*1834–46*) *re* Spain 103, 104, **Docs. 19, 20**; (*1839–41*) *re* Mehemet Ali 122, 123 and n., **Doc. 30**; (*1841*) *re* humanitarianism in Greece **Doc. 24**; (*1848–9*) revolution in France **Doc. 38,** Italy 163–5, 168, Hungarian refugees 178, 180–1; (*1852*) Malmesbury on 189; (*1856*) **Docs. 98, 99**; effect of annexation of Savoy and Nice on (*1859*) 204–5, **Docs. 61, 62,** 256; (*1864–5*) **Docs. 102, 103**; (*1881–2*) *re* Egypt 417; (*1886*) complaint of Rosebery's attitude *re* colonies 441; (*1893*) Siam dispute 471; alienation between 477, 480; (*1894*) colonial questions and 488, **Docs. 190, 191,** 490; Nile and Niger Valleys and (*1895*) 501–2, **Docs. 196, 197**; Fashoda incident and (*1898*) 505–6, **Doc. 198,** 509–12, 517; growth of *entente* 521–2

and Greece, Anglo-Franco-Russian treaty (*1827*) 85; (*1841*) 112, **Doc. 24**

and Italy (*1805*) 12; (*1813*) 33; (*1815*) 35; (*1859–60*) 203–5, **Docs. 61, 62**; (*1860*) **Doc. 66,** 220, 221, **Doc. 68**; (*1867*) **Doc. 118 d**

and Luxemburg (*1866–7*) 309

and Poland (*1863*) 236–8, **Docs. 72, 73, 77**

and Prussia (*1788*) 1; (*1805*) 17–18, 19; (*1815*) 35; (*1830–1*) 89, 91, 92; (*1859–63*) **Doc. 81**; (*1869–70*) 318–19, **Doc. 124**; (*1870*) 323–4, **Doc. 125**

and Russia (*1792*) 9; (*1838*) Palmerston on importance of 101; (*1852–3*) Holy Places dispute 138, **Doc. 34**; (*1859*) 201, 202; (*1893–4*) growth of Franco-Russian understanding 470, 471, Rosebery on 478, 482, 484; (*1898*) Fashoda Incident 517

and Scheldt (*1792*) 5–7, 8; (*1813*) 30

and Schleswig-Holstein question 248–9, 253, **Docs. 85–7, 91**

and Spain (*1807*) 22–3; (*1822–3*) 64, 68, 69, 81; (*1856*) 287

and Spanish America 68–9, **Doc. 8**

and Turkey (*1839–41*) 122–3, 124, **Doc. 30,** 130, **Doc. 31**; (*1853*) **Doc. 34,** 145

FRANCIS II, KING OF THE TWO SICILIES, 1859–60
194, 212, 214, 215–17, 224–5, 227

FRANCIS JOSEPH, EMPEROR OF AUSTRIA, 1848–1916
accession of (*1848*) 154, 170; campaign in Italy 165; minute by 466

FRANCO-RUSSIAN ALLIANCE *v. sub* TREATIES

FRANKFURT PARLIAMENT
153

FREDERICK VII, KING OF DENMARK, 1848–63
and Schleswig-Holstein question 260–1; patent issued by (*Mar. 1863*)
261, 265

FREDERICK WILLIAM IV, KING OF PRUSSIA, 1840–61
constitution granted by (*1848*) 153, 154

FRENCH REVOLUTION
decrees of (*Nov., Dec. 1792*) 3, 4–5, 8; Chauvelin's interpretation of
4 n.; attitude of Convention to England (*Jan. 1793*) 8
Pitt and 1–8, **Doc. 1**

GAMBETTA, LÉON, FRENCH PRESIDENT OF THE COUNCIL, 1881–2
and Egypt 417

GARIBALDI
expedition of 194, 212, 215–17
Napoleon III and 215
Palmerston and 215, **Doc. 65**
Russell and 215–17, **Docs. 66, 67**

GENOA
Pitt's proposals *re* (*1805*) 13–14; Castlereagh's proposals *re* (*1813*) 28, 33

GERMAN CONFEDERATION AND GERMAN STATES
organization of, Pitt on (*1805*) 19; Canning on (*1807*) 25, **Doc. 3**;
Castlereagh on (*1813*) 33
situation in (*1820*) 62–3
and Luxemburg (*1867*) 309
and Schleswig-Holstein question 260–1, **Doc. 88**, 265; exclusion of
from final settlement 277

GERMANY (*v.* also *sub* PRUSSIA)
and Austria (*1871–3*) 343–4, 347; (*1875*) 352, 353; (*1881–2*) 390–1,
(*1890*) 465
and Egypt (*1884–7*) 423–4, **Doc. 166**, 426, 452; (*1887*) **Doc. 179**
and France, war scare (*1875*) 351–2, **Docs. 137, 138**; (*1887*) 445–6
and Great Britain, Bismarck's overture (*1874*) 347, **Doc. 136**; War
Scare (*1875*) 351–2, **Docs. 137, 138**; overture (*Feb. 1876*) 354–5,
Doc. 139; beginning of colonial question (*1884*) 423–5, **Doc. 166**;
Salisbury's relations with (*1885*) 429; Mediterranean agreements
(*1887*) and 446, 448, 449, 455–8, **Doc. 181**; peak period of Anglo-
German cooperation (*1887–90*) 462; attempts to solve colonial
differences (*1887–90*) 462–3; African problems and (*1894*) 488,
Docs. 190, 191, 490, **Docs. 192, 193**; Near East and (*1895*)
494–5; growing difficulties between (*1894–7*) 517; overtures for
alliance (*1898, 1901*) 517–18, **Doc. 200**
and Near East, policy of disassociation from (*1893–5*) 484, 489, 495

and Russia (*1871–3*) 343–4, 347; (*1875*) 351–2, **Doc. 137**; (*1881*) 390–1, 411–12, **Doc. 159**; (*1884*) 426, 430, 442; (*1887*) 454–5, 457–8, 459; (*1897*) 499–500

GLADSTONE, WILLIAM EWART, PRIME MINISTER, 1868–74, 1880–5, 1886, 1892–4

principles of policy 317, **Doc. 123**, 390–1, **Doc. 149**, 474; on Conservative principles (*1852*) **Doc. 52**; on annexations (*1870*) 323–4, **Doc. 125**; on arbitration 327–8, **Doc. 126**; on the rule of law 328, 330–1, **Doc. 127**; on the fleet 472; on guarantees **Doc. 129**; on sanctity of treaties 336–7, **Docs. 130, 131**; on territorial aggrandisement 198

and Austria-Hungary 409, 410, **Doc. 159**, 471, 476

and Egypt (*1882–5*) 416–17, 420, 421

and Greece (*1886*) **Doc. 172**

and Naples (*1851–2*) 191–5

and Near East, disapproval of Black Sea clauses of Treaty of Paris (*1856*) 330, and cancellation of (*1870–1*) 330–1; and Cyprus Convention 397, 398, 399, **Docs. 153, 154**, 405, **Doc. 155**, 406–7, 414, **Doc. 161**; and enforcement of Treaty of Berlin 394, 407, **Docs. 156, 157**, 409–10, **Doc. 158**, 411; attitude to Turkey (*1894*) 483

and United States, his preference for Union **Doc. 107**; his speech *re* making a "nation" (*Oct. 1862*) 296–7; his belief that recognition must come soon 299

GORČAKOV, PRINCE, RUSSIAN CHANCELLOR, 1870–82

circular from *re* Black Sea (*9 Nov. 1870*) 330–1, **Doc. 127**

Disraeli on 389

GORDON, MAJOR-GENERAL, CHARLES GEORGE

423

GRANVILLE, GEORGE GRANVILLE LEVESON-GOWER, 2ND EARL, SECRETARY OF STATE FOR FOREIGN AFFAIRS, 1851–2, 1870–4, 1880–5

general policy of (*1851*), instructed by Russell to prepare a memorandum *re* 182–3, text (*12 Jan. 1852*) **Doc. 47**; (*1880–5*) 390–1

and Austria-Hungary (*1871–2*) 343–5; declines Andrássy's overture **Doc. 134**

and Belgium, action with Gladstone *re* (*1870*) 317, 335–7, **Doc. 130**; quoted in Belgian Chamber (*1887*) 446

and Egypt, on previous commitments 416–17; explains dispatch of ships to Alexandria (*23 May 1882*) **Doc. 162**; instructions for Constantinople Conference (*21 June 1882*) **Doc. 163**; bombardment of Alexandria 420, explanation of attitude **Doc. 164**; attitude to Soudan 421–2, **Doc. 165**; against defence of Khartoum 423; difficulties with Bismarck 423–5, who uses Egypt to bargain on colonial questions **Doc. 166**; *re* British occupation 426, **Doc. 167**; Turkey protests to Salisbury *re* liberal policy **Doc. 168**

and France, unwillingly acknowledges obligations *re* Tunis 413–14, **Doc. 160**

and Germany, disagrees with Gladstone over Alsace-Lorraine 323–4, **Doc. 125**; relations with Dreikaiserbund (*1881*) 411–12; (*1884*) 426

GRANVILLE, GEORGE GRANVILLE LEVESON-GOWER, 2ND EARL *continued*
    and Near East, formulation of policy by (*1880*) 394, **Doc. 150**; private
        explanation of policy **Doc. 151**; desire to cancel Cyprus Conven-
        tion 399, annoyance of Queen with **Doc. 154**, 405, discussion of 406
    and Portugal, upholds pledges (*Jan. 1852*) 186; acknowledges Ancient
        Treaties (*1873*) 341–2, **Doc. 133**
    and Russia, Black Sea clauses (*1870*) 330–1, **Doc. 127**; on Tripartite
        Treaty of (*1856*) 331, **Doc. 128**
    and Spain, advises a constitutional policy (*1852*) 186, **Doc. 48**

GREECE (*v.* also *sub* GUARANTEES)
    Anglo-Franco-Russian Treaty *re* (*1827*) 85, 206
    boundaries of, Palmerston and (*1832*) 117; Salisbury and (*1878*) 368–9,
        Doc. 146; Granville and (*1880*) **Doc. 150**; Salisbury and (*1885*)
        432; Rosebery and (*1886*) 434, **Doc. 172**
    constitution of (*1841*) 107–8, **Docs. 22–4**
    revolt in (*1821*) 47, 64
    Austria and (*1841*) 107, **Doc. 22**
    Russia and (*1853*) 135

GRENVILLE, WILLIAM WYNDHAM, BARON, SECRETARY OF STATE FOR
    FOREIGN AFFAIRS, 1791–1801
    character 1–2, relation to Pitt 3 and n.
    policy of, pledge to Holland (*13 Nov. 1792*) 2; on French aggression
        (*26 Nov. 1792*) 2 and n.; dispatch of (*31 Dec. 1792*) **Doc. 1**; declares
        Le Brun's explanation "insufficient" (*12 Jan. 1793*) 8; dismisses
        Chauvelin (*24 Jan. 1793*) 2; letter to Whitworth distinguishing two
        sorts of intervention (*29 Dec. 1792*) 9; sketch of European concert
        or League (*12 Oct. 1792*) 9, n.

GREVILLE, CHARLES
    182–3

GREY, SIR EDWARD, later VISCOUNT GREY OF FALLODON UNDER-
    SECRETARY OF STATE FOR FOREIGN AFFAIRS, 1892–5; SECRETARY
    OF STATE FOR FOREIGN AFFAIRS, 1905–16
    and Belgium and Luxemburg (*1914*) 316
    and Cyprus Convention (*1913*) 407
    and Niger and Nile Valleys (*1895*) 501–2, **Doc. 196**, 506, 511

GUARANTEES
    collective guarantees, discussion of 315–16; Bismarck on 315–16; Law
        Officers on (*1870*) **Doc. 132**
    returns of Treaties of Guarantee (*1859, 1871, 1899*) 407, 514
    Tripartite Treaty (*1856*) and 315, **Docs. 128, 129**
    Argyll, Duke of, and 315
    Canning and, general views on, 81–2, **Doc. 10**, 88
        refusal to guarantee constitutions to Spain and Sicily 81; proposal
        for *re* Cuba 81; *re* free navigation of Rio de la Plata 82; *re* Portugal
        82, 85, 86 and n., 342; refusal of, *re* Greece 82
    Castlereagh and,
        proposed guarantee of European settlement (*1814*) 28–9; of Spain
        and Portugal against France 30; absence of in Treaties of Paris
        and Vienna 40; to France (*1814–15*) 43; refusal of for thrones 81

Clarendon and, 305, 315–16
Derby (14th Earl) and (*1867*) **Doc. 120,** 315–16
Derby (15th Earl) and, general views on, 315–16
 guarantees of Treaty of Vienna worthless 306, **Doc. 118a, b**; *re*
  Luxemburg (*1867*) 306, 309, **Doc. 119,** 311–12, **Docs. 121–2;**
  re Belgium 310, 347, 350–1; *re* Portugal (*1875–6*) 342, 512–13
Gladstone and, general views on, 157, 330–1, **Doc. 129;** *re* Belgium
  335–7, **Doc. 131;** *re* Portugal 342
Granville and, general views on 315; *re* Tripartite 330, 331, **Doc. 128;**
  re Belgium 335–7, **Doc. 130;** *re* Portugal 341–2, **Doc. 133,** 512
Grey and (*1914*) 316
Malmesbury and (*1859*) 197–8
Metternich and **Docs. 16, 17,** 124, **Doc. 32**
Palmerston and, general views on, **Doc. 16,** 124, **Docs. 32, 36,** 157,
  164; *re* Greece (*1841*) 107, 111–12; *re* Turkish integrity (*1841*)
  131; *re* Belgium (*1848*) 155, 157; *re* Lombardy (*1848*) 155; *re*
  Rhineland (*1848*) 155; *re* Saxon Prussia (*1848*) 155, 157; *re*
  Switzerland (*1847–8*) 155, 157
Pitt and, proposals for guarantee of European settlement (*1805*) 10, 11,
  18–19; proposed guarantee treaty between England and Russia 10;
  19
Rechberg and, proposed guarantee to Austria against French attack
  (*1859*) 197–8
Russell and (*1859*) **Doc. 37,** (*1867*) 315
Salisbury and, *re* Belgium (*1887*) 445–6, **Doc. 177;** *re* Portugal (*1899*)
  342, 514–15, **Doc. 199** (*v.* also *sub* TURKEY, TREATIES, CYPRUS
  CONVENTION)
Belgium *v. sub* BELGIUM
Denmark, settlement of (*1852*), not guaranteed 260
Greece, Anglo-Franco-Russian, discussions of (*1841*) 107, 111, 112, 132
Luxemburg (*1867*) *v. sub* LUXEMBURG
Polish constitution, discussions *re* guarantee of (*1831–2, 1863*) 232–4, 242
Portugal, House of Braganza guaranteed their throne (*1810*) 81,
  Ancient Treaties, British interpretation of (*1820*) 52; (*1825–6*)
  82, 85, 342; (*1852*) 186; (*1872–3*) 341–2, **Doc. 133,** 512; (*1875*) 342,
  512–13; (*1899*) 342, 514–15, **Doc. 199**
Savoy 155
Saxony 155, 305
Switzerland (*1815*) 35, 155
Turkey, integrity not guaranteed (*1841*) 131, 132–3, 134; Tripartite
  Treaty (*1856*) 315, 331, **Docs. 128, 129,** 516; Cyprus Convention
  (*1878*) 365, 366, 381, 383, 397, 399, **Docs. 153, 154,** 405, 406–7
GUIZOT, FRANÇOIS PIERRE GUILLAUME, FRENCH MINISTER FOR FOREIGN
 AFFAIRS, 1840–8
 and constitutionalism in Greece **Doc. 23**
 and humanitarianism in Greece **Doc. 24**
 and Princess Lieven 190

HAMMOND, EDMUND, later BARON, PERMANENT UNDER-SECRETARY OF
 STATE, 1854–73
 and constitutionalism 284

HANOVER
  accession of territory to (*1815*) 35
HARDINGE, SIR CHARLES (BARON HARDINGE OF PENSHURST), PERMANENT
    UNDER-SECRETARY OF STATE FOR FOREIGN AFFAIRS, 1906–10;
    VICEROY OF INDIA, 1910–16
  on Belgian Treaty 155 n., 337
  on Mediterranean Agreements 472
HATZFELDT, COUNT, GERMAN AMBASSADOR AT LONDON, 1885–1901
    445, 446, 449, 457, 465, 466, 471, 489, 491
  conversations with Salisbury (*July–Aug. 1895*) 494
HELIGOLAND
  cession of, to Britain, Castlereagh and (*1813*) 31
  Heligoland-Zanzibar Treaty (*1890*) 463
HOLLAND (*v. sub* NETHERLANDS)
    2 n.
HOLY ALLIANCE *v. sub* TREATIES
HOLY PLACES DISPUTE, 1852–3
    138, **Doc. 34,** 144–5, 151
HUNGARY
  refugees from (*1849*) 177–9, **Docs. 45, 46**
  revolution in (*1848–9*) 158–9, 169–71, 173–4; Palmerston and 170–1,
    Docs. 43, 44; Russia and 169–71, **Doc. 43**

IDDESLEIGH, SIR STAFFORD NORTHCOTE, 1ST EARL OF, SECRETARY OF
    STATE FOR FOREIGN AFFAIRS, 1886–7
  supports Salisbury *re* Near East 441; death of 441
IGNATIEV, COUNT, RUSSIAN AMBASSADOR AT CONSTANTINOPLE, 1864–77
    and Salisbury (*1876–7*) 357
INTERVENTION (*v. also sub* NON-INTERVENTION)
  in Greece (*1841*) 107–8, **Docs. 22–4**
  in Spain (*1835*) 104
  Grenville distinguishes two sorts of (*1792–3*) 9
  Palmerston contemplates, to stop Spain from invading Italy (*1860*)
    Doc. 69, 285
  Russell and, *re* Italy (*1860*) **Doc. 68,** 227
IONIAN ISLANDS
  cession of, to Greece 291
ITALY (*v. also sub* NAPLES, PAPAL STATES, SARDINIA, etc.)
  revolution in (*1848–9*) 162–5; Palmerston and 164–5, **Docs. 41, 42,** 170
  union of, France and 203–5, **Docs. 58, 61, 62**; Prussia and 222, 226–7;
    Russia and 222, 225, 226–7; Spain and 221, **Doc. 69**; Palmerston
    and 203, **Doc. 69,** 228–9, 254–5, 257, 291; Russell and 203–5,
    Docs. 58, 59, 214, **Docs. 66, 67,** 221–2, **Doc. 68,** 226, 228–9
  and Austria (*1805*) 10, 15–16, 17; (*1813*) 33; (*1821*) 64; (*1848–9*) 162–5,
    Doc. 42; Russell on (*1860*) 218–19, 220, 225, 226–7, 229, **Doc. 70**;
    (*1867*) 308; (*1919*) 234
  and France (*1805*) 12; (*1813*) 33; (*1815*) 35; (*1860*) **Doc. 66,** 220, 221,
    Doc. 68; (*1867*) **Doc. 118 d** (*v. also supra,* union of)
  and Great Britain, Pitt and (*1805*) 10, 12, 13–14, 15–16; Castlereagh
    and (*1813*) 28, 33, (*1815*) 35; Russell's friendship for 221–2;
    overtures of (*1887*) 446–7, **Docs. 175, 176,** 455–8, **Docs. 181,**

182; growth of Anglo-Italian friendship 470–1; Parliamentary criticism of (*1888–90*) 471 (*v.* also *supra*, revolution in, union of) *and* Prussia *v. sub* PRUSSIA *and* Tyrol (*1919*) 234

JAPAN
    Palmerston and 284
    policy of Anglo-Japanese Alliance 521–2

JOHN, ARCHDUKE OF AUSTRIA
    154, 168

KÁLNOKY, COUNT, AUSTRO-HUNGARIAN MINISTER FOR FOREIGN AFFAIRS, 1881–95
    and Mediterranean Agreements (*1887*) 446–7, 456–8, **Doc. 181**
    and Straits' question 466–7
    and Rosebery 472–3, **Docs. 186–9**

KÁROLYI, COUNT, AUSTRO-HUNGARIAN AMBASSADOR AT LONDON, 1878–88
    and Mediterranean Agreements (*1887*) 447–8, 450

KIMBERLEY, 1ST EARL OF, SECRETARY OF STATE FOR FOREIGN AFFAIRS, 1894–5
    general policy, in accordance with Rosebery's on relations with Triple Alliance and question of Straits (*1894*) 487; position *re* Germany and Russia defined (*21 Nov. 1894*) **Doc. 193**
    and Nile and Niger Valleys, maintains attitude of watchfulness to Germany in colonial questions (*1894*), and asserts British interests as regards France (*1894*) 488, **Docs. 190, 191**; (*1895*) re-inforces Sir E. Grey's warning (*1895*) **Doc. 197**

KITCHENER, GENERAL SIR H. H., later EARL KITCHENER, SIRDAR OF THE EGYPTIAN ARMY, 1892–9
    and Fashoda incident 506, **Doc. 198**, 509–12

KOSSUTH, FERENCZ
    169–70, 177, 193

LACAITA, SIR JAMES
    215–16

LAMARTINE
    policy of (*1848*) 153

LANSDOWNE, HENRY CHARLES KEITH PETTY-FITZMAURICE, 5TH MARQUIS OF, SECRETARY OF STATE FOR FOREIGN AFFAIRS, 1900–5
    policy of, *re* alliances 521
    and Anglo-German negotiations (*1901*) 517–18, **Doc. 200**

LAYARD, SIR A. H., BRITISH AMBASSADOR AT CONSTANTINOPLE, 1877–80
    appointment of (*1877*) 360; correspondence of Disraeli with (*1877–8*) **Doc. 141**, 361, of Salisbury with (*1878*) 365, 383; recall of (*1880*) 397 and n.

LAW, RULE OF
    Gladstone and 317, **Doc. 123**, 324, 329, 330
    Malmesbury and 197
    Palmerston and 283
    Pitt and 18
    Russell and 246, 279, 283

LEOPOLD I, KING OF THE BELGIANS, 1831–65
and Brazil arbitration (*1863*) **Doc. 113**

LEOPOLD II, KING OF THE BELGIANS, 1865–1909
and Congo Treaty (*1894*) 490–1, 509, 511

LIEVEN, PRINCESS
and Grey 239
and Guizot 190

LOMBARDY AND VENETIA
Pitt's proposals *re* (*1805*) 10, 16; Castlereagh's proposals *re* (*1813*) 28
Austria and (*1814–15*) 35; (*1848–9*) 162–5, **Doc. 42**; (*1859–60*) 203, 216,
Docs. 70, 71

LOUIS XVI, KING OF FRANCE, 1774–93
execution of 8

LOUIS PHILIPPE, KING OF THE FRENCH, 1830–48
accession of 89; abdication of 153, 158, 159
and Belgium (*1831*) **Docs. 12, 14**, 101
and Egyptian question 122–4, **Docs. 30, 31**

LUXEMBURG
neutrality of, guaranteed by the Powers (*1867*) 306, 309–10
    Derby on **Doc. 120**
    Grey on (*1914*) 316
    Stanley on (*1867*) 306, **Doc. 119**, 311–12, **Doc. 121**, 315–16
and Belgium (*1831*) 90–1
and France, Napoleon III's designs *re* (*1866–7*) 309
and Netherlands (*1839*) 309
and Prussia, garrison of Prussian troops in (*1839*) 309; Bismarck's
    attitude to French designs (*1867*) 309–10, **Doc. 119**

MACKINTOSH, SIR JAMES
and Spanish colonial trade (*1824*) 523

MAHMUD II, SULTAN OF TURKEY, 1808–39
Mehemet Ali and 117–20, 121–4, **Docs. 26, 28, 29**

MALET, SIR EDWARD, BRITISH AGENT AND CONSUL-GENERAL IN EGYPT,
    1879–83; AMBASSADOR AT BERLIN, 1884–95
and Egypt (*1881*) 416
and German colonial questions (*1884–5*) 424–5; (*1894*) 491
and Mediterranean Agreements (*1887*) 449, 456, 457

MALMESBURY, JAMES HOWARD HARRIS, 3RD EARL OF, SECRETARY OF
    STATE FOR FOREIGN AFFAIRS, 1852, 1858–9
general policy, statements of objects of British policy (*1852*) **Doc. 49**;
    (*1861*) 197; proposal for disarmament (*1859*) 197, for neutrality
    of Adriatic and Baltic (*1859*) 202; repudiation of desire to annex
    Sicily (*1859*) 202; Palmerston on 198
and Austria (*1852*) **Doc. 50**; (*1859*) proposal for mediation 197–8, **Doc.
    55**, 201
and France (*1852*) **Doc. 49**
and Switzerland (*1852*) **Doc. 49**

MARCHAND, CAPTAIN
mission of 506, **Doc. 198**, 509–12

MAZZINI, GIUSEPPE
  and revolution of (*1848*) 163, 193
MEDIATION
  British mediation, Spanish request for, in colonial dispute (*1810*) 72,
    523, 526 and n.; proposals for, in American Civil War (*1862*) 294,
    296, 297–8
  provisions of Treaty of Paris (*1856*) *re* invoked by Malmesbury (*1859*)
    198, **Doc. 55,** 201
MEDITERRANEAN
  alleged British designs in (*1852*) 198
  status quo in *v. sub* MEDITERRANEAN AGREEMENTS
MEDITERRANEAN AGREEMENTS
  proposal for (*1878*) 382–3; (*Feb., Mar. 1887*) 1st proposal for maintenance
    of *status quo* in Mediterranean area **Docs. 175, 176;** conclusion of
    446–8, **Doc. 176;** (*Dec. 1887*) negotiation and conclusion of 2nd
    454–8, **Docs. 181, 182**
  Austria-Hungary and (*1887*) 446–8, 455–8, **Doc. 182;** proposals for
    renewal (*1893*) 470–3, **Doc. 187;** (*1896–7*) 495–6, **Doc. 194**
  Germany and (*1887*) 446, 449, 455–6, 457–8; (*1893*) 473
  Italy and (*1887*) 446, 447, 448, **Docs. 175, 176,** 455–8, **Doc. 182;**
    preservation of (*1892*) 470–1
  Blanc and 455, **Doc. 181**
  Calice and 455–6, **Doc. 181**
  Corti and (*1878*) 383; (*1887*) 447, **Docs. 175, 176**
  Crispi and 456–8
  Currie and 470 and n., 472
  Derby and (*1878*) 382
  Deym and *v. supra* Austria-Hungary and
  Hardinge and (*1907*) 472
  Kálnoky and *v. supra* Austria-Hungary and
  Károlyi and *v. supra* Austria-Hungary and
  Kimberley and 487
  Malet and 449, 456
  Paget and (*1878*) 383, 446–7; (*1887*) 457, 470 n.; (*1893*) 472, 473, 475
  Rosebery and (*1893*) 437, 470–3, **Doc. 187**
  Salisbury and (*1887*) 447–8, **Docs. 175, 176, 180,** 455–8, **Docs. 181,**
    182; (*1892*) 470–1; (*1896–7*) 495–6, **Doc. 194**
  White and 455, **Doc. 181**
MEHEMET ALI, PASHA OF EGYPT, 1805–49
  117–20, 121–4, **Docs. 26–30**
MENŠIKOV, PRINCE
  144–5, 149
METTERNICH, PRINCE, AUSTRIAN CHANCELLOR, 1809–48
  general policy, Vienna settlement (*1815*) 34–9; attitude to constitu-
    tionalism 109, 111; interpretation of guarantees **Doc. 17,** 124,
    Doc. 32; Canning on (*1824*) 87; resignation of 153, 163
  and Bavaria (*1815*) 35
  and Belgian guarantee (*1837*) 95, **Doc. 17**
  and Greece, Palmerston and (*1841*) **Doc. 22**
  and Naples (*1814–15*) 35

METTERNICH, PRINCE *continued*
  and the Straits (*1832*) 118; (*1841*) 124, **Doc. 31**
  and Turkey (*1841*) **Doc. 32**

MEXICO
  position in (*1823*) 68; British recognition of 69, 76
  and United States, Palmerston's fears of its absorption (*1855*) 294, **Doc. 104**

MILAN PROCLAMATION, 1859
  Doc. 58

MOLDAVIA AND WALLACHIA
  exchange for Venetia contemplated (*1863*) 231
  occupation of, by Russia (*1848*) 158; (*1853*) 145
  Prince Couza in 257

MONROE DOCTRINE
  69–70

MONTENEGRO
  defence of (*1853*) 140
  frontiers of 394, 395–6 and n., 407, **Doc. 157**, 409–11

MÜNSTER, COUNT ZU, later PRINCE, GERMAN AMBASSADOR AT LONDON, 1873–85
  and Derby (*1874*) **Doc. 136**; (*1875*) 351, **Doc. 138**
  and German colonial question (*1884–5*) 424–5

NAPIER, CAPTAIN, later ADMIRAL SIR CHARLES
  capture of Dom Miguel's fleet (*1833*) 102
  concludes convention with Mehemet Ali (*1840*) 123

NAPLES
  conditions in (*1820*) 47; (*1848–60*) 163, **Doc. 41**, 190–2, 193–4, **Docs. 51, 52**, 212, **Doc. 68**
    Aberdeen and 191, **Doc. 51**
    Gladstone and 191–2, 193–4, **Docs. 51, 52**, 212
    Palmerston and **Doc. 41**, 191, **Doc. 65**, 257
    Russell and 215–17, **Docs. 66, 67**
  Metternich and (*1814–15*) 35
  Pitt and (*1805*) 12, 13

NAPOLEON I
  national resistance to, Pitt on 22; Canning on 24
  Treaty of Alliance against (*25 Mar. 1815*) 41, 45 n.

NAPOLEON III, EMPEROR OF THE FRENCH, 1852–70
  accession of 254; position of (*1863*) 253; Aberdeen on 289; Clarendon on **Doc. 99**; Palmerston on **Doc. 98**
  and American Civil War 294, 296, 298
  and Belgium 336
  and Crimean War 145
  and Italy (*1859*) 203–5; British attitude to 204–5, **Docs. 58, 61, 62**; (*1863*) desire to restore Kingdom of Two Sicilies 257
  and Mexico 253
  and Poland (*1863*) 236–8, **Docs. 75, 77**
  and Russo-Prussian *entente* (*1863*) 236

and Schleswig-Holstein question, his proposal for a Congress (*1863*) 253, **Docs. 85–7**; his unreadiness to fight **Doc. 91,** 268

NATIONALITY, PRINCIPLE OF (*v.* also *sub* Self-determination)
  Burke and 24
  Canning and 22–5; on German nationality 25, **Doc. 3**
  Castlereagh and 22
  Gladstone and 193, 194
  Palmerston and 283; *re* Italy (*1848–9*) 164, **Doc. 42,** 193, 194, (*1860*) **Doc. 69**; *re* Germany 168
  Pitt and 9, 22
  Russell and **Doc. 67,** 283
  in Germany 25, **Doc. 3,** 271
  in Italy 162, 164, **Doc. 67**

NAVAL DEMONSTRATION
  Granville and 410
  proposed *re* Schleswig-Holstein (*1864*) 266; *re* cession to Montenegro (*1880*) 407, 410; *re* Greece (*1886*) 434

NAVAL STRENGTH *v. sub* DEFENCE, NAVAL AND MILITARY

NAVY
  British and French navies compared (*1859*) 289–90, 291

NESSELRODE, COUNT, RUSSIAN MINISTER FOR FOREIGN AFFAIRS, 1822–56; CHANCELLOR, 1844–62
  and Crimean war 145, 146–52
  and Poland 234–5
  and revolutions of (*1848–9*) **Docs. 38, 40**

NETHERLANDS (*v.* also *sub* BELGIUM, independence of)
  defence of (*1805*) 19–20
  union of, as barrier against France (*1805*) 16–17; (*1813*) 30, 31, 32–3; (*1814–15*) 35, 36; Pitt's proposals *re* (*1805*) 9–10, 12, 14; Castlereagh's proposals *re* (*1813*) 28, 32

NEUTRALITY AGREEMENTS AND DECLARATIONS (*v.* also *sub* BELGIUM, GUARANTEES)
  Adriatic and Baltic, Malmesbury's proposal for neutrality of (*1859*) 202
  British neutrality in Polish question (*1863*) **Doc. 73**; in Schleswig-Holstein War (*1863–4*) 259–62, **Doc. 88,** 264–5, **Docs. 90, 91,** 267–8, **Doc. 92**; in Austro-Prussian War (*1866*) **Doc. 118**; in Russo-Turkish War (*1877–8*) 357–9, **Doc. 140,** 361–2

NICHOLAS I, TSAR OF RUSSIA, 1825–53
  conversations with Aberdeen (*1844*) 134–5, 138 n.
  conversations with Seymour (*1853*) 134–5, 138 and n.
  memorandum to Paskievič (*1853*) 134–5
  and Crimean war 145
  and France, proposals for Anglo-Russian secret alliance against (*1841*) 134, **Doc. 33**
  and Polish refugees in Turkey (*1849*) 178
  and revolutions of (*1848–9*) 158–9, **Docs. 38, 39**

NIGER BASIN
  negotiations *re* (*1894*) 488, **Docs. 190, 191**; (*1895*) 501, **Doc. 196**

NILE VALLEY (*v.* also *sub* FASHODA INCIDENT)
  negotiations *re* (*1894*) 488; (*1895*) 501–2, **Docs. 196, 197**; (*1897–8*)
    505–6, **Doc. 198,** 509–12

NON-INTERVENTION
  Aberdeen on intervention in Naples (*1850*) 191, (*1851*) **Doc. 51**
  Canning and, 48, 65–6, 86, 88, 90, 104, 107; instruction to Wellington
    re Spain (*1823*) 64, **Doc. 59**
  Castlereagh and, 47, **Docs. 6, 59**; *re* Spain (*1821*) 64
  Derby (14th Earl of) and, 305, 306
  Gladstone and (*1870*) 317–18; (*1893*) 474
  Granville and (*1852*) 183, **Doc. 47,** 186, **Doc. 48**
  Lamartine's declaration *re* (*1848*) 153
  Malmesbury and (*1852*) **Doc. 49**; (*1861*) 197
  Palmerston and, generally 90, **Docs. 13, 15,** 107–8, 159, 175–7, 285;
    departure from, *re* Spain (*1835*) 103, **Doc. 18**; *re* Greece (*1841*)
    107–8, **Doc. 24**; *re* Naples (*1856–60*) 212, **Doc. 63,** 226–9; *re*
    Italy (*1860*) **Doc. 69,** 285
  Russell and (*1859*) **Doc. 59**; (*1860*) 212, **Docs. 66, 68,** 226–9; (*1864*)
    272, 273
  Stanley (later 15th Earl of Derby) and 305–6, **Docs. 117, 118,** 308, 309

NORWAY
  union with Sweden (*1814–15*) 25, 35–6

NOVARA, BATTLE OF, 23 MAR. 1849
  163–4

ORLOV, COUNT
  119

PAGET, SIR AUGUSTUS, BRITISH AMBASSADOR AT VIENNA, 1884–93
  and Mediterranean Agreements (*1887*) 446–7, 470 n.
  and Near East (*1886*) 442, **Doc. 174**
  and the Straits (*1890–1*) 466, **Doc. 184**
  Károlyi on (*1887*) 447
  speech by (*1893*) 472, **Doc. 186,** 475

PALMERSTON, HENRY JOHN TEMPLE, 3RD VISCOUNT, SECRETARY OF STATE
    FOR FOREIGN AFFAIRS, 1830–4, 1835–41, 1846–51; PRIME MINISTER,
    1855–8, 1859–65
  and Queen Victoria 163–5, 178, 182, 203, 227, 267, 272, 279, 282–3;
    and Cabinet 282; *and* public opinion 285–6
  relation to Canning 88, 90, 107, 176, 228, 284–5; Salisbury's error *re*
    Palmerston and Canning 84 and n.; policy praised by Disraeli
    121–2; compared by Count Apponyi to Kaunitz 278, with Russell
    281; criticized by Derby (*1852*) 187–8; no system of policy 88;
    Cabinet (*1859–65*) complains of 282
  General
    alliances, on nature of (*1856*) **Docs. 98, 99,** criticized by Clarendon
      Doc. 99
    congresses, European, refuses one *re* Spain (*1837*) **Doc. 20**; on (*1849*)
      205, **Doc. 60**; (*1862*) 205 and n.; desire for (*May 1863*) 241; on
      general functions of (*1863*) **Doc. 85**; particular objections to
      (*1863*) **Doc. 86**

constitutions and constitutionalism, general 100–1, 144–5, 190–1, 283–4 (*v.* also *sub* BELGIUM, GREECE, HUNGARY, ITALY, POLAND, PORTUGAL, SPAIN)

defence, naval and military, 284, 288–91, **Docs. 102, 103**

guarantee, on value to Saxon Prussia (*1848*) 155; on value of, to Belgium (*1833*) **Doc. 16,** 155; Palmerston argues with Metternich on value to Turkey and Greece (*1841*) **Doc. 32**; distinction between guarantee and treaty **Doc. 36**; Palmerston will not defend Prussian Rhineland nor Austrian Lombardy (*1848*) 155

nationalism (*1849*) **Doc. 60**; (*1864–5*) 276–7, 283

non-intervention, departure from, in Belgium 90, **Docs. 13, 15**; in Portugal 100–4, 107; in Spain 103, **Doc. 18**; *re* Italy 285

Vienna Treaty of (*1814–15*), views on **Docs. 36, 37,** 251, **Doc. 85**

and Austria (*v.* also *infra* Hungary) *re* Belgium, Metternich and Guarantee (*1837*) **Docs. 16, 17,** 101; in Spain 103; and Turkey, joint note of Four Powers *re* (*1839*) 122, 128; Palmerston argues with Metternich *re* Guarantee (*1841*) **Doc. 32**; situation over Vienna Note (*1853*) 145, 146, 148; Palmerston and revolution of (*1848*) 153–5; will not defend Austrian Lombardy (*1848*) 155; general attitude *re* Austrian Italy (*1848–9*) 162–5, recommends a constitution (*1848*) **Doc. 41,** criticizes Austrian rule **Doc. 42**; criticizes Austria *re* Hungary (*1849*) 169–71, but declares Austria an essential element in the Balance of Power (*1849*) 172; Palmerston's attitude towards, in Italy (*1860*) and Garibaldi 203–5, denounces Austrian rule in Venetia (*1860*) **Doc. 70,** advises Austria to sell Venetia (*1862*) 229; Palmerston's attitude towards, in Poland (*1815*) 232, (*1863*) 238, *re* amnesty (*1863*) 239, Palmerston suggests independent Austrian Archduke (*1863*) 241, **Doc. 75**

and Belgium, general 89–90; on French designs in (*7 Jan. 1831*) **Doc. 12,** on need for French evacuation (*17 Aug. 1831*) **Doc. 14**; on guarantee to, and value of **Docs. 16, 36**

and Denmark and Schleswig-Holstein (*v.* also *infra* France), Palmerston on the treaty of (*1852*) **Doc. 89**; Palmerston's warning to those who attempt to attack Denmark (*July 1863*) **Doc. 84,** 259; advice to Denmark (*Jan. 1864*) **Doc. 90**; fears expressed to Queen Victoria (*8 Jan. 1864*) 279; fears German invasion of Copenhagen (*Feb. 1864*) 267; warns Austria against sending fleet to Baltic (*May 1864*) **Doc. 92**; argues with Queen Victoria 272; comments on Russell's plan (*May 1864*) **Doc. 96**; summarizes results to Russell but prefers a strong Prussia (*Sept. 1865*) **Doc. 97**; on self-determination 228

and Egypt, Mehemet Ali's attack (*1832*) 117–18; Palmerston refuses to intervene (*1832–3*) 118–20; Wellington's action (*1835*) 120–1; Mehemet Ali's renewed threat (*1838*), Palmerston's warning (*1838–9*) **Docs. 26, 29**; warns the Sultan (*1839*) **Doc. 28**; Palmerston's policy defeats Mehemet Ali (*1840–1*) 122–4, praised by Disraeli 121–2; Palmerston and Metternich on value of Guarantee to Turkey (*1841*) **Doc. 32**; intervention in Persian Gulf (*1838*) **Doc. 27**

PALMERSTON, HENRY JOHN TEMPLE, 3RD VISCOUNT *continued*

    and France, Palmerston's relation to, over Poland (*1831–2*) 233, 235; and Louis Philippe over Mehemet Ali crisis (*1839*) **Doc. 30**; his treatment of France (*1840–1*) 122, 123 and n.; Palmerston and Metternich on Straits' Convention (*1841*) **Doc. 31**; Palmerston recommends humanitarian policy over Greece (*1841*) **Doc. 24**; his decision to recognize revolutionary government in France (*1848*), explained to Russia **Doc. 38**; Palmerston and France in Italy (*1848–9*) 164–5, 168; and France over Hungarian refugees (*1849*) 178, 180–1; joint action with, *re* Naples (*1856*) 212; and Napoleon III, on alliance with (*1856*) **Doc. 98**; differences over Italy and French annexation of Savoy and Nice (*1859–60*) 203–5; French proposal to stop Garibaldi landing on mainland (*1860*) defeated 215–16, 218; Palmerston's belief that French military strength is superior to Prussian (*1860–3*) 250–1; Poland and Napoleon III (*1863*) 236, 244–5, 249, 286; opposes Napoleon's idea of a Congress (*Nov. 1863*) 253, 259, in general **Doc. 85**, and in particular **Doc. 86**; Palmerston's failure to secure joint action with, over Schleswig-Holstein (*1864*) 260, 264, on French refusal to use force **Doc. 91**, 268, 279–80

    and Greece (*1832*) boundaries of 117

    and Hungary (*1848–9*) Palmerston's general policy misunderstood 169–71; on Austrian policy to (*1849*) **Doc. 44**; on Hungarian refugees in Turkey 177–9, **Docs. 45, 46**

    and Italy, and Garibaldi (*1860*) 214–15; danger of French intervention 215–16; Palmerston justifies Garibaldi (*1860*) **Doc. 65**; warns off Spain from interference **Doc. 69**; Palmerston justifies revolution of 228–9, denounces Austrian rule in Venetia (*1860*) **Doc. 70**

    and Naples, Palmerston breaks relations with (*1856*) 212; denounces King (*1856–7*) 212, **Doc. 63**; opposes union with Sicily (*1860*) **Doc. 67**

    and Poland (*1831–2*) 232–5; protests against Austria's occupation of Cracow (*1849*) 208; suggests Russia giving home rule to (*1848*) 161; on Austria and (*1849*) 174; Polish and Hungarian refugees (*v.* also *supra* Hungary) (*1849*) 179; question of Poland at Congress of Paris (*1856*) 235; revolution of (*1863*), Palmerston agrees with Russell *re* 232, 236; relations with France 233, 235; urges amnesty (*Feb.*) **Doc. 72**; (*May*) **Doc. 74**; deprecates war (*Ap.*) **Doc. 73**; suggests independence under Austrian Archduke (*May*) **Doc. 75**; advises Russell to be moderate (*12 Oct.*) **Docs. 77, 78**; thinks a Congress *re* futile (*Nov.*) **Docs. 85, 86**

    and Portugal, Palmerston sanctions British intervention (*1833*) 100–4, (*1847*) 107

    and Prussia, danger to Belgium from (*1830*) 89, 95; Palmerston on British pledge to Saxon Prussia (*1848*) 155, 157; on Bismarck and Prussia (*1862–3*) 248–9, **Docs. 81–3**; on Schleswig-Holstein and Denmark (*q.v.*) (*1864*) 259–64; Palmerston on treaty obligations of *1852* **Doc. 89**; on Prussia's relation to (*1865*) **Doc. 97**

    and Russia, Palmerston and Belgium (*1837–9*) 89, 95–6; Palmerston and policy of, in Spain (*1834*) 103; Palmerston and, in Greece (*1841*) 107–8; Palmerston and Turkey and Unkiar Skelessi (*1832–3*) 117–19, 123, Palmerston refers to (*1839*) 129; on overture of

Nicholas (*1841*) **Doc. 33**; on Tsar's overture (*1853*) 135, general 138–46; revolution of (*1848*), Palmerston's *entente* with, over 158–60; will not be drawn into war with (*Dec. 1848*) 162; Tsar decides to aid Austria against Hungary (*May 1849*) 170; Russian victory 171; Palmerston's attitude towards 171, **Docs..43, 44**; question of Russia and Hungarian refugees (*1849*); Palmerston resolves to protest 177–9, **Docs. 45, 46**; Palmerston on Russian designs in Asia (*1860*) 247

and Spain, intervention in (*1833–47*) 102–4, **Docs. 18–21**; warned off by Palmerston from armed interference in Italy (*1860*) **Doc. 69**

and Switzerland, Palmerston reserves freedom to act *re* (*1847*) 155, 157

and Straits, Palmerston and Wellington (*1834–6*) 118–21, importance of latter's move **Doc. 25**; Palmerston and Metternich on Straits' Convention (*1841*) **Doc. 31**

and Turkey (*v.* also *supra* Egypt, Russia), integrity of Ottoman Empire (*1839–41*) 116–33, 134; (*1849*) 177–81; (*1853–4*) 135; (*1860*) 285; (*1860, 1865*) 285 and n.

PAPAL STATES
restoration of (*1813*) 33; (*1814–15*) 35; French troops in (*1848*) 163; invasion of (*1860*) 223–4; conditions in 224

PARIS, DECLARATION OF, 1856
Palmerston and 300

PARLIAMENT
Canning and, supported by 65, 66; publishes State Paper of (*5 May 1820*) 47; speech *re* non-intervention 48
Castlereagh and 65; *re* Parliament and British obligations (*1820*) 63
Derby and Stanley, speeches of *re* Guarantee 312, 313
Gladstone and, *re* Belgian neutrality 336, speech *re* **Doc. 131**; *re* Alabama Arbitration **Doc. 126**; *re* Egypt 421
Granville and, *re* Tunis 414; *re* Egypt 421
Grey and, *re* Nile Valley 501–2, **Doc. 196**
Palmerston and, generally 248, 283; *re* Denmark and Schleswig-Holstein 259, 260, 278, 283; *re* Parliament and British obligations 134, 137
speeches, *re* Austria (*1849*) 171, **Doc. 44**; *re* Canning and British interests, 88; 'civis romanus sum' 171; *re* constitutional states 101; *re* failure of Kings to grant constitutions 100; *re* power of opinion 100
Rosebery and, *re* Batoum 436, **Doc. 173**; *re* Mediterranean Agreements 475–6
Russell and, speech *re* Savoy and Nice, 205, **Doc. 62**
Salisbury and, *re* Bulgaria 431; *re* British obligations 519–20; speech *re* British obligations (*1871*) 516
Italian, first (*1860*) 204
Prussian (*1863*) 248–9
Turkish, Gladstone and **Doc. 152**

PENJDEH CRISIS
390, 426, 427, 429, 437, 457

PERSIAN GULF
    control of, Palmerston's determination *re* (*1838*) 124, **Doc. 27**; Derby
        on British interests in (*1877*) 358
    danger to, from Russia (*1878*) 363
PIEDMONT (*v.* also *sub* SARDINIA)
    Pitt's proposals *re* (*1805*) 10, 12, 13, 15, 16; Castlereagh's proposals *re*
        (*1813*) 28, 33; acquisition of Genoa by (*1814–15*) 35
PITT, WILLIAM, THE YOUNGER, PRIME MINISTER, 1783–1801, 1804–6
    (*v.* also *sub* GRENVILLE)
    general, inaugurates a new foreign policy (*1783*) 1; connexion with
        Grenville 2–3, Castlereagh 9–10, Canning 22; ideas of guarantee
        of concert, and of a European League to enforce peace, first sketch
        (*1792–3*) 9–10; more fully developed in memorandum for settlement
        of Europe (*1805*) 10, **Doc. 2**; his policy anti-nationalistic 9–10, 13
    and Balance of Power 10–21
    and Austria (*1805*) 10, 13, 14–15 (*v. infra sub* Italy), to seek compensation
        in Italy 15–16
    and Austrian Netherlands (*1793*) 8, thinks Austria unable to hold
        (*1805*) 14, to be transferred to Prussia 10, 16
    and Germany (left bank of Rhine, Luxemburg, etc.) disposal of (*1805*)
        10, 14, 16, 18
    and Holland (*1788*) 1; (*1792–3*) 2 and n., 3, 5, 7 n., 8; his resolve to
        recover (*1805*) 9–13, 16
    and Italy, ideas as to future of Austrian influence in (*1805*), to have
        Lombardy, Modena, Tuscany and Venetia, 10, 12–13, 15–16;
        Genoa 13–14; Naples 12; Piedmont and Sardinia 10, 12–13, 15–
        16; Savoy 2, 7 n.; Tuscany 10, 13; Venetia 10
    and Netherlands, Austrian, *v. supra* Austria
    and Netherlands, Dutch, *v. supra* Holland
    and Prussia, Pitt's concert with (*1788*) 1; his proposals for increasing
        her territory (*1805*) 9–10; left bank of Rhine 10; Holland 16;
        and inducements to annex Low Countries as barrier against
        France 14–16
    and Russia, Oczakov incident (*1791*) 1; reply to her proposed inter-
        vention in France (*1792*) 9; reply to Tsar Alexander's proposals
        (*1805*) 9; foreshadows a guarantee system 10–12
    and Spain, and Canada (*1790*) 1; disapproves of compensation to, in
        Italy (*1805*) 14; attitude towards national rising against Napoleon
        22
    and Switzerland, on re-establishment of independence of (*1805*) 12
PLEBISCITES
    re Central Italy 204
    re Savoy and Nice 204
POLAND
    Alexander I and 232–3
    conference proposed *re* (*1863*) 238–9
    constitution of (*1815*) 232–3, 234, 242; alteration in (*1831*) 233, 234–5;
        Palmerston recommends (*1848*) 161; destruction of (*1863*) 233
        Clarendon and (*1856*) 235
        Nesselrode and (*1832*) 234–5

Palmerston and (*1831–2*) 233–4, 235; (*1848*) 161, 235; (*1856*) 235;
  (*1863*) 235–6, **Docs. 75, 77, 78**
Russell and (*1848*) 235; (*1863*) 232, 235–9, **Docs. 73, 76, 78**
Satov, legal views of, 235
misgovernment of 255
partition of, Burke on 24
rebellion in (*1831*) 233–4
refugees from, in Turkey (*1849*) 177–81
restoration of, Canning and 25
revolution in (*1863*) 236–47, 251
  Austria and 237–9, **Docs. 73, 75, 76, 78,** 285
  Napoleon III and 236–8, **Docs. 75, 77**
  Palmerston and 236–7, **Docs. 72, 75, 77, 78, 82**
  Russell and 237–9, **Doc. 73**
Russia and (*1805*) 9; (*1815*) 34, 232–3, 242; (*1830–2*) 234–5; (*1848–9*)
  158–9; (*1863*) 232–47
Treaty of Vienna and 232–3, 235, 237, 238, 242; Stanley on out-worn
  character of obligations of Vienna Treaty (*1868*) 306, **Doc. 118**

POLIGNAC, PRINCE DE, FRENCH AMBASSADOR AT LONDON, 1823–9
  Polignac memorandum **Doc. 8**

PONSONBY, SIR JOHN (VISCOUNT PONSONBY), BRITISH AMBASSADOR AT
  CONSTANTINOPLE, 1832–7
  'discretionary order' *re* fleet given to (*1834*) 119–20; revocation of
  Doc. 25

PORTUGAL
  colonies of, question of application of guarantee to, Canning and 82;
    Granville and 342, 343; Derby and 512; Salisbury and 342, 514–
    15, **Doc. 199**
  conditions in 303–4, 513–14
  negotiations (*1876–7*) *re* Goa 512; (*1887–91*) *re* East Africa 513;
    (*1898*) Anglo-German negotiations *re* 514; (*1899*) Anglo-
    Portuguese declaration and 514–15, **Doc. 199**
  slave trade and slavery in **Doc. 114**
  treaty with Transvaal (*1875*) 513, 515
  constitutionalism in 85–6, 102, 103, 284
  revolt in (*1820*) 47; (*1832–4*) 102, 103, 107
  and France, Napoleon I and 22
  and Great Britain, Ancient Treaties with
    Canning and (*1825–6*) 82, 85, 186, 342
    Castlereagh and (*1820*) 52
    Derby and (*1875–6*) 342, 512–13, 514
    Granville and (*1852*) 186; (*1872–3*) 341–2, **Doc. 133,** 512, 514
    Salisbury and (*1899*) 342, 514–15, **Doc. 199**
    guarantee of succession of House of Braganza (*1810*) 81
  and Spain (*1826*) 66–7, 85; (*1833*) 102, 103; (*1852*) 186; (*1873*) 341–2
PRESS
  British
    Churchill (Randolph), support of (*1886*) 441
    Malmesbury on strictures of, against governments in alliance with
      Britain 188

PRESS *continued*
Palmerston's connexion with 88
Vienna note (*1853*), leakage of 145
Globe, publication of Salisbury-Shuvalov memoranda in 389 and n.
Morning Chronicle Palmerston and 88; praise of Canning in 88
Standard, article by 'Diplomaticus' in (*1887*) 445–6, 451
Times, declaration in, that Britain would not fight over Savoy (*1860*)
211; advises giving up of Crete (*1867*) 306; publishes Benedetti
letter (*1870*) 336 and n.; article supporting rumour that England
had joined Triple Alliance (*1887*) 462

German
Berlin *Post* "war scare" headline (*1875*) 351
Hungarian
grant of freedom to (*1848*) 169

PRUSSIA (*v.* also *sub* BISMARCK, GERMANY)
constitution in (*1848*) 153, 154
military strength of **Doc. 81**, 318–19, **Doc. 124**
Canning and (*1807*) **Doc. 3**
Castlereagh on (*1814*) 25 n.
Pitt and compensation of (*1805*) 14–15, 17–18
Russell and, his view that there could be no Germany without Prussia
(*1863*) 252
and Austria (*1805*) 17; (*1815*) 35; (*1860*) 226–7; (*1863*) **Docs. 82, 83**;
(*1866*) 305, **Doc. 118**; (*1870*) 320
and Belgium (*1831*) 89, 95; (*1870*) 336–7
and France (*1788*) 1; (*1805*) 17–18, 19; (*1815*) 35; (*1830–1*) 89, 91, 93;
(*1860–3*) **Doc. 81**; (*1869–70*) 318–19, **Doc. 124**; (*1870*) 323–4,
Doc. 125, 335–7
and Italy (*1860*) 222, 225, 226–7; (*1867*) 308
and Luxemburg (*1839*) 309; (*1867*) 309–10, **Doc. 119**
and Netherlands (*1805*) 15, 16
and Russia, Canning on (*1807*) 27; (*1863*) 236; (*1870*) 320
and Schleswig-Holstein question, her acceptance of a Congress (*1863*)
253; attitude to Christian IX 261; ultimatum to Denmark 262, 264–
5; establishment of condominium with Austria in Duchies 278–9
and Spain (*1820*) 49

PUBLIC OPINION
Canning and 65–6, **Doc. 7**, 84, 285
Castlereagh and 65
Gladstone appeals to, *re* Naples Atrocities 192
Palmerston and 170, 171, 175–6, 179, 245, 248, 285–6, 291
Pitt and 1, 2, 3
Russell and 221, 226, 286
Salisbury and, *re* Turkey 407, 497–9
and Crimean War, pressure real cause of English entry 138
and French Revolution 2
and Garibaldi and Italian unity 226
and Hungarian refugees 179
and Hungarian revolution 170, 171
and Menšikov mission (*1853*) 145

and Poland 239, 240
and Sardinia (*1859*) 198–9

RECOGNITION
Canning and, *re* South American States, commercial recognition of 65, 69 and n., 76, political recognition of 76, 206; general theory *re* 77, **Doc. 9,** 88, 159, 228
Castlereagh and, *re* South American States 68
Gladstone and recognition of South in American Civil War 297, 299; Cabinet and 282
Lewis, Sir G. Cornewall and, *re* South in American Civil War 297
Napoleon proposes recognition of South in American Civil War 294, 296, 298
Palmerston and, *re* French Republic (*1848*) 153, 159, **Doc. 38**
Russell on British principles *re* 207
American view *re* (*1823*) 76
Spanish view *re* (*1823*) 76–7

REFUGEES
in Britain 196
Hungarian in Turkey 177–9, **Docs. 45–6**
Polish in Turkey 178

REVOLUTION OF 1688
cited by Russell *re* Naples (*1860*) 214, 221, 223–4, 225, 227–8

REVOLUTION OF 1830
89, 160

REVOLUTIONS OF 1848–9
153–5, 158–60, 162–77, 177

RHENISH PROVINCES
and France (*1859–63*) **Doc. 81**

ROME (*v. also sub* PAPAL STATES)
and Italy (*1863*) 255, 257

ROSEBERY, ARCHIBALD PRIMROSE, 5TH EARL OF, SECRETARY OF STATE FOR FOREIGN AFFAIRS, FEB.–JULY 1886, 1892–4; PRIME MINISTER, 1894–5
general policy, continuity of foreign policy, statement to Count Hatzfeldt (*1886*) 512 n.; speech on (*12 Oct. 1898*) 511–12; on continuity in Near East, statement *re* Greece (*Feb. 1886*) 434, **Doc. 172;** doctrine of the binding force of engagements (*1886*) and attitude in (*1893*) 437, 472
differences with Gladstone over fleet 472, **Doc. 188;** relations with Kimberley 487
and Africa, Congo Treaty with King Leopold II and withdrawal of Art. III 490–1; threat to return to policy of free hand (*June 1894*) **Doc. 192;** Nile Valley 488, Editors' Note 493, attitude towards (*29–31 Mar. 1895*) 502; speech at Epsom over Fashoda crisis (*12 Oct. 1895*) 511–12
and Austria, discussion *re* Constantinople (*1893*) 472–3, **Docs. 186, 189;** refused to give binding assurances but ready to defend Straits alone against Russia (*31 Jan. 1894*) **Doc. 189,** (*26 Feb. 1894*) 487; threat to withdraw assurances (*1894*) 492; discussion *re* colonial question (*1894*) 490–1

ROSEBERY, ARCHIBALD PRIMROSE, 5TH EARL OF *continued*
    and France, quarrel over Siam (*1893*) 471
    and Near East, *re* Greece 434, **Doc. 172**; his attitude to Constantinople
        Docs. 186, 189, 487, 492; his attitude to Mediterranean Agree-
        ments (*1893*) **Docs. 187–9**
    and Russia, severe dispatch *re* Batoum (*13 July 1886*) 436–7, **Doc. 173**;
        and Russian Mediterranean fleet (*1893–4*) 471–2, 478, 481–2;
        might defend Straits alone against Russia (*1894*) 487

ROUMANIA *v. sub* MOLDAVIA AND WALLACHIA

RUSSELL, LORD JOHN, 1ST EARL, PRIME MINISTER, 1848–52, 1865–6;
        SECRETARY OF STATE FOR FOREIGN AFFAIRS, 1852–3, 1859–65
    instructs Granville to draw up memorandum on foreign policy for the
        Queen (*1851–2*) 182–3; relation to the Queen 165, 182, 283;
        weakness of his ministry (*1852–3*) 183; assumption of office (*1859*)
        203, 214; methods of (*1859–65*) 281–6; belief in nationalism and
        constitutionalism 283; in importance of naval strength **Doc. 101**;
        attitude to arbitration 284, 300; and reaction against Palmerston
        (*1865–6*) 305; his connexion with instructions to Stratford de
        Redcliffe (*Feb. 1853*) **Doc. 34,** 138 n.; his application of Palmer-
        ston's principle of Guarantee to Cracow (*1841*), to Parma and
        Modena (*1859*) 157; on importance of consent of governed (*1859*)
        Doc. 58; on Congresses since (*1815*) 180–1, **Doc. 59**; compared
        with Palmerston 207, 214, 282
    and American Civil War **Doc. 109**
    and France 286
    and Italy (*1860*) 204; cession of Nice and Savoy **Doc. 62**; better in-
        formed than Palmerston 214, 282; friendship for Italy 221–2; on
        Union 214–15, **Doc. 67**; on Garibaldi's expedition 215–16, **Doc. 66**;
        dispatch of (*27 Oct. 1860*) 221, **Doc. 68,** 226–9; on Venetia **Doc. 71**
    and Poland *v. sub* POLAND
    and Revolution of (*1688*) *v. sub* REVOLUTION
    and Russian designs in Asia 247
    and Schleswig-Holstein question *v. sub* SCHLESWIG-HOLSTEIN

RUSSELL, LORD ODO (LORD AMPTHILL), BRITISH AMBASSADOR AT BERLIN,
        1872–84
    mission to Bismarck *re* Black Sea question (*1870*) 330, 334
    overture of Bismarck to (*Jan.–Feb. 1876*) 554–5

RUSSIA
    attitude of (*1805*) 9, 12–13, 20
    European alliance and (*1813–15*) 36–7; (*1818*) 37–9; (*1820*) **Doc. 6**
    settlement of Vienna and 34–5
    and Afghanistan, Penjdeh crisis *re* (*1885*) 390, 426, 427, 429
    and Asiatic expansion (*1860*) **Doc. 79**; (*1877–8*) 360, 363–5, 369, 370–1,
        381, **Doc. 145** (*v.* also *sub* CHINA)
    and Austria *v. sub* AUSTRIA
    and Black Sea (*1791*) 1; (*1870–1*) 330–1, **Docs. 127–9**; (*1886*) 436–7,
        Doc. 173
    and Egypt (*1832–3*) 118–20; (*1839–40*) 122; (*1844–5*) 426; (*1853*) 135;
        (*1887*) 452

and France, overture for intervention in France (*1792*) 9; Holy Places dispute (*1852–3*) 138, **Doc. 34**; Crimean War with 144–6, **Doc. 35**; relations with (*1859*) 201, 202; Fashoda incident (*1898*) 517; growth of Franco-Russian understanding and alliance (*1893, etc.*) 445, 470, 471, 484; Rosebery on possibility of Franco-Russian combination (*1893*) 478, (*1894*) 482, 484; (*1898*) 517

and Germany, connexion with, in Dreikaiserbund (*1871–3*) 343–4, 347, (*1881*) 390–1, 411–12, **Doc. 159**, (*1884*) 426, 430, 442; war scare and (*1875*) 351–2, **Doc. 137**; policy of Reinsurance Treaty (*1887*) 454–5; Bismarck's ill-temper with (*1887*) 457–8, 459; cooperation with, in China (*1897*) 499–500

and Greece, Anglo-Franco-Russian treaty *re* (*1827*) 85; (*1832*) 107, 111, 132

and Great Britain, Anglo-Russian discussions (*1805*) *re* guarantee 10–12, *re* peace terms **Doc. 2**; (*1807*) Canning on use of Russia to check Prussia 27; (*1813–15*) question of guarantee of settlement 28–9, peace terms 34–5; (*1815*) Holy Alliance 36–7, 47; (*1815–18*) Congress System 37–9, **Doc. 5**; (*1820–3*) question of Spain 47, **Doc. 6**, 65–6; (*1821*) Greek question 64, (*1827*) 85, (*1841*) 107–8; (*1831–2*) Poland 232–5; (*1831–9*) Belgian question 89, 95–6, 101; (*1832*) danger of Franco-Russian alliance 101; (*1832–9*) Near Eastern crisis 117–19, 122–3, 129; (*1841, 1844, 1853*) Anglo-Russian conversations 134–5, **Doc. 33**; (*1848*) Poland 161; (*1848–9*) 158–60, 162, 170, 171, **Docs. 43, 44**; (*1849*) Hungarian and Polish refugees 177–9, **Docs. 45, 46**; (*1852–3*) Holy Places dispute 138, **Doc. 34**, 144; (*1853*) Vienna negotiations 145–6, **Doc. 35**; (*1860*) Asiatic expansion 247; (*1863*) Poland 232, 236, **Docs. 72–4, 77, 78, 85, 86**, 249, 251, 258; (*1864*) Schleswig-Holstein question 267, 275; (*1865*) Palmerston on 280, 284, 290; (*1866*) Austro-Prussian War **Doc. 118 b**; (*1870–1*) Black Sea question 330–1, **Docs. 127–9**, 345; (*1870*) Belgium 337; (*1875*) cooperation *re* war scare 351–2, **Docs. 137, 138**; (*1877*) 357–8, **Docs. 140, 141**; (*1877–8*) 361–2, 363–5, **Docs. 143, 144**; Berlin 381, **Docs. 145, 148**, 412; (*1880*) 408, 409–10, 411; (*1881*) 412; (*1885*) 390, 426, 434; (*1886*) 434, 436–7, **Doc. 173**, 441; (*1887*) Second Mediterranean Agreement an anti-Russian document 455; (*1893*) Russian Mediterranean fleet said to be directed against Britain 472; (*1893–4*) Rosebery on attitude to Russia and to Franco-Russian combination 471–2, 473, **Docs. 186, 189**, 487; (*1894*) effect of improved relations on British policy towards Triple Alliance **Doc. 193**; (*1895*) alleged British arrangement *re* Constantinople 494–5; (*1898*) British overture to 499–500, **Doc. 195**

and Hungary, Russian intervention in (*1848–9*) 169–71, **Doc. 43**; question of Hungarian refugees in Turkey 178–9, **Docs. 45, 46**

and Italy (*1860*) 222, 225, 226–7

and Near East (*1821–8*) Greek War of Independence and 64, 85; new policy towards Turkey (*1829*) 118; alliance with Turkey (*1833*) 118–19, 128, 134; attitude in Egyptian crisis (*1839–40*) 122, 123–4; Tsar's proposals for re-settlement (*1853*) 134–5; Stratford de Redcliffe and Russo-Turkish relations **Doc. 34**; Russian claims and outbreak of Crimean War 144–6, **Doc. 35**; denunciation of

RUSSIA *continued*

Black Sea clauses (*1870*) 330–1, **Docs. 127, 128**; Russo-Turkish War (*1877–8*) 357, 360, 361, 362, 363–5; peace settlement 381, 382; enforcement of Treaty of Berlin 409–10, 411; Bulgarian crisis (*1885*) 429–31; Greek question and isolation of Russia (*1886*) 434; alteration in status of Batoum (*1886*) 436–7, **Doc. 173**; suspected Russian move in Balkans (*1886*) 441, **Doc. 174**; development of Bulgarian crisis (*1887*) 445; policy of Reinsurance Treaty (*1887*) 454–5; negotiations for commercial treaty (*1893*) 471, and rumours of Russian move 471–3, 474, 480, 481, 483–4, 485; (*1894*) 493; alleged discussions with Britain (*1895*) 494–5; Salisbury's overture for a 'partition of preponderance' (*1898*) **Doc. 195**

and Poland (*1805*) 9; (*1815*) 34, 232–3, 234, 242; (*1830–2*) 234–5; (*1848–9*) 158–9, Polish refugees in Turkey 177–81; (*1863*) 232–47

and Prussia, Canning on 27; (*1863*) 236; (*1870*) 320

and Spain (*1820*) 51, 55–6, 59; (*1834*) 103

and Straits question (*1829–33*) 118–20; (*1853*) 135; (*1878*) 364, 426; (*1891*) 466–7, **Docs. 184, 185**; (*1893*) 471; (*1894*) **Docs. 189, 193**; (*1897*) 496–7

SALISBURY, ROBERT CECIL, 5TH MARQUIS OF, SECRETARY OF STATE FOR FOREIGN AFFAIRS, 1878–80, 1885–6, 1887–92, 1895–1900; PRIME MINISTER, 1885–6, 1886–92, 1895–1902

general questions, alliance policy, development of (*1871*, *1875–8*, *1887*) 516; *entente* relationships 516; *v. also sub* MEDITERRANEAN AGREEMENTS; growing tendency to isolation 517–18; doctrine of (*1901*) **Doc. 200**; general results of 521–2

conferences, definition of functions (*1885*) 430; refusal of conference or arbitration on Portuguese colonial question (*1890*) 513

constitutions, Canning and Palmerston on, Salisbury's comment 84 and n.

and Belgium (*1887*) 445–6, **Doc. 177**

and Bulgarian crisis, refusal to act alone (*1885*) 429; acceptance of Conference of Constantinople 430, **Docs. 169, 170**; policy in a new departure 431, **Doc. 171**; (*1886*) 441–2, **Doc. 174**

and Central Powers, friendly overture (*1885*) 429; Mediterranean Agreements (*1887*) 446–8, **Docs. 175, 176**, 452, **Docs. 179, 180**, 454–8, **Docs. 181, 182**; (*1895*) 494–5; (*1896–7*) 495–6, **Doc. 194**; *v. also infra* Germany

and China, overture to Russia *re* (*1898*) **Doc. 195**

and Egypt (*1885, 1887*), attempt to find solution in Wolff Conventions 452; views on evacuation **Doc. 178**; dependence on Bismarck **Doc. 179**; reconquest of Soudan 506

and Germany, relations with (*1885*) 429; (*1887*) 446, 448, 449, 455–8, **Doc. 181**; peak period of Anglo-German cooperation (*1887–90*) 462; colonial negotiations (*1887–90*) 462–3; Near East and (*1895*) 494–5; difficulties with 517; alliance proposals (*1898, 1901*) 517–18, **Doc. 200**

and France, Fashoda incident with (*1898*) 505–6, **Doc. 198**, 511–12

and Near East, policy at Conference of Constantinople (*1876–7*) 357; proposals for partition (*1877*) 357; views on settlement of Eastern

question (*1878*) 363–5, **Docs. 142–4**, 381–4, **Doc. 145**; new departure in policy (*1885–6*) 431, **Doc. 171**, 441–2, **Doc. 174**; Mediterranean Agreements and the *status quo* (*1887*) 446–8, **Docs. 175, 176**, 454–8, **Docs. 181, 182**; insistence that Austro-Hungarian interests were greater than those of Britain (*1887*) 458; development of policy (*1895*) 494–5; completion of change of policy (*1897*) **Doc. 194**; overture to Russia *re* (*1898*) **Doc. 195**
    and Nile Valley, warning to France (*1897*) 506, 508; Fashoda incident 506, **Doc. 198**, 511–12
    and Russia (*1875–8*) *v. sub* EASTERN CRISIS; (*1895*) rumoured approach to 494–5; (*1898*) overture to 499–500, **Doc. 195**
    and Straits' question (*1878*) 362, 364, 366, 369, 381–2, **Doc. 147**, 437; (*1887*) *v. sub* MEDITERRANEAN AGREEMENTS; (*1891*) 466–7, **Docs. 184, 185**; (*1896–7*) 495–6, **Doc. 194**
    and Tunis (*1878*) 383, 413, 415

SAMOA
    Anglo-German agreement *re* (*1889*) 462–3

SARDINIA
    conditions of, in revolution of (*1848–9*) 162–5; constitution in (*1848*) 162, 166; Lombardy, annexation of 203
    and Austria (*1859*) 197–8, **Docs. 54, 55**; war with Austria (*1859*) 203–5, **Docs. 61, 62**
    and Great Britain (*1859*) **Doc. 54**

SAVOY AND NICE
    and Pitt 2, 4, 7 n.
    annexation of, by France 204, **Docs. 61, 62**, 253, 254, 286

SAXONY
    Prussia and (*1814–15*) 35

SCHELDT
    French decree for opening to navigation (*1792*) 2, 3, 5–6, 7; Castlereagh on exclusion of French naval establishments from (*1813*) 30

SCHLESWIG-HOLSTEIN QUESTION
    analysis of 259–62, 267–8, **Doc. 93**; Conference of London on 268, settlement of 277–9
    Austria and, 260–2, **Docs. 88, 92**; ultimatum to Denmark by 262, 264; reluctant assent to invasion of Jutland (*Mar. 1864*) 267; establishment of condominium with Prussia 278
    France and 248–9; Congress proposal 253, **Docs. 85–7**; unreadiness to fight (*Jan. 1864*) **Doc. 91**, 268; increased bellicosity (*Feb. 1864*) 267
    Russia and, refusal to join naval demonstration (*Feb. 1864*) 267
    Bismarck and 248
    Clarendon and, his mission to Paris 268; comment on Russell's plan (*May 1864*) **Doc. 94**
    Palmerston and, his failure *re* 248–9; his warning to Europe **Doc. 84**; on desirability of incorporating Schleswig in Denmark 255; on obligations of Treaty of (*1852*) **Doc. 89**; advice to Denmark **Doc. 90**; Cabinet decision not to use force (*Jan. 1864*) **Doc. 91**, 267; decision not to send the fleet to Copenhagen despite Palmerston's views 267; criticism of Austrian policy **Doc. 92**; comment on

SCHLESWIG-HOLSTEIN QUESTION *continued*
Russell's plan (*May 1864*) **Doc. 96**; effect of result on his prestige
278–9; attitude to Convention of Gastein 279, **Doc. 97**; importance of differences in Cabinet 282–3
Russell and, comments on situation 251–2; French proposal for a
Congress (*1863*) 256; account of Cabinet decision to refuse **Doc. 87**;
share in pacification of (*1842–52*) 259–60; the 'Gotha' dispatch
(*1862*) 261; views on the crisis (*Dec. 1863*) **Doc. 88**; proposals for
naval demonstration 267; his compromise scheme (*May 1864*) 272,
Doc. 93; definition of British policy after Conference of London
(*June 1864*) **Doc. 95**; protest against Convention of Gastein (*Sept.
1865*) 279

SCHWARZENBERG, PRINCE, AUSTRIAN CHANCELLOR, 1848–52
154, 170, 180, 192, 193

SELF-DETERMINATION (*v.* also *sub* Nationality)
Burke and 228
Canning and 228
Clarendon and 276
Gladstone and 323–4, **Doc. 125**
Palmerston and **Doc. 38**, 164
Russell and **Doc. 58**; British proposal for, *re* Central Italy (*1860*) 204;
Napoleon III and 204; **Doc. 67**, 221, 272, 273

SERVIA
Austria–Hungarian alliance with (*1881*) 430, 431
Russia and (*1853*) 135
Settlement of Berlin and 364

SEYMOUR CONVERSATIONS, 1853
134–5, 138 and n.

SHUVALOV, COUNT, RUSSIAN AMBASSADOR AT LONDON, 1874–9
Derby and, note to (*6 May 1877*) 358; (*17 July 1877*) **Doc. 140**; (*13 Dec.
1877*) 361
Disraeli and (*1877*) 357
Salisbury and, negotiations with (*1878*) 364–5, 381, 389

SIAM
Anglo-French dispute *re* (*1893*) 471

SINOPE
destruction of Turkish squadron at (*30 Nov. 1853*) 146

SLAVE TRADE AND SLAVERY
Aberdeen Act (*1845*) *re* **Docs. 114, 115**
Brussels Conference and (*1889*) 463
Brazil and 284, 302, 303, 304
France and 256, 304
Portugal and 303
Spain and 256, 303
Palmerston and, his idea of emancipation as a war measure against the
Southern States 294, **Doc. 106**; execution of Aberdeen Act (*1863–4*)
Docs. 114, 115; on Spanish and French attitudes to (*1863*) 256,
303–4; on slave trade in Brazil 302, 303, **Doc. 116**

SOCIALISM
  Malmesbury on **Doc. 49**
SOLFERINO, BATTLE OF, 24 JUNE 1859
  203, 214
SPAIN
  colonies of, in South America, British mediation proposed (*1810*) 72 and
    n., 523; British trade with 72–3, 523–6; Congress proposals *re*
    (*1823*) 65, 69, 75 and n.; inability of Spain to recover 68, 71, 73;
    recognition of, attitude to 76, 80; situation in (*1823*) 68
    Argentine, Chile etc. *v. sub nom.*
  constitution of (*1812*) 55, 83; constitutionalism in, failure of 102, 103,
    284; Granville and (*1852*) 186, **Doc. 148**
  marriage question (*1846*) 190
  recognition of republic 350
  revolution in (*1820–3*), Castlereagh and 47, **Doc. 6,** 64; Canning and
    64–5, 66–7, 68, 206; French intervention in 64, 68–9, 81, 83;
    Carlist revolt (*1833–9*) 102–3, **Docs. 18–21**
  rising against Napoleon, Pitt and 22; Canning and 22–4
  and France (*1807*) 22–3; (*1823*) 64, 68–9, 81, 83; (*1856*) 287
  and Great Britain (*1807–9*) Canning and 22–4; (*1814–15*) settlement of
    35; (*1820–3, 1833–9*) *v. supra,* revolution in; (*1852*) Granville and
    186, **Doc. 48**; (*1860*) Palmerston and, *re* Italy 221, **Doc. 69**;
    (*1873*) Granville and, *re* Portugal 341–2, **Doc. 133**
  and Italy, King's interests in, not entitled to consideration (*1805*) 14;
    relations with (*1860*) 221, **Doc. 69**
  and Portugal (*1826*) 66–7, 85; (*1833*) 102, 103; (*1852*) 186; (*1873*) 341–2,
    Doc. 133
  and slave trade (*1863*) 303
  and Tripartite Treaty of (*1856*) 334–5

STANLEY, EDWARD HENRY, LORD, LATER 15TH EARL OF DERBY, SECRE-
    TARY OF STATE FOR FOREIGN AFFAIRS, 1866–8, 1874–8
  character, Beust on relation to Disraeli 347; relation to 14th Earl of
    Derby (*q.v.*) 306–7
  and guarantees, thinks guarantees of Vienna Treaty worthless (*1866*)
    Docs. 118 a, b; Brunnow and Apponyi on 308
    on guarantee to Luxemburg (*1867*) 309–10, **Doc. 119**; and Bismarck
      311–12; Derby's speech interpreting guarantee **Doc. 120**;
      Stanley's authoritative statement defining **Doc. 121**; Bernstorff
      and **Doc. 122**; collective doctrine of, contested by jurists 315,
      adopted by Grey (*1914*) 316
  on non-interference and intervention 305–6; Apponyi on **Doc. 117**;
    application to Austro-Prussian War (*1866*) **Doc. 118,** and to Italy
    308
  and Austria-Hungary (*1866*) **Doc. 118**; overture of (*1874*) **Doc. 135**;
    negotiations with (*1877*) 357, 364
  and Belgium, prepared to maintain integrity of (*1874*) 347, 350–1
  and Eastern question (*1876–7*) 357–9, 364; defines British position to
    Russia (*17 July 1877*) **Doc. 140**; his policy of *laisser faire* opposed
    by Disraeli 360; the *double politique* and resignation of Derby (*Mar.*
    1878) 361–2; results of Salisbury's accession 363

STANLEY, EDWARD HENRY, 15TH EARL OF DERBY *continued*
    and Germany, overture from *(1874)* **Doc. 136,** *(Feb. 1876)* 354–5,
        Doc. 139; war scare *(1875)* 351–2, **Docs. 137, 138**
    and Portugal *(1875–6)* 342, 512–13

STOPFORD, ADMIRAL SIR ROBERT
    capture of Beyrouth and Acre *(1840)* 123, 130

STRAITS OF BOSPHORUS AND DARDANELLES
    dispatch of fleets to Dardanelles, proposal for *(1849)* 178, 180
    passage of British fleet through *(1832)*, Stratford Canning's request for
        fleet to be sent to Constantinople 118; 'discretionary order'
        to Sir Josias Rowley *(1834)* 119–20; revocation by Wellington
        (1835) 120, **Doc. 25**; renewal of order *(1836)* 120; instructions sent
        by Aberdeen and Clarendon to Stratford *(1853)* 145, **Doc. 35**;
        Beaconsfield's instructions for fleet to pass through Dardanelles
        (Jan. 1878) 362; their cancellation and renewal 362; Emperor
        William's remarks *re (1895)* 494
    passage of Russian fleet through, occupation of Constantinople *(1833)*
        118; Russian Volunteer fleet *(1890–1)* 466–7, **Docs. 184, 185**;
        rumours of Russian move *(1893)* 471, *(1894)* 480–1, 482; Austria-
        Hungary and **Docs. 186–9**, 496, **Doc. 194**
    proposals for opening, British Cabinet Committee and *(1878)* 364, 369;
        Salisbury and *(1878)* 364, 366, to Britain only 381–2, **Doc. 147,**
        (1891) if open, open to all 466–7, **Doc. 185,** Count Metternich
        on *(1911)* 467, *(1896–7)* Salisbury's desire to open 496, opposition
        of Austria-Hungary expected 496, **Doc. 194**
    Rule of the Straits, statements *re* in Treaty of Unkiar Skelessi *(1833)*
        119; in Straits' Convention *(1841)* 123, **Doc. 31,** 469; Russian
        proposals *re (1853)* 135; in Treaty of Paris *(1856)* 469; in Treaty
        of London *(1871)* 331, 469; at Congress of Berlin *(1878)* 362, 364,
        381–2, **Doc. 147,** 426, 469; in Reinsurance Treaty *(1887)* 454–5;
        in Mediterranean Agreement *(Dec. 1887)* 455, 456, 460, 461
        Aberdeen and *(1853)* 145
        Clarendon and *(1853)* 145, **Doc. 35**
        Derby and *(1877)* 358, 361–2
        Disraeli and *(1878)* 361, 362
        Granville and *(1870)* 330
        Palmerston and *(1834–8)* 119–20, **Doc. 25**; *(1841)* **Doc. 31**; *(1849)*
            178–9, 180
        Rosebery and *(1886)* 437; *(1894)* **Doc. 189,** 487
        Salisbury and *(1878)* 362, 364, 365, 366, 369, 381–2, **Doc. 147,** 426;
            (1887) 460, 461; *(1891)* 466–7, **Docs. 184, 185**; *(1896–7)* 495–6,
            Doc. 194
        Wellington and *(1835)* 120, **Doc. 25**
    Stationnaires in *(1895)* 494–5

SUEZ CANAL
    Beust on *(1874)* 348
    Derby on *(1877)* 358
    Disraeli and *(1875)* 390
    Rosebery and *(1886)* 441

SUEZ CANAL CONVENTION
  and Anglo-French relations (*1887*) 459
SWEDEN
  Castlereagh's proposals *re* (*1813*) 31
  Palmerston's fears of absorption of Denmark by (*1864*) 278
  union with Norway 25, 35–6
SWITZERLAND
  independence and guarantee of 35, 155, 157
  Malmesbury and (*1852*) **Doc. 49**
  Palmerston and (*1847–8*) 155
  Pitt's proposals *re* (*1805*) 12
SYRIA
  Holy Places dispute (*1850–3*) 138, **Doc. 34,** 144–5, 151
  Mehemet Ali and (*1832–41*) 117–19, 122–4, 132

TAHITI
  Aberdeen and dispute with France *re* (*1844*) 190
TENTERDEN, CHARLES STUART AUBREY, 3RD BARON, PERMANENT UNDER-
  SECRETARY OF STATE FOR FOREIGN AFFAIRS, 1873–82
  notes on Treaty of San Stefano 388
TREATIES, ALLIANCES, ENTENTES, ETC.
  Adrianople, Treaty of (*14 Sept. 1829*) 118
  Alvensleben, Convention of (*Feb. 1863*) 236
  Anglo-Austrian, Austrian overtures for alliances (*1871–2*) 343–5, **Doc.
    134**; (*1874*) 347, **Doc.135** (*v.* also *sub* MEDITERRANEAN AGREEMENTS)
  Anglo-Portuguese Treaties (*1343–1661*) 52, 82, 342, **Doc. 133,** 514–15,
    516; Anglo-Portuguese Declaration (*14 Oct. 1899*) 515, **Doc. 199**
  Anglo-Russian, Russian overture for alliance against France (*1840*) 134;
    Salisbury's overture *re* Turkey and China (*Jan. 1898*) 499–500,
    Doc. 195
  Austro-German Alliance (*7 Oct. 1879*) 458
  Austro-Russian Balkan Agreement (*8 May 1897*) 499
  Austro-Servian Alliance (*28 June 1881*) 430
  Berlin, Treaty of (*13 July 1878*), British policy at Berlin Congress 381–4,
    Docs. 147, 148; enforcement of terms (*1880–1*) 390, 394, **Docs.
    150, 151,** 407, **Docs. 156–8,** 413; and the Bulgarian question
    (*1885–6*) 429, 431, **Doc. 171;** and Greece (*1886*) 434, **Doc. 172;**
    and Batoum (*1886*) 436–7, **Doc. 173;** Salisbury's recognition of
    British obligations under (*1887*) 445
    Articles XXIX 407, LIX 437–8, LXI 400, 404, LXIII 469
  Chaumont, Treaty of (*1–9 Mar. 1814*) 34, 38, 41, 42
  Cyprus Convention (*4 June 1878*), conclusion of 365, 366, 381, 448;
    interpretation of 383; Gladstone and Granville and 397, 398,
    399, **Docs. 153, 154,** 405, **Doc. 155,** 406–7, 414, **Doc. 161;**
    Grey and 407; Salisbury and 407
  Dreikaiserbund (*1871–3*) 343, 347; (*1881*) 390–1, 411–12, **Doc. 159;**
    (*1884–7*) 426, 430, 442
  Franco-Russian Alliance (*1891–3*), development of 445, 471, 484
  Gastein Convention (*14 Aug. 1865*) 278–9
  Holy Alliance (*26 Sept. 1815*) 36–7, 47, 86

Treaties, Alliances, Ententes, etc. *continued*

Kutchuk Kainardji, Treaty of (*1774*) 145, 149–50, 377

London, Declaration of, *re* Treaty engagements (*17 Jan. 1871*) 331, 376, 439, 440

London, Treaty of (*19 Ap. 1839*) *re* Belgium 89, 157, 336, 337, **Docs. 130–2**

(*15 July 1840*) *re* Egypt 122, 130, 135–6, 139 and n.

(*8 May 1852*) *re* Schleswig-Holstein 260, 262, 263, 264, 265, **Doc. 89,** 266, 267, 272

(*8 May 1867*) *re* Luxemburg 311–12, **Docs. 120, 121**

(*9, 11 Aug. 1870*) *re* Belgium 336–7

(*13 Mar. 1871*) *re* Black Sea clauses 330–1, 469

Mediterranean Agreements *v. sub nom.*

Mediterranean League, proposal for (*1878*) 382–3

Paris, Treaties of (*1814–15*) 36, 39, 41, 42–3, as binding Europe collectively, Castlereagh on 39–40

(*30 March 1856*) Black Sea clauses, Gladstone's disapproval of (*1856*) 330, cancellation of (*1870–1*) 330–1, **Docs. 127–9**; provisions for mediation invoked by Malmesbury (*1859*) 198, 201

(*15 Ap. 1856*) Tripartite Treaty, proposal that Germany and Italy should join (*1870*) 330–1, 334, 335; Gladstone on (*1870*) **Doc. 129**; Granville on (*1870*) **Doc. 128**; Russia and 334, 335

Quadruple Alliance (*20 Nov. 1815*), conclusion of 37; character of 41, 43–4; effect of Conference of Aix-la-Chapelle on 37; interpretation of, by Alexander (*Oct. 1818*) 38, by Castlereagh (*Oct. 1818*) 38, 45–6, by Canning (*1823*) 65–6

Quadruple Alliance (*22 Ap. 1834*) 103, **Doc. 18**

Reinsurance Treaty (*18 June 1887*) 454–5

San Stefano, Treaty of (*3 Mar. 1878*) 363–4, **Doc. 143**

Straits' Convention (*13 July 1841*) 123–4, 130, **Doc. 131**, 134, 469; violation of (*1853*) 145, **Doc. 35**

Suez Canal Convention (*29 Oct. 1888*) 459

Tripartite Treaty *v. sub* Paris, Treaty of

Triple Alliance (*1882, 1887, 1891*), conclusion of (*20 May 1882*) 391; rumours that England had joined (*1887*) 462; English relations with (*1893–4*) 474, 489, 490–1, **Docs. 192, 193**; effect of Bismarck's fall in increasing importance of Austria-Hungary in 465

Unkiar Skelessi, Treaty of (*8 July 1833*) 119, 134

Vienna, Treaty of (*25 Mar. 1815*), against Napoleon 41, 45 and n.

Vienna, Treaty of (*9 June 1815*), as binding Europe collectively, Castlereagh on 39–40, 59; citations of 228, 232–3, 234–5, 236–8, 241, 242, 244, 258, 305; uselessness of appeal to (*1866*) 307, 308; modifications and violations of 204, **Docs. 60, 82,** 254–5; summary of provisions 28, 34–6

Villafranca, Preliminaries of (*11 July 1859*) 203, 254

Wolff Convention (*22 May 1887*) 452, **Doc. 178**

Treaty Engagements

Declaration *re* (*17 Jan. 1871*) 331; cited by Salisbury (*1878*) 376, by Rosebery (*1886*) 339, 340

Russia and (*1866*) **Doc. 118 b**